Library / Media Center
Carroll Community College
1601 Washington Road
Westminster, Maryland 21157

WITHDRAWN

The German Left

D0209281

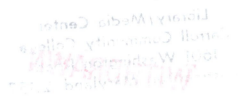

Europe and the International Order

Series Editor: Joel Krieger

The dramatic events of 1989, perestroika and post-perestroika developments in the Soviet Union, and the apparent end of the Cold War, European integration, and the aftermath of the war in the Persian Gulf marks a period of extraordinary volatility in Europe. This series considers the causes, dimensions, and consequences of these new transitions in European politics. It includes books which transcend the divisions of East and West, challenge narrow disciplinary approaches, and examine the connections between international and domestic politics.

Published

R. J. Dalton and M. Kuechler (eds), *Challenging the Political Order*
A. de Swaan, *In Care of the State*
P. Hall, *Governing the Economy*
J. A. Hellman, *Journeys among Women*
L. Holmes, *The End of Communist Power*
J. Jenson, E. Hagen and C. Reddy (eds), *Feminization of the Labour Force*
J. Krieger, *Reagan, Thatcher and the Politics of Decline*
A. Lipietz, *Towards a New Economic Order*
A. S. Markovits and P. S. Gorski, *The German Left*
F. Fox Piven (ed.), *Labor Parties in Postindustrial Societies*
G. Ross, S. Hoffmann and S. Malzacher, *The Mitterrand Experiment*

Forthcoming

J. Keeler, *The Scope and Limits of Democratic Reform*
C. Murphy, *Global Governance and Industrial Change*
G. Ross, *The Construction of Europe*

The German Left
Red, Green and Beyond

Andrei S. Markovits and
Philip S. Gorski

Oxford University Press • New York
1993

Oxford University Press

Oxford   New York   Toronto
Delhi   Bombay   Calcutta   Madras   Karachi
Kuala Lumpur   Singapore   Hong Kong   Tokyo
Nairobi   Dar es Salaam   Cape Town
Melbourne   Auckland   Madrid
and associated companies in
Berlin   Ibadan

Copyright © 1993 Andrei S. Markovits and Philip S. Gorski

First published in 1993 by Polity Press
in association with Blackwell Publishers

First published in North America by Oxford University Press, Inc.,
200 Madison Avenue, New York, New York 10016

Oxford is a registered trademark of Oxford University Press

All rights reserved. No part of this publication may be reproduced, stored in
a retrieval system, or transmitted, in any form or by any means, electronic,
mechanical, photocopying, recording, or otherwise, without prior permission
of Oxford University Press.

CIP data for this book are available from the Library of Congress.

ISBN 0-19-521051-4 (cloth)
ISBN 0-19-521053-0 (paper)

Printing (last digit): 9 8 7 6 5 4 3 2 1
Printed in Great Britain on acid-free paper

Contents

Preface and Acknowledgments   vii
List of Abbreviations   xi

Introduction   1

Part I   Predecessors   29
1   Reconstruction, Rearmament and Reintegration:
    The Emergence of the Extraparliamentary Left   33
2   "Anabaptists in the Affluent Society": The New Left and
    the Student Revolt   46
3   Revolutionary Cadre Politics and Terrorism   59
    With Gregory Wilpert
4   Revolution, Retreat, Reform: To APO and Back . . . to
    Parliament   79

Part II   Ideology and Policy   113
5   Ideology: The World Imagined   115
6   Policy: The World Desired   152

Part III   Politics   187
7   Politics: The World Experienced   189
8   The East German Greens: From Underground Opposition
    to Bundestag Representation   237
    With Susanne Altenburger

Conclusion   265
Appendix   290

Notes   296
Bibliography   364
Index   383

To the memories of our fathers,
Ludwig Markovits and Saul B. Gorski;
and to Dovi, Andy's eternal friend and partner

Preface and Acknowledgments

It is only fitting that I am writing these words of reflection and appreciation in Santa Cruz, California, where the first concrete steps toward this book originated. As stated in the preface to my monograph on West German labor (*The Politics of the West German Trade Unions: Strategies of Class and Interest Representation in Growth and Crisis*), much of my research agenda as a scholar of European politics concentrated on two questions: (1) What made the Federal Republic different from previous political formations in twentieth-century German history? And (2) How firmly rooted were these differences in the institutions and values of contemporary Germany to guarantee a future free from the horrors of the past? I then went on to say that my work on the German trade unions constituted the first part of what was to be a scholarly trilogy which sought to find some satisfactory empirical answers to these questions. The second, on which I had already broken ground by 1986, was to be a book-length study of the Left in the Federal Republic, particularly concerning its intellectually original and politically varied manifestations following the epoch-making events of the late 1960s. This book represents the product of my endeavors.

Nobody has been more instrumental and supportive in the creation, implementation and completion of this project than my dear friend and esteemed colleague Joel Krieger. We had both been invited by my current colleague Michael Brown to a conference on "The Unraveling of the Welfare State?" which Michael had organized at the University of California, Santa Cruz, in early June 1985. Joel was to present the British case at the conference and I the German. We shared a room in a Santa Cruz hotel, which was extremely fortuitous since we had numerous opportunities not only to discuss each other's conference papers but also to speak extensively about a topic which had been at the center of each of our identities as scholars, academics and participants: the fate of the Left in the United States and Europe. It was in the course of these wonderful discussions that Joel learned about my intentions to write an extensive study of the Left in the Federal Republic, especially in its post-1968 and green incarnation. From that June in 1985 in Santa Cruz until the book's completion nearly eight years later, Joel remained a singular source of encouragement. Not once did he waver in his support of the project, and never did he convey any impatience when I was repeatedly tardy about deadlines. Since meeting Joel at the Center for European Studies at Harvard University in October 1975 I always knew him as a first-rate scholar, a keen student of British politics, a prolific writer, a dedicated teacher and a trusted friend. But only in the course of writing this book was I made aware of Joel's admirable qualities as an academic coach, whose perseverance, empathy and thoughtfulness made the completion of this project possible.

As in every aspect of my intellectual and personal life, the Center for European Studies at Harvard played a pivotal role in the creation and completion of this study as well. It was the Center's unique ambience – so brilliantly concocted and maintained by its chairman Stanley Hoffmann, its director Guido Goldman and its associate director Abby Collins – which accorded me the opportunity to flourish as a student of European politics. Part of this flourishing included encounters with talented students – both undergraduate and graduate – whose commitment to the study of European affairs led them to join me in various collaborative endeavors over the years. One of these talented students was Philip Gorski, the co-author of this book. I met Phil in January 1985 when he sought me out at the Center to help him formulate some thoughts on the German Greens for a short project which he wanted to conduct over the summer in Germany, with the possibility of expanding it into his senior honors thesis at Harvard College. From our very first meeting at the Peasant Stock, appropriately then one of Cambridge's "green" restaurants, now alas defunct, Phil and I established an intellectual and personal rapport which continues unabated eight years later. By supervising Phil's honors thesis and working on similar topics myself, we concluded by the late spring of 1985 that we both understood the emergence and importance of the Greens and their milieu in similar terms, that is as a consequence of a political transformation of the German left rather than as a result of an ecological crisis of capitalism. It was Joel's encouragement in Santa Cruz which catapulted Phil's informal collaboration with me into a full-fledged book project.

A Fulbright grant and a fellowship from the National Science Foundation enabled Phil to spend two years in Germany, during which he studied with Jürgen Habermas in Frankfurt and also gathered materials for our book. Early drafts circulated back and forth between Cambridge and Frankfurt, with my frequent forays to Germany serving as brief but useful brainstorming sessions, sometimes held in one of the lounges at the Frankfurt airport. With Phil's move to Berkeley and his obligations to an exacting doctoral program in sociology and my usual distractions common to a professorial existence, the project lay dormant for a while, though – very much on account of Joel's unabated encouragement – it never became moribund.

The Center for European Studies once again proved the ideal place for various reactivating maneuvers which – as is evident – proved successful. Its library full of the most current German publications, its visitors from Germany, its permanent associates, its academic guests from other American universities provided such an intellectually vibrant atmosphere and scholarly support that it was a pleasure for me to return to this project at various times over the past few years. Above all, the Center served as a superb place for the recruitment of top-level student talent, whose assistance helped in the completion of this project. Here I would like to mention Karen Donfried, who, during the course of her doctoral studies at the Fletcher School of Law and Diplomacy at Tufts University, proved immensely valuable in the categorization of hundreds of newspaper clippings and other sources of information. Gregory Wilpert from Brandeis University co-authored the chapter on the K-groups and terrorism. Susanne Altenburger, also from Brandeis University, did the same for the chapter on the East German Greens.

The book would not have been completed without the wonderful assistance on the part of two extremely talented young women. Both, Beth Noveck, then of Harvard now of Oxford University, and Manik Hinchey of Yale University, combined superb talents as budding professional social scientists and exacting editors in helping Phil and me merge our various drafts across a continent, write new parts where necessary and rewrite old ones which needed revision. Through their association with this volume, both women have become close personal friends and remained collaborators on current projects. Beth has co-authored with me a book-length chapter on the tormented relationship between Germans and Jews since the Second World War, which will appear in a series under the auspices of the Holocaust Memorial Center, edited by David Wyman and published by Johns Hopkins University Press. This study will furnish the third part of my promised trilogy on postwar Germany and key aspects and institutions of its democracy. Alas, it will also be the least optimistic of the three. Manik continues to conduct research with me on Germany's hegemonic role in the new Europe, which, too, seems to offer little cause for elation. Beth's and Manik's intellect, industriousness, humor and dedication serve as constant reminders of those rare moments when being a teacher appears truly a privilege and joy. I would like to express my deep appreciation to the Program for the Study of Germany and Europe at the Center for European Studies at Harvard University, whose financial generosity made it possible for me to hire these talented young people to participate in various stages of this project.

Lastly, I would like to thank the wonderful people at Polity Press in England. David Held's encouraging faxes, Debbie Seymour's and Gil Motley's managerial competence coupled with a wonderful sense of humor made all forms of transatlantic communication enjoyable as well as efficient. I owe a special gratitude to Ann Bone, whose editorial skills were so impressive and meticulous that – far from finding her comments and queries annoying or tedious – I marveled at their ability to improve the text in style and clarity by levels I had never experienced before. I also appreciated Ann's consistent good cheer and friendly demeanor in our countless telephone conversations regardless of the day and hour when they occurred. David Roll of Oxford University Press in New York also proved a thoughtful and encouraging editor. He, like all others mentioned in these acknowledgments, deserves much of the credit for this book's merits. Its shortcomings, however, remain my sole responsibility.

Andrei S. Markovits

Abbreviations

AD Action Directe – Direct Action
AGDF Aktionsgemeinschaft Dienst für Frieden – Action Community Service for Peace
AL Alternative Liste – Alternative List
ALB Air Land Battle
APO Ausserparliamentarische Opposition – Extraparliamentary Opposition
ASF Aktion Sühnezeichen/Friedensdienst – Action Sühnezeichen/ Service for Peace
AStA Allgemeiner Studentenausschuss – University Student Council
A3W Aktion 3. Weg – Action for a Third Way
AUD Aktion Unabhängiger Deutscher – Independent Germans' Action
BBU Bundesverband der Bürgerinitiativen für Umweltschutz – Federal Association of Citizens' Initiatives for Environmental Protection
BDA Bundesverband der Deutschen Arbeitgeberverbände – Federal Association of German Employers' Federations
BUF Bundeskonferenz Unabhängiger Friedensgruppen – Federal Conference of Independent Peace Groups
BUU Bürgerintiative Umweltschutz Unterelbe – Citizens' Initiative for Environmental Protection on the Lower Elbe
BuVo Bundesvorstand – Federal party executive committee
CCC Cellules Communistes Combattantes – Communist Fighting Cells
CDU Christlich Demokratische Union – Christian Democratic Union
CI Citizens' Initiative
CSU Christlich Soziale Union – Christian Social Union
DA Demokratischer Aufbruch – Democratic Awakening
DBD Demokratische Bauernpartei Deutschlands – German Democratic Farmers' Party

DFG/VK Deutsche Friedensgesellschaft/Vereinigte Kriegsdienstverweigerer
– German Peace Society/United Conscientious Objectors
DGB Deutscher Gewerkschaftsbund – German Trade Union Federation
DKP Deutsche Kommunistische Partei – German Communist Party
DSU Deutsche Soziale Union – German Social Union
DVU Deutsche Volksunion – German People's Union
EDC European Defence Community
EKD Evangelische Kirchengemeinschaft Deutschlands – Council of
German Evangelical Churches
FDP Freie Demokratische Partei – Free Democratic Party
FRG Federal Republic of Germany
Fundis Fundamentalists
GAL Grüne Alternative Liste – Green Alternative List
GAZ Grüne Aktion Zukunft – Green Action Future
GDR German Democratic Republic
GIM Gruppe Internationale Marxisten – Group of International Marxists
GLU Grüne Liste Umweltschutz – Green List for Environmental
Protection
GNU Gesellschaft für Natur und Umwelt – Society for Nature and
Environment
GSG-9 Bundesgrenzschutzgruppe 9 – Border Protection Unit 9
GVP Gesamtdeutsche Volkspartei – All-German People's Party
IDJ Initiative Demokratie Jetzt – Initiative Democracy Now
IFM Initiative für Frieden und Menschenrechte – Initiative for Freedom
and Human Rights
Jusos Jungsozialisten – Young Socialists
KAB Kommunistischer Arbeiterbund – Communist Workers' Federation
KB Kommunistischer Bund – Communist Federation
KBW Kommunistischer Bund Westdeutschlands – Communist
Federation of West Germany
KdA Kampf dem Atomtod – Campaign Against Nuclear Death
KfA Kampf für Abrüstung – Campaign for Disarmament
KfDA Kampf für Demokratie und Abrüstung – Campaign for Democracy
and Disarmament
K-groups Communist groups
KOFAZ Komitee für Frieden, Abrüstung und Zusammenarbeit –
Committee for Peace, Disarmament and Cooperation
KPD Kommunistische Partei Deutschlands – Communist Party of Germany
KPD-AO Kommunistische Partei Deutschlands–Aufbau Organisation –
Communist Party of Germany–Reconstruction Organization)
KPD-ML Kommunistische Partei Deutschlands–Marxisten Leninisten –
Communist Party of Germany–Marxist Leninist
KPW Kommunistische Partei Westdeutschlands – Communist Party of
West Germany
LDPD Liberal-Demokratische Partei Deutschlands – Liberal Democratic
Party of Germany

MSB-Spartakus Marxistischer Studentenbund–Spartakus – Marxist Students' League–Spartakus

NATO North Atlantic Treaty Organization

NDPD National Demokratische Partei Deutschlands – National Democratic Party of Germany (East Germany)

NOW National Organization for Women

NPD Nationaldemokratische Partei Deutschlands – National Democratic Party of Germany (West Germany)

NRW North Rhine-Westphalia

OPEC Organization of Petroleum Exporting Countries

PCF Parti Communiste Français – French Communist Party

PDS Partei des Demokratischen Sozialismus – Party of Democratic Socialism

PFLP Popular Front for the Liberation of Palestine

PSP Pacifistisch Socialistische Partij – Pacifist Socialist Party

PSU Parti Socialiste Unifié – Socialist Union Party

RAF Rote Armee Fraktion – Red Army Faction

Realos Realists

RGO Revolutionäre Gewerkschaftsopposition – Revolutionary Union Opposition

RZ Rote Zellen – Red Cells

SALZ Sozialistisches Arbeiter- und Lehrlingszentrum – Socialist Workers' and Apprentices' Center

SB Sozialistisches Büro – Socialist Office

SDS Sozialistischer Deutscher Studentenbund – Socialist German Students' League

SED Sozialistische Einheitspartei Deutschlands – Socialist Unity Party of Germany

SHB Sozialdemokratischer Hochschulbund – Social Democratic University League

SPD Sozialdemokratische Partei Deutschlands – Social Democratic Party of Germany

SPK Sozialistisches Patienten Kollektiv – Socialist Patients' Collective

SPÖ Sozialistische Partei Österreichs – Austrian Socialist Party

Spontis Spontaneists

SPV Sonstige Politische Vereinigung–Die Grünen – Miscellaneous Political Union–The Greens

SRP Sozialistischer Reichs Partei – Socialist Reich Party

Taz *Die Tageszeitung*

UFV Unabhängiger Frauenverband – Independent Womens' League

USP Umweltschutz Partei – Environmental Protection Party

WEU West European Union

WG Wohngemeinschaft – Living commune

WGA Wählergemeinschaft Atomkraft, Nein Danke! – Voters' League, . Nuclear Power, No Thanks!

Introduction

We see the central task of this book as providing some answers to a few rather simple questions: Why have the Greens substantially transformed politics in the Federal Republic of Germany during the course of the 1980s? How have they managed to transform the style and output of the German Left to such an enormous degree? And finally, what has made the German Greens the most prominent and potent expression of a new politics in the advanced capitalist states, a politics often characterized as "postmodern," denoting the diminution of traditional categories of political thinking and action? Put simply, what rendered the Greens into the most influential anti-establishment party in Europe, possibly in the industrial, capitalist world?

As is evident, our complex of issues requires a comparative approach. We propose to examine the development of the German Greens on both a general and a particular level. In this chapter, we will focus mainly on the former. It is possible, in our estimation, to discern a cluster of independent variables which contributed to the rise of green politics in most economically developed states.[1] Despite considerable variations in strength and orientation, green parties have succeeded in altering the political discourse and "political space" throughout the countries of the advanced industrial world, including Japan. Indeed, these green parties and movements seem to have effected lasting changes in the social cleavage schemes and political party structures which dominated politics in these societies from the end of the First World War.[2] Although the main fault lines of politics there still run along the old axis of the owner–worker cleavage (that is, essentially the management of the industrial conflict concerning production and (re)distribution), a new set of "postindustrial" conflicts has emerged, centering primarily on the improvement (or preservation) of the environment, quality of life, and the politics of (no) growth.

While the development of green political potential can in part be traced back to a set of secular trends, the institutionalization of this potential was deeply influenced by domestic political circumstances. Thus, in the second part of this introduction, we will seek to explain why in the course of the 1970s and 1980s – the green movement's golden era – green parties became important political players in some countries and not in others. In other words, we will attempt to isolate those factors which contributed to successful green "party formation."

In the third part of the introduction – as well as much of this book – we turn to an in-depth examination of the Greens in the Federal Republic of Germany and in particular of their Germanness. By Germanness, we mean first of all, the peculiarities of German political development since the Second World War. But we also mean the fearful historical legacy left by the war itself. Boldly put, we believe that there are direct – if usually hidden – links between Auschwitz and the Greens. It is this connection, we believe, that has made the German Greens so complex, misunderstood, uncanny and contradictory, both for participants and observers, and which has, in fact, added to their political significance both inside and outside the Federal Republic. In a sense, then, we view the Greens as a particular historical expression of the German Left and, as such, as yet another complicated facet of the perennial "German question." Bespeaking the complexity of German history in the twentieth century and its continued legacy to this day is the fact that the entity of "Germany" was not decided definitively until October 3, 1990. From May 1949 until October 3, 1990, the zones occupied by the United States, Great Britain and France following the defeat of the Nazis comprised what became known as the Federal Republic of Germany, also conveniently called West Germany. In response to the Western creation of the Federal Republic, the former Soviet-occupied eastern zone became the German Democratic Republic in early October 1949, also known as East Germany. With the disappearance of this entity and its absorption by – or implosion into – the former West Germany, the term "Federal Republic of Germany" – once denoting only West Germany – now applies to both previous Germanies, East and West. In most of our analysis the "Federal Republic" will refer to West Germany alone. Yet, in numerous instances, it will also mean the recently unified East and West Germany. We believe that the reader will have few problems discerning the difference between the two since the contexts in which the term will be used will serve in a clarifying manner. Nevertheless, the occasional confusion and double entendre of the text serve as excellent replicas of their parallels in reality where a country's name such as the "Federal Republic" is indeed ambiguous. Telling of the partly unresolved complexity of the "German question," there are no equivalent ambiguities concerning the names of "France," "Italy," the "United States" or "Mexico," for example. Such are the trials and tribulations of German identity and politics in the twentieth century of which the Greens are an essential part.

Throughout the book, we are concerned with describing and analyzing the changing face of one of the most important and traditional Lefts in Europe. Before the advent of the Greens, the Left in Germany and elsewhere pursued a politics of "progress" defined by the goals of social equality and political justice. Though its goals were universalistic, the Left looked principally to the working class for their realization. Indeed, left-wing intellectuals had regarded the working class as the chief agent of historical change since the nineteenth century. In Germany, the birthplace of Marxian socialism, this symbiotic relationship between class interest and social progress was especially meaningful. Nazism itself was in part a backlash against the growing political power of the working class in Germany. But while the Nazi episode deeply affected the outlook of the German Left, it was not until the 1980s that the axiomatic link between the Left and the workers' movement was seriously challenged. The "greening" of the German Left did not mean the disappearance of "red" politics. Henceforth, however, the German Left was to become increasingly "multicolored."

In part at least, the declining hegemony of the red Left was caused by changes in capitalist production which antedated the rise of green challengers. As early as the late 1960s, fundamental structural transformations were underway, which left the working class increasingly fragmented. At the same time, the rapid changes in the nature of production changed the social composition of the working class. Thus, the shift from the previous system of regimented assembly-line mass production, often referred to as "Fordism," to a more group-oriented and flexible manner of production called "post-Fordism" entailed a concomitant shift within the working class. "Classical" or "Fordist" workers – mainly blue-collar, skilled, male and in heavy industries – became less prominent at the cost of "post-Fordist" workers comprised of professionals, clerical employees and state-sector people. All these formed what became known as the "new class" which, in its social composition, political aspirations and cultural expressions, was profoundly different from its "old," industrial predecessor. A new milieu of working-class politics emerged in the wake of the transition from Fordism to post-Fordism.

While this transition caused considerable dislocation in the West, it contributed to an already increasing economic stagnation of the East. Although the precipitous collapse of Eastern European Communism in 1989 was long in the making, its timing surely had something to do with this system's inability to adapt to changes in global capitalism.

The deepening crisis of Leninist-style Communism itself had a profound effect on the West European Left as a whole. But here, too, Germany occupied a unique position. No other western country was so directly and so deeply affected by the revolution in Eastern Europe as was the Federal Republic. Conversely, in no other East European nation were leftist visions and projects so hegemonic "after the fall" as in the German Democratic Republic. Indeed, academics and intellectuals in the new Germany were themselves united by their hopes for a "third way" between capitalism and state socialism.

What Were the Structural Preconditions for the Emergence of Green Issues, Politics and Movements in Advanced Capitalist Societies, or the Greening of Progressive Politics in the First World?

The 1960s experience As attested by the many 20-year anniversary celebrations and retrospectives in the US, France, Italy, Germany and elsewhere, the "sixties" marked a watershed in the political history of the West. It is not by chance that people still speak nostalgically or derisively about this period, for the late 1960s brought a deep change in values, ideology and politics among a large segment of the public.

The sixties, however, evoke not only a time but a generation. In 1968 – as in 1848 – a new political generation arrived which, through its political activism and outlook, posed a direct challenge to the establishment. The "sixty-eighters" – or *soixante-huitards* – were first of all a demographic phenomenon. Born in the late 1940s and early 1950s, they were products of the baby boom which followed the Second World War. Demographics alone, however, did not define them; instead, it was their common life experiences which constituted them as a generation.[3] Reared in an era of unprecedented affluence and stability, this generation revolted against the perceived conformity and complacency of its parents. It urged a new daring and optimism in all things, but especially in politics.[4]

The new class The last 25 years have witnessed a radical change in the class structures of the advanced capitalist societies. On the one hand, the traditional working class – that is, the male, blue-collar worker – has experienced rapid decline. On the other, the expansion of the service sector has swelled the ranks of white-collar workers dramatically. As the social basis of the traditional Left shrank, increasing attention was focused on the political orientation of this "new class."

By the late 1960s, a vast literature had already arisen concerning this question.[5] While most authors agreed about the magnitude of the change, few concurred about its political implications. Optimists contended that the "new working class" would infuse a radicalizing element into an "old" working class that was increasingly adopting bourgeois values and lifestyles. The end of the "end of ideology" was at hand.[6] A monotonous and heteronomous work environment, they argued, made the "new middle class" more alienated than its predecessors. This, in addition to the higher level of education attained by the members of this class, rendered it less docile and compliant than the traditional working class had apparently become.

A more pessimistic interpretation saw this "new class" as a deradicalizing and de-ideologizing influence.[7] Drawing on findings in which upward mobility and white-collar work seemed to encourage conformity and moderation, this analysis focused on the centrist impetus of this social development.[8] This argument held that the self-consciously middle class identity of the new white-collar workers distanced them from traditional, working-class concerns. This in turn would increase the quiescence of the blue-collar workers.

Closely related to the foregoing developments was the enormous expansion of higher education during the 1960s. The quantitative pressure exerted by the baby boomers, the demand for qualified workers and the educational policies of reformist governments all played a role in this process. Colleges and universities, which had long been the providers of a classical education to the scions of a small, ascriptive elite, now increasingly became purveyors of technical training and vocationally oriented curricula geared towards a larger, quasi-meritocratic cadre of managers and bureaucrats. This trend towards the massification and Taylorization of the university was met with concerted – and often successful – resistance by the students themselves. Educational reform was therefore both a cause and a consequence of the sixties.

By the later 1960s, it had become unclear what place universities occupied in these societies. Were they first and foremost the primary loci of basic research in these countries, untainted by the political activities of their respective governments? Or, by virtue of their growing involvement in applied research, had they become partners, albeit junior ones, in the domestic and foreign policies pursued by these governments? (This was a major issue in the student rebellion in the United States and the Federal Republic, but of lesser importance in France and Italy.) Were universities primarily teaching or research institutions? What were the appropriate curricula for a rapidly expanding and socially more diversified student body? Were universities to remain the bastions of a classical humanist education or were they to become the purveyors of vocationalism? Who was to make such decisions? The struggle over the university opened into a wider set of issues, politicizing many students.

Historically, of course, students have been in the vanguard of many social movements.[9] But they attained unprecedented importance in the 1960s. This was due, first of all, to their sheer numerical weight. However, it derived also from the importance of post-secondary education in advanced capitalist societies. The "megaversity" had become increasingly indispensable – as a locus of research, teaching, training, strategizing, integrating, weaning and deciding in modern society.[10] Indeed, one of the distinctive features of modern capitalism has been precisely the presence of an extensive and diversified system of higher education.

Whatever else universities became in the course of the 1960s, they most certainly became more bureaucratic. As such, they exhibited the dialectics of all modern bureaucracies. On the one hand, by including hitherto excluded social groups, the bureaucratized university fulfilled an important democratizing task in these countries. Especially in Europe, it was in the course – and the wake – of the sixties and its reforms that the children of the middle and lower middle classes as well as at least a somewhat respectable number of working-class representatives entered universities as students rather than custodians. (This is not to suggest that universities became egalitarian institutions. Nor is it to deny the existence of tracking mechanisms – themselves the result of curricular reforms – which helped perpetuate and legitimate existing inequalities.[11])

Nevertheless, bureaucratization changed the mission, shape and entire habitus of the university – and the very experience of higher education. For in breeding size, distance and impersonality, bureaucracy increased alienation among students, and even faculty. To many, the "megaversity" seemed but another branch of the "culture industry." Like the state, multinational companies, political parties, churches, and unions, the university was another bureaucratic institution oriented toward controlling the minds of individuals.

Yet it was precisely in such bureaucratic institutions and especially in the state that many of these new university graduates found employment during the early 1970s. They served as teachers, administrators, health and social workers in the rapidly growing and diversifying public sector, forming the core of a growing category of workers whom Claus Offe and others have perceptively termed "decommodified" labor.[12] As we will see, it is precisely from this milieu that the Greens in West Germany and elsewhere drew the majority of their activists, members, voters and sympathizers.[13] Thus, in this sense, too, the rise of the Greens was inextricably tied to the expansion of the welfare state and the etatist reforms of enlightened technocrats in the wake of the student revolts.

Post-Fordism and the end of the social-democratic compromise   The "material basis" for reforms in higher education and the expansion of the state sectors during the late 1960s and early 1970s was a global economic boom. Prosperity nurtured rising expectations. In countries such as the Federal Republic and Italy, labor became restive. Led by unions, workers demanded major wage hikes to keep pace with the surge in profits. The September strikes in West Germany and the Italian "hot autumn," when union-led strikes and working-class militance attained unprecedented gains for organized labor, established a certain theoretical as well as strategic link between the causes of the old blue-collar and the new white-collar Left. It was to a large extent this successful mobilization of labor which revived old Leninist ideas for the faltering student movements and infused their successors with a variety of Leninist interpretations of Marxism which were concretized in the communist "groupuscules" in cities such as Berlin, Paris and Milan.

During the late 1960s, the unions achieved the highest wage packages in the postwar era.[14] In this, they were surely aided by general prosperity and a tight labor market. But the success and character of this labor mobilization also owed a good deal to the student rebellions. Student radicals joined labor's ranks as staff economists or in some other intelligentsia-type role, changing labor's agenda in the process. As always, the relationship between Marxist intellectuals and union administrators remained tense, but the influence of the intellectuals led labor to emphasize new issues in its collective bargaining and its demands vis-à-vis the state. Issues such as quality of work life, workplace democracy, worker participation in decision making and worker control of production began to receive serious attention in most of Western Europe and – to a lesser extent – in the United States.[15]

At the same time, however, the very nature of capitalist production was undergoing a deep restructuring. However one chooses to label it – "post-industrial," "technetronic" or otherwise – there can be no doubt that a new epoch in the history of capitalism had begun.[16] Of key importance to this process was the increasing centrality of information and knowledge. These new developments not only altered the social composition of the work force (as discussed above); they changed the consciousness of citizens, disturbed established divisions between private and public, and eventually affected the entire form and content of politics. It was a period of boundless optimism which was to end with the crisis of the mid-1970s.

The collapse in 1971 of the Bretton Woods arrangement, which had defined the framework of international trade and finance through the entire postwar period, marked the end of an era. Suddenly, the Keynesian paradigm, which consisted of a policy of full employment based on the primacy of consumption and a strategy of demand-led growth – a policy that had proven so complementary to the social-democratic compacts of the 1960s – began to run into serious trouble on all fronts. The boom of the late sixties and early seventies, coupled with American expenditures in connection with the Vietnam war, fueled global inflation. More importantly, perhaps, the underlying motor of Keynesianism – sustained, demand-led macroeconomic growth – came to a sudden halt in the wake of the first oil shock of late 1973/early 1974, and never regained its previous vigor and consistency. Various austerity measures implemented by (neo)corporatist conflict management schemes replaced Keynesianism as the hegemonic economic strategy of most capitalist countries. These corporatist arrangements witnessed a close institutional cooperation among elites representing the interests of capital, labor and the state respectively. This tripartite relationship assumed both formal and informal dimensions just as it affected a wide range of policy areas, from economic and social to foreign and cultural. With growth either stuck or sluggish, the generous distributive policies so essential to social democracy's political success became increasingly more difficult to implement. Ironically, belt-tightening measures hit hardest among social democracy's strongest supporters. Workers were asked to reduce their wage demands and lower their reformist expectations vis-à-vis the state. With austerity the order of the day, certain social expenditures, which were to benefit the less endowed socioeconomic strata in these countries, were either substantially cut or eliminated altogether.[17] In addition to the working class, it was also "social democracy's children," to use Willy Brandt's apt characterization, who suffered from these cutbacks. For the reduction of public-sector expenditures also squeezed health and social workers, teachers, welfare-state bureaucrats, students on state loans and scholarships. Decommodified labor, largely a creation of social-democratic reformers, suddenly found itself a victim of social-democratic budget slashers. (Although social-democratic parties did not govern everywhere, for example,

Italy and France, this was an age of social democracy in the sense that social democracy was an economic arrangement rather than simply the formal exercise of state power on the part of a social-democratic or socialist party.)

At the same time, social-democratic etatism was under attack from the right. In its stead, conservatives proffered various neo-liberal and neo-conservative economic strategies which emphasized the primacy of the market as the major locus and motor of economic production and allocation. Following the second oil shock of 1979, virtually every capitalist country's economic strategy began to tilt toward the market. While anti-etatist rhetoric was most strident in Margaret Thatcher's Great Britain and Ronald Reagan's United States, market-led and monetarist policies were quietly pursued on the Continent, regardless of the party in power.

The economic malaise – and the apparent lack of panaceas – also sparked a critical response on the left. The oil shocks made it clear to many in the West that the very commodity which had (literally) fueled postwar industrial growth was in limited supply and beyond the political control of the First World. The recognition that economic growth had inherent limits issued into a powerful normative critique of growth itself.

A central episode in this process of rethinking on the left was the accident at Three Mile Island in March 1979. Precisely at the moment when technocrats were trumpeting nuclear power as a potential replacement for oil and the basis for the capitalist world's energy independence, this incident served to underscore the worries that the public had long harbored vis-à-vis nuclear power. The delegitimation of nuclear power led many to question both the feasibility *and* the desirability of sustained economic growth, which had long been the central rallying point for social democrats of all stripes.

The question of growth – its potential role in the achievement of a better society – became *the* central issue separating the ranks of the "old" (red) and the "new" (green) Left. Thus, in the course of the late 1970s and the early 1980s, the anti-capitalism of many sixty-eighters increasingly found expression in an opposition to unbridled economic growth. At the same time, the wave of anti-growth sentiment swept a new generation of protesters (and sometimes older generations as well) into the environmental and anti-nuclear movements. The most committed and vocal segments of the Left were quickly "going green."

This internal, ideological shift within the Left corresponded in certain ways to changes which were occurring within the structure of capitalism itself. On the one hand, markets were becoming increasingly global. On the other, industrial production assumed a growing regionalization. These two movements – one from above, the other from below[18] – were rapidly undermining the etatist political and economic strategies of the old Left. Bureaucracy was not only undemocratic. It had become ineffective as well. Managing a "post-Fordist" economy necessitates social and political arrangements different from the Keynesian welfare state and industrial mass production. Like neo-conservative "market-led" strategies, the green call to "think globally and act locally" can be seen as a response to a post-Fordist world.

The exhaustion of classical ideology The great ideologies which have dominated the postwar era – liberalism, Marxism-Leninism and social democracy – were all born during the nineteenth century. In the battle against fascism, they forged a shortlived alliance whose collapse ushered in the era of Cold War confrontation. Liberalism, represented by America, opposed Marxism-Leninism, embodied by the Soviet Union, with social democracy geographically and politically squeezed between the two. Especially during the last decade, these ideologies have each been challenged by profound – in some cases even lethal – crises.

The crisis of liberalism has been inextricably linked to the crisis of America as the leader of global democracy. The United States suffered its first loss of legitimacy during the Vietnam war. This, as well as subsequent foreign adventures of shorter duration and smaller scale, made clear to many that a country domestically governed by liberal democracy could very well behave in an imperial(ist) fashion in its external relations. But this decline in prestige was largely confined to a comparatively narrow strata of students, intellectuals and radicals. The various political scandals and social ills which beset America in the 1970s and 1980s – Watergate, Irangate, the proliferation of urban crime, drugs, the death of America's inner cities, homelessness, poverty, and a general decay in civic culture – spread disillusionment and even cynicism among the wider population as well. By the mid-1980s, America also found its economic hegemony in decline. Towering and seemingly intractable deficits in payments and trade, and the economic successes of Japan and the "four tigers" in Asia, also seemed to accentuate the weaknesses of the American political system.

It remains to be seen whether this signifies a crisis of the American political economy or of liberalism *per se*, but there can be no doubt about the ignominious and utter demise of Marxism-Leninism. With the collapse of the Soviet Union in December 1991, Marxism-Leninism as a model of economic, political and social development lost its empirical reference point. Disillusion with Soviet-style Communism among – admittedly limited – elements of the European Left began much earlier. Indeed, by the time the Red Army brutally crushed the Prague Spring in 1968, the Soviet Union had already become an anti-model for proto-green segments of the left. Despite a small and shortlived resurgence of Communist sectarianism (see below), the 1970s witnessed a decisive delegitimation of the Soviet Union as a model for anything among most western progressives. Democratic rhetoric thinly cloaked an unresponsive gerontocracy which crushed personal choice, freedom of the individual and critical thinking beneath a clumsy and inefficient bureaucracy. Following its early advances in industrialization – achieved through forced collectivization at the expense of millions of lives – and technological development (symbolized by Sputnik), the Soviet Union limped sorely behind the West, excelling only as a prolific polluter and a producer of nuclear power. If the Left's hatred and antipathy towards Communism was perhaps less marked than its negative feelings toward liberalism, it was not until the peace initiatives of Mikhail Gorbachev that this Left found anything to admire about the Soviet Union. Apart from blemishing the world "socialism" for decades to come, the collapse of the Soviet Union resulted in few positive legacies for the Left in Europe and the advanced industrial world. As we have already seen, social democratic reform efforts were slowed, halted and even reversed during the mid-to-late 1970s by a long and severe economic crisis. And given the subsequent structural changes in the world economy – the transition to post-Fordism – it remains unclear whether the old recipe of Keynesianism and redistribution is still viable.[19] Whatever the case, by the early 1980s, substantial segments of the Left had turned their attention to "postmaterial" issues such as peace, the environment, and individual autonomy, most of which seemed beyond the immediate "material" purview of conventional "bread and butter" concerns. Green critics did more than merely introduce new foci. They not only questioned social democracy's policy mix but its very world-view, with its trust in bureaucracy and technology, its focus on prosperity and security, and its vision of progress and universalism. Thus, as we will see, in its most trenchant expressions, green thinking began to attack social democracy at its Enlightenment roots.

Postmaterialism and the new social movements   During the 1970s, researchers detected a dramatic shift toward what came to be called "postmaterial" values, preferences, lifestyles. Of special consequence politically were changing attitudes vis-à-vis the relationship between the private and the public. The traditional boundaries, so essential to the modern liberal order, were either becoming blurry or were altogether redrawn, heralding a consciously confusing arrangement of values and traditions which was later to be labeled "postmodern." Postmaterial value orientations – and with them, new understandings of the public and the private – seemed most pronounced among the (growing) minority of university educated, decommodified young people. While their origins and character remained a subject of debate, postmaterial values[20] – most researchers agreed – were directly opposed to the very materialist values of social-democracy. Thus, it is not surprising that postmaterialism found its most potent political expression outside the established Left in the motley configuration of "new social movements."

A vast literature has emerged around the "new social movements."[21] Not surprisingly, it is richest in those countries where the movements have been strongest such as in the Federal Republic.[22] Perhaps the most interesting aspect of this literature is the debate concerning the "newness" of these movements, that is, how they differ from "old" movements and especially the labor movement. Rather than recount the debate in its entirety, we will simply enumerate some of the features of these movements which scholars[23] have identified as new.

Unlike old movements, which concentrated on the expansion of rights, the new social movements devote their energy to the expansion of "autonomy." Using T. H. Marshall's trilogy of civil, political and social rights, one could array the old movements along a spectrum: the battle for civil and political citizenship was fought by the liberal bourgeoisie, while the struggle for social rights was the work of the workers' movement. While the new social movements – and especially the women's movement – continue to strive for the expansion of these rights and their extension to all citizens, their overriding concern is the establishment of group (as well as individual) autonomy vis-à-vis the state, the economy and all large organization. The goal of these new movements is the complete sovereignty of the individual in action and thought. The concern with autonomy – just like their preoccupation with the avoidance of "dread" (*Angst*)[24] – does not lend itself readily to the politics of interest and compromise, favoring instead a politics of emotions and morality (*Gesinnungspolitik*).[25] In contrast to the old politics of material distribution, the new politics of autonomy tends to be zero–sum.

In contrast to the socialist movements, the new social movements generally eschew comprehensive visions or theories. Instead, they tend to prefer an often incoherent and sometimes contradictory catch-all construct of complaints, frustrations and demands which do not amount to a unified whole. While this may not be tantamount to a postmodern "anything goes" relativization, it certainly conveys the new social movements' deepseated suspicion towards any of the old – or for that matter old new – Left's belief in all-encompassing ideological constructs. It is precisely for this reason that members of the old Left as well as staunch sixty-eighters have on occasion accused participants in the new social movements for being too atheoretical or even anti-theoretical.

The new social movements are rarely interest based. Instead, they tend to be preoccupied with the preservation and enhancement of collective goods. For them, collective purpose always overrides private interests. This is why the level of professionalization in green parties (or parties anchored in green movements) is so low. As a rule, the green parties include few if any apparatchiks or "notables" who live "off" or "for" politics. Instead, the parties are usually run by "postmaterialist entrepreneurs," whose incomes derive from some combination of parttime work (often in the grey market), non-specific party employment, public remuneration (for electoral office), the state bureaucracy or social assistance. In a word, they live within the decommodified interstices of advanced capitalism. Thus, in contrast to traditional politicians who seek to accumulate wealth and power in the course of a political career, green "entrepreneurs" are motivated principally by "ideal interests," seeking wealth mainly as a material basis for their political activities.[26]

Typically, participants in the new social movements do not define the collectivity in class terms, as has been the case with all expressions of the labor movement and most manifestations of the Left. (Nor, of course, do they define it in the racial or ethnic terms of fascism.) Rather, they understand the collectivity in one of two ways: either as the "species" (*Gattung*), that is, humanity as a whole; or as a "milieu," grounded in face-to-face interaction and shared lifestyle. They seek to reconcile these two notions of collectivity through a belief in "unity in diversity" via a "politics of identity."

The new social movements' major opponent is not a class of owners but the state, the mega-organization, the mega-bureaucracy, the mega-machine. All of these institutions of modern life are evil and dangerous by virtue of their size, which necessarily renders them undemocratic, unresponsive, irresponsible and heteronomous. Their size and built-in bureaucratic rigidity distance these institutions from their original mandate, which was first and foremost to serve people and their needs. Thus, to adherents of the new social movements, nuclear energy is evil not only because it involves a product which is dangerous to the community's health but because it is, by its very nature, large-scale in expenditure, in organization, in deployment. Nuclear installations, precisely because of their importance to a country's energy sources and defense-related industries, need a big apparatus of protection. Thus, to the activists of the new social movements, there exists a compelling link between the evils of the "nuclear state" (*Atomstaat*) and those of the "security state" (*Sicherheitsstaat*).[27]

Unlike earlier post-second World War movements of the 1950s and even the 1960s (peace, anti-nuclear, ban-the bomb, student movements) the "new" social movements were neither created by nor in any way dependent on any resources of the established political parties (although they may now profit from the public resources controlled by the green parties). Hence the activists of the new social movements have not been absorbed by various institutions of the established Left as was previously the case with student radicals and other activists who, following their "movement" days, often found employment in the ranks of the parties and unions comprising the established Left. Thus, the new social movements have created a political infrastructure outside of that maintained by the established parties.

Participants in the new social movements do not perceive themselves as revolutionary – at least not in the strict Leninist sense of an avant-garde party. Typically, they insist on using mainstream channels to broadcast and achieve their political goals. Thus, new social movements have always been involved in electoral politics, run candidates for office and in general pursued their "civic duties" as conventional pressure groups. At the same time, they have sought to legitimate new kinds of political participation and expression, particularly extraparliamentary and extrainstitutional forms of involvement, with their corresponding strategies of civil disobedience, demonstrations and the physical occupation of sites in dispute to further their cause.

Participation in new social movements entails both a personal as well as political transformation. Indeed, it is a *sine qua non* that both occur simultaneously and with substantial commitment. Membership and activism inside new social movements is quite different from, say, membership in religious sects which make no overtly political claims or, conversely, membership in conventional political organizations such as trade unions and established parties which demand no personal transformation. The new social movements see transformation on the macro and the micro level as inextricably linked. Participation in the new social movements demands a weakening of the strict separation of public and private, one of liberalism's – and modernity's – most sacred tenets. Here, the women's movement and the politics of gender have played a pivotal role. For in marked contrast to the old Left as well as the old New Left, both of which devoted much verbal encouragement and theoretical support to the equality of women but failed to translate this emancipatory idea into the daily praxis of their organizational lives, activism in the "new" social movements has certainly meant an all-encompassing effort to eradicate sexism in the public and private lives of movement members and sympathizers.

New social movements strive for what the West German Green Party activist Joschka Fischer calls "dynamic interaction" with the political mainstream. New social movements exist on the cusp between establishment and antinomy. Poised on this thin dividing edge, a movement forfeits its existence as a movement as soon as it goes too far toward the political mainstream and away from making external challenges to it. But, by the same token, if the movement ceases to draw support from society's mainstream and fails to participate in establishment politics, it will devolve into a sect. Thus, new social movements have generally welcomed the participation and support of conservative elements such as farmers or housewives whose "value conservatism" they perceive as a direct challenge to the imperatives of state bureaucracy, commodified capitalism and the industrial machine. The "establishment" and "mainstream" do not, in and of themselves, constitute negative concepts for the new social movements in the way that they clearly did for the "new" Left as well as for the "old" Left in its "countersociety" or "ghetto" phase, which lasted well into (and even beyond) the 1950s in most advanced capitalist countries. On the other hand, new social movements have been self-conscious about retaining their "movement" character and their system-challenging nature. Therefore, new social movements are continuously compelled to walk this tightrope between systemic challenge and cooptation.

New social movements rely very much on their own milieu, just as the working-class movement in its early phases did. Encompassing the realms of production as well as reproduction, these movements have created their own subsocieties with alternative repair shops, groceries, daycare centers, newspapers, clubs, clothing stores, medium-sized companies, language and habits. The new social movements have vastly expanded this alternative lifestyle (which was started during the hippie phase of the late 1960s and thus was very much a corollary of the New Left) and institutionalized it into an autonomous political milieu.

Lastly, new social movements attempt to formulate a non-reactionary and universalistic critique of modernity and modernization by challenging institutionalized patterns of technical, economic, political and cultural rationality. At the same time, they seek to avoid romantic idealizations of traditional institutions and arrangements such as family, small property, community, and nation. Of course, the question as to their success in this area remains an empirical – and open – one.

We have now reached the end of the first part of our introduction. In it we established some shared characteristics of all "new" social movements of the advanced capitalist world. We also sketched some of the generally shared reasons which led to the rise of these movements all over the liberal capitalist West. In the next section, we will try to highlight some of the commonalities of those countries where these movements became small but important, political parties and significant political innovators in the course of the 1980s. Thus, if the task in this section was to concentrate on the Greens as a movement and as an expression of a ubiquitous postmaterialist phenomenon, the subject matter in the next section will focus on the Greens as small but successful political parties.[28]

Why Did Successful Green Parties Develop in Some Countries and Not in Others?

Herbert Kitschelt has aptly characterized the emergent green parties as "left-libertarian."[29] Their mistrust of the marketplace, private investment and the ethic of accumulation place these parties solidly within the tradition of the Left, as do their broadly egalitarian orientations. However, in sharp contrast to the old Left, they are libertarian insofar as they reject the bureaucratic and etatist strategies of socialism for an emphasis on participation and democracy. In sum, left-libertarians accept important aspects of the socialist agenda while dismissing its political means and production-based identity.

Ferdinand Müller-Rommel speaks instead of "new politics" parties.[30] These parties, he contends, have had two distinct feeders. The first are "small left-wing parties" such as the Radical Party in Italy, the Pacifist Socialist Party (PSP) in the Netherlands and the Socialist Union Party (PSU) in France. These are typically New Left parties, hailing from the student movement of the mid-to-late 1960s. From their very beginning, these parties profiled themselves explicitly as left-wing alternatives to established socialist, social-democratic and communist parties. Their supporters were predominantly leftist rather than postmaterialist. While their members and supporters hailed mainly from the decommodified realm, these parties were definitely more "red" than "green," more "socialist" than "oppositionist," more "productivist" than "ecological."

In contrast to these small left-wing parties, Müller-Rommel discerns a second group of "newly founded green parties" which are creations of the mid-to-late 1970s. While the composition of their membership is quite similar to those of the new politics parties, the newly founded green parties exhibit a greater ideological heterogeneity. In particular, they show a more pronounced affinity for postmaterialism and a distancing from all varieties of socialism. Although still part of the Left, these newly founded green parties were a good deal more suspicious of, in certain cases even hostile to, Marxism of the old or new Left than were the small left-wing parties of the late 1960s. These two party types merged formally, creating the uneasy alliance which Müller-Rommel terms "new politics" parties. It is this symbiosis which has dominated the discourse of reform in certain European countries during the late 1970s and the 1980s.[31]

If we look at the countries where green parties entered the legislatures on a local and national level (ignoring for the moment less salient elections such as the ones for the European parliament) in the late 1970s and throughout the 1980s, we will note that almost without exception they had been situated in the north-central tier of Europe: Austria, Belgium, Denmark, Iceland, Luxembourg, the Netherlands, Norway, Sweden, Switzerland and West Germany. In two countries, Finland and Italy, new politics parties emerged but failed to attain anywhere near the political importance gained by their counterparts in the previous group of countries. Lastly, in all other nations of the First World, including specifically the United States, Canada, Australia, the United Kingdom, Japan, France and Spain, green parties or any others hailing from the world of the new social movements remained insignificant, even irrelevant. It is well to remember that we are here concerned with the *origin* of green party formation, not its later development. Thus, for example, by the early 1990s green parties also emerged in Spain, Greece and France. Indeed, in the latter there were two. But tellingly, these "belated" green parties had little in common with the original green parties except the name. They were either simple anti-system protest parties or ecological interest groups which decided to contest national elections. None of the green parties belonging to the latter group of countries ever attained the political significance and innovative power which characterized the emergence of their predecessors of the late 1970s and 1980s in the countries forming the first group. Whereas the nature of politics was substantially changed by the emergence of green parties in, say, Germany and Austria, this has decidedly not been the case in, say, France and Italy.

In the remainder of this section, we will seek to explain this pattern by examining several features that distinguish the first group of countries, which, for reasons that will become apparent, we will call "democratic-corporatist," from countries belonging to the other two groups.

In every single country where new politics parties attained significance, social-democratic parties either shared or exercised sole governmental power, either during the emergence of these new social movements and/or during their subsequent successful institutionalization as green parties. Kitschelt corroborates this very elegantly by demonstrating that his "left-libertarian" parties entered the political arena successfully in countries with few strikes and little labor strife. Conversely, in countries with high labor strife (as measured by lost working days per annum), such as Australia, the United States, Canada, Ireland, the United Kingdom, left-libertarian parties barely emerged and most certainly failed to attain political significance.[32] This is highly suggestive because, as Walter Korpi has demonstrated in his original work on the comparative strength of labor movements in western liberal democracies, labor strikes less in countries where it has successfully attained state power and more where it has not.[33]

Partly as a consequence of labor's strength, class conflict in these countries has become highly institutionalized in the course of the post-Second World War settlement. Replete with many "parapublic" institutions, the capital–labor contest has developed into a highly ritualized, institutionally regulated and mediated procedure in which neither side has the desire or the ability to score a knock-out victory over its opponent.[34] In these countries corporatist forms of conflict mediation are among the most important venues of political life, be it the tripartite (state–capital–labor) top-down, centralized arrangement which pervades all important aspects of the Austrian, Norwegian and Swedish political economies; the banker-led corporatism of an all-party-inclusive Switzerland; or the carefully balanced religious "consociationalism" of the Netherlands, its language-based counterpart in the Swiss case and its class-based equivalent in Austria. All these countries have developed a finely tuned extraparliamentary and paraparliamentary system of conflict resolution whose main characteristic lies in its inclusive nature. Though still saddled with the role of "countervailing power," labor has become both a major player and a key beneficiary of this deal-based system. This "pact," whose informal rules are even more important than its formally codified ones, has made labor, via its social-democratic institutions, a central actor in the "organizing" of capitalism.[35]

Due in part to labor's strength – as well as to conservative paternalism – these countries developed a tightly knit net of social protection which has become central in legitimating the political system as a whole. By cushioning the inequities of the market, the welfare state has served as the chief dispenser of collective justice. Where more pristinely capitalist societies such as the United States enshrined the value of mutual aid within the private sphere (described by George Bush as "a thousand points of light"), in these countries the state became the chief agent of collective solidarity. Here, citizens looked to state-led reforms rather than individual initiative, to provide increased individual opportunity and material security. The state did this, not only by providing a "floor" for the weakest and poorest, but by guaranteeing education, healthcare, old-age benefits and a wealth of other social services to everyone. In order to administer these programs, these states hired veritable armies of white-collar and pink-collar workers. As benefactor and as employer, then, the state created a vast decommodified realm sheltered from the rules of the market.

Propelled by the economic growth of the early 1970s, several social-democratic parties – most notably in Sweden, the Federal Republic and Austria – sought to extend the reform process into new domains. In Willy Brandt's famous phrase, they tried "to dare more democracy" by expanding individual rights, enhancing the power of labor in the workplace and liberalizing their foreign policy. The Kreisky–Brandt–Palme axis among the leaders of Austria, West Germany and Sweden contributed to a general opening of public discourse, spawned a climate of optimism and served as a forerunner and pacesetter for the new politics parties which would develop a few years later.

Beginning in the mid-to late 1970s, the social democratic reforms turned sour. Henceforth, the social democrats led a schizophrenic existence where, *qua* party of government, they slashed the very programs upon which their support, *qua* party of movement, depended. Redistributional reforms were

quickly undone and even those reforms which had altered the basic structures of capitalist accumulation – such as collective bargaining and public
ownership of major industries – quickly came under attack. In a word, social
democratic governments sought to master the economic situation largely by
forcing their own supporters to bear the costs of restructuring. Not surprisingly, this cost social democracy the support of activists of the "new" Left and
the decommodified milieu as a whole.[36] Social democracy was losing its hold
over the reform space of progressive politics in all these countries and its
supporters – whether instrumentalists or idealists – were beginning to look
for alternatives. Some would find such alternatives in the neo-conservative
resurgence, while others would form the core of the "new politics" parties.

Many in the latter group were especially concerned about the weakening
of parliamentary democracy, a potential "side-effect" of corporatism. As top-
level deal-making between organized interest groups becomes more important, the importance – and power – of parliaments and legislatures is almost
unavoidably diminished. Hence, while corporatist "pacts" provide excellent
models for the technocratic management of complex economies, and even
for the achievement of greater material equity, they also bring a decrease in
democratic accountability. Indeed, corporatist arrangements discourage participation by "disorganized" groups (that is, those which do not lie along
established social cleavages) and exclude "nonmaterial" interests (those lying
outside the realms of production and distribution). Thus, in the long run,
social democratic rule has its own de-democratizing and alienating effects.

In every single country in which "new politics" parties came to the fore in
the late 1970s, communist parties were either nonexistent or played a "junior"
role. The marginalization of communism in these countries opened a "gap"
to the left of social democracy which remained unoccupied until the arrival
of the green parties in the 1980s. In countries with strong – or even dominant
– communist parties such as Finland, France, Italy, Greece, Portugal and
Spain, new politics parties remained weak. There, communism served as the
main focus of protest and the chief alternative to social democracy.

"First-past-the post," "winner-take-all" electoral systems, such as those in the
US and Great Britain, provide an almost insurmountable barrier for the
legislative representation of new parties. In fact, all the countries where green
parties emerged in the 1980s use some sort of electoral system based on
proportional representation to choose representatives. The British Green
Party, for example, is the oldest in Western Europe. Since their founding in
1973, the British Greens have garnered considerable support, particularly
in elections to the European parliament during the late 1980s, with tallies
approaching 15 percent. Thus their failure to send a single member of parliament to Westminster can be attributed only to the hurdles presented by
the electoral system.[37]

With the exception of Belgium and Austria, all the corporatist democracies
have large Protestant majorities. In the Federal Republic of Germany, for
example, the Green Party was more successful politically and more radical
ideologically in Protestant as opposed to Catholic regions.[38] There is also some

evidence which suggests that Protestants may have been more active in the "new social movements" in Germany.[39] While more study would be necessary in order to specify the nature of the relation between religious background and political radicalism, it is evident that some association exists between Protestantism and the "new politics."[40]

This concludes the second part of the introduction. In it we suggested a number of factors which we believe explain why new social movements evolved into successful and effective new politics parties only within the corporatist democracies of north-central Europe. Within this group, the German Greens occupy a special role, for they became the most prominent and influential green party in the world. No doubt, this has something to do with the Federal Republic's sheer size and economic might, but we believe there are also other factors at work, peculiar to Germany's political history.

Why the Prominence of the Greens in the Federal Republic, or the "Germanness" of the Green Phenomenon

At first glance, the answer to the prominence of the Greens in the Federal Republic would appear to be deceptively simple. Yet we believe that the most salient reason for the Greens' political and moral significance in the public life of the Federal Republic in general and of the Left in particular is deeply connected to what one could term the "Holocaust effect." Included therein is an array of enormously sensitive issues which have lain beneath the surface of political discourse and repeatedly exploded into public life since the end of the Second World War. Whether discussed openly or not, publicly acknowledged or concealed, the burden of Germany's past impresses its potent legacy on many key aspects of contemporary Germany politics and society.[41] Central to our argument is the fact that among all comparable industrial societies, this weight of the past, in its ubiquity and gravity, has remained unique to Germany. All countries have experienced momentous events in their history which continue to remain contentious and divisive long after their conclusion. In France, even after two hundred years, the French revolution still evokes very different emotions and leads to diametrically opposed interpretations. The more recent French involvement in Algeria has left an imprint in the popularity of an openly anti-immigrant (that is, anti-Arab and de facto anti-Algerian) movement and party. With the collapse of the Soviet Union, the people of Russia and the other former republics seem poised for their own major debate concerning the legacies of Lenin and Stalin. The American Civil War by and large reached its end with the inclusion of the South into the national agenda during the course of America's economic development and as a result of the civil rights policies pursued by the Johnson administration in the mid-to-late 1960s. But the legacy of the Vietnam experience is far from over. Despite the seemingly successful conclusion of the

Gulf war and President Bush's smug declaration that America had once and for all "kicked the Vietnam syndrome," it continues to be an open wound, fostering conflict between "hawks" and "doves," right and left. Israel has its own "historians' debates" about the reception of Holocaust survivors in the Yishuv (pre-state Jewish settlements) and the events of 1948 involving the expulsion/willing departure of the Arabs. Austria's two large political "camps" (Lager) still interpret the civil war of February 1934 quite differently and the whole Anschluß question continues to raise tempers on either side of the political divide. Japan, along with Germany the major loser of the Second World War, has been deeply engaged in a national debate about the wartime role of the country's military institutions and ideology, and its relations with other Asian countries as a result of this war. Yet nowhere are events of the recent past as unresolved, painful and thus – we argue – politically meaningful as in Germany. Here, of course, one has to draw a clear distinction between the former West Germany and the former East Germany. No matter how inadequate and incomplete West Germany's coming to terms with the German past has been, it still could claim that certain events occurred in its 40-year history which fostered a public debate of this painful and irresolvable topic. The Auschwitz, Treblinka and Majdanek trials, the repeated controversy about the statute of limitations concerning National Socialist genocide, the screening of the TV soap opera "Holocaust," the Bitburg incident, the "historians' debate" and the Gulf war all raised extensive and painful debates about the German past and its relevance in West Germany. Whereas the West German state and the political class "instrumentalized" the Holocaust by depicting it as the tragic result of a madman's aberrant behavior, thereby exonerating all previous German history and the role of German (and European) capitalism, West German civil society experienced a few key incidents which made the Holocaust a known reality in the daily political presence of the Federal Republic. Most West Germans tried to avoid the subject, felt embarrassed by it, angry at it and perhaps even guilty about it; but few could deny its weighty legacy in contemporary German life even if they tried. In short, faulty as its way was, West Germany nevertheless dealt with its Nazi past in some inadequate but genuine fashion.

This process of collective reflection, it should be noted, had no parallels in the former East Germany. There, the exculpatory mechanism was rather simple: National Socialism, like any other form of fascism, was regarded as nothing but a particularly acute manifestation of capitalist class rule. Since capitalism had been superseded by socialism in the German Democratic Republic (GDR), the burdens of fascism and National Socialism had been "historically transcended." They were a problem only for the capitalist West. A policy of *verordneter Antifaschismus* (antifascism by fiat) exculpated the East Germans wholesale, by state decree "from above." This approach made Nazism a problem only of capitalism and not of Germany, particularly the "good" Germany of peasants and workers who now had "their" state in the form of the GDR. This forty-year lie was perhaps the only one which the citizens of the GDR welcomed with open arms. It conveniently made East Germans the "better" of the two kinds of Germans. East Germans might have been materially poor, economically disadvantaged, politically constrained, geographically confined and individually stymied when compared to their West German brothers and sisters but they at least had the immense satisfaction of being the anti-Nazis, the antifascists, the anticapitalists, in short the morally superior Germans. Any lie, as Goebbels so diabolically understood, becomes truth provided it is repeated with sufficient frequency. This is *a fortiori* the case with lies whose content enjoys immense legitimacy among their recipients by virtue of their exculpatory character. Thus, for example, it was not uncommon for schoolchildren in the GDR to believe that it had been an alliance of Soviet and East German troops which defeated Hitler's evil regime. Similarly, this policy of state-decreed antifascism had the GDR claim that it – unlike, of course, the Federal Republic – had successfully extirpated any form of anti-semitism. Jews were never recognized as special victims of the Third Reich. Only as "antifascists" did the few Jews who remained in (or returned to) the GDR after the war enjoy certain recompensatory benefits at the hands of the state. Needless to say, the GDR never found it necessary to engage in any restitution, material or otherwise, vis-à-vis the Jewish community collectively, be it in Israel or elsewhere. Instead, the viciousness of anti-Zionism emanating from the GDR in a systematic and massive manner for over two decades, especially after the Six-Day War of June 1967, remains perhaps unparalleled in postwar European history.

The mendacious character of this exculpatory antifascism by fiat became obvious soon after the Berlin Wall's disappearance. The brutal attacks on foreigners by neo-Nazi youths and – much more telling – the East German citizenry's tolerance, indeed approval, of these dastardly deeds clearly convey to the world that forty years of Communist dictatorship had failed abysmally to have East Germans come to terms with Germany's Nazi past. With the demise of the Communist dictatorship which – as was known to all but the most gullible believers – had its own tales of horror, there exists the real danger of yet another "crowding out" of dealing with the Nazi past in a comprehensive way in the new, united Germany, particularly in its eastern provinces which comprised the former East Germany. With the need to address the failings – and crimes – of the Communist regime, there have already emerged a number of telltale signs which lead one to fear that the "other" past – that is National Socialism – will yet again be marginalized. Particularly disturbing are clear tendencies which equate communism and National Socialism with each other. Under the guise that both were dictatorships and that both committed atrocities, there exists the movement and desire to "relativize" both, thereby coming to terms with neither.

What makes the German situation unique is the confluence of a number of potentially discrete problems, none of which have yet been fully resolved. There were many fascist movements, even governments, in Europe. None, however, killed six million Jews in a bureaucratically systematic way mandated by government policy. There were a number of losers in the Second World War; none, however, suffered the ignominy and pain of being divided as a nation for over forty years. Among the several participants in the Cold War, none were in such frontline proximity as the Germans. In short, Germany's political and moral predicament since 1945 has not only been unique among all advanced capitalist countries, but it has also created a singular atmosphere wherein the politics of the new social movements attained a particularly keen significance. In the following few pages, we would like to present some factors which have contributed to this German predicament and which, by constituting what we have termed the "Holocaust effect," have rendered the German Greens the most important "new politics" party among all green parties in Europe, indeed in the world.

The acuity of the generation gap in the Federal Republic   Cross-national surveys convey clearly that the generational cleavages in the Federal Republic are more pronounced than in other comparable liberal democracies.[42] The gap is particularly clear between the sixty-eighter generation and its parents. The parents formed the backbone of what has become known as the "silent generation," that is, the last generation to have participated fully in the German war effort as young adults. It was this generation which proved "unable to mourn" and which tried to sublimate its guilty conscience by remaining silent about the past while busily (re)constructing the Federal Republic's economic prosperity. The sixty-eighters were the first to confront their parents massively both in private and in public. Indeed, the public aspect of the student revolt in the Federal Republic has to be contextualized first and foremost as a critique of the complacency and accommodation of the Bonn republic's institutions and political culture vis-à-vis the Nazi regime. The students and their few intellectual allies outside the academic realm blamed the university, the state's bureaucracy, the market fetishism of a capitalist society and some of the country's policies for continuing the Nazi regime's very essence without its worst excesses. Not by chance, it was at this juncture that the bulk of the social science literature on "fascism," in which most authors tried for the first time to relate this concept to their country's past, appeared in the Federal Republic.[43] Significantly, the emergence of this literature and of fascism as a topic of concern to the New Left was in good part triggered by the sudden electoral successes of a far-right, crypto-Nazi party, The National Democratic Party of Germany (Nationaldemokratische Partei Deutschlands, NPD) in the wake of the Federal Republic's first recession in 1966.[44] Thus, fascism and the Bonn republic seemed quite compatible to many student activists; to some they indeed became coterminous. Hence, in notable contrast to student revolts occurring simultaneously in other advanced capitalist countries such as France, the United States and Italy, the West German New Left protested against two regimes: the current Bonn republic and its Nazi predecessor. In a mediated and frequently myopic way, this was the first time that massive protests erupted on West German soil against Germany's Nazi period. It was a flawed and belated, though none the less sincere, attempt on the part of a visible segment of the West German public to come to terms with Germany's uniquely murderous past.[45] Along with Willy Brandt's justly famous kneeling at the memorial to the Jewish victims of the Warsaw ghetto revolt, and his rapprochement with Germany's eastern sufferers through his Ostpolitik, the New Left's massive criticism of German national socialism and the Bonn republic's quiescence about it helped – perhaps indirectly, though no less decisively – to create an atmosphere of contrition, if not repentance, about the German past. This – at least until German unification in 1989 – contributed to the acceptance of the Federal Republic as a completely "normal" member of the European and global community of nations.

Confronting two regimes made the generational break more pronounced in the Federal Republic than elsewhere in the advanced capitalist world. This phenomenon is partly responsible for the continuing longevity of the student movement's legacies in the politics of the West Germany Greens. There has existed in West Germany since the late 1960s a politicized counterculture which formed the world of the new social movements and continues to surround the Greens. While this world became relegated to the realm of culture, and thereby to political irrelevance, in the case of many an activist history of the late 1960s (such as that of the American New Left), the counterculture and the sixties in West Germany have stayed alive and well in part as a consequence of the generation gap's political significance in that country.

The Federal Republic's geopolitical and geographic situation   Unlike any of the other countries with important "new politics parties," West Germany has been in the frontline of all East–West confrontations. Although Austria also bordered on Warsaw Pact countries, it has never been a member of NATO nor has it ever been divided, thus giving it a substantially different role from that of the Federal Republic in any potential war involving Eastern and Western Europe. Contrary to the increasingly frequent assertions of the West German Left and Right in the late 1980s, it is questionable whether any European war would have made only the Germans its victims ("the shorter the missiles, the deader the Germans").[46] Nevertheless, there was little doubt in the pre-1989 world that *any* war involving all but the most geographically marginal European countries (say Turkey and Greece) would inevitably involve Germany in a substantial way. Hence, pacifism – a rather widespread ideology among all of the "new" social movements – attained a clear existential dimension in addition to its moral one in the Federal Republic's "alternative" scene. West Germany's proximity to Eastern Europe and the Soviet Union, that is, its border status vis-à-vis the Warsaw Pact, rendered it the most appropriate country in which to deploy the largest number of medium-range nuclear weapons, most notably land-based Cruise and Pershing II ballistic missiles. Indeed, among the European allies of the United States, the highly accurate Pershing II missiles were deployed only in the Federal Republic. It was in part the Federal Republic's geographic location which accounted for the particularly active, massive and committed peace movement that arose in West Germany in the early 1980s in opposition to NATO's double-track decision in favor of deploying intermediate-range nuclear weapons in a number of European countries. While peace movements gained much attention in Great Britain, Holland and Belgium, nowhere did they attain the domestic as well as international centrality that they did in West Germany. The centrality of "peace" as a particularly Germany issue was corroborated convincingly during the Gulf war of 1991. While there exists ample evidence that the first German peace movement of the 1980s – the one protesting the deployment of intermediate-range nuclear missiles on German soil – had a strong, if in part still hidden, national (indeed nationalist) agenda, there can be no doubt that this movement was very European in scope since its Belgian, Dutch, Italian and British counterparts were equally active and vocal in their demands.[47] Yet, barely eight years later, the goal of peace as an ultimate end had become a virtual monopoly of the Germans. In no other European country did the Gulf war engender such fear, concern – one might say hysteria – on such a massive level in virtually every social group as it did in the newly united Germany. Reaching well beyond the countercultural milieu of the demonstrations which dominated the peace movement of the early 1980s, this "second" movement engulfed members of all political parties, and rallied a substantial number of Germany's intellectual leaders, political elite and opinion makers comprising the Federal Republic's establishment. One of the unifying themes centered on the notion that because of the thorough lesson which their terrible history had taught them, only the Germans could really appreciate and fully cherish peace. In contrast to what many Germans perceived as the inherently bellicose western powers such as Great Britain, France and above all the United States, Germany appeared to these people as a morally superior nation by reason of its sanctification of peace above any other virtue.[48] More than the randomness of the country's geographic location proved responsible for this prominence of the West German peace movement. Let us now turn to a discussion of three additional factors which we see as salient in this context.

The unresolved national question   It needs to be established from the outset that the centrality of the national question to the postwar German debate and its recent manifestations in the public realms of both East and West Germany have little to do with any nationalist sentiments on the part of Green Party members or others inside the new social movements. Indeed, there is much evidence that shows the Greens and their ancillary milieu to be the least overtly nationalistic constituency in all of the Federal Republic. Not only do activists in this milieu perceive themselves as internationalists by virtue of their preoccupation with such international issues as ecology, feminism and the exploitation of the Third World, to mention only the most prominent, but they have also been the only politically prominent group in the Federal Republic which has consistently pushed for an immediate and unconditional extension of German citizenship to all so-called "guest workers" and "foreigners" currently living in the Federal Republic. The Greens and their movement cousins have also been the most liberal in terms of opening the Federal Republic's doors as wide as possible to those seeking asylum and to other refugees, most of whom have hailed from the Third World and the poorer part of Eastern Europe.[49] Thus it would be misleading to brand the Greens and their allies as left-wing nationalists whose political agenda rested on a reunification of the two Germanies based on the old nationalist sentiments of pre-1945 Germany with some minor modifications.

Indeed, the Greens' vehement anti-nationalism led to their poor electoral showing in the first all-German Bundestag election of December 2, 1990, with the result that the West German Greens failed to attain parliamentary representation. This left the Greens' legislative role in the Bundestag to a handful of East German Greens and their allies who – as a consequence of the opposition of the Greens (both East and West) to German unification – contested this election as a separate entity apart from their larger and politically more seasoned western cousins. It is precisely because nationalism has been such an uncomfortable (perhaps even an unimportant topic) for the Greens and their milieu that one can understand the Greens' open reluctance to embrace German unity with its inevitably national – if not nationalist – overtones. One could not help but have the feeling after the fall of the Berlin wall in November 1989 that the Greens in particular and the German Left in general were somehow ashamed of, indeed opposed to, the momentous events, which began with the GDR's failure as a socialist experiment on German soil and ended with German unification.

The Greens' – and the Left's – misgivings about German nationalism went beyond caution and fear. They disclaimed it all and, more importantly, simply could not relate to it. Tellingly, the Greens and their milieu had become the most pronounced representatives of the postwar German order which – at least nominally – had become perhaps one of the least national(ist) in Europe. The West Greens were prototypical representatives of the West German Left and its milieu: more at home in the Toscana, Berkeley and Nicaragua, than in, say, Leipzig or Rostock. For the East German Greens, too, nationalism was either neutral or negative. To them, just as to the West German Left, its salience paled compared to issues such as ecology, women's (and personal) liberation, the struggle against all forms of heteronomy and – most important – the upholding of the true socialist project untainted by the bureaucratic brutality of "real existing socialism" East-German style which cynically abused the concept of "socialism" for its own inhuman ends. Indeed the Greens' reluctance to accept the new national reality and their decision to contest the December 2, 1990 election as two separate entities – East and West – contributed directly to the West Germans' failure to overcome the 5 percent hurdle exacted by the Federal Republic's electoral laws as a minimum amount of electoral votes which are necessary for representation in any legislative body, be it local, state or federal. Had the Greens campaigned in a unified manner, as all the other parties did (after all, the country had united on October 3, 1990), the electoral arithmetic would have allowed them to participate in the first all-German Bundestag as a complete party, instead of as the eastern fragment which they willy-nilly became.

However, we submit that there is some connection between German nationalism and the prominence of the West German Greens, although the Greens themselves have certainly not been nationalists. Rather, we see the importance of the West German Greens and the staying power of the new social movements in the Federal Republic in good part as a consequence of the murkiness of German identity since 1945. In no other European country – with the notable exception of East Germany – have millions belonging to the postwar generations grown up with uncertainties and stigma attached to their national identities. Swedish, Danish, Dutch, Swiss, Belgian, even Austrian, youths were not necessarily educated in a chauvinist atmosphere in which they were taught to extol everything belonging to their country at the expense of what was foreign, but they were certainly not uncertain or ashamed of their national identity. With the disappearance of hypernationalism as a politically salient factor in the Western Europe of the post-Second World War era, nationhood, as distinguished from nationalism, continued to play a role as one of many ingredients determining public identities of citizenship in liberal democracies. Thus one could be unequivocally Swedish, Danish or Dutch without at the same time representing or advocating Swedish, Danish or Dutch nationalism. In most of Western Europe, national identity just existed, stronger in some countries, less so in others. But nowhere did it result in anything like the burdens, troubles, uncertainties and ignominy that it did in the Federal Republic. Anti-communism and a rather feeble pan-European internationalism hoped to serve as viable ersatz national identities in the Federal Republic of the 1950s and 1960s. Ostpolitik shattered the former, while lengthy bureaucratic battles regarding agricultural subsidies and steel quotas dimmed the latter, with German nationalism barely becoming more acceptable in the meantime. One could not find anything comparable anywhere else in Europe. Our argument then is *not* that the Greens reintroduced nationalism as an acceptable discourse in the Federal Republic's public debate, but that the salience of the Greens and that of their "alternative" milieu in West Germany was partly shaped by the political and psychological climate in which uncertainties and difficulties associated with national identity have consistently played a key, yet – because of their nature – often unspoken, role.

The Federal Republic's relationship to the United States Whereas the United States has assumed the position of first among equals with respect to all of Western Europe since 1945, there can be no question that its position vis-à-vis the Federal Republic has been structurally rather different. In a role somewhat comparable to that which it played in relation to Japan, the United States has been the Federal Republic's creator, liberator, occupier, role model, protector, ally, rival, and bully all rolled into one.

German-American relations – in contrast to, say, Franco–American, Anglo–American or Swedish–American relations – have not only been the "normal" bilateral relations between two states with all the accompanying difficulties, strains and rewards. Beyond the manifest level of German–American relations hovers a submerged iceberg of domination, submission, gratitude, jealousy, overprotection, fear of abandonment, friendship and rivalry which is much more pronounced in this relationship than in any other the United States has had in postwar Europe. Americanism and anti-Americanism have attained a qualitatively different meaning (both positive and negative) in the Federal Republic from elsewhere in Europe. The complexity of this relationship remains inextricably tied to the continuous and widespread perceptions in the Federal Republic that – at least until October 3, 1990 – it suffered from a deficit in political sovereignty, especially vis-à-vis the United States. Thus, the West German peace movement protesting the deployment of American medium-range missiles, the Greens' desire to sever West Germany's ties to NATO, and the massive and explicitly anti-American protests engulfing this milieu during the Gulf war do not only manifest disagreements about policies and strategies between two random countries, in this case Germany and the United States. Unlike parallel developments in Britain and Spain, for example, these options also signify a battle over sovereignty, memory, history and identity. It is in this context that the American presence in the Federal Republic's existence has given the politics of protest and antinomy a particular content hardly visible in any other West European country.[50] We thus argue that the special salience of the West German Greens and their ancillary milieu, when compared with parallel developments in the previously mentioned group of north-central European countries, is inextricably tied to America's involvement in postwar German history.

Some special ingredients in the German intellectual tradition   Many Western – especially French, British and American – observers of recent political developments in the Federal Republic have emphasized the German traditions of romanticism, love of nature and antimodernism as keys to a proper understanding of the Greens' strategies and desires.[51] While we find these explanations to be somewhat simplistic and certainly reject any analyses of the Greens which try – even implicitly – to push them into an affinity with the Nazis by virtue of focusing on their shared preoccupation with nature and their common dislike for modern rationalism, there can be no doubt that some key strains in the German intellectual tradition have found their way into the Greens' *Weltanschauung*. Indeed, it would be strange not to find elements of German antinomian thought in a protest movement anchored by German intellectuals. The "new" social movements in all advanced capitalist countries comprise a head-on attack on the very premises of industrial modernization such as economic growth, bureaucratic authority, representative government and the logic of rationality. There is no difference here between German or Vermont Greens. What makes the former a good deal more potent in their respective political environment is – among many other factors delineated in this introduction – the salience of a political tradition which has advocated similar demands in the past, although frequently in completely different contexts. Thus neither of two relativizations – one cross-cultural, the other historical – seems appropriate here: it is not that antimodern thoughts and movements do not exist in advanced industrial societies other than Germany; nor is it the case that the Greens are like the Nazis by virtue of their common antimodernism (that is, that green equals brown). What we perceive as important in this context is the salience of a particular German intellectual tradition which has expressed itself with very different political voices under very different socioeconomic conditions at very different historical conjunctures.

In the body of the book, we will present an in-depth study of the Greens as a phenomenon of the Left in Germany. Although we concentrated our initial research on the old Federal Republic, the momentous events of 1989–90 led us to include an analysis of the East German Greens and their milieu. What has made this aspect of our project so exciting was to observe the fundamental similarities as well as the glaring differences between these two political entities which emerged on either side of the Berlin wall. While the book's empirical material concentrates more on the West Greens than on their East German counterparts, the latter's presentation should not be construed as an afterthought. Rather, it should illustrate how certain common issues emerged in two very different socioeconomic systems which gave rise to similar expressions of political dissent and critique. At the same time, the East German case will highlight the particularities of the West German Greens, who emerged from the very specific context of the postwar Federal Republic. We have organized our material into three parts. In part I, entitled "Predecessors," chapters 1 through 4 present a historical overview of what we perceive as the Greens' forerunners in the Federal Republic. Here we discuss key developments of the "old" as well as "new" Left which we find important for a proper understanding of the Greens. In the next part, called "Ideology and Policy," chapter 5 looks at the main pillars of green thought in a historical and comparative context. It is here that we spend some time investigating the exact nature of the Greens' antimodernism as well as other aspects of their *Weltanschauung*. Chapter 6 looks at the actual policy proposals and strategic innovations defining the political reality of the Greens. We investigate their views on issues like defense, the economy, ecology and foreign relations. Part III, entitled "Politics," provides a detailed account of the actual developments informing the Greens' political life throughout the decade of the 1980s. In chapter 7, we look at the internal debates among various factions of the party, examine how much the reality of a party has changed (and been accepted) by the movement, and assess the conflicts surrounding the party's relationship to other political actors, most notably the established representative of the "old" Left, the venerable Social Democrats. Chapter 8 examines the rise of the East German Green movement, its role in the downfall of the Communist regime, and concludes with an analysis of the East German Greens' complex relationship with their western counterparts. Our volume ends with a detailed conclusion in which we assess the Greens' importance to the changing nature of the Left, to the politics of Germany, and, by proxy, to the advanced capitalist countries in general. Our appendix offers some helpful electoral results and two graphic presentations of the genealogy of the West German and East German Greens respectively.

Part I

Predecessors

Since their appearance in the late 1970s, the West German Greens have swiftly captured both critical and sympathetic interest throughout the West, above all because of their "newness." For political scientists weary of the stability of Western Europe's party landscapes, for sociologists disillusioned with traditional Marxist categories, or for leftists caught between the increasing moderation of traditional social democratic organizations and the impotence of extraparliamentary protest, the emergence of the Greens seemed to signal a dramatic change. Observers have described the Greens as a "party of a new type," harbingers of "postindustrial" or "postmodern" politics, the representatives of "the new class," the end of the "Left/Right spectrum" and the product of a world ecological crisis. Such characterizations are not unfounded, for as we will see later, the ideology, praxis and political behavior of the Greens has been self-consciously unorthodox, unpredictable and at times even erratic. It is equally clear that the political style and concerns of the Greens have differed radically from those of postwar social democracy in Europe, not least of all because they embody responses to a very recent constellation of problems.

But for the student of German politics there is something unmistakably "German" about the Greens. The increasingly ruthless factional and ideological battle throughout much of the 1980s between "fundamentalists" (Fundis) and "realists" (Realos) concerning the relative merits of fundamental opposition and reformist gradualism recalls historical debates within German social democracy during the period of the Second International (particularly the turn-of-the-century *Massenstreikdebatte*, concerning the usefulness of strikes as a strategy for social change). Likewise a certain romanticization of nature, yearning for simplicity in lifestyle and communal feeling are reminiscent of German Romanticism, as well as the *Wandervögel* and Youth Movement of the 1920s. Moreover, the irony, imagination and spectacle which have

characterized green political praxis and behavior cannot be understood apart
from their roots in the German student movement of the 1960s. In some
respects the element of continuity between the Greens and their predecessors on the German Left is almost as astonishing as their "newness."

By no means do we wish to deny the innovativeness and novelty of the
Greens or the ways in which the causes for their emergence and their ultimate ramifications extend beyond the boundaries of Germany. But it would be
just as mistaken to overlook their roots in the specific national political culture
and unique institutional environment of the West German Left. As we argued in the introduction to this volume, we see the formation of the German
Greens as a consequence of the larger socioeconomic and political developments which transformed all industrial societies since the late 1960s as well
as particular German factors.

This section will focus on the latter. It is our thesis that a closer historical
and empirical examination of the political culture of the German Left and
its institutional arrangements is able to explain several things of central importance not well articulated by many systems-theoretical or simpler Marxist
accounts: in particular, why the Greens' diverse concerns were organized
around the concept of ecology and why they adopted the unorthodox form
of organization they did.

The analysis will focus principally on postwar events. We believe that one
can identify clear predecessors of the Green Party within the context of the
postwar German Left. Most directly, the Greens emerged as strictly electoral
alliances of groups disgruntled with both the Social Democratic Party of
Germany and extraparliamentary tactics: the women's, ecology, anti-nuclear,
peace, "alternative" and other movements loosely called "new social movements"; the many "citizen's initiatives" organized to reach a single political
goal in a local arena (such as the preservation of a park, the prevention of
building a highway, a runway, a dam, a thoroughfare, or the creation of
neighborhood associations); the remains and legacies of various revolutionary
Marxist splinter-parties or "K- (for Communist) groups."

However, to understand the anatomy of these direct predecessors of the
Greens, one must go back further. One must look not only at the student
movement of the 1960s but at the evolution of German social democracy in
the 1950s, taking as our starting point the Social Democratic Party of Germany (Sozialdemokratische Partei Deutschlands, SPD), the country's oldest
political party and its longlived representative of the interests of labor as well
as of the established Left. We will examine the extraparliamentary organizations which emerged from the party during the 1950s, their development and
divergence during the 1960s and 1970s, always with an eye towards their
reconvergence into the Greens during the 1980s. Two key questions we will
continually seek to address in the following chapters are: *why* segments of these
groups eventually aligned with one another in a parliamentary party, given
their rather diverse goals and interests, and their generally shared aversion
to parliamentary politics; and how such a comparatively significant segment
of the German population, especially among the young, the educated, the

urban and the politically engaged, was either actively drawn into them or, conversely, comprised a passive pool of sympathetic onlookers. The principal aim of this section, then, will be to reconstruct the developments in the political culture, institutional environment and problem constellations of the extraparliamentary opposition and the Left as well as of the SPD which eventually paved the way for a parliamentary alliance known as the Greens.

In the following we will roughly divide this process into four phases, each of which corresponds to an integral and autonomous upswell of protest dominated by particular organizations, characterized by certain strategies and aimed at distinct goals: the first phase of protests against German rearmament (1950–61); the rise of the New Left and the student movement (1961–9); Marxist/revolutionary cadre politics and terrorism (1969–77); and the growth of the new social movements (1975 to the present). We will attempt to show that the emergence and character of the Greens can in large part be regarded as an understandable and logical result of this chain of radical protest and activism in German postwar history.

1

Reconstruction, Rearmament and Reintegration: The Emergence of the Extraparliamentary Left

Three characteristics have long distinguished the German Left: its propensity for rigid (party) organization, its parliamentary orientation and its domination by the Social Democrats.[1] Even those who succeeded in formulating a shortlived, albeit credible, challenge to this hegemonic pattern – independent socialist groups such as the USPD and communist parties like the KPD – soon found themselves preservers of the very characteristics which they had so vigorously criticized as social democracy's primary flaws. But none of these pre-1945 challengers to the SPD could be labelled "extraparliamentary" in any meaningful sense of that term. Even the Communists, who were deeply hostile to parliamentarism in theory, remained deeply committed to parliamentary activity in practice and, in general, "fixated" on the state. Moreover, the German Left had never entirely abandoned the Kautskian dream of someday attaining an electoral majority. It was against this historical background and in the wake of Germany's defeat and dismemberment, that the German Left began its own auspicious reconstruction in 1945.[2]

Following the war, the political climate appeared uniquely favorable for the German Left. The overwhelmingly anti-fascist, anti-militarist climate of public opinion gave the Left a credibility bonus over the Right and allowed the SPD and KPD to imagine themselves heir apparent to the occupying powers.[3] Moreover, socialism's main opponent, capital, seemed weak and discredited because of the role which some of its most powerful representatives had played in the Third Reich. As the occupying powers sought to "liberalize" and "democratize" the country through strict denazification and political reeducation programs, their only appropriate and acceptable partners were on the Left.

Yet, despite these initially encouraging circumstances, the 1950s were a decade of repeated electoral defeat, dwindling support, and escalating internal conflict for the Left. In the elections of 1946, 1949, 1953 and 1957, the

SPD won, respectively, 35 percent, 29.2 percent, 28.8 percent and 31.8 percent of the vote, while the Christian Democratic Union (Christlich Demokratische Union, CDU), the Federal Republic's leading conservative party, was able to convert the "bourgeois coalition" it had forged in the first two elections of the Federal Republic (1949 and 1953) into an absolute majority of the Bundestag seats by 1957.[4] The Moscow-oriented, Marxist-Leninist KPD incurred even heavier losses than the Social Democrats. The rapid consolidation of Communist-totalitarian dictatorships under Moscow-controlled parties in Eastern Europe, the founding of the GDR, the outbreak of the Korean conflict, in a word, the Cold War, fanned a violent anti-communism in West Germany. In 1954, the KPD gained a mere 2.2 percent of the vote, down from 9.4 percent in 1946.

Worse was yet to come. On August 17, 1956, the Federal Constitutional Court (Bundesverfassungsgericht) ordered the dissolution of the KPD, declaring it a threat to the "basic order of freedom and democracy" (*freiheitliche, demokratische Grundordnung*) guaranteed by the Basic Law.[5] Hence even the relative stability of the SPD electorate deceptively veiled an overall decline in support for the Left. And with social democracy's shortcomings at the polling place, the voice of moderate reformers within the SPD grew stronger, culminating in the 1959 Bad Godesberg program in which the SPD shed its traditional status of a "class" or "workers" party for that of a "mass" or "people's" party (*Volkspartei*). Thus, in the Federal Republic, political space to the left of accommodationist social democracy was becoming available during the 1950s.

However, electoral deficiencies alone do not explain the SPD's momentous Godesberg decision. It is also important to recognize that the 1950s were not just a decade of defeat but of deeply disappointed expectations for the German Left. The unqualified destruction of National Socialism and Germany itself had left a great institutional and political vacuum, nurturing the Left's hopes for restructuring and democratizing the economy in a reunified, disarmed and pacifist Germany. The Left's vision contained four focal points: codetermination; a state-directed economy in which the market was to play a significant but circumscribed role; eastern policy *(Ostpolitik)*/reunification; and, finally, disarmament. Indeed, there is good reason to believe that this vision was more or less shared by the overwhelming majority of the West German population.[6]

Yet by 1958, a pronouncedly conservative course and irreversible defeat for the SPD had been accomplished on each of these issues. Far from having codetermination dominate the Federal Republic's industrial relations system, the country's unions suffered serious defeats in the course of the 1950s, which relegated this vaunted system of worker control of management to the Federal Republic's declining coal and steel industries.[7] Indeed, instead of a nationalized (or "socialized," to use the terminology preferred by the Left) economy, the Federal Republic was rapidly becoming the free market's most ardent advocate and most envied success story. In relations with the East, the GDR was a daily reminder of the country's division and its occupation by foreign powers. Even concerning disarmament, the Left's tally seemed woefully inadequate. Not only did the Federal Republic obtain its own army, but it integrated this army into the western alliance of NATO and allowed the stationing of American nuclear weapons on German soil. All in all, this was far from the auspicious situation which the Left had envisioned for Germany immediately following the end of the war.

Furthermore, the laws and institutions established by these decisions irrevocably defined the parameters of further development in the Federal Republic. Karl-Werner Brand, Detlef Büsser and Dieter Rucht contend that: "In these three dimensions of diluted or abandoned original hopes for a radically new beginning ... lay the specific crises and potential for delegitimation which provided the soil for the extra-parliamentary protest movement in the course of the 50s and 60s."[8] The SPD's decision to break with its thorny path of opposition and work toward the model of the *Volkspartei*[9] was not just an attempt to increase its share of the vote but a recognition of and acquiescence to the prevailing political, social and economic order.

Yet not all could be expected to accept stoically these disappointments, and those opposed to the new system could no longer find their political home in the SPD. Thus was extraparliamentary opposition born in the Federal Republic.

Let us now briefly examine the three major episodes of political protest during the 1950s which occurred over codetermination, rearmament and atomic weapons respectively.

Labor's Battle for Codetermination in Industry and Socialization of the Economy

The first episode of protest against the emerging postwar order of the Federal Republic was the battle of the German trade unions for socialization and co-determination of key German industries. In the political climate of the time, these goals were not as radical as they might appear in hindsight. At least initially, they had the support not only of the working-class parties, the SPD and the KPD, but of the main bourgeois party, the CDU, and of a large share of the German population.[10] In the aftermath of the war, German capital was deeply delegitimated because of its close association with National Socialism.

But if capital was weakened, plans for socializing key industries and introducing codetermination had two other formidable enemies during the late 1940s and 1950s in the US military government and CDU leader and federal chancellor Konrad Adenauer.[11] With the onset of the Cold War, the Americans were primarily committed to maintaining an economically healthy bulwark toward the Soviet-dominated East and deemed this most readily achievable through a revitalized free market economy in the Federal Republic. Thus reform plans for Germany were subordinated to foreign policy goals, and the United States restricted its reorganization of the German economy to dismantling excessively cartellized and concentrated branches of German industry.[12] This policy found resonance with Konrad Adenauer and his economics minister Ludwig Erhard, whose concept of the "social market economy" had been elevated to the official party doctrine of the CDU before the 1949 election.[13]

In fact, the CDU and the US military government had already initiated steps to block or suspend the implementation of certain codetermination and socialization measures as early as 1948. As denazification efforts were quietly abandoned, most of the capitalists and managers who had supported Hitler's war machine experienced a *de facto* – if not *de jure* – rehabilitation.[14] Even though the Basic Law, passed in 1948, contained a number of formulations which explicitly addressed workers' rights and welfare, the end result did not fulfil the hopes labor and the Left had held for it. Thus Walter Freitag, IG Metall's chairman, ominously warned: "Should the old owners who bear the responsibility for our misfortune acquire status and dignity once again, then the iron and steel workers will feel the need to apply their fullest powers to bring the factories to a standstill."[15] Yet, as so often during this critical period, the unions did not support their radical rhetoric with decisive action. Thus, by 1952, at the very latest, Freitag's fears concerning capital's restored power had already been entirely realized.[16]

But the unions did achieve one notable victory in 1951 during this otherwise unbroken series of fatal rollbacks for labor and the Left in West Germany. Considerable (and justified) apprehension arose within union ranks concerning the Adenauer government's intention to dismantle the existing system of codetermination in the iron and steel industry. Labor feared the disappearance of its one significant postwar achievement, the so-called *Montanmitbestimmung* (codetermination in the coal and steel industry). Underlining the symbolic importance of this institution for labor, the DGB (Deutscher Gewerkschaftsbund – the German Trade Union Federation), IG Metall (the metalworkers' union), and IG Bergbau und Energie (the miners' union) appeared ready to mount concerted defense. The leadership was supported in its protests by the union rank-and-file.[17] Adenauer, sensing the imminent danger of a major strike, offered himself as mediator. Last-minute negotiations and the CDU's affirmative vote in the Bundestag codified the existing codetermination system into law. But the main form of attack on labor's position by the conservative government and industrial elites was not so much open confrontation as willful neglect and quiet sabotage of existing laws.[18]

In an exchange of letters during the early 1950s, DGB chairman Hans Böckler and Adenauer debated the role of unions in a liberal democracy. Böckler advanced the view, held by unions since Weimar, that economic democracy was a prerequisite for political democracy. Adenauer, on the other hand, contended that parliament alone was the focus of democratic participation. This, he argued, precluded the influence of interest organizations, such as that of the unions, from the political process.[19] It was this disagreement which colored the debate, beginning in 1950, over the prospective passage of an all-embracing Works' Constitution Act (*Betriebsverfassungsgesetz*).

If passed, such a union-weakening measure would have been devastating to the unions' shopfloor power and their presence inside the Federal Republic's firms and factories. This bill designated "works' councils" the sole representative of workers on the shopfloor, thereby excluding the unions from this critical layer of working-class organization. It also legally constrained the works' councils, prescribing that their "primary loyalty" be to the firm rather than the union or the workers. In addition, far from granting "full parity" co-determination, the bill provided that labor receive only one-third of the seats on company advisory boards (rather than half, as existed under the provisions of the *Montanmitbestimmung* scheme). After deliberations by a joint committee of unionists and managers (the so-called "Hattenheim negotiations") broke down in 1950,[20] the DGB succeeded in stalling the bill in committee and in temporarily delaying its parliamentary passage for nearly two years. But during this lengthy reprieve, the unions failed to devise a counterproposal or alternative strategy. By 1952, this led to yet another costly and unsuccessful legislative struggle by labor and the Left in the Federal Republic. Conservative forces, led by a parliamentary majority which consisted of the dominant CDU and its small coalition partner the Free Democratic Party (Freie Demokratische Partei, FDP) – a laissez-faire oriented party in the classical style of European liberalism – passed the Works Constitution Act. Labor was thereby excluded from all decisions regarding powers within the firm, thus weakening the German unions' shopfloor presence in a massive manner.

By the summer of 1952, labor had suffered a nearly total defeat of its agenda for economic restructuring and political change. In 1946, the unions and SPD had reserved for themselves an exclusive role as the sole capable heirs of a viable democracy on German soil. However, Adenauer had cunningly disinherited labor of this claim by redefining "democracy" as a strong parliamentary executive centered around the chancellor (so-called *Kanzlerdemokratie* or Chancellor's Democracy). There were, no doubt, several points at which more radical union tactics might have blocked Adenauer's course. But an ambivalence about directly challenging the Federal Republic's parliamentary institutions seems to have caused hesitation on the part of the union leadership. This tacit recognition of parliamentarism as the most legitimate and feasible exercise of democracy, though exploited in an unfortunate way by Adenauer, was a momentous step in the history of the German Left. To be sure, the Left – especially in its hegemonic social-democratic version – had long been a defender of etatist institutions and the state itself. Indeed, it could well be argued that it was primarily through social democracy's unmitigated support that the Weimar Republic survived for as long as it did. Yet during the Weimar Republic, the SPD supported parliamentary democracy and the state for lack of a better alternative. It was only during the 1950s, that the German Left began actively to embrace parliamentarism and develop a positive identification with republican institutions. But precisely for this reason, social democratic and union leaders remained deeply suspicious of extraparliamentary movements and tactics, which they found reminiscent of the Brown Shirts of Hitler's SA.

Germany: Rearmed and Divided

If in 1945 a fundamental reorganization of the German economy seemed perhaps desirable, the rearmament of Germany appeared altogether impossible. Exhaustion, defeat and occupation evoked a mood (or at least a posture) of pronounced anti-militarism among the German population. In 1946, Adenauer himself expressed a wish for German "neutrality," and his future defense minister, Franz-Josef Strauß warned that "whoever wants to take a rifle in his hand again – his arm should fall off."[21] The victorious Allies, especially France and the Soviet Union, seemed determined to neutralize German military might forever.[22]

It was principally, though not exclusively, a convergence of German and American interests in the changed climate of the Cold War which gradually turned the tide on this issue. The announcement of the Truman doctrine and start of the Marshall Plan in 1947; the Berlin blockade and the Allied airlift in 1948; and the beginning of the Korean war in 1950 all marked another temperature drop in the Cold War. With each escalatory event, voices to integrate a rearmed Germany into the western alliance grew louder.[23] For the United States, Germany's geopolitical situation and (potential) military strength made its inclusion into an American-led alliance indispensable. For Adenauer, a German military contribution was the only readily available bargaining chip which he could use in his quest to reestablish German political sovereignty.[24] In his view, a smaller republic anchored in the West was not only more politically possible but actually more morally desirable than a united Germany "floating" between East and West.

Given this community of interests, West Germany's rearmament and integration into the West were bound to proceed quickly. And they did. Adenauer began establishing the machinery of the defense ministry long in advance.[25] In May 1952, the Federal Republic signed a treaty for the building of a European Defence Community (EDC) under a supranational command. By way of exchange, the Federal Republic was promised its return to full sovereignty by the Allied powers in the so-called General or German Treaty.[26] In February of 1954, the Bundestag passed a military amendment (*Wehrergänzungsgesetz*) to the Basic Law, which gave military services a constitutional and legal basis.[27] When the EDC pact failed to pass in the French National Assembly in 1954, a new package of agreements which addressed French objections, the so-called Paris Treaties, were drafted.[28] Like the EDC agreement, they also included a General Treaty providing for Germany's national sovereignty. The Bundestag ratified the package in early 1955. As we will see in the following section, the first American atomic weapons were stationed in the Federal Republic just three short years later. Adenauer thereby implicitly gave priority to securing the existence of the Federal Republic, a path which would fast extinguish hopes for a united Germany. Adenauer was convinced that only via a sound – and unalterable – anchoring in the West would Germany's destructive vicissitudes finally come to an end. Adenauer favored the establishment of a stable, parliamentary democracy on

German soil, for which he was ready to sacrifice the country's national unity. Nowhere was Adenauer's greatness as a political leader more pronounced than in his readiness to abandon the sanctity of national union for economic stability and political democracy. This was all the more remarkable since Adenauer was, after all, the leader of a conservative party and the chancellor of a right-of-center coalition government.

The chain of developments culminating in West German rearmament met the categorical opposition of the organized left – KPD, SPD and DGB – and unleashed a storm of extraparliamentary protest with varying connections to the unions and parties. It is therefore in the years between 1950 and 1956 that we can properly date the emergence of an independent extra-parliamentary Left in the Federal Republic.

In order to understand the form assumed by extraparliamentary opposi-tion to rearmament, it is important to examine the strategy of opposition practiced by the SPD during this period, specifically Kurt Schumacher's "politics of intransigent opposition." With its massive party apparatus, powerful ancillary organizations and totalizing Marxist world-view, the SPD had long presented itself as the sole viable representative of any comprehensive systemic opposition. But the new strategy was more subtle.

While Schumacher did not completely condemn or reject the Federal Republic, he never regarded it as permanent. He was fond of referring to it as a "provisorium" or transitional entity. The Federal Republic was a divided and occupied Germany, and in the eyes of Schumacher and the Social Democrats, a Germany without its sovereignty and unity was no Germany at all. There was in the SPD's stance a thinly veiled patriotism, a kind of left-nationalism, a feeling that Germany had suffered sufficiently, that Germany comprised not just Nazis but exiles and opposition fighters, and – as a con-sequence – did not deserve national division as "punishment."[29] Theo Pirker summarizes this sentiment rather well: "the goal of [Schumacher's] intran-sigent opposition was in no way a change of government (*Regierungsumbildung*) as much as a restructuring of the form of government (*Regierungsneubildung*) with a consequent alternative policy at the end of which was to stand the transformation of the provisional bourgeois state into a permanent socialist German Reich."[30]

It was toward this vision of a reunited, sovereign and socially renewed Germany that Schumacher oriented the SPD.[31] It was this vision which, in turn, shaped the SPD's stance towards German rearmament.

"Intransigent opposition" entailed much more than simple "parliamentary opposition." However, it did not imply absolute, systemic opposition to all existing institutions of state and society,[32] for Schumacher was firmly com-mitted to parliamentary democracy.[33] Indeed, there were two things which Schumacher did not regard as "provisional" about the Federal Republic: its parliamentary institutions, and above all its constitution or Basic Law. In Schumacher's view of democracy there was as little room for "experiments" with "radical" or "grass roots" democracy as there was for Leninist "demo-cratic centralism." For him, plebiscitary or movement politics were strongly reminiscent of Nazism and therefore illegitimate as a political strategy.

Schumacher's commitment to parliamentarism was also based on a strategic calculation. He firmly believed that the failure of the CDU's free-market policy on the one hand and social democracy's commitment to German national unity on the other would soon rally a majority of West German voters to the SPD. Once the social democratic strongholds in the East were reunited with the Federal Republic, an electoral majority for the SPD would be all but a foregone conclusion.[34]

It is important to emphasize that the SPD's stance against rearmament was not based on pacifism. For Schumacher, parliamentary democracy was worth defending – with German arms if necessary.[35] In Schumacher's words, "the indissoluble attachment of Germany's fate with that of western democracy" in itself provided sufficient ground for German rearmament.[36] Schumacher's anti-communism and commitment to the West outweighed his anti-militarism.[37] But, unlike Adenauer, Schumacher was not willing to forgo political sovereignty in a united Germany for a rump Germany's subordinate integration into a western defense alliance dominated by the United States.[38]

Thus, the first rumblings of extraparliamentary protest against German rearmament did not emanate from the SPD, but from religious, pacifist and communist organizations. In the fall of 1950, following vigorous, open debate on rearmament in the Protestant church (Evangelische Kirchengemeinschaft Deutschlands, EKD) the prominent theologian and church leader, Martin Niemöller, addressed a widely circulated, open letter to Adenauer, suggesting the chancellor call new elections or conduct a plebiscite on rearmament.[39] At the same time, large parts of the population were seized by a spontaneous mood of pacifism which rallied around the slogan "without me" or "without us" ("ohne mich" or "ohne uns").[40] Isolated episodes of labor protest also erupted.[41] During 1950 and 1952, the KPD founded several peace organizations and conducted peace conferences in Berlin.[42]

A more moderate grouping under the leadership of Gustav Heinemann who had resigned as Adenauer's Minister of the Interior over the rearmament issue, brought forth the non-partisan Emergency Society for European Peace (Notgemeinschaft für den Frieden Europas), whose activities centered around a massive petition campaign.[43]

In line with Schumacher's views on democracy, the SPD joined the CDU in staunchly opposing Heinemann's plebiscite plan.[44] In the spring of 1952, the SPD went so far as to declare membership in Heinemann's Emergency Society and membership in the SPD as incompatible.[45]

Rejecting extraparliamentary tactics, the SPD instead sought to block the treaties by challenging them in the Federal Constitutional Court,[46] and by seeking to veto them in the Bundesrat.[47] Adenauer succeeded in defeating both ploys.

Not until the eve of the legislative and judicial defeat, and just before the passage of the Paris Treaties, did the SPD desperately join with the extraparliamentary opposition and even then, only with the greatest reluctance. In the spring of 1955, the SPD, DGB, EKD and various intellectuals invited a thousand selected guests to an organized weekend of lectures and presentations against rearmament to be staged, symbolically, in Frankfurt's Paul's Church, one-time home of the 1848 National Assembly. The slogan of the Paulskirche Bewegung, the "Paul's Church movement," as it came to be called, was "Rescue unity, peace and freedom! Against communism and nationalism!" As its "German manifesto" emphasized, the movement opposed the Paris Treaties only because they were an obstacle to reunification.[48] With the passage of the Paris Treaties several months later, the Paul's Church movement faded away quietly. Its form of organization was neither suited nor intended to mobilize sustained public opposition to rearmament.[49] On the contrary, the Paul's Church movement was largely designed to dampen and contain radical currents within the DGB and SPD which were calling for a general strike.[50]

As we have seen, neither the SPD's stance on rearmament nor its interpretation of democratic participation at this time could be reconciled with a pacifist, extraparliamentary movement. Thus it should not be surprising that the one organization which tended in this direction was founded by Gustav Heinemann. After Adenauer prohibited his petition campaign, Heinemann founded the shortlived All-German People's party (Gesamtdeutsche Volkspartei, GVP), which emerged out of his Emergency Society in time for the 1953 federal elections. What made the GVP historically exceptional and accounted for its modest success was its resemblance to later, more developed forms of mobilizing and organizing protest: it had a clear message (one might say a "theme") in that it called for the prevention of rearmament; it had a discernable goal in that it strove to unseat Adenauer; and it was willing to combine both parliamentary and extraparliamentary tactics. Perhaps the greatest weakness of the GVP was its inability to reach leftists whose positions on rearmament more nearly resembled the GVP's than the SPD's. Such a historic alliance had to wait for another 25 years.

In sum, during the first half of the 1950s potential opposition to rearmament was great while organized opposition to it remained small. This was due at least in part to the SPD's stance on extraparliamentarism. This, in turn, was not just a reflection of social democratic phlegmatism or ineptness. Rather it also conveyed the party's commitment to parliamentarism, albeit in a relatively restricted sense. The resultant inability on the part of the SPD to articulate completely its alternate vision of Germany not only frustrated certain currents of the party, but also alienated it from potential electoral supporters. Still, had a subsequent wave of protest not occurred during the second half of the decade, the SPD might nevertheless have fully integrated its oppositional tendencies into the Federal Republic's extraparliamentary ones of the time.

"A Refinement of the Artillery": the Battle against the Nuclear Plague

The drive to station American nuclear weapons on German soil began even before the ratification of the Paris Treaties and stretched over a period of nearly four years. Following NATO deliberations beginning in 1954[51] and a preparatory press campaign by the Adenauer government in 1955,[52] the United States formally offered to station "tactical" nuclear weapons and warheads on German soil in late 1957. Seizing the moment, the CDU pushed a bill through the Bundestag in March 1958 to "equip the armed forces of the Federal Republic with the most modern weapons. . . ."[53] In many ways both the arguments and fronts of conflict were similar to the battle over rearmament, with one important difference:[54] the plan to station atomic weapons on West German soil evoked protests which were substantially broader, deeper and more sustained than those against rearmament several years before. Undoubtedly, the most important reason for this notable difference was the direct involvement of the SPD in organizing the opposition against the stationing of nuclear weapons. Moreover there existed a certain residual capacity in mobilization and organization from the protest against rearmament. As a consequence, protest opposing nuclear weapons was organized more intensively and effectively.

The origin of the West German ban-the-bomb movement was a specific cluster of events in the spring of 1957. Several months before the parliamentary elections, the SPD introduced a "grand inquiry" (*grosse Anfrage*) in the Bundestag in an attempt to expose the Adenauer government's semi-secret deliberations with the United States.[55] Adenauer ineptly sought to downplay the issue by characterizing tactical nuclear weapons[56] as a mere "refinement of artillery" (*Weiterentwicklung der Artillerie*).[57] This distortion stirred 18 of Germany's most prominent nuclear physicists to sever private discussions with Adenauer and publish a general statement, the "Göttingen declaration," which was in essence a cursory description of the bomb's destructive potential, the impossibility of protecting oneself from it, and a clarification of the general confusion (encouraged by Adenauer and his defense minister Strauß) regarding the meaning of "tactical" nuclear weapons.[58] The declaration had astounding resonance. The DGB, IG Metall and the Protestant church all issued statements of support.[59] Local action committees burst spontaneously into existence, and opinion polls recorded a rapid hardening of public opinion against the Adenauer course.[60]

In spite or perhaps because of the approaching elections, the SPD proceeded cautiously in mobilizing this opposition.[61] In its "Ollenhauer plan" (named for its author, SPD chairman Erich Ollenhauer, Kurt Schumacher's successor), the SPD attempted to link nuclear disarmament to its goal of reunification through a Continental "system of collective security" which was to be guaranteed by the superpowers in a sort of organizational merger of NATO and the Warsaw Pact toward the end of general security.[62]

In the electoral campaign, Adenauer attacked this plan with his customary tactic: he sought to discredit social democrats as communist sympathizers and juxtaposed the prosperity of the *Wirtschaftswunder*, the "economic miracle," to East Germany's economic woes. In this way, he succeeded in neutralizing the issue of the bomb. In June, the CDU and its Bavarian sister party, the even more conservative and staunchly Catholic Christian Social

Union (Christlich Soziale Union, CSU), received 50.2 percent of the votes (the sole instance in the history of the Federal Republic – indeed any German democracy – when a party obtained an absolute electoral majority). This was despite the fact that, according to opinion polls, some 70 percent of the population was categorically opposed to the stationing of nuclear missiles on German soil.[63] Clearly, Adenauer had succeeded in defining the election's character around the issue of economic prosperity rather than rearmament.

The gloom among social democrats and their sympathizers following the SPD's third trouncing in as many elections held in this young republic was broken by the Polish Secretary of State, Adam Rapacki. His plan for creating a demilitarized zone in Central Europe (including both parts of Germany) as the basis for a collective security system was received enthusiastically by the SPD and American liberals.[64]

However, the brief optimism of the Left was crushed as a NATO conference in Paris in December affirmed the alliance's commitment to stationing nuclear arms in the Federal Republic. Since all Adenauer needed was the Bundestag's approval of NATO's authorization, parliament became the inevitable focus of this conflict.

This time, the SPD sought to coordinate its parliamentary tactics with extraparliamentary mobilization. In January, the party called another foreign policy debate in the Bundestag.[65] It also submitted a bill to ban the manufacture or stationing of atomic weapons in the Federal Republic.[66] Erich Ollenhauer announced an "information campaign" in order to initiate a "broad wave of opposition against nuclear death." Right from the beginning, the campaign, "Battle against Nuclear Death" (Kampf dem Atomtod, KdA) was conceived as a genuine mass mobilization beyond the boundaries of the Social Democratic Party and the established channels of parliamentary politics. The organizers included the entire spectrum of the opposition from 1954.[67] The SPD's massive party machinery was set in motion to circulate petitions, organize local KdA committees and sponsor mass rallies throughout the Federal Republic. The KdA achieved the first coordinated mass mobilization in the young republic: within two weeks demonstrations occurred in more than half of all German cities with populations over 200,000.[68]

In the end, the Adenauer government succeeded in constructing legal and political blocks to all the SPD's and KdA's efforts.[69] However, the course of this extraparliamentary mobilization was marked by several pivotal events which proved to have long-term significance from the perspective of our analysis.

First, despite an initially positive response[70] from the SPD,[71] the union rank-and-file[72] and the general public,[73] the DGB leadership ultimately shied away from initiating any major strike activity in support of the KdA. In the end, the DGB's priorities lay elsewhere, most notably in wage hikes and the vexing issue of automation's potentially adverse effects on the job security of its members; above all, the union leadership was unwilling to jeopardize the unions' newly won public credibility as a reliable "social partner" in the construction of a successful social market economy in the Federal Republic. The

DGB's decision was part of a larger development in which organized labor essentially agreed to "depoliticize" its activities and restrict itself to "material" issues. This development signaled the first break in the established alliance between left intellectuals and organized labor since the fall of National Socialism.

The second matter concerned the SPD's handling of the KdA after Adenauer's victory. While KdA leaders were inclined to continue and expand the campaign even after passage of the NATO communiqué and the Federal Constitutional Court's rejection of the popular referendum, moderate SPD leaders began to dismantle the movement and its extraparliamentary structures. The SPD's aim in founding the KdA had been strictly to exert pressure on the powers that be in case of a parliamentary conflict. The party never intended to establish an independent extraparliamentary opposition to atomic weapons. Tellingly, Herbert Wehner argued that the danger of continuing the KdA lay in "awakening sentiments and gathering people with whom Social Democracy cannot be identified at all after a certain point – since this [identification] could demolish [the SPD's] appeal to the so-called man in the street in the process."[74] In essence, Wehner replicated the DGB's position by distancing himself and the SPD from the concerns of middle-class radicals and independents in order to concentrate on the achievable, material goals of "the man in the street."

This was no isolated incident, of course, but part of a larger process of social democracy's fundamental reorientation during the 1950s culminating in the Godesberg program of 1959. Godesberg embodied an immensely significant juncture in the evolution of the extraparliamentary opposition in the Federal Republic for several reasons. First, social democracy's conscious de-ideologization rendered it unserviceable as a nexus for creating and reproducing utopian aspirations, or for that matter, for providing any systematic criticism of the *status quo*. Second, the party's firm commitment to parliamentarism and to interest mediation compelled it to renounce any extraparliamentary forms of agitation and politics.

The third turning point signaled by the KdA centered on the structure of the theme over which protest erupted. Most notably, there occurred a marked shift in the KdA's rhetoric. Its appeals were not addressed to a particular group, much less a class. Nor did they represent the struggle as one between two opposed interests. Rather the KdA saw it as involving humanity in general on the one hand, and a detached, heteronomous and menacing bureaucratic force on the other.[75] Opposition to atomic weapons failed to fit into the traditional scheme of capital–labor conflict, thus making the conventional tools of traditional socialist politics all but irrelevant.

In a word, the bond between middle-class radicalism and working-class socialism was cracking, as was the link between middle-class intellectuals and organized labor. This process was graphically represented in the departure of the KdA from the SPD and DGB. Although it withered considerably once severed from the SPD, the KdA campaign was the first shoot of the vigorous extraparliamentary opposition which blossomed during the 1960s. The KdA engendered a widespread public mobilization, not only in the sense of "consciousness raising" but also in that of creating a group of committed and experienced potential opposition leaders. Indeed, to stretch the metaphor a bit, one might rightly say of the KdA that it sowed seeds – knowledge, tactics and personal moral commitment – which germinated only years later.

2

"Anabaptists in the Affluent Society": The New Left and the Student Revolt

In 1963, Adenauer resigned his chancellorship after well over a decade in office. The Bundestag elected his popular economics minister, father of the "social market economy," Ludwig Erhard as chancellor. Thus ended the venerable "Adenauer era," which witnessed the reconstruction of the West German economy and the establishment of a parliamentary democracy in the Federal Republic. The country had emerged astoundingly prosperous; it had also developed into a trusted partner of the West and a stable democracy. Furthermore, the general population, including the average worker – in good part due to the unions' considerable leverage in certain aspects of collective bargaining – began to share increasingly in this unprecedented wealth and security. The Germans observed with considerable satisfaction that their success had not escaped the attention, indeed admiration, of the rest of the world. Under Adenauer's leadership the Federal Republic had become a respected and powerful nation, in spite of the haunting – and unforgettable – specter of National Socialism. Adenauer's program of economic and political reconstruction had, with the significant exception of reunification, been realized.

The stability of the Federal Republic promised to be more than superficial. The new social and political formation genuinely appeared to have capped the traditional well-springs of conflict and unrest: material inequality and authoritarian political structures. First, the postwar compromise between capital and labor largely neutralized class conflict in its militant manifestations in most parts of the Federal Republic and helped make labor an important, albeit junior, partner in West Germany's political economy. Second, despite Adenauer's heavy-handed style of leadership, parliamentarism and basic democratic values had become firmly established in the young republic. The infamous "Spiegel affair," in which the defense minister at the time, Franz-Josef Strauss, ordered an illegal search-and-seizure action in the offices of the

Federal Republic's most prominent news magazine, provided an acid test of the viability and vibrancy of the country's democratic institutions and political values.[1] And yet, despite these apparent grounds for contentment and satisfaction with the status quo, the 1960s were an age of unprecedented unrest.

As we have seen in the preceding chapter, the two giants of the Left, the SPD and DGB, had become so firmly integrated into the social and political system of the Federal Republic by the early-to-mid 1960s that they could no longer represent or absorb the utopian aspirations of middle-class radicals. Instead, the energies of this group found an outlet in what came to be known as the *außerparlamentarische Opposition* (extraparliamentary opposition) or APO. The term APO never designated a single organization or tendency. Rather, APO was a loosely constituted *negative alliance* between a diffuse array of groups united against a shared "opponent." Nevertheless, two groups were particularly ground breaking and influential within APO: the "Easter March" movement, which evolved eventually into the Campaign for Democracy and Disarmament, and the Social Democratic Students' League or SDS. One can also differentiate three relatively distinct developmental phases in the evolution of APO. The first (1959–66) was a period of organizational and theoretical consolidation, during which APO came to operate and view itself as an autonomous force on the left, independent of organized labor and social democracy. The second (1966–8), marked by the beginning of student unrest in West Berlin, was a period of political opposition, during which new and now familiar forms of political praxis (such as sit-ins) were invented and diffused. The third (1968–9) consisted of a brief period of all-out opposition, characterized by self-reinforcing dynamics of escalating confrontation with the state and an increasing radicalization of the protests' participants. This stage also witnessed major mobilization of protesters and their sympathizers. It was the "failure" of this third phase which led to the subsequent fragmentation and eventual dissolution of APO.

From Ostermarsch to KfA

To uncover APO's roots we must first return briefly to the Adenauer era, specifically to the years 1959–61, when we discover a remarkable and direct continuity between APO and the "ban-the-bomb" movement. After the SPD "betrayed" the cause of KdA[2] many of the movement's "homeless" activists and supporters opted to leave the SPD and join other organizations. In fact, a majority of KdA's executive committee found its way into the Hamburg-based "Easter March of the Opponents of Atomic Weapons" (Ostermarsch der Atomwaffengegner), one of several small movements remaining from 1958. The Easter March movement was lead by the pacifist and conscientious objector Hans-Konrad Temple and owed its name to the form of its ritual protest – a silent, four-day march held every Easter.[3]

During the early 1960s, the Easter March movement underwent

transformations in its self-conception and organization which were groundbreaking for APO's development. Under Temple's leadership the Easter March movement had remained primarily an "ethical-pacifist milieu," conservative in its overall outlook and hostile to communists. Its "demonstrations were directed not against a particular political opponent but indeterminately against 'war' and 'the bomb.' "[4] But by 1961, a consensus had developed within the Easter March's leadership circle that, in Temple's words, a "concretization and associated reformulation in [Easter March's] basic goals (*Zielsetzung*)" was necessary. Whereas in 1960, the Easter March slogan had simply been "against the means of nuclear destruction of every sort and every nation," three years later in 1963 the organization demanded that the "statesmen" render Central Europe "nuclear free" and make it a demilitarized zone of international détente.[5] Thus began a process of self-reflection through which the movement's goals and political program became more comprehensive, and which made it more accessible to larger segments of the sociopolitical "environment." Gradually, the Easter March's vague ethical opposition to atomic weapons gave way to a well-defined social critique of militarism within capitalist society. Reflecting this evolution in radical consciousness, the name Easter March changed, first to Campaign for Disarmament (Kampf für Abrüstung, KfA) and then to Campaign for Democracy and Disarmament (Kampf für Demokratie und Abrüstung, KfDA).

In a parallel process, the organization and activity of the movement were both broadened and intensified. Previously, Temple had restricted participation to non-Communists.[6] Similarly, he had sought to underline the strictly moral roots of the campaign by prescribing and enforcing silence and nonviolence during the marches.[7] At the movement's first national conference in the fall of 1961, a circle of its leaders openly challenged him. They felt it was necessary "to win approval for a particular political position from all possible sides."[8] By 1963, this current had prevailed and led to a series of changes, including the first change of name to Campaign for Disarmament (KfA). The new KfA central committee cautiously opened debate to Communists and began to court support and participation more actively from other organizations on the left, including the left wings of the SPD and DGB. Thus the KfA was evolving towards a heterogeneous, "single-issue" movement.

Reflecting their manifestly political character, the Easter marches shed their funereal sobriety and became loud, festive, and affirmative day-long celebrations, since, as one leader put it, "the march isn't just a demonstration against war; it's a demonstration for life."[9] While the Easter march remained *the* central event, organizers expanded the radius of activities to include marches on "Hiroshima Day" (August 6), international conferences on disarmament, and more spontaneous demonstrations in response to particular political events. As one movement leader argued rather pointedly, it would be "necessary" for the KfA in its quest for new supporters "to proceed according to the laws of modern advertising psychology (*Werbepsychologie*)."[10] The success of this novel approach is graphically demonstrated by the abrupt jump in participation in 1963 and 1964 illustrated by the table.

Table 2.1 Participation in the KfA, 1960–1964

Year	Participants	Rallies
1960	1,000	n.k.
1961	23,000	n.k.
1962	50,000	n.k.
1963	100,000	130
1964	130,000	280

Source: Hans Karl Rupp, *Außerparlamentarische Opposition in der Ära Adenauers*, Cologne: Pahl-Rugenstein, 1970, p. 147.

Obviously, this success did not emanate from an "objective" deterioration in the arms race. Rather it resulted from the invention of a new form of organization which could mobilize opposition to it. Since the arms race did not impinge immediately on any particular group's interest but represented, instead, a general and abstract threat, any movement against the build-up of weaponry would have to represent this development in near apocalyptic terms in order to secure significant popular support against it.

One key precondition for the extraparliamentary opposition embodied by APO was its break with mobilization models invented by labor. These models were no longer appropriate, because the KfA was a movement based on shared value commitments rather than a common set of interests. The heterogeneity of the participants – the KfA included Christians, pacifists, "old" and "new" leftists, SPD and DGB leaders among others – meant that mobilization had to be selective and specific. This was accomplished principally through limiting the campaign to a negative program based on a minimal consensus. The organizational model developed by the KfA became the example toward which many movements of the late 1960s would orient themselves.

SDS: From Party Training Corps to Intellectual Avant-Garde

The second germ cell of APO was SDS (Sozialistischer Deutscher Studentenbund). Unlike its US counterpart of the same acronym, the German SDS did not begin as a radical extraparliamentary experiment of the New Left. In fact, it was established by the SPD as the youth organization of the party to contest university student council (Allgemeiner Studentenauschuß, or AStA) elections, represent SPD positions in university affairs, and season recruits for the party.

Like KdA, the "Battle against Nuclear Death," SDS was severed from the SPD in 1959 at the behest of moderate and reformist forces within the party unhappy with SDS's restive left wing.[11] SDS's participation in the Berlin

Student Congress against Nuclear Arms,[12] in which Communists participated, provided the pretense for disciplinary action. In response, the SPD halted its financial support of SDS. Over the next two years SDS slowly disintegrated. Its right wing joined a rival socialist student organization created by the SPD, the Social Democratic University League (Sozialdemokratischer Hochschulbund, or SHB); in 1961 party leaders forbade simultaneous membership in SDS and SPD.[13]

SDS could not have survived without the financial support of the Socialist Aid Society (Sozialistische Förderergesellschaft) founded by a circle of leftist professors in early 1961.[14] After the SPD also decreed membership in the SFG as incompatible with belonging to the SPD, many SFG supporters left the SPD to form the Socialist League (Sozialistischer Bund). A second group of ex-SPD members had been excluded from the party because of entertaining overly intimate contacts with East Germany's governing party, the Socialist Unity Party (Sozialistische Einheitspartei Deutschlands, or SED). They formed the Union of Independent Socialists (Vereinigung Unabhängiger Sozialisten) in 1960. Thus, the SPD's "Godesberg turn" ultimately resulted in the alienation and exclusion of several generations of radical socialist intellectuals from the parliamentary spectrum of the Federal Republic's left politics.

It is certainly interesting to speculate about the unintended and unforeseen impact which the constitutional court's decision in 1956 to declare West Germany's Communist Party (the KPD) unconstitutional had on these events. Had the KPD still existed in 1960, it seems logical that a fair share of these disillusioned Social Democrats might have migrated to it. Had they done so, the radical left intelligentsia might well have remained integrated into the Federal Republic's parliamentary system. However, with no parliamentary alternative to the SPD's left, extraparliamentary articulation of politics became a structural necessity for these leftist critics. Indeed it was the only way for them to remain politically active and true to their convictions.

It did not take SDS long to realize this. In the fall of 1962, SDS explicitly identified itself as a "theoretical avant-garde organization which in the long run wanted to win over the bourgeois intelligentsia for its [SDS's] emancipatory goals."[15] Debate within SDS increasingly revolved around the political role of the academic intelligentsia in advanced capitalism with the working class receiving only secondary attention.[16] The "anti-authoritarian" current (which, beginning in 1965, won the upper hand under the leadership of Rudi Dutschke and Bernd Rabehl) saw an objectively depoliticized mass society which only marginalized groups and outsiders could reinvigorate politically. This serves as an excellent case in point for the ideas developed about the New Left in the introduction to this volume. It will be recalled that we argued that one of the New Left's main characteristics was its substitution of students and other decommodified – often marginalized – groups for the traditional Left's working class as the subject of history.

Very much in line with the thinking of their idolized theorist Herbert Marcuse, SDSers ceased to regard the working class as the "subject of history" and the key agent of progressive change. They contended that labor had been "bourgeoisified" and corrupted and could no longer serve as the social basis for radical opposition. Thus, SDSers transferred their political hopes for a fundamental transformation of capitalism on to a coalition of radical intellectuals, Third World liberation movements and various *Lumpen* elements in the First World (such as prisoners and other déclassés).

SDS's role in and contribution to the West German student movement was very different from that of the KfA. In sharp contrast to the latter, SDS was never a mass organization. Nor did it want to be. Even at the apex of the student movement in 1968 its membership numbered only slightly more than 2,000.[17] In notable contrast to its namesake, the Students for a Democratic Society (SDS) in the USA, with its membership of about 45,000 in 1968–9, the German SDS always remained essentially a small group of a few independent New Left radicals.[18] As such, it was much more cerebral, theoretical and ultimately monolithic than its more motley and amorphous American counterpart. As the single most important focus of theoretical debate and discussion, SDS exerted an influence on APO and the student movement entirely out of proportion to the actual size of its membership. What KfA embodied on the organizational front, SDS had become on the theoretical front: a trailblazer for left-wing politics and progressive change in the Federal Republic of Germany.

The Spark of Protest: the Student Revolt in West Berlin

Until about 1967, most activities of SDS and the West German student movement were concentrated in West Berlin. There were a number of reasons for this. One was the fact that residents of the city were exempt from the draft due to the city's special status in the postwar arrangement. This meant that West Berlin developed into the Federal Republic's mecca of youth and alternative culture. The other reasons concern the special nature of the Free University. Founded with American help in the late 1940s, when Berlin's established university, the Humboldt University, fell under Communist influence due to its location in the eastern part of the then divided city, the Free University became the Federal Republic's most Americanized institution of higher learning, thus making it far and away the most liberal and democratic university in Adenauer's Germany of the 1950s and early 1960s. In addition, the so-called "Berlin model" gave the student government at the Free University unusual latitude and self-determination. It was the "Berlin model" which became the nodal point for the first eruption of widespread protest on the Free University campus during the 1965 summer semester. Until then, SDS's activities had consisted mostly of "congress politics": small work and discussion circles, and the yearly delegate conferences. The first concrete political action SDS took was a campaign to reform the authoritarian German university system, the so-called *Ordinarienuniversität* in which a handful of senior professors determined virtually every aspect of university life. Since the so-called Humboldtian reform of the early nineteenth century, full professors had exercised total control over curricular content and all matters related to teaching, research and accreditation in their universities.[19] Student support for this system was centered in the dueling fraternities and conservative student organizations such as the Christian Democratic Students' Circle (Ring Christlich Demokratische Studenten). In 1963 SDS launched a campaign to unseat the latter and wrest control of the Free University student council. Buoyed by its increasing popularity, the SDS succeeded in winning over the council within two years. Soon, student government at other West German universities also turned "red."

The goals of the movement began to assume a wider – indeed a global – scope as SDS began to see events as fitting into what it took to be an ominous and alarming pattern.[20] In 1964, the uncomfortable presence of Germany's National Socialist past was abruptly thrust into the light of public debate by the Auschwitz trials held in Frankfurt.[21] Controversy erupted over a proposed amendment to the constitutional statute of limitations, without which all Nazi war criminals would soon be immune from prosecution.[22] Underscoring the tension, the ultra-rightist National Democratic Party of Germany (NPD), with links to former Nazis, was founded that year. To make matters worse, the NPD gained entrance to several state legislatures two years later by easily surmounting the Federal Republic's 5 percent electoral barrier.[23] All this helped remind left-wing intellectuals that the Federal Republic had not yet fully shed its anti-democratic culture and Nazi past. Fascism may not have been a matter of the past for the Federal Republic after all.

The Left responded with demands for a thorough "coming to terms with the past" (*Vergangenheitsbewältigung*) and an end to the older generation's reign of silence concerning the era of National Socialism.[24] To the left, particularly in its academic incarnation, Adenauer Germany's coming to terms with its past seemed shallow and false. Instead of really getting to the roots of what constituted the origins of fascism, West Germany was busily constructing a self-serving ideology of rabid anti-communism. This credo, so the Left believed, had blocked the process of democratic reform in West Germany. Just as anti-communism had replaced democracy in this "feel good" Germany, so too did general prosperity mask the immense social costs of capitalism.[25] It was necessary, the Left argued, to confront the brutal facts of the past head on, not just to renounce Nazi crimes but to recognize their sources in German history, culture and consciousness itself. It was this concern with the German past which spawned a rather prolific (though often simplistic) literature on fascism within the West German Left. Yet, in a certain sense, the Left itself continued the exculpatory practices of the West German establishment by subsuming the singular brutality of Germany's Nazi past and its systematic annihilation of the Jews under the generic term and "structural" concept of "fascism." Seen from this vantage point, the Left altered the Right's approach to the German past much less than it imagined. Ultimately, the Left, too, remained carefully silent and frightfully negligent about Nazism's unique – and most defining – characteristic: the destruction of European Jewry.

But as the Federal Republic entered its first postwar recession during 1966 to 1967,[26] the Left had other reasons to suspect that the Adenauer formula was dissolving from within. The blow was not only material but psychological. The bubble of spiraling economic growth and affluence burst. The reappearance of unexpected labor unrest[27] and economic stagnation proved that the essential instabilities of the major capitalist economies had not been solved. This shortcoming led to a revival of Marxism and proletarian socialism in certain leftist circles.

Chancellor Ludwig Erhard proposed to counter the crisis through his plan for an "organized society" (*formierte Gesellschaft*).[28] But to the Left, Erhard's words were just gloss on another layer of centralized, authoritarian structures. To the Left the zealous persecution of Communists by the CDU-led government and the SPD's post-Godesberg swing toward the political center were two prongs of a general campaign waged against all radical opposition by the conservative establishment. The entrance of the SPD into a "grand coalition" with the CDU/CSU in 1966 only confirmed the will of the powers that be to cement the existing institutions and power relations of the Federal Republic, thereby eliminating any radical alternatives. To the extraparliamentary left, the formation of the grand coalition was yet further evidence of the SPD's hopeless move to the right and the conservative establishment's endless abilities for cooptation. It was this dissatisfaction with the SPD which catapulted the extraparliamentary Left into action and colored its reaction to two pivotal issues of the day: the Vietnam war and the so-called "emergency laws."[29]

In 1965 American bombing of the civilian population in Vietnam was widely publicized for the first time. As a group of prominent student leaders would attest some years later: "No political event played so decisive a role in the discussion and in the politicization of the students as the Vietnam war."[30] This "imperialist war" waged against an indigenous "national liberation movement" under the banner of freedom and democracy seemed to the German students – as well as to their American counterparts – the acme of hypocrisy. Radical students identified with the Vietcong and Ho Chi Minh, often seeing themselves as an integral part of a global battling against repression.[31] German students found a theoretical justification for this heroic self-conception of themselves as the "revolutionary subject" in the widely studied works of Frankfurt School Philosopher Herbert Marcuse.

Fall 1965 was the "Vietnam semester" at the Free University of Berlin. It began when KfA published an influential and elaborately researched "Vietnam Report"[32] and the Free University's SDS-controlled student council distributed an appeal for "peace in Vietnam." Throughout the course of the winter at the Free University, a flurry of activities focused student attention on Vietnam – exhibitions of pictures and documents, films, weekly press reviews, podium discussions and demonstrations.[33] The tone of student criticism grew ever sharper. SDS accused the American government of committing "genocide emanating from imperialist political and economic interests"[34] and attacked the West German government's tacit support of US policies.

By early 1966, student demonstrations against the "dirty war in Vietnam" were moving toward open confrontation with the state.[35] Through the use of sit-ins and other tactics of passive resistance borrowed from the American civil rights and student movements,[36] student protesters garnered increasing media attention. The press, however, was almost universally negative in its attitudes towards the students and their activities. In particular, the popular tabloids controlled by media magnate Axel Caesar Springer went on the offensive.[37] Springer was to become the focus of mounting animosities between the students and the mainstream media.

In the spring of 1966, a nationwide SDS-sponsored congress under the title "Vietnam: Analysis of an Example" occurred at the University of Frankfurt. Virtually all of West Germany's most prominent leftist intellectuals were among the 2,200 participants.[38] The Vietnam congress represented the acme of SDS's "congress politics." Swept up by the anti-Vietnam war campaign, the SDS executive committee urged that the congress mobilize a "'cadre' for broader agitation."[39]

But already at this juncture splits were beginning to emerge. One group, clustered around Marcuse's position, called for "work on the emancipation of consciousness" as a "material basis for the overthrow of the existing order."[40] A second current of opinion, opposed to Marcuse, argued that protest should aim at more pragmatic and readily achievable goals. In the Vietnam protest and student movement, it was the former, "anti-authoritarian" course which would emerge victorious.

Let us now turn to a discussion of the Emergency Laws, the second focus of extraparliamentary activity. The Emergency Laws consisted of a package of legislation and constitutional amendments which aimed at expanding the government's power in the event of severe internal unrest. The idea for this constitutional revision and legal offensive emanated from the ranks of both the Christian Democratic and the Free Democratic parties, who felt that the Federal Republic's constitution, the Basic Law, as originally drafted, failed to give the government sufficient executive power in cases of national emergencies. Drafts of the amendment were introduced in the Bundestag in 1960 and 1962. The centrists and Godesberg adherents within the SPD quickly realized that this provided a good opportunity for them to underscore the Social Democratic Party's new image of moderation by supporting these revisions, while at the same time trying to eliminate and tame some of their harsher provisions. The SPD's Left, the country's activist unions led by powerful IG Metall and, of course, the intelligentsia of the Federal Republic dominated by the New Left vehemently opposed these measures. Were they to be enacted into law, these critics feared a serious infringement of democratic rights and freedoms by an increasingly dirigiste and authoritarian state. The battle over the Emergency Laws raged throughout much of the 1960s. The Bundestag finally enacted them with the help of the Grand Coalition in the spring of 1968. Even though the Social Democrats and the trade unions succeeded in rendering the final version of these laws a good deal less dictatorial than their conservative creators had envisioned them originally, the very fact that these laws could become reality only with the SPD's legislative support enraged the student Left and their supporters. Perhaps more than any other action by the Social Democrats in the Bonn republic, it was their ultimate consent to the creation of the Emergency Laws which convinced many leftists of the SPD's total conversion to becoming a faithful servant of the established capitalist order. Hardly to anyone's surprise, the New

Left and its allies mobilized massively in opposition to these troubling developments.

In several respects, this mobilization was different from the protest against the Vietnam war. First, student radicals did not dominate this movement. Second, the issue itself was more limited and clearcut: enactment of the Emergency Laws required a two-thirds majority in the Bundestag, which could be achieved only with the votes of the SPD. Third, the forces of social democracy and labor, including moderates, had long been opposed to the "Emergency."[41] Hence it was an issue around which a broad, leftist coalition could easily converge.

Rumors that the SPD agreed to pass a moderate version of the Emergency Laws in return for entrance into a grand coalition with the CDU/CSU served as a particular catalyst for leftist mobilization on this issue.[42] A heavily publicized appeal signed by over 1,000 intellectuals and ministers called on the unions and the public to oppose the Emergency measure.[43] Having voiced its opposition to the Emergency Laws several years earlier,[44] SDS undertook a massive publicity campaign during the spring of 1965.[45] SDS also initiated and organized[46] a congress under the title "Democracy's Emergency" ("Demokratie vor dem Notstand").[47] "Democracy's Emergency" brought together the two major strands of the extraparliamentary Left. Initiated by SDS[48] it was planned and executed by a special committee of the KfA.[49] Thus, the KfA's technical-organizational competence was put into the service of APO. Not least of all through the KfA's prowess, this congress, which was held in Frankfurt, proved immensely successful.[50]

Indeed, the entire campaign was – at least temporarily – a triumph. Under leftist pressure, the SPD's leadership withdrew its support for the Laws for the time being. Grass-roots committees including students, unionists, leftist intellectuals, church officials and even SPD officials organized throughout the Federal Republic in opposition to the Laws,[51] thereby helping to consolidate the disparate forces of the Left in the Federal Republic.

The experience of cooperation between the unions, radical students and left intelligentsia during this campaign revived the hopes of reestablishing an alliance between intellectuals and the working class among "orthodox" SDS activists.[52] Some radicals even considered the Emergency Laws as "part of comprehensive, overall, political-military-social strategy"[53] on the part of capital and the state in their ever-consistent battle against labor and the Left. This interpretation of conditions in the Federal Republic was to become particularly prominent in the Communist groupuscules of the 1970s.[54] But other opponents of the Emergency Laws perceived themselves as a complement to parliamentary democracy, a corrective when parliamentary majorities no longer reflected the popular will and abandoned their circumscribed mandate in an act of megalomania and hybris. This tendency would later become the foundation for radical activism within the SPD.

Before turning to a closer examination of the various post-APO groupings, it is important to look at how the internal dynamics of the movement evolved during the late 1960s. As we have seen, the movement's frame of reference had become steadily more systemic and global in its orientation. A near-apocalyptic mood took hold among activists, lending a deep sense of urgency to the tasks confronting the movement. Every event and action seemed charged with significance. The sense of crisis on the one hand and expectation on the other produced a volatile mixture.

Escalation and Dissolution of APO: "From Protest to Resistance"

The explosion occurred during the summer of 1967 in West Berlin. The spark which set it off was the fatal shooting of Benno Ohnesorg, a student, on June 2 by a policeman during a protest against a visit by the Shah of Iran. This incident represented a key turning point in the movement, which "unleashed a sharpened escalation of violence and counterviolence between the state apparatus and the students".[55]

The students and the Left did not see Ohnesorg's death as a tragic accident, the result of human error. Instead they interpreted it as a political murder, the inexorable consequence of the callous actions of an oppressive system. Though Ohnesorg was in reality little more than a sympathetic bystander, militants immediately heralded him as a martyr. The intransigence of the authorities did nothing to discredit this interpretation of events. It is at least possible that an official apology or an expression of regret might have dampened the subsequent outcry. But police, politicians and the mainstream media presented a uniform wall of silence.[56]

In the following week, over a hundred thousand students throughout the Federal Republic demonstrated.[57] The student movement, until that point simmering feverishly in Berlin, precipitously boiled over into West Germany. Student activists represented Ohnesorg as "the accidental victim of a planned attempt to oppress an extraparliamentary opposition."[58] SDS declared: "Student Benno Ohnesorg's death at the hands of the police is the first political murder of the postwar period."[59] The language of civil war underscored the perception among militants that APO had now become an emancipatory "insurgency movement" within the Federal Republic.

The same dramatic shift in consciousness was evident one week later at a congress entitled "University and Democracy" ("Hochschule und Demokratie"). Discussion centered on the question of when – rather than if – "illegal action" and violence were legitimate means of opposition in a modern capitalist society ruled by parliamentary democracy, just like the Federal Republic. A hardened core of radical students began to emerge, bent on a course of all-out resistance and physical struggle.[60] These students saw themselves as part of an international guerrilla movement. This became apparent in the slogan, which first appeared during these months: "Vietnam is the Spain of our generation."[61]

The first focus of attack, however, was not the state apparatus as represented by Bonn or the Bundestag, but capital's shrillest voice, as embodied by the press empire of Axel Caesar Springer.[62] But planning for the anti-Springer campaign was harshly overtaken by a second incident of homicidal violence. This time the target was SDS leader and movement figurehead, Rudi Dutschke. In the spring of 1968, Dutschke was shot three times in a near-fatal attack on the Kurfürstendamm, West Berlin's main boulevard. In a flyer distributed the following day, SDS declared: "Regardless of the question as to whether or not comrade Rudi Dutschke was the victim of a political conspiracy: it can surely be said now, that this crime is only the consequence of the systematic provocation which the state and the Springer corporation have to an increasing degree inflicted upon the democratic forces in this city."[63] That same evening, a spontaneous demonstration in front of the Springer corporation's main office building in West Berlin escalated to an unprecedented level of violence and vandalism.[64]

The following weeks until the end of May, known as the "Easter unrest," marked both the high point and watershed for APO. In the "spirit of the people's front,"[65] students and workers marched shoulder to shoulder.[66] The annual Easter march, once an outpouring of pacifist sentiment, witnessed brutal, violent clashes between masses of demonstrators and the police.[67] The "Star march" in Bonn against the Emergency Laws mustered some 50,000 protesters, including a heavy turnout of unionists. As students and workers banded together elsewhere in Europe,[68] West German student radicals were not the only ones who believed (mistakenly) that this temporary alignment signified the fulfillment of their long-awaited hopes for a lasting alliance between students and workers.

In the summer of 1968, seemingly at its moment of greatest power, APO reached a strategic and moral impasse which it proved unable to surmount. It became glaringly apparent to SDS and other APO organizations that clashes with the state (as represented by the police) employing current forms of action (such as confrontational demonstrations) were hopeless.[69] There were essentially four possible responses to this dilemma.

One was to broaden the base of opposition by "organizing the masses." This was the path undertaken by the KPD-AO (Kommunistische Partei Deutschlands–Aufbau Organisation), which opened the floodgates for the wave of "avant-garde workers' parties" established mostly between 1969 and 1971 "to mobilize the proletariat" for the violent overthrow of capitalism. Those who chose the path of revolutionary communism remained committed to the means of violent confrontation, but realized that a small contingent of student radicals could not wage civil war. Thus, they sought a traditional ally: the working class. Realizing that the form of organization employed by APO, a loose solidarity based on common rituals, was inadequate for their political aim, those forming the KPD-AO opted for the strict hierarchical organization regulated by discipline and centralized planning characteristic of Leninist parties.

The second response was to use armed violence in order to unleash a "civil war" without seeking the immediate support of the working class. The tiny minority which was willing to cross the threshold of violence but had less patience for as well as less faith in the laboring classes than those comprising the previously mentioned category found its way eventually into the Red

Army Faction terrorist organization or one of its circle of sympathizers and abetters such as the Red Cells. The followers of this path exhibited few scruples about using violence against inanimate objects and – eventually – human beings as well.

The third response was to retreat from politics – and mainstream society – to initiate and accomplish personal transformation within the context of a utopian community. The most significant of the groups which rejected violence or were frustrated by political activism and confrontation with the system and thus retreated into their own subcultural milieu was West Berlin's legendary Kommune 1. Rather than destroy the existing society, a majority of Kommune 1 and other organizations of its kind in the Federal Republic tried, in their words, to "drop out" of society (*aussteigen*, in the suggestive German phrase) and construct a radical, "alternative" version instead. In the formula of the day, APO was torn between "hashish and revolution."

The lines between the "drop out" response and its armed counterpart remained quite porous throughout the late 1960s and early 1970s. Thus, as will be seen later, while West Berlin's Kommune 1 was most representative for the "drop out" option, it also had a more violent side to it, which, indeed, transformed some of its members and sympathizers into terrorists. The two traditional sides of anarchism — passive resistance and active confrontation – were well represented in the milieu of the West German post-APO Left. Both sides, of course, shared a marked disdain of and hostility toward established authority and the state.

Finally, the response of the Jusos (Jungsozialisten, Young Socialists) was to achieve "radical reform" through the transformation of existing institutions – particularly the SPD. These four responses defined the major directions of post-APO politics during the 1970s.

This era, then, witnessed a remarkable – and rare – confluence of cultural transformation "from below" and social reform "from above." If APO failed to achieve its stated goals, it succeeded in breaking down the conservatism of public and private discourse in the Federal Republic. In this way, it unwittingly paved the way for social democracy's arrival in state power. Social democratic power, in turn, freed institutional space and public resources for the radical Left. From the beginning, then, the scions of APO and the patriarchs of the SPD stood in a curious relation of mutual dependence. Thus began a long and arduous symbiosis between a state-anchored SPD and an increasingly fragmented extraparliamentary Left which defined the existence of the West German Left until the early 1980s.

In the years after 1968, APO disintegrated into a multiplicity of splinter groups. The united front of the Left, which shone through for brief moments in the late 1960s, had become all but impossible by the early 1970s. The Greens emerged as the outgrowth and legacy of this turmoil. Preceding them, however, was nearly a decade in which APO's successors were a good deal more troubled. It is to a discussion of these forces, beginning with the numerous communist groups on the one hand and terrorism on the other, that we now turn our attention.

3

Revolutionary Cadre Politics and Terrorism

With Gregory Wilpert

The Communist Groups in West Germany (the K-groups)

The "K-groups" of the late 1960s and early 1970s attempted, above all, to institutionalize APO as a permanent social force and expand its "popular base" into the working class. As a result of disagreements about how to achieve revolution – a debate which had begun during the late sixties within the socialist faction of APO – the universe of the K-groups split between Marxist-Leninists and non-Leninist socialists. Prompted by the disappointments of 1968 – as well as the hopeful moments of worker-student solidarity – students left their universities in order to approach the "masses" and organize grass-roots groups (*Basisgruppen*), city groups (*Stadtteilgruppen*) and workplace groups (*Betriebsgruppen*) in search of building the institutions of grass-roots democracy. While these activists soon split into warring ideological factions – Leninists, Spartacists, Trotskyists, Maoists and anarchists – they were all united in the traditional vision of the working class as "revolutionary subject."

Departing from the New Left perspectives of the Frankfurt School which had dominated APO, they reverted to the orthodoxies of the old Left. Indeed, they reveled in "pure" Marxism – or rather, their particular version of it. This was the time when *Das Kapital* study groups and *Grundrisse* workshops proliferated in the Federal Republic's university towns such as Heidelberg, Göttingen, Marburg and Tübingen, in addition to such traditional movement bastions as Berlin and Frankfurt. Of course, this is not to say that these sites were interchangeable or identical. Indeed, it is interesting to note how each one of these locations created its own radical milieu which differentiated it from other movement locales. Thus, for example, among Germany's traditional university towns, Marburg – home of the legendary Marxist scholar Wolfgang Abendroth – assumed a much more "orthodox" line than the equivalent milieu of, say, Tübingen or Heidelberg, where more unconventional forms of radical politics became hegemonic among leftists. Such differences also informed the formation of leftist subcultures of the big cities, notably Frankfurt and Berlin. Whereas the latter remained a bastion of "spontaneous," anti-orthodox radicalism based in an anarchist and grass-roots oriented interpretation of Marxism and its political offspring, Berlin's leftist scene developed in a much more orthodox direction, anchored in a conventional interpretation of Marxist socialism, mainly of the Leninist kind.

The fundamental difference between the Marxist-Leninists on the one hand, and the non-Leninist socialists on the other, was that the former placed a major emphasis on the central role of a vanguard-type party in the process of progressive transformation; the latter, on the other hand, leaned toward Maoism in one form or another, with its emphasis on mass cultural transformation.

Deutsche Kommunistische Partei (DKP)

History and organization The DKP was the successor of the old Kommunistische Partei Deutschlands, disbanded by Hitler during the 1930s and brutally repressed thereafter until 1945. The KPD was reestablished after the Second World War, mostly by former members of the prewar party. But in August of 1956, the KPD was declared unconstitutional on the grounds that its party platform violated the "free democratic order" of the Federal Republic of Germany. At the time of its prohibition, the KPD had about 70,000 members. Some 7,000 of them participated in the formation of the Deutsche Kommunistische Partei (DKP) in 1968.[1] Prompted by the positive events of the 1960s, which witnessed the possibility of genuine revival of a Left in West Germany that was clearly to the left of social democracy, the old members hoped to create a vital and open communist presence in the Federal Republic. To this end, several leading functionaries – Karl Schabrod, Franz Ahrens, Kurt Erlebach, Richard Scheringer and Manfred Kapluck – started an "initiative committee for the legalization of the KPD" in March of 1967.[2] However, Minister of Justice Gustav Heinemann ruled legalization of the KPD impossible, making establishment of a new party the only alternative. The official founding of the DKP thus occurred on October 27, 1968 in Essen.

Many members of the new DKP had belonged to the original KPD.[3] In the decade after 1969, the DKP's membership doubled from 22,000 to 46,500.[4] By 1976 the party had about 300 cells in factories and offices, about half of which belonged to the metal industry,[5] but the DKP's university support group, the MSB-Spartakus, had in many ways become the party's most visible representative. For the most part, these activities were sponsored financially by the GDR.[6]

Ideology and activities The DKP was careful to avoid phrases such as "revolution" and "dictatorship of the proletariat," for it did not want to run the risk of being declared unconstitutional like the KPD. But while the DKP welcomed participation in parliamentary politics, it viewed this as merely ancillary to the true struggle, which in a bourgeois system had to be extraparliamentary by definition. The DKP saw the Federal Republic as a country dominated by monopoly capital, where the power of the monopolies controlled the state apparatus and thus all important aspects of politics and society. This rigidly instrumental interpretation of the workings of the Federal Republic led the DKP to be in the vanguard of an analysis of capitalism known as "state monopoly capital" (*Staatsmonopolkapitalismus*), best known under the abbreviation *Stamokap*.

The GDR was the DKP's main model of a good and just society. In order to achieve a "socialist victory" in the Federal Republic as well, the party dedicated itself to promoting the interests of the working class. Concretely, that meant pursuing an activist role in the Federal Republic's unions, particularly those with a reputation for radicalism, such as the metalworkers (IG Metall), printers and paperworkers (IG Druck und Papier), and bank, insurance and retail workers (Gewerkschaft Handel, Banken, Versicherungen).[7]

Like its ideological model, the GDR, the DKP developed into a stagnant and unattractive bastion of the old Left. Almost irrelevant electorally – the party never attained even 1 percent of the vote in a parliamentary election[8] – the DKP remained a throwback to the 1950s in its theoretical outlook and political strategy. The DKP never attained a pro-active significance in either the politics of the Left or the politics of the Federal Republic which would have led it beyond the drab greyness of its apparatchik existence.

But not all orthodox Marxist groups had been passed by the events of the 1960s. Others, whose roots were in the New Left, were much more radical and innovative.

Kommunistische Partei Deutschlands (KPD)

History and organization One example of this reinvigorated orthodoxy was the new KPD, which shared only its name with the old KPD outlawed in 1956. The new KPD was founded in early 1971 in Berlin by two former SDS activists, Jürgen Horleman and Christian Semler. Efforts to build a new KPD had begun in the late 1960s under the auspices of the Kommunistische Partei Deutschlands–Aufbauorganisation (KPD-AO). Most of its members hailed from the Red Cells in Berlin, especially those at the Free University (see below, pp. 73–5).

Soon after its founding the party came under police investigation because its members had been involved in violent activities at demonstrations.[9] However, these investigations were halted when allegations of criminal activity by the party could not be substantiated.[10]

As of 1977, a very rough membership estimate attributed about 800 full members and approximately 4,500–5,000 sympathizers to the KPD. The party had six regional committees, which together consisted of about 75 cells, 40 of which were organized in plants.[11]

Ideology and activities The new KPD was avowedly Maoist. This meant committed support for Chinese politics and especially for the "cultural revolution." Like most Maoist organizations, the KPD denigrated the Soviet Union as a retrograde and dangerous force against the spread of truly progressive politics on a global level. Indeed, this anti-Soviet animosity was so prevalent that the KPD supported the West German defense forces and even NATO as bulwarks against Soviet imperialism. Following Mao's death, the KPD remained dedicated to Maoist politics and ideology as represented by the Gang of Four in China, particularly by Mao's widow.

The KPD's main strategy was to draw attention through spectacular and violent actions at demonstrations, usually focusing on local issues such as increases in cost of public transportation, nuclear power plants and squatted houses. Another important area for the KPD was its union work, where it tried to separate the "inherently progressive" union membership from its "inherently reactionary" leadership who, so the KPD believed, were "necessarily" little more than stooges of monopoly capitalism. In order to foment grass-roots revolution within labor, the KPD founded an intra-union opposition group called Revolutionary Union Opposition (Revolutionäre Gewerkschaftsopposition), whose acronym of RGO harkened back to Weimar days when, in a more militant period of the German class war, the then powerful KPD challenged the social democrats' hegemony on the German shopfloor by initiating a radical revolutionary opposition of the same name. Needless to say, this RGO revival by the new KPD proved an even greater failure than its earlier incarnation led by the KPD's legendary namesake.

Kommunistische Partei Deutschlands/Marxisten-Leninisten (KPD/ML)

History and organization The KPD/ML was founded in Hamburg on December 31, 1968 by Ernst Aust, a former functionary of the pre-1956 KPD. The party's goal, which it failed to achieve, was to organize all Marxist-Leninists into one party. Although the KPD/ML participated in the Hamburg elections of 1974, it boycotted subsequent electoral campaigns. The party, later centered in Dortmund, was present in five federal states, where it organized in 40 communities. Its membership was estimated at 700–800. Several attempts were made to unite the KPD and the KPD/ML, but due to personal rivalries and international developments in Marxism, this proved to be impossible.[12] The only time a coalition was formed with other Communist groups was for a demonstration in Bonn on October 8, 1977, when the CDU/CSU proposed to outlaw all new (that is, post-APO) Communist parties.

Ideology and activities Although the KPD/ML and the KPD waged bitter battles against each other in their respective publications, including repeated threats of violence, the two parties remained virtually indistinguishable from each other as far as their ideologies and views were concerned. The KPD/ML – just like the KPD – extolled all the Marxist/Leninist and Maoist doctrines, most notably democratic centralism, the dictatorship of the proletariat, the role of the vanguard party, and opposition – pursuant to Maoism – to Soviet and GDR "revisionism." The main difference between KPD/ML and KPD was that the former remained Maoist well into the late 1980s, whereas the latter shifted to the new Chinese line by the mid-1980s. The KPD/ML's model society was Enver Hoxha's Albania, with which the party maintained very close relations. Like the KPD, the KPD/ML advocated the use of violence to attain a socialist revolution; and like the KPD its failures inside the unions were abysmal.

Kommunistischer Bund Westdeutschlands (KBW)

History and organization With about 2,800 members, the KBW was the strongest Maoist and Marxist-Leninist party in West Germany.[13] The KBW was founded on June 12, 1973 in Bremen through a consolidation of numerous smaller, independent Communist groups. Its driving spirit and general secretary was Joschka Schmierer, a former SDS activist from Heidelberg. In 1977, the KBW moved its headquarters from Mannheim to Frankfurt in order to underline its seriousness as a party instead of a student organization. Concomitant with this move, the party changed its name to Kommunistische Partei Westdeutschlands (KPW), dropping the informal "Bund" for the formal "Partei".[14] The KBW bragged about being the only post-1968 Communist K-party to have placed an elected official into a position of governmental responsibility. (Helga Rosenbaum was elected to the Heidelberg city council in May 1977.) The party existed in about 50 communities and had about 250 cells in factories, schools and universities.

Ideology and activities Like the other Maoist parties, the KBW was dedicated to Marxism-Leninism and its associated doctrines. It, too, idealized China and Albania. The KBW also viewed revolutionary violence as being crucial for its strategy, as evidenced by its actions during a demonstration in Heidelberg in the summer of 1975. The KBW proved successful at organizing inside anti-nuclear power groups and in urging them to use violent forms of protest at nuclear power plants. In contrast to the KPD and the KPD/ML, the KBW was never intent on destroying the Federal Republic's existing unions, preferring to reform them. It did not try to organize opposition groups within the unions, concentrating its efforts on winning elections instead. In this sense, the KBW participated in general elections as well as union elections. Exhibiting a modicum of modesty and a rare sense of reality otherwise woefully absent in this milieu of post-APO radical activism, the KBW never considered itself a genuine Communist party since it lacked massive working-class support.

Kommunistischer Bund (KB)

History and organization   Founded in Hamburg in 1971, the Kommunistischer Bund (KB), just like the KBW, was a conglomeration of smaller
Communist groups, such as SALZ (Sozialistisches Arbeiter- und Lehrlingszentrum) and KAB (Kommunistischer Arbeiterbund). With its membership concentrated in northern Germany, the KB was perhaps the most
obscure among the K-groups of the 1970s. Its membership, ranging between 800 and 1,500, was organized in cells and followed the doctrine of
democratic centralism. Yet the KB proved relatively successful in its union
work and in some cases it attained 33 percent of the vote in the works
councils elections of 1975 and 1978. By the late seventies, the KB had over
a hundred of its members elected to various works councils in the Federal
Republic.[14] The KB's university group met with moderate success as well,
gaining, for example, representation on the student government in
Göttingen in 1976.[15]

Ideology and activities   The KB, too, pursued an orthodox Marxism-Leninism of the Maoist variety, which it rigidly upheld, even after Mao's death.
Just like the KBW, the KB believed that the time had not yet been ripe for
the creation of a full-fledged political party due to the working class's
continued adherence to various reformist ideologies. The KB distinguished
itself from all the K-groups with its rallying cry of "fascism," by which it
referred to the counterrevolution that it saw emerging all over the Federal
Republic.

Gruppe Internationale Marxisten (GIM)

History and organization   Founded in 1969 and headquartered in Frankfurt, the GIM has remained the largest and only Trotskyist organization
(out of about ten) in the Federal Republic to have participated in elections. The GIM has been officially part of the Fourth International, which
was founded by Trotsky in 1938. GIM's membership had been estimated
at 400–600,[16] with about 51 chapters throughout the Federal Republic in
the late 1970s, and early 1980s. Even though GIM experienced a decline
in membership and influence in the Federal Republic's leftist milieu
throughout the 1980s, this group – unlike its K-group cousins and rivals
– never disappeared completely from the West German political scene,
proving perhaps yet again Trotskyism's impressive staying power.

Ideology and activities   GIM has considered the state and the bureaucracy
as the main obstacles to socialism because these prevent workers from
attaining self-determination. Democratic centralism as an organizational
principle has meant something slightly less centralized for GIM than it has

for the K-groups in that it is supposed to ensure that decision making occurs from below to be combined with the enforcement of discipline from above. Compared to the K-groups, GIM has been amenable to making compromises with capitalists and managers who offer better work conditions. Other foci of activity for GIM have centered around guaranteed job security, decreasing working hours, rejecting unions because they suppress strikes, and opposing the armed forces of the Bundeswehr because they represent the bourgeoisie's instrument of power. GIM also criticized the Soviet Union, its East European satellites and China, because production in all these places remained state controlled and thus was never granted to the workers, rendering it, in GIM's estimation, non-participatory and non-democratic.

Terrorism

One of the most complex and troubling phenomena in the post-1968 Left has been terrorism. Though it never accounted for more than a few hundred core activists and sympathizers, terrorists were able – largely through their spectacular actions and the state's merciless reaction to them – to attain an importance within the West German Left not warranted by their numbers. This was because terrorism represented, albeit in extreme form, values deeply held by many in the West German Left: constant confrontation with a repressive state; an active role for intellectuals in pushing for social change; disgust with a "complacent" and "bourgeoisified" working class; a conviction that peaceful protest was a weak and limited means for attaining reform; and a rejection of existing institutions, including those of the traditional Left, as a meaningful arena for political activity.

Although the number of those who actually committed acts of terrorism was quite small, they enjoyed at least some support from a wider group. A case in point was the obituary for Siegfried Buback, the federal prosecutor-general assigned to the Baader-Meinhof case, who was murdered by terrorists in April 1977. It was written by a student under the pseudonym "Mescalero,"[17] and in it, the author claimed that he could not conceal his "clandestine joy" over Buback's death.[18] The obituary was reprinted by a group of 43 professors, who rejected terrorist acts, but who claimed the freedom to publish the obituary. Their action was an illustration of the extent of the tacit support of many on the Left for the aims of the terrorists, although not for their actions. (More importantly, however, the professors' action challenged the excessively repressive laws enacted to combat terrorism.) The prolonged and painful discussion concerning political violence which ensued was critical in spreading the commitment to peace and non-violence which became a mainstay of the new social movements and eventually of the Greens' political platform as well.

West Germany's leftist terrorist organizations have been very diverse in terms of their membership, organization, and background. The four main terrorist groups that emerged between 1967 and 1985 were the June 2 Movement (Bewegung 2. Juni), the Red Army Faction (Rote Armee Fraktion, RAF), the Socialist Patients' Collective (Sozialistisches Patienten Kollektiv, SPK), and the Red Cells (Rote Zellen, RZ). Some of these have been very tightly organized, such as the RAF, and others somewhat more loosely, such as the RZ. Their timespans of activity vary; June 2 and SPK were active only in the early 1970s, RZ in the 1980s, and the RAF persisted throughout the early 1970s and into the 1990s. Common to all of them is the fact that their roots lay in the social upheavals of the student movement and counterculture of the late 1960s. Their membership exhibited mainly an upper middle-class background, with a large majority of activists hailing from the milieu of the communes and the student-dominated subcultures around universities.[19]

As we have seen, the collapse of the student movement spawned a mood of desolation and despair among many of the sixty-eighters. Among those who held fast to the dream of revolution, there were two groups. One placed faith in the workers and migrated to the K-groups. Another decidedly smaller group, disillusioned with the proletariat, reached for more radical means. It assumed the cause of "armed struggle" against the state, which its members perceived as the only realistic way of fomenting revolution.

Bewegung 2. Juni

One of the first terrorist organizations was the June 2 Movement, a regional movement concentrated in West Berlin. It emerged from a loosely organized group called the Hash Rebels (Haschenrebellen), rooted in various Berlin communes. 1969 witnessed a spate of bombing and arson attacks throughout the Federal Republic.[20] The Hash Rebels – whose members were Georg von Rauch, Michael "Bommi" Baumann, Heinz Brockmann, Annerose Reiche, Angela Luther, Peter Knoll, Thomas Weissbekker, and Ralf Reinders – were responsible for a number of such attacks in West Berlin, including bombings of the Berlin Jewish community center, the city court director, the city attorney general and various cars bearing American license plates.[21] A wave of arrests brought many of these activities to a halt. But when one of the leaders of the Hash Rebels, Georg von Rauch, was shot by the police in late 1971, the group metamorphosed into a much more tightly knit, secretive organization, calling itself the Bewegung 2. Juni in memory of the day when – as will be remembered – a policeman killed the student Benno Ohnesorg.

Originally, Bewegung 2. Juni envisioned a *modus operandi* different than the RAF's. Its members wanted to confine their activities to Berlin and work mostly on local issues, such as opposing fare increases in Berlin's public transportation and offering support to workers in conflicts with management. However, as its actions escalated, the June 2 Movement needed increasing logistical support in the form of apartments, cars, weapons, documents and money. It received some of these from the RAF.

A main source of the group's inspiration in terms of its strategy and tactics was a handbook of sorts entitled the *Mini-Manual of the Urban Guerilla*, authored by the Latin American Carlos Marighella. It recommended two main goals: the "physical liquidation" of the bosses and their helpers in the armed forces and the police; and "the expropriation of wealth and the means of production that belong to the government, the monopoly capitalists, the land owners, and the imperialists." Bank robberies were considered especially suitable towards achieving this second goal. This handbook included, among other things, instructions as to the manufacture of bombs and the stealing of cars.[22] The June 2 Movement touted the Tupamaros of Uruguay as real-life models for this type of urban guerrilla force.

The group incurred its first casualty in February 1972 during the bombing of the British yacht club in Berlin. In a subsequent statement, the June 2 Movement admitted that losing one of its member's lives bespoke an error in the group's overall strategy. This, in addition to other disagreements with the RAF concerning the latter's intensified bombing campaign during that year, led to the severing of the June 2 Movement's cooperation with the RAF. The June 2 Movement was consistently decimated by police arrests, partly due to an informer in its ranks; on his discovery, he was killed by the group on June 5, 1974. Later that year, on November 9, the highest judge of the city of Berlin, Günter von Drenckmann, was shot in his home by the June 2 Movement, apparently in a failed kidnapping attempt by the terrorists.[23]

Subsequently, in order to free its imprisoned companions, the June 2 Movement kidnapped Peter Lorenz, the chairman of the Christian Democratic Party of Berlin on February 25, 1975. In preparation for this kidnapping, the group robbed two banks, collecting over DM 100,000. At this time the core of the group consisted of Fritz Teufel, a graduate of Kommune 1 activities of 1969, Ralf Reinders, Ronald Fritsch, Gerald Klöpper, Till Meyer, Inge Viett (who became an RAF member in 1977), Juliane Plembeck and Gabriele Rollnick. Their demands were the freeing of six terrorists, including the attorney Horst Mahler, a former RAF member. They also demanded a Boeing 707 to fly them to a city of their choice. On March 2, the police decided to accede to their demands and flew the prisoners (except for Horst Mahler, who refused to participate in the action) to South Yemen. The June 2 Movement then released Peter Lorenz on March 4. In subsequent leaflets the group stated that it considered its actions as being in self-defense and that it saw itself as a revolutionary vanguard. A month after the kidnapping, the police made its first arrests in the case.[24] By 1977 the group had been so decimated that it disbanded. Its remnants joined what had by then become the "second generation" of RAF activists.

Rote Armee Fraktion

The RAF also had most of its roots in the West Berlin of the late 1960s. The burning of the Brussels department store "À l'innovation" and the destruction of its display of American goods on May 22, 1967, inspired the violence-oriented members of Kommune 1 to produce a leaflet asking, "When will the Berlin department stores burn?"[25] Less than a year later, on April 5, 1968, Gudrun Ensslin, Andreas Baader and two others were arrested for having set two Frankfurt department stores on fire three days earlier.

Gudrun Ensslin, one of the RAF's founding members, was a minister's daughter. She had studied philosophy, German and English at the Free University in Berlin. She had spent one year studying in the United States, where she adopted the ideas of the Weathermen, one of the American SDS's most radical successor organizations. In 1967 Ensslin met Andreas Baader, who was a drifter. He had dropped out of high school and subsequently abandoned an apprenticeship as a potter in order to move to Berlin and study art. Baader had always been considered a "problem child" and before he moved to Berlin at age 20 he had already committed numerous car and motorcycle thefts. The previously apolitical Baader became politicized by Ensslin, who had been involved in SDS circles for some time, and by the shooting of Benno Ohnesorg on June 2, 1967. Baader joined Horst Mahler's Republikanischer Club and established ties with Kommune 1, where he was admired for being a person of action. A little later he and Ensslin drove to Frankfurt with two Kommune 1 members, where they hoped to activate the masses by burning the department stores. Otto Schily, later to become one of the most prominent Greens and one of their most outspoken Realos, and Horst Mahler, who was later to join the RAF, were two of the lawyers who defended the four arsonists. The four were sentenced to three years in prison.

Horst Mahler, a respected and successful attorney in the early 1960s, was co-founder in 1966 of the Republikanischer Club in Berlin, a communication and contact center for the extraparliamentary opposition. During the student movement he was the attorney for many important leaders of the movement, notably Rudi Dutschke, Fritz Teufel, and Andreas Baader. Gradually he also became one of the student movement's main theoreticians. During the arson trial of Baader and Ensslin, Mahler faced a trial of his own because of his participation in the demonstrations against the Springer press conglomerate which occurred in the wake of the assassination attempt on Rudi Dutschke.

After spending 14 months in prison, Baader and Ensslin were released on June 13, 1969. While awaiting the result of their appeal, they both began working at an education and training center for juvenile delinquents. When their appeal failed, they fled to Paris. After receiving word that a new militant leftist group was about to be founded, they clandestinely returned to Germany. The founders were Fritz Teufel and Dieter Kunzelmann; Kunzelmann had trained with Al Fatah in Jordan (and would be elected to the West Berlin parliament as a member of the Alternative List (AL), the Greens' Berlin party 13 years later). But Kunzelmann and Teufel were not radical enough. Ensslin and Baader decided to join another group being formed by Manfred Grashof and Petra Schelm. Baader quickly became the leader of this group. Thus the RAF was born.

With the help of an informant, the police arrested Baader on April 4, 1970. Immediately the RAF began devising a plan to free him, and it was successfully implemented on May 14, 1970, while Baader was on a furlough supposedly doing research for a book with the help of Ulrike Meinhof, a new member of the RAF. In the course of the escape, however, a police officer was critically wounded.

Ulrike Meinhof (born 1934) grew up with an adoptive mother, a committed pacifist who adopted Ulrike as a child following the death of her parents. After her studies, Ulrike became active in the nuclear disarmament campaign. It was there that she met her husband, the publisher of *Konkret*, a prominent left-wing magazine, alleged at the time to have had some financial ties to the GDR. The two of them joined the (then illegal) Communist Party (KPD). Writing for *Konkret*, Meinhof attracted national attention with her highly critical and iconoclastic articles. After her divorce in 1967, she moved to Berlin, where she continued working for *Konkret*, while at the same time beginning to write for the *Rote Presse Korrespondenz*, a main organ of the New Left. Meinhof also joined Rudi Dutschke in editing a new left-wing publication called *Konkret Berlin*. In Frankfurt, Meinhof met Baader and Ensslin at their experimental education center project.

Shortly after freeing Andreas Baader, the group flew to Jordan, where they hoped to receive training in guerrilla warfare from Al Fatah. Following conflicts with the Palestinians, the group decided to return to Berlin. There the group dedicated itself to the pursuit of the "underground struggle." Cars and apartments were purchased. By September 29, 1970 the group had carried out three bank robberies in Berlin, acquiring DM 220,000.[26] But on October 8, the police apprehended Horst Mahler and several others.

After spending some time trying to figure out how to free Mahler, the group decided to relocate to West Germany. Shortly thereafter, Ulrike Meinhof produced a position paper in which, for the first time, the group called itself the Rote Armee Fraktion. This was the prelude to a series of attacks throughout West Germany which culminated in the notorious triple bombing on May 11, 1972 at the headquarters of the V. Corps of the US army in Frankfurt. It was quickly followed by bomb attacks on sites in six other cities, which left several innocent people dead and numerous wounded: at the Bavarian criminal investigation office in Munich; in Karlsruhe, where the target was a federal judge whose wife suffered serious injuries in the attack; at the Springer publishing house in Hamburg; and in Heidelberg at the European headquarters of the US army, where two soldiers were killed and five seriously wounded. Finally, on June 1, 1972, the police managed to track down and arrest Andreas Baader, Holger Meins, and Jan-Carl Raspe after a shoot-out in Frankfurt. That same day Gudrun Ensslin was taken into custody in Hamburg. Ulrike Meinhof and Gerhard Müller were caught in Hanover two weeks later.

During these early years of the 1970s, the RAF published a variety of pamphlets and leaflets detailing its political ideology and strategy. Unlike the June 2 Movement, which operated in secrecy, the RAF seemed eager to develop a public profile. It argued for the primacy of praxis, and claimed that armed struggle was the highest form of Marxism-Leninism. The fundamental correctness of armed struggle, argued Meinhof, was never to be doubted. Its truth depended only on its feasibility.[27]

This did not mean that existing efforts to organize the working class should be abandoned: because "the organization of armed illegal opposition forces cannot replace the legal proletarian organizations . . . the armed struggle was no substitute for political work in the factory and in the community".[28] But, Meinhof insisted, only an armed struggle could unite the workers in order to topple the system.[29] Meinhof rejected the theorizing of the New Left. She argued that it was not theory, but armed struggle that was the only means to forge a historical alliance between workers and intellectuals. Success, not theory, was the only standard of an action's correctness. Various groups of the New Left criticized this attitude for being a "vulgar trial and error" strategy. While there was consensus within the RAF about the necessity of armed insurgency, there were disagreements about "revolutionary strategy and tactics." Mahler felt that the fight against imperialism in the Third World was paramount. He envisioned the RAF as an urban guerrilla force, which would seek to destroy physically the instruments of imperialism with the logistical support and backing of the general population. Meinhof on the other hand felt that the class war in Germany was most important. She argued that RAF first had to develop support within the general population through spectacular revolutionary actions that would provide the RAF with a psychological victory over the state by showing that the state was far from invincible and could in fact be intimidated by terrorism. Meinhof's standpoint was the more radical insofar as it combined the use of terror with psychological warfare, while Mahler favored a more limited strategy of obstruction and sabotage. It was Meinhof's position which ultimately emerged victorious.

According to Meinhof, the revolutionary struggle was to occur in three phases: first, the population would be shown that armed groups can in fact develop and fight the state; second, exemplary attacks would be conducted to demoralize the ruling class; and third, general popular war would be initiated against the oppressive system. The RAF was to serve as the catalyst igniting the first phase.[30]

Following the arrest of the RAF's core members, the police assumed that the terrorist scene had been destroyed. They were mistaken. The RAF reappeared in many places, though no longer in the major cities. Its activities in 1973–4 consisted mostly of bombings of foreign offices (such as the Iranian and Chilean embassies, as well as the Israeli tourist office), US army bases, members of the judiciary, and police departments. On April 24, 1975, the "Commando Holger Meins", a squad named after one of the RAF members who died in prison because of a hunger strike, stormed and occupied the West German embassy in Stockholm. Six hostages were taken, including the ambassador himself. After shooting one of the hostages in order to get the police to leave the building, the terrorists demanded the release of 26 imprisoned RAF activists (including the RAF leadership) and an airplane in Frankfurt. The government, under Helmut Schmidt's leadership, refused to accede to any of the demands, even though the terrorists threatened to shoot one hostage every hour after their deadline passed unfulfilled. After one of the hostages was shot and the police were about to storm the embassy, one of the terrorists' bombs exploded accidentally, giving the police the opportunity to save all the other hostages and arrest the terrorists.

In 1976, another terrorist group formed around attorney Siegfried Haag and his friend Roland Meyer, dubbed the "Haag-Meyer gang." The group itself continued its operations even after the arrest of Haag and Meyer on November 30, 1976, due in large part to the influence Baader and Ensslin exerted on its members from their prison cells with the help of their attorneys. In prison, while court proceedings were underway against them, Baader and Ensslin prepared Brigitte Mohnhaupt to take control of this group once she had completed her prison term. As soon as she was released she reorganized the group and renamed it RAF, thus denoting a clear continuity between the organization's first and second incarnations. On May 8–9, 1976, Ulrike Meinhof hanged herself in her prison cell halfway through the court case against her. In the course of this year the police registered about 150 bombings and arson attempts in over 50 cities throughout West Germany by the RAF and other left-wing terrorist organizations.

During 1977 two sensational assassinations placed the RAF at the center of public attention. On April 7, in Karlsruhe, members of the RAF assassinated the Federal Republic's attorney general, Siegfried Buback, in the middle of the street, also killing his driver and one other person in the car. The RAF described the action as an "execution" because of Buback's role as an "agent of the system," for being the "nodal point between the judiciary and the news organizations" and for his alleged complicity in the deaths of Ulrike Meinhof, Holger Meins, and Siegfried Hausner (who was killed in the Stockholm embassy raid).

The second attack came on July 30 when Jürgen Ponto, the chief executive of the Dresdner Bank, was killed in his home by RAF members after a failed kidnapping attempt. The group managed to gain entrance into Ponto's home by having Susanne Albrecht, the daughter of one of the Ponto family's closest friends, pretend to make a casual visit.

An even more dramatic plot was foiled the following month, when the police found an RAF-constructed homemade rocket launcher, armed with 42 rockets and aimed at the attorney general's office in Karlsruhe. The contraption malfunctioned.

The RAF struck again in Cologne on September 5, 1977. In a daring action, a group calling itself the "Siegfried Hausner Commando of the RAF" attacked Hanns-Martin Schleyer, a powerful industrialist and then president of the Bundesverband der Deutschen Arbeitgeberverbände (BDA), one of the three most powerful employers' associations in Germany. The terrorists abducted Schleyer, killing three police escorts and a driver in the process. In exchange for Schleyer's release, they demanded freedom for 11 imprisoned RAF members (including Baader, Ensslin, and Jan-Carl Raspe), each of whom was to receive one hundred thousand marks. Just as in the Stockholm embassy hostage crisis, the government refused to succumb to any of the terrorists' demands.

Six weeks later, on October 13, Palestinian terrorists hijacked a Lufthansa airplane and commandeered it to Mogadishu in Somalia, demanding the release of the same 11 terrorists, as well as two Palestinians held in a Turkish prison. After delaying tactics by the German government, a special anti-terror force (GSG-9) stormed the airplane and freed all passengers unharmed, killing three Palestinian terrorists in the process. A couple of hours after this action, Baader, Ensslin and Raspe were found dead in their prison cells. An investigation determined that their deaths were suicides, although the mysterious circumstances led many to dispute this finding. The day following the terrorists' deaths, the police found Schleyer's dead body in the trunk of a car near the French border.

The events of 1977 proved to be very demoralizing to the RAF. Many of the participants in theses actions were arrested not so long afterwards and the RAF seemed all but defeated. Those who were not arrested either left the country or quit the organization. However, in 1979, the RAF started a new recruiting phase. Three years after their previous bank robbery, RAF members robbed a bank in Bochum, acquiring DM 124,000. That year the RAF also implemented a failed assassination attempt of then NATO commander, Alexander Haig, in Brussels. Subsequently, in September 1981, a RAF anti-tank projectile barely missed US General Frederick Kroessen's car.[31]

According to RAF plans found by the police in 1984, the RAF had a three-step plan which it hoped to implement in 1985. First, key NATO military positions were to be bombed. Second, the imprisoned RAF members were to start a hunger strike that would be accompanied by RAF attacks throughout the country. Finally, "representatives of repression" were to be killed. The RAF implemented this plan in December of 1984, when RAF prisoners went on a hunger strike. At the same time bombing attacks occurred throughout Europe. For example, on January 25, 1985, the French general René Audran was killed; on February 1, the chief executive of the Motoren-Turbinen-Union, Ernst Zimmerman, was fatally shot; and on August 8, 1985, the RAF bombed the US air force base in Frankfurt, killing two Americans and wounding 11 others. The police found evidence that the RAF had begun to cooperate with both the French terrorist organization Action Directe (AD) and the Cellules Communistes Combattantes (CCC) organizations in Belgium.[32]

Even though substantially weakened, the RAF continued to alert the German public with spectacular assassinations of key public figures throughout the rest of the 1980s and into the 1990s. In the fall of 1989, the RAF assassinated the chief executive of the Deutsche Bank, Alfred Herrhausen, arguably among the best known and most prominent German businessmen. Barely 18 months later, in the spring of 1991, the RAF once again proved successful in killing yet another key German industrialist. This time, the terrorists aimed at Detlef Rohwedder, formerly the chief executive of Hoesch, one of the Federal Republic's leading steel companies; he was a well-known supporter of the SPD, and at the time of his death the head of the Treuhandanstalt, the public agency entrusted by the Federal government with the privatization of the newly merged East German economy. In both cases, the RAF succeeded in assassinating people who were prototypes of the RAF's prime enemies: powerful but enlightened business leaders with close connections to both the public and private sectors of the German political economy.

Sozialistisches Patienten Kollektiv – Heidelberg (SPK)

Three months before Baader was freed in February 1970, a certain Dr Wolfgang Huber founded the SPK in Heidelberg. Despite constant problems with that city's university clinic, where he was working, he managed – through hunger strikes with his students – to keep rooms at the university for his therapy group. According to the SPK, the economic and social conditions of the Federal Republic made people sick, and the only way for them to be cured was to destroy the system itself.[33] Therapy which healed the individual without changing the system that caused the problem in the first place was no cure at all. For its theoretical underpinnings, the group referred to the writings of R. D. Laing.

SPK had an inner circle of around 12 people, who were supposed to act as therapeutic and political leaders. The existence of this inner circle was kept a secret from the other 300 members. Various working groups were organized, including one for radio technology, one for bombing technology, and one for karate. Huber believed that about 1,000 members would be sufficient for a well-organized revolution, which he planned for 1972–3. When the organization was started, it comprised about 30 members. By March 1971, membership had increased to 300. SPK also tried to establish contacts with other extremist groups, notably the RAF.[34]

The group continued to attract a great deal of attention, particularly in the psychiatric community. It continued its regular operations even though it had begun to organize bombing attacks against public buildings, bridges and military installations. By the summer of 1971, the group acquired weapons, explosives and ammunition, which it obtained mostly through its contacts with the RAF. When Huber and his wife were arrested at the end of July 1971, the group disintegrated.[35] However, many of its members joined other existing terrorist organizations. Ralf Reinders, for example, joined Bewegung 2. Juni and was one of the Lorenz kidnappers, and Hana Krabbe participated in the occupation of the German embassy in Stockholm.

Revolutionäre Zellen (RZ)

The RZ groups emerged from the same left-wing student scenes of the post-1968 milieu as did the RAF and the Bewegung 2. Juni. However, unlike the latter two, which originated in West Berlin, the RZ groups began in Frankfurt. The RZ had always been critical of the RAF for its elitist and hierarchical style. As opposed to the RAF, the RZ was loosely organized into many small (three to five person) cells. It had two branches, one whose members attended to their violent activities parttime while still living normal civilian lives, and another whose members lived in the underground and operated as revolutionaries on a fulltime basis. Some major activities of the RZ groups involved the Entebbe hijacking, conducted together with Palestinian terrorists in mid-1976, and the taking of hostages of OPEC ministers in Vienna in December 1975, also with the help of Palestinians. The close ties which some RZ cells maintained with the Progressive Front for the Liberation of Palestine (PFLP) involved them in attacks on Israeli targets in Germany.

The group started developing around 1973, when leftist groups began splintering in the aftermath of the RAF bombings of 1972. RZ's members tried new tactics of living legal lives as long as possible, confining their subversive activities to their "leisure hours". Indeed, other radical groups derided the RZ as "after hours guerrillas" (*Feierabend Guerilla*). The RZ drew their members from various anarchist and communist organizations (such as the Black Help, the Red Help, the Anti-Imperialist Struggle and the Revolutionary Struggle) and provided a sort of umbrella group for various revolutionary movements.

The RZ first attracted national attention in 1974 because of its involvement in numerous strikes. This was in consonance with their professed goal of politicizing and radicalizing social problems. Unlike the RAF, however, the RZ regarded violence against persons and illegal actions only as a very last resort. Instead, they chose forms of radical resistance which lay in legality's gray zone, such as factory occupations, activities on behalf of lower public transportation costs (mostly vandalism), so-called "free shopping," sabotage at construction sites, terror-inducing phone calls, and spray-painting political graffiti. The cells operated almost completely independently of each other as no central coordinating body existed. In 1977, when the RAF murdered Buback, Ponto and Schleyer, the RZ distanced itself from the RAF, considering these actions irresponsible and counterproductive. The group's ideology was propagated in its publication *Revolutionärer Zorn* ("Revolutionary Wrath").

A booklet that appeared in 1981 called *Guerilla Diffusa* described how RZ-type groups should be organized. It argued that a diffusion of small autonomous guerilla groups was much more effective in overthrowing the existing social order than a tightly knit Leninist-style vanguard cell because the police had greater difficulty in tracing such a loose association of activists. The booklet continued to state that activities should focus on Molotov cocktail attacks on banks and department stores, as well as involve bomb scares designed to harm businesses, instead of killing people.

Main areas of activity for the groups were Berlin, the Rhine-Main area, the Ruhr region, and occasionally Hamburg and north-west Germany. By 1982 the federal criminal investigations office (Bundeskriminalamt) estimated that RZ groups had been responsible for 132 bombings or arson attacks, causing about DM 50 million in damage. The number of cells was estimated at 50–100 with a total of about 300–500 members. Although they opposed pacifist-inspired peace and anti-nuclear groups, most of their members were in fact recruited from these groups. Both the diffused guerrilla groups and the RZs were quite successful in implementing their numerous acts of terror, while the authorities remained quite ignorant as to who they really were, how they operated, and what their members' background was. In terms of the simple quantity of operations, the RZs far surpassed both the RAF and the June 2 Movement.

The state's reaction to terrorism

One of the most troubling features of the outbreak of terrorism was the reaction of the state. Sensitive to the criticism of the CDU and CSU that it was being "soft" on terrorism,[36] the governing coalition between the SPD and the Free Democrats pushed for tough amendments to the criminal code with the intention of curbing terrorism. Between 1974 and 1978, the Bundestag passed a series of amendments to the criminal code, which included allowing the government to forbid lawyers to defend certain clients if the lawyers were suspected of passing communications from their clients to the outside, and permitting authorities to monitor telephone calls of lawyers who were suspected of supporting a criminal organization. In 1978, legislation was passed which authorized police to ask persons in public places for identification, even if they were not suspected of having committed a crime. If they failed to produce satisfactory identification, they could be detained for up to 12 hours while the police tried to establish their identity.[37]

Perhaps the most controversial legislation of the period was the Contact Ban Law (Kontaktsperre-Gesetz). After the kidnapping of Hanns-Martin Schleyer in September 1977, federal and Länder ministers of justice ordered that a number of prisoners accused of either membership in or support for a terrorist organization be barred from receiving newspapers, listening to the radio, sending or receiving letters and corresponding with their lawyers. The Bundestag legalized the actions of the justice ministers, and on September 29, 1977, passed the Contact Ban Law, which granted authorities the right to bar prisoners accused or found guilty of terrorist activities from having any contact with each other, their lawyers or the outside world for 30 days. After 30 days, the ban could be renewed.[38]

To some it seemed that the Contact Ban Law was an unjustifiable restriction of civil liberties. Four SPD deputies voted against the bill, claiming that they were upholding the free social and legal foundation of the liberal-democratic state. Twelve other SPD deputies and four FDP deputies abstained from the vote. Their actions provoked an angry response from SPD parliamentary leader Herbert Wehner, who upbraided the dissidents for their breach of party discipline. Two hundred SPD deputies signed a letter in support of Wehner for upholding the principles of democracy in the Bundestag.[39]

Many in the SPD, particularly the so-called *Kanalarbeiter* ("sewer workers"),[40] who were in leadership positions in the "accommodationist" trade unions, enthusiastically supported the anti-terrorist laws. However, others on the left saw these laws as a further revelation of the SPD's "subservience to the state" (*Staatshörigkeit*) – a harkening back to the Weimar period when the SPD Minister of the Interior Gustav Noske had used the army to suppress the Spartacist uprising.[41] The controversy over the anti-terrorist laws conveyed the widening split between the old and the new Left, especially concerning the relationship of the state to society.

Terrorism accentuated the worst aspects of the German Left. It highlighted its dogmatic streak, which shows no tolerance for discussion and debate, let alone dissent. It manifested a certain underlying elitism, which came to the fore repeatedly in the notion that all the masses needed was activist leaders who showed them the way. This "vanguardism," though inherent to any small, cell-like and clandestine organization, was particularly pronounced and self-justified in the case of the German terrorists. As we now know from a number of interviews with ex-terrorists, they really believed that they were morally superior to everybody else. This sense of "calling," of politics as a strictly moral category also appears among all terrorist groups in the world. Yet there is a particular side to this political discourse which renders it not unfamiliar to various traditions of German politics. In that sense, terrorism also addressed the German condition well beyond the confines of the German Left, no matter how broadly construed.

It is in this context that one has to evaluate the intimate relationship between the German terrorists and their Palestinian colleagues. Once again, it is well known that various camps operated by Al Fatah, the PFLP, the Democratic Front for the Liberation of Palestine (DFLP), the PFLP-General Command, As Saiqua and others helped train terrorists from many countries during the 1970s and early 1980s. Thus the Germans who came to these camps were in many ways not particularly special. And yet one cannot help but see a very distinct pattern in the affinity of certain German leftists to organizations whose most sought-after desire at the time was the obliteration of the state of Israel. One of the ugliest (and still unrecognized) moments of post-Holocaust German history was the incident in which German terrorists helped Palestinians in Entebbe to "select" Jewish passengers from others during the highjacking of an El Al plane in the summer of 1976. For German leftists to engage in precisely the same activity that was perpetrated by their parents on Jews barely 30 years before bespeaks of a cruelty which must rest in the younger generation's total rage against its elders. One of the most fundamental pillars of legitimation for the new Federal Republic was its "special" relationship to the Jews and, above all, to Israel. Few things could render one's contempt for this republic more pronounced than spurning the "specialness" of this relationship. Lest there be no doubt about this position of antinomy, one then went ahead and formed an active alliance with those who made it their policy to destroy Jews once again, 30 years after Auschwitz.

Just as ugly as terrorism itself was the state's response to it. Violating its own values of civil liberties and due process, the West German state mobilized forces of repression and surveillance well beyond the proportions necessary for an appropriate response to the challenges exacted by the terrorists. The state's excessive vigilance not only undermined the Federal Republic's democratic order. It also failed to eradicate terrorism. Above all, the state's measures seemed inappropriate, due to the fact that any kind of left-wing extremism, let alone of the terrorist sort, enjoyed absolutely no support among the population as a whole.

Contrast to this the German state's belated and meek response to the serious right-wing terrorism which endangered the public peace and exacted a number of lives 15 years later in the newly united Germany. Repeated firebombings of foreigners by right-wing extremists in the former East Germany as well as in cities and towns of the old Federal Republic led to a de facto tolerance on the part of the repressive apparatus of the state in 1992. Not until numerous voices from abroad let it be known that Germany's public image may once again be seriously tarnished did the government deploy the state's necessary might to curb the activities of right-wing extremism and terrorism. Thus, it took the potential threat to the Federal Republic's most prized possession – its exports – to have the German state respond to a situation which, in terms of representing a danger to the democratic order, was far more acute and serious than any of the challenges posed by the terrorist activities of the Left in the 1970s and 1980s. The reason for the marked difference in the state's respective responses is abundantly clear: being a democracy, political actors in the Federal Republic – just like elsewhere – follow public opinion. And that has been unmistakably clear in this case: while virtually nobody in West Germany supported the aims or the tactics of left-wing extremism of the 1970s and 1980s, this, alas, cannot be said about right-wing extremism of a decade later. To be sure, a vast majority of Germans emphatically reject the tactics of right-wing extremism and terrorism. However, an equally impressive majority agree with these terrorists' aims, which in this case mean to keep foreigners away from entering Germany as refugees and asylum seekers. The success of right-wing terrorism was in fact swift in coming. In the fall of 1992, the conservative-liberal coalition government – with the help of the social-democratic opposition – forged a new law which severely curtailed access to Germany for all potential refugees and asylum seekers. Left-wing terrorism could not even remotely fathom, let alone concretely claim, a victory of such a kind in its 20-year existence.

Lastly, yet another aspect of terrorism rendered it so central to contemporary German events. Among the many startling revelations which accompanied the disappearance of the German Democratic Republic was the one about the active support that the GDR's regime rendered to the Federal Republic's left-wing terrorists virtually throughout their entire existence. In addition to providing financial and logistical help, the GDR also offered a safe haven to terrorists seeking refuge from West German authorities. This was a particularly disillusioning revelation for many on the German Left, for whom terrorism was clearly not a real political option but for whom the terrorists did in fact represent a legitimate antinomy to the much-despised Federal Republic. That these tarnished but nevertheless legitimate heroes of the anti-Leninist Left, these veterans of 1968 and APO, emerged among others as de facto collaborators of the bankrupt GDR was a serious disappointment to many a former sixty-eighter. But 1968 had a happier legacy as well. It is to that we now turn.

4

Revolution, Retreat, Reform:
To APO and Back . . . to Parliament

At the outset of the 1970s, there were essentially three tendencies within the Left: revolution, retreat and reform. At this stage of disparity, it would have seemed rather unlikely to the historical actors themselves that these initially divergent and often warring tendencies which we delineated in the preceding two chapters would or could be (re)united one decade later. Yet by the late 1970s and early 1980s a relatively unified constellation of protest had emerged, centered around the anti-nuclear and ecology movements. This green protest movement subsequently formed the platform for the emergence of the first green electoral lists and parties on the local and state levels in 1977 and 1978. In this chapter, we will focus on the green movement (leaving the party to subsequent chapters) by trying to reconstruct a twofold pattern of development: on the one hand, the "greening" of the radical "leftovers" from APO, the so-called "sixty-eighter generation," and, on the other, the mobilization and radicalization of liberal or moderate elements of the "educated middle class" (*Bildungsbürgertum*). To comprehend the historical significance of the Greens as well as the concomitant greening of the German Left (openly in the West and clandestinely in the East), it is essential to understand this alliance between what one might in an anticipatory way designate as a "post-Marxist" radical Left and a "postmaterial" reformist middle class.

The background for both these sets of developments lies in the failures of social-democratic reform politics during the 1970s. If the 1960s were a decade of disillusion for the radical Left, then the 1970s were a decade of disappointment. The prospects for fundamental reform following the formation of the Brandt-Scheel government in 1969 seemed so bright to many that the phrase "reform euphoria" was coined to describe the mood of the times. The SPD's membership grew substantially during the early 1970s, above all among younger voters, including ex-APO disciples attracted by the increasingly radical Young Socialists or Jusos.[1]

The "social democratic compromise," the strategic vision and social settlement which underlay social-liberal reform politics of the SPD/FDP coalition during the 1970s, is worth recalling here briefly. Its outline was simple: economic growth, stabilized through Keynesian measures, would provide a social surplus large enough to fund wage increases for the working class and social reform programs for the liberal middle class without threatening corporate profits or decreasing investment levels. The flaw in the equation was the assumption of unlimited economic growth. The economic woes caused by the substantial increase in the price of oil as a consequence of the Yom Kippur war of 1973 between Israel on the one hand and Egypt and Syria on the other and the global recession of 1977 undermined the theoretical premises and material bases of the social-democratic reform program. Seeing the clear choice of aborting social reforms or suffering economic decline, the Schmidt government chose the former.

For the radical Left in and near the SPD, these were unacceptable priorities. As in 1959 (the Bad Godesberg program) and in 1966 (the Emergency Laws and the formation of the Grand Coalition), leftists felt betrayed by the SPD and, as a consequence, many of them invested their hopes in the politics of extraparliamentary movements. At the same time, the once compelling vision of the social-democratic "growth society" (*Wachstumsgesellschaft*) suffered a broadside from the famous 1973 report, *Global 2000*. Authored by an eminent group of international and interdisciplinary experts on behalf of a large association of scholars, politicians and intellectuals concerned with global development known as the Club of Rome, it postulated ecological limits to growth. Paradoxically, social-democratic reform politics failed just where it had previously succeeded. On the one hand, the SPD's reliance on economic growth and its infrastructure policy inadvertently unleashed deleterious environmental and ecological side-effects by promoting industrial expansion and construction programs which further accelerated the contamination and destruction of nature. On the other hand, the centralized administration and bureaucratic execution of these plans triggered increasing discontent and opposition among liberal-minded citizens with the idea of more participatory democracy.

The protest potential contained in ecological issues even for moderate middle-class citizens was manifested throughout the Federal Republic during the 1970s in the spontaneous appearance of hundreds of "citizens' initiatives" (*Bürgerinitiativen*).[2] Increasing opposition to nuclear energy beginning in the mid-1970s helped weave the scattered strands of the citizens' initiative movement into a unified, national ecology movement, which in turn became the banner under which the diverse and fragmented forces of the Left gathered with political moderates and middle-class newcomers. Concomitantly, a "new" women's movement coalesced around the issue of abortion. Finally, the "new" peace movement which formed around opposition to the euromissiles during the late 1970s and early 1980s and an alliance with the ecology movement brought a critical mass of support for the burgeoning green movement and its emerging "parliamentary arm" – the nascent green parties.

Willy Brandt's poignant description of the Greens as the "SPD's lost children" perfectly summarized the predicament faced by the Social Democrats during the 1970s. The economic crisis forced the party to choose between its governing mandate and that of its grass-roots constituents. Put differently, the SPD had to make a painful choice between two identities: one as party of government, the other as party of movement. It was the former which triumphed. This strategy could well be labelled "economic Noskeism," with social democracy's sense of order and ultimate subservience to capitalist accommodation once again prevailing over its impetus for social change and systemic transformation; just as Gustav Noske's SPD opted for a defense of the newly established, bourgeois Weimar Republic against the revolutionary ambitions of portions of social democracy's rank-and-file, so too could one interpret the Schmidt government's austerity measures designed to alleviate the economic crisis as an obvious attempt to stymie social democracy's potential for reform in favor of stabilizing the status quo.

It should be apparent that the complex process by which the green protest movement evolved confronts the analyst with a difficult task. Unlike the student movement, the green movement does not lend itself easily to metaphors of diffusion and intensification – such as "mobilization" or "radicalization." It did not "spread" from a central location – such as West Berlin – or a central organization – such as SDS or KfA. Rather it possessed the character of a "crazy quilt," gradually sewn together out of a multitude of smaller leftovers and scraps of "new material," whose end product was not a fully monolithic organization (like traditional leftist parties) but a heterogeneous coalition whose eclectic origins were clearly manifest. The political colors represented were equally motley: the red of the SPD and K-groups, the green of both "eco-freaks" and "eco-farmers," the jet black of the anarchists and "autonomists" (*Autonomen*), as well as the more traditional black of CDU-oriented "value conservatives."

The narrative itself must reflect the nature of this process. Consequently, rather than proceed in a strictly chronological fashion, we will portray each of the six constitutive pieces in the patchwork of the green movement in turn, beginning with the three post-APO tendencies – resignation, reform and revolution – and concluding with the three most significant new movements of the 1970s – the women's, ecology and peace movements. Through the analysis, we will try to discover the timing and structure of the processes which led to the highly contingent and hardly inevitable convergence of these factors into a "green" protest movement.

The Alternative Scene and the Spontis: Infrastructure of a New Politics

The "alternative movement" originated out of tendencies within APO and the student movement toward subcultural retreat and mass cultural revolution.

The alternative movement sought to present a radical alternative to all aspects of established society: consumer culture, the capitalist market economy, the bourgeois family, and indoctrination by the mainstream media. Some scholars define the movement as "the context of all attempts . . . to practice social change directly through self-organized forms of work and collective living arrangements."[3] But the alternative daily, *Die Tageszeitung*, placed the location of "alternative" differently: "the point is not to change society but to have a house where you can live differently."[4] Both tendencies, outward looking and inward looking, revolution and resignation, cohabited in an uneasy symbiosis within the alternative movement.

Because of its many fissures, lack of clear boundaries and diverse membership, the actual topology of the alternative movement is somewhat more complex than its self-representations allow. One must differentiate between rural and urban segments of the movement. However, the influence of the first, the "rural flight" and "commune" movements, has been basically confined to a tiny and politically insignificant band of converts. More interesting from our perspective have been the urban, alternative, subcultural milieus within the Federal Republic's major metropoles such as West Berlin, Frankfurt, Cologne, Munich, Hamburg and Dusseldorf.

The alternative movement had no formal organization, structure or membership. It has been more cultural than political.[5] Consequently, it is difficult to distinguish what or who "belongs" to it. It is much simpler to schematize the movement as a set of concentric circles involving varying levels of organization and commitment:[6] (1) the alternative milieu and culture at the individual level; (2) the alternative public and "scene"; (3) alternative projects and parties. Each of these levels also corresponds to a stage of the movement's historical development and growing public influence. Between approximately 1970 and 1975, the movement consisted of scattered, diffuse and unassociated projects, individual experiments and local politics. Then until about 1977 distinctly unconventional publications began to take shape, a blossoming network of alternative writings linked together by clearly delineated urban "scenes" inhabited by alternative activists and intellectuals, and defined by their own ways of speaking, dressing and behaving. In the final phase from 1977 to 1980, a mass of alternative projects such as joint working/living experiments based on alternative principles were founded. In this uniquely differentiated yet surprisingly informal and porous milieu, a diverse collection of leftist forces began to gather beneath the umbrella of alternative politics.

Let us now examine in more detail each of these phases and the respective segment of the movement which each helped create.

The alternative movement began with the rejection of organized action by disillusioned sixty-eighters and their retreat into the private sphere. These disheartened activists initiated a localization and privatization of politics. As one APO leader suggestively put it: "What does Vietnam have to do with me? I've got orgasm problems!" At first, these shattered remnants of the "anti-authoritarian revolt" were unified only by vague new currents of ideas – "new sensuality," "new spirituality"[7] – and a rejection of rallies, meetings and organizations, collectively labeled "APO-crap".[8]

In time, however, the alternative milieu became an institutional fixture of the West German metropolis. In many cities, a distinct alternative quarter evolved – Berlin's Kreuzberg and Schöneberg, Frankfurt's Bockenheim and Nordend, Hamburg's St Pauli – dotted with meeting points, which could be cafés, bars, discos, galleries, shops, clubs, or movie theaters, all catering to the alternative clientele of the city and its surrounding areas. Each quarter was criss-crossed by a matrix of niches or submilieus. One significant division emerged between "Müslis" (German granola) and "Mollies" (from Molotov cocktail). Sixties music, potted plants and coarse, "organic" peasant-style furnishings suggested a "granola" or "old new Left" hippie-ized crowd, while black decor, modern art, art-deco furnishings and progressive new-wave or punk music characterized the avant-garde, slightly younger, post-1968 tendency. Hitherto "marginal groups," particularly women and homosexuals, created their own scenes as well. A rich sampling of underground films, theater and music, and a lightly politicized Bohemianism rounded out these alternative cultural offerings.

Mediated by mainstream culture, the practices, habits, thoughts and places of the alternative culture and milieu reached well into the wide world of Germany's students and enlightened middle-class. The appeal was far-reaching, encompassing in one form or another 61 percent of the general population aged 22 to 25, 45 percent of all SPD voters and 49 percent of all FDP voters.[9] The marketing boom and proliferation of "alternative" staples (bio-bread, raw leather sandals, peasant furniture, overalls, roll-your-own tobacco) and subsequently of punk fashion (black, leather, extreme haircuts, jewelry and make-up) gave witness to the unmistakable appeal of alternative, radical chic.

For those within its inner circles, the alternative milieu also formed a material infrastructure for the reproduction of radical political potential within the Federal Republic. The well-known, well-established and expansive alternative milieus in Berlin, Frankfurt and other cities recruited students, socio-economic drop-outs (*Aussteiger*) and marginals. Once integrated, it became psychologically easy for them to stay. One could maintain a sparse but bearable existence on 500 dollars, 400, with thrift and ingenuity even 300 dollars a month. The Federal Republic's comparatively generous student assistance program[10] and the abundance of parttime work in this milieu have made an alternative existence both a long-term possibility and an attractive option for many German youths and young adults. This scene, which eventually became firmly entrenched in the social landscape of the Federal Republic, has been – and continues to be – an abundant reservoir for radical political activists for the simple reason that the premises of its creation in the late 1960s and throughout the 1970s still pertain: a deep dislike of capitalism; an equally passionate disdain for the Federal Republic; contempt for all established institutions of politics and administration; and a fervent desire to be different, remain apart, and start something new.

A smaller, more committed circle in this alternative milieu has adopted alternative living arrangements in the form of the *Wohngemeinschaft* or WG, "communal apartments" or "living communes." Household chores, purchases and furnishings are usually shared, distributed and owned equally by the WG members. Members are most often single students, but others have jobs and there are also couples, married and unmarried, and children (not infrequently of single mothers). While WGs first appeared as radical arrangements of household and sexual practices in the late 1960s, the pragmatic motive of saving money on rent and of sharing household duties became an equal priority as WGs proliferated in the 1970s and 1980s. Many APO graduates and their followers also adopted the WG as a way of unifying their political and private lives. Today, whether the WG setting serves as an intimate, familial sphere or as a laboratory for radical social experiments depends strictly on its inhabitants.

A central medium through which each scene defines its boundaries and identity is provided by the various "city magazines," which summarize and comment on local cultural and political events. Most often the established city magazines grew conceptually and often literally out of local city papers and information sheets. After enjoying a brief heyday in the early 1970s these sporadically published tabloids gave way to ones which made ideological concessions to the necessities of marketing. The success of the city magazines has been documented by their longevity and consistently high circulation (an estimated 1.6 million copies a week).

A similar process can be observed in the gradual institutionalization of alternative book publishing. During the late 1960s and early 1970s, hundreds of tiny, low-budget leftist presses were established to break the "monopoly of the bourgeois press and publishing conglomerates." Today only a handful of successful enterprises remain. In addition to supporting left-leaning social theory and historical scholarship for an academic audience, these alternative publishing houses distribute a wealth of literature on what one might call "pop politics."[11] Leftist debates, current events, and spirituality are packaged and propagated for a wider audience of sympathizers. Thus books on toxic chemicals like dioxin, the Chernobyl nuclear accident, the German peace movement, revolution in Eastern Europe, the Sandinistas in Nicaragua and feminism, emanating from the countercultural milieu, have made it on to the display tables of even the most middle class book stores.

Without a doubt, the crowning achievement of the leftist "counterpublic" (*Gegenöffentlichkeit*) was the establishment of the Federal Republic's first alternative daily newspaper, *Die Tageszeitung* or *Taz*. Following one-and-a-half years of public planning and discussion and local initiatives in the major German cities, the *Taz* commenced regular operation in the spring of 1979, with a start-up edition of 38,000 copies a day, reaching approximately 50,000 by the mid 1980s and hovering around 100,000 in 1991. This is quite an achievement considering the repeated failures of rival publications appearing over the years. Thus, for example, *Die Neue*, which – just like *Taz* – was first published in the early spring of 1979, and – again like *Taz* – attempted to become the alternative milieu's daily paper, folded barely one year later. One reason for its failure was its much more rigidly ideological editorial policy which essentially toed the "Stamokap" or "state monopoly capitalism" line advanced by the DKP, the left Jusos, IG Metall and IG Druck und Papier. The *Taz* does not exhaustively cover the daily news *per se*, nor does it strive to do so.[12] Instead, the paper has consistently aimed to be an explicit critic of the German Left's legendary dogmatism and notorious humorlessness by maintaining an openness to new ideas of the decidedly spontaneous and witty variety. In its effort to be iconoclastic and unpredictable, the *Taz* has repeatedly printed editorials and stories which much of its readership – the leftist urban milieu – has rejected as conservative, reactionary, even blasphemous.[13]

This is entirely in keeping with the intent of the founding editorial collective, which proclaimed that "the *Taz* will again have ears for melodies played beyond the Left."[14] The *Taz* was inspired by an increasing perception of the Left's fragmented discourse and the need to unify it, if not in actual politics, at least in its nationwide reading habits. Indeed, the *Taz* has provided a unique and important national forum for debate and discussion which, by the early 1990s, reached well beyond the Left's alternative milieu.[15] As perhaps the single institution of the German Left never to have succumbed to any dogma or ideological faction, the *Taz* has provided a rare forum of intellectual give-and-take which otherwise does not exist in this milieu. As such there can be no doubt that the *Taz* ranks among the most impressive, lasting legacies of the West German New Left.

To the extent that a characteristically alternative form of politics and a discourse distinct from other leftist currents developed in this period, it was in the "spontaneist" and "undogmatic" "grass-roots groups" which emerged in the mid-1970s. The self-characterization of "undogmatic" represents a rejection of the ideological, organizational and tactical dogmatism of the "orthodox" K-groups.[16] Spontaneity meant just that: an idealization and pursuit of direct, unmediated, uncalculated and unpredictable forms of action and interaction. Johannes Schütte describes three basic components of spontaneism's "morphological structure":

a   Rejection of and protest against hardness, molding, creeping forms, on practical as well as "theoretical" levels;
b   Sensit(ive)(ized) non-cooperation and retreat to experiential contexts capable of harmony;
c   Departure from the existing order and explorative, speculative searching for the indeterminately different.[17]

Adherents to this spontaneity, the so-called Spontis, rejected and retreated from the "system's" demands for achievement, in order to focus – often to an obsessive degree – on repairing the damage these demands had done to the lifeworld of their inner psyches and interpersonal relationships. One popular sponti slogan captured this view rather poignantly: "A bit more pleasure principle can't hurt!"

Informal sponti grass-roots groups (*Basisgruppen*) existed as early as 1973, but undogmatic and spontaneistic politics first won significant influence on West German campuses beginning in 1975 with a rapid influx of new supporters from reformist-socialist groups. Among them were some of the SPD's Young Socialists or Jusos, as well as some supporters of the Sozialdemokratischer Hochschulbund (which, as will be recalled, served as the SPD's counter attraction for the radicalized SDS in the early 1960s) and even some formerly orthodox Communists from the DKP and K-groups.[18] In an effort to maintain their momentum and counter the growing influence of the orthodox Marxist groups, Spontis and undogmatic Leftists allied on many campuses and ran jointly in student council elections.[19]

Sponti demonstrations emphasized ritual and celebration to the exclusion of strategy and content. Unlike APO, the Spontis were ironic to the point of self-denigration, whimsical to the point of nonsense.[20] Dancing, street theater and flowers for the police all belonged to their repertoire. A climactic event in the sponti movement and one of considerable import for the alternative movement as a whole was the Berlin "Tunix meeting" (literally, "do nothing" meeting) in early 1978. The publicity flyer called all "freaks" to "sail off to Tunix Beach," an imaginary, humorously described alternative utopia "beneath the cobblestones of this country."[21] Attended by some 17,000–20,000 young people,[22] the meeting was covered under the slogan "departure from model Germany"[23] and included theater of the absurd, dancing and other festivities.

Viewed against the backdrop of Marxian socialist political culture as it had existed for a century in Germany, spontaneism had a deeper significance. More than empty ritual, self-indulgence or plain nihilism, spontaneism represented an intellectual openness which attained programmatic status. Spontaneism was perhaps a necessary antidote or catharsis against an orthodoxy of theory and organization which – especially in the milieu of the post-APO K-groups – had become more constraining than beneficial in a rapidly changing world. The spirit of spontaneism, improvising and recreating politics, was best captured in the phrase, "experiment without knowing where you'll land!"[24] Insofar as spontaneism could be placed into a programmatic mold at all, its central axiom was caught by that venerable slogan of the Parisian students during their demonstration in May 1968: "Power to the imagination."[25] At the same time, however, spontaneism exhibited some ugly excesses, particularly of the anti-intellectual sort.[26]

Nevertheless, by divesting themselves of the past, spontaneists were often able to reopen political discourse so as to render it receptive to new sorts of problems and praxis. Spontaneists rejected principles or theories as guideposts, acting instead out of *unmittelbare Betroffenheit*, that is, that which directly affects, impacts and upsets.[27] Correspondingly, in sponti usage, the ideal of "emancipation" was dropped in favor of "autonomy" or the "fulfillment of needs." Spontis also searched for forms of group interaction which would eliminate informal as well as formal power structures. The result was "grass-roots democracy" (*Basisdemokratie*): "radical democratic, decentralized organization in interrelated, autonomous groups."[28] Though it nurtured some anarchist extremists,[29] the main effect of the sponti movement was to break ground for a pragmatic, leftist, radical-reformist politics. The concepts of *unmittelbare Betroffenheit* and autonomy made it possible to organize grievances and discontent on issues such as ecology or the rights of "marginal" groups which a political system based on the articulation of class cleavages and material interests would not have processed or even registered. In a word, spontaneism suggested a passable avenue toward a post-Marxist radicalism, a politics disentangled from the German Left's "dialectic of defeat" of verbal radicalism and practical failure. The Spontis opened a perspective for the radical Left in Germany that was to help it break out of a vicious circle of radicalization, defeat and resignation which had plagued it since the 1848 revolution and the First International.

The New Women's Movement

Like so many changes in the German Left, the women's movement, too, had its roots in the contradictions of APO and the German student movement. It began abruptly and with symbolic flourish on September 13, 1968, at the 20th SDS delegate conference. Following dismissive remarks from the (all male) podium regarding a speech by Helke Sander of the newly founded Berlin Action Committee for Women's Liberation (Berliner Aktionsrat zur Befreiung der Frau),[30] "comrade" Sigrid Röger angrily hurled a tomato in the face of SDS theoretician Hans-Jürgen Krahl.

Shortly after the now-famous tomato-throwing incident, the first "broads' committee" (*Weiberrat*) – named partly in irony, partly as a polemic – was established in Frankfurt. In 1969, broads' committees from the entire Federal Republic met in Hanover under the slogan, "liberate the socialist eminences from their bourgeois dicks!" Yet these women remained socialists first and women second. For them, as for August Bebel in his *Women and Socialism* published nearly one hundred years before, capital's struggle with labor was still the "main contradiction" subsuming all other contradictions, including those concerned with gender, which were regarded as secondary. "Since under capitalist relations of production all regions of social and private life are marked by class antagonism, the theory and practice of the women's movement also has a class character."[31] Tellingly, the Frankfurt broads' committee filed *en masse* into the Communist Party (DKP), and the Berlin Action Committee renamed itself the Socialist Women's League of West Berlin.[32] These organizations had the character "more of Marxist school courses for women than emancipation groups. The women were supposed to receive tutoring in political economy in order to elevate them to the men's level of knowledge."[33]

The "autonomous" or "radical feminist" current of the German women's movement – as opposed to its Marxist counterpart – first emerged in the summer of 1971 in the wave of protest against the anti-abortion clause of the

German criminal code known as Section 281. "Action 218" and women's liberation were thrust into the public eye through a spectacular media event organized by journalist and publicist Alice Schwarzer, who was to become one of contemporary Germany's best-known and most controversial feminists. Following the example of the Parisian Movement de la Liberation de la Femme, Schwarzer assembled 374 women, some prominent, some ordinary, whose names, photos and signatures appeared in the June 1 cover story of the German weekly *Stern* entitled, "I had an abortion!"[34] The powerful popular response which followed permanently altered the character of the German women's movement by mobilizing support and activity well beyond the narrower intellectual avant-garde and socialist university milieu. In the same month, the first delegate conference of Action 218 occurred in Dusseldorf.[35] And a mere six weeks after the appearance of the *Stern* article, 2,345 additional women publicly reported their abortions and 86,000 declarations of solidarity had been received.[36] In Ute Frevert's words: "That things did not remain in the realm of theory in the academic ghetto and that a women's movement with its own action program and political goals developed, was essentially due to the ... debate about Section 218."[37]

It is worth briefly digressing to explore why. In contrast to, say, wage discrimination (one of the empirical cornerstones of the orthodox socialist analysis),[38] which affects women severely but not exclusively, the issue of abortion revealed a gender-specific oppression "without class content." It was a matter not of inequality in production but of regulation of reproduction, here, significantly, in the most individual, literal and physical sense. We will return to this issue at the end of this section. For now, it is important to see how the character of the abortion issue shaped the "new women's movement." First, for socialist women it potently challenged the "secondary contradiction" theorem of Bebel and of Friedrich Engels, confronting women with the choice of being principally socialist or principally feminist, and propelling them in many cases toward a conversion to radical feminism and a switchover to sponti or autonomous women's groups.[39] Second, the abortion issue harbored vast protest potential, for it ultimately touched all women, not just students but otherwise "apolitical" women in the home as well. In that sense, a particularly female concern served as a universalizing agent in the consciousness raising of women as a politically potent collective.

Throughout the 1980s, abortion remained a major catalyst for feminist politics in the Federal Republic. Indeed, abortion became one of the most contentious issues surrounding unification in 1990. This was the case because abortion was completely legal in the former East Germany. The continued legality of abortion in the five new eastern Länder of Germany was perhaps the only instance where a former East German arrangement was not dismantled by or adapted to West German conditions. It led to the awkward situation whereby a woman could have a completely legal abortion in one state, say Saxony, and be liable to criminal prosecution in another, say Bavaria. This anomalous situation was resolved in June 1992, when the Bundestag voted to adopt a modified version of the East German arrangement for the Federal

Republic as a whole. Since then, conservative forces have mobilized to have this legislative decision reversed by the courts, though – at least until January 1993 – to no avail.[40]

The passionate debate initiated by the Section 218 controversy introduced a hitherto completely unrecognized cluster of discrimination into the reality of German politics. Gender-specific oppression in the sphere of reproduction was never again to be the same as it was before the advent of the women's movement. The abortion issue had ramifications well beyond the immediate concerns at hand. It helped politicize the private, sensitize an entire society to the problems of home life and issues related to sexuality and childraising, and opened a vast and unexplored area for thought, discussion and action in the discourse of progressive politics in the Federal Republic of Germany.

The first federal women's congress held in March 1972 in Frankfurt ushered in the new women's movement and initiated a phase of feverish and innovative political activity. Four work groups were organized: "reasons for the self-organization of women"; "the situation of the employed woman"; "the function of the family in society"; "action Section 218."[41] An extensive catalogue of demands was drafted, including parttime work for men and women, equal wages for equal work, a "baby year" of paid leave for both mother and father, and the creation of autonomous – that is, men-excluding – women's organizations.[42] The target of the measures was the double burden for women of domestic responsibilities and public career. Especially engaged discussions ensued on the limited nature of any "liberation" which focused on employment to the exclusion of the domestic realm. Thus, many women argued, full equality with men in the labor market via identical remuneration in employment still did not address the realm of the home, where women performed unpaid labor, usually for the benefit of men. Pressure on these issues, as well as others, did not remain confined to the construction of theories and the delivery of speeches. Actions accompanied these words. Provocative and attention-grabbing demonstrations were the order of the day. Beauty pageants were disrupted, entrances to pornography shops walled shut, church membership publicly renounced *en masse*, pigs' tails (*Schweineschwänze*) distributed to doctors at the Hartmann League convention (the West German medical association). "Behind the slogans 'Together, women are strong' and 'The personal is political,' an entirely new understanding of organization and politics was revealed. . . ."[43]

The spring of 1972 also saw the emergence of the first women's magazine and handbook in the Federal Republic: Grunhild Feigenwinter's *Hexenpresse* "Witches' Press") and a women's handbook published by the Bread and Roses group in Berlin. West German women, comparatively late in starting their own movement, also devoured translated imports from the already sizable stock of American feminist literature.[44]

Although various new topics in feminist politics began germinating at this time, most activities in 1973–4 remained centered around Section 218. After the safer, more efficient "suction method" of abortion had been demonstrated in the Federal Republic for the first time at a women's congress in Munich on February 11, 1973, this method itself became a subject for agitation on the part of women.[45] In 1974 the social-liberal coalition presented its draft for a reform of Section 218 in the form of the so-called "term solution" (*Fristenlösung*). This proposal was to permit abortions within the first three months of pregnancy under certain (bureaucratically defined) conditions. In response, the women's movement established "Action – Last Chance" (Aktion letzer Versuch) and proclaimed March 16 a national day of protest. To present their plight and status graphically, women throughout the Federal Republic marched wearing the garb of deceased victims of illegal abortion clinics, bandaged their mouths shut or wore papier mâché balls and chains. In a characteristic turn of phrase, the *Spiegel* proclaimed an "uprising of the sisterhood."

Yet even before the SPD/FDP abortion reform bill passed the Bundestag in 1974, substantially stilling feminist agitation in the Federal Republic in the process, harbingers of the second phase of the new women's movement, the so-called "introspective turn" (*Wende nach Innen*) had already emerged. In 1973, women students in Heidelberg established the first of what would eventually become many "CRs" (for consciousness raising) or "self-experience" groups.[46] On March 3, 1974, the first women's festival, the "Rockfest im Rock" (Rockfest in skirts) took place on the campus of Berlin's Technical University, attracting, not the expected 200 women, but 2,000, for an evening of all-women's dancing, drinking and socializing.[47] As women discovered women socially and sexually, and phrases such as "the new tenderness" and "women love women" made the rounds, two lovers, Judy Andersen and Marion Ihns, went on trial for murdering the latter's husband. Slanderous press sensationalism and shoddy legal procedure let lesbianism become the real issue for both sides.[48] This ugly confrontation with patriarchal power increased the numbers of women declaring themselves as lesbians, kindled tense but productive disputes among and between heterosexual and homosexual women about sexual politics, and sparked the experiments of "movement" lesbians. Beginning in 1974 at Berlin's Free University, permissions to have women's study groups, seminars and professorships were wrested from the (usually resistant) university administration. By the spring of 1974, 12 women's centers had been established in the Federal Republic[49] for the purposes of exchanging information and experiences, holding meetings and dispensing medical advice.[50]

In 1975 the United Nations proclaimed an "international year of the woman," and Alice Schwarzer published the first "women's lib" bestseller, in the Federal Republic entitled *Der kleine Unterschied und seine grossen Folgen* ("The Little Difference and its Big Consequences"). The book's topic focused on the patriarchal appropriation of female sexuality as a means of controlling reproduction. The positive public debate stimulated by the book and an unparalleled baiting campaign by the press against Schwarzer drew mass attention to the women's movement for the first time. During the second half of the 1970s, increased media exposure, combined with the introspective turning away from agitation, lured droves of women who had previously been hesitant into the movement. In contrast to the veteran APO sixty-eighters, ex-Communists and anarcho-Spontis, these women brought no political experience to the movement with them; instead they mostly wanted to talk about everyday problems, their problems. Not being interested in or knowledgeable about Marx, these women sought a suitable forum for their problems in the CRs and self-experience groups. Proceeding from their own subjective concerns (*Betroffenheit*), they typically addressed themes such as childhood, sexuality, career, family life, relationships, identity and feelings toward other women. But when these women had finished speaking their minds, they often disappeared again. The CR/self-experience groups therefore had transient memberships with high turnover and very short lifespans, few of them lasting over a year.

As in the second phase of the alternative movement, the threads of a feminist public emerged in this phase of the women's movement. In 1976, the first women's publishing house, Women's Offensive (Frauenoffensive) was founded in Munich, to be followed in short order by half-a-dozen others throughout the country. Women's bookstores in Berlin and Munich also opened their doors that year. And in 1977, two national women's magazines, *Emma* and *Courage,* appeared on the shelves and at newsstands, and together quickly reached a circulation of over 200,000. Moreover, every year since 1976 a "women's summer university" has been held in Berlin, each year with a different theme.[51]

But the development of the women's movement differed from that of the alternative movement in one significant respect: organization. The women's movement had attained dimensions which could no longer be coordinated through the personal contacts of activists. In notable contrast to the ecology, peace and anti-nuclear movements, the women's movement lacked an umbrella organization which could suitably coordinate activities on a nationwide basis. There were two principal causes for this: first, the fact that all problems related to the reproductive sphere came to be thematized on the level of the "personal" and "non-political," both of which were inherently unsuited to any conventional strategy of mass agitation; and second, that the primacy of "autonomy," which opposed contact with other, typically patriarchal, political organizations, also impeded concrete steps toward the acquisition of cross-gender support.

That these characteristics did not necessarily emanate from the nature of feminist politics *per se* can perhaps best be understood with the help of a comparative example, in this case the engagement of the US women's movement through the National Organization for Women (NOW) in the battle for the Equal Rights Amendment. Regardless of the concrete outcome of the struggle, which in this instance resulted in an actual defeat for NOW and American women's rights, NOW succeeded in mobilizing a huge number of America's women, who became part of the women's movement even if they never developed an active feminist consciousness. The flexibility and tolerance of the American political system allowed an antinomian challenge to that system a much broader range than was the case in Germany. Briefly put, their different respective environments and histories made organizing for similar causes a fundamentally different experience for women in the United States and the Federal Republic.

The West German women's movement's comparative deficit in formal organization did not prevent the transmission of its concerns into the alternative parties. But it did contribute to the fact that the heterogeneous concerns of the new social movements were organized under the banner of a "green" party and were thereby burdened with an ecological identity not always in line with the constellations of problems and interest they sought to represent – such as those of women.

In the period from 1977 to 1980, the main attention of the women's movement, like that of the Alternative Movement, was focused mostly on project-related undertakings. In part, the projects provided the foundation for an expanding feminist counterculture. In addition to the efforts toward creating a feminist public through the publishing houses, magazines and bookstores mentioned above, women's bars, restaurants, psychotherapy centers and even driving schools emerged. A code of clothing and insider slang allowed feminists to identify one another. And for gay and straight alike, women's communes enjoyed a brief flourishing beginning in 1976–7.

Next to publicity work, "women's houses" were perhaps the most widespread variety of projects during this period. By offering shelter, support and therapy for battered women and their children in a communal environment, these houses not only aided victims but helped to tear the veil of silence previously cast over violence in the home by the authorities. The first West German women's house was opened in Berlin in 1976, and by 1979 women's houses existed in 14 cities in the Federal Republic.[52] Women's health centers sought to work against the estrangement of women from their own bodies, promoting self-examination and offering gynecological education and counseling.

Active and aggressive campaigns against rape and violence toward women, organized, propagated and discussed with an intensity reminiscent of Action 218, complemented these self-help projects. On March 1, 1977, women in Berlin took to the streets to protest a rape and murder, and on April 30, in the first "take back the night" march in defense of women's safety, bands of women armed with pots and pans careened and clattered through the streets. The first rape-crisis hotline also appeared that spring.[53] The theoretical capstone was laid by the publication of the German edition of Susan Brownmiller's feminist critique of rape, *Against Our Will*.

Beginning in 1979–80, the women's movement cautiously searched for commonalities with the other new social movements. In a declaration, "Violence Against Women," drafted at its second national conference on October 6–7, 1979, in Dusseldorf, the Democratic Women's Initiative group drew connections between sexual violence against women, "structural violence" in the workplace, the arms race and ecological destruction.[54] Other groupings, such as Women for Peace (Frauen für den Frieden), addressed pressing global issues from the women's perspective.[55] At the Women's Congress against Nukes and Militarism on September 15–16, 1979, Sibylle Plogstedt spoke of the "man against man battle mentality," making the connection between violence and patriarchy yet more explicit.[56]

Concurrent with this seeming repoliticization, a new constellation gravitating around phrases such as "new motherliness" and "new femininity" polarized the ideological fronts within the women's movement. In a representative text of the sort published in the Women's Yearbook 1977, Eva-Maria Stark argued that "the desire for a child can come from deep within one's belly," and praised the strengths of motherhood, the "peaceful mother–child relation," "the affection and willingness to sacrifice," the "needs and rhythms of our bellies."[57] Four years later, Monika Jaeckel reemphasized in yet more unambiguous language, that motherhood was the essence of womanhood: "Women long to affirm and live that which concerns and comprises them. . . . We women want to begin unfolding the social potential of being a mother as part of a strong and unified women's movement."[58]

In certain respects this romanticization of the corporeal dimension of motherhood and the menstrual cycle represented the search for "equality with difference," the attempt to reclaim a feminine identity from the desire for absolute equality. But the depoliticizing dynamics immanent within the "new femininity" manifested themselves most dramatically in the brief popular renaissance of witchcraft, moon cults, paganism and other premodern spiritualist and irrationalist tendencies. Radical feminists aimed their attacks above all at the new femininity's patent biologism, its equation of female needs with hormonal drives. They objected that it ignored socialization in the shaping of gender roles and perceived this new femininity as providing an apolitical picture of women which played all too easily into the hands of traditional male conservatives.

The women's movement in the late 1970s displayed a contradictory complexion. On the one hand, signs of politicization were evident in the unfolding anti-violence and rape campaigns. Attempts to center feminist theory and praxis within an overarching "revolt of the reproductive sphere against the conditions of the productive sphere,"[59] and a "greening" of the women's movement beginning in 1979, emerged in organizations such as the German Women's International and Women for Peace. This was also the first time that future green politicians such as Petra Kelly emerged as activists in the feminist, peace and ecology movements. In the eyes of many feminists, particularly in the radical camp, the chief obstacle to a unified, politicized women's movement was the lack of a "concrete utopia," an imaginative vision of a future feminist society which could serve as a horizon for the orienting of everyday politics. The mysticist, spiritualist revival was alas not serviceable as a "concrete utopia," an imaginative dramatization of long-range political ideals. Much more, it revealed a latent antimodernist tendency present in all the new social movements which made them susceptible and attractive to certain rightist, "reactionary" politicians. This antimodernism was to resurface later in the "fundamentalist" wing of the Greens as well. Its complexity once again reaffirmed the immense difficulty of formulating a viable reformist politics in the reproductive arena.

Jusos: the Failed Project of Radical Reform

Another key group in the green alliance of the late 1970s and early 1980s consisted of disappointed SPD, and to a lesser extent FDP, voters, especially the block of students and young, educated members of the "new middle-class," the same constituency whose votes had brought the Social Democrats to power in the late 1960s.[60] Often APO activists or sympathizers, this group flocked to the SPD particularly during the years between 1965 and 1969, a period in which over half of all new party members were under 35. In setting its hopes on the SPD, this group "expected . . . the merger of a pointedly conceived reform strategy with a long-term, anti-capitalist trajectory. . . ."[61] Since all SPD members under 35 are automatically Jusos (for Jungsozialisten, Young Socialists), the party's youth organization grew to proportions reaching some 180,000 members by 1980, 25 percent of whom – that is, 45,000 – were politically active in the sense of attending meetings, working for the party in some voluntary capacity, and participating generally in political life beyond voting.[62] Between 1969 and 1979, the Jusos transmitted vital oppositional impulses into the SPD, stimulating the first theory discussion inside the party since Godesberg and forming the nucleus for internal opposition within the party. This decade of Juso history provides instructive insights not only into the difficulties confronting radical reformism within the SPD but also into the process by which a radicalized middle class voting block was set adrift and washed on to the shores of the Green Party.

From their (re)founding in 1945 until 1968–9, the Jusos were a passive cadre organization, a loyal source of logistical support and future leadership for the mother party. In part, the Jusos' abrupt transformation from a party "mailman for the young generation" to a "progressive group for pushing through necessary reforms"[63] reflected a general change within the SPD. This process of radicalization was driven largely by the ideological and personal influence of APO and APO activists. By 1967, in traditional left-SPD strongholds such as South Hessia, Schleswig-Holstein, and certain quarters of Berlin, left-wing Jusos had gained control of the party's youth organizations, passing resolutions critical of the Grand Coalition. By 1968, a leftist majority existed both among the Jusos' rank-and-file and in the Juso steering committee at the federal level.[64] Following advance talks among left Jusos, a peaceful putsch against loyal party rightists and a ceremonious impeachment of then Juso chairman, Peter Corterier, were staged at the Munich Juso congress on December 5–7, 1969.[65] In the congress's closing statement, entitled "The Situations and Task of the SPD," the Jusos strongly criticized the SPD's gradual cooptation through its catch-all "people's party" image. The Jusos demanded the "democraticization of all areas of life in society" and the gradual transition to a socialized economy. They described their own role in politics and society as a "mediator between non-organized youth and party members."[66]

All this led to an uproar. The Jusos' ex-chairman decried the Jusos as "APO's bridgehead inside the SPD,"[67] SPD rightists called for disciplinary measures and the press widely publicized the Jusos' leftward course. However, there was also approval of this change during 1970, when ex-APO activists streamed into the Jusos, helping to consolidate their already dominant left wing.[68] In the following years, a "mobilization and expansion of the leftist grass roots,[69] especially among young voters, reached historically unprecedented heights: in 1972, a total of 107,000 new party memberships were issued, 65 percent to people of Juso age.[70]

The purpose of this section is not to recount or account for the transition from Brandt's "reform euphoria" and "dare more democracy" to Schmidt's "Modell Deutschland" and "stabilization of the achieved." But whether one regards the Schmidt era as success or failure, realism or sell-out, the fact remains that it represented a bitter disappointment for the aspirations for radical reform placed in the SPD by thousands of its new members. By the late 1970s, these disappointed aspirations had swelled into a massive reservoir of distrust toward social democracy and parliamentary politics in general. Simultaneously, these activists constructed a negative ideal of party structure and political strategy which was to influence the Greens decisively. In the following, then, we will outline the Juso program in the SPD in order to illuminate a set of formative experiences and theoretical premises which were to shape considerably the historical dimensions of the green project.

The Jusos' most distinguishing innovation and lasting legacy was their "double strategy" aimed at combining "mobilization, politicization and organization" of the population, on the one hand, with "intensive cooperation on all levels of the party," on the other, including the aim of internal party reform. The first leg of this double strategy, the *Basisbein* or grass-roots leg, was planted in the arena of local or community politics. The Jusos established its guidelines at their "community politics workshop" in Mannheim on April 24–5, 1971. It was also at this conference that the phrase "double strategy," soon a Juso shibboleth, first appeared.[71] Under the "fields of work" for "community politics," the Jusos included the following: (1) urban planning, building and renewal; (2) living and renting; (3) transportation; (4) leisure facilities; (5) community-based economic promotion; (6) community-based home improvements; (7) community-focused health and social services.[72] At this level, the Jusos reasoned, where political decisions had immediate and grave ramifications for those affected, it might be possible to awaken and politicize apathetic citizens. By stimulating an active cooperation among those directly involved, the Jusos sought to realize in their own way Brandt's famous promise to "dare more democracy." At the same time, by actively involving themselves at the local level, the Jusos hoped to cement an electoral basis for radical reform politics which would ultimately attract young voters to the SPD and help push the party toward the left.

The Jusos initiated and participated in numerous local campaigns. Among other things they mobilized against rent increases, real-restate speculation, freeway expansions, and the destruction of neighborhood playgrounds. In many cases, they cooperated with other political organizations in these campaigns, including both Communists and citizens' initiatives. Indeed, these coalitions proved successful in a number of cases.[73]

The other leg of the double strategy, the intraparty leg, still needed to have its democratic reflexes revived. The Jusos therefore sought to introduce "better and constant controls of public office holders and party functionaries by the membership, the dismantling of the usual accumulation of positions and the fundamental separation of the holding of public positions from party offices.[74] The Jusos sought first of all to subjugate elected officials and party functionaries to some form of "imperative mandate," making their actions in one way or another answerable to the party rank-and-file or perhaps even the party's congresses.[75] In a number of cases, the Jusos were also able to force powerful SPD politicians, such as Hans-Jochen Vogel, then mayor of Munich and chairman of the Bavarian Social Democrats, to renounce either their party position or their public office. Beginning with the 1972 Bundestag elections, the Jusos initiated a rather successful campaign to repoliticize the highly routinized process of nominating the party's Bundestag candidates. The Jusos saw to it that in all cases, even the most hopeless ones, a leftist or progressive candidate at least contested the party's nomination. Each local Juso chapter drafted or was furnished with a specific, well-designed catalogue of questions with which it sought to stimulate debate between the two candidates for the party's nomination on matters of urgent popular concern. Even where Juso candidates were trounced, their sheer efforts of running proved fruitful in democratizing the party's nomination process, since this new procedure – a sort of informal primary – provoked intraparty discussion and bred controversy. Moreover, in many cases, Juso-sponsored left-wing candidates did, in fact, win. The efficacy of this strategy seemed to be borne out by the doubling in size of the left-wing representation of SPD members of parliament, the "Leverkusen circle," in the 1972 Bundestag from 25 to almost 50.[76] The Jusos hoped that their double strategy would lead to an "elimination of the technocratic approach to administration and the dismantling of informal, unofficial power cliques," which the Jusos perceived as being dominated by the conservative "sewer workers" (*Kanalarbeiter*) and party apparatchiks, to the detriment of a reform-minded SPD.[77]

Another Juso target was the unreflecting "pragmatism" which had overcome the Social Democrats since they had embarked on their post-Godesberg "course of conformism." So deep had the party's theoretical deficit become that Juso-sponsored "theory discussions" involved a wholesale appropriation of New Left ideas.[78] For the Jusos, theory aimed not at the construction of utopias but at "the awareness of social contradictions and conflicts" and the contribution of "models for a stronger humanization of social and political life."[79] Only through precise knowledge of the enemy could the battle for systemic change be won. A blueprint for such a change was first delineated at a Juso strategy congress held in Hanover on December 11–12, 1971, just months after the community politics conference.[80] The results were the so-called Fifty Theses on the analysis of society, loosely unified under the notion of a "strategy of system-transcending reforms." This non-revolutionary concept for systemic change tried, "proceeding from the spaces of autonomy and/or the unions' adversarial positions . . . , to 'refunction' the multiplicity of necessary, system-immanent changes ('reforms') in such a way, that they first tend to question the foundations of the capitalist system or partly transcend them, and thereby make it possible to capture further adversarial positions of social and political reorder."[81]

But this was rather more an idea than a strategy, and it is therefore not surprising that different groups within the Jusos chose to interpret these theses differently. Three doctrinal forces diverged in their interpretations and subsequent policy proposals: the majoritarian reformist line, also called the "executive committee" faction; the Stamokaps, so named for their theory of state monopoly capitalism; and the anti-revisionists, who, like the DKP and the K-groups, claimed to uphold a traditional, orthodox Marxism. One hotly contested question (a holdover from APO days) concerned the class composition of the revolutionary subject: was it to be a coalition of wage labor and petty bourgeoisie or wage labor all by itself? Even more arcane was the long-winded discussion as to whether the state merely *acted* like the archetypal capitalist or whether in fact it *was* the archetypal capitalist.[82]

But despite this dogmatic turn in the Juso theory discussion, these debates proved fruitful for the party as a whole. Driven by the Jusos, the SPD's Left issued common aims for the representation of socialist positions at the party convention in May 1973. At the congress itself there were a few promising results, one of which centered on the decision "to appoint a commission to work out, based on the Godesberg program, a long-term, social policy program, which had to be concretized and quantified."[83] This mandate in turn resulted in the SPD's "Long-term Program: 1975–1985," also known as Orientation Guideline '85 (*Orientierungsrahmen*), issued under the chairmanship and supervision of Helmut Schmidt. While this program had little actual policy impact during Schmidt's chancellorship, it nevertheless marked a turning point in the SPD's internal history since it was the first major party document which originated with the Jusos and saw them as important proto-partners throughout all phases of this program's formulation.

But the heyday of the Jusos proved as shortlived as the Brandtian reform euphoria which had fueled them. The year 1974 saw both plummet into the jaws of crisis. Incessant internal feuding began to undermine the ability of the Jusos to act as a source of intra-party opposition. At the Juso congress on January 25–7 in Munich, a series of highly theoretical exchanges flared.[84] The party executive committee, breaking with its habitually lax policy, retorted with great severity that diverging opinions within the party would be tolerated only insofar as they did not disadvantage the party's competence to act. The executive committee was especially miffed at Stamokap hints that the social–liberal coalition in Bonn acted as an "agent of monopoly capitalism."

Observers noted that, with the executive committee decision in relation to the Munich federal congress, a harsher tone was introduced toward the Jusos.[85] And on June 28, 1974, some six weeks after Schmidt's assumption of the Federal Republic's Chancellorship,[86] a second executive committee decision regarding work groups, including all Juso organizations, placed further limits on their powers. It emphasized that work group decrees, unlike party convention decisions, were not binding, could not contradict party agreements, and that in those cases where work group functionaries *had* sought to countermand party rulings, they could be expelled from the party.[87] In subsequent weeks, this arrangement was broadened to include an executive committee privilege of censorship; and the definition of a work group was shaped so as to encompass individual party members, granting the party, in effect, the right to silence the Juso functionaries.[88]

The second phalanx of the executive committee attack paraded under the banner of anti-communism. Particularly through their community politics program, the Jusos found themselves sporadically engaged in alliances of convenience with the DKP and K-groups. As early as November, 1970 the SPD executive committee, executive council and control commission passed a resolution forbidding Jusos to participate in rallies, publications or flyers in which the DKP or any of its numerous ancillary organizations also participated.[89] With this, the Jusos faced the choice of either clearing the field where starting points for political activity appeared *and* the DKP was active, or sliding into a major conflict with the party and confronting a multiplicity of party proceedings, whose echo would affect the actual goals of their grass-roots activity.[90]

Karsten Voigt reacted by sponsoring a discussion in which the Jusos defined themselves apart from – and in opposition to – the Communists, delineating under what circumstances they would work with and could not work with the DKP and its ancillary associations.[91]

Despite the Jusos' openly critical attitude toward the DKP, the SPD – ever worried about being perceived as too close to communism–introduced disciplinary proceedings and even reclaimed party membership books from several Jusos, especially those involved in community organizing and grass-roots activities.[92] Quite rightly, many on the Left were inclined to see these executive committee decisions as a further dimension of an SPD campaign designed to splinter and marginalize the radical Left, indeed to render it illegal. In the history of the Federal Republic, few government actions have created a controversy as emotional, polemical, and long lasting as the ministerial decree of the Brandt–Scheel government of 1972 concerning "radicals" employed in public service. Entitled Basic Principles on the Question of Anticonstitutional Personnel in the Public Service, it has become known more simply as the Decree against Radicals (*Radikalenerlass*) or, by its opponents, the Ban on Careers (*Berufsverbot*). Aimed primarily at Communists, the decree prohibited from civil service posts anyone whose loyalty to the state was suspect to the governmental authorities. Enactment of the measure led to a massive loyalty check of 3.5 million individuals, the rejection of

2,250 applicants for political reasons, disciplinary proceedings against 2,000 public servants, and the dismissal of 256. It also spawned international protests and legal actions that continued well into the 1990s. Suffice it to say that this sorry episode of abusing state power to enforce an allegedly threatened law and order was arguably one of the most ignominious acts committed by the German social democrats since 1945.[93]

In the preceding résumé of Juso activity, we glimpse a concentrated pattern of collective development which no doubt had countless individual parallels in the broader arena of post-APO sympathizers with the SPD. Under Brandt, the vast leftist potential mobilized in the late 1960s and early 1970s was successfully channelled into hopes for deep-reaching democratization and radical reform projects. Under Schmidt, hopes for reform foundered on the worldwide recession. This alone would not have destroyed the SPD's credibility in the eyes of the radical Left; but Schmidt did not choose to stick by Brandt's (expensive) reform promises and face the (perhaps devastating) economic and electoral consequences. The anti-democratic clamp-down on radicals, inside and outside the party, qualitatively deepened the estrangement of the Left from the SPD. Not just the policy, it appeared, but the party itself was undemocratic and uncommitted to reform. The lasting bitterness, mistrust and disgust of many Greens toward the SPD can only be understood with reference to these "betrayed hopes."

The alternative for those with radical democratic and reformist claims was clear: extraparliamentarism or a new party. The following sections explore why the latter course was chosen.

From "Citizens' Initiatives" through "No Nukes" to the Ecology Movement

Although the followers and concerns of all the movements in this section may now be found in the ranks of the Greens, it is from the ecology movement that the party received its name, identity and public image as an "eco-party." Thus, while it would be erroneous to underestimate the influence which the predecessors already treated in this chapter had in shaping the Greens, the party's relationship to the ecology movement assumes special significance. In the following, we will attempt to reconstruct how an extraparliamentary alliance between middle-class, reform-oriented voters; the radical Left; and the "new" movements of the mid-1970s coalesced around the issue of ecology. The question as to why ecology, instead of any other salient problem (such as gender divisions, class inequalities or race relations between Germans and foreigners, to name but a few), created the bonding agent which unified these different fragments of political potential will be the subject of subsequent chapters.

The ecology movement developed in three increments. During its first phase (1969–75), grass-roots "citizens' initiatives" combatted local bureaucratic interventions in community life, thereby establishing a critical link between ecology and participatory democracy. During the second phase (1975–7), political protest erupted against nuclear energy, effecting an endemic radicalization of the movement. In the third phase (1977–80), these diverse segments of protest and opposition were increasingly unified under the rubric of "ecology." Let us look at these three segments in some detail.

The first phase, 1969 to 1975

The 1970s term "citizens' initiatives" (CIs) can be traced back to the idea of "citizen's initiative" used in the late 1950s and early 1960s, when it connoted individual civic activity.[94] Then, through the Social Democratic Voter Initiatives founded in 1967–8, the term came to signify a particular form of political organization.

Both senses of the term, the participatory and the formal-organizational, became enmeshed during the course of the 1970s as the CIs multiplied into a CI movement. In reality, the CIs were structurally heterogeneous, assuming forms as various as the circumstances and problems which surrounded and occasioned their development.[95] Nevertheless, a certain idea – or rather ideal – of the CI as a "principle of form" crystallized. Principally, CIs were non-hierarchical, democratic organizations, dominated by the grass-roots, allying socially and ideologically diverse individuals against a threatening project or administrative plan. Their principal enemy was not so much the ruling class of the rich but rather the bureaucrats of the state and the managers of large, impersonal organizations. CIs perceived their primary mission as one of combating technocracy instead of capitalism, the megamachine instead of the market.

During their formative phase from 1969 to 1972, the CIs had several well-springs. One came from those segments of the student movement (such as the Juso community politics advocates or early Spontis treated above) who, in the wake of APO, turned to neighborhood projects (*Stadtteilarbeit*), environmental initiatives or other kinds of local politics. The opening of West Germany's political culture in the late 1960s had also shown ordinary citizens how much "pressure could emanate from unconventional, direct actions."[96] The CIs were above all an expression of awakening activism among the Federal Republic's middle class not only in their role as citizens but as bourgeoisie. Data on the CIs suggest that their membership and potential was above all drawn from the educated middle class.[97] In particular, 36.4 percent of the CI membership hailed from the professional sector; 27.3 percent came from the rank of civil servant, usually of the higher echelons and in possession of advanced university degrees; and 24.2 percent were employed in managerial positions in service industries and other clerical segments of the German economy.[98] Indeed among CI leaders these class-based and education-based correlations appear to be even more pronounced than among CI regulars.[99] Like the ban-the-bomb protest of the early 1950s and late 1960s, the CI movement was thus a manifestation of grass-roots, middle-class radicalism.

While their relative financial security and education undoubtedly made CI activists sensitive to new sorts of problems,[100] the problems themselves – at least in these activists' view – originated in good part through the increase in macroeconomic steering and centralized infrastructure planning by the state under the technocratic aegis of the SPD-led coalition. "As a rule, grievances and errors in the development and implementation of social and environmental policy offer[ed] the motive for the spontaneous rise of CIs."[101] They were particularly active during the 1970s in the transportation sector, energy, large-scale manufacturing, and urban development. These were the CIs' principle loci of activism and protest.[102] Typical CIs might oppose the construction of an expressway or power plant, seek to secure government funding for a school, try to implement stricter measures against problems of noise pollution, or attempt to block rezoning laws or uphold rent control. In the main, a majority of CIs aimed at hindering a project or impeding an installation.[103] As such, they were primarily opposed to technocratic solutions to what they perceived as deeper social problems.

In line with the social composition of a majority of these members, most CIs were moderate and sought constructive dialogue with the state even though they opposed its technocratic mission and character. The offices to which they overwhelmingly addressed their grievances were state or local agencies and authorities, which under the SPD had been increasingly transformed from executive agencies (*Vollzugsverwaltungen*) to planning bureaucracies (*planende Verwaltungen*).[104] At least in the beginning, CI activists most often wished to act as a cooperative, plebiscitary complement to the official technocratic bureaucracy.[105]

The broader significance of the CIs for the development of the green movement was therefore twofold. First, although the ideal of the CIs only corresponded to reality during the initial phase of the movement (1969–72), when they were truly a "conglomeration of single-issue activity,"[106] the concept of political participation and democracy which they represented heavily informed the new social movements later in the decade.[107] Second, the CIs prefigured a synthesis of participatory democracy and the political defense of the reproductive sphere which formed the basis for an alliance of the reformist middle class and the radical Left. This was an important precondition for the subsequent electoral success of the Greens.

The second phase, 1975 to 1977

The forces behind the CIs first acquired a radical, unified, national organization and perspective as the anti-nuclear movement burst on to the scene in 1975. However, the ground was fertilized for this development by several developments between 1972 and 1975.

First, the Club of Rome report, *Global 2000*, on the "limits of growth" and the worldwide oil crisis seemed to suggest, indeed confirm, that it was not so much individual, bureaucratic planning errors but the entire policy of uncontrolled expansion and growth that were the root of the ills which the CIs sought to address. This was complemented by a wide-ranging discussion of the "quality of life" which questioned whether growth and its fruits – namely, an abundance of consumer durables – could serve as a benchmark for human happiness and social justice.

Second, media coverage and academic debate concerning the CIs buttressed public support for their activity, and a "clear tendency toward progressive cooperation and coordination of the local groups" became evident.[108] In 1972, the first CI umbrella organizations appeared: 15 CIs joined in forming the Federal Association of Citizens' Initiatives for Environmental Protection (Bundesverband der Bürgerinitiativen für Umweltschutz, BBU), soon to become the largest and most significant ecology organization in the Federal Republic. A second merger that same year, the Upper Rhine Action Committee against Environmental Endangerment through Nuclear Power Plants (Oberrheinisches Aktionskomitee gegen Umweltgefährdung durch Kernkraftwerke) marked the opening salvo in the battle against nuclear energy, a struggle which would dominate, drive and ultimately transform the CI movement during the next two years.

The first phase of the anti-nuclear movement began in 1972 in the town of Wyhl (in the state of Baden-Württemberg) in the upper Rhine area of Bad-Elsass, where there existed a precarious symbiosis of industrial parks and picturesque vineyards. Several CIs were already present in the region[109] when Wyhl was announced as one of several potential sites for a planned reactor that year.[110] But it was not until the spring of 1973 that the local citizenry, the most affected group, learned – on the radio no less[111] – that bureaucrats were considering Wyhl for the construction of a nuclear power plant! When Wyhl was in fact selected as the final site several months later, the Citizens' Initiative Weisweil was founded. Over the next nine months, numerous petitions were circulated and over 100,000 signatures collected opposing the planned construction.

Formal legal hearings in the summer of 1974[112] collapsed under the weight of revelations that four members of the state examining committee were also members of the power company's board of directors.[113] The damage wrought by the exposure of these conflicts of interest could not be rectified by subsequent information campaigns,[114] or by attempts to discredit the CIs and local scientists. Later that summer, 2,000 demonstrators marched to the proposed construction site, where they founded the International Committee of the 21 Citizens' Initiatives of Bad-Elsass[115] and agreed to occupy the plot should it prove necessary. They also read an angry and lengthy statement condemning the graft, corruption and undemocratic tactics of the representatives of the government and the power company, and – more significantly – declared their general opposition to all use of nuclear energy.[116] Here, as elsewhere in the rapidly forming anti-nuclear movement, the haughty tactics and corrupt behavior of politicians and businessmen were pivotal in transforming moderate, regionalist protests into a national opposition front against the Federal Republic's nuclear program. Local initiative and self-interest soon waxed into demands for enhanced democracy and socially responsible energy planning.[117]

Through dubious maneuvers and a tightly contested referendum at province level, however, local politicians and the power company together succeeded in acquiring the building site.[118] Despite continuing opposition and ongoing proceedings, construction was begun on February 17, 1975.[119] The next day, 30 CIs held a joint press conference, and immediately afterwards several hundred participants occupied the reactor site and successfully halted all construction work. Two days later, 650 policemen cleared all demonstrators from the site. The resultant publicity aroused such support for the demonstrators that three days later, on February 23, 28,000 people – among them protesters from France and Switzerland – once again swarmed into the construction area. The demonstrators, determined to hold the area occupied, erected a small, "alternative" settlement. One month later they built a "friendship house" and an adult education center.[120] These activities were crowned with success in late March, when an administrative court ordered a halt to construction.

The victory at Wyhl was a decisive moment in the formation of the anti-nuclear movement. It developed into a catalyst and symbol for protest in the rest of the Federal Republic. The tactic of occupying the construction site and converting it into an alternative colony was a provocative – and constructive – model which found frequent imitation in subsequent conflicts. Moreover, it was at Wyhl that a cadre of mobile, hard-core protesters, including many Communists and anarchists, made their first appearance in this scene of anti-nuclear activists.

Their presence was of great significance in the second chapter of the anti-nuclear movement, which occured on the lower Elbe in a tiny village in Schleswig-Holstein called Brokdorf. The construction of an atomic energy plant there was announced in the fall of 1973. The first CI, the Citizens' Initiative for Environmental Protection on the Lower Elbe (Bürgerinitiative Umweltschutz Unterelbe, BUU), was founded some two weeks later.[121] As in Wyhl, the power company and state government first sought to buy off the local community with lavish public works projects.[122] But this time, a referendum failed to support the plant.[123] This, however, did not deter the power company from proceeding with construction as originally planned.[124]

The ensuing conflict at Brokdorf reached a qualitatively higher level of polarization and brutality than at Wyhl. Extremists intent on violent confrontation with the state slipped into the ranks of peaceful protesters. The police in turn applied force with singular determination and little discrimination. The CIs were harassed, spied on by the authorities and tricked.[125] Before construction began, "Fort Brokdorf" emerged – complete with moat, fence, and barbed wire – in order to prevent a repetition of the Wyhl occupation.[126] Four days later, some 30,000 to 45,000 protesters appeared for a rally under the slogans "Where justice becomes injustice, resistance becomes a duty" ("wo Recht zu Unrecht wird, wird Widerstand zur Pflicht") and "No nukes in Brokdorf or anywhere else."[127] Following the obligatory speeches, 2,000 demonstrators pressed through police lines, bridged the moat, tore down a segment of the wall under the barrage of water cannons and occupied a section of the construction site. This act, having crossed the threshold of open violence, unleashed a rapid escalation in the intensity of confronta- tion, first at Wyhl,[128] then in demonstrations the following year against planned reactors in Grohnde and Malville, France, where clashes between the police and demonstrators resulted in fatalities on both sides.[129]

The "battles of Brokdorf, Grohnde and Malville" and the terrorist acts during the "hot autumn" in 1977 pushed the anti-nuclear movement's mod- erate majority into a phase of reflection: "Within the anti-nuclear movement a transformation now set in. It had become obvious, that the instrument of occupying the construction site . . . under the changed conditions was entirely unsuitable. The quasi-military parade favored provocations and excesses on both sides. Violent actions brought the aims of the CIs into discredit among the broader population."[130] In order to stem the violence without fragmenting the movement, the CIs responded by raising non-violence to a first principle without, however, categorically distancing themselves from the small minority of violent anarchists and Communists.[131]

The message from the protestors did not go unnoticed by politicians. In 1975, two highly influential books on the "ecological crisis" were published by Erhard Eppler (SPD) and Herbert Gruhl (CDU) respectively.[132] For a brief moment during 1976–7, unsettled by the escalating conflict between the state and the anti-nuclear protesters and a sudden swing of public opinion against nuclear power,[133] the SPD leadership even struck a receptive pose.[134] However, an alliance among party technocrats (like Chancellor Helmut Schmidt), conservative functionaries and wage-oriented unionists ultimately prevailed in continuing the SPD's traditional policies of "material" concerns based on technocratic crisis management, unfettered economic growth and increased wages.

Thus one of the most significant political developments during 1977 consisted in the SPD's simply missing the boat on the crucial issue of ecology, thereby disqualifying the party for at least a decade from being a major player in the construction of this particularly central area of progressive politics in the Federal Republic. The haughty authoritarianism and unre- sponsive posture on the part of all authorities (federal, state and local) to the CIs and anti-nuclear movements disappointed a large segment of the edu- cated professional middle classes and led to their disaffection vis-à-vis the state and the established parties, particularly the SPD.

The third phase, 1977 to 1980

Although the concerns and arguments of both the CI and anti-nuclear movements could be said to revolve round ecology, it was not until 1977 that their respective supporters and activists began to perceive themselves as part of an "ecology movement" *per se*. In a path-breaking document which foreshadowed much of the Greens' first program, the BBU – by the late 1970s a powerful consortium encompassing nearly 400 CIs in its sphere of influence[135] – insisted that an "ecological economy" could not be effected through "single-issue, individual measures in the area of technical environmental protection . . . but only when the requirements of ecology become the foundation of economic and social policy in their entirety."[136]

The "ecological alternative," as it was repeatedly formulated during these years,[137] rested on two concepts. The first was "qualitative growth": "a middle path . . . which above all requires a reduction of growth rates in the consumption of resources and the environment but not in the level of demand already achieved."[138] The second was the vision of an "ecological economy of circulation" (*ökologische Kreislaufwirtschaft*), in which production would occur in harmony with the "natural balances" of the environment. In this scheme, production was always to replace fully what it took from nature, never adding more to nature than it could recycle. In short, production – according to this view – was to emulate the ecological balance of primitive economies of hunters and gatherers.

Alongside this vision of an ecological reform project, a nascent eco-ideology also emerged. This was reflected in the increasing penetration and permeation of political vocabulary by ecological principles – or rather naturalist analogies – such as "unity in diversity" (*Einheit in der Vielfalt*) and the sudden vogue of an ecological lifestyle, spartan in material claims and environmentally conscious in everyday practice.

More important for our analysis was the fact that many of the radical and reformist tendencies, as well as movements of the 1970s, began to examine the role and relation of ecology vis-à-vis their own concerns. Many analysts from the Communist/socialist spectrum, ranging from orthodox members of the DKP and various K-groups to left-wing social Democrats and Jusos, began to reexamine critically the narrow focus in the positive stance of Marxian socialism toward growth, technology and the exploitation of nature.[139] The discussion of "eco-feminism" began in 1975.[140] The eco-feminists' argument centered on the view that women had a different, healthier, more wholesome relationship to nature than men, who had been distanced from nature through their instrumental and linear thinking as well as their alienating and exploitative activities. Therefore, so the eco-feminists believed, the ecological crisis was the obvious result of patriarchy. Only a feminized society provided the requisite preconditioning for sound and lasting ecological reforms leading to an ecological society worthy of the name.[141]

During this period, too, various "anthroposophic" societies which advocated a third way between capitalism and socialism (and played a significant role in the formation of the Green Party) began to formulate theories of "ecological humanism," which linked together the environmental crisis, the arms race and the north–south conflict as a challenge to the species.[142] Nothing short of a moral and ethical revolution could avert the certain catastrophe emanating from this miserable predicament. Moreover, Christians, especially within the German Protestant church, cast in a critical light the biblical maxim that humanity subject the natural world to its will. They chose to emphasize the role of Christians as guardians of the Creation instead.[143]

It was therefore the concept of ecology which forged the bond among the disarrayed forces of the Left during the late 1970s. This broadly understood notion of ecology served as a hub around which diffuse interests and commitments to the natural and social structures of physical and cultural reproduction could coalesce. Although, as we will see later, this ecological synthesis presented a thorny set of problems for the theory and practice of reform politics, it at least established a minimum consensus as a foundation on which to pursue the concerns, both old and new, of the Left during the 1970s. However, whereas eco-socialism, eco-feminism and eco-Christianity contributed substantially to the subsequent formation of the Greens, another alliance, "eco-pax," proved most important for their eventual success. It is to a discussion of the new peace movement that we now turn.

The New Peace Movement

In the years 1980–1, the "new peace movement" abruptly swelled into the largest, most heterogeneous mass movement in the history of the Federal Republic, dwarfing its predecessor in the late 1950s and exploding to dimensions vastly exceeding those of the CI, anti-nuclear and ecology movements. The confluence of factors in its emergence was as dense as its supporters were diverse. However, the common focus of the movement was the stationing of American Pershing II ballistic missiles and Cruise missiles; its binding agent was opposition against them.

The catalyst was "missile chancellor" Helmut Schmidt, who claimed two leading roles for himself in this drama. The first was as a principal strategist in the rethinking of NATO's defense policy during the late 1970s, which led to the "double-track decision" that coupled Soviet-American arms reduction talks to the deployment of euromissiles; the second was as a key statesman and politician in bringing national and partisan support into line behind the planned deployment of the euromissiles. In assuming the latter role, Schmidt drove the wedge between the SPD, on the one hand, and the reformist Bildungsbürgertum and students, on the other, deeper than the "hot autumn" and Brokdorf ever had. Moreover, it was this fundamental cleavage between pro-deployment forces allied with Chancellor Schmidt and an ever-growing number of anti-deployment pacifists opposed to the chancellor which divided the SPD against itself to a degree from which it had not yet recovered in the early 1990s. This estrangement between the center-right of the Social Democrats, holding governmental power, and its Left in virtual opposition to this power – between the party of government and the party of movement – was the final leg in the development of an "autonomous, non-partisan and extraparliamentary grass-roots and mass movement."[144] This split within an increasingly factionalized social democracy represented the final and perhaps decisive factor which proved responsible for sending a last and critical contingent of voters into the green/alternative electoral camp.

The West Germany peace movement passed through essentially four phases in the decade between 1975 and 1985. Despite a slight increase in the number of demonstrations and activities beginning in 1975–6, the peace movement remained in the state of dormancy into which it had fallen after APO's demise until the NATO double-track decision awakened it again in 1979. A period of agitation and mobilization followed, culminating in its first mass demonstration in the fall of 1981. This introduced the phase of maximal mobilization, which continued until the actual stationing of the euromissiles was approved by the Bundestag and deployment began in November 1983. While moderate forces retreated, militant supporters entered on a campaign of violent resistance and obstruction, which culminated in the fragmentation and collapse of the peace movement in 1985.

The first period, 1975 to 1979

During the era of detente in the early 1970s, venerable pacifist organizations such as the German Peace Society/United Conscientious Objectors (Deutsche Friedensgesellschaft/Vereinigte Kriegsdienstverweiger, DFG/VK, founded in 1882) and the German Peace Union (Deutsche Friedensunion) upheld peace activities at a low level. They were joined by Christian groups such as the Action Community Service for Peace (Aktionsgemeinschaft Dienst für den Frieden, founded 1968) and the Action Sühnezeichen/Service for Peace (Aktion Sühnezeichen/Friedensdienst), all of which would later assume leadership functions in the new peace movement. The first bud of the autonomous or grass-roots element of the new peace movement was the Democratic Women's Initiative, founded in 1975.[145]

This was supplemented by government-sponsored peace research.[146] A significant addition to the roster came in 1974 with the establishment of the Committee for Disarmament and Cooperation (Komitee für Abrüstung und Zusammenarbeit, KOFAZ), which, in spite of, or perhaps because of, its close ties to the DKP[147] and its lock-step with Soviet foreign policy,[148] first sought to organize support for détente and disarmament on the broadest possible basis, thereby securing itself a leading role in the new peace movement.[149] It was KOFAZ which revived street demonstrations and reactivated extraparliamentary opposition inside the peace movement. Following the success of a peace rally in Bonn in the spring of 1976,[150] KOFAZ began to organize several well-attended demonstrations every year, which later provided a convenient point of entry for new opposition forces.

The second period, 1979 to 1981

The new peace movement began with the NATO security conference in Brussels in December 1979. The double-track decision was narrowly passed with the aid of an indispensable affirmative vote from West Germany. In the strained climate of international relations during the late 1970s, there was good reason to view the new missiles to be trained on Europe from both east and west as more than another unimportant and technical chapter in the arms race.[151] The election of Ronald Reagan, the most hawkish US president in decades, radically decreased the trust in the United States felt by moderate and liberal West Germans.[152] Last, but certainly not least, there was the special role of the Federal Republic as NATO's forward defense barrier, should the Pershings and Cruise missiles be employed in the sort of limited nuclear exchange in Europe for which some strategists envisioned these weapons systems, and – much more important – for which millions of Germans rightly or wrongly took them to be intended.

Let us now examine the configuration which emerged within the peace movement during the years immediately after the double-track decision for each of the five groupings which were later to develop into key green constituencies.

Conservative converts Given the technical nature of the debate and the special national threat it represented for the Federal Republic, it is not surprising that the first informed criticism of the euromissiles emanated not from left-leaning pacifists but from conservative military leaders such as Alfred Mechtersheimer and Gert Bastian.[153] They argued that, following deployment of these weapons, "the chances for the Europeans' survival, given a failure of deterrence . . . equaled zero!"[154] Many peace researchers also attacked the defense "expertocracy," challenging the premises of its strategic models and developing proposals for non-nuclear "alternative defense" schemes.[155] Clearly, the fact that "the goals of the peace movement [were] grounded first of all in military and security policy" was one of the main features which distinguished it from the vague moralism of the ban-the-bomb movement of the 1950s.[156]

Eco-pax alliance Interaction and cooperation between the ecology movement and the new peace movement developed rather rapidly. In the words of eminent students of the Federal Republic's new social movements: "It was not a long path from the self-understanding of the ecology movement as a life movement (*Lebensbewegung*) to the peace movement as a survival movement (*Überlebensbewegung*)."[157] Particularly instrumental in forming a real alliance were Jo Leinen, chairman of the BBU (the federation of citizens' initiatives for environmental protection), on the one hand, and Roland Vogt and Petra Kelly, peace activists, on the other; together they pursued their vision of an "eco-pax" movement based on the "principle of life."[158] The eco-pax synthesis was cemented through an array of congresses and grass-roots cooperation all through 1979–80.[159] The eco-pax activists thematized many points of overlap in the concerns of the ecology and peace movements: the pernicious relationship between the "peaceful" and military uses of atomic energy and its proliferation into the Third World;[160] the exploitation of[161] and potential for military conflict over natural resources;[162] and, on the most general level, the functional and systematic connection between "the threat of nuclear war" and the "creeping destruction of nature through uninhibited industrialization", offering an ecologized interpretation of the military-industrial complex.[163] It is important to understand that the synthesis of the ecology and peace movements had as much an intellectual basis as it did an existential one.

Christian organizations A third, highly influential strand of the new peace movement emerged from various religious groups. Two of the most significant ones, ASF and AGDF, founded respectively in 1958 and 1968, had actively represented pacifist positions in the Federal Republic for some time. Christian pacifists first took a political turn in May 1978, when the initiative, Live Without Armaments (Ohne Rüstung Leben), began circulating a petition, eventually signed by 13,000 Christians[164] who declared themselves "ready to live without the protection of military arms."[165] Following the model of the Dutch Protestant churches, the ASF organized a peace week, held in October 1980 in 350 locations in the Federal Republic under the slogan "Make peace without weapons" ("Frieden schaffen ohne Waffen"),[166] with such great success that it was repeated annually in subsequent years.[167]

The left wing Given the substantial internal opposition within the SPD to the double-track decision, many among the party's left wing either joined the peace movement and its activities openly, or supported it and its milieu in a quiet, though resolute, manner. Prominent intellectual and cultural figures who were members of the SPD signed the 1980 Bielefeld appeal, challenging the seriousness and therefore the validity of the disarmament talks conducted by the superpowers.[168] In June 1981, under the auspices of the party's moral conscience, the so-called Gustav Heinemann Initiative (named after the popular SPD leader and president of the Federal Republic, Gustav Heinemann), SPD members and sympathizers, among them two powerful left-wing party officials, Erhard Eppler and Oskar Lafontaine, issued a statement on security policy whose elegant and subtle wording barely failed to conceal its radical core: a rejection of deterrence through strategic parity, and allusions to Germany's historical and constitutional obligation to peace.[169] At their federal congress several weeks later, the Jusos passed a yet more radical statement.[170]

Grass-roots organizations The "independent" or "autonomous" organizations, as they were called, did not have an organizational mouthpiece in the new peace movement until March 1982, when the Federal Conference of Independent Peace Groups (Bundeskonferenz Unabhängiger Friedensgruppen, BUF) was established. It comprised mainly anarchists, anti-imperialists and anti-militarists, who advocated radical forms of opposition, particularly civil disobedience.[171] Because of their extreme tactics and positions, as well as diffuseness, these groups remained relatively marginalized, coming to the forefront only in the final phase of the movement.

Representatives of all these currents joined for the first time at the Krefeld forum, held under the slogan "Nuclear death threatens us all" in the fall of

1980. The result, the Krefeld appeal, pegged the minimal consensus of the peace movement at a non-negotiable opposition to the stationing of the Pershing IIs and Cruise missiles on German soil.[172] Within six months, some 800,000 West German citizens had signed the Krefeld appeal, and after a year and a half the figure had swelled to well over two million.[173] The appeal marked the high point of the peace movement's mobilization phase.

The third period, 1981 to 1983

The next milestone for the new peace movement was the great mass demonstration in Bonn in October 1981. Spurred by a spontaneous peace march after the Protestant church convention the previous summer,[174] a meeting of 22 prominent peace activists representing the spectrum of the movement (excepting the "autonomists")[175] was held to discuss the demonstration. To counter the government's practice of discrediting the movement as Communist controlled and infiltrated, the demonstration was sponsored by the ASF and AGDF.[176] To maximize participation, a follow-up meeting including some 95 organizations was held in mid-July.[177] In their flyer, the organizers not only demanded that the "governments of NATO's member nations withdraw their approval of the decision to station new middle-range missiles" in Europe, the peace activists also incorporated the Russell Peace Foundation's call of the previous summer for the establishment of a nuclear-free Europe.[178] Attendance soared beyond the 50,000 projected by the organizers to some 300,000, making it what was then the largest demonstration ever in the history of the Federal Republic.[179] Its success was largely due to the unity and political savvy of the organizers and the careful framing of their appeal.

The impact of the demonstration was enormous and immediate. In its wake, nearly half the population of the Federal Republic expressed a positive attitude toward the peace movement, and nearly a quarter of those aged 18 to 29 expressed a willingness or desire for active participation in it.[180] The small circle of organizers was so encouraged by the results that it not only decided to continue meeting[181] but in the spring of 1982 formed an official coordinating committee to steer further activities of the peace movement.[182] Over the next two years, the committee conducted seven "action conferences." It not only administered and organized a series of major demonstrations, but managed relations to the press, issued statements and position papers on current events and, in general, carefully manicured the image of the peace movement.[183]

The period from spring and summer of 1982 until the Bundestag voted to begin deploying these weapons in November 1983 represented the acme of the movement's demonstration phase. The euphoria of the Bonn demonstration, the consolidation of the coordinating committee, the beginning of the US–Soviet negotiations in Geneva in November 1981, all these had lent the peace movement tremendous momentum entering 1982. For the first time since 1968, nationwide Easter marches were organized, drawing an estimated

500,000 participants in 1982, 650,000 in 1983.[184] The NATO summit held in Bonn in the summer of 1982, on the occasion of which Ronald Reagan delivered a speech before the Bundestag, attracted some 400,000 demonstrators to the capital, thus surpassing the record set during the previous October.[185]

The fact that the March 1983 Bundestag election, called after the collapse of the social-liberal coalition in September 1982, fell in the midst of the "hot phase" of the new peace movement was of great importance for the eventual success of what was to become the new social movements' parliamentary representation in the form of a new party called the Greens. Though Helmut Schmidt's would-be successor, Hans-Jochen Vogel, declared himself ready to do everything in his power toward the success of the Geneva negotiations in order to render the stationing of the euromissiles "superfluous," the Greens were to benefit tremendously from the votes of those who unequivocally opposed the double-track decision.[186] The activity of the peace movement appeared to have effected a significant turn of public opinion against the euromissiles since the 1981 Bonn demonstration.[187]

The fourth period, 1983 to 1985

The fourth and final phase of the peace movement, one of opposition and resistance, began in the summer of 1983 during demonstrations against a visit by George Bush, then US vice-president, at a German-American Friendship Festival in the small town of Krefeld. Intricate planning by both police and militant "autonomists" were the prelude to violent militant confrontations on a par with the anti-nuclear demonstrations of the "hot autumn" of 1977.[188] As it became clear that the superpower negotiations in Geneva were doomed to failure, "autonomists" and "independents" began planning "resistance actions" against the stationing of missiles for months in advance.[189] The highlight was a concerted attempt to disrupt and obstruct the Bundestag debate and vote on approving the missile deployment in November.[190] December brought the first act of planned sabotage.[191]

Then as earlier, the line of the autonomists and independents remained a minority position at best. Very few were willing to carry on the struggle following the Bundestag vote. Even among those who were the most committed representatives of the coordinating committee, an increasing polarization between "demonstrators" and "blockaders" developed.[192] The unity of the peace movement was also threatened from another direction. Since the minimal consensus underpinning it had centered around preventing the deployment of the missiles, and that had become a *fait accompli*, the established basis for cooperation had disappeared. Nor was the search for a new one in slogans such as "out of NATO," in campaigns like "people's plebiscite" against the missiles, or in actions such as "human chains" particularly successful. But while the peace movement's leadership proved capable of finding new compromise formulas to preserve the unity of the coordinating committee, it appeared unable to establish broad-based support for the movement's new campaigns. The elaborate activities planned for the fall of 1984 were implemented only by small bands of militants.[193]

This, of course, was far removed from the mighty peace movement which attained its importance on the basis of establishing an impressive coalition of disparate forces. It was the diversity of this political movement which was to congeal into the Green Party of the 1980s.

Part II

Ideology and Policy

Having established a rather extensive genealogy of the West German Greens in the four chapters comprising the first part of our book, we now proceed to a discussion of what we believe to be the most pronounced characteristics of this new political formation. We have decided to divide our presentation of these characteristics into two parts. The first will concentrate on an analysis of what we have termed the Greens' ideology. Concretely, chapter 5 offers an overview of what we judge to be the main ideological strains of this complex and motley movement. Since the Greens have rightfully claimed much credit for being heterodox, any analysis of their ideology will by necessity fall short of reality's complexity. Clearly, there exist traits in many a Green's *Weltanschauung* which our presentation in chapter 5 does not even mention. Following the logic of our presentation in the first part of the book, our analysis in chapter 5 is also historically informed in the sense that we relate the main ideological clusters discussed in this chapter to preceding ideologies which shaped German politics. Thus chapter 5 is not intended to be a comprehensive treatment of all ideologies which affected the daily world of the Greens as party and movement; nor is it an up-to-date account of the newest developments in green thinking; instead, chapter 5 offers a detailed discussion of the major ideological pillars on which the Greens' calling rested at the most critical junctures of the party's formative period.

The second dimension of the Green's contemporary characteristics which we analyze pertains to their policies. This is the subject of chapter 6. In a sense, we view policy as applied (or middle-level) ideology. If ideology comprises abstract principles and ordering categories, policy tries to apply these to the quotidian aspects of politics. It is precisely because we see a close relationship between the Greens' ideologies and policies that we decided to present them together in part 2. Chapter 6 concentrates on presenting key aspects of the Greens' policies in certain issue areas which we thought important in two respects: first, in terms of their salience in the Federal Republic's political reality; and second, as defining moments of green identity.

Policies can be gauged on the input as well as the output side of the political system. Given the fact that the Greens have remained a "milieu" party throughout their existence – never attaining a majority in any legislature and thus never having exercised executive power by themselves on any level of the German governmental system – green policies cannot be measured as "output" with any degree of certainty. Thus the analysis in chapter 6 is based entirely on the "input" dimension of green policy. In other words, we focus on what the Greens say, write, want and hope, rather than on what they actually do.

This, of course, is not to argue that the Greens' smallness in size has barred them from having any effect on the output side of the German political system. Quite to the contrary. As we will argue in part 3, as well as in the conclusion, perhaps the most salient aspect of the Greens has been their ability to transform the political debate in the Federal Republic; this in turn has had a major impact on policies and their implementation, as well as fundamentally altering the form and content of progressive politics in Germany.

5

Ideology: The World Imagined

The three preceding chapters have been organized around the contention that the Greens must be viewed as part of the West German Left and, more particularly, in their relation to German social democracy. We have tried to show that understanding the Greens along their most critical dimensions – their historical emergence, the political landscape in which they operate and the set of policy concerns which they attempt to address – requires, above all, situating them within the development and dilemmas of Germany social democracy. Thus, our analysis places the Greens in the tradition of the larger context of the German Left. In line with this analysis, this chapter will develop the thesis that green ideology in all its variants has been defined by the attempt to develop a theoretically grounded synthesis of ecological and socialist politics. Put differently, green ideologues aimed to reconstruct Marxian socialism.[1] In the party's early years, many green activists would have angrily rejected this assessment. Their conviction that the Greens were inventing a completely new politics, organizing a historical coalition of the entire species and preparing a new society beyond the tired alternatives of the established political spectrum were embodied in the then popular slogan, that the Greens were "neither left nor right but ahead."

In retrospect, this claim seems exaggerated (and even a bit ironic) in light of the leftist pedigrees which most green activists and supporters earned in the SPD, the K-groups or the "undogmatic" Marxist organizations of the 1970s. Having already excluded the moderate and conservative ecologists around Herbert Gruhl (see chapter 7), by the early 1980s the party had drifted into the empty political space left of the SPD. We can think of political space as the opportunities for legitimate mobilization within a polity not monopolized by established linkage mechanisms.[2] It was not until the mid-1980s, however, that the Greens' self-understanding began to catch up with the leftist image, politics and allegiances of the party.

Nevertheless, while the Greens have occupied roughly the same position in the West German political landscape that the French and Italian communist parties have traditionally assumed in their countries – that is, on the left margin of the "respectable" political spectrum – it would be erroneous to characterize the Greens exclusively as "radical socialists" (a label which, in any event, most Greens would surely eschew). Even though the historical genealogy and sociological composition of a majority of the Greens' leadership as well as their activist following hailed from the world of post-APO socialism, the ideology of the Greens has indeed been profoundly informed by "radical ecology" as well. How this synthesis emerged will be the subject of this chapter. As to its success as a viable option for quotidian politics in contemporary Germany, the reader will have to await the verdict offered in the "Politics" section of this book.

On a theoretical level, the attempt to reconcile ecology with *reformist* socialism proved particularly difficult. This is because radical ecology introduces naturalistic terms and metaphors ("survival," "cycle," "diversity"), both as means of interpreting the social world and as standards for evaluating political action. The naturalism of radical ecology is strongly at odds with the world-view of reformist socialism, which is deeply informed by the traditional categories of Enlightenment radicalism ("humanism," "reason" and "liberation"). In many respects, the green strategy debate of the 1980s was in fact a struggle between this radical ecology and reformist socialism, just as the departure of the so-called Fundamentalists from the party in the 1990s was to represent a failure on a practical level to achieve a lasting synthesis between the two.

In this chapter, we will begin by arguing that there have been four principle ideological streams within the Greens, each of which represents a distinctive approach to reconciling socialism and ecology. We will then show how these ideological differences fed into and informed the green strategy debate (and ultimately short-circuited attempts to overcome them). We will go on to examine each of the four tendencies in more detail, focusing at length on the most challenging (and troubling) of them: radical ecology. This will enhance our understanding of what was at stake in the debates of the 1980s and what was lost by the departure of the Fundamentalists (Fundis) in the 1990s. In addition, we hope that this presentation will also serve to illuminate the dilemmas facing any ecological reconstruction of socialist ideology, as well as make clear how necessary such a project is if a viable and vibrant Left is to survive beyond the collapse of "real, existing socialism" into the twenty-first century.

The Four Main Ideological Currents: a Typology

In the various efforts to synthesize ecology and socialism within the German Greens, it is possible to discern four principal impulses. From Marxian socialism come the *dogmatism* of revolutionary strategy and belief in the inevitable nature of social and material progress, as well as a *humanism* which

Marxian socialism

	HUMANISM	DOGMATISM
REFORMISM	A	C
NATURALISM	B	D

Ecology

places emancipation and liberation at the center of political praxis. Both of these tendencies are ultimately rooted in the political thought of the Enlightenment. From ecology come both a *reformism* aimed at repairing environmental damage and restructuring industrial production to eliminate its causes, and a *naturalism* oriented toward redefining the "good society" in ecological terms. One might envision the potential permutations of these major components of green ideology in terms of the two-by-two grid above.

Of course, like all four fold typologies, this one should only satisfy the most basic forms of schematization of frequently complex relationships. No reformist humanism (A), for instance, would be conceivable without first modifying western society's objectifying, "value free" and ultimately exploitative relation to nature (that is, borrowing from D). Nor could dogmatic naturalism (D), in its quest to preserve and/or recapture the original state of the environment, ever eliminate the question of human emancipation and social progress in its entirely. What defines the boundaries of this fourfold typology is a division over the Enlightenment notion of inevitable, universal, material and moral progress as transmitted to the Left from Kant through Hegel and Marx. Theoretically, two avenues of response emanate from this ecological critique: one may either attempt to ecologize socialism (reformist humanism) or seek to socialize ecology (dogmatic naturalism). While the former represents an attempt to *reconstruct* the socialist interpretation of the Enlightenment's vision of progress and liberation through reason, the latter embodies the urge to *reject* this vision altogether in favor of an ideal of naturalistic wholeness and harmony drawn from premodern and non-western cultures and religions. Roughly speaking, these four ideological tendencies correspond to the four factions and the coalitional strategies which emerged within the German Greens during the 1980s. These are set out in the first box overleaf.

The realists and the fundamentalists represent the larger, more powerful factions, while the eco-libertarians and the eco-socialists are smaller groups allied with one of the larger groups, as indicated by the arrows. It is important to note that the cross-cutting alliances are based on the issue of "strategy" rather than the question of "goals". Rearranging the matrix of humanism/dogmatism and reformism/naturalism to reflect the bipolarity of "strategy" and "goals" instead of the previous "ecology" and "Marxian socialism," we

Marxian socialism

	HUMANISM	DOGMATISM
REFORMISM	realists	theoretically possible but not an empirical reality in the world of the Greens
NATURALISM	eco-libertarians ⌐ eco-socialists ➤ fundamentalists	

(left label: Ecology)

Goals

	NATURALISM	HUMANISM
REFORMISM	eco-libertarians ◄─►	realists
DOGMATISM	fundamentalists ◄─►	eco-socialists

(left label: Strategy)

arrive at the useful graphic categorization of the four main green factions, their strategies, goals, and alliances, in the second box above. The eco-libertarians are inclined toward a policy of reform which therefore allied them rather frequently with the realists. The eco-socialists, in turn, have been linked to the fundamentalists through their shared commitment to a strategy of "fundamental opposition" even though the former's intellectual anchor in the humanistic tradition of reason and emancipation placed them in an uneasy alliance with the fundamentalists' unquestioned belief in naturalism. This pattern of alliances and interactions reveals the anatomy of blocked development which has consistently plagued the Greens throughout their existence. While the fundamentalists ultimately proved incapable of forming a majority alliance based on naturalist dogmatism, they repeatedly succeeded in subverting the lasting establishment of a reformist–humanist coalition between eco-liberals, eco-socialists and realists.

Thus, the Greens' search for an ideological identity fusing socialism and ecology revealed two grave dangers for the young party. The first was the possibility (very real at several junctures in the party's development) that the radical Left might be reconstructed around naturalistic categories which hearkened back to romantic and anti-western traditions of German thought. The second and more imminent danger stemmed from the political paralysis of (and declining electoral support for) the party, which resulted from on-going but inconclusive confrontation between the four tendencies. We now turn to an examination of the "strategy debate" which raged during the 1980s, and of its ideological roots.

The Green Strategy Debate: a Case of Blocked Development

The Fundi/Realo dispute appears to have originated in 1982 in Hessen as the "Fischer/Cohn-Bendit gang" wrested control of the state party from Frankfurt fundamentalists around Jutta Ditfurth and Manfred Zieran. The controversy quickly focused on the question of the Greens' allying with the SPD. This preoccupation came to overshadow every substantive policy issue and question of content within the federal party. As we will see in our "Politics" chapter, this controversy intensified during 1984, following the emergence of the first red–green coalition in Hessen. It reached a crescendo after the Greens' electoral defeats in North-Rhine Westphalia and the Saar in the spring of 1985. While the conflict abated briefly in the wake of the party's euphoria following its excellent showing in the Bundestag election of January 25, 1987, it returned in full force later that year. By the late 1980s, the interfactional strife had begun to threaten the political survival of the Greens. It was only in the wake of the great party finance scandal of 1989 that the fundamentalist faction began to crumble. Its final departure from the party did not occur until the early 1990s, thus giving its main rivals, the much-despised realos, a good run for their money. While the Fundi/Realo dispute possessed – just like any other intraorganizational conflict – many important (and aggravating) facets, the one concerning the Green Party's optimal strat-egy surely played an especially central role.

To be sure, strategy debates have been a staple of socialist politics in Germany since Karl Marx, not least because of Marx's own ambiguous po-sition on the role of political praxis. Thus the Greens' interfactional feuding stands within a certain tradition stretching from the great revolution vs re-form debate of Rosa Luxemburg and Karl Kautsky during the Second Inter-national, to the conflict between the Juso concept of "system-transcending reforms" and the orthodox Leninist politics of the communist sect groups during the 1970s. The debate which occurred between fundamentalists and realists, like earlier debates, proved costly to progressive forces, severely sapping the strength and support of party and movement.

Yet the historical link does not completely conform to the terms of the Fundi/Realo conflict, since this strategy debate within the greens was not about revolution versus reform *per se*. The "crisis of the Left" and the dissolution of the K-groups during the late 1970s discredited the orthodox concept of revolution in the milieu of the West German Left. Eco-socialist Eckhart Strattmann insisted he was speaking for the whole party when he emphasized that "reform strategy instead of revolutionary nonsense enjoys a consensus; parliament as an instrument of decision does as well. . . ."[4] But the "consensus," while embracing reformist tactics, still clung to revolutionary aims. Said Realo, Helmut Wiesenthal, citing his Fundi arch-rival, Rainer Trampert: "On this point, all currents within the Greens are agreed: the most important goal is not the improvement of the status quo but rather a fundamental change in this society. . . ."[5]

On the surface, the problem in the Fundi/Realo debate was whether or not entering an alliance with the SPD (where red–green majorities emerged) offered a viable route to "fundamental" change. The immediate background of the debate was not theoretical but historical. The Greens in general and the fundamentalists in particular harbored a deepseated mistrust of the Social Democrats. Historically, the radical Left's image of the SPD had been one of cooptation and betrayal. Radical leftists saw direct continuity between the SPD which voted for the war credits in 1914 and helped kill Karl Liebknecht and Rosa Luxemburg in 1918, and its postwar successor which gave the country repressive anti-terrorist laws and NATO's much-hated double-track decision, among other acts of cowardice and accommodation.

Fundamentalists regarded the SPD in its contemporary form as an unacceptable political partner.[6] This was so in part because fundamentalists claimed to see a "thoroughgoing overlap in identities between the two big parties, the CDU and SPD" with respect to their actual policies, if not their rhetoric.[7] But most of all, fundamentalists rejected any partnership on the part of the Greens with the SPD out of a visceral dislike for Social Democrats and a substantial mistrust of their motives: "The function of Social Democracy was always to integrate social movements, progressive movements. . . ."[8] Nevertheless, since Rudolf Bahro's exaggerated hopes for a green majority[9] lost credence outside the party, most fundamentalists conceded that, in the long run at least, the SPD remained the only visible coalition partner for the Greens. However, for the fundamentalists, a red–green alliance always presupposed a radical internal transformation of the SPD. The fundamentalists believed that this could best be achieved through a complete renunciation of compromise. While, according to the Fundi view, the Greens might have been permitted a strictly tactical divergence from this course by entering into a temporary and informal single-issue cooperation with the SPD (based on a reluctant toleration of social democracy) in order to "get people to see certain substantive issues (*Inhalte*) as important" and "unmask" the SPD's political bankruptcy and moral poverty, this faction's world-view would never have condoned a strategic alliance between Greens and the SPD for any reason.[10] Whereas this exclusionary strategy would make it difficult to present tangible policy successes to the voters – at least in the short run – the fundamentalists contended that it was simply paramount for the Greens to remain uncompromising and radical on questions of principle. It was precisely the Greens' upholding of "radical contents" which, so the Fundis argued, established the movement's "political foundation" in the eyes of the world.[11]

While the realists shared this basic mistrust and skepticism toward the SPD, they differentiated rather precisely between the apparatchik (*Kanalarbeiter*) faction of the SPD Right and "green" Social Democrats such as Oskar Lafontaine, Gerhard Schröder or Peter Glotz. In Realo eyes, the best route to transforming the SPD was an alliance with the Greens which, so many Realos believed, would inevitably strengthen the position of the SPD Left among the Social Democrats. Within the context of a formal coalition, the SPD would be forced, in the Realos' view, to cooperate with the Greens on issues such as nuclear energy and disarmament, where the position of the SPD electorate was close to that of the Greens. Failing to do so would discredit the SPD with its increasingly restive and critical constituency. The Realos argued that so far as the Greens succeeded in extracting reforms from the SPD, the public would recognize and reward the Greens for being a necessary corrective, thereby strengthening the Greens' position in German politics. Ultimately, in the view of the Realos, the legitimacy of the Greens did not rest on "mere verbal radicalism," but on the party's ability to effect concrete and visible (if gradual) reforms. In the long run, failure to do so would only undermine the party's popular support.

In sum, while the realists maintained a critical but differentiated stance toward the SPD, the fundamentalists were apt to dismiss the Social Democrats entirely. The realists wished the Greens to play the role of an ecological corrective and have them supply socialism with new impulses. The fundamentalists' objective on the other hand was to attack, fragment, and eventually destroy social democracy and to use the ruins as raw materials for building a green majority. If the realists wished to rebuild socialism through green influence, the fundamentalists hoped to destroy it to make room for green domination.

At another level, the dispute over the coalition question involved the relative weight given to parliamentary reformism and movement protest in a strategy of radical social change. It was on this deeper level that the Greens were haunted by the ghosts of the past strategy debates within the German Left. For many fundamentalists, like Jutta Ditfurth, the Green double strategy meant seeking a "path between reformism and armed militancy."[12] The fundamentalist position was perhaps best expressed in Petra Kelly's well-known soccer analogy: the movement is the standing leg (*Standbein*) and the party is the kicking leg (*Spielbein*). In Kelly's words:

> For us, parliaments are a place like the market square or the construction site where we can speak, introduce our standpoints and depart with information. . . . I would like a strong grass-roots movement such as ours to have a voice and vote in parliament . . . Parliament is not a goal but part of a strategy. We are the anti-party party . . . the most important thing is to work on the grass roots, to change at the grass roots.[13]

Fundamentalists contended that the possibility for fundamental social change through parliaments was limited, since the decisions which actually shaped society – such as on arms, nuclear power, industrial production – occurred in government bureaucracies, cabinet meetings and corporate boardrooms, never in legislatures.[14] Social movements, on the other hand, could alter relations directly in civil society and exert legitimation pressures on the "real" loci of power. The fundamentalists believed that the Greens' parliamentary power could be most effectively used for the tactical and logistical support of the social movements, supplying them with needed public relations, money and organization. Instead of striving for hopeless and premature reforms through coalitions, the Greens should first work to organize a broad basis of social opposition. Thus eco-socialist Thomas Ebermann: "We are in a phase in which we are collecting the forces which are prepared for change, in which we enlighten in order that this preparedness expand. . . . It is ridiculous to see the question of power as comprising the incendiary point in a time when many people are not even convinced of the necessity of fundamental change."[15] The question of power becomes salient only when a majority of the population "realizes" that the position of the Greens is correct. The moment for fundamental social reform can come only after this massive transformation of consciousness has been completed.

The realists, in contrast, maintained that reforms themselves must form the first steps in a strategy for fundamental social change. The idea of this strategy was captured in phrases such as "radical reform with a fundamental intention" or "system-transcending *realpolitik*," a policy of gradual step-by-step reform guided by and ultimately directed toward the radical ideal of a new society. In the assessment of the realists, a mass social movement might help legitimate green demands or put pressure on other parties, but any "realistic assessment of the relations of power in the Federal Republic" showed that real power lay within the established institutions. Hence, "real" social change could be reached only along the "reformist path, the path of participation in power."[16] While the realists did not claim that parliament was the only locus of social power, they insisted that it was a new and "relevant" one for the radical Left.[17] As what Joschka Fischer called the "parliamentary arm of the movement", the Green Party concentrated on moving those levers of social power located in parliament. Toward that end, it was necessary that one "differentiate between the tasks of a movement and the tasks of a party. . . . movements . . . are – where they are really strong – radical in such a way . . . that the Greens, when they want both, will break down on this issue in the long run."[18]

In essence, the realists advocated a sort of political division of labor between the green movement and the Green Party. The realists contended that the fundamentalists' emphasis on "the movement" stemmed from an infantile and antiquated fascination with the ghetto of oppositional subculture, which led the fundamentalists to overlook the seriousness of Germany's social and environmental problems. Environmental reforms were not only pressing, urged the realists, but could "create the necessary space" for "autonomous developments in society, culture and economy to unfold."[19] Moreover, since parliamentary reform necessitated a legislative majority, the realists felt it imperative that the Greens seek an alliance with the Social Democrats.

The fundamentalists' dogmatism was of the simple, quasi-chiliastic variety characteristic of orthodox Marxism. Little wonder then that ex-Communists weighed so heavily in their ranks. In essence, the fundamentalists believed that they possessed the right answers and best solutions to contemporary social problems and consequently regarded political concessions as "mendacious compromises" (Ditfurth). As Petra Kelly put it: "In certain questions, the Greens cannot enter into any compromises. There is not just a little bit of death, a little bit of annihilation, a little bit of cancer, a little bit of war or violence!"[20] Indeed, in the final analysis, the fundamentalists saw no need for compromise, dialogue or discussion, for they believed that truth was on their side. They regarded the triumph of their position as essentially inevitable. In the Fundis' view, the Greens needed only to wait and to keep the faith in doctrinal purity in order to claim their role in ushering in the ecological millennium.

And yet, the "blocked development," of which the strategy debate was symptomatic, had not been caused solely by fundamentalist dogmatism. After all, the fundamentalists rarely comprised a majority of the party leadership and were certainly in a minority position in the green electorate. It took the realists, in turn, a decade to lead their reformist–humanist coalition to a quasi-hegemony within the party. This, in a sense, proved a pyrrhic victory because it exacted from the realists their own brand of dogmatic reformism. The realists had been forced to devote so much effort to defending constructive parliamentary activity against the arguments of the fundamentalists that they had all too often become narrowly, almost obsessively, focused on the coalition issue. This excessive emphasis on the coalition question had in turn blocked processes of creative policy thinking and theoretical reflection. The repeated fundamentalist charge that realist leaders such as Joschka Fischer were nothing but "macho power politicians"[21] had become something of a self-fulfilling prophecy, for a certain cynicism regarding the content of politics and a concomitant obsession with governmental power as a political panacea had unquestionably taken hold of the realist camp. The realists' dogmatic reformism rendered the strategy of parliamentarism into a fetish.

The roots of the blocks in the Greens' ideological and political development reached well below the structure of the Fundi/Realo conflict. They constituted two figures of thought derived from Marxism which were unthinkingly, perhaps even unconsciously, incorporated into green ideology and analysis. The first concerned the idea of "radical social change." Most Greens have continued to speak in terms of a "systemic" or "structural" transformation of society, that is, an embracing, all-encompassing reordering of state, economy, society and culture, reaching from the structure of collective decision-making to the aesthetic of individual lifestyles. In this, the greens have clearly remained influenced by the concept of a "social totality" transmitted from Hegel through Marx and Lukàcs; since real, radical social change must be total, all strategies aimed at limited or incremental improvements – that is, reforms – can only be justified insofar as they fit into a program or strategy for promoting systemic transformation. Therefore, the rationale fundamentalists tended to offer for the Greens' existence as a parliamentary party was their ability "to promote continually what the movement mostly calls forth only as a spontaneous effect and after-effect, a change of the consciousness of great masses."[22] Even the realists felt compelled to emphasize that "parliamentary work" contains a "system-transcending option."[23]

The second thought motif frequently invoked by Greens, and especially by fundamentalists, was the idea of "crisis." Insofar as voluntaristic, political action appears insufficient to provoke systemic change, a conviction strongest among fundamentalists, trust must be placed in the play of "objectives forces" to create such change. Many Greens share the "conclusion that without deepreaching 'survival reforms' in the next 15 years, no human perspective for life beyond the year 200 is thinkable."[24] It is this belief in the imminence and transformative power of crisis which has often led the Greens to the same passive *attentisme* and "waiting for the worst" characteristic of radical revolutionary socialism.

The result of this unreflecting appropriation of the Marxian concept of totality and theory of crisis was that any discussion of political praxis had to be automatically framed in terms of opposition vs integration. Thus, any compromise made with "the system" – even where it may have obvious, positive results – has necessarily been viewed as unwitting cooptation or a conscious sell-out. This sort of argumentation was mustered by fundamentalists to reject categorically almost every proposal or attempt to deploy or increase the Greens' political influence be they participation in a governing coalition, professionalization of the party, expansion of the electoral basis or countless other issues. This attitude was well exemplified in Petra Kelly's fear: "I am sometimes afraid that the Greens will suddenly get 13 per cent in an election and turn into a power-hungry party (*Machterwerbspartei*). It would be better for us to stay at 6 or 7 percent and remain uncompromising in our basic demands. Better to do that than have green ministers."[25]

It is by virtue of this logic that powerful fundamentalist leaders and media stars like Rainer Trampert and Jutta Ditfurth were long able, in good conscience, to characterize the Greens' most devastating electoral defeats, if not as successes, then certainly not as failures.

As was often the case, the basic premises of fundamentalist thinking were articulated in their purest and clearest form by Rudolf Bahro, for whom there were only two alternatives with regard to industrial society: to "get in" or "get out."[26] The starkness of this choice meant that fundamental opposition in parliament regarded only its failures as successes.[27]

Thus, the Green Party's malaise of blocked development occurred on three mutually reinforcing levels. The first was the dogmatism of the fundamentalists. The second pertained to the obsessive reformism of the realos, which fetishized the otherwise valuable political venue of parliamentarism. The third consisted of the Fundi/Realo debate itself, which focused on the issue of achieving fundamental social change through parliamentary reform. It centered on the metatheoretical level of the debate, above all on the importance of the concepts of "radical social change" and "crisis." In many ways, the Greens' attempt to repair or move beyond the tradition of Marxian socialism remained both superficial and inadequate. While abandoning the outmoded categories and utopian goals of class struggle and violent revolution, the Greens retained certain Marxist dogmas, axioms and categories which paralyzed their efforts to create a viable politics of ecological reform. Hence two of the critical challenges for any politically effective green ideology had to be the invention of a non-totalist concept of social change and a description of eco-social dysfunctions which did not rely on the idea of apocalyptic crisis. In a subsequent section of this chapter, we will examine the work of several intellectuals within the green purview who have addressed these deficits and attempted to "reconstruct" received leftist wisdom by incorporating impulses from sources such as systems theory and liberalism.

Before turning to this topic, however, we wish first to address another tendency within the Greens, which did not seek to overcome green dogmatism but rather to ground it "scientifically" in ecology. Rather than reappropriating the humanism in Marx, this current of "radical ecologists," more or less identical with the fundamentalists, wished to replace this Marxist humanism with naturalism. While it is important to emphasize that these were never the predominant, let alone the sole, impulses within the Greens, even the sympathetic observer must be somewhat alarmed to see the German Left flirting with ideas whose historical legacy is so tragic. In the following section, we will explore the relationship of green thinking to these non-socialist, anti-Enlightenment (and at times proto-fascist) movements and thoughts.

Dogmatic Naturalism: Ecology, Utopia, Apocalypse, and the New Spirituality

We have seen how a fundamentalist dogmatism, ultimately rooted in certain categories of Marxism, stunted the project of ecological reformism. Let us now turn to the second well-spring of green ideology, ecology. In the following section, we will explore the other half of the fundamentalist synthesis, a *naturalism* rooted in ecology and hostile to the humanist legacy of Marxian socialism. The end-product, a *dogmatic naturalism,* eventually undermined the construction of a successful and viable reformist eco-socialism.

The architects of dogmatic naturalism reached outside the tradition of the Enlightenment, and often of western civilization itself, for their inspiration. In particular, they relied on the following four sources: a generalized ecology; romantic utopianism; so-called New Age spirituality and eastern religions; and visions of the apocalypse. Despite their apparent unconnectedness, these pseudo-theories were linked together in radical or social ecology by a web of elective affinities (*Wahlverwandtschaften*). In spite of their deepseated connections and obvious relations to each other, most tenets of green thought

remained scattered across the wide spectrum of books, pamphlets and publications comprising something akin to a green "canon." Only in the works
of Rudolf Bahro did this constellation of ideas attain the coherence of what
one could call a genuine theory or ideology of dogmatic naturalism. At first
glance Bahro's marginal position within the Green Party until the mid-1980s
and his eventual departure in 1988 could lead one to argue that by using his
writings as an ideal type for dogmatic naturalism, we are overestimating the
significance of this *Weltanschauung* for the party. We do not believe so. While
Bahro had few political allies inside the party, he most certainly had many
spiritual and intellectual ones, particularly in the ranks of the fundamentalists.
Thus it seems to us not only reasonable to reassemble the fragments of
radical ecology beneath the rubric of dogmatic naturalism, but to treat Bahro
as the theory's most consistent proponent.[28]

But even if there existed no single, coherent dogmatic naturalist synthesis
such as Bahro's theory, one could still justify this approach from a historical
vantage point: after all, dogmatic naturalism fits into an established pattern
of thought which enjoys almost as much tradition and intellectual prestige
in Germany as it does in Marxism. For an Anglo-American audience, this
tradition may be unknown and even perplexing, for it was born in a long
dismembered (and now perhaps renascent) intellectual and geographical
entity known as Central Europe or *Mitteleuropa*,[29] peopled by thinkers barely
read outside of contemporary Germany such as Novalis, Friedrich Schlegel,
Ernst Bloch, Walter Benjamin and Theodor Adorno. As in the case of dogmatic
naturalism, this tradition's two previous flowerings, early German Romanticism (ca.1790–1810)[30] on the one hand and revolutionary Jewish messianism[31]
and conservative *Kulturkritik* on the other (ca.1890–1940),[32] were also reactions against "progress," particularly against the rationalizing influences of
the Enlightenment and French revolution and the rapid industrialization of
Germany during the late nineteenth and early twentieth centuries.[33] If
nothing else, the perilous career of these ideas is certainly cause for reflection about their usefulness in rebuilding the contemporary Germany Left. As
we will see, they have already attained a certain influence in the Federal
Republic's political discourse that is not always apparent to the casual
observer.

What links these anti-Enlightenment currents of the past – particularly
those of the early twentieth century – with the Greens, is the belief, as expressed by Fritjof Capra, that "we find ourselves in a state of profound, worldwide crisis ... whose facets touch every aspect of our lives ... a crisis of
intellectual, moral and spiritual dimensions; a crisis of a scale and urgency
unprecedented in recorded human history."[34] The crisis is perceived to be an
epochal, global crisis of western civilization, with a total character that does
not permit "partial solutions."[35] It does not require change but a "transformation"[36] with the magnitude and form of a universal religious conversion.
This conviction of impending upheaval rests only to a slight (if varying) degree
on historical analysis, and much more on historical allegory – usually invoking
Arnold Toynbee or Oswald Spengler[37] – of the inevitable, cyclical "genesis,

growth, breakdown, and disintegration"[38] of civilizations. All those who espouse these views agree that western civilization is past its bloom, whether
they believe the West's seed to have been planted with the transition from
the neolithic village to a commercial society, the triumph of the Judeo-
Christian religious tradition, the scientific revolution of Newton and Descartes
or the Enlightenment of Kant and Voltaire.

In the following section, we will treat the four images of ecology, utopia,
apocalypse and spirituality as they appear in the green discussion, paying
special attention to the various levels of their interconnectedness and concluding with treatment and criticism of Rudolf Bahro's work on new spirituality
as a *pars pro toto* to stand for the rather pervasive view of the world in many
circles of the Greens and their sympathizers.

The uses and abuses of ecology: "nature as politics"

Ecology is simultaneously the most pregnant and vexing word in the green
vocabulary. The vagaries and downright contradictions with which it is used,
however, are highly instructive. Strictly speaking, of course, ecology is just the
subfield of biology concerned with studying the interrelationships between
different organisms in the natural environment.[39] However, many Greens and
hard-core environmental activists have sought to broaden its scope. In Germany, this "social" understanding of ecology can mostly be traced back to
Carl Amery, whose book *Nature as Politics* arguably influenced the discourse
of the German ecology movement more than any other single work. In it,
Amery christened ecology the "new queen of sciences" (*neue Leitwissenschaft*),[40]
the place first held by philosophy, and in modern times occupied by physics.

Originally, this claim for ecology was founded in discoveries of the "new
physics," which propelled many scientists to an understanding of the universe
that resembles ecology's conception of nature. "In modern physics, the image
of the universe as a machine has been transcended by a view of it as one
indivisible, dynamic whole whose parts are essentially interrelated and can
be understood only as patterns of a cosmic process."[41] To some, this shift in
scientific theory suggested ecology as a new paradigm for thinking about the
dynamics of the material – and social – world. Fritjof Capra, the maverick
physicist, suggests that ecology's emphasis on interdependence, holism and
dynamic change will make ecology, like physics and philosophy before it,
the model and ideal toward which other fields of knowledge will orient
themselves.

In fact, Capra's prediction has been partially vindicated by attempts to
develop a general systems theory.[42] Systems theorists contend, in essence, that
physical, biological and social phenomena can all be studied with the same
set of general principles, namely those relating to the functioning of complex
systems. "The reality, in which all life occurs . . . is an interconnected system"
joined together by processes of "action and reaction" and structured by
complex "cycles" and "exchanges".[43] Within the epistemological framework

of systems theory, biological systems and their study – that is, ecology – are frequently regarded as *the* quintessential example,[44] a fact which explains why green vocabulary and argumentation are so permeated by its language and maxims. Thus, Greens and radical ecologists who envision a universally valid science based on an ecological paradigm have felt justified in invoking both physics and sociology in support of their claims.

But the Greens, again following Carl Amery, often try to take this privileging of ecology one step further, essentially transforming ecology from a heuristic device into a metaphysics of morals. Amery begins with the contention that all life – even in the most developed, industrial societies – ultimately rests on the functioning of the eco-system. From this premise, he draws the bold (if logically erroneous) conclusion that "myths, systems, states, institutions do not stand outside natural laws and cycles, they are not self-defined units. They are much more ecological species of the second, third or fourth order."[45] Having thus subjugated society to the "laws" of nature embodied in the "eco-system," Amery proceeds to derive various political imperatives from the functional principles of ecology. Appropriately, he calls his theory of nature and politics "ecological materialism," for he regards it as the heir to Marxian political economy. "For [ecological materialism] the interaction of nature and history is central." It regards "natural history as social history."[46]

In Amery's ecological materialism, the driving contradiction of human history is the parasitic exploitation of nature. Through this development, individuals become estranged from their nature as "predator[s] of the third or fourth order."[47] Human nature is defined by its assigned functional role in the "natural cycles" of the eco-system. This harmony was disrupted by successive ruling elites or "central powers" who, in order to secure their own domination, erected ever more destructive systems of "artificial cycles" in place of the natural ones. Modern, industrial society is the most powerful of these systems and therefore the most destructive. To maintain power, the industrial elites engage in self-perpetuating activities which disrupt and destroy the natural cycles of the environment. Thus, concludes Amery in his quasi-religious language, the "central power itself turns into the ally of the desert."[48]

Since the artificial cycles imposed on nature by human production are the cause of the ecological crisis, the most consistent remedy would be to return to a pre-agrarian, hunter-gatherer society. As Amery puts it, "the form of production most compatible with life (*lebensfreundlich*) would be – no production."[49] This is not to suggest that humanity also "return to the para-primitive" state of mind.[50] People must continue to think and be conscious. But feeling must replace reason as a guide for action. We, as human beings, cannot return to the state of natural balance and cycles, but we can consciously *restore* this state by making the principles of nature into principles for political action. For example, Amery suggests that the ecological principle of a stable population be used as the criterion for population policies."[51] In what is not his only but his most patently Hitlerian turn, Amery proposes that evolution be set in motion again: the "mutation of *homo sapiens*" into "*sapiens et perfectus*," says Amery, is "more than overdue."[52] By subsuming the human into the natural world, Amery subtly transforms heuristic devices such as balance and cycle into natural facts and uses them to deduce normative prescriptions. Amery's ecological materialism contains a deep antipathy toward the principles of the Enlightenment. Not only humanism and "anthropocentrism,"[53] but ethics too must give way to "natural" norms: "Reconciliation with the earth: that is the necessity out of which the consequent materialism grows and acts. Not the end of estrangement, not the bounty of goods for people, these cannot be its goal."[54] Not freedom or justice or equality but "life" is the value around which politics must be oriented, and since the "industrial system is in the final analysis humanity's opting against life and for the desert," there is but one course of action conforming with the principle of life: "The logic of humanity's survival . . . requires the fastest possible destruction of the industrial system and indeed at almost any price."[55] Amery's vitalism leaves no room for compromise.

Few Greens would accept crypto-fascist conclusions such as these, but Amery's thought is strongly echoed by radical ecologists within the green milieu. In particular, two basic ideas constitutive of Amery's view have become commonplace among fundamentalist Greens. The first idea, held by "the large majority of the ecology movement," is that of "ecology as a normative science that not only determines what is so and why it is so, but also says what should be,"[56] in the political as well as the natural realm. As the green ex-parliamentarian Manon Maren-Griesbach put it unabashedly, ecology is a foundation for action and politics: "And since [ecology] has a *scientific* basis, precisely provable, testable, exactly satisfying the demands of western, rational science, no one can fiddle around with it."[57] It is peculiar, if not ironic, that the Greens' skepticism about the infallibility of science should be suspended on this one point.[58] The second constitutive principle, bearing more than slightly vitalistic overtones, is the transformation of "life" into a moral axiom, which we will examine in more depth later.

The power of these axioms in shaping green thinking can be seen directly in several peculiarities of the Greens' political praxis: first, in the practice of representing questions of environmental policy as "questions of survival" where no compromise is possible; second, ecological "principles," or rather images, are often carried outside their proper realm of application and used to deduce and legitimate policy stances. Thus, concepts such as "balance," "natural cycle," "stability through diversity" or "unity in diversity" appear in almost limitless political contexts. In this way, fundamentalist Greens seek to skirt (or suppress) serious political debate and to challenge the liberal model of politics itself, in which the policy-making process is structured around compromises between conflicting interests and values.

But while the Greens and the German ecology movement often try to legitimate their goals and policies scientifically through ecology, their picture of ecology has little in common with the principles and practices of actual ecologists.[59] As Trepl puts it: "Ecology today is above all *Weltanschauung*, taking a political stand . . . the [ecology] movement understands itself as a millennial event . . . the fact remains that for a large and growing number of people, ecology bundles together all the hope for which words such as paradise, the messianic age, communism and other [hopes] just short of salvation . . . once stood."[60]

Ecology represents at once *Zivilisationskritik* and a new blueprint for society (*neuer Gesellschaftsentwurf*). For the "true believer" ecology is not principle, program or science, but "the alternative," a basis and a matrix for a spiritual, utopian and perhaps apocalyptic transformation of society.

"*Ecotopia*"

Closely associated with this vision of radical, ecological transformation is the idea of utopia. Thrust into disrepute by Marx, the concept was rehabilitated by the German philosopher Ernst Bloch and, largely through his influence, has come to occupy a central and positive place in the discourse of the German Left, especially that of the Greens. To a certain extent, the resurrection of the utopian idea simply reflects the Greens' efforts to reopen and re-enliven a pluralistic discussion over social ideals in order to arrive at a set of positive images which reach beyond the staid, antiquated ideas of socialism and integrate an ecological perspective into progressive politics. The Greens often cite utopian images as a necessary ingredient in motivating, guiding and sustaining a long, wearying struggle for social transformation, which inevitably will always meet with setbacks, compromises and disappointments. In describing the kind of utopia for which they strive, the Greens have been fond of Ernst Callenbach's fanciful neologism, "ecotopia."

The Greens' ecotopia is restorative. It emphasizes the return to a lost, original harmony, wholeness and oneness with nature, self and others, the radical transcendence of all heteronomy among individuals and between the human species and nature. It regards "the history of 'civilization'" as a "steady process of estrangement from nature that has increasingly developed into outright antagonism."[61] To ground their ecotopias, green thinkers reach back in time and social evolution toward an "original," "natural" state or situation. Often, "organic" societies such as those of the Native Americans or African tribal cultures are held up as models.[62] According to green thinking, such societies lived in an ecological balance or harmony with nature. They gave back as much as they took from the environment, so that their reproduction did not require the progressive exploitation and destruction of nature.

Still more central is the notion that these societies possessed an unblemished wholeness supposed to have given human experience an integrity, immediacy and authenticity lost in the transition to modern society.[63] The texture of experience was different because organic society predated the countless divisions characteristic of modern life (such as those between subject and object, ruler and ruled, the individual and nature, work and play), which have since torn asunder the basic "connectedness of body and mind."[64] An ecological society would, insofar as possible, strive to re-enchant and reanimate an objectified, commodified nature. Moreover, by healing the division between humanity and nature, an ecological society would also help to reintegrate the individual into a web of solidaristic, caring relationships.[65] Murray Bookchin (one of the very few US thinkers to enjoy a positive reception among the German Greens) pleads that we "frankly acknowledge that organic societies spontaneously evolved values that we can rarely improve on," namely the values of "mutuality," "consociation," and "usufruct."[66]

This admiration for the values of premodern, preindustrial cultures has not led the Greens to propose "a return to the stone age," as some German conservatives have charged. Science, technology and industrial production need not be abandoned in a wholesale fashion.[67] But the impact of technology must be "internalized" in the economic and political decision-making process.

Ecotopia need not be a regression in historical development. On the contrary, by situating human development within the framework of the "biological springs of life" and the "natural history of the species," some green theorists argue, it is possible to pick up the lost thread of human and natural evolution. As Dieter Duhm puts it, "the estrangement of today's individual is a biological one in the deepest sense."[68] In ecotopia, neglected human faculties such as "desire, longing, will, feelings, soul" could be revived and nurtured.[69] Humanity could shed the truly "Neanderthal" remnants left in its behavior, such as fear, anxiety and competition, which modern society not only preserves but encourages. The final "mutational leap" in the "evolution of humanity"[70] would be the achievement of a genuinely *aufrechter Gang* (connoting both "upright gait" and "dignified bearing").[71] The transformation to ecotopia would be more than a reform of society or even a redirection of civilization. It would be tantamount to reentry into the evolutionary process.

The ecotopian project, it is argued, does not abandon progress but redefines it. "Mind" is the highest expression of the self-organizing principles inherent within nature itself: "we are the very 'knowingness' of nature, the embodiment of nature's evolution into intellect, mind and self-reflectivity."[72] Humanity, then, can realize the *telos* of nature. The problem is that modern society has denatured reason into a set of heteronomous technological and bureaucratic forces. Ecotopia represents the reabsorption of society into an expanded ecological totality whose forces of development, diversification and unity attain consciousness in human subjectivity, which in turn is liberated not only from physical necessity but from the instrumentalist, functionalist form of reason used to overcome it. Ecotopia represents a "biological humanism" (Duhm) or an "ecology of self-realization" which are not realized against the natural world but through the conscious and critical reappropriation of "life." Social ecology can (re)open the horizon of a world in which "ethics, values, and with them, social relationships, technics and self-cultivation can . . . become self-forming, guided by intellect, sympathy and love."[73]

Ecotopia replaces the "outmoded" notions of progress and instrumental rationality with the ideals of biocultural evolution and ecological restoration. This makes ecotopia a very different sort of utopia from that of the socialists. As a utopia of restoration and renewal, it does not measure itself against an idea of human freedom but against nature itself. Nor does ecotopia project its ideals on to a future society but instead retrieves them from an anthropologically postulated, natural-historical past. The horizons of utopia are removed from the temporal axis and set within the bounds of space and geography. Since the contours of ecotopia can only be defined within the limits of an existing, national landscape, the ecotopian is of necessity conservative. For, unlike the Marxist, for whom conflict, violence, and destruction are the gateway to utopia, the overriding interest of the ecotopian must be in preserving an existing, natural totality.

In a word, ecotopia represents a sort of radical conservatism. It replaces the idea of progress with the longing for restoration. It dethrones reason and imagination as arbiters of the future and sets function and nature in their place. It does not seek revolution but devolution – or at least, "balance." Thus one cannot trust in the laws of social evolution to create ecotopia. Indeed, erecting the ecotopian regime requires that social laws be abolished and natural laws set in their place.

Why should human beings willingly accept the rule of nature? The answer is necessity. If humanity contravenes the laws of nature, it will be visited with cataclysm. The species is compelled to accept the laws of nature or face an apocalypse.

Apocalypse now?

In the discourse of radical ecology, the dialectical opposite of ecotopia is apocalypse. The image of an eco-nuclear Armageddon appears to have entered political discourse in the Federal Republic through the environmental horror scenarios and nightmare visions of "nuclear winter" outlined in the *Global 2000* report and various scientific journals. From there, they rapidly passed into the media of popular culture, where – no doubt due to Germany's particularly grave ecological problems and precarious position in the East–West nuclear confrontation – they have taken especially deep root in political discourse and public consciousness in the last twenty years.

If some interpreted the danger of an apocalypse in literal terms, for many others it assumed the character of a quasi-millenarian belief. They felt that the cosmic "yin and yang," the equilibrium between the "forces of production" and those of "destruction" had been upset. The most widely discussed and influential version of this argument was the one centered on the concept of "exterminism" put forth by the British Marxist historian, E. P. Thompson.[74] Thompson argued that the category of imperialism was no longer adequate to describe contemporary developments.[75] In its place he suggested "exterminism," which designates these characteristics of society . . . which thrust it in a direction whose outcome must be the extermination of multitudes. . . . Exterminism is a configuration . . . whose institutional base is the weapons-system, and the entire economic, scientific, political and ideological support-system to that weapons-system – the social system which researches it, "chooses" it, produces it, polices it, justifies it and maintains it in being.[76]

Though Thompson made some attempt to ground his analysis geopolitically in the dynamics of bloc confrontation and the power structures of opposing nations, exterminism was ultimately a metahistorical category connoting a "perhaps irreversible direction" in history or "last stage in civilization."

This viewpoint had already been anticipated by the German philosopher Günther Anders, whose influence on the peace and ecology movements in the Federal Republic has been substantial. Anders argued that the bomb had to be situated on a "metaphysical" level, as both the symbol and culmination of the destructive forces in western civilization. If Auschwitz represented an age where "all humans can be killed," the bomb represents one where "humanity as a whole can be killed."[77] The bomb is the centerpiece, the "pyramid" of an "age in which we . . . ceaselessly set forth the production of our own demise."[78] Particularly telling of a certain strain in postwar German thinking akin to both the Left and the Right is a blithe relativization of Auschwitz. To many Germans of this "apocalyptic" milieu, Auschwitz has lost its historically accurate meaning as a place where Germans committed genocide against Jews according to the principles of industrial production, and instead becomes a generalizable concept for all mass destruction. The Jewish (as well as German) specificities of Auschwitz are conveniently universalized. Auschwitz thus becomes a synonym for the horrors wrought by modernity instead of the particularly heinous locus of a very concrete aspect of German history. But then, of course, to German fans of the apocalyptic outlook of human development, Jews – as representatives of modern rationality – have always been rather suspect, if not indeed evil.

Anders saw the bomb as but one, albeit most destructive, component of the "macroapparatus," "the system of apparatuses" which "use our 'world,' "[79] albeit the most destructive component. The macroapparatus represents the endpoint of social heteronomy, for neither it nor its innumerable parts can be considered means anymore.[80] Indeed, they have achieved perfect "mediality," reducing everything else in the world, including people, to "raw material."[81] The bomb is the perfect expression of this, since a machine cannot be a means to anything – and surely not to security or defense. It is an end in itself. It is *the* end.[82] In its threat, indeed its promise to wipe out humankind, it makes clear that "technology has now turned into the subject of history with which we are only 'co-historical.' "[83] The bomb not only represents the end of history as the chronology of humanity, but as the product of humanity. It represents the "antiquatedness of man."

Lewis Mumford, another thinker of decisive (if indirect) influence on green ideology,[84] translates this image of society as a machine on to a metahistorical plane. In *The Myth of the Machine*, Mumford spans millennia to explain the (re)emergence of a specific "power complex," the "megamachine," born in the Egypt of the pharaohs and reincarnated in contemporary America. "The megamachine . . . is not a mere administrative organization: it is a machine in the orthodox technical sense, as a 'combination of resistant bodies' so organized as to perform standardized motions and repetitive work."[85] While "profit," "productivity," "prestige," "political power," and "property" are the slogans of the "pentagon of power," the "purpose" of the modern megamachine, if it can be called such, is power plain and simple. It is a total apparatus, including and utilizing every available resource as a component. Its "bodies" or parts of the megamachine are "mechanical, electronic, chemical" – and human.[86] Since the megamachine puts all things, living and material, at its own service, it is also an apparatus of total domination. It "can command obedience and exert control through a vast battery of efficient machines."[87] Individuals are not its servants but its instruments and slaves and, insofar as they are not "serviceable," they are replaced, eliminated or adapted. Though a human creation, the megamachine no longer serves its human creators. It completely "ignores the needs and purposes of human life in order to fortify the power complex and extend its dominion."[88] The megamachine is an "underdimensioned system,"[89] in which an excessively narrow notion of progress, the "equation of mechanical with moral progress,"[90] was institutionalized. By thus reducing the idea of what constituted improvement to a single quantitative axis of power, natural limits on change were removed. Thus, underlying the megamachine is the belief "that there are no desirable limits to the increase of knowledge, of material goods, of environmental control, that quantitative productivity is an end in itself and that every means should be used to further expansion."[91]

However, the limitless expansion of power does not ignore humanity's moral and spiritual dimensions; it does not even comport well with the species' biocultural fundament. The megamachine is not programmed to differentiate between life-preserving and life-destroying forms of power. Indeed, it is hostile to life insofar as it interferes with the mechanical functions of power. In its universal catalogue of capabilities, self-annihilation must be included, not as an accidental but as a quintessential expression of power. "Once complete and universal, total automation means total renunciation of life and eventually total extinction."[92] The machine, concludes Mumford, is not merely a central instrument of our society but the central myth of our culture. Moreover, the religion based on this myth is a death cult, not unlike that of the Egyptians. But – and this is the key thought – because of the total character of the megamachine, its unlimited scope and power, the cult is an apocalyptic one whose highest rite is not individual sacrifice but collective suicide. Mumford waxes poetic on this theme: "Over the entire Pentagon of Power . . . hovers Aragnarok, or Twilight of the Gods . . . : a world consumed in flames, when all things human and divine would be overcome by the cunning dwarfs and the brutal giants."[93] Fundamentalist Greens fully accept this vision. They add little to this contemporary, secularized version of Revelations but the idea of the global eco-system. Through its material exchanges with the economy, nature becomes one more component in the megamachine.

Since the apocalyptic threat is total, it requires a total response. An "apocalyptic politics" can know no compromises for it does not seek to balance different interests and values but to defend the ultimate and universal interest of the species in survival. There are only two alternatives in an apocalyptic politics: total change or total annihilation. Therefore, political action can only assume two forms: business as usual; or reversal, transformation, turnaround. Likewise, political actors are of two varieties: those who "go along"; and those who "get out."

Not only does the apocalyptic threat make political action absolute. It renders it desperately urgent. For the fundamentalist Green, the clock is stuck at "five to midnight," just shy of the hour of destruction. The task is as great as the time is short. Any sort of quotidian political action is desperately inadequate yet absolutely necessary. The inherent volatility of a movement based on apocalyptic politics is obvious: it must continually walk a knife's edge between complete mobilization and utter despair.

This dialectic between hope and doom has been evident from the earliest days of the green movement. Paradoxically, it was in the wake of ecological catastrophes such as the nuclear disaster at Chernobyl that spirits were highest among green fundamentalists. Only through such apocalyptic events, it was reasoned, could a general conversion of the population be set in motion. Many Greens believed (wrongly) that the supposed "silent revolution in values" or emergence of "postmaterialist consciousness" touted by social scientists during the 1980s provided a "scientific basis" for these expectations of a revolution in mass consciousness.

Many Greens perceive an "ethical lag" in modern society. They believe that technological development has dramatically outpaced its human and moral counterparts. As Anders states it: "We as feeling [beings] are still stuck in the rudimentary cottage-industry phase, while as killing [beings] we have already reached the proud state of mass production."[94] In fact, the situation has become so unbalanced that "today, the moral imperatives emanate from technology."[95] This retardation in moral development manifests itself at several different levels. The most elementary one is a lack of institutions or even criteria with which to determine the appropriate quantity and quality of technology and change required for the "good life," for it has become apparent that technology is not salutary in unlimited quantities. Certainly one barrier to developing such a sensibility is our "promethean shame" (Anders) before the perfection of our own products. Indeed, so great are the destructive powers of our products that their physical capabilities far exceed our moral sensibilities, leaving us "apocalypse-blind."[96] "Before the thought of the apocalypse, the soul goes on strike."[97] The scope of humanity's apocalyptic powers encompasses not only the entire earth but all of future history. Consequently, the compass of moral responsibility must also be extended to include coming generations: in a popular green aphorism, "We only borrowed the earth from our children." Anders concludes: "The decisive task for today . . . consists of training the moral imagination."[98]

Some social thinkers, such as Jürgen Habermas, argue that the ethical lag can be overcome by recovering western humanistic values embodied in the

Judeo-Christian tradition and the Enlightenment.[99] Others, such as Ernst Bloch, adopt a more radical stance, which perceives humanistic values as part of a mechanical or Cartesian view of the world. As such, these humanistic values form in the eyes of these thinkers part of a repression and exploitation common to modernity instead of representing a force for liberation and enlightenment. In this interpretation, what is needed is a complete moral and cultural renewal of western civilization, preferably one drawing on non-western spiritual traditions. While it would be somewhat exaggerated to assert that the majority of German Greens adhere to the latter viewpoint, many have in fact entertained some sort of belief in the need for a "new spirituality" whether of an exotic or homegrown variety.

Apocalypticism is by no means confined to the green milieu. On the contrary, it has penetrated the consciousness of broad segments of the population in the Federal Republic. Two examples will illustrate this point. The first concerns the mobilization against the deployment of euromissiles on German soil between 1981 and 1983 (see part I). Within this variegated mass movement (perhaps the largest in the history of the Federal Republic) it was not exceptional to hear voices which identified the stationing of the missiles with the inevitable end of Germany, Europe and civilization. Deployment meant certain destruction.[100]

An even more pronounced (if decidedly less justified) upsurge of apocalyptic fear swept the Federal Republic during the Gulf war in early 1991. Protest against the war was quantitatively and qualitatively more pronounced than in any other country in the advanced industrial world. Apocalyptic images of nuclear winter and ecological disasters caused by the explosion of Kuwaiti and Saudi oilfields were commonplace. What made this fear unusually interesting was the fact that it identified Germany – instead of the immediately affected Gulf region – as the helpless victim of irresponsible politics and the extremist logic of the modernization process.[101]

Also interesting in this argument was the identification of the western powers[102] – led, of course, by the United States – as the driving force behind the military confrontation. In notable opposition to the "linear rationality" and "technological infatuation" of the "war-happy" western powers, many in the German peace movement and beyond welcomed the Germans' emotional pacifism and proudly expressed collective fear.[103] One leading German feminist, Alice Schwarzer, even proclaimed that she was proud to be German, which she saw as morally superior to being, say, English or American, by virtue of the Germans' categorical pacifism.[104] Some went so far as to see this widespread pacifist sentiment as a welcome feminization and emotionalization of Germany, which they juxtaposed favorably with the macho bellicosity of the western powers. To this milieu, the lessons of the Holocaust were crystal clear: *total, unmitigated, non-negotiable, ubiquitous peace* was the primary goal. Regardless of the costs – repression, loss of freedom, loss of lives, loss of country – peace had to be maintained. Hans-Christian Stroebele, one of the Green Party's leading figures, argued in an interview with the *Jerusalem Post* that "the Iraqi missile attacks are the logical, almost compelling consequence of Israeli policies," and that Israel was at fault because of its past treatment of the Palestinians and the Arab states, including Iraq. For Stroebele, peace was even worth the lives of one million Jews.[105] The fact that this man had to resign his position in the party when sentiments such as these and others became public is less important than the numerous letters received by *Taz* from people belonging to the alternative milieu, supporting Stroebele's position.

While it is clear that Stroebele's views were perhaps a bit too extreme in tone (though much less in content) for most members of Germany's leftist milieu, it is equally clear that his real crime was to have expressed such views in public, where anti-Semitism still has a certain stigma attached to it. Sadly, Stroebele's views were the result of an immensely successful post-APO socialization process which made the hatred of Israel and the extolling of the Palestinians arguably one of the most accepted – and exacted – social norms of this milieu. It was after all a key representative of this milieu, the green fundamentalist Jürgen Reents, who exculpated his Germany from the bane of Auschwitz by declaring the Palestinians the "victims." It was in this milieu, too, where "Israel" and "Zionism" had become pejorative concepts tantamount in their dread to Nazism and fascism. (One would be hard put to come up with a more potent insult in the world of the German Left than "Zionist.") It would be well beyond the scope of this book to demonstrate how Israel (and even the Jews on occasion) assumed characteristics in the eyes of the German Left which it – and the world – associated with the Nazis. Suffice it to say that to a considerable segment of the German post-APO Left the quickest and most convenient path to a reconciliation with its parents' in-volvement in the crimes of the Third Reich was to develop a visceral hatred of Israel, indeed to render it the equivalent of Nazi Germany. With the Jews in Israel assuming the role of Nazis, the Germans (past and present) could no longer be accused of having committed a singular crime. It was clear for all to see: The Jews were just as evil as the Germans.

The perfect relativization of history which equates Israel with national socialist Germany is, to be sure, not the only view of this complex subject among the German Left or within the Greens. There exists a variety of versions milder in tone, if not necessarily in content. We find particularly loathsome the multitude of those criticisms of Israel which attempt to legitimate themselves by prefacing their diatribes against the Jewish state by granting the Jews their right to have a state of their own, by allowing them in essence to live. When barely 40 years after Auschwitz parts of Germany's most prolific and intellectually original segment of the population only reluctantly and perfunctorily agree to let the Jews survive, it is obvious that German–Jewish reconciliation is nothing but a chimera. Stroebele disappeared as a leader of the Greens in the wake of the explicit nature of his comments. The essence of his sentiments, alas, has not. They remain alive and well, especially in fundamentalist circles, where – in marked contrast to the world of the realos – hatred of Israel continues to receive particular pride of place.

Not only had peace, by 1991, become a total value and a non-negotiable moral category in the battle against the impending apocalypse, but – in notable contrast to a decade before – it had also become German. The peace movement of the early 1990s used decidedly "German" categories to present its case. (Note, for example, the constant reference to the western powers as *Alliierten,* especially when referring to their bombing raids. Also remarkable in this context was the constant parallel between contemporary Iraqi cities and their German counterparts during the Second World War both suffering as a result of "Allied bombing.") It did so obviously to emphasize its own (that is, German) virtues in juxtaposition to the vices and transgressions of the modernist, imperialist, rational West. Moreover, also in contrast to the peace movement of the early 1980s, these sentiments were deeply shared – and articulated – by a vast number of Germans well beyond the immediate confines of the Greens and the peace movement *per se.* The fact that the Gulf war gave Germans an opportunity to display their peace-loving and virtuous nature created a coalition which began with the country's president and extended deeply into all political camps, black, blue, red, and green. For some, the total burden of Auschwitz seemed to have been finally overcome by a new – this time less lethal, though equally problematic – totality: the militantly pacifist German.

This was not a pretty sight. What rendered it particularly ugly was the selectivity and specificity which this phenomenon, despite its holistic and totalitarian veneer, exhibited when analyzed over time. For, curiously enough, barely six months after the Gulf war, when the flames of a brutal war were in the process of destroying the former Yugoslavia, which is, after all, virtually on Germany's doorstep, the militant pacifists had miraculously disappeared from the streets of Germany's cities to the comfort of their living rooms. Gone were the masses of school-age children marching in candle-light parades, praying for Armageddon to spare them. But then again, the brutalities of the Yugoslav war involved neither Americans nor Israelis, thereby rendering the matter uninteresting for German pacifists. It seems clear: militant pacifism, though continuing to be very much present in the green and left milieu as part of an apocalyptic vision of world politics, remains latent until it is rendered manifest by two forces – the United States and Israel. Short of the engagement on the part of these two countries, the German Left's apocalypse-based militant pacifism seems to remain confined to the realm of latency and the private sphere.

New Spirituality – Bahro's Logic of Salvation: a Green Synthesis?

While these four themes – ecology, utopia, apocalypse and spirituality – recur throughout the green-oriented literature, Rudolf Bahro represents perhaps the only theorist who made a systematic attempt to synthesize them. As we have mentioned before, Bahro's earlier patriarchal relationship to the Greens has dissolved into one of mutual distance and distrust, even vis-à-vis once sympathetic fundamentalists. However, it has been frequently asserted – and this is our position – that Bahro became untenable to the fledgling party principally, if not solely, because he developed the fundamentalist position too rigorously and stated it in too impolitic a fashion. Consequently, while one could not assert that Bahro's most central work, *Die Logik der Rettung* ("The Logic of Salvation") is officially condoned by or even openly discussed within the Green Party, a closer examination of it may nevertheless reveal a great deal about underlying connections and developmental tendencies within the fundamentalist ideology. Indeed, what we will find is a deep hostility to the essential values of the Enlightenment – democracy, equality, humanism, reason, and progress – which structure political activity in the western, industrial democracies.

Despite his ongoing quarrels with his ex-party compatriots, Bahro has continued to claim the title of "fundamentalism" for his views. Having thus liberated it from the arena of parliamentary politics, Bahro was free to posit a concept of fundamentalism which represents a radical spiritual, cultural and political agenda rather than just a partisan strategy for radical reform.[106]

Bahro extends the boundaries of his critique beyond the socioeconomic system to encompass the whole of western civilization and culture. To describe western civilization, Bahro adopts Mumford's metaphor of the megamachine: science, technology, capital and the state are fastened into a single central power.[107] But while he accords capital a central role in the "grand machine," he insists: "The relationship of capital is not the last cause but rather only the most recent means of expansion."[108]

Clearly Bahro does not view the "totality" of western civilization primarily in functional terms. "The megamachine does not function but is death oriented."[109] Bahro sees this "exterminist" drive in western civilization as having been present in each of six successive sociohistorical "sediments." They are, in Bahro's order, "genotype (*conditio humana*)," "patriarchy," "European cosmology," "dynamic of capital," "industrial system (megamachine)," and "exterminism."[110] According to Bahro, each one of these layers deepened and reinforced the destructive, anti-life tendencies of western civilization, with no single one, however, proving decisive.

Bahro's self-proclaimed task is to trace the "logic of self-extinction" back to its deepest sources in western culture. Not surprisingly, it is to be found in the "human condition" itself.[111] The developmental problem inherent in the "human genotype," argues Bahro, is inherent in the biological fact of our large brain (*Großhirn*), which gives each human individual identity and imagination.[112] The whole of western civilization and culture are, in essence, a response to this situation: "History is psychodynamics. The logic of self-extinction is a breaking of the human soul. . . . It is all culture, second nature created by us. It is that with which we have not come to terms (*das Unbewältigte*) in our human, our physical existence."[113] The structure of western civilization represents but one possible response which the eternal dilemmas posed by our "species essence" as large-brained animals.

The logic of self-extinction stems from the primacy in western culture of "human, all-too-human maxims of the self-assertion principle."[114] Whereas

eastern civilization chose to follow the "path of self-awareness, the path in-
wards,"[115] the West elected the opposite course: the separation of the self from
nature, the path of rational analysis and control of the external world, and,
ultimately, self-sufficiency of the individual human ego. This led to a situation
in which the "subjective meaninglessness and insignificance of individual
existence" became more terrifying than "physical death."[116] Cultural life and
second nature have become so completely divorced from their basis in physical life and origins in biological nature that they are no longer merely destructive but apocalyptic.

Like the problem, the solution must be total. The "logic of rescue" "begins
by our being ready to let go of everything,"[117] that is, our entire way of life,
including all the individual creature comforts and all the "substitute
satisfactions" with which the megamachine rewards its operators. The next
step is a complete transformation of consciousness, ego and personality,
which have been programmed by the megamachine. While the megamachine
has "scattered" our consciousness, it also provides a "crack" between conscious
and unconscious structures where the process of integration can begin, a
"reunification of our living spirit with its natural roots, with the wells of
culture. . . ."[118] Any involvement in the external world, even in oppositional
politics aimed at subverting the megamachine, is doomed to failure, for in
the struggle against the megamachine, "the fronts do not run so much between people as inside [them]."[119] Yoga, not organizing, is the well-spring of
rescue politics.[120] Only by returning to the "godliness in ourselves" can we
find the energy necessary to effect social transformation.

The immediacy of the apocalyptic threat requires stop-gap measures, a
"rescue government," whose task would be to assure "that life continues."[121]
This government, submits Bahro, must be invested with absolute moral and
political authority. It would be an emergency government, to be dissolved at
the end of a transitional period. Echoing the maxim of the dictatorship of
the proletariat, he argues that "there is no period of transformation without the state."[122]

What form would this transitional state assume? Representative, parliamentary institutions give too much weight to short-term, egoistic interests, and
"are insufficient for the state's present task."[123] The rescue government would
have to be a "prince of ecological transformation," both in Machiavelli's sense
of a legislator or lawgiver, a founder of new institutions, and in Gramsci's
Leninist sense of the embodiment of an avant-garde revolutionary party
effecting fundamental cultural transformation in the name of universal
interest. The popular basis of this fearsome hybrid would be an "invisible
church," a diffuse, worldwide spiritual community and union, the rebirth of
"the old idea of the godly state (*Gottesstaat*)."[124] The functionaries of this
mixture of tyranny, one-party rule and theocracy would be an enlightened
minority,[125] a heretical band of technocrats who disavowed their allegiance to
the megamachine and joined the rescue movement.[126]

Few Greens, even amongst the most militant fundamentalists, would have
openly agreed with Bahro's conclusions. But many radical ecologists, in fact,

shared his basic premises. What distinguished Bahro was not so much his basic assumptions, but the logical rigor with which he thought them through and his unwillingness to modify or disguise his conclusions for the sake of political expediency

As we have endeavored to show, Bahro's writings provided the logical systematization of the four *leitmotifs* interwoven in Green fundamentalism: ecology, utopia, apocalypse and spirituality, with a special emphasis on the latter. We have implicitly argued that, at least as they are understood within the Greens, these concepts were never serviceable points of political orientation. Their totalizing, uncompromising character made them hostile to any form of quotidian political praxis, while providing the soil for unbending moral fanaticism, thereby leading their adherents into a tragic, unstable dialectic of defeat and disappointment. Nor could they provide a suitable foundation for the reconstruction of leftist politics in the Federal Republic. Bahro, again, was perhaps the most candid in this regard when he boldly asserted that "no more leftist project is possible" within the bounds of fundamentalism. Socialist politics ultimately owes a great deal to the principles and ideals of the Enlightenment. Fundamentalist politics categorically discards these principles and ideals. Readers versed in German intellectual history will recognize this fundamentalist error as "typically German." Indeed, it is no coincidence that fundamentalists share more with early Romanticism than a passing hostility to the Enlightenment. Both pursue a concept of politics which is as arresting in theory as it is inadequate, even dangerous, in practice. One might have hoped that the tragic failures that these ideas brought German progressives (in 1848 and 1933 to mention but two of the most obvious cases) might have permanently inoculated the German Left against a return to anti-western Romanticism. But the events of the 1980s and early 1990s suggest that such hopes may be premature.

Nevertheless, to paraphrase former SPD chief Hans-Jochen Vogel, even if they gave the wrong answers, the fundamentalists often asked the right questions. Certainly any reconstructed leftist politics had to reevaluate its productionist ethic in light of ecological problems, particularly in the Federal Republic. Likewise, the myopic fixation of politicians and voters on economic performance figures had to give way to a broadened sense of political and social responsibility toward the natural environment and future generations. Moreover, the inadequacy of consumer culture as the basis for a good society had to be squarely faced.

We now turn to other currents within the Greens which sought to address these questions by contemplating but not dismissing the Enlightenment tradition itself.

Reformist Humanism: Anatomy of a Coalition

In the two preceding sections, we subjected Green fundamentalism to a critical examination. We concluded first that fundamentalist dogmatism accounted for the Green Party's "blocked development", and second that the dogmatic naturalism of the fundamentalists was profoundly at odds with the historical values and agendas of the Left. Thus, in our estimation, only by rejecting fundamentalism could the Greens become a leftist, ecological reform party. While it took them a decade of much turmoil and anguish to accomplish this feat, they had indeed done so by 1991.

In this section we will examine representatives from each of the three other currents within the party and their efforts to incorporate ecological politics into socialist ideology. In their work, we argue, can be seen the anatomy of a potential reformist humanist politics, which could not only serve as the basis for the identity of the party but for the sustenance of a viable political coalition dedicated to ecological reform.

Realism *beyond* realpolitik

As we noted earlier, realism itself was drawn into a vicious circle of debate with fundamentalism through its tacit acceptance of the idea that reform could only be legitimated by the fundamentalist intent of totalist system-change. These terms of debate reduced realism to *realpolitik*. Parliamentary reform could be represented only as a necessary evil and legitimated only by cynicism associated with power politics. This, in turn, made it possible for the fundamentalists to style themselves as the defenders of the party's basic values and true identity.

The then "Bielefeld sociologists" – Helmut Wiesenthal, Norbert Kostede and Claus Offe – tried to restore the positive sense of realism by founding it not on cynicism but on a social-scientific analysis of the changing dynamics of social conflict and change. Wiesenthal and Kostede (though certainly less well-known than Offe outside of Germany) were both active realists in the party and held important positions on the Greens' federal executive committee.[127] All three could be categorized as neo-Marxists, but their revision of realism had been strongly influenced by systems theory, especially via the pathbreaking work of their Bielefeld colleague, Niklas Luhmann.

With characteristic timeliness and intellectual acuity, Offe was one of the first social theorists to analyze how eco-pax issues challenged traditional leftist strategy. The goals of the eco-pax movement – preserving nature and ending the arms race – were negative ones, oriented toward the "preservation of valuable entities, not effecting 'progress.'"[128] In describing this new politics, Offe employed Walter Benjamin's metaphor of revolutions, not as the "loco-motive of history," but as something more akin to the entire human species "reaching for the emergency brake." Since their politics were no longer (solely) guided by the logic of progress, the Greens required a new sort of political rationality. Offe proceeded to identify three problems which the politics of "maintaining the already attained" (*Bestanderhaltung*) created for the rationality of a parliamentary party. First, "politics which follows this type of rationality tends to become layperson's politics, protest politics, politics 'in the first person.'"[129] Secondly, it made political compromise or middle solutions more difficult, since issues tended to take the form of "yes or no" rather than of "more or less" or "sooner or later."[130] Both of these dynamics presented difficulties for a small party which was organized around the principle of representation and could achieve its goals only through political compromise. However, Offe offered no solution to these dilemmas, concluding only that "hardly any theoretical models or suitable political forms of organization" had, as of then, been developed.

Resuming where Offe's analysis had desisted, Wiesenthal tried to rethink green strategy in terms of the new, eco-pax issues. Wiesenthal based his strategic concept on an examination of how the structure of the new, green social and political conflicts differed from that of the old Left/Right battle over material distribution. In his analysis, Wiesenthal identified three key contrasts. First, the sheer variety of conflict themes could not be "reduced to a simple formula." Second, "there is no mechanism lying in the . . . objective character of the themes which tends to the continuity of the conflicts. . . ." Third, because of the "heterogeneity of the participants" and their often limited form of engagement (based on a single issue), there was also no mechanism which automatically aggregated interest and goals into a coherent ideological or organizational framework.[131] This landscape of multiple conflicts characterized by "diversity, uncertainty and participation" diverged sharply from the Marxist picture determined by the economically rooted centrality of class-based conflict. Thus, concluded Wiesenthal, the proper role and most effective organization for the Green Party must be different from those of a traditional, leftist working-class party.

The fragmentation of the new social conflicts and green movements suggested an obvious role for a parliamentary party:

> For the creation of continuity, the accumulation and preservation of experiences, and the protection of demands emanating from conflicts which are interest based and thus attempt to distort and displace, there surely arises the need to have an organization which not only can handle these conflicts but which also can navigate among these conflicts [in an optimal manner].

The Green Party, in short, could harness for itself the political power arising from constant conflicts in the political arena, which it was better at solving than its political rivals. This "niche" approach, or flexible specialization, could, in turn, enhance the Greens' organizational and ideological unity, which proved particularly difficult for the party – let alone the movement – to sustain over a significant period of time. Moreover, by dint of its overarching perspective, the Green Party could help the individual movements by targeting "weak points in the system as appropriate starting points for making their influence felt in a goal-conscious way."[133]

Wiesenthal's revised strategy rested on the simple insight of systems theory that in a complex, highly differentiated society, power tends to be widely (if unequally) dispersed in the largely autonomous subsystems of state, society and economy. The sense of combining parliamentary and extraparliamentary activity was to disperse opposition accordingly. Where there was no single, decisive locus of power (such as economy or state), there was also no hope for total change. Hence, by the very standards it set itself, a totalist or fundamentalist strategy would *always* fail – worse yet, it would regard its real failures as successes. Thus a socially homogenous *Weltanschauungspartei* oriented toward a single social conflict no longer furnished an adequate model for radical, leftist politics and pluralistic organization. Above all, it also failed to offer a recognition of the limits of parliamentary politics in effecting social change.

Wiesenthal's reformulation of the issues would make it possible to escape some of the false dilemmas of the strategy debate. By reshaping and limiting the role of the party, his concept permits a redefinition of political success in such a way that it would no longer be judged by its contribution to systemic change (which by definition always renders it inadequate) but rather by the extent to which it increased options for political activity and opposition at all levels.[134] This shift in perspective also permits the viewing of reformist legislation as a triumph rather than a "dirty compromise" or "sell-out." By correcting false hopes, Wiesenthal's concept also eliminates the "false disappointments" which have so often and unnecessarily impeded green political activity and cooperation. Wiesenthal's perspective also skirts the dead-end debate over "party vs movement" by suggesting a functional division of political labor. Party and movement are here no longer conceived as two prongs of a single, total strategy but as forms of organization and opposition which correspond to the very different arenas of state and civil society.

Indeed, the unspoken faith that one could gain control of *the* levers of power by winning a majority of the population, whether through electoral or through movement politics, still has more adherents in the green camp than one might suppose. In fact, as we have seen, it was the belief that one or the other of these majorities would be sufficient to effect a program of radical reforms which underlay the strategies of both realists and fundamentalists during the 1980s.[135] As the repeated failures of various red–green coalitions have clearly suggested, both are likely mistaken.

In essence, then, Wiesenthal argued for a green politics guided by a flexible, open strategy oriented toward the principles of "emancipation and of maintaining the already obtained."[136] On the one hand, the pursuit of Wiesenthal's scheme would abandon the remnants of dogmatism, attentisme, totalism and fixation on the state which the Greens inherited from the Marxian tradition of historical materialism and revolutionary state socialism. On the other hand, it would positively transcend the central emancipatory goals of socialism, expanded to include an ecological component. Much like the neo-Kantian strain of socialism of the early twentieth century, it would be oriented toward mobilizing diverse activities around the universal imperative of emancipation rather than organizing a central apparatus around the historical inevitability of revolution.

The eco-libs

A second, equally sharp critique of Marxist dogmatism in the Greens emanated from the so-called "eco-libs," who combined elements of both libertarianism and liberalism. The centerpiece of the eco-lib program was an attack on centralized state-bureaucratic authority, which the "eco-libs" contended, undermined the autonomy of representative institutions. In contrast to most Greens, the eco-libs unabashedly defended the institutions of liberal democracy. Unencumbered by the baggage of "proletarian" or "revolutionary" culture, the eco-libs have never had any qualms about "bourgeois" politics or the political center. Thus, while allied with the realists in their commitment to reform, the eco-libs consistently advocated opening the Greens to moderate issues and middle-class voters. This, of course, is not to say that the eco-libs wished to make the Greens the new party of the political center. Instead, the eco-libs wanted to see the Green Party at the political center of a new politics which was based on "the extended interests of the Left."

The latter phrase was coined by the eclectic editor and brilliant publicist Thomas Schmid, formerly of West Berlin, later of Frankfurt, probably the best known and most intelligent spokesperson for the eco-libs.[137] Both anarchist and bourgeois, Schmid's disdain for Marxism had two obvious points of support. As he put it: "The leftist world picture, ultimately always rooted in Marxism, appears to me . . . outmoded and inapplicable for a future-oriented politics."[138] Four years before the opening of the Berlin wall and the collapse of Soviet-style "socialism" in Eastern Europe, Schmid unequivocally equated socialism with the "structural tyranny, centralism and inherently flawed economies" of eastern bloc state totalitarianism. He argued: "The socialist design has proved itself inapplicable for a better society."[139] Nevertheless, while Schmid maintained that the "theoretical and political instruments of the Left are not very useful any more," and attacked the "conservatism of the Left," he sustained a crucial aspect of the Left's heritage by extolling the concept of emancipation which seemed perfectly congruent with the ideals of the Enlightenment and the subsequent incarnations of progressive political praxis.[140]

The new goals of the Left must be sought in the "embracing crisis" of industrial society. As the eco-libertarian manifesto proclaimed: "Industrialism is as of now the latest and most destructive heritage of a history in which humanity rendered itself the lord of the world."[141] The eco-liberals and eco-libertarians perceived this will to domination, this "self-consciousness of the maker,"[142] as not so much rooted in capitalism or western culture itself but in the "centralism of large institutions."[143] Thus, in their view, the bureaucratic, "Jacobin" politics of the modern welfare state were just as much to blame for social and ecological woes as the massive, multinational corporations.

For Schmid and the eco-liberals, the only route to emancipation – and a healthier environment – was to combat hierarchy and centralism wherever it was found and to strengthen democratic, parliamentary institutions, including the existing ones.[144] Despite the imperfections and limitations of parliaments, the eco-liberals saw them as legitimate, profoundly democratic institutions worthy of nurturing instead of scorn.[145] Naturally, eco-liberals felt strongly that parliamentary democracy had to be consistently complemented by grass-roots activity, in order to stay – or, better still, to become more – democratic. Short of totalitarianism, fundamental social change could never be effected from the top down, for the mechanisms which reproduce existing social arrangements are dispersed into the daily lives of countless individuals. In Schmid's words: "Not only those on top but also those on the bottom bear responsibility for things being the way they are. There is no Archimedean point."[146] Here Schmid refers to a comment attributed to Archimedes, who allegedly stated that with a lever long enough and a point to stand upon he could move the world.

Like Wiesenthal, Schmid argued that social conflicts were too fragmented and dispersed to be fought on any one front, be it parliamentary or extraparliamentary. "Capital does not exist, any more than the working class, the liberation and the alternative."[147] To Schmid, these were merely useless and reified abstractions which, far from illuminating social realities, helped obfuscate them. The idea for any kind of alternative politics had to rest on a demystification of the subject and its reality. Politics did not operate on an abstract whole. Consequently, there could never be just one single movement (as claimed by the fundamentalists). The idea of *the* movement, Schmid charged, was the invention of leftist intellectuals who wished to monopolize the power and space of the radical Left for themselves. Schmid never concealed his contempt for this self-styled avant-garde intelligentsia; he quoted Hans Magnus Enzensberger: "So far as the species is capable of surviving, it will not owe its continued existence to a bunch of outsiders but rather to very normal people."[148] The hostility and smugness of the leftist elite towards the "little people" was, in Schmid's view, not only self-righteous but also self-defeating, for ordinary citizens often wrestled with the same dilemmas that concerned the elite, albeit in a quiet and "non-political" manner. The Greens, argued Schmid, had to abandon outmoded political taboos and open themselves to this new potential.

While these arguments were obviously directed at the fundamentalists, Schmid was equally unsparing in his criticism of the realists. Above all, he abjured their "Jacobinism" – not only their obsession with coalitions but their very idea of politics as massive reform from the top down. For Schmid, comprehensive reform packages such as the Greens' reconstruction program smacked too much of Lenin's totalitarian equating of truth with the vanguard party and its praxis.[149] Instead, Schmid pleaded for a more open, pluralistic society, which actively fostered communal but also *individual* experimentation.[150]

In sum, Schmid's eco-liberalism and eco-libertarianism exhorted the Greens to open the party on several levels: first, on the level of constituency, where Schmid hoped for a genuine opening of the party's middle-class potential, and discouraged the Left's self-indulgent "love affair with the ghetto" of revolutionary politics and cultural underground; second, on the level of issues and ideology, where Schmid argued for an active search for new issues, even in areas which had traditionally been severely neglected by the Left (such as family politics). In short, Schmid offered concepts for the Greens' electoral extension into areas of potential new support. His ideas were also conceived as political expansion in that they raised issues not previously addressed by any of the Federal Republic's established parties. Schmid's was not a vision of a 5 percent party based on moral purity but of a 10 percent party based on political innovation.

Eco-socialism between revision and retreat

Unlike realism and eco-liberalism, eco-socialism did not just constitute a faction inside the Greens. Rather, it represented a loosely bounded school of thought which had well-known proponents in the social-democratic camp as well, such as Ossip K. Flechtheim, Johanno Stasser, and (with some allowance) even ex-party manager and former minister Erhard Eppler. Among the Greens, eco-socialism was most strongly associated with fundamentalists Thomas Ebermann and Rainer Trampert, former K-Group leaders from Hamburg.[151] What both groups – Social Democrats and Greens – had in common was a commitment to developing an "ecologically enriched socialism" which "joins the essential, human intentions of socialism with ecological requirements."[152] What divided them were their attitudes towards red–green cooperation. But before touching on this latter point, let us first examine the eco-socialist project in more detail.

The central tenet of eco-socialism consisted of the view that the fundamental framework of Marxian political economy could still account for the emergence of the ecological crisis during the 1970s. This crisis, insisted Ebermann and Trampert, was basically explicable in Marxian terms, namely as a result of the requirements of capitalist competition: "Without overcoming this competition . . . this process of the destruction of the natural foundations of human existence cannot be contained."[153] Thus, they concluded, because the ecological problem was structurally rooted in the dynamics of the capitalist economy, it required a leftist solution."[154]

However, this solution could not be of the *traditional* leftist variety. In the eco-socialists' view, state socialism and social-democratic reformism had not only failed to address ecological problems but had, in fact, been their central cause. In the West it was only via the corporatist compact constructed by the unions and social democrats with capital, based on the premise of "industrial mass production, diversity of products, continually growing mass productivity,"[155] that the "institutionalized growth compulsion" could be maintained so effectively and with such devastating consequences for the environment.[156] Thus the eco-socialists concluded that the first step in alleviating the ecological crisis was the withdrawal of the working class from this pernicious "growth coalition."

While eco-socialists chastened the trade unions and the labor movement for their phlegmatic, even hostile, attitude toward ecological movements and issues, they perceived the working class essentially as the victims of a "false utopia" of spiraling mass production and mass consumption propagated by capital.[157] The task of eco-socialist revisionism was therefore to uncover the roots of this false "productionist" utopia in Marxism itself.[158]

The principal target of eco-socialist revisionism was Marxism's naive faith in the objective, neutral and emancipatory character of science, technology and production.[159] Ebermann and Trampert argued that the exploitation of nature was programmed into the very methodological and epistemological framework of western science: "The 'natural sciences' offer no theoretical explanation of the diversity of appearances in nature and their complex interaction. Rather they reduce and simplify nature to its measurable, quantifiable dimensions."[160] The narrow band of information which scientific analysis provides reduces the natural world to a means, an object for exploitation. In Bloch's aphorism: "Single-science reason was always an imagination grown clever through harm."[161] Moreover, the eco-socialists saw the scientific community itself as embedded in the "technostructure" of the productive apparatus.[162] Far from being neutral, the scientific community tends to encourage the production of everything it discovers[163] – including the consumer's need for it.[164]

The eco-socialists also challenged the messianic image of technology in western Marxism as the provider of infinite riches and the deliverer from the "kingdom of necessity." Society's single-minded obsession with technical innovation as a means to increase output and consumption has blinded socialism to the labor process, the *how* of production, and human needs.[165] The progressive "rationalization" of the production process has served to make work increasingly routinized and monotonous, less qualified and meaningful. The experience of what has become known as real, existing socialism has shown that this alienation in work does not result from the social relations of production but from the technologized production process itself.[166]

Growing alienation in the work process has been compensated by increasing leisure-time consumption. The satisfaction derived from consumption's abilities to compensate, replace and replenish has become a substitute for meaningful work: "It is not on the basis of [the individual's] personal dreams and desires, but above all on the basis of [the individual's] place, rich in renunciation, in a division of labor which allows no more room for the unfolding of such personal desires and wishes, [that] new needs take shape."[167] Thus, the technologization of the labor process has a built-in social safety mechanism: any increase in worker alienation is compensated by a commensurate increase in worker productivity and consumption. Through this dialectic of alienation and consumption, technology therefore generates a need for what it creates.

This consumer ethos, in turn, tends to legitimate the policies which lead to the intensification of the labor process in the first place: policies oriented toward ever-increasing production. Thus a vicious circle is closed, where increased alienation, increased production and increased consumption lock together in an embrace which strangles human needs and desires. The working class has been lured into the embrace of productionism by its own fetishization of science and technology. Socialism, once caught in this vicious cycle, has lost sight of its "original intent" – as well as content – namely the emancipation of wage labor not only *from* but also *in* the production process.

Eco-socialist revisionism sought to reappropriate this original intent and content by adding a new ecological dimension to socialism. The eco-socialist program focused on three fundamental concerns: (1) the need for a new, non-dominating relation of society to nature; (2) the need to subject the effects and application of technology to concerns of the environment, and, in the workplace, to political scrutiny; (3) the need for new standards and criteria of production and measurement of economic success other than growth. These goals could never be realized in a "proletarian state" or by a social-democratic technocracy. Instead the eco-socialists advocated a decentralized, democratic solution to the present crisis.

Insofar as practicable, the eco-socialists desired the reincorporation of political and economic power into the local community. Only by investing local government with the responsibility for social and economic planning could the malaise of centralized control be avoided. Restoring autonomy to local communities would not only allow self-administration, but also create room for "spontaneously experienced solidarity" and communal "self-serving through a community-related morality."[168] The eco-socialists recognized that alienation was not just rooted in the division of labor and the private appropriation of capital, but also in the industrial compulsion toward ever larger unity in the areas of production and reproduction and the continually growing demands on human, geographic and social mobility.

Thus the eco-socialists, who until the early 1980s considered themselves the heirs of Lenin and Mao, changed their views in the course of that decade toward espousing the decentralization of power as a key step toward socialism. The political agenda underlying eco-socialism was to forge an alliance between organized labor and the new social movements based on the shared goals of ecologizing and humanizing production. As the ranks of the working class shrink and those of the enlightened middle class grow, this alliance, so the eco-socialists reasoned, would become the only viable coalition for any meaningful reform. Short of either an outright red or green majority, only a red–green alliance offered a possibility to concretize such politics in reality.

While the SPD eco-socialists were resigned to the necessity of just such a red–green alliance, the green eco-socialists, at least under the leadership of Ebermann and Trampert, pursued a strategy of fundamental opposition. In this way, they hoped in the long run to transform the working class into an acceptable coalition partner. Their aim was a moral and political conversion of the working class from red to green. Ultimately, however, the actions of Ebermann and Trampert did not lead to the achievement of ecological reform, but only to the preservation of fundamentalist dogma.

What bound the green eco-socialists to the fundamentalists was not revisionism but dogmatism. In the final analysis, the Ebermann/Trampert camp proved more interested in incorporating ecology into Marxian dogma than adapting socialism to the task of ecological reforms. With the departure of Ebermann and Trampert from the Greens, there is a good chance that the temperamental and strategic alliance which these two had forged with the fundamentalists will loosen and eco-socialism will move closer to the realists' camp of democratic humanism, with which it always had a much closer affinity, in terms of outlook and content, than with the anti-socialist world of fundamentalism. For there can be no doubt that the future success of green politics lies in a rejuvenated alliance between the progressively reformist middle class and substantial parts of the working class.

The only escape from the fundamentalist cul-de-sac is a coalition between realists, eco-liberals and eco-socialists based on a reformist humanism. As we have endeavored to show, each of these tendencies contained an impulse essential to the political realization of reformist humanism. From realist Helmut Wiesenthal came a strategic concept which transcended the trap of "totalizing" the idea of reform. Thomas Schmid rightly insisted that the real political possibilities for the Greens lay in the enlightened middle classes. He showed how their members could potentially be tapped by the Greens through the thematization of new issues. The eco-socialists, in turn, outlined the basis for an alliance between the middle class and organized labor. Only by combining these three elements could the Greens ever hope to fulfill the three tasks of a political party: to implement their program, to expand their support, and to share in power. Whether or not they will ever achieve this – particularly in the wake of their halting and inadequate response to the events of 1989 and the political failures they experienced in the early 1990s – remains an open question.

Conclusion

The Greens have always squirmed within the constraining cloak of party existence. From the beginning, they have conceived themselves as an "epochal" phenomenon, the germ cell of a new politics or the prototype of a party of a new type. We are now perhaps in a position to evaluate in what this newness consists. While it is clear that the emergence of the Greens opens a new period in the evolution of the European Left, our analysis leaves little room for the contention that the eco-party marks the advent of a new state in civilization. Of course, it is a typical (perhaps inevitable) error of utopian movements to exaggerate their own significance.

Nevertheless, our analysis laid the lion's share of the blame for the Greens' misfortunes at the doorstep of the fundamentalists. Through a combination of political obstructionism and distorting rhetoric, they blocked the creation of a leftist reform alliance, a modernization of leftist politics as well as policies and the reconstruction of socialist ideology, while slavishly repeating the old errors of the German Left: self-marginalization, utopianism and dogmatism. That, indeed, was the great irony of green politics in the 1980s: in no instance did the old politics of the Left prove more detrimental to the emergence of a new politics than in the words and deeds of the fundamentalists, who made the sweeping claim that they were the only ones to have transcended the past.

Still, it is important to give the fundamentalists their due. Without doubt, they represented one of the most colorful and creative tendencies to emerge from the postwar German Left. Their metaphors and slogans not only helped to rejuvenate political discourse in Germany but were critical in the mobilization process. So long as the costs of political commitment outweigh the immediate personal benefits – and this is almost always the case in radical, social movements – visionaries will be necessary.

The 1980s and early 1990, made it clear that the Greens could not survive with the fundamentalists. The question for the mid-to-late 1990s is whether they can revive and survive without them.

6

Policy: The World Desired

Three social currents converged in the formation of the Greens: reformist SPD voters; remnants of the various post-APO groups from the late 1960s; and the "new" movements of the mid-1970s. The Green Party understood itself as a "coalition of green, multicolored and alternative [electoral] lists and parties . . . bound to all those who work together in the new democratic movement: the life, nature and environmental protection associations, the citizens' initiatives, the peace, human rights, women's and Third World movements."[1] Since the Greens originally saw themselves primarily as the parliamentary arm (or representative) of "the movement," their first policy statement, the Saarbrücken program of 1980, was in large part simply a *pot pourri* of the concerns of the different movements – and hence of the historical concerns of the Left, especially in its Marxist variant.

Despite its obvious continuities with the traditional Left, the party derived much legitimacy from its claim to be inventing a completely "new politics" which transcended old issues. Using the ideas of life and ecology rooted in the eco-pax or "life/survival" movement, the Greens sought to incorporate a variety of new issues – environmentalism, peace, feminism – into the political discourse of the Left and distinguish themselves from all representatives of the "old politics," especially the SPD. Thus from the very beginning the Greens sought to be not just a single-issue ecology party but an *ecological reformist* party, encompassing a broad range of social, political and cultural concerns.

Tellingly, questions of ecology actually comprised only a small fraction of the Saarbrücken program.[2] Instead, it sought to define a comprehensive new politics around "four pillars": ecology; grass-roots democracy; social welfare; non-violence. Ecology was not then, nor has it ever been, the sole or even dominant intellectual theme or political preoccupation of the Greens. Rather, it served as the conceptual underpinning of green policies and, above all, as the ideological legitimation for a reconstitution of radical politics. In chapters 5 and 7 of our study, we contend that the centrality of ecology in the green synthesis has not been inherent to green policies, but instead resulted principally from the historical circumstances and timing of the Greens' emergence. In our view, the common denominator defining green policies is the defense of the reproductive sphere. This included "ecological" policies aimed at maintaining what the Greens reverently refer to as the "natural bases of life" (*natürliche Lebensgrundlagen*). But it also contained policies aimed at preserving the integrity of *sociocultural reproduction*. Under rubrics such as "autonomy" and "self-realization," many green policies have aimed to defend the lifeworld, the realm of relationships, personality and expression, from distortion by the forces of the state and the imperatives of the market. Thus, what distinguished – and continues to distinguish – the green program from the traditional social-democratic agenda was not so much the environmental concerns of the ecology movement as a libertarian/anarchist defense of individual autonomy vis-à-vis capital, large bureaucracies, impersonal institutions, and the state.

The Greens have consistently argued that the problems besetting advanced industrial societies stem not only from the irrationalities of the market but also from technocratic attempts to master them. While unanimously suspicious of economic growth and affluence, the Greens have remained ambivalent with respect to the larger question of whether social "progress" is possible at all. Since modern industrial societies appear unable to master (or limit) the detrimental side-effects of their very essence, some argue, perhaps a return to "natural balances" and "cycles" is the only solution. Or perhaps it is possible to reclaim the ideal of progress in its original form as set forth during the Enlightenment, namely progress as increasing collective self-determination and individual freedom. The ecological identity of the Green Party has often disposed it toward the former, romanticist response, but its leftist heritage has kept alive the Enlightenment vision of progress. This deep and as yet unresolved conflict between the Romantic and Enlightenment ideals becomes concretely evident in the policy statements of the Greens.

In the following, then, we will not only attempt to summarize green policies (based primarily, though not exclusively, on the party's programmatic statements) but to reveal some of their underlying tensions. We will begin this task with a review of the Greens' ecological, economic and energy policies. We will then try to unearth the hidden conflicts and historical residues beneath the policy prescriptions and programmatic statements.

While the history of the Greens as a party spans only a little over a dozen years, their policies and programs have a longer history. They contain the traces of the German Left's entire historical development. In them, we will encounter ideas from the Battle against Nuclear Death, Easter Marches, the New Left, K-groups, Spontis, Jusos and, of course, the New Social Movements. Upon closer scrutiny we will even discern some of the dilemmas reminiscent of the Golden Age of German Social Democracy, the era of Rosa Luxemburg and Karl Kautsky.

Our discussion will be organized into four sections, in which we will seek to examine both the historical roots and internal development of green policies. The first section discusses policy proposals for ecology, the economy and society; the second section is concerned with green policy regarding peace; and, the final section is a representative sampling of green policy proposals taken from the Greens' electoral platform for the 1990 Bundestag elections, a case study of sorts.

Ecological, Economic and Social Policy

The three areas of the economic, the ecological and the social cannot be separated from one another in a discussion of green policy for the Greens view them as inherently interconnected. Solving contemporary economic, ecological and social problems, they argue, requires a comprehensive conversion of industrial society which will prevent ecological catastrophe in the short run and generate systemic change in the long run.

The policies proposed by the Greens are not only aimed at protecting the environment. They are aimed at remedying the wider socioeconomic ills which began during the crisis of the 1970s and were, they believe, compounded by the subsequent political responses to it. By the early 1980s, when the government led by Helmut Schmidt collapsed, slow growth had led to an unemployment rate in double figures. While growth revived under Helmut Kohl's stewardship during the mid-1980s, it failed to stimulate employment significantly.[3] At the same time, budget-cutting by the conservatives loosened the Federal Republic's social safety net (still tight by American standards), creating an underclass of the under- or unemployed, an underprivileged third excluded from the prosperity and opportunity enjoyed by the rest. "Ever larger groups are squeezed to the edge of society and out of the purview of politics: the long-term unemployed, the elderly ... welfare recipients, foreigners. The word 'two-thirds society' characterizes reality: two-thirds of society profit from the developments or come to terms with them, one-third suffer under them."[4] An alliance of capital, of (unionized, well-paid) labor, and of government – a construct known to an admiring world as "Modell Deutschland" but derided by the Greens as a particularly devious and pernicious institution of the status quo – was, so the Greens believed, profiting at the direct expense of marginalized, less productive groups.[5] Rejecting the language of class struggle, the Greens nevertheless still maintained the Marxist maxim that industrial society was inherently unjust and crisis-ridden, benefiting the rich and powerful at the expense of the poor and weak.

But the Greens also departed from the traditional Left. For them, the underclass was not the only victim. The two-thirds society also rested on the exploitation of nature. According to the Greens, the "two-thirds growth cartel" was extracting its wealth not only from the have-nots but from the natural environment. Ecological and social forms of exploitation, the Greens contended, were linked by the consumerist "mentality of waste" and "dominating relations toward nature" inherent in modern capitalism.[6] The dysfunctionality of capitalism, in turn, derived not merely from "an economic crisis (cyclical and/or structural)" but rather from "fundamental disturbance in the development of capitalist industrial society."[7] Industrialists and politicians, the Greens argue, have failed to include the ecological costs of production into their calculations.[8] Meanwhile, these costs – in the form of air and water pollution and food contamination – have become so great that they often outweigh the benefits of increased production. Moreover, while the benefits have been appropriated by a few, the costs have been displaced onto the many.

Because the exploitation of nature has assumed such enormous dimensions and because it has a social component, "environmental protection" and repair measures alone do not provide a satisfactory remedy.[9] In a well-known green phrase, "ecology is more than environmental protection": it means "putting politics on an ecological foundation."[10] In order to attack the socioecological crisis at its roots it is necessary to alter both the external incentives driving material accumulation and the cultural values legitimating it. Ecologizing the economy means using political and legal means to ensure that "the unavoidable interventions of human production in nature proceed in a way that considers the laws of our world's natural household and protects nature, the foundation of our life."[11] Pointing to irreparable environmental catastrophes, such as the Chernobyl nuclear disaster or the contamination of the Rhine – at the hands of large corporate and state organizations[12] – the Greens contend that the ecological crisis does not just threaten the environment, but life itself.

On this level, ecology necessarily becomes a "species question" rather than a class issue. On the one hand, the risks posed by environmental disasters are peculiarly democratic;[13] they are no respecters of persons or of class, wealth or status. On the other hand, their causes had little to do with forms of ownership or the class of the culprits. They resulted from the logic of big technology and economic growth. Thus the crisis of modern capitalism can no longer be understood solely in terms of economic contradictions. Increasingly it is rooted in the natural limits of the environment.

"The natural foundations of life: air, soil and water"

The Greens' first ecological program begins with the "natural foundations of life," that is, air, soil and water. These basic elements must be decontaminated, managed and conserved if life on the planet is to continue. Environmental protection, reducing pollution output, provides the necessary starting point.

But the Greens argue that technological means must be combined with political ones. The financial and material incentives and the technological and institutional conditions governing production must be systematically altered so as to discourage pollution and waste. For example, the Greens suggest the introduction of a "contamination tax" (Schadstoffabgabe) levied on industry, automobile owners and farmers to be commensurate with the amount of pollution they cause. These monies, in turn, would be pooled into ecological research funds in order to improve production techniques and anti-pollution devices. In accordance with the "delinquency principle" (*Verursachenprinzip*), individual firms rather than the government would be liable for bearing the costs of cleaning up pollution and environmental accidents which they caused in the past and present.[14]

Rather than imposing standards only on waste and end-products, the usage of certain dangerous substances in manufacturing processes would be controlled or forbidden altogether. According to the Greens the avoidance of dangerous substances must have priority over the technical protection of the environment. The Greens also demand the establishment of an "ecological accounting" system in industry, in which environmental transactions would be recorded as a means of monitoring and controlling the use of resources and the production of pollution. New products would be subject to rigorous tests regarding their ecological compatibility and any potential health threat they might pose. The Greens also support an ecological "structure policy" aimed at promoting small and medium-sized firms better able, because of their scale, to exist harmoniously with the environment than large companies. The Greens encourage the expansion of an "ecology sector" including, for instance, "renewable energy sources" and public transportation as a replacement of the currently private.

On the demand side, the Greens hope to complement the conversion program with an active consumer policy. Consumers would be provided with comprehensive information on the "production process, [as well as] components and effects" of commodities.[15] The success of the program, however, "presumes a value transformation."[16] Consumerism, which measures personal satisfaction in commodities and social progress in GNP, must be replaced by a new mentality oriented toward an "ecologically supportable style of life and consumption"[17] and "qualitative growth." By qualitative growth – a catchphrase also used by the SPD and the unions – the Greens mean a shift away from purely quantitative criteria of economic progress to ones governed by "genuine human needs."[18] Economic development would focus on increasing the overall quality of life rather than just the quantity of output.[19]

To gain a clearer understanding of how qualitative growth would be implemented in practice, let us briefly examine the Greens' reform program for the German chemical industry,[20] which is one of the largest economic sectors in the Federal Republic and one of the least regulated industries in the advanced, capitalist societies.[21] In their three-point program, the Greens demanded the "conversion (*Umbau*) of existing chemical production toward one bearable for nature and health; the dismantling (*Abbau*) of especially dangerous lines of production; and the construction (*Aufbau*) of soft chemistry."[22] As immediate measures (*Sofortmaßnamen*), the Green decontamination program (*Entgiftungsprogramm*) envisioned a ban on the manufacture and export of especially toxic substances.[23] In the next phase, regulatory agencies and controls were to be greatly expanded.[24] The legal rights of citizens and accident victims vis-à-vis the chemical industry would be enhanced.[25] Fees would be fixed for the usage of certain chemicals, and the revenues derived therefrom would in turn be funneled into a massive clean-up campaign, coordinated by an expert "decontamination committee" of scientists, industrialists, unionists, environmentalists and consumers.[26] Finally, positive financial incentives would be created to encourage the development of "soft chemistry."[27]

Alternative energy policy

From its inception, green energy policy was constructed on the cornerstone of categorical opposition to nuclear energy. Historically speaking, this reflected the influence of the anti-nuclear movement. Building on this base,[28] the greens have articulated a comprehensive agenda for alternative sources of energy provision.

The Greens differed – and still differ – from other parliamentary parties not only in their opposition to nuclear energy (which is shared in principle by a sizable faction within the SPD) but in their demand for an "immediate exit" from nuclear power.[29] But what has really set the Greens' position apart is the argumentation underlying it, which defies the traditional categories of "conservative" and "progressive" politics.[30] Even more than their ecological argumentation, the Greens' anti-nuclear critique does not proceed so much from existing dysfunctions as from future risks.[31] Of course, nuclear power also involves ongoing risks; leakage of low-level radiation from nuclear power plants and waste dumps pose immediate health hazards.[32] But since Chernobyl the Greens have focused on a less probable but more apocalyptic scenario, the so-called "super-GAU"[33] or total meltdown. As the Greens put it, nuclear power represents a "mortgage on future generations:"[34] it provides limited benefits for the present in exchange for incalculable risks for the future.

It should be noted that the nuclear issue presents a major challenge to the conceptual and political logic which has governed debate and conflict over the welfare state.[35] While distributional issues are typically resolvable via a politics of bargaining – give and take or a more or less – all matters concerning nuclear politics are in the Greens' eyes categorical and existential, thus not subject to bargaining and compromise.[36] Of course, the risks of nuclear power can be reduced to a statistical distribution for a given population. But the "costs" cannot be redistributed among individuals. Nor, for that matter, can the overall costs be clearly calculated, for they extend into an indefinite and uncertain future. Using cost–benefit calculations – as is often done in social policy – to make decisions about nuclear energy raises both ethical and technical difficulties. But viewing nuclear energy in existential terms makes political compromise impossible.

While an immediate exit from nuclear power remains its foremost priority, the Greens' energy policy proposes a fundamental restructuring of the institutions and attitudes surrounding energy production and use:[37] "maximal utilization of energy-saving potential . . . a prioritative expansion of soft-energy techniques and . . . the most environmentally sparing utilization of domestic energy sources possible. . . ."[38] Efforts to make existing power plants cleaner and more efficient comprise the first step.[39] But in the long run, energy conservation would require a change in public attitudes. Energy, the Greens argue, must no longer be conceived as a purchasable, wastable, object-like "commodity" available in unlimited quantities. It must be seen as a service: "'warm spaces,' 'power and light'."[40] Public information and reeducation would be introduced to promote energy conservation.[41] In addition, the structure of energy provision would be radically decentralized. The Greens have advocated "energy policy from the bottom up" through a "recommunalization of energy provision."[42] Finally substantial government support would be provided for the development of alternative or soft energy technologies, notably of the solar, wind and bio-mass variety.[43]

The Greens realized that this global transformation of the technologies, institutions and attitudes involved in the production and consumption of energy could never be achieved through parliamentary reform alone. An "unprecedented political mobilization on all levels of society"[44] would be necessary to break through the "'unholy alliance' of energy concerns, industry and bearers of state power" – the "megawatt clan" – which supports the status quo: "Now as ever, it is not the optimal use of energy, the securing and increasing of the quality of life with reduced energy use, which determine the energy system's goals in the Federal Republic, but the encouragement of increased energy consumption, expanded profit and the maximal valorization of capital."[45]

The Greens, by contrast, believe that the essence of the problem fundamentally challenges the very "paradigm of industrial civilization": a way of thinking based on a constantly growing scale of centralization, capital intensity and technologization of production which associate progress with increased production and consumption.[46]

Green Sozialpolitik

For Germans the concept of *Sozialpolitik* has much broader connotations than the English "social policy." German *Sozialpolitik*, since its birth under Bismarck, has had a dual structure which in the Federal Republic today encompasses: (1) social security (*soziale Sicherung*), a comprehensive system including old-age pensions, national health insurance, accident insurance and a work-promotion policy (*Arbeitsförderung*) including vocational and secondary education, and unemployment compensation and child support (*Kindergeld*); and (2) an institutionalized system for the "balancing of social interests" (*sozialer Interessenausgleich*), including the right to collective bargaining (*Tarifautonomie*), codetermination (*Mitbestimmung*) and a works constitution (*Betriebsverfassung*) regulating industrial relations at the plant level.[47]

Over the last hundred years, the German welfare state has grown continuously but resisted efforts at comprehensive reform efforts by both conservative and social-democratic governments. It is administratively decentralized and subject to a number of legal jurisdictions. Moreover, its funding derives from a complex web of private and public contributions. Likewise, since the "institutionalized balancing of interests" is, in essence, a product of a hundred years of class conflict, it too is composed of numerous ambiguities and compromises.

Since Bismarck, the attitude of the German Left has been divided on the issue of *Sozialpolitik*. Some have seen it as a particularly devious device of social control, while others have hailed it as a major attainment of social progress and distributive justice. In the Federal Republic, the debate has crystallized in the constitutional issue of the relation between the *Rechtsstaat* and the *Sozialstaat*, for example in the question of whether the Basic Law, the country's constitution, merely foresees a material redistribution while preserving a realm of "bourgeois freedoms" (property) protected from state intervention; or whether it delivers a "mandate for activist social policy" (*soziale Formierung*) in which efforts to achieve social justice transcend the sacrosanctity of private property.

When the Greens espouse themselves as *sozial* or as proponents of a "social economy," they implicitly place themselves in the latter, socialist tradition. But while the Greens retained the basic Marxist critique of the exploitation and alienation of labor under "capitalist relations of production,"[48] they reject the means Marx suggested to remedy them.

> We Greens emphasize: An essential precondition for individual freedom is private property in objects which serve the shaping of one's own life or the securing of one's personal existence. . . . We reject the familiar forms of nationalization since they do not allow grass-roots democratic control. . . . We Greens hold *market mechanisms* to be an important means of steering the economy. But shaping the ecological and social conditions of the economic process with the help of state policy (*Vorgaben*) and interventions must correct and complement the deficits of the market mechanisms.[49]

For the Greens, the economy also had to be "grass-roots democratic," for, as the Stalinist variety of "real, existing socialism" in Eastern Europe and National Socialist "totalitarianism" in Germany had shown, an all-powerful, centralizing state is as inimical to free self-determination and self-realization as is an unfettered market. Unlike traditional socialists, the Greens do not see the *Sozialstaat* and *Sozialpolitik* in their present incarnation as transitional stages toward a socialized, planned economy, but as flawed fixtures which have to be reformed and modified according to principles of social amenability, collective justice and grass-roots democracy.

Let us then turn to the Greens' program for restructuring the German social security system, for it is here that the Greens' sensibility to new structural problems has been most acute and the novelty of their suggestions the greatest.

In contrast to ecological issues, the "crisis of the *Sozialstaat*" was not first thematized by the Greens. Indeed, an emotionally charged, highly complex debate on this subject emerged in the Federal Republic beginning in the early 1980s, involving Left and Right and both academics and policy makers.[50] Already during the last few years of the Schmidt government, some of the Federal Republic's extremely generous welfare packages were being substantially cut. The Kohl government undertook further reductions in social spending with the battle cry of "achievement has got to pay again!"[51] At the same time, critics on the Left implicated social democracy in the development of a serious "legitimation crisis"[52] and "fiscal crisis"[53] of the German state. Prompted by these developments, major discussion began in the SPD and DGB concerning the "limits of the *Sozialstaat*."[54] It is principally this debate which formed the basis of the Greens' own contribution to the problem.

The Greens attributed the cost explosion of the late 1970s to the slowdown of growth and the emergence of structural unemployment. They rejected conservative arguments which rendered an alleged demand-related inflation and a supposed laziness of the work force responsible for Germany's economic crisis and dismissed the conservative prescription for "reprivatizing" social problems and restoring the free play of market forces. At the same time, however, they also opposed a return to the traditional tactic of throwing more bureaucracy and money at social problems in the traditional style of the Social Democrats. The *Sozialstaat*, they contended, addressed symptoms and not causes; moreover, its very growth was itself becoming a source of social problems. Increasingly intensive forms of capitalist growth, they argued, were valorizing and denaturalizing sociocultural reproduction. For example, tasks previously performed in the context of communal and private life were being replaced by commodified goods and services.[55] Interventions by state and social service agencies aimed at undoing damage within the private sphere were themselves disturbing processes of "symbolic reproduction" by their own bureaucratic imperatives, a "colonization of the lifeworld."[56] As the Greens put it, "the highest possible budgetary expenditures for social policy are not an adequate criterion for social security or the quality of life ... bureaucratization and juridification (*Verrechtlichung*) are mere reflexes from the lack of direct opportunities to shape work and living conditions. The more compensatory measures must be undertaken, the more complicated the social system becomes."[57]

The Greens, in short, did not simply criticize the number of social programs or the level of welfare spending; they questioned the very idea of equating such programs with "social security." "Properly understood *Sozialpolitik* must have above all a *preventive* character. It must go far beyond the traditional understanding of social security and take the *sociocultural side* into consideration" (emphasis added).[58] A green *Sozialpolitik* would involve shielding the sphere of sociocultural reproduction against the intrusions of the capitalist market without subjecting it to the distortions of bureaucratic regulation.[59]

The Greens suggest several steps toward achieving this delicate balance. First of all, the existing system which awards benefits for specific conditions (disability), reasons (such as unemployment) or contributions (such as old-age pensions) should be replaced by a universal, "need-oriented basic security system" (*bedarfsorientierte Grundsicherung*).[60] "Through the social security system, every member of the population whose basic existence is not secured for whatever reason should be guaranteed an income at a level which covers minimal needs in a form which is not degrading."[61] Making basic income a fundamental and unquestionable right would both simplify administrative procedures and reduce the stigma and humiliation usually associated with them. The entire insurance system would be unified and need would be made the sole criterion for receiving aid. Existing inequities, particularly vis-à-vis women, would be abolished.[62] Multiple agencies would be eliminated[63] and degrading inquiries to determine neediness would be eliminated.[64]

To prevent these new super-agencies from evolving into instruments of social control, they would be organized in a decentralized and democratic fashion. Public oversight would be maintained and private, profit-oriented enterprises excluded from providing social services.[65] At the same time, decentralized self-help groups would be promoted and financed by the government. "Experiments with 'small social networks,' in which neighborhoods assume a share of the educational tasks, the supervision and care of elderly people and the sick, are to be supported by the community via the availability of space, living quarters and land."[66] These structures, unlike those of the traditional *Sozialstaat,* would be suited to deal with the "sociocultural aspect" of social security.

Green *Sozialpolitik* retains the socialist ideals of distributive justice[67] but primarily as a means of attaining the "self-determination and free unfolding of the individual."[68] For the Greens (as for orthodox socialists) self-determination means, first of all, "work as a free, self-determined activity," but also (as for traditional liberals of the J. S. Mill sort) the free development of the individual personality through "leisure time" and "self-determined [cultural] activity."[69]

A central target of the green reform plans was the national healthcare system. They proposed that payments be fixed at a uniform percentage rate of a person's gross monthly income in order to ensure that the well-to-do did not escape paying a "fair" share.[70] Private insurance coverage for civil servants, professionals and the self-employed would be eliminated and membership in the public insurance system made mandatory.[71] Likewise, various rationalization and cost-cutting measures such as limiting claims by "expensive" patients would be eliminated. Instead, attempts should be made to contain costs by eliminating incentives for unnecessary hospitalization and treatment.[72]

The Green reforms would go beyond assuring an equitable and cost-effective delivery of services: "Our health is also threatened by the healthcare system itself."[73] In the Greens' view, the profit-oriented marketing techniques of the pharmaceutical industry promoted the proliferation and use of unnecessary medicines. The Greens suggested that testing standards, which had become quite lax in Germany, be tightened and that prices, which were above European levels, be controlled. Like the "chemicalization" of industry, the "pharmacization" of medicine had become part of the problem instead of being its solution.

Another focus of green healthcare policies was patients' rights. In order to make patients better able to defend themselves against unnecessary medical procedures or excessive medication, the Greens demanded the protection of basic "constitutional and human rights": "Treatments and dispensing of aid . . . cannot impinge on constitutional rights. The [patients] concerned must have access at all time to charts, files and findings."[74] Patients' complaints would be handled by "independent and publicly financed grievance offices (*Beschwerdestellen*)."[75] Greater patient involvement, the Greens believed, might itself serve as a form of preventative medicine.[76]

But genuine prevention, they argue, must also take account of the social and environmental causes of illness. To the Greens, pollution, poor working conditions and poverty are public health issues.[77] Moreover, the healthcare system itself is controlled by a "power cartel" – "the physicians' lobby, the medical instrument industry, the pharmaceutical industry and the large welfare associations" – which has an interest in monopolizing the treatment of illness.[78] Indeed, the Greens go so far as to suggest that this "medical-industrial complex" with its "aggressive dispositions to expansion,"[79] has an inherent interest in the reproduction of illness.

Hence, health itself needs to be defined in more holistic terms. Hospitals could be largely replaced with comprehensive health centers and outpatient clinics which would combine various branches of the health profession – nurses, physicians, osteopaths, physical therapists, psychologists, nutrition specialists – under one roof. These integrated healthcare providers would then be controlled by local health initiatives, autonomous patient groups or cooperatives.[80]

We now turn to a brief analysis of the Greens' social security scheme. Its foundation would be basic income, which would be available to anyone who for any reason did not receive a salary above a certain level. It would also be available to every citizen regardless of whether the person is employed or not. The Greens pride themselves on pursuing a policy which decouples remuneration from employment. This would provide all members of society with a minimum of material safety. But it would not assure them of satisfying work, significant cultural activity and an engaging private life. That is the goal of the Greens' labor relations policies, which lie within the second division of *Sozialpolitik*, namely the institutionalization of collective interests, to which we turn.

To understand the Greens' position in this area, it is important to elucidate the Federal Republic's industrial relations system. The German state does not as a rule engage in much direct, centralized planning typical of "state corporatist" countries such as Sweden and Austria, and also practiced in a different context by France. Nor, despite one half-hearted and failed attempt, does the German state exercise a concerted incomes policy.[81] The Federal Republic's meso-corporatist governmental arrangement[82] rests on a dualistic system of interest representation: on the one hand, exclusive bargaining rights in the form of *Tarifautonomie* (bargaining autonomy) are accorded to the two "social partners," the trade unions and the employers' associations; on the other hand, the Works Constitution Act delineates clearly between capital–labor relations on the shopfloor and outside the factory gates. The law, both in its original version of 1952 and its revised form of 1972, basically excluded unions from the Federal Republic's shopfloors by empowering works councils as the sole – indeed quite powerful – representatives of the work force on matters related to everything excepting the negotiation of wages. State intervention is thereby restricted to setting the "normative conditions" for industrial relations.[83]

In practice this has meant that industrial conflicts have been subjected to increasing legal regimentation and restriction over the course of the postwar period. This process of juridification (*Verrechtlichung*) has been neither welcomed nor opposed by the unions. Nevertheless, it is, as Rainer Erd aptly concludes, "the (surely unintentional) product of a development consciously promoted by the unions,"[84] the consequence of a "cooperative labor politics"[85] in which the unions actively strove to become a "factor of order" in alliance with business. The high degree of labor–business cooperation has resulted in low strike activity, high wage gains (which, however, lagged behind productivity growth) and a tendency to accept stressful workplace conditions in return for added remuneration. In comparison with some of its poorer and/or strike-ridden European neighbors,[86] the Federal Republic could hold up its industrial relations as a model, a successful embodiment of the "social democratic compromise."[87] Of course, Modell Deutschland also experienced episodes of tension and turmoil. And during the 1970s and 1980s, the German labor relations system was repeatedly tested by economic crises.

The formation of the social–liberal coalition revived old agendas of union reform, involving the expansion of codetermination and the revision of the repressive Works Constitution Act of 1952. At the same time, business, reeling under the blow of the "oil shocks," struck a more aggressive pose; and the much discussed slowdown in world economic growth diminished the social surplus available for transfer payments and wage hikes, the core of the "material base of consent." Finally the "paradigm of production" around which the system of industrial relations had been forged, namely *mass* production,[88] underwent a revolution based on electronically steered "flexible technologies" and the expansion of the service sector. In the 1970s, many developments conspired to challenge the premises, foundations, institutions and practices of the West German industrial relations system, prompting increased industrial conflict[89] and rendering the triangular relationship between labor, capital and the state more delicate. Tellingly, however, none of these crises ever became so severe as to impede the proven functioning of this interaction.[90]

The green movement emerged amidst this crisis and many leftist Greens were politically weaned by the unions. Hence, it is not surprising that green labor and industrial relations policies largely mirrored those of organized labor's activist wing, as constituted notably by IG Metall and IG Medien (formerly IG Druck und Papier).[91] The Greens' policies on labor issues rested essentially on the following four demands: (1) introduction of a 35-hour working week to combat mass unemployment; (2) a program for the "humanization of work"; (3) a rescue program for crisis-ridden industries, especially steel producers; and (4), further revision of the Works Constitution Act policies. All these issues were important to the unions.

But despite the Greens' outspoken support for union goals, relations between the eco-party and organized labor were anything but friendly. Substantively, all the fierce debates and frequent misunderstandings between Greens and unionists have in one way or another hinged on the economy versus ecology controversy: whether an unavoidable trade-off exists between the two, as the established union leadership has repeatedly contended[92]; or whether both can be productively reconciled with each other, as the Greens insist.[93] Is the relationship between economy and ecology zero–sum as labor contended throughout much of the 1970s and well into the 1980s, or is it in fact positive sum as the Greens have consistently believed?

On another level, the complex and difficult interaction between the unions and the Greens stemmed from a clash between two fundamentally different milieus. One, profoundly anchored in the blue-collar world of industrial life, represented the "material" values of the old Left. The other, rooted in the university-trained intelligentsia, embodied the "postmaterial" values of the new Left. Tellingly it was not until 1987 that a leading German unionist, IG Metall's Hans Janssen, in change of the union's collective bargaining division, could openly attend and address a green party congress. Perhaps equally revealing is the fact that this union official resigned – or was made to resign – from IG Metall's executive council shortly after his appearance at this congress. Nor have the Greens succeeded in garnering significant electoral support among blue-collar industrial workers. Barring farmers, among no other sector of the German population have the Greens been burdened with as little success as among the traditional working class. Workers and hippies just do not seem to mingle. Yet, despite these obvious conflicts between the Greens and the unions, there can be no doubt that to the former the working-class – if not organized labor – represents a humanizing and democratizing force whose political struggle has brought objective progress and whose plight deserves the full support of all radical reformers. As such, the Greens have always perceived labor as a somewhat alien but all the more worthy and ultimately reliable ally.

Let us now turn to the question of unemployment. Despite its deserved reputation as Europe's industrial dynamo, the unemployment rate in the Federal Republic since 1980 has been embarrassing at best.[94] The emergence of permanently high levels of unemployment was not solely the result of the world economic crisis;[95] it was compounded by responses of the Schmidt and Kohl governments to it.[96] Business, for its part, pursued a policy which tended to marginalize young, old, female, foreign and handicapped workers.[97]

The phenomenon of high unemployment and the failure of state policies to combat it convinced the radical and alternative Left in the Federal Republic that "a politics of reducing working hours . . . is the only half-way promising strategy . . . for combating growing mass unemployment once the traditional means of anti-cyclical policy have either exhausted their economic effectiveness or proved themselves politically incapable of being implemented."[98] This alternative is also ecologically more desirable, since growth rates sufficient to achieve full employment might well wreak havoc on the environment.[99] The Greens (along with IG Metall[100] and the socialist intelligentsia[101]) advocate the immediate introduction of a 35-hour working week:[102] "For the Greens . . . the distributional effects of work-time reduction assume unquestioned priority;"[103] a decrease in the length of the working week to 35 hours is the "labor policy variant from which the greatest employment effects can emerge."[104] However, these expected employment effects could only be achieved if there were rapid implementation.[105]

The 35-hour week could only be introduced through an agreement between the "collective bargaining partners," the unions and employers' association. But the Greens have proposed a number of "flanking measures" which would buttress such an agreement.[106] They propose, among other things, that the legal working week be reduced to 40 hours (it still stands at 44) and to restrict "surplus work" (*Mehrarbeit*)[107] and overtime by awarding additional leisure time instead of additional monetary compensation for them, and by sharply regulating "flexi-time" schemes.[108]

The Greens depart sharply from the unions in their call for a "redistribution of work" not only within the firm, but between firm and household, men and women. Under the existing "patriarchal employment system," they argue, "socially necessary work" is divided into two categories: public production which is remunerated and performed chiefly by men, and private reproduction which is unremunerated and is performed chiefly by women.[109] The Greens first proposed a radical cure for this problem in their 1985 anti-discrimination bill.[110] Its aim was no less than the end of patriarchy,[111] an ambitious goal in any society but especially in one such as Germany where women's rights on both the legislative and constitutional level still remain among the most backward in Western Europe.[112] The bill included major revisions in existing laws concerning abortion, rape and social security. It also contained three measures pertaining to labor.

The first component was a general clause prohibiting all "discrimination against women".[113] "Discrimination in the sense of this law exists when a woman is disadvantaged or promoted less than a man on the basis of her sex, her ability to bear children or her form of life."[114] The second and more controversial element[115] of the bill was the so-called "Quota Law" (*Quotierungsgesetz*), a radical, affirmative action program for women which demanded that "all employers in the private economy and civil service are obliged to favor women in filling training slots, in hiring, promotion, retraining, continuing education and other such measures until women are represented to the order of 50 percent at all levels and areas in which they are [now] underrepresented.[116] Although men would have been enormously disadvantaged in the short run,[117] most women in the Greens felt that such drastic steps were necessary to rectify historical discrimination against women[118] and that for the present "men's legal rights must take a back seat."[119] The law would also have established a sizable administrative machinery – run by women – to implement and enforce the law.[120]

The aims of the proposed law went beyond a "corporate-style feminist adaptation by women to male norms and values."[121] It also sought to change men's values. The transformation of working life would make it possible for men to assume equal responsibility in the household.[122] For example, men would be allowed to take extended childraising leave. The intent of the bill, then, was not only to incorporate women more fully into production but also to incorporate men more fully into reproduction.

The Greens have consistently supported a redistribution of social labor between the spheres of production and reproduction, "in order to release available social quantities of time in a socially bearable way for work which is completed outside the received relations of remunerative labor and serves the comprehensive needs of society and general welfare."[123] In the Greens' vision, lived and practiced in the alternative milieu, a share of the overwhelming social and psychological resources concentrated in production must be transferred to nurturing and regenerating tasks and into leisure time necessary for the pursuit of individual self-realization through educational and cultural activity.[124]

However, while the Greens might have liked to diminish the centrality of work and production in modern society, they also remained committed to the Marxian ideal of "emancipatory labor." The Greens therefore supported organized labor's demand for a "humanization of work."[125] In the wake of the radicalization of a good part of the West German Left in the aftermath of 1968, the unions, too, experienced major challenges to their traditional positions of collective bargaining. While conventional and quantitative bread-and-butter issues defined the unions' strategy of bargaining until the early 1970s, the post-1968 wave of radicalization introduced new and "critical" dimensions into the unions' logic, among them concerns pertaining to the larger "quality of life."[126] These demands were, of course, reinforced by the introduction of new technologies and other measures of intensified rationalization which, most visibly in industries such as steel and automobile production, lead to a considerable restructuring of work often accompanied by serious job losses and a deskilling of formerly skilled workers. As one of the DGB's "action programs" put it, the humanization of work "has to do with no less a goal than securing a further fulfillment of human capabilities in worklife."[127]

Pursuing these union demands, the Greens put forward a number of measures designed to relieve the monotony and stress of traditional industrial work.[128] However, realizing that such a program would be impossible without greatly expanding the influence of organized labor on the organization of production itself, the humanization of labor issue subsequently merged, both for the unions and the Greens, with demands for expanded codetermination rights in production and the economy, and increased democratization of society and the state.

Both by law and by structure, further changes lay within the purview of the "social partners."[129] However, in the existing scheme of legal relations, labor had few means, barring certain rights of consultation and refusal, to determine effectively the organization of production. The Greens therefore demanded that labor become a completely equal partner with capital in deciding on "all measures for the introduction of new technologies, products and processes,"[130] because "the participation of employees and their representative organs in the planning phase for . . . new technologies, processes and products or commensurate developments in the service sector is the precondition for social and ecological criteria being adequately taken into consideration."[131] Accordingly, the Greens proposed a series of changes in the Codetermination Act of 1976 and the Works Constitution Act of 1972. If implemented, they would activate the more extensive form of "parity codetermination" anchored in the Codetermination Act of 1951,[132] which, though a persistent dream of Germany's organized labor, has eluded it in real life.

The Green democratization program would also extend to the workplace basic constitutional rights, such as freedom of opinion and conscience and the right to physical integrity (*körperliche Unversehrtheit*) among others.[133] In addition, the works councils would fall under the mandate of the plenary works assembly (*Betriebsversammlung*)[134]; furthermore, the areas subject to codetermination through the works council would also be expanded.[135]

The intention of the Greens' policy was not a continuation of the process of juridification, of depoliticizing conflict – sheathing the strike weapon and shelving the "systemic question" – in return for the legalization of collective rights.[136] For the Greens, laws could by definition never reconcile the opposed interests of labor and capital but only organize them.[137] Juridification only helped integrate the working class into the existing relations of domination.[138] The Greens, exhibiting an orthodox Marxist view on this point, were determined to revive the politics of class conflict by lifting legal restrictions impinging on labor activity.[139] Given capital's "structural dominance" in industrial conflicts, the Greens believed that only an improvement in the unions' position vis-à-vis management could lead to a modicum of fairness in the Federal Republic's industrial relations system.

Peace Policy: Against All Military Conflict, Exploitation and Repression

Were this an analysis of a conventional party, this section would be entitled "foreign policy" and bear subtopical headings such as "security," "development" and "strategy." But so radical are the Greens' views on these matters that they themselves present these concepts in quotation marks as a reflection of their skepticism, even cynicism, toward the conventional view of global affairs. "Radical" should not, however, suggest that their views are entirely new. In fact, both as models of thought and programs of action, antimilitarism, anti-imperialism and internationalism, the three paradigmatic elements of Green "foreign policy", are at least as old as the Third International. The Greens, however, have appropriated only the analytical fundament of this "old left" legacy, not its positive ideological content of pacifism, communism and class solidarity.

While the framework of their thinking is drawn from the orthodox Marxist tradition, the Greens' vision of international relations has been framed by the great divisions of postwar geopolitics: the old East/West or superpower conflict; underdevelopment and repression in the Third World, the North/South divide; and the previous division of their own nation into two Germanies. As the Greens saw it, these three conflicts have not been isolated problems but reflect a set of international, social and cultural relations that perpetuate war, oppression and violence. At the root of their vision is a faith – in stark contrast to political "realism" – that violence and conflict can be eliminated from human social relations. Thus the Greens have contended that "deterrence" in the East/West conflict, "stabilization" of repressive governments, "suppression" of national upheavals in the Third World, and the maintenance of "law and order" at home do not safeguard peace, development and order but themselves perpetuate an unsafe, unstable and unfree world.

The Greens are also vehement opponents of having women join the Bundeswehr in any capacity. Rejecting the American feminist position of seeing equality of men and women in terms of having women as full participants in all aspects of the armed services, the Greens perceive their feminism as abolishing *all* armed services. Thus, for them, it is not a question of arming women, but of disarming men.[140]

Genuine peace, in their view, does not just mean the absence of open, violent conflict but the cultural transcendence of aggression. The first step toward peace is universal disarmament, followed by universal recognition of the right to national self-determination and the implementation of non-violent mechanisms for balancing conflicting interests. Ultimately, though, peace could only be guaranteed by eliminating the root causes of military conflict, which they see as material inequality and political repression. Lasting peace, in other words, is possible only in a fair and democratic world. We will now seek to outline the Greens' plans and policies for achieving global peace. We will also present their arguments as to why their radical vision is both practical and realizable.

The Greens' strategy for neutralizing the East/West conflict was among the most detailed and developed policy proposals they presented. While the gist of these proposals has been largely (if not entirely) eclipsed by the collapse of East European Communism since 1989, the Greens' concepts in this area still represent the broadest and most detailed statements concerning their peace policy.

The green position on peace owed much to the peace movement, with which, as we saw earlier, the Greens were closely connected by institutional and personal ties. During the battle over the euro-missiles, both the peace movement and the Greens tried to engage US and NATO defense experts on their own terms. Thus, whatever the ultimate verdict on them may be, the

Greens' position on international security has gone beyond a simple-minded pacifism right from the beginning.

The development of green policy mirrored the many twists and turns taken by East/West relations during the 1980s. Their longstanding first priority, the "immediate and unconditional removal of the Pershing II and Cruise missiles" (still maintained in the 1987 programs[141]) has since been realized. But the Greens continue to favor unilateral initiatives over a tit-for-tat style of negotiated arms reductions; the creation of a European "nuclear-free zone"; and the exit of Germany from NATO.

The disaffection of the Greens with NATO did not result from the missile question alone but from a perceived transformation in the rhetoric and strategy of the alliance of which the missiles were but an expression. In the estimation of the Greens, these changes pointed above all to an alarming increase in the militancy of the United States. US military planners and hawkish politicians seemingly no longer avoided the prospect of nuclear war but spoke of it in the early 1980s (during President Reagan's first term) as "limitable," "wageable" and "winnable." To the Greens it appeared that America was not only developing the capability for a first strike against the Soviet Union and a nuclear war on the European continent but was planning to fight one – on German soil!

The more bellicose American rhetoric stemmed from what was called the "crisis of deterrence,"[142] which first manifested itself in changes in US defense policy under the Carter administration.[143] West German peace activists and Greens were particularly alarmed by the well-known "presidential directive 59," which officially endorsed the "counterforce" principle (hitting enemy missiles in their silos[144]), and the "Carter doctrine," which called for the defense of "vital" US interests – such as the Persian Gulf and Central America – with military means. The two policies were linked by the principle of "horizontal escalation," which implied, as then Secretary of Defense Harold Brown put it, that such a defense would be undertaken where the US chose it, meaning not necessarily at the location of the conflict but possibly at the locus of US strength. To make this new strategy credible, it was inevitable and essential – at least in the Greens' eyes – that the US government maintain the prerogative of a first strike and of limiting conflict, to Europe for instance.[145]

The assumption of power by Ronald Reagan signaled the beginning of the most hawkish United States administration since the Second World War, and only intensified green fears. When US policy papers containing statements on the feasibility of limited nuclear war in the "European theater" were leaked to the European press,[146] the Greens' worst suspicions seemed to be confirmed.

Though the intention behind the euromissiles had originally been to "recouple" Western Europe (and above all West Germany) to the American nuclear guarantee,[147] the deployment of these missiles was interpreted by the Greens as part of an American strategy to achieve complete hegemony over Europe, and especially Germany. They regarded justifications of the euro-missiles as a response to the Soviet SS20s as a smokescreen for American power. For the Greens there was never any doubt that it was the United States which was the driving force behind the arms race and the real potential aggressor.[148] Years of anti-Americanism coupled with a genuinely aggressive US foreign and defense policy proved a potent mix in rendering the United States – and most things American – the most hated enemy for the German Greens.

The Greens sought to substantiate this position with respect to the technical capabilities of the euromissiles, especially the Pershings. With their short flight trajectory (no warning time) and pinpoint accuracy, they were ideal for destroying enemy silos. And because they were stationed above ground, they had to be deployed ("use or lose") before an enemy attack was launched on them. The Pershings and cruise missiles, they contended, were "counterforce" or first strike weapons. Since the Soviets were surely aware of this implied threat of "nuclear blackmail," the euromissiles, so the Greens believed, actually served to destabilize the superpower confrontation.[150]

More disturbing to the Greens was the fact that in their view US efforts to render nuclear strategy credible again were actually "lowering the psychological barrier to pulling the nuclear trigger" and making war morally acceptable.[151] In order to "restore the credibility of the nuclear deterrent," objected the Greens, millions of human lives were being wagered. And life, after all, was ultimately more important than security or the alleged freedom which official Western ideology kept touting incessantly.

Accompanying this unequivocal prioritization of life, however, was a hard calculation of European and especially German interests. The NATO strategy, the Greens believed, imposed a unique and enormous risk on the German people. In part, the explanation was geopolitical: since the iron curtain coincided with the German–German border, the German people – pursuant to the Greens' analysis of the situation – were bound to become "hostages," even "sacrificial victims" in any superpower conflict conducted in Europe.[152] Moreover the Greens argued that under the American strategy of horizontal escalation and limited war, the German population might be sacrificed or forsaken to maintain US hegemony elsewhere in the world, for instance in the Persian Gulf. Thus, concluded the Greens, there can be no security for the Federal Republic under any conditions set by NATO and exacted by US strategy. As Petra Kelly put this, "What, then, are the realistic, political conditions for protection against war . . . in a Federal Republic which, in the role of a forward-based colony, is now made into a nuclear launch-pad?"[153] For the Greens, the Federal Republic existed in a quasi-colonial status (exemplified by the leftist epithet, "Bananenrepublik Deutschland"), for its government did not ultimately answer for the lives and security of its people. Hence "it is bitterly necessary for [the Greens] to lift the taboos on the question of neutrality"[154] so that the Federal Republic could regain its national sovereignty. In the Greens' eyes, the Federal Republic's fight for neutrality from American bondage was equivalent to any colony's war of national liberation.

It is interesting to note that such a subjectively a-nationalist – even anti-nationalist – group of people as the Greens and their milieu pursued such an objectively nationalist course in the context of German–American relations.

In notable contrast to the vehement opposition to the United States's involvement in Vietnam on the part of APO and SDS, whose members – despite their political antagonisms vis-à-vis the United States – still admired and copied many things American, the Greens and the peace movements of the early 1980s (euromissiles) and early 1990s (Gulf war) despised all things American. Above all, in marked distinction to their predecessors of 1968, who viewed the Federal Republic as an accomplice of the United States in the evil scheme of imperialism, the movements of the 1980s and 1990s perceived Germany as a victim of American imperialism. In opposition to their forebearers of the 1960s, many Greens of the 1980s and 1990s are less likely to speak English well, less likely to have visited the United States, and more prone to think of the United States as a "decadent culture" and of Americans as "obsessed with consumption." Coupled with this, the essence of the green Left, concerned as it is with issues of ecological destruction at the hands of a fetishized culture of consumption and an unbridled belief in technology, contains a critique of modernism and industrialism of which the United States is the leading embodiment. (The opposition of much of the green Left to industrialization itself, and not just to capitalist industrialization, stands in marked contrast to the favorable disposition toward industrialization along socialist lines held by many leftists during the 1960s.) Moreover, in their commitment to antimodernism, many Greens have embraced aspects of anti-Americanism traditionally associated with the German Right. No wonder, then, that people such as Mechtersheimer could seamlessly make the transition from the far-right CSU to the Greens, all the while maintaining, indeed intensifying, their hatred of America and their view of Germany as an exploited colony of the United States.

At the same time, the German policy establishment itself began to perceive a serious conflict between American and European interests in NATO.[155] German experts questioned the wisdom of the euromissile deployment, albeit from a different angle than that of the Greens. For conservative and moderate German politicians, the Federal Republic's national security still depended on the American commitment to West Germany's defense, indeed on America's technical capability and political will to be the first to use nuclear weapons.[156] Confronted with the need to render its defense options in Europe more flexible,[157] the US became convinced of the necessity for a conventional military build-up of sufficient strength to repel a Soviet attack without resorting to theater nuclear weapons.[158] This consensus was soon to spread over Europe.[159] Part of this strategic overhaul was predicated on the US military's development of a new war-fighting strategy dubbed Air Land Battle (ALB).[160]

Strategically speaking ALB translated the rhetoric of "conventionalization" on to the battlefield level. It outlined the hardware and logistics for a highly mobile fighting force capable of rapidly waging and winning limited conflicts at any point on the globe – be it in Europe, the Persian Gulf, or Southeast Asia.[161] ALB openly embraced the "spirit of the offensive," emphasizing that "the offensive is the decisive form of war," and that "in order to win, one must attack."[162]

Particularly after the first euromissile deployments in 1983, the peace movement, the Greens and the alternative Left in the Federal Republic made a concerted effort to shift the focus of their opposition toward ALB.[163] As in the case of the euromissiles, the Greens attacked ALB as inherently destabilizing and as placing disproportionate risks on the Europeans.[164] The Greens also challenged ALB's underlying assumption, namely that once begun, a military conflict, could be rationally planned, limited and controlled. Said Marie-Louise Beck-Oberdorf: "American military planners appear to me to be indulging in an illusion when they actually proceed from the assumption that a war would behave itself so rationally that it would play itself out as a limited conflict on European soil."[165] Once ignited, a limited conflict would not behave rationally but escalate into a full-scale nuclear conflagration. And "if the aggressive, militarized US policy, in and of itself, already increases the danger of war, then it places the risks associated with such a policy to a disproportionate degree on the Europeans."[166] In the final analysis, the Greens have always perceived the Federal Republic's alliance with the United States as a threat to rather than a guarantee of Germany's and Europe's security interests.

In the Greens' eyes, the alliance with the United States also represented a threat to the security interests of the rest of the world. The ALB constituted a profound "militarization of foreign policy." The Greens consistently interpreted the American commitment to counter "Soviet aggression" and protect American interests anywhere on the globe as a "displacement of the East–West conflict on to the Third World."[167] And they flatly denied the validity of the argument which portrayed the United States as the "defender of freedom and democracy."

It is difficult to overlook the fact that the Greens' analyses tend to place the lion's share of the responsibility for the arms race on the US and the capitalist West.[168] For the most part, the Greens attribute the ostensibly higher level of aggressiveness of the West, and especially of the United States, to crude economic interests which, in their view, have become inextricably coupled with brute imperialist designs. America's effort to enhance its military power, the Greens argue, stems from the need to compensate for the declining competitiveness of its economy and the decay of its global hegemony.[169] Thus the role of the US as global policeman helps restore America's political and economic hegemony over the Atlantic alliance and the industrial West.[170] Nothing confirmed this view of the United States on the part of the Greens more forcefully than the American-led engagement against Iraq in 1990–1. The issue appeared simple to most Greens and their allies: The United States conducted this predatory war against an abused and misunderstood Third World country in order to continue exercising American hegemony over oil. By so doing, the United States could maintain its domination of all worlds: First, Second and Third. Beneath this analysis lie the conventional and "old left" postulates of the Leninist theory of capitalist imperialism,[171] mingled with a strong dose of cultural anti-Americanism not uncommon to the German Right and Left.[172]

Whatever its defects, the Greens argued, the Soviet social and political system lacked the American's equivalent of a "systemic" or "structural" impetus towards expansion.[173] To be sure, the Prague Spring, the repression of Solidarity in Poland and the Soviet war in Afghanistan made it somewhat difficult for the Greens to absolve the Soviet Union entirely of responsibility for the arms race. Indeed, a small faction within the party and the peace movement assigned the Soviet Union equal blame for the escalation of the arms race and for pursuing an aggressive foreign policy. But on the whole the Greens painted the Soviet leadership as passive reluctant participants in an arms race led by America,[174] while seeing the Soviet people as peace-loving in contrast to the inherently belligerent and imperialist Americans. The Greens' feeble attempt to introduce the Soviet Union as the other culprit in endangering global peace and threatening the German people's well-being was nothing but a smokescreen for their otherwise clear conviction that the real bully was the United States alone.

Just how great the Greens' mistrust of anything American had become by 1985 can be seen in the response of green "peace specialists" to Ronald Reagan's Star Wars (SDI) program.[175] In part, their criticisms of SDI echoed those of governmental, military and scientific circles who charged that Star Wars was too expensive,[176] too easily and cheaply subverted by the Soviets[177] and technologically unfeasible. More than this, though, the Greens perceived SDI not as a defensive system but as part of an offensive strategy to attain a first-strike capacity. To the Greens, SDI was yet another example as to how the bellicose Americans were using their technological superiority to intimidate the world and defeat the peace-loving Soviets.

Yet it would be a mistake to see green peace policy simply as a manifestation of the Greens' pronounced, sometimes even vicious, anti-Americanism. Thus the Greens also opposed the French plan for a European missile defense system (EUREKA) and spoke out against the various proposals for a "Europeanization of defense" espoused by many social democrats, including leading figures in the SPD. In fact, the Greens reject all military defense and alliance strategies. Instead, they advocate developing national policies of civil, social or alternative defense, resting on "resistance with non-violent, non-military means against a military aggressor from within (Putsch, coup d'etat) or without (intervention, invasion)."[178] As the Greens openly concede, their ideal of peace cannot be fully realized by government or governments, but requires a "new culture of peace from below," carried by a "grass-roots mass movement," for like all their programs it aims at a fundamental social and personal transformation, which legislation and policy can only set in motion but never attain.

Policy: a Representative Microcosm

Nowhere do a party's policies receive a clearer articulation than in its electoral platforms. Perhaps even more than a party's official programs, its platforms highlight its political wishes in the issue areas the party deems important. Electoral platforms are like political hit parades. They highlight the political orientation which the party tries to sell successfully to the voters at large as well as to its own clientele of sympathizers and members. As such, electoral platforms represent a distilled overview of a party's policies at a given time. They offer an excellent snapshot of the substance and form of the politics which, given the opportunity by the voters, the party wants to implement. Thus electoral platforms are especially appropriate documents to offer insights into the "input" side of a party's policies.

With this in mind, we thought it useful for an understanding of the Greens' policies to present a detailed discussion of the Green Party's electoral platform for the Bundestag election of December 2, 1990, which, as will be recalled, was the first free and fair election in a unified Germany since 1932. Following this presentation, the reader might perhaps have a better understanding as to why the Green Party failed to overcome the 5 percent representational threshold which, in turn, led to the party's virtual disappearance from the first all-German Bundestag after a stint of nearly eight years as the parliamentary representative of the post-APO German Left. Addressing a wide array of fascinating issues with often innovative policy proposals, the Greens had virtually nothing to say about the mindboggling events which obliterated another German state next to the Federal Republic, caused the collapse of Soviet domination over Eastern Europe, led to the eventual disappearance of the Soviet Union itself as a political entity, and created a fundamentally new paradigm for global politics, German affairs and, of course, the Left. In other words, the Greens had completely missed a political earthquake which changed the world around them. Yet, with all its sins of omission and commission, this document encapsulated the essence of the Greens as the prototypical representatives of Germany's progressive Left at the beginning of a new political era.

Appropriately labeled "Bundestag Election 1990: the Program," this 43-page document comprises one preamble and six sections. The preamble bears the optimistic title "Green is necessary – Green is achievable". It extends over four pages and provides a concise overview of the Greens' visions and priorities. Tellingly, the document begins with the scandalous conditions of the environment. It sees the ecological crisis as much more than the soiling of beaches and the polluting of air. Instead the document argues that this ecological crisis is but the most stark expression of the fundamental bankruptcy of the modernization process as implemented by bourgeois culture. Thus ecological policy is ultimately a policy of complete reculturation, of a fundamental rethinking and reordering of values, structures and behavior. Far beyond the incremental instrumentalization which others might be suggesting, any ecological policy worthy of the name would have to entail a comprehensive restructuration of industrial society, the democratization and pacification of all human relations and lifeworlds, the feminization of society and the establishment of multicultural tolerance.[179]

The preamble explicitly rejects any piecemeal solutions of this crisis, a policy which – according to this document – the other parties have come to advocate by stealing "green ideas" for their rhetoric and, even worse, by applying them in the compartmentalized style of "technocratic management." The preamble stresses all the well-known green values: hostility toward the West, solidarity with the Third World, anti-militarism, radical feminism, anti-etatism, anti-capitalism, anti-industrialism. While these themes recur repeatedly in the more concrete sections of the document, there is one remaining issue in the preamble which is never repeated in any of the subsequent sections: German unification. Beginning with a self-congratulatory paragraph in which the Greens proudly announce that they had always criticized the model of "real existing socialism" and sided with the dissidents of Eastern Europe, this very brief section then proceeds to attack the West German government by labeling it a "pimp" which is coercing the former East Germany (and Eastern Europe) into prostituting its existence and identity for money. This section concludes by deriding the fact that the "Anschluss policy" of the West German government and people is justified and legitimated by invoking nationalist sentiments and making chauvinist appeals.[180] So much for unification! The greens' electoral platform of 1990 has only three brief paragraphs on the most momentous events in postwar history, events which, after all, altered the very political space in which the Greens and their allies would henceforth operate. None of the following six sections had anything to say about German unification, let alone offer any policy proposals. As will also be evident in subsequent sections of this book, the revolutions of 1989–90 were simply not relevant to the Greens and their world, beyond a sheepish silence, followed by total confusion and a helpless flailing against the evils of the Kohl government. Small wonder, then, that the Right had a virtual monopoly in formulating and implementing policies which shaped this new "German order."

Section 1 of the document is devoted to ecology. Entitled "The Greenhouse Effect: the Hole in the Ozone Layer," and subtitled "The Ecological and Social Restructuring of the Industrialized Countries," this section offers a ten-page concretization of the ecological themes raised in the platform's preamble. Policy proposals abound. Here is a selection of the most interesting ones. The realization of an international policy which would see to it that the average global temperature would not rise by more than 2 degrees centigrade by the year 2010. This, so the argument states, would be the absolute limit in an increase in global warming which the eco-system could still sustain without incurring further damage. According to the Greens, this international policy would have to mandate, among other things, a 50 percent reduction in carbon dioxide emissions; an immediate stoppage of the production of all nuclear energy; the cessation of the burning of any fossil fuels by 2010; and the immediate and complete prohibition of the production and consumption of any chemical products which contain materials detrimental to the ozone layer.[181]

Turning to the Federal Republic, the green platform presents concrete policies in the areas of ground and air transportation, chemical production, genetic engineering, agricultural production, ecological garbage disposal and recycling, and nature conservation. The demands are interesting. In terms of implementing their policies regarding an ecologically improved transportation, the Greens demand: (1) that by 1995 all passenger cars be required to have a fuel efficiency which permits them to cover 100 kilometers on four liters of gas; (2) that the three-way catalytic converter become a requirement; (3) that a speed limit of 100 kilometers an hour be introduced on the German superhighways, the famed *Autobahnen*, which currently have no speed limits; (4) that driving be limited, and cycling and walking be given priority at all times; (5) that gasoline taxes be raised; (6) that the Swiss model of "rail and bus 2000" which is clearly designed to displace automobile transportation in the long run be adopted in Germany as well; (7) that supersonic air travel be banned; (8) that all military air traffic be prohibited; (9) that any air travel below the distance of 800 kilometers be forbidden; (10) that air travel be much more heavily taxed.[182]

Demands for what the Greens term "soft chemistry" are at the core of their environmental policy.[183] Crucial here is the party's desire to have all products banned immediately which in any way harm the ozone layer. Thus the Greens have been the vanguard in educating the German public against the use of plastic cutlery, plates, tables, chairs, toys, packaging, plastic shopping bags and other disposable items common to any consumer-oriented capitalist society. With Germany adopting Europe's – indeed the world's – strictest environmental protection laws in 1992, in which many aspects of the Greens' soft chemistry policy were prominently featured, it is safe to say that in this area the Greens' policies did not remain confined to the "input" ledger of the German political system.

The Greens demand a five-year moratorium on all areas of genetic engineering, including genetic research.[184] Concerning agricultural production, the Greens attack all aspects of agribusiness, demanding small and ecologically sound farming instead. It is especially in this policy area that the Greens revert to an idealized glorification of preindustrial life which – at least in our interpretation based on reading these passages in the context of the horrible legacy of Germany's recent history – borders on the reactionary. The document argues that traditional farming, as exercised by the preindustrial peasantry, created an ecological, as well as productive, harmony between the land and its tillers which modern capitalism destroyed.[185] The text extols traditional farming and peasant-based agricultural production to the point where it is clear that their reinstatement has become part of the Greens' policy agenda.

In terms of waste disposal, the Greens' policy opposes burning or depositing of waste in landfills. Instead, the Greens argue for a policy of garbage prevention and massive recycling.[186] Lastly, the Greens oppose the current system of nature conservation, which they see as too restrictive and ghettoized in the sense that it concentrates almost exclusively on nature parks, nature preserves and other protected areas, while leaving the rest of the land open to the rapacity of industrial capitalism. Green policy on this issue pursues a more holistic approach which would be part of the much larger aspect of ecologically sound engineering, ecologically sensitive landscape architecture and environmentally conscious planning.

Section 2 of the document deals with peace. Entitled "Disarmament Now! For a Europe without Military Blocs," it delineates the Greens' policy on disarmament and related security matters in four pages. Concretely, in this segment the Greens articulate their demands concerning unilateral disarmament, Germany's immediate withdrawal from NATO and its abstention from any military pact that might replace it such as the Western European Union, a nine-nation European military consortium.[187] Green policy also includes demands for the abolition of all nuclear, biological and chemical weapons on German soil; the dismantling of the German army, the Bundeswehr; the conversion of all military production to civilian and ecologically sound goods and services; the immediate cessation of all low-level flights over the territory of the Federal Republic; annulment of the Wartime Host National Support agreement with the United States, which permits the United States the stationing of six divisions on German soil during peacetime as well as the usage of depots, matériel and technical assistance in a crisis situation or during war. In the Greens' eyes, this agreement renders Germany complicitous with any American military action against third parties, who, so the Greens believe, will inevitably be countries of the Third World. Green policy also demands the immediate cessation of all exports of German military products, a highly lucrative business which by 1990 had rendered the Federal Republic the fifth largest exporter of military goods in the world.

Concluding this section of the platform is the Greens' belief in the internationalization of security. Their policy supports the vaunted, though nebulous, "common European home" and approves of the Conference for Security and Cooperation on Europe as the best body to implement and safeguard this new internationalized security arrangement. Being independent of any military bloc does not mean that the Greens intend to pursue a policy of selfishness and autarchy. Aware of the dangers of nationalism, they thus demand that Germany – like all other European countries – be embedded in a collective European security arrangement which should prevent the outbreak of hostilities among its members as well as vis-à-vis countries beyond its proper area.[188]

Section 3 of the document addresses social policy. Bearing the title "Social Rights: the Shaping of Work," it deals with five issues in seven pages. The first topic concerns the Greens' policy of universalizing social protection as a matter of right rather than privilege. The mainstay of their argument pertains to the view that social security and protection should occur independently of work and employment. Thus, green policy demands the payment of DM 1,200 per month for anybody regardless of whether they have ever worked in their lives.[189] Income in the Greens' view has to become independent of work. Income is a fundamental right which society owes its citizens regardless of their ability or desire to work. The Greens, as already argued, view this "decoupling" of social protection from the world of labor and production as particularly urgent in an era when the brutal exigencies of capitalist accumulation are in the process of dividing Germany into a rich, highly qualified "two-thirds" in the middle and at the top of the social structure, with a poor, increasingly unemployable, often foreign and disproportionately female "one-third" at the bottom of it.[190] Add to this the unexpected social costs of the unification process, and the urgency of social policy as a corrective and challenge to the existing capitalist system becomes even more compelling.

The second topic within section 3 concentrates on work. This section combines, on the one hand, a number of policy areas which the Greens share with the German labor unions with, on the other hand, policy proposals which remain much too New Left for organized labor. As to the former, the most prominent ones pertain to the Greens' demand for a drastic reduction of the weekly working hours, favorably mentioning the 35-hour work week as we discussed above, but already demanding its 30-hour successor.[191] The Greens demand this shortening of working hours not only for the conventional reasons associated with the trade union movement for over a century, but also to alleviate the patriarchal division of labor in which women have been relegated to the "private sphere" of reproduction while men have constituted the "public sphere" of production. By reducing working hours in such a significant way, the Greens' policy is to alter the conventions of the "normal" workday, thereby facilitating the much-needed role reversal in which men become active in the domestic area while women have the opportunity to hold jobs in the public sphere.[192] To that end, Green policy stresses the need to treat parttime work as the exact legal and contractual equivalent to fulltime employment. The clear preference given to the latter by employers and the legal system has, in the eyes of the Greens, as well as of labor, further corroborated the unequal treatment of men and women in Germany's labor market. Still in full conformity with the unions, the Greens have emphatically rejected any models of flexibilization or deregulation which would permit work to be conducted on weekends, holidays, nights and other periods. In notable contrast to some Social Democrats – Oscar Lafontaine in particular – who seemed willing to introduce certain deregulatory measures for the purpose of making working time more flexible, the Greens sided with the unions on this issue in defending the sanctity of certain work-free time (weekends, nights, holidays) as a space of collective decommodification free of the exigencies of the capitalist accumulation process.[193]

Concerning the Greens' work demands which go beyond the current policy horizons of the trade unions, the policy on affirmative action stands out as previously mentioned. Featured under the German term of *Quotierung* – thus using the word "quota" in this context in a way which has remained anathema to the US equivalent of the Greens' progressive stand – Green affirmative action policy is explicit. Following their own practice in which women hold at least 50 percent of all official party positions, the Greens demand that all jobs in Germany as well as positions in vocational training programs be occupied by women to a minimum of 50 percent.[194] It is important to mention in this context that the Greens' policy in terms of demanding this rigid quota of complete job equality for men and women pertains as much to the state sector as it does to private industry.

The third topic in section 3 focuses on what the Greens call "solidaristic health policy." Starting with the premise that health is socially stratified and that "poverty sickens," the Greens center their health policy on the prevention instead of the treatment of illness. "Green health policy has to begin with a serious consideration of social and ecological questions. This, in turn, means that green health policy is inextricably linked to labor, social, housing, transportation, energy, recycling and agricultural policies."[195] Especially prescient is the Greens' criticism of how illness – that is the failure to protect health – is valorized by the medical establishment and the pharmaceutical industry, both of which are among the wealthiest sectors in German society. Characteristic of the Greens' libertarian-anarchist streak is the opinion voiced in the ensuing paragraph of the document which denounces "the compulsion to be healthy" that is exacted by the uniformization process of advanced industrial capitalism, and extols instead the right to be ill. This view is a bit disturbing in that, in its attempt to be fair and helpful to sick people, it declares illness to be normal to the point of rendering it almost a matter of choice, where some people might in fact opt to be ill rather than healthy. Among the most salient demands of the Greens' health policy is the democratization of the health system; the widening and strengthening of patients' rights and privacy, which of course are part of this democratization; and the preservation and expansion of various natural therapies which, in the Greens' view, form the cluster of a "soft medicine" in opposition to the high-tech, high-chem version of the medical establishment.

The fourth topic in section 3 concentrates on housing policy. Here the Greens' policy emphasizes the necessity to intensify the construction of low-income housing. Moreover, their policy also demands strict ceilings on rent; legislation against speculative purchases of real estate; the abolition of tax breaks for the acquisition of older housing; and a prohibition against constructing in metropolitan areas single-family houses suburbstyle, on the one hand, and large apartment complexes, on the other.[196] Rather, the Greens would like to see housing construction occur on vacant lots or in unused industrial areas.

These demands link up with the fifth and final topic delineated in this segment of the electoral platform, democratic and ecologically oriented urban planning. Much skimpier in content than the other policy areas of this section, the Greens underline their belief in having citizens participate in every phase of planning and development likely to alter their community's structure and space.[197]

Section 4 of the document is dedicated to women. Entitled "Emancipation and Self-Determination for Women," this section documents in seven pages the Greens' deep commitment to policies of feminist politics. Short of their unmitigated engagement on behalf of environmental protection, there is nothing in the Greens' policy catalogue which even approximates the passion aroused by feminist politics. For the Greens, feminist politics forms the core for the emancipation of humanity and not just the liberation of a particular group. The Greens have thus universalized one of the most fundamental credos of their politics, which could potentially have remained ghettoized in a gender-specific and ascriptive milieu. As a picture in the document of a graffito on a male statue poignantly amplifies: "The future is female or not at all."

The long-term policy goal of the Greens is the abolition of patriarchy. To that end, they have formulated three clusters of policies and strategies which are to make women into autonomous and independent beings, not reproduce them as "parts" of structures, be they the family, the division of labor or other domains of patriarchal power. The first cluster focuses on the right to material independence. Here, the Greens reiterate a number of points which are featured parts of their social policy. Prominent among them are the call for a 50 percent female quota for all jobs in Germany; the introduction of the six-hour working day which amounts to a 30-hour working week; the demand for a three-year, fully paid leave of absence with complete job guarantees for parents (not just mothers) with children up to the age of 12; the abolition of job-sharing arrangements and home employment both of which, in the Greens' view, severely disadvantage women; and the equal treatment of fulltime and parttime work. In the context of material independence for women, the Greens also demand the recognition of prostitution as a fully legitimate form of employment. While not illegal in the Federal Republic, the earnings received for sexual services are deemed "immoral," which renders the labor performed beyond the regular purviews of taxation, social benefits and – most important – the country's very powerful labor laws. The Greens' policies to protect the prostitutes by making them fully integrated participants in the labor market also include the demand that the currently existing compulsory health examinations, just like the specially designated "red-light districts," be abolished.[198]

The second cluster centers on policies designed to guarantee the right to autonomous lifestyles. First, the Greens want to have marriage as a privileged institution of cohabitation abolished. Since the privileges always accrue to the husband, the Greens see marriage, at least as constituted in the Federal Republic, as one of the bastions of male dominance in society. Second, Green policy aims at making lesbian lifestyles and forms of cohabitation completely acceptable in Germany. Discrimination against lesbians, still widely practiced in virtually every aspect of German public life such as housing, the labor market and the granting of children's custody, forms the core of this policy area.[199]

The third cluster concerns the right to the integrity and autonomy of women's bodies. At centerstage here is the Greens' unmitigated support for women's reproductive rights, meaning, of course, their opposition to any intervention by the state in terms of impeding, let alone criminalizing, a woman's decision to have an abortion. Surprisingly, the Greens go to some length to state that they recognize the validity, even necessity, of having unborn life protected in some manner. But this, so they argue, is not within the purview of the state. Instead it pertains to the women alone, along with responsible behavior by men, who would have to become fully fledged partners in an enlightened policy of contraception and family planning.

The Greens are adamant opponents of any kind of surrogate motherhood and high-tech manipulations of fertility. They also reject sterilization and abortion as measures of population control, particularly in the Third World. Above all, they have been the most vocal protagonists against any kind of sexual violence committed against women and girls. The Greens' policies have been in the forefront in establishing houses for battered women throughout Germany. Largely as a consequence of the Greens' feminist engagement, issues such as domestic violence, pornography and sex tourism have emerged in the open and form part of the public debate in the contemporary Federal Republic. In terms of the expression of sexuality, the Greens want to arrive at a point where women can enjoy pleasurable, emancipated sex without being subjected to the sexual exigencies of male domination.[200]

Section 5 of the document deals with policies concerning the larger areas of democracy and justice. Entitled "Ecological Restructuring with Radical Democracy," this four-page segment reveals the Greens' radical orientation to the problems of state–society relations, focused on the grass roots and plebiscitarian in style. Democracy to the Greens "is a method of constant and renewed struggle for freedom via interference, protest, civil disobedience and social mobilization in opposition to all structures of power."[201] This German equivalent to the African-American "fight the power" approach to politics characterizes the core of the Greens' relations to political order, at least in terms of the input side of their policy formulations. Invoking the popular, though largely peaceful, revolutions which toppled the Stalinist order in 1989–90, the Greens believe that such movements, coupled with their western predecessors of the late 1960s, 1970s and 1980s, will also help democratize western European societies as well.

The first segment of section 5, entitled "Basic Rights," is a fundamental reaffirmation of civil society's autonomy and the individual's rights vis-à-vis permanent encroachments by the state. "A liberal democracy," according to the platform's statement, "does not need any protection by the state. Instead, it needs public contestation on the part of its citizens regarding the correct political road. Secret services and Verfassungs'schutz' have to be dissolved without any further ado."[202] The most salient policy proposals concentrate on issues such as the decriminalization of all forms of drug consumption and non-violent crimes, the reduction of all prison sentences, and the complete alleviation of lifelong jail terms. Moreover, they demand an expansion of the powers and rights of defendants and the defense in criminal trials, and the curtailment of all police powers. Above all, the Greens demand the immediate introduction of much more stringent controls concerning the immense proliferation of personal data and their availability to employers and, of course, the state. Green policy has been very committed to fighting what has become known in Germany as the "transparent citizen" (*gläserner Mensch*). Rather, the Greens want a "transparent state" (*gläserner Staat*) instead.[203]

It is precisely this transparent state and a concomitant democratization of all power centers of the economy as well which form the core of the next segment of this section, entitled "Democratization of State and Economy." The Greens demand the creation of access by all citizens to files and information kept on them by the state. They call for the abolition of the 5 percent cut-off clause which has proven a formidable and, in the Greens' view, undemocratic obstacle to the successful formation of small parties in the Federal Republic, thereby obstructing the people's will and distorting the parliamentary representation of Germany's genuine political topography.[204] The Greens seek the abolition of the state's emergency laws, whose passage in the mid-to-late 1960s helped create, as will be recalled, the West German New Left, that is, the Greens' direct predecessors.

In terms of democratizing Germany's economy, the Greens once again pursue policy proposals which are very close to those of the unions. The Greens demand the expansion of all existing forms of codetermination, be it on the shopfloor, in the boardroom or at the level of macropolitics. Labor has to be given decision-making powers in all matters concerning the introduction of new technologies in the production process. Moreover, the Works Constitution Act, which is mainly responsible for regulating most matters concerning firm-specific dimensions of German industrial relations, should be made to become much more sensitive to ecological issues and punitive in case of their disregard by the employers. One of the most interesting, daring – and, of course, profoundly unrealistic – of the Greens' policies in this issue complex is their demand to have Germany's large industrial corporations become much more decentralized. By asking that the participation and ownership of the German banks in the country's leading companies be "reduced to zero," the Greens' policy represents nothing less than a head-on challenge to what arguably has been the most essential – and successful – pillar of capitalism, German style.[205]

The last segment in this section is entitled "multicultural democracy." Here, the Greens demand a policy of open doors and open borders, meaning that anybody should be able to travel, work and live wherever she/he wants. Given the burdens of German history which the Greens – true to their leftist bent – still refer to by the generic "fascism" instead of the more specific "national socialism," Green policy would be to grant asylum in the Federal Republic to anybody fleeing from any adversity, be it political persecution, sexual discrimination, torture or any other human rights violations, which for the Greens include economic deprivation and material indigence.[206]

This issue, perhaps more than any other, highlights certain politically frustrating, maybe even objectively retrograde, aspects of the Greens' unbending (fundamentalist) idealism. In their admirable vision of universal human rights, the Greens dismiss the reality of citizenship based on currently existing nation-states, with the possible exception of the Third World, notably Palestine. The Greens dismiss the reality (let alone the validity) of identities based on citizenship in particular nation-states in Europe. Above all, they have nothing but contempt for any kind of official identification with the German state as constituted in the Federal Republic. In short, the Greens' aversion to the nation-state has led them to base their policies on an elusive notion of global (or European) citizenship, in which political identities are not defined by borders and passports, but by a complete liberty to travel and settle anywhere anybody chooses. True to their anti-statism and anti-nationalism, the Greens basically refuse to recognize the political sovereignty and reality of nation-states. Thus, in their inclusionary zeal, the Greens continue to insist that the Federal Republic's generous asylum practices, which have been guaranteed by Article 16 of the Basic Law, not be changed under any circumstances; meaning, in essence, that anybody arriving in Germany can claim political asylum. This constitutional provision hails from the immediate postwar period when the framers of the Basic Law consciously countered the rabidly racist and exclusionary practices of the Third Reich by giving the new Federal Republic far and away the most welcoming constitutional framework concerning asylum seekers anywhere in Europe. However, this constitutional generosity toward asylum seekers was not accompanied by an equivalent magnanimity toward the extension of the most basic political rights in a liberal democracy, namely the granting of citizenship. The criteria for the latter remained inextricably tied to the racist notion of biological origin based on blood ties (*jus sanguinis*) or, less important, to the cultural exclusivism of belonging to the community of the German *Volk* in some manner (by having graduated from a German school in Romania, for example, or by demonstrating proficiency in the German language).

The fact that the Greens have consistently demanded the immediate cessation of this exclusionary manner in bestowing German citizenship deserves nothing but praise. Yet, their totalistic – and unrealistic – approach to this problem has also led the Greens to oppose any kind of legal initiative which would introduce to the Federal Republic an American-style immigration law based on quotas of admission. To the Greens, the Federal Republic is to remain open to anybody who wants to come and settle there. Regardless of its moral rectitude and "political correctness," this has become an irresponsible position in post-Communist Europe, where borders are more open than ever and income differentials more pronounced as well. This led to the potentially untenable situation of having 438,191 asylum seekers arrive in the Federal Republic in 1992 alone. Making matters worse, existing German law would render it virtually impossible for all but a handful of these asylum seekers ever to obtain full German citizenship, thus enhancing and prolonging an untenable state of ambiguity and limbo. To its great credit, the Social Democratic Party led the effort to institutionalize some kind of immigration law based on official quotas of admission. In a much more ignominious vein, the SPD also agreed as a *quid pro quo* with the conservative Kohl-led government to curtail concomitantly the previous liberal asylum practices. True to their totalism, the Greens (wrongly) rejected the SPD's attempts to introduce some kind of immigration law in Germany, yet also (rightly) denounced the Social Democrats' agreement to the tightening of the country's liberal asylum practices. Thus, to the Greens, immigration and a multicultural society ultimately remain non-political: to them, these are not issues of citizenship based on concrete realities of existing political sovereignties embodied by nation-states, but acts of voluntary inclusion based on affect and a desired universalism. To the Greens, multiculturalism can be willed by decent men and women rather than enacted by states. Thus, the Greens see it as a centerpiece of their multicultural policy to enlighten the German population about its racism and xenophobia. It is interesting in this context – and yet another instance of the Greens' libertarian streak – that they are against any state measures which would declare representatives of the radical Right such as the Republikaner and the Deutsche Volksunion illegal, let alone unconstitutional. According to the Greens, these right-wing groups have to be fought in civil society and not by state fiat exacting their prohibition. Only when they resort to violence to fulfill their political aims should the state, in the Greens' view, respond with punitive measures against the radical right.

Section 6, the last of the Greens' electoral platform, deals with matters concerning global politics and international relations. Entitled "For an Ecologically Solidaristic World Economy," the Greens repeatedly demonstrate their solidarity with the Third World. Among the most salient policies formulated in this section are the demand to have all Third World debt rescinded; to compel the rich First World countries to donate a minimum of 1 percent of their gross domestic product to an "international climate fund" whose main task would be to help Third World countries in the financial plight they suffer as a consequence of the destruction of their environment; to prohibit industrial countries from offering public monies to subsidize their private corporations in order to export ecologically detrimental products to the Third World; to have the European Community's restrictive agricultural protectionism stopped in order to give much-needed help to agricultural exports by the poor southern countries; and to impede the ruthless and uncontrolled exploitation by multinational corporations of most Third World countries.

Postulating a direct link between exploitation, ecological destruction and patriarchal domination, the Greens see their international engagement as part of their struggle for the cultural, political and economic emancipation of all women. In this context, Green policy is bitterly opposed to any kind of artificial population control – thus the control of women's bodies – as often suggested by agencies such as the World Bank and the International Monetary Fund. Women everywhere should be free to have as many children as they want. Sterilization is anathema to the Greens. Instead, they demand proper education and family planning.

The Greens affirm that the United Nations is the medium of a world society and appeal to its further strengthening. They call for the United Nations' Conference on Trade and Development to be established as the guarantor of the interests of the South, for the General Agreement on Tariffs and Trade to be incorporated in the structure of the United Nations and for the World Bank to be dissolved into development funds for Africa, Latin America and Asia.

The document concludes by stating that the eventual liberation of the South from the North is part of the same global liberation struggle as the one by women against men. As behooves their essence as prototypical representatives of the New Left and the new social movements, the Greens have thus transformed the link which Lenin postulated between the working classes of the First World and the exploited nations of the Third World into an alleged alliance between the women of both worlds.

Part III

Politics

Following the presentation of the Greens' genealogy in part I and their ideology and policies in part II, we now proceed to a narrative of their actual politics in part III of our book. Chapter 7 offers a detailed account of the Greens' fate as a party in the West Germany of the 1980s. Organized chronologically, the story takes us virtually full circle from the Greens' early beginnings as a negligible, marginalized entity representing the new social movements and their milieu, to their painful defeat in the first all-German elections since the fall of the Third Reich. And yet, as the narrative in chapter 7 amply demonstrates, this is by no means a story of failure. Indeed, we believe that quite the opposite has been the case. The decade of the 1980s witnessed the transformation of the New Left from the world of movement politics to that of parliaments and parties. Even though this decade ended with the Greens' temporary departure from legislative politics at the federal level, it at the same time witnessed their entrenchment at the state and local levels of German politics. In short, by the early 1990s, the Greens had indeed become part of Germany's political establishment.

This process of institutionalization took an immense toll on the Greens. Always mindful of their origins in movement politics, the Greens never became fully comfortable with their new-found role as a political party. The bitterly divisive and ultimately internecine struggle between the party's "realist" and "fundamentalist" wings is accorded special attention in the chapter. This is not primarily because they highlight a number of political conflicts which have come to identify the essence of the Greens and that of the Left in general. Rather, these conflicts are ultimately about nothing less than the full-scale transformation of progressive politics. Here the Greens' relationship with social democracy and the labor movement are of particular relevance, as are the struggles associated with feminism and ecology, to name but some of the salient ones. By forming an essential part of the restructuring of the

West German Left, the Greens have also played a crucial role in the alteration – we would argue augmentation – of democracy in the Federal Republic.
Thus the intra-Green battles depicted in chapter 7 are not only testimony to
human vanity and querulousness. More important, in our view, they represent a genuine struggle in search of a new progressive reality within and
outside the Greens. This search has gained in urgency since the miraculous
events of 1989–90 which changed the context, substance and form of what
it means to be progressive in a post-Leninist world.

For these reasons, we have devoted an entire chapter to the fascinating
story of the East German Greens. Again proceeding in chronological order,
chapter 8 narrates the (still) incredible rise of the East German Greens and
their allies in the late summer of 1989, from insignificant dissenters in a
Stalinist dictatorship to the unquestioned vanguard of what became the one
and only successful German revolution in history. The story traces the origins
of this East German dissident milieu to the semi-autonomy of the Lutheran
church under the Communist regime. It then proceeds to detail this milieu's
leading role in the "velvet" revolution which defeated one of the most repressive regimes in modern Europe, leading to the disappearance of East Germany as a separate state. A particularly tragic tale in this chapter is the fact
that the progressive elements who led the successful East German revolution
were simply no match for the West German juggernaut's takeover of the
former German Democratic Republic. Once again the East German Greens
and their allies would find themselves in the role of dissenters. This pertains
even to their relations with the West German Greens. While eastern and
western Greens share many things, the chapter makes amply clear that there
are substantial differences which will continue to divide them even after the
formal unification of these two green parties in the spring of 1993.

7

Politics: The World Experienced

In chapters 1 to 4, we looked at the green movement within the context of the Federal Republic's postwar political history, examining its sources in a unique convergence of protesters and activists searching for a parliamentary voice, on the one hand, and Social Democrats disillusioned with the politics of the Schmidt government, on the other. We have seen how the diverse strands of the peace, anti-nuclear and women's movements, the local citizen's initiatives, elements of the extraparliamentary Left and the K-groups were woven together into a loosely unified milieu which in its politicized version was to yield an entity known as the the Greens. We also discussed the fact that the Greens' emergence was not only an act of commission on the part of this post-APO world of decommodified leftists, but also an act of ommission on the part of representatives of the established Left, most notably the Social Democratic Party.

The rise of the Greens was meteoric, surprising sympathizers and alarming critics. Grass-roots green electoral lists at the community and county levels first appeared in 1977, the year of Germany's "hot autumn," in which the state responded with particularly repressive measures to the acuteness of terrorist activities. The first regional green party, the Environmental Protection Party (Umweltschutz Partei) was founded in Schwarmstadt, Lower Saxony, by Karl Beddermann in the same year. In 1978, green parties contested a number of elections in which they attained considerable successes, but failed to overcome the "5 percent threshold" necessary to attain parliamentary representation on any level (federal, state and local) in the Federal Republic. However, this breakthrough occurred only one year later, when the Greens received 5.1 percent in the city-state of Bremen. In less than two years, this motley crew of environmentalists, sixty-eighters, radical leftists and disillusioned social democrats forged a political coalition which was poised to change the landscape of German politics and the Left. Inspired by these victories, Greens ran for the European parliament as the Miscellaneous Political Union

–The Greens (Sonstige Politische Vereinigung–Die Grünen, or SPV), garnering 3.1 percent of the vote despite a hastily organized and poorly publicized campaign. Shortly thereafter, in 1980, encouraged by these results, a spectrum of green political groups founded the federal party, The Greens (Die Grünen), in Karlsruhe to contest Bundestag elections in that year. Although the Greens failed to tally the necessary 5 percent the first time, they succeeded in 1983 when, with 5.3 percent of the vote, they received 27 seats in the Bundestag. Represented by this time in 5 of 11 state parliaments and numerous local bodies (where they had occasionally polled more than 15 percent), the Greens appeared unstoppable by the middle of the decade.

During this same period, red–green coalition governments became mathematically feasible in two important state parliaments – Hamburg and Hessen. Subsequently, SPD leaders Klaus von Dohnanyi and Holger Börner began negotiations with a party they had previously either ignored or despised. The change in attitude appeared most dramatic in Börner's case, for his vitriol toward the Greens and their milieu had become legendary in the violent conflicts over the construction of the new west runway at Frankfurt airport. This opening toward the junior party occurred with the explicit sanction of the SPD's top brass. Party patriarch Willy Brandt boldly discerned "a majority this side of the Union" (that is, to the left of the CDU/CSU) in the Federal Republic. Even though negotiations collapsed in Hamburg and became bogged down in Hessen, it seemed the Greens had established themselves as a permanent fixture on the left margin of the West German party system.

Yet with the same abruptness which had characterized their political ascent, the Greens plunged into a period of deep crisis in 1985. Following six months of intensive effort, red–green negotiations in Hessen collapsed. Furthermore, the streak of green electoral successes disappeared in the Saarland and North-Rhine Westphalia despite very different campaigns. The Saarland's mercurial, iconoclastic, and left–leaning Oskar Lafontaine, arguable the greenest SPD leader at that moment, had not only promised the voters a coalition with the Greens should the SPD emerge as the strongest party after the election, but also demanded that the Greens become active members of his coalition by assuming ministerial posts instead of passively "tolerating" an SPD minority government. This was a bold step in the political climate of the FRG at the time. At social democracy's helm in the Federal Republic's largest state, North-Rhine Westphalia, stood Johannes Rau, a popular and paternal man of the SPD's center who categorically refused to work with the Greens and openly campaigned for an absolute majority for the SPD, in good part to keep the Greens from the helm of government. Remarkably, these diametrically opposed approaches by the Social Democrats to the green challenge led to identical results: the Greens failed to clear the 5 percent hurdle and the SPD gained an absolute majority in both states. While impressive achievements, these social-democratic victories were also the result of green blunders.

The Greens themselves were quick to draw the conclusion that these defeats had been "home-made debacles." As the cement of the previously effortless successes dissolved, the gap between realists, who advocated coalitions with the SPD, and fundamentalists, who were set on a strategy of opposition through the movement, widened dangerously. At a special party convention called in Hagen during the summer of 1985 to evaluate the defeats in North-Rhine Westphalia and the Saarland, tensions exploded into open polemic. Despite repeated attempts at reconciliation over the next six years, the Greens continued to hover in a permanent state of division, a crisis of orientation.[1] Until the early 1990s, the party was riven by repeated purges, departures and splits.

The election of 1986–7, when the Greens boasted victories in Hamburg (10.4 percent) and Hessen (9.4 percent) as well as an expansion of their representation in the Bundestag (8.3 percent), seemed to signal an electoral restabilization in the Greens' favor. While the success temporarily restored a certain camaraderie between the warring factions, the showing at the polls did not alter the party's fundamental lack of unity and direction. This became painfully evident the following spring. In Hessen the red–green coalition, the model experiment in the politics of the realists, dissolved following much acrimony between red and green coalition partners. And the conservatives rode the "red–green experiment" to an electoral triumph for themselves, yielding a Bonn-style CDU/FDP government in Hessen as well. Meanwhile in Hamburg, the obstructionist policies of the Greens, a model for the politics of the fundamentalists, drove Mayor Klaus von Dohnanyi to seek a coalition with the FDP, and prompted disappointed potential green voters to give him the necessary majority to attain his goal.

Taken together, these events signaled a portentous shift. The apparent inability of the Greens to achieve concrete results as a party of either opposition or government seemed to have exhausted the patience of both their voters and their only possible ally, the SPD. The crisis of orientation during which the course of action was debated among the Greens within a stable environment of steady electoral support and continuing dialogue with the Social Democrats, seemed to give way to a period of stagnation when the options of pure opposition, the Hamburg model, and of coalition, the Hessen model, were – for the time being, at least – unattainable.

Based on this cursory sketch of Green political history, we can distinguish five essential phases of development.

1 The period of formation, bounded roughly by the Hot Autumn of 1977 and the formation of the SPV to run in the 1980 European elections, during which a politically heterogeneous array spanning from left to right sought to organize green potential into various local and state electoral initiatives.

2 The period of struggle for the political fate of ecology between Left and Right, concentrated during the first six months of 1980 when the federal party was founded and its first program drafted. The leftist red-greens skillfully machinated an alliance with the centrist green-greens, and they together set the new party on a political footing unacceptable to the Right.

3 The period of electoral expansion which began shortly after the Greens' defeat in the 1980 federal election and continued until the defeat in the Saarland in March, 1985.

4   The period of the orientation crisis, which began properly with the formation of
    the fundamentalist and realist factions in 1982, intensified first around red–green
    coalition negotiations in Hessen in 1984, and were further exacerbated following
    the losses in the Saarland and North-Rhine Westphalia.
5   The period of political stagnation and marginalization, subsequent to the Greens'
    defeats in Hamburg and Hessen during the spring of 1987 and culminating in
    their relegation from the Bundestag following their electoral debacle on Decem-
    ber 2, 1990. While the Green share of the vote appeared to stabilize above the
    5 percent survival mark, it seemed impossible to expand this margin without a
    credible commitment to a pragmatic reform policy. At the same time, the only
    viable partner for such reforms – the Social Democrats – seemed to turn their
    back on the Greens. The segments of the SPD Left which had fought for an
    opening toward the eco-party joined forces with the party's Right in the cam-
    paign to capture an absolute majority or reestablish the social–liberal coalition
    with the FDP. Even if many Social Democrats continued to admire the content
    of the Green's demands, they were frustrated and disheartened by their unpre-
    dictable and "irresponsible" tactics.

In the body of this chapter, we will examine these five phases, paying
particular attention to the last two.[2] We wish to investigate the phases of crisis
and stagnation in more detail because they seem to represent a developmental block in the evolution of the Greens into a leftist, parliamentary party
with an identity distinct from the SPD but open toward constructive cooperation with it. We will seek to explain this block not only in terms of internal developments and strife within the Green Party, but with reference to
the SPD and the experiences of the Left during the late 1960s and the 1970s.
As we will see, the informal rules and principles governing the Greens' internal
relations, the consuming, unproductive Fundi/Realo conflict, a sometimes
paranoid mistrust of the SPD often combined with the latter's own phlegmatic,
anachronistic policies, and a deep ambivalence toward parliamentarism and
reform – all these factors converged in an unfortunate way in the years
between 1985 and 1987. These internecine battles left the Greens – and by
political osmosis, the SPD as well – immensely weakened in their ability to
find any appropriate responses to the momentous changes wrought by the
events of 1989–90. Nowhere in the West was the Left as ill prepared for these
immense changes as in the Federal Republic. In our conclusion, we will
outline the consequences of these developments for the Left as a whole.

Formation and Cooptation:
From Red to Green to Red Again

During the formative years stretching from 1977 to 1980, numerous local
and regional green electoral movements were founded. Loosely organized
and highly decentralized, the various slates and parties encompassed an
astonishingly broad political spectrum. While the extreme and moderate left
groups which eventually ended up controlling the party and defining its

identity throughout all of the 1980s until today were quick to organize, the initial impetus for a green party came principally from conservatives: most notably, ecologically oriented Christian Democrats such as Herbert Gruhl, "value-conservatives" such as the colorful farmer-activist Baldur Springmann, and moderate anthroposophic organizations such as August Hausleiter's Independent Germans' Action (Aktion Unabhängiger Deutscher, AUD), the Action for a Third Way (Aktion 3. Weg, A3W) and the Achberg Circle. While some nationalist and neo-fascist groups close to the NPD tried to infiltrate the Greens and establish a parliamentary beach-head, their efforts were frustrated early on. Members of the Federal Republic's neo-Nazi fringe were immediately exposed and expelled by these early green organizations. The superficial affinities between the Greens' precursors and those of National Socialism – Romanticism, love of nature, dislike of liberal capitalism, anti-western attitudes – were insufficient to prevent the expulsion and marginalization of neo-Nazi tendencies, an encouraging symptom of the democratic and anti-authoritarian attitudes which had taken root in West German political culture since the war.

Several of the key figures during the early years of the eco-party, such as Petra Kelly and Alexander Schubert, were disgruntled ex-SPD activists. Some found their way into the Greens via the new social movements; others through the rapidly disintegrating "orthodox" revolutionary, Marxist cadre parties or the scattered groupings of the "undogmatic" Left aligned with the Socialist Office (Sozialistisches Büro, SB) headquartered in Offenbach or the Frankfurt Spontis. But they were a minority. The principal initiative at the time came from the Right.

This was evident during the formative phase of the Green List for Environmental Protection (Grüne Liste für Umweltschutz, GLU) in Lower Saxony. The Environmental Protection Party (Umweltschutz Partei, (USP),[3] founded in early 1977 by Karl Beddermann, was *the* predominant regional eco-party, which in one way or another influenced the founding of all the rest. The struggles surrounding the three nuclear sites at Grohnde, Wyhl and Gorleben climaxed in 1977. These conflicts politicized many otherwise conservative farmers and middle-class people, especially via citizens' initiatives.[4] However, while the citizens' initiatives clearly fertilized the soil, the party "did not emerge out of a broad discussion of the citizens' initiatives, but rested on the initiative of individuals" such as Beddermann. The USP's founders and first members were anything but young radicals. Indeed, they were hostile towards the *Chaoten*, the longhaired radicals with whom they had little, if anything, in common, and whose participation they perceived as detrimental to their cause. The USP advocated a solution to ecological problems from within the system (*systemimmanente Lösung*).

Its members' motives for establishing a party were principally strategic. Most of them were not so much interested in "new politics" as disgruntled by the SPD's neglect of their cause and the maltreatment of the citizens' initiatives by the bureaucracy. They aimed not at the establishment of a "long-term party with the broadest possible base, but the most effective form of protest."[5] The idea was not to replace the citizens' initiatives[6] but to draw the attention of established politicians, without fundamentally challenging the political system. The USP proclaimed its goal as sending warning signals (*Denkzettel*) to the established parties.[7]

By the time of the local elections that fall, two other groups had also entered the running. The first was the GLU, a pure ecology group which sought to offer a "total socioeconomic alternative" to the established parties.[8] The second comprised a leftist citizens' initiative, the Voters' League, Nuclear Power, No Thanks! (Wählergemeinschaft, Atomkraft, Nein Danke!, WGA). While both succeeded in garnering a small percentage of votes and winning some local posts, none reached the critical 5 percent mark which would have given them parliamentary representation. But encouraged by their recent success and electoral pragmatism, the USP and GLU merged in December 1977, assuming the latter's name.

Naturally the Left was irked by its exclusion from the GLU. The WGA demanded that the GLU open itself and become the representative of all forces in the extraparliamentary movement. It invoked the principle of a rainbow coalition (*bunte Liste*) as it had been developed in Hamburg in the fall of 1978 largely through the influence of the communist KB.[9] Meanwhile, unhindered by the exclusionary declaration which the GLU passed against its members in March 1978,[10] the KB in Lower Saxony pursued its Leninist tactic of infiltrating and influencing the GLU. However, while the KB's machinations undoubtedly planted a fundamentalist germ in the GLU, the door was opened to the Left through a more subtle dynamic.

Party debates over the participation of the radical Left, and attempts to unite programmatically the currents already within the GLU, promoted the coalescence of a strong centrist faction[11] in which moderate organizations such as the AUD, Achberg Circle and traditional environmental groups gained considerable influence.[12] The Right subsequently made an effort to reconsolidate its predominance in the GLU, with Herbert Gruhl's newly founded Green Action Future (Grüne Aktion Zukunft, GAZ) playing a pivotal role. GAZ functioned "as a crystallization point for those who did not work toward a fundamental alteration of democratic forms of participation but were rather inclined toward an authoritarian style of leadership. . . ."[13] This, however, directly conflicted with core principles of the centrist groups, making an alliance with the Left seem more attractive, despite considerable disagreements over economic and social policy. In Lower Saxony as elsewhere, the Right lost its battle with the Left for the favored position of the center over the issue of participatory democracy.

Given the central importance of radical democratic principles, why did the GLU continue to present itself as an ecology party? While ecology obviously possessed a high priority for the activists, it attained centrality largely for reasons embedded in the strategic situation and developmental history of the party. The party contained politically heterogeneous groups which disagreed on many policy issues. In order to break the 5 percent barrier, it was imperative that the various currents find some ground for cooperation. At the same time, the party leadership began to feel that a more comprehensive program was necessary if the GLU was to be transformed from a "protest party" to a "program party." Ecology answered to both the strategic and programmatic needs. "The more widely the concept of ecology was grasped, and the more strongly the primacy of environmental conflicts over traditional dimensions of politics was affirmed, the higher was the integrative power of the young party."[14] The primacy – and ambiguity – of ecology served as a unifying formula for both Right and Left, a lowest common denominator between two otherwise hostile camps.

By contrast, in city-states such as Berlin and Hamburg, with a larger, more lively leftist political culture, ecology did not become as central. There the Left had an open field and was able to assert its control more quickly. Thus, rather than develop a "green" party, Berlin gave birth to an "alternative list,"[15] Hamburg to a "rainbow list"; in both, ecology was but one component of an extensive list of mainly traditional socialist concerns.

As the process of regional party formation spread and accelerated throughout the Federal Republic during 1978 and 1979, the battle between Left and Right for the fate of the green electoral movement became more pronounced. In North-Rhine Westphalia (NRW), one of the few open spots left on the political map of budding ecology parties, Friedrich Wegener, a disciple of Gruhl, founded a skeletal GLU-NRW in hopes of heading off the leftist rainbow lists which had already emerged further in university towns such as Cologne, Bielefeld, Bochum, Bonn, and Essen. The process of party formation was now being driven more by competition of nationally organized, political tendencies than by the grass-roots evolution of the citizens' initiatives.

The stakes in this race for control over green politics increased in 1979 when the possibility of constituting a green slate for the upcoming European elections became a subject of active discussion.[16] The Left was initially skeptical. This opened the field to center-right forces.[17] On March 17, 1979 in Frankfurt an alliance of GAZ, GLU, AUD and the Green List Schleswig-Holstein founded the Miscellaneous Political Union or SPV, which was to become the pilot organization for the federal Green Party. A ten-person organizational and program committee had negotiated the alliance in the face of protest emanating from leftist groups such as the Bremen Green List, Rainbow List of Hamburg and the Alternative List-Berlin.[18] In the elections for the European parliament held on June 17, the SPV tallied 3.2 percent of the vote.

Encouraged by this result, the SPV called an open program congress on November 4, 1979 to discuss the program and strategy of a possible federal green party. Many leftists were in attendance, but the conservatives successfully implemented a measure – aimed primarily at the Communists – denying voting rights to individuals who were already members of other parties or party-like organizations. This effectively excluded the Left from the process. The first strategic victory in the battle for the federal party was therefore won by the Right.

However, the Right was forced into retreat at the program congress in Saarbrücken on March 21–3. While basic agreement was quickly achieved on ecological issues, the discussions of social and economic policy soon degenerated into a Left–Right confrontation. Particularly explosive were the issues of homosexuality and immigration. (Curiously, though, there developed quite a bit of convergence between Left and Right on issues related to peace and foreign policy.) The Left also advanced standard proposals from the union agenda such as qualitative economic growth and a 35-hour working week, and embraced the feminist demand for abolition of the Federal Republic's highly restrictive abortion law as represented by "Section 218" of the country's criminal code.

In this instance the Left prevailed. The attack was spearheaded by the Communists. Employing classic Leninist tactics they "infiltrated" the program committee. Allying with the centrist groups like the GLU and AUD, alternative and rainbow groups from Berlin, Hessen, Bremen, Hamburg and NRW gained admission to the committee. The center-left majority then pushed through a draft program which was clearly unacceptable to the Right. Thereafter, committee member Marie-Luise Beck-Oberdorf said, "one soon didn't trouble oneself any more to create a consensus but ignored the demands of the moderates and declared the proposals of the Left as the program."[19] Beck-Oberdorf concluded, not too surprisingly, that this underhanded maneuvering was largely the work of former members of K-groups long schooled in conspiratorial politics.

The Right felt itself sorely used and demanded that a new program be drafted. The Left did then proffer an olive branch in the form of a moderate electoral platform at the congress in Dortmund on June 21–2. But the conservatives received a final, intolerable slap in the face when, in the elections to the federal executive committee, the assembly twice refused to elect Gruhl to one of the committee's three offices. Members of GAZ, Green List Schleswig-Holstein and AUD walked out of the congress. The Right had lost and the left-center coalition had captured the green electoral movement. Emerging from this unexpectedly easy victory, the Left proceeded to consolidate its position permanently.

The most important turn of events during the formative phase was the triumph of the center-left coalition in the regional and federal parties and the Right's concomitant exclusion. While some conservative ecological organizations, especially Gruhl's GAZ, continued their bid for power, they met with no success and their influence plummeted with astonishing speed. However, other principles and practices, often the result of historical particularity and circumstance, were also established during this period and proved to have a significant impact during the ensuing years of crisis and conflict. We have seen that the centrality of ecology in the green movement in part reflected the need for unity and identity in a politically diverse organization struggling to establish itself against existing parties. It did not result directly from its objective or material importance. The arguments for democracy, openness and the protection of minorities which the Left had so skillfully used to seize influence over key green organizations, as in the cases of the GLU and the SPV, would later be deployed by similar "agile minorities" within the party, often ex-Communists turned fundamentalist, to prevent majority criticism or to legitimize the blatant undermining of democratic processes. Finally, the Greens continued to claim that they represented interests which cut across the political spectrum and which, so the Greens argued, were "neither right nor left but ahead," long after this claim ceased to correspond to the actual reality informing the party. In sum, as is so often the case with political organizations, principles and practices stemming from the Greens' formative phase assumed an aura of universal validity and legitimating power long after the disappearance of the particular historical circumstances in which they were grounded.

The Phase of Expansion: "Grün und kein Ende?" – Green and No End?

During most of the postwar period, a variety of factors had conspired to make the political landscape of the Federal Republic seem the impregnable preserve of the SPD, FDP and CDU/CSU. Surrounded by a legal shield, most notably the 5 percent clause, these three parties successfully "oligopolized" all political life in the Federal Republic from the mid-1950s. Compared to some of its stormier neighbors in Europe, notably France and Italy, the Federal Republic had earned the laurel of being a stable democracy, where governmental shifts were rare, where the differences between Left and Right were quite small in action, if not in rhetoric, and where a continuity was all but guaranteed by virtue of the participation of the Free Democrats in every governing coalition. Indeed, the electoral stability and continuity were so high that all three instances of governmental change in the Federal Republic's 44-year existence – 1966, 1969 and 1982 – were the results of shifts in coalitional allegiances rather than of substantial changes in the political preference of voters. It is important to keep this in mind in order to understand just how remarkable and unsettling was the green electoral success at the time.

Shortly after the Greens' first feeble steps, when the 5 percent hurdle still seemed insurmountable, the party began not only to clear this barrier, but to do so with a comfortable margin. As already mentioned, the first major green electoral breakthrough materialized in the city-state of Bremen, where the party garnered 5.1 percent in 1979. Further encouraging results occurred with the Alternative List's 7.2 percent in West Berlin in May 1981 and the 7.7 percent of the Hamburg Green Alternative List (GAL) in June of the following year. That fall, the Hessian Greens reached the 8 percent mark. And in March 1983 the Greens leapt the highest barrier of all, the one into the German federal parliament, the Bundestag, capturing 5.6 percent of the vote and 27 seats. There were, of course, also failures during this period. Interestingly, however, these occurred exclusively in relatively conservative provinces with more moderate green parties, such as Bavaria (October 1982, 4.6 percent) Rhineland-Palatinate (March 1983, 4.5 percent) and Schleswig-Holstein (March 1983, 3.6 percent). The center-left model appeared better poised to mobilize a larger basis of electoral support than its center-right counterpart.

As many observers both within the party and outside of it noted during this period, there was a certain automatism in the Greens' expansion. Success seemed to have curiously little to do with what green candidates and leaders did or said. In fact, the four principal reasons for the Greens' string of electoral victories were external, though it must certainly be added that the Greens capitalized effectively on the opportunities provided.

First, the West German peace movement reached its climax during just this period between 1983 and 1984, when the NATO double-track decision was ratified by the Bundestag. The Greens were the only party to have unequivocally opposed the euromissiles and supported the peace movement in the preceding years, and they became the main electoral beneficiaries, as well as benefactors, of this development. Moreover, the Greens were strongly identified with the peace movement through the many important figures from the latter who had become green leaders, among them Petra Kelly and Lukas Beckmann.

Second, the images of the established parties had been badly tarnished by the Flick scandal, which implicated top leaders of the CDU/CSU, FDP and SPD in accepting illegal contributions and pay-offs in return for special tax breaks for their parties.[20] The affair was made all the more sordid by its historical resonances, for the Flick family had been deeply entangled with the Nazi regime and had profited greatly from it. Had the newly elected green Bundestag delegation not demanded the establishment of a parliamentary investigative committee, the whole Flick affair would likely have been swept under the carpet. It was only the tireless legal prodding of lawyer Otto Schily, green delegate to the investigative committee, that kept the scandal in the limelight. The considerable corruption of the "saleable republic" which he uncovered let the Greens sparkle with moral superiority. Pointing to the unbroken political influence of the Flicks since Hitler, Schily together with his colleague and ideological compatriot, Joschka Fischer, raised the more disturbing question of subtle and hidden continuities between the Nazi regime and the Federal Republic.

But most of all, the Greens benefited from social democracy's considerable troubles during the early 1980s. Unavoidably, the gradual rightward slide of the Social Democrats under Schmidt had alienated voters, especially on the party's left wing. The departure of the Social Democrats from office signaled not just the collapse of a government but of an entire policy, for which the SPD had no ready or immediate replacement. Among those seeking a clearcut alternative to the Kohl government and disaffected with the SPD, the Greens were the party of choice.

The Federal Republic also experienced an upsurge of popular ecological consciousness beginning in the late 1970s. These concerns were ignored, if not outright rejected, by the mainstream parties. Hence, for the ecologically minded voter, the Greens were the only real choice.

All these factors, visibly expressed in the Greens' increasing share of the vote, forced their supporters and detractors alike to take them more seriously. Having demonstrated their ability to cross the 5 percent hurdle, the Greens represented more than a throw-away vote for a protest party. The simple numeric shift from a three-party to a four-party system made other parties, especially the SPD, take notice of the Greens as parliamentary newcomers. The Greens' arrival in the Bundestag changed the political topography and arithmetic of party politics in the Federal Republic.

Of course, right from the beginning, the relationship between the reds and the greens went much beyond merely tactical and arithmetic considerations. If, as Willy Brandt was fond of saying, the Greens were the "lost children of the SPD," they were sufficiently unruly children to foster considerable disagreement in the "mother party" about what to do with them. Before the fall of the social–liberal coalition in 1982, SPD strategists and thinkers such as Peter Glotz confidently and repeatedly pronounced the Greens to be a temporary phenomenon not to be taken seriously. Furthermore, the SPD, according to this argument, was not in search of a coalition partner.

The end of the SPD's passive disregard for the Greens was signaled in February 1982 shortly before the break-up of the coalition. The SPD's Commission on Basic Values, chaired by Erhard Eppler, Hermann Rappe and Richard Löwenthal, published a paper encouraging discussion with Greens and alternatives.[21] Debate quickly flared up. Chancellor Helmut Schmidt sternly warned the Social Democrats not to flirt with the Greens and flatly rejected the possibility of a coalition with them.[22] A particularly influential argument against red–green convergence was contained in a much-discussed paper by Richard Löwenthal which appeared in a number of social-democratic and trade union journals.[23] In this essay, Löwenthal clearly and brilliantly delineated the choice faced by social democracy in the 1980s: opting for its traditional milieu of largely blue-collar, industrial workers, or choosing the world of the new social movements. Löwenthal made it plain that in his view pleasing both would be virtually impossible, and that a choice for the latter option would irreconcilably alter the party for the worse, while simultaneously enhancing the Greens in stature and importance.

Other social-democratic intellectuals, such as Erhard Eppler, disagreed with the Löwenthal-Schmidt line. Eppler argued that social democracy's future lay precisely in embracing green issues and voters. For these Social Democrats, the Greens constituted a welcome rejuvenating agent not only of social democracy, but of German politics in general. An alliance with the dynamic newcomers, they contended, represented the only realistic chance which the SPD had to topple the conservative coalition in Bonn. Together with the Greens, they believed, it was possible to assemble a majority to the left of the CDU/CSU, perhaps even to that of the coalition government of CDU/CSU and FDP.[24]

Hence, according to this logic, it was only a matter of time before a red–green coalition would become mathematically possible and thus change the nature of politics in the Federal Republic. Even before the emergence of just such a coalition, the leader of the SPD opposition in Lower Saxony insisted, with an eye on the March 1982 state elections, that were it numerically feasible he would seriously have to consider a red–green "cooperation."[25] The first opportunities, however, emerged not in Lower Saxony but in Hamburg and Hessen. These two provinces would come to represent two opposed models for green politics.

From Expansion to Crisis: the Hamburg and Hessian Models

Hamburg

The June 1982 elections in the independent Hanseatic city-state of Hamburg opened the way for the first red-green experiment. Following the elections to the city parliament (Bürgerschaft), a red–green alliance was the only mathematically feasible majority other than a "grand coalition" between the CDU and SPD.[26] In a move soon imitated by other green organizations, the Hamburg GAL offered to enter into a cooperation (but not a coalition) with the SPD in June if it agreed to meet some of the GAL's "unconditional demands." The price for GAL cooperation was not exactly modest: an emergency program against unemployment, annulment of all budgetary austerity measures and an "immediate exit from atomic energy."[27] At its party convention the following week, the SPD voted for further attempts at reconciliation with the GAL. While the SPD Left saw its position as differing from that of the Greens only in the assessment of what was realizable in the short term, the SPD Right was considerably more skeptical of the Green demands.[28]

The ice was broken when the GAL joined the SPD in voting down a motion of no confidence proposed by the CDU. Jörg König invited the GAL to begin formal negotiations. The watchword in the SPD was that the GAL was "maturing." Playing on this, the colorful GAL leader and ex-KB insider Thomas Ebermann hung a sign on the party's office door which proclaimed "Quiet! We're becoming politically mature so that the SPD will like us – GAL."[29] Despite the high spirits, many spoke of a "historical hour."[30] Commented the *Frankfurter Rundschau*: "Hamburg is something of a model case. . . . If it comes to a stable agreement with the GAL, the left social democrats will receive breathing room. If the attempts at compromise fall apart, the line of [SPD rightists] Franke, Renger and Börner will steamroll them."[31] Indeed, during the first week of July, a few weeks into the discussions, the Work Group for Employee Affairs, a reformist circle in Hamburg, began organizing to force new elections.[32] At the same time, Hamburg's SPD mayor, Klaus von Dohnanyi, had to defend his discussions with the GAL against heavy fire from national leaders such as Helmut Schmidt and Hessian prime minister, Holger Börner.[33] It was evident that the Greens were not negotiating with one single SPD but with two warring factions within it.

A slight improvement in the negotiating climate followed when the GAL helped pass a temporary credit authorization during the third week of August to enable Dohnanyi's administration to cover current expenses.[34] But things worsened again abruptly after an incident in which GAL leader Ebermann participated in the occupying of a house by a group of Hamburg squatters. The SPD opened the next round of discussion by declaring that it would continue to clear squatted houses. Though the SPD retreated slightly from this position in subsequent negotiations, the stalemate on central programmatic issues continued unabated.

In the spirit of "unpredictable" and "imaginative" politics, the GAL submitted a proposal to declare Hamburg a nuclear-free zone at the first plenary session of the city parliament after the summer recess. This exacerbated deep tensions within the SPD. Right and Left denounced and defended the idea with equal vigor. In the end, a diluted statement reiterating the formulation of the Munich decision of the 1950s was adopted – a nuclear-free zone was to be a goal, but only a long-term one.[35] SPD rightists tightened ranks yet further. In the meantime, Ebermann challenged the "capability and willingness for peace" exhibited by the CDU and the SPD Right.[36] Here he had gone too far. Even Bodo Schumann, a moderate leftist in the SPD, began to question whether the GAL proposal might not really have had the tactical aim of splitting the Social Democrats.[37] Ignoring this signal, Ebermann sought to drive the wedge even further into the SPD by demanding that the city government employ all its available resources against the pending deployment of the euromissiles.[38]

A virtual impasse had been reached on two issues – atomic energy and an SPD program to expand the city's harbor. Despite the worsening of the situation, Dohnanyi emphasized commonalities between GAL and SPD in ecology and labor market policies during an interview and declared that calling new elections would be avoiding the problem.[39] Shortly thereafter, in early October, Dohnanyi presented a 33-page assessment of the negotiations approved by the party.[40] The Greens voiced their disappointment the next day. They accused the SPD of orchestrating the breakdown of negotiations and of being neither "prepared to compromise" nor "capable of learning."[41] Later that week, a special SPD congress passed a motion by Dohnanyi and the executive committee calling for new elections.[42] The discussions had failed. The shortest legislative period in the history of Hamburg, 196 days to be precise, had come to an end. The GAL lent the SPD motion its votes allowing it to pass against the CDU[43] but declared that it would renew its offer for a possible coalition pending a repetition of the election results.

A week after the SPD's decision to call a new election, the GAL published a paper which stated its ambivalence concerning this move. Playing on Brandt's – as well as Eppler's – phrase, it argued that a "new majority requires a new politics" and implicitly attributed the failure to attain this majority to social-democratic rigidity: "Our door remains open for an SPD ready to compromise."[44] The GAL ran its campaign under the somewhat inflammatory slogan, "Create more pressure: vote GAL."[45] At the same time, its tone was moderate compared to its previous presentation of "unconditional demands."[46]

The GAL's posturing was for nought. The SPD unexpectedly scored an absolute majority, but not in the way one might have expected. Interestingly, the SPD drew its new votes almost exclusively from the bourgeois camp, the CDU and FDP, while the GAL fell just below 7 percent, a hair's breadth shy of its previous result.[47] Unimpressed, the federal Greens expressed shock and amazement, having fully expected a significant increase in their local colleagues' share of the vote.[48]

This reversal, though it ultimately pivoted around very small voter movements, was unexpected for the Greens. Indeed, the entire GAL strategy, masterminded by Ebermann and his sympathizers, aimed at augmenting the already existing cracks within the SPD. By forcing public debate on issues which were controversial within the senior and established party of the traditional Left, the Greens hoped to divert leftist elements from the "concrete faction" of the right and "unmask" the party's essentially "reactionary" stance on green issues. This newly formed eco-socialist red–green block could then gradually gather all forces of the Left behind it and attack the conservatives.

This appeared like a realistic strategy to the Hamburg Greens because of the way they and many other Greens interpreted the "automatism" of the party's and the movement's appeal during the period of expansion. For them, these positive developments were not just the consequence of a favorable, if temporary, alignment of circumstances but the result of a deepening social crisis in the Federal Republic and advanced capitalism. In order to expand their base of support, then, the Greens believed that they needed to do only two things: first, to increase consciousness about the crisis, and second to make it clear that only they represented a progressive solution to it. Dialogue, negotiations or cooperation with the SPD were useful only insofar as they furthered this end. Thus the interest which the Hamburg Greens displayed in compromise and the value which they placed on competition within the political arena were both particularly low. While this strategy was viable under the conditions of automatic expansion, it would not be relevant for a number of years yet to come. And, in any event, the GAL's tactics of divide and conquer underestimated the rapidity with which the SPD would reorient itself and the forces that held the Social Democrats together.

This is not to say that controversy among SPD leaders over the Greens was not heated. The SPD leadership had carefully observed events in Hamburg. Public dissension had emerged among the party's leadership at the beginning of the Hamburg negotiations during the first weeks of July. North-Rhine Westphalia prime minister Johannes Rau voiced his belief that no formal or informal cooperation should occur between the SPD and the Greens, for it would irretrievably damage the SPD's hold on the political center. "We should not pass ourselves off as greener than we can be," he quipped.[49] Schmidt moderated his tone, claiming that the Greens found themselves "in a process of maturation."[50] At the same time, the SPD's Left argued in highly restrained terms for an alliance with the Greens. Brandt reiterated that some red–green cooperation could – and should – not be ruled out for all time. Lafontaine implored that the debate be conducted on substantive rather than tactical grounds because the Greens' electoral mandate could not be ignored.[51] Brandt finally succeeded in capping dissent within the SPD by reaching a temporary truce when he intervened with a "declaration of principles" concerning the Greens and their relation to social democracy: Even though the Greens were not yet ripe as a *bona fide* partner for the SPD, experiments in collaborating with them were certainly in social democracy's long-term interest. Patience became the operative watchword.

Hessen

Such was the mood in the SPD and among the Greens as the site of the "red–green experiment" shifted from Hamburg to Hessen. Comprising large cities such as Frankfurt as well as university towns like Marburg, Hessen has traditionally been one of the "reddest" German states. But its then prime minister Holger Börner belonged to the SPD's moderate wing and during the course of his career had developed a visceral dislike for "chaotics," "vandals" and "alternatives" – that is, Greens. Following a violent confrontation with anti-runway demonstrators at Frankfurt's airport in May 1982, he proclaimed: "I regret that my high government office forbids me to pop these [demonstrators] one in the face myself. It used to be that you took care of things like this on the construction site with a two-by-four (*Dachlatte*)."[52] Not surprisingly, Börner opposed any cooperation with the Greens.

However, the Hessian Greens ranked as one of the most moderate of the green state parties. A circle of fundamentalists around the "radical ecologists" Jutta Ditfurth and Manfred Zieran had briefly dominated the green fraction in the Frankfurt city council. But during 1982, pragmatic currents from the Socialist Office and the "Sponti scene" mobilized to displace them. A group around the future member of parliament and cabinet minister Joschka Fischer, the expatriated French student leader and publisher of *Pflasterstrand*, Daniel Cohn-Bendit, and ex-SPD politician Karl Kerschgens refashioned the Hessian Greens into a bastion for "realism."

Nevertheless, at the beginning of the 1980s the level of red–green rapport in Hessen did not appear significantly higher than in Hamburg. In their 1982 electoral statement, the Hessian Greens did not directly rule out cooperation with the SPD but insisted, instead that "We cannot establish any common ground with a party which, when wielding governmental powers, has not shrunk from implementing civil-war like methods, has completed projects such as [Frankfurt Airport's] West Runway with brutal police violence against the will of the population, and criminalized citizens' initiatives."[53] The reference to the west runway of the Frankfurt airport pertained to the fierce confrontations between the state authorities and demonstrators hailing from the Greens' milieu regarding the extension of the Frankfurt airport by an additional runway. The Greens and their sympathizers opposed this extension of the airport on a number of grounds, all of which were central to their mission and identity. To the Greens, the runway represented a modern, industrial, state-led encroachment on a piece of pristine nature. Few items symbolized the ills of modern industrial capitalism more starkly to the Greens than airports: impersonal, transient, concrete-based industrial structures, serving high-flying business elites and their political minions in their quest to make money, they demolished cherished traditions such as community, contemplation, leisure and nature in the process. Adding a further incentive to the Greens' opposition to the extension of the Frankfurt airport was the fact that it was also designed to augment Frankfurt's role as a military hub for NATO forces, thus, of course, for the United States air force and army. Therefore, in the Greens' eyes, the extension of the airport also symbolized the increased militarization of Germany. Most important, however, it denoted the continued subservience of Germany to American interests. Thus, in addition to violating the sanctity of nature, the Frankfurt airport's west runway was further evidence to the Greens that Germany was not an independent country. Once again, one should not underestimate the centrality which issues pertaining to political sovereignty and autonomy played in the mobilization of the Greens and their sympathizers.

In an official clarification of their position at a state congress later that year, the Greens declared that they were prepared for "cooperation on objective issues" with the SPD but "would make no compromises on questions of life and survival" with the Social Democrats. The Greens ruled out both a coalition with and a "toleration" of any SPD-led government.[54]

Despite this unfavorable climate, the elections on September 26, 1982 again yielded a mathematical majority for a red–green coalition.[55] Börner was thus trapped between his electoral promise and personal determination to shun the Greens, and the need for a parliamentary majority to run the government. Rather than enter negotiations with the Greens immediately, Börner decided to propose a budget first, which would be drafted single handedly by the SPD but which he hoped would be so politically irreproachable that the Greens could not but vote for it.[56]

Meanwhile Börner found his position under heavy fire from the SPD Left, which had traditionally maintained a strong position in Hessen, especially in the south. In September, one month before the election, the SPD's Left denounced Börner's stubborn rejection of a political partnership with the Greens.[57] Pressure mounted further. Immediately after the election, the Greens formally offered "discussions" over programmatic commonalities, and hinted they might help elect Börner to the post of prime minister of Hessen, not by actively voting for him in the legislature, but rather by tolerating him passively in that the Green delegates would not vote against him.[58] Three weeks after the elections, Börner completed a momentous personal and political turnaround. He suddenly shed his previously held "contact phobia" with the Greens, among whom he now claimed to discern "a lot of thoughtful young people, not just troublemakers."[59] Börner even hinted that he might reevaluate his position on atomic energy and reexamine his approval for a third nuclear reactor to be added to a plant at Biblis.[60] But, at bottom, he was motivated mainly by a sense of mission for the party and loyalty to its "lost children." His change of heart did not really extend to his political convictions. Though he was no longer "two-by-four Börner," he was at this time still "concrete Börner."

Unlike the GAL, the Hessian Greens entered preliminary discussions with the SPD without any unconditional demands. Börner remained in office as "chief parliamentary executive."[61] For reasons of electoral timing[62] and due to pressure from the party's Left, Börner declined to call new elections until the fall of 1983. But while he shelved his old anti-Green convictions, Börner felt politically compelled to implement his promised emergency program against unemployment. Green support for the program, enlisted after six negotiating sessions and SPD concessions, was the first turning point in Hessen's red–green experiment.[63] For the first time in the Federal Republic, a significant piece of Social Democrat legislation had been passed with the help of green votes. The Green Party had finally had its say in governmental policy.

However, there still remained several stumbling blocks on the path to the bargaining table. In March 1983, the Greens, encouraged by their success in the federal elections, refused to pass the SPD's budget proposal, and Börner, encouraged by the SPD's defeat of the GAL in Hamburg, decided to call new elections. Following Dohnanyi's lead in Hamburg, Börner campaigned for an absolute SPD majority. "I don't want a coalition, I want a majority, I want a clearcut situation," he proclaimed.[64] In hopes of recapturing the voters it had lost to the Greens, the SPD adopted an "ecologically oriented business and jobs program," which borrowed heavily from the eco-party. This practice of coopting green positions, popularly referred to by the Greens and their friends as "issue rip-off" (*Themenklau*) was to become increasingly common among the established parties.

The rhetoric was more than just campaign strategy. Since the failure of the budget, Börner was again under heavy pressure to resist any overtures by the Greens, this time from the SPD's Right. Some members of this faction went so far as to contest Börner's leadership.[65] But at the same time, the SPD Left and green realists moved even closer to a rapprochement. The Jusos openly defied the SPD leadership and met with the Greens to discuss strategies and issues of "new politics."[66] The SPD's powerful leftist district of South Hessen brusquely dismissed the desirability of the SPD's attaining an absolute majority, and openly discussed the possibility of a coalition with the Greens.[67] Ultimately, though Börner's words remained sharp, the party refused to rule out officially any cooperation with the Greens.[68]

By election time, the events of the previous months and Börner's Hamburg tactics led to a slight reshuffling in the Hessian Landtag;[69] the SPD failed to attain an absolute majority. Thus the only viable solution continued to be a red–green one. The two parties would have to settle their differences.

It was a green initiative which broke the ice. In a surprise reversal of the party's campaign stance, a party congress voted by a large majority to offer the SPD something termed "continuous cooperation" (*kontinuierliche Zusammenarbeit*).[70] Shortly thereafter, an SPD party congress reciprocated the offer by an almost unanimous vote. In a brilliant and lengthy speech in favor of the motion, Börner elaborated on the significance of a red–green coalition. It was not, he insisted, resignation to circumstance but a historical initiative. Hessen would act as a counterweight to Bonn, meaning, of course, that a red–green coalition in Hessen would act as a genuinely progressive corrective to the conservative-liberal bloc furnishing the federal government. The most pressing political task of the day, Börner continued, was to reconcile economy and ecology, and Hessen "was always a state in which problems and developments preceded their appearance in the Federal Republic as a whole."[71] In essence, though Börner had not presented his views in such detail before, this had been his position since his initial turn to the Greens. It presented a commitment to a new alliance but not to a new politics. A ten-person committee of Social Democrats and Greens promptly began negotiations. Between the red and green sides of the table lay good intentions and mutual solidarity but grave differences in principle. Börner expressed determination to bid adieu to the SPD's hitherto technocratic and growth-oriented policies.[72] But the SPD's key points of negotiations remained within the accepted frame of social-democratic reform politics.[73]

The Greens, of course, had higher ambitions. Moreover, they would not be made into "the creators of a majority just for peanuts."[74] High on their "wish list" were the immediate stoppage of use of the west runway at the Frankfurt airport and the unconditional discontinuation of the Biblis nuclear plant, both, it must be remembered, built by Social Democrat governments. This presented an obvious dilemma for the would-be partners. Giving in on all political issues pertaining to "questions of life and survival," like the runway and nuclear power, would have been tantamount, for the Social Democrats, to admitting the falsity of their previous policies in Hessen. On the other hand, it was precisely on these issues that even the most pragmatic Realo had to either draw a line or risk losing all support in the Green Party. Nevertheless, the first round of negotiations concluded with a basic agreement: the Greens were to tolerate the SPD government at least as far as voting to approve the 1983 and 1984 budgets was concerned.

Though the green Landtag delegation voiced thorough satisfaction with the agreement, the party constitutions required that it be presented to the rank-and-file for approval at a state convention. In January, the convention gave permission to approve the 1983 budget, but, to the disappointment of the SPD, they balked on the "double budget." While voicing its agreement with the principles of grass-roots democracy, the SPD argued that submitting a state budget to an assembly of a small contingent of one party's members was a rather different matter. SPD grumbling about the "dictatorship of the base" within the Greens was to grow substantially in the future.

But for the moment, the SPD shared in the elation. It declared itself "backing Börner without a hitch."[75] Hans-Jochen Vogel, the SPD's parliamentary leader, went so far as to proclaim Börner the party's "man of the year."[76]

The honeymoon between Social Democrats and Greens was brief, however. When Börner presented his draft of the 1984 budget in March of that year, the Greens felt their concerns had been omitted. Thus, they affixed a set of "imperatives" to their approval of the budget.[77] Another back-and-forth process of concessions and demands followed.[78] Börner responded with a conciliatory letter with further promises emphasizing his steadfast will to continue the cooperation agreement.[79] Though a high degree of mutual trust and even personal rapport had been established, it was not founded on substantive consensus. Both the Greens and the SPD had entered into co-operation largely as an experiment. But the political capital already invested in this alliance and the symbolic value of its success began to make continued cooperation important in and of itself. Hence, though the points of conflict remained unresolved, the Greens conceded, and passed the proposed budget.

At its own party congress in June, the SPD also overwhelmingly approved the alliance (though not without increasing signs of dissent).[80] In July, the SPD and Greens finally reinstated Börner as prime minister and confirmed his cabinet after more than 19 months of minority rule. Börner declared the alliance to be the "architecture of a new politics" and an answer to the "concentration of social, economic and ecological problems" generated by Bonn's policies.[81] For many this partnership was motivated by pragmatic and instrumental concerns: an exclusionary strategy toward the Greens would have been "irresponsible."[82]

Early in the fall, the alliance was shaken by a dispute over two nuclear projects, NUKEM and ALKEM.[83] In October, another Green Party convention made a continuation of the alliance between the SPD and the Greens conditional on cancellation of approval for a new NUKEM II fuel rod factory and of an ALKEM order for weapons-grade plutonium set for delivery to unspecified Third World buyers. "No hopping aboard the plutonium economy," warned the ultimatum.[84] Certain green principles, argued fundamentalists, stood above any compromise. The red-green experiment appeared to be over.[85]

In the SPD and the Greens, the alliance was threatened not only by disputes between the parties but also by quarrels within each party, as well as by the flagging support of their respective national leaderships. Increasingly, the real alliance was between SPD Left and Green realists, for whom an end to cooperation between these two parties of the left would have meant a dramatic loss in power and prestige within their own respective parties.[86]

Thus, in order to save the red–green experiment, the green realists and SPD Left began pushing for a formal coalition.[87] The alliance was sealed when Börner – acting personally and unilaterally[88] – offered the Greens a coalition and the post of Minister for Environmental and Energy Policy in May. In exchange, he demanded passage of the 1985 budget as well as a "double budget" for 1986–7. He declared that "the integration of young and environmentally conscious strata of voters . . . benefits the legitimacy of our democratic state because it binds the voter strata represented by the Greens into our political system and opens up to them perspectives for a constructive reform politics."[89] The Greens in parliament rejected the "double budget" plan; and the Fundis demanded two ministries and two high-ranking cabinet points. As negotiations progressed, they further insisted that nuclear energy be included under the jurisdiction of the green minister and that a Ministry for Women be created.

The SPD executive committee resisted the pressure tactics. The final compromise provided for separate deliberations on the two budgets with, however, both to be passed within a year: one designated a green Minister of the Environment and the other a green advisor on women's issues within the Ministry of Health, Family and Education. The three governmental posts which the Greens had gained were occupied respectively by Joschka Fischer, Karl Kerschgens and Marita Haibach.

The protracted and tumultuous negotiations deflated the initial euphoria. The Hessian SPD began to paint the alliance as an unavoidable cohabitation rather than as a historic opportunity. The national leadership of the SPD went even further, proclaiming that Hessen represented a "purely instrumental alliance" which "did not offer any kind of a model whatsoever" for the federal party.[90]

Similarly, the federal Greens saw "no model for the federal level" in Hessen.[91] Many fundamental differences of outlook and method had just not been sufficiently ironed out to forge real common policies or a new consensus. As one SPD member of the negotiating team said, "respecting all relevant topics of negotiation" there had not been even "the sighting of a compromise on the horizon."[92]

Thus, as the first full-fledged red–green coalition came into being in Hessen in 1985, several areas of instability were already clearly visible. It was a new coalition which did not rest on a new politics. The tactic of neutralizing or containing controversial issues like NUKEM/ALKEM by postponing or tabling them for further discussion could only stave off the Fundis and SPD rightists for a limited period of time. The motivations of the two parties for entering the alliance also mitigated against the development of a substantive consensus. While some SPD leftists clearly appeared eager to abandon their technocratic, growth-oriented politics and develop some sort of eco-socialism, Börner and others still aimed only at "integrating" the Greens, so as to tap into and perhaps coopt their electoral potential for social democracy. And all this made it easier for Fundis in the Green Party and SPD functionaries (*Kanalarbeiter*) to sabotage the alliance from within through obstructionism. Yet, while the SPD possessed enough discipline and organization to contain internal opposition, the Green's commitment to minority protection and extensive veto power of the rank-and-file made Joschka Fischer's Realos much more vulnerable.

The Period of Crisis and Contraction – the Saarland/ NRW Debacle and its Aftermath

Despite persistent troubles in Hessen, the fall of 1984 was a dizzying highpoint for the Greens. The *Frankfurter Rundschau*, the Federal Republic's leading left-liberal paper, opined the question "Green and no end?"[93] The SPD suffered heavy casualties against the newcomers in the state election in Baden-Württemberg and local elections in North-Rhine Westphalia. At this point, the SPD Left was still enthusiastic about the idea of red–green cooperation.[94] Yet just months later the positions of the two parties were reversed. In the SPD a consensus coalesced around the view that social democracy not only should but could go it alone in the 1987 federal election. By September this party consensus had become official party policy: there was to be no coalition with the Greens; the campaign was to be conducted so as to gain maximum support from the middle of the electorate; lastly, the SPD's strategy was to attain an absolute majority. This posture vis-à-vis the Greens was the same as the one Johannes Rau had successfully employed in NRW to win an absolute majority for the Social Democrats in that state and once again to leave the Greens without seats in the Dusseldorf Landtag. The meager 4.6 percent of the vote which the NRW Greens collected in this important state election was not only a disappointment but a major turning point in the entire party's mood and the attitude of German voters toward it.

The loss was all the more devastating because it came so unexpectedly. At the beginning of the campaign, the Greens were still on the offensive and the SPD in retreat. After all, the Greens were being courted by many prominent Social Democrats – Oskar Lafontaine among them – not only as temporary junior partners in a red–green coalition, but as long-term companions in the exercise of state power. During the fall of 1984, it was Lafontaine and not Rau who seemed more realistic. The continued electoral expansion of the Greens appeared an irreversible fact.

The Greens' campaign in the NRW election of 1985 began at an auspicious moment. In the European elections of June 1984, green delegates from NRW were returned to Brussels with a convincing 8.2 percent of the vote. This very respectable result was topped by the 9.1 percent which the party attained in local elections several months later. A June 1984 survey by the *Hessische Allgemeine* newspaper found 7–8 percent support for the Greens at the state level.[95] In another survey, an astonishing 26 percent of voters gave the NRW Greens "good marks."[96] The green candidates were confident, even cocky.[97] In an internal position paper, party headquarters boasted that "never before in NRW was a campaign mapped out so early as this one."[98]

The meticulous preparations which began in December 1983 were a reflection of the importance which a win in NRW would have for the Greens' strength and image nationwide. NRW is by far the most populous German state, comprising about one-third of the pre-unification Federal Republic's total area and population. Its core is the Ruhr area, the major concentration of industry in West Germany. Consequently it possesses a strong working-class vote. A win there would have given the Greens a new and significant aura of legitimacy and recognition in two areas central to their concern and future identity. If they attracted a significant number of blue-collar votes, the Greens could then rightfully claim to have developed into a genuine left-wing party which offered a viable alternative to the accommodationist SPD. After all, the Greens' failure to attract working-class voters still represented the missing link to becoming a *bona fide* political representative of the Left. It is interesting how in this sense the working class continued as a special category even for the post-APO New Left and its political and intellectual successors. Moreover, a respectable showing in NRW would have demonstrated to the German public that the Greens had some appeal in the eyes of the "average German" and not just in those of Berlin "alternatives," Frankfurt "intellectuals" and university students in Tübingen, Freiburg and Marburg. It was not to be. The Greens failed to clear the 5 percent hurdle, and were thus not represented in NRW's new parliament.

What caused this electoral debacle? First, in contrast to Hessen and Hamburg, neither the realist nor the fundamentalist tendency was able to gain control of the party. A realist faction close to party headquarters in Dusseldorf agreed with party manager Martin Pannen's view that "it is probably necessary to enter alliances" but not ones following the Hessian model.[99] However, a powerful eco-socialist wing lead by MP Eckhart Strattmann strongly opposed any sort of formal cooperation with the Social Democrats. The two factions sought to mend their differences in a series of party congresses during the thick of the election campaign. The result was a painstakingly detailed and longwinded catalogue of demands (including the immediate shut-down of all nuclear plants in NRW).[100] The tome-like program was unavailable to the public until a few days before the election.[101] The *Frankfurter Rundschau* quipped that "the Greens' whole election program comprised 500–600 pages. Nobody has counted them exactly from cover to cover – nor read them either most probably."[102] The Green program also included an unfortunate passage, inserted at the behest of a small contingent of homosexuals at the program convention, describing sex with children as a "pleasant, productive, encouraging development, in short: positive."[103] The passage soon made headlines in sensationalist tabloids[104] and the SPD Right gleefully pounced on what was already known as the "child-sex scandal."[105]

The Greens' image was seriously tarnished by their defeat in NRW. The incessant bickering between the two factions made the Greens look disunited and incompetent. Moreover, the party's formidable catalogue of demands before a red–green majority even existed made such demands appear unrealistic and arrogant. This was especially the case since all the Greens offered the SPD for agreeing to the conditions of coalition was to help vote Rau into office.

Within the party, there were competing explanations for the defeat. Realists blamed it on the obstructionism of the fundamentalists. Jakob Sonnenschein of the *Taz* bitterly charged that

> Those people who basically don't want a toleration of the SPD and don't say this openly, but set the barriers for a toleration so high that a cooperation with the SPD is made impossible right from the start, must come out of the closet here. An unholy alliance of Realist politicians with fundamentalist intentions and leftist Fundamentalists and Bahro followers has emerged. . . . Whoever in NRW demands . . . the "immediate exit" from atomic energy as a quasi precondition [to governmental cooperation], but simultaneously swears allegiance to such a cooperation is not playing according to the rules.[106]

The fundamentalists blamed it on the poor campaign management of the realist executive committee. Christa Nickels and Antje Vollmer of the Greens' Bundestag delegation contended that "90 percent of the debacle in NRW was homemade. . . . The main failing was that the state executive committee did not have the trace of an idea as to what a state campaign really is."[107] But neither fundamentalist obstructionism nor realist blunders had hampered the Greens in the past.

In fact, the Greens' NRW defeat appeared to fit into a broader developmental trend. After all, it followed closely on the heels of an even greater loss in the Saarland one month before, where the Greens tallied a disappointing 2.5 percent. Tellingly, just like NRW, the Saarland was also an industrial province, the other center of German steel production, and even more economically troubled than NRW. Despite their high hopes, it appeared that the Greens seemed to have failed to attract any support in the working class for their "new" politics of protest and autonomy. This lacuna in their electoral appeal was to accompany the Greens until the very present.

The *Richtungswahl*: Lower Saxony

It was Heiner Geissler, then the flamboyant and provocative CDU general secretary, who dubbed the June 15 state election in Lower Saxony a *Richtungswahl*, an election which would delineate the direction of coming events in the political landscape of the Federal Republic. Since Lower Saxony's socioeconomic composition is that of the Federal Republic writ small, this last major election before the national contest possessed a certain power to influence and forecast the federal campaign, which was due exactly seven months later on January 25, 1987. In fact, due to a confluence of events, the Lower Saxony elections became "the most closely watched state contest in West Germany in years."[108] At least for the Greens, its impact was to equal that of federal elections.

Much depended on its outcome. Chancellor Helmut Kohl was widely seen to be experiencing a crisis of confidence, and a conservative defeat in Lower Saxony might have jeopardized his government. Moreover, the chances seemed high that Gerhard Schröder, the SPD's dynamic and progressive young candidate in Lower Saxony, could replicate the impressive victories of his colleagues Oskar Lafontaine and Johannes Rau. And a Schröder victory could potentially have generated critical momentum in the SPD's Bundestag campaign.

For the Greens, too, the election seemed pregnant with possibility, not least because of Schröder, who, true to his progressive background as one of the SPD's most visible Juso leaders, had long declared himself open to a red–green coalition. Although he backpedalled during the spring of 1986 (largely in order not to break ranks with the SPD's Rau strategy) most Greens were confident that Schröder would be "available" for them if the numbers for a red–green coalition proved auspicious. So confident were the Greens of such a favorable outcome that they unconditionally offered the SPD the formation of a coalition well in advance of the election. Several other factors made this seem a genuine possibility. During the course of the campaign in Lower Saxony, the first fully fledged red–green coalition was inaugurated in Hessen and Joschka Fischer was sworn in as the first Green Party minister, albeit in tennis shoes. Moreover, the warring factions in Bonn declared a temporary cease-fire. Carefully avoiding the word coalition, the federal Green party formally declared an openness to "cooperation" but forbade discussing its form except where the numerical preconditions actually emerged.

Overall conditions for a replication of "Hessian circumstances" seemed positive. To many Greens, Social Democrats, indeed German citizens, it seemed that red-green could be transformed from a dream to a practicable political alternative to the ruling center-right coalition within the short span of a year. Even the conservative *Frankfurter Allgemeine Zeitung* queried: "Hessen, maybe Lower Saxony, later Hamburg or Bonn?"[109]

The wild card in this unstable, even volatile political constellation was the Soviet reactor catastrophe in Chernobyl. By confirming their dark vision of an eco-apocalypse, the Chernobyl disaster greatly strengthened the position of the fundamentalists within the party, while the gradualist stance of Hessen's "Fischer gang," by contrast, was called into question.[110]

The changed intraparty balance among the green forces was evident at the extraordinary federal party congress on May 16–19 held in Hanover, the capital of Lower Saxony. Rather than discussing revisions to the newly drafted 1987 federal election program as originally intended, the congress quickly devolved into a debate over green "fundamentals," "essentials" and "principles." Fundi hardliner Jutta Ditfurth set the tone early: "Chernobyl is everywhere"[111] . . . "After the 28th of April, 1986, the day of the nuclear disaster in Chernobyl, our life is no longer as it was. We will have to redefine what a normal life is. It is a moment in history of which we must say, that we could not wish more that we had not been right in this case."[112] Fundamentalists decried a "nuclear mafia" of "terrorists" and "murderers" (encompassing everyone from the SPD to the plutonium processors) who knowingly prepared a radioactive wasteland for profit. Said Rainer Trampert dramatically, "All 374 nuclear installations on earth are declarations of war against us."[113]

This "verbal radicalism" had only one practical target, namely Fischer's newborn red–green coalition in Hessen. Because of the moratorium on discussion of the coalition question, Fischer could not be attacked directly. But he could be put under considerable pressure to take "concrete steps" toward a nuclear-free Hessen: "exit now, without negotiations," demanded Petra Kelly.[114] Lukas Beckmann warned, "If the SPD in Hessen doesn't move and if there's no success in making Biblis and Hanau[115] into shutdown monuments, then there's only one thing left for us: departure from the coalition."[116] In fact, however, neither Fischer nor the Hessian state government had any legal authority to effect an "immediate exit" from nuclear power. Jurisdiction over nuclear plants lay solely in the hands of the federal government in Bonn.[117] Under attack by the fundamentalists Fischer retorted that "concrete measures and effective implementation, not just testimonials" were necessary.[118]

Mikhail Gorbachev's proposals to reduce nuclear armament also rekindled a third issue for the Greens: their longstanding demand that the Federal Republic "get out of NATO." This tenet was challenged for the first time from two directions within the party: first, by a small but "relevant minority" which advocated setting an East/West arms treaty at the head of green priorities;[119] and second by realists, who fought to strike the anti-NATO clause which identified the West and the United States as the "warmongers" principally responsible for the arms race.[120] They succeeded in changing the party platform slightly but not significantly.[121] The other parties were quick to exploit the Greens' controversial position.[122] Johannes Rau commented: "What's been decided by the Greens at their party congress is obviously a victory for those called the Fundamentalists . . . I feel myself reinforced in the opinion that on the federal level, cooperation with such unreasonable people is impossible."[123]

Of course, the Greens were not the sole force on the Left electrified by the Chernobyl disaster. Protest around the construction sites for the nuclear reprocessing plants in Wackersdorf, Bavaria, and Brokdorf, Lower Saxony, flared dramatically – and violently. In scenes "resembling civil war," helmeted, leatherclad troops of the anarchist Autonomen armed with sling-shots, Molotov cocktails and flare guns clashed brutally with the police, who employed water cannons, helicopters and CS gas (officially banned for use against civilians). Frequent calls for extraparliamentary protest during the Hanover congress brought the Greens into an unfortunate alliance with violent demonstrators. Indeed, according to a malicious rumor, disproved after the election,[124] the news that over a hundred policemen had been injured in Wackersdorf was supposed to have provoked "cheering" and "wild applause" among green delegates.

While it surely exploited the Greens' ambivalent relation to violent protest and their continued uncertainty and reluctance to recognize the state's legitimate monopoly on deploying violent means in a liberal democracy, this rumor, or at least its propagation, was part of an aggressive conservative campaign directed against the Green Party and its milieu. *Der Spiegel* went so far as to suggest that police strategy at Brokdorf, following orders from above, consciously provoked violent clashes in order to discredit protesters – and the Greens. Whatever the truth of these speculations may be, there can be no doubt that CDU tacticians had revised their previous strategy of ignoring the Greens in the hope that they would disappear. CDU politicians conducted an "unprecedented propaganda campaign"[125] against the Greens, denouncing them as child murderers (because of their abortion stand) and terrorists, and warning that a "red–green chaos" would bring the "ruin of the nation."[126] This aggressive media campaign was not in vain: the election in Lower Saxony was decided by a hair's breadth in favor of the Bonn coalition partners.

The CDU/FDP coalition retained a slim one-seat majority in the legislature. The SPD especially could claim considerable credit, because it had gained over 5 percent since the last election, almost solely at the expense of the CDU. On the evening news, SPD candidate Schröder sorrowfully concluded: "We won, but we didn't prevail."[127] An important signal for the federal election had been sent. SPD party manager Peter Glotz evaluated the result as a "tailwind for the federal election" and a confirmation that the SPD's course was correct.[128]

If the winner was hard to ascertain, the loser was not. It was clearly the Greens, who not only tallied fewer votes than in the previous election, but whose arrangements with the SPD were not accepted by their potential supporters and clients, let alone the population at large. The Greens confronted "broken dreams"[129] (or was it inflated expectations?) for the official electoral analysis concluded that, in fact, the voters in Lower Saxony "oriented themselves . . . more strongly toward familiar models than many observers would have thought possible."[130] The decisive voter movements occurred in the last weeks of the campaign – and not in the wake of Chernobyl.[131]

It was just this, the normality of the election and the absence of the confidently expected "Chernobyl effect," which occupied green leadership in the weeks following the election and plunged the eco-party into what was until then the deepest crisis of its short history. The reaction of Bonn delegate Ludger Volmer to the election would be repeated in varying forms and with uniform bewilderment by his party colleagues in the following weeks: "People found the horror of a red–green coalition more terrible than the nuclear clouds from Chernobyl."[132]

Of course, analyses of why public outrage and upset over the catastrophe in the Ukraine did not translate into Green votes varied according to familiar factional lines. The Fundi-controlled federal executive committee blamed the realist coalition course of the Lower Saxony Greens. Eco-socialist and party speaker Rainer Trampert insisted that the Greens "should not always go begging after the SPD."[133] On the whole, fundamentalists attached themselves to the fatalistic argument that 7 percent was the "optimum that could be attained by a leftist party in the Federal Republic."[134] In other words, the cost of maintaining doctrinal purity had to be a limited electorate. Realists like Joschka Fischer seized on this point and drew a different strategic lesson: the Greens needed "to move closer toward the people,"[135] his words for increased credibility and greater electoral success. The election in Lower Saxony was not only a "referendum on Chernobyl," where a vote for the Greens denoted only a vote against Chernobyl. Observed Lukas Beckmann, the Greens' former party manager: "Whoever is afraid of nukes can at the same time conceive of NATO as a protective power, be afraid of women's liberation and be against foreigners."[136] Votes were complex composites of overarching decisions, which incorporated more than one question. Fischer concluded that the "verbal radicalism" of the Fundis, exemplified in the Hanover NATO debate, had "repelled voters, who actually share our opinions."[137] The fundamentalists' rigid view of the world and their compartmentalization of complex issues into simplistic categories impeded the Greens' appeal to a pool of potential supporters at the ballot box.

However, more was required than simply toning down green debates and moderating election programs. For the Greens to become a credible reform party instead of a protest party, those voters who agreed with all green policies had to be convinced of the party's competence to implement its ideas. In the opinion of many Realos, the "performance of the [Greens'] wrecking-ball faction"[138] at Brokdorf and its impact on the election had proven once and for all that a rapprochement with "normal voters" would require a clearcut and official rejection of all violence by the Green Party. The alternative to addressing larger segments of the population would be a dangerous stagnation into a "stronghold party in the domain of the college educated"[139] and a confinement to the Left's most ghettoized milieu, known as the "scene." Thus, both Joschka Fischer[140] and Gerhard Schröder[141] concluded that the problem in Lower Saxony was not the Realo course itself, but the deficit of voter trust caused by a lack of resolve and predictability on the part of the Green Party in pursuing this trust. In short, Fischer's analysis pointed to a green credibility gap.

This conflict between Fundis and Realos in Lower Saxony followed a simple but familiar pattern: dormant after victories but animated by defeats. Nevertheless, the electoral loss in Lower Saxony represented a significant juncture not only in the evolution of this factional conflict, but in the historical development of the German eco-party and the Left in general. The strategies espoused by both factions before the election were informed by a certain vision of the Green Party. The fundamentalists perceived the Greens as a historical movement, which would absorb ever greater segments of the population as they awoke to the dangerous direction of socioeconomic developments inevitably assumed by a crisis-ridden capitalism. For the Fundis, the role of the Greens was to be a vanguard, agitating to raise the consciousness of citizens and to act as their organizational center. In the view of the Fundis, it was therefore essential for the Green Party to maintain doctrinal purity and resist political integration so that the Greens would eventually become a genuine mass movement, indeed – so the Fundis believed – a movement of the majority which could overturn the existing social system from within. After Lower Saxony, the Fundis, nonplussed by the failure of Chernobyl to have the predicted "consciousness-raising effects," retreated to a self-righteous 7 percent sectarianism. Their attitude was: if the majority of voters remained too stupefied (*verdummt*) to see the light even after Chernobyl, that was hardly the fault of the enlightened few.

The realists, on the other hand, sought to promote the evolution of the Greens from a radical movement into a leftist reform party. The Realos believed that the aims of the Greens could not be realized through extraparliamentary pressure alone. In the Realos' view it was necessary for the Green Party to participate directly in the country's governing process and effect incremental steps toward reform. The only hope toward fulfilling this strategy of sharing power was to align with the SPD. In particular, the Realos believed that it was indispensable for the Greens to issue clearcut, unambiguous coalition offers to the SPD, especially in states with progressive SPD leaders such as Lafontaine in the Saarland, von Dohnanyi in Hamburg, or Schröder in Lower Saxony. The more red–green coalitions were established, so the Realists hoped, the more the position of the SPD Left and green realos would be strengthened in their respective parties. Public anxieties and mistrust vis-à-vis the Greens would be stilled.

As became clear in Lower Saxony, it was a grave error on the part of the realists to imagine that a coalition offer, in and of itself, was sufficient to secure the credibility and eligibility of the Greens. This could not be done without redefining the party's relation to the movement, especially the latter's violent, anarchist "wrecking-ball faction." It also necessitated a major revision of the realists' relation to the fundamentalists on substantive issues. The realists had become so fixated on the "question of power," narrowly conceived as "red–green," that they had neglected to develop concrete policy positions. The result was that practically all the Greens' programmatic statements, and most of their public debates, bore the handwriting of fundamentalists and eco-socialists to the disproportionate exclusion of the Realos."[142] In their quest for respectability, the realists had forgotten the connection between positional power and ideological convictions in politics.

By the late 1980s, the line of factional conflict between Fundis and Realos was no longer drawn between movement and party, but between two sorts of parties. The Fundi version could best be summarized as a radical, leftist, socialist ecology party more concerned with maintaining its doctrinal purity and its links to the leftist, urban milieu of protest movements than with enlarging its share of votes in the legislatures via the electoral process. In this Fundi vision, the Green Party was to occupy a gap in the Federal Republic's party space which had been filled by communist parties in other European countries. Instead of the usual Third International communism characteristic of most conventional communist parties, the Fundis envisioned the Green Party to offer an overhauled, ecologized Marxism as its strategic and ideological base.

In contrast, the Realo image of the Greens envisioned a pragmatic, progressive reform party willing to appeal to moderate, employed, middle-class Germans insofar as they supported an ecologically and socially informed restructuring of industrial society. The party, so the realists hoped, would fill a political space created by the inability of traditional Social Democrats to integrate demands for enhanced democratization and participation with the organizational exigencies necessary to administer the complexities of a modern industrial society.

While these competing visions differed radically, they were part of a painful maturation process in the fledgling party. Gone was the sense of zeal and historical mission transmitted by the new social movements. Gone too were certain fundamental illusions about the possibilities of party politics in parliamentary democracies. But in reproducing – rather than eliminating – the internal structural tension between movement and party at a higher level, the two competing green factions had at least managed to avoid their worst respective nightmares: "cooptation" into the ranks of the established parties for the Fundis; and a return to the "ghetto" of sectarian, cadre politics and extraparliamentary protest for the Realos.

The 1987 Bundestag Election: Stabilization . . .

The election in Lower Saxony had a complicated and perhaps even positive impact on the Greens' Bundestag campaign in the fall of 1986. Even though most Social Democrats knew that an absolute majority was unattainable, the party dutifully fell into line behind its candidate. The SPD's candidate for federal chancellor in this election was – as will be recalled – the prime minister of NRW, Johannes Rau, who, among other feats, succeeded in gaining an absolute electoral majority for the SPD in NRW by pursuing a decidedly exclusionary strategy vis-à-vis the Greens. Rau's rejection of any red–green coalition, however, did not resolve the coalition debate among the Greens. But it did produce an interfactional ceasefire, which allowed the party to present a superficially unified facade during the critical months of the campaign. As the "Brokdorf effect" superseded the "Chernobyl effect," the Realos appeared to be on the upswing again. The cool, controlled character of the campaign cannot be ascribed only to the Realos, however. Genuine anxieties about the survival of the party engendered an unusual degree of cooperation and unity within the party leadership.

The first signal of a new professionalism within the Greens was the "silent end of rotation." The intense (and often misplaced) anxiety about "elites" and "career politicians" had slowly given way to a recognition of the value of political experience and public recognition. Even the new faces on the green ticket were often well-known and savvy political players, such as Gray Panther leader Trude Unruh and peace researcher Alfred Mechtersheimer. Moreover, around a dozen prominent Greens, so-called "promis," once again emerged in "promising" spots on the state electoral lists, among them media figures like Otto Schily, Antje Vollmer, Christa Nickels and Waltraud Schoppe. Even Petra Kelly, the only Green who had refused to rotate during the previous legislative period, was put on the Bavarian party slate.[143]

The "ghost of Lower Saxony" haunted the federal party congress in Nuremberg on September 26–8. Delegates on the sidelines muttered, "anything but not another congress like Hanover."[144] Issues likely to spark controversy within the party or its electorate, such as the party program on abortion,[145] were either deleted from the agenda or simply ignored.[146] The decision whether to sign a petition in protest against the Wackersdorf nuclear reprocessing plant in Bavaria was quietly delegated to the state party,[147] in full knowledge that it would decline its support for such a measure.[148] There was, in short, a concerted effort to avoid negative publicity. Gone were the ruthless name-calling and vitriolic polemics which had characterized earlier congresses. A peaceful atmosphere with a new spirit prevailed: "compromises instead of radical demands, reaching agreement instead of factional infighting, reconciliation instead of division."[149] The Greens, so it seemed, had at last learned how to behave like a "normal" party.[150]

As regards the coalition debate, some 22 position papers had been submitted.[151] The statement which was ultimately adopted was written by Antje
Vollmer, an ex-pastor and party iconoclast. Though generally compromising
in its tone, Vollmer's letter struck several new accents. It portrayed the Greens
as "advocates of life" and the "first pacifist and emancipatory party" in postwar German history.[152] And rather than attacking the SPD or offering lengthy
analyses of issues, it stressed the negative consequences, the "reversal into a
closed society,"[153] which would inevitably be the outcome if the Greens did
not retain their seats in the Bundestag. In sum, the letter not only displayed
a strategic reserve but a new self-consciousness of the party as a bulwark and
an institutional fixture in the German polity.

In terms of the coalition question itself, the letter to the voters adopted an
open and flexible stance. In contrast to past resolutions, it contained no
minimum requirements or preconditions for coalition negotiations. At the
same time, it did not exhibit an explicit coalition offer either, but in the
event of a red–green majority left a decision on the form of governmental
cooperation by the Greens to a party congress to be held after the election.[154]
The strength of this compromise was twofold. First, it left the path for negotiations open while maintaining factional peace. Second, its wait-and-see
attitude prevented Rau from leaving the overanxious bride waiting at the
altar as he had in 1985. In this way, the Greens managed to cast themselves
in a favorable light as flexible, compromising and sincere, and the SPD, in
turn, as rigid, narrow and manipulative.

The new party professionalism was also evident in the conduct of the
campaign itself. For the first time, the Greens thematized issues with an eye
to the voters rather than out of allegiance to "the movement" or "the scene."
In contrast to past practice, no symbolic resolutions were passed concerning
the fundamental aims of the party (such as disarmament, opposition to nuclear
power, ecology). Instead, the Greens strategically chose to emphasize, first of
all, their liberal stance toward political asylum seekers and their support of
voting rights for foreigners, in response to the conservative camp's alarmingly
xenophobic and racist policy proposals, spearheaded predictably by Bavarian
Prime Minister Franz Josef Strauss.[155] The second focus was women's rights,
the green issue least successfully colonized by the established parties at the
time and the one most successful in reaching crossover voters from the
CDU/CSU and FDP as well as the SPD.

In addition to presenting their draft of an anti-discrimination law, the
Greens passed a "women's statute" according female party members several
special rights and privileges. In nominating Bundestag candidates, state delegations were required to observe a "zipper process," alternating female and
male candidates, and awarding women the odd numbers in the rankings,
thus always guaranteeing them first place.[156] Women delegates were given a
"veto right." Any decision directly affecting women could be challenged and
subjected to a veto by a women's caucus, requiring that the decision be
reintroduced and newly debated at the next congress. By focusing on these
two issues, the Greens addressed two topics which had been salient to a large

constituency of progressive Germans well beyond the immediate confines of the green milieu. By maintaining the radical nature of their programmatic statements and by eschewing debate over controversial issues, the Greens prudently avoided alienating their movement support, yet generated no bad publicity to frighten away moderate SPD voters.

This promising campaign received a second boost from the state elections in Bavaria and Hamburg in mid-October. In Franz-Josef Strauss's conservative and Catholic Bavaria, the decidedly realist wing of the Greens polled the "grandiose result" of 7.5 percent, thereby clearing the 5 percent hurdle for the first time by an unexpectedly healthy margin.[157] Moreover, in the traditional SPD bastion of Hamburg, the fundamentalist GAL, running on an all-female ticket, surged from 6.8 to 10.4 percent.

Weeks later, in early November, another environmental tragedy boosted the green campaign. Just months after the massive Hoechst chemical spill into the Rhine, a second spill occurred in Basle caused by the Swiss firm, Sandoz. The manmade scourge poisoned all but the simplest macrobiotic plant life in the mythical Teutonic river. Dead fish were hauled away by the truckload in many of the Rhine's port cities.

Meanwhile, the SPD was scrambling to control the political damage from a highly publicized scandal surrounding the subsidized housing corporation, Neue Heimat, owned by the DGB. Trade union leaders, most of whom were prominent members of the Social Democratic Party, were caught not only enriching themselves to the company's detriment, but mismanaging one of the labor movement's most prized possessions to the brink of bankruptcy.[158] As the "hot phase" of the election campaign began, all SPD leaders, excepting Johannes Rau himself, confessed that 45 percent would be a "fine result" for the Social Democrats. The futility of Rau's continued pursuit of an absolute majority became the inside joke and open secret of the campaign, gravely undermining the man it aimed to support.

The Greens interpreted Rau's approach as part of a long-term SPD strategy whose aim was to eliminate the Greens in 1987 in order to prepare the way for an absolute majority in 1990.[159] (The strategy, as it turned out, worked only in part: the Greens were indeed eliminated from the Bundestag in 1990, but the SPD, far from attaining a majority, slipped dangerously close to its pre-Godesberg 30 percent). However, the moderate and traditionalist Rau was better suited to raid the political middle than to recapture leftist SPD members who had migrated to the Greens. Greens such as Antje Vollmer deftly turned the tables on Rau: "At the moment the SPD is, in our view, neither ready for nor capable of an alliance."[160] The Greens had thus managed to assume a remarkably attractive pose for the key contingency of leftist voters caught between red and green: in the case of an SPD majority, the Greens seemed the more reliable and determined coalition partner; yet in the case of the Kohl government's victory, the eco-party appeared to be the most determined and competent opposition in the critical areas of peace, ecology and women's rights.

The old disorganization of the Greens had not been entirely supplanted by their new professionalism. The Fundi-controlled federal executive committee had dissolved the 20-seat Realo-dominated election committee without replacing it,[161] resulting in a "decentralized," even anarchic campaign organized mainly through the appointment books of individual "promis" and activists.[162] Nevertheless, Greens with national name recognition, above all Fischer, Schily and Kelly, consistently played to packed halls in large cities,[163] while less well-known candidates filled taverns even in the provinces.[164] The only centrally directed green electoral push was the showboat tour "Winter Magic." The eight-stop revue comprised a three-hour alternative entertainment revue – a Nicaraguan band, Swiss graffiti artist Harald Naegeli, and "Blutrote Kamille," a women's theater group – punctuated by one-liner election speeches by green public figures. The Greens were cleverly trading on the popular appeal (even the bohemian chic) of alternative culture.

In a final spurt down the home stretch, two weeks before the election on January 25, the Greens released their summary report assessing their Bundestag experiment. Their marks were contradictory. In the drive for public enlightenment, green diligence left the other parties far behind in both relative and absolute terms: 367 proposals, 53 bills, 87 "grand" and "small inquiries" and a daunting output of press releases in four short years of parliamentary activity.[165] Their legislative balance sheet was decidedly more meager: the Greens could attest to only one successful measure, a ban on the import of sea turtles into the Federal Republic. Still the party leadership rightly argued that they had succeeded in changing the dynamics of German politics. Said Ludger Volmer: "The parliamentary delegation was able to establish the green position as a long-term, critical opposition, thereby making its presence known in a hitherto vacant space in the topography of German party politics."[166] On the deficit side, the report noted the growing distance to "the movement" and the Greens' increasing "professionalization."

The final election result vindicated the pollsters and not the pessimists: 8.3 percent and 44 seats for the Greens, which was a major increase from the previous Bundestag election of March 1983, when the party attained 5.6 percent of the vote and 27 seats in the federal parliament. Complementing the 17 additional seats was the fact that the party's Bundestag delegation included 25 women.[167] The federal executive committee characterized the outcome as a pathbreaking result and called it a "historic election."[168] But Greens from left to right, uncomfortable with success, suspicious of power, and distrustful of euphoria, commenced with their habitual attacks and bickering at the very moment of their most notable political triumph, railing against the CDU/CSU's "new nationalism" (Ditfurth), the "shitty strategy of the SPD" (Vollmer) and the "conservative block" (Trampert).[169] The cease-fire among the various factions of the Greens was over virtually before it had begun.

The Greens' apparent stabilization proved in reality to be a deadlock. By the following spring, it had already become clear that the success, and even the very survival of the party, required more than time. It demanded a fundamental reorientation.

... and Paralysis: the Demise of the Red-Green Block in Hessen and Hamburg

During the four-year period bounded by the 1983 and 1987 Bundestag elections, a new alignment had come to define the political cleavage structure of the Federal Republic. Two distinct blocs emerged, divided by ideology, social composition and political "color": one red-green (SPD-Greens), which represented the country's political Left, and the other black-yellow (CDU/CSU and FDP) which encompassed the Federal Republic's center-right. (In the German – indeed Central European – tradition, where political parties are identified with colors, the FDP liberals have been assigned a combination of blue and yellow, with the latter, however, clearly the dominant of the two.) While this development was neither intended nor desired by any of the concerned parties, most notably in the red-green camp, it seemed nearly inevitable for a number of reasons. First, despite setbacks and slumps, the Greens had steadily expanded and then stabilized their share of the vote throughout the entire period, upsetting predictions and hopes that they would disappear. Second, the Greens, at least in the eyes of the voting public, had come to represent strategies and policies which were neither "ahead" nor "centrist," as the Greens once claimed, but quite simply left, indeed distinctly left of the SPD. While the two left parties in this new red-green bloc could safely rely on core voters, they found themselves increasingly locked in battle over a contingent of independent leftist voters, largely composed of the young and upwardly mobile, the "new" middle class and women. These floating voters comprise anywhere from 1 to 6 percent of the electorate in the Federal Republic. Third, this in fact meant that the SPD could not entertain a realistic hope of attaining an absolute majority other than in states such as NRW and the Saarland where the milieu of postindustrial groupings was especially weak and the core of a blue-collar working class still a considerable social force. With the memories of the Free Democrats' desertion of the SPD-led coalition in 1982 still very fresh, and any coalition with the Christian Democrats completely unacceptable to a majority of Social Democrats, the Greens had advanced *faute de mieux* to becoming the SPD's sole possible coalition partner. This had an obvious impact on interparty competition and dialogue: while the two blocs competed for absolute shares of the West German vote as a whole, the parties within each of the blocs competed for relative shares. Indeed, much of the interesting political dialogue in the Federal Republic occurred *within* the ruling and opposition blocs rather than *between* them. This intrabloc competition was particularly keen between the SPD and the Greens.

Between 1983 and 1987 red–green relations were riven by two deep tensions, one structural, the other political. The first was the transformation of the Greens "from the typology of protest and movement politics to that of 'party politics,' "[170] a change which evoked a deep sense of identity crisis and moral anguish within the party. The second was the determination of both the SPD Right and the fundamentalist wing of the Greens to undermine and sabotage efforts at red–green cooperation wherever they emerged. Until the Bundestag elections of 1987, these dilemmas had remained unsolved. But as the initial euphoria and "automatic success" of the early years subsided, a mood of paralysis set in. The German Left was comprised of two parties which could neither rule nor coexist, alone or together.

In the spring of 1987, events in Hessen and Hamburg set in motion a violent struggle over the identity of the Green Party and indeed over the entire direction of the Left. The impending crisis was first signaled by elections to party posts within the Bundestag delegation. Since this conflict provided an illuminating example of the paradoxes of green-style party democracy, it is worthy of a brief review.

All internal party elections had been governed by a set of unwritten rules based on the green principles of minority protection and gender parity quotas, meaning in practice that even where Realos or men possessed a majority of the votes, both wings and sexes in the party had to be represented in proportion to their numbers. In this case, this meant that of the three speakers, two had to be women and one a fundamentalist. Only a dozen of the 44 green Bundestag delegates could be counted unambiguously among the party's fundamentalist wing, hardly sufficient to help the Hamburg Green and ex-KB leader Thomas Ebermann, the Fundis' "dream candidate," attain another victory. This was rendered all the more difficult since Ebermann, whose positions, especially on the use of violence, were radical even by green standards, was pitted against Otto Schily, rivaled only by his realist colleague Fischer in public acclaim and general popularity.

Tactics for the subversion of majorities by minorities are, of course, a staple of Leninist practice and formed an essential part of the political socialization of Ebermann and his entourage in communist cadre parties delineated in chapter 3. And indeed, Ebermann's ultimate victory over Schily was the work of shrewd tactics. Ebermann's machinations unleashed a wave of accusations in the Greens' Bundestag delegation, ranging from "dirty tricks" (Kelly)[171] to "damage to the whole party" (Schily).[172] The criticisms of the otherwise coolheaded Schily took a highly unfortunate personal bent. Schily charged Ebermann with representing "an eccentric and to some extent adventurist position" and denounced "excessive pluralism"[173] in the party in such a manner as to suggest, at least to his enemies, that he (Schily) as "crown prince" possessed prerogatives and rights sufficient to override a democratic election. Schily's bruised ego and temporary political marginalization inside the Green Party, if not in the landscape of German politics, led to his gradual disengagement from the Greens, until in the fall of 1989 he left the party and joined the SPD.

To Ebermann's victory was added another major setback for the Realos. On February 8, three days after Schily's defeat, Joschka Fischer received a pink slip dispensing with his services from his boss, Hessian Prime Minister Holger Börner. The immediate cause for the break-up of the red–green coalition was a renewed dispute over the plutonium factories in Hanau,

NUKEM and ALKEM. Since the expiration of their charter permits in 1975, these plants had operated and even expanded production in a dubious state of semi-legality. In the wake of the Chernobyl congress in Hanover, Fischer and the Hessian Realos had assumed a more rigid posture on the closing of NUKEM/ALKEM. It remained unclear at this point whether the Hessian state government had the constitutional authority to close the plutonium factory's doors without Bonn's consent.[174] So when Ulrich Steger, Hessian Minister of the Economy, promised Bonn that he would issue a limited operating permit for the Hanau concern, the Greens revolted. Fischer and Jochen Vielhauer, who was chairman of the Greens' Landtag representation, demanded withdrawal of Steger's written promise. At a Green Party congress two days later, Jutta Ditfurth and the Frankfurt fundamentalists escalated matters by formulating an official party demand which made continuation of the coalition contingent on immediate retraction of the Steger offer.[175] In complete exasperation, Börner not only fired Fischer[176] but resigned as prime minister and announced his retirement from political life.[177]

Ironically, however, while Börner's departure initially appeared to be a major victory for the Fundis, it ultimately played into the hands of the Realos. The former prime minister had always stood for the "old SPD." His coalition government had always been founded more on personal rapport with certain Realos than on substantive agreement with the "new politics."[178] The Hessian Realos therefore represented the break-up of the Börner government as an opportunity for greater participation and responsibility on the part of the Greens.[179] They demanded from the SPD two ministerial posts, and the deputy prime ministership, which traditionally had been the due of "junior partners."[180] They sought the "continuation of the red–green coalition, but this time on an improved foundation" firm enough to make it not an experiment but the "normal case."[181] Marshaling their grass-roots supporters, the "Fischer gang" held the fundamentalist candidates to a fifth of the available spots on the Greens' Landtag slate,[182] violating the Green party's unwritten rule of having each of the factions represented proportionally. In this way, the vote was transformed into a barometer of public support for the realist course.

Several other factors combined to make the elections into a virtual plebiscite pitting the red–green model against the CDU-led Bonn coalition. First, the SPD left no doubt about its intention to enter a coalition with the Greens in the case of a red–green electoral majority.[183] This represented the first such pre-electoral statement by the SPD in Hessen (or anywhere else for that matter). Second, the CDU chose the federal Minister of the Environment Walter Wallman, as its candidate for the post of prime minister of Hessen. The very fact that a CDU-led government deemed it important (as well as politically prudent) to establish a ministry responsible for environmental matters and ecological problems in the Federal Republic bespeaks the immense cultural and institutional effect which the Greens attained in the politics of the Federal Republic during the 1980s. Clearly, their influence far exceeded the numerical presence of their parliamentary delegations, party activists, electoral supporters and milieu-based sympathizers. In his ministerial capacities, Wallman not only represented the CDU's practice of "environmental protection" which it devised in response to the popular salience of green issues, he was also responsible for overseeing the Federal Republic's nuclear plants. Hence it was he who stood in the front line for Chancellor Kohl in the repeated and highly publicized scuffles between Bonn and Wiesbaden over NUKEM/ALKEM. Thus the Hessian election was not so much a race between four parties as between two blocs, and to a certain degree between two opposite visions of the Federal Republic.[184]

In this complicated, multidimensional contest, the Hessian realists won, but the red–green coalition lost. The Greens bettered their 1983 margin dramatically from 5.9 percent to 9.4 percent. The SPD, however, plummeted by 6 percent to 40.2 percent. CDU and FDP together captured 49.9 percent of the vote, giving the Bonn coalition partners a two-seat majority in the Landtag in Wiesbaden. Among potential SPD voters who cast their ballots for the CDU/FDP, the majority were opposed to the SPD/Green Party alliance.[185] While it would be inappropriate to draw hasty conclusions from such a narrow defeat, the election demonstrated clearly that the real weakness of a red–green coalition did not lie on the left but in the political center.

Needless to say, this placed the SPD in a difficult position. By ignoring or shunning the Greens, the Social Democrats would lose voters to their left; by allying with the Greens, they risked diminishing their support in the center. It appeared that the SPD was in an unenviable bind: it could not return to power with the Greens or without them.

No leader had been a greater victim of this dilemma than Hamburg's SPD Mayor Klaus von Dohnanyi, whose city had become virtually ungovernable since he lost his absolute majority in November 1986 to the strong showing of the GAL's "women's ticket." After nearly four months of unsuccessful discussions between the CDU and SPD on the formation of a grand coalition, the Hamburg city parliament was dissolved and new elections set for May.[186] Several weeks later, Dohnanyi renewed his offer of coalition negotiations to the GAL, which promptly countered in its usual fashion, by issuing a 12-point catalogue of preconditions for a "toleration" of an SPD government by the GAL.[187] Dohnanyi's intent, as the GAL was well aware, was principally tactical, for his real aim was the formation of an SPD/FDP coalition.[188] He therefore concentrated his campaign on demonstrating the GAL's "repudiation of reform politics," and its "incapacity for reform," in short, its inability and unwillingness to assume the responsibilities of government.[189] Dohnanyi's strategy was to recapture reform-oriented voters from the fundamentalist GAL.

The defeat of the Hessian coalition in April suddenly gave the Hamburg contest a new and greater significance. Should the GAL make a strong showing, fundamentalism and the Hamburg model could lay claims to being more successful than realism and the Hessian model. On the other hand, a Dohnanyi victory and a subsequent SPD/FDP coalition would set a powerful precedent, and strengthen the hand not only of the realists but of those in the Federal Republic who claimed that the Greens were simply not viable coalition partners, not *koalitionsfähig*. Even though the GAL's electoral loss of 3.4 percent (from the previous 10.4 percent to 7 percent) at the Hamburg polls could have signalled the Fundis' demise, it did not. Instead, a tug of war between Fundis and Realos ensued, which stalemated the party for the next three years. Neither of the two factions was strong enough to knock out its rival definitively, yet each mustered sufficient energy to place major obstacles in its competitor's path. This internecine struggle was to contribute significantly to the curious situation in which a party that had been largely responsible for the shaping of an entirely new discourse in German and European politics misgauged so hopelessly the events of 1989–90, which were fundamentally to alter the postwar order.

Waxing or Withering? The Greens in the Late 1980s and Early 1990s

In the late spring of 1987 the Fundis, who had emerged with much momentum since the Bundestag election of January 25, managed to gain a temporary upper hand in their struggle with the Realos. By placing three of their key figures, Jutta Ditfurth, Regina Michalik and Christian Schmidt, on the federal party's executive committee (the Bundesvorstand, BuVo), the Fundis were well situated to define the political content and form of the party's internal debates and its external positions. Meanwhile, the Realos remained far from powerless, expanding their influence in their parliamentary positions, especially in the Bundestag. Thus the lines were drawn for what was to become a brutal and relentless internecine struggle between the radical, extra-parliamentary Fundis, relying on their strength in the party's executive committee, on the one hand, and the reformist, parliamentary Realos based in the Greens' Bundestag delegation on the other. The Federal Republic's frequent elections on the state and local levels provided ample opportunities to keep these animosities alive.

State elections on May 17 in Hamburg and Rhineland-Palatinate offered openings for mutual accusations and recriminations. Hamburg's Fundi-dominated GAL, home of the radical eco-socialists Ebermann and Trampert, suffered an ignominious defeat, largely at the hand of the Social Democrats. Whereas the Greens obtained 100,000 votes (10.4 percent of the electorate) in the 1986 elections for the Hamburg legislature (the Bürgerschaft) and augmented this already impressive number by 14,000 in the Bundestag election of January 1987, they barely attained 69,000 votes (7.0 percent) in the election of May 17.[190] The Realos blamed the Fundis' obstreperousness and poor strategic thinking for this electoral debacle. Fischer, Schily, Schoppe and others in the realists' camp accused the Fundis of political immaturity and adventurism. The Realos believed that views such as the one expressed by Christina Kukielka, one of the GAL's Fundis, arguing that "stones can also serve as arguments," could at best be seen as immature, at worst counterproductive to the Greens' cause.[191] Fischer and his allies interpreted the electoral outcome not as an achievement of the Hamburg SPD led by the popular mayor Klaus von Dohnanyi but rather as a manifestation of the voters' disgust with a Green Party dominated by irresponsible Fundis and their immature political allies.

In response to the Realos' accusations, the Fundis were anything but apologetic. They attributed the party's poor showing to the SPD's attempt to "buy" votes by promising to take over 40,000 apartments from Neue Heimat, the previously mentioned scandal ridden construction company owned by the trade unions and based in Hamburg. Moreover, the Fundis also argued that the Realos' accommodationist course helped deradicalize the Greens' image and the true nature of their clientele, leading to a self-fulfilling prophecy in which deradicalized people opted for the real thing, that is, the SPD.[192] The intraparty disagreements and bickering reached such dimensions by late May that a number of commentators began to describe the Greens as two parties masquerading as one. The word *Spaltung* (splitting) began to make the rounds in public discussions of the Greens. Even the party's success in the Rhineland-Palatinate elections, in which the Greens managed to gain representation in that Land's parliament for the first time, could not hide the deep divisions which informed the party's public persona. With the Fundi wing in ascendance in Rhineland-Palatinate, early summer looked rather bleak for the Realos. Had it not been for their continued prominence in the party's Bundestag delegation in Bonn, the Realos might possibly have succumbed for good to their radical rivals at this juncture. Instead the stalemate continued with neither side being strong enough to deliver a decisive blow to its intraparty rival.

The Greens' continued travails at the polls did not help matters either. Following the habitual summer lull, the election season picked up full steam in the fall. On September 13, voters in Bremen and Schleswig-Holstein, the Federal Republic's northernmost Land, went to the polls. Once again, the results were very disappointing to the Greens. First and foremost, the party's 4 percent in Schleswig-Holstein once again fell short of the 5 percent minimum required by the Federal Republic's electoral law for gaining representation in the legislature. Even the 10.5 percent in Bremen, which, as will be recalled, was the cradle of the Greens' parliamentary presence in German politics, represented a defeat of sorts: the result was simply not good enough to dislodge the Social Democrats from their absolute majority in Bremen's legislature. Since this was one of the Greens' publicly declared goals of their campaign in this city-state, the election results represented an obvious shortcoming for the Greens from this perspective. Despite this fine performance at the polls, the Greens once again had to make do with being in the opposition. Moreover, this otherwise very respectable "double digit" result still embodied a numerical setback when compared to the Greens' electoral showing in Bremen during the Bundestag campaign of January 25, when they attained 14.5 percent.[193]

With the polls hardly closed, the ritual of mutual recriminations was once again in full swing. The Realos blamed the Fundis for mismanaging the campaign and marginalizing the party with their radical methods and messages, while downplaying the fact that the party's natural base was weak in Schleswig-Holstein, with its rural social structure and absence of large cities and university towns. The Realos conceded that the SPD might have benefited from the "sympathy bonus" credited to its smart and progressive candidate Björn Engholm, who had just emerged as the only hero in the otherwise sorry Barschel affair.[194] (Engholm became the leader of the SPD following the party's electoral debacle in the first all-German Bundestag election in December 1990. To the surprise and consternation of the German Left and social democracy, Engholm resigned all his party positions in May 1993 as a result of the unexpected rekindling of the long-dormant Barschel affair, in which Engholm apparently was not merely the victim as had been previously assumed.) However, the Realos pointed to Fundi intransigence and immaturity as the major cause of the party's problems. By rejecting any coalition possibilities with the SPD, the Fundis had – in the Realos' eyes – once again failed to accept political responsibility. Adding insult to injury, an internal squabble in the party's executive committee between the Realo minority and the Fundi majority led the former to accuse the latter of employing "Stalinist practices."[195]

As usual, the Fundis were hardly retiring in their countercriticisms. The party's major problem, so the Fundis claimed, was its seemingly inexorable drift toward the SPD, which had meant in effect that the Greens had become indistinguishable from the Social Democrats. The Realos' obsession with sharing governmental power in coalition with the Social Democrats had attained such paramount importance that what once had been merely a question of tactics had all but replaced other issues in the Greens' public identity; by being enamored with power and "hot to govern" (*regierungsgeil*) the Realos had – in the Fundis' eyes – undermined the party's very essence as a radical, movement-type alternative to the Federal Republic's corrupt and bankrupt political and economic institutions. Whenever voters rejected a CDU-led government, as was the case in this Schleswig-Holstein election, they turned to the SPD with a vengeance rather than bother with voting for a weak imitation.[196] Again the debate remained inconclusive.

But the bitterness lingered. Even a cursory reading of Germany's political reporting makes it apparent that by the late 1987 the Greens had ceased to act or function like a party. Words such as "wrath," "depression," "warfare," "splitting," "betrayal," "blackmail," "manipulation," "psychoterror" dot the articles in which the Greens were discussed. Even though there can be no question that some of the acerbity of these continuing altercations had to be taken with a grain of salt, it is quite clear (given the benefit of hindsight) that these internecine struggles worked to the party's detriment.[197] Three factors proved largely responsible in saving the party's nominal unity: First and foremost, the knowledge on the part of every Green – Fundi and Realo – that any splitting of the party would mean its end. Thus the leaders of both tendencies realized full well that their political survival depended on a continued, albeit rancorous, cohabitation. A second factor which served to hold the party together was a major revolt by the party's grass-roots. Storming a six-hour party meeting in Bonn in late November, rank-and-file activists expressed their disgust with the leadership's constant internal bickering in no uncertain terms. "We have had enough," declared one poster, another proclaimed, "Resign or we will," a third stated "Your quarrels truly disgust us."[198] The third factor in saving the party were the integrative efforts and personal commitment of Antje Vollmer.

"Small, quiet, shy, but a political heavyweight: that is Antje Vollmer" is how one magazine described this important green politician.[199] It will be recalled that Vollmer had formulated the compromise statement on the "coalition question" for the 1987 Bundestag elections. By January of 1988, it had become clear to Vollmer that something concrete had to be done to prevent the Greens from self-destructing. Toward that end she and 13 of her green Bundestag colleagues formed Aufbruch '88 (New Beginning '88) whose aim was to create a bridge (or at least some sort of middle ground) between Fundis and Realos. An explicit attempt at offering dialogue and being an integrating element in the party, Aufbruch '88 hoped to salvage some of the political content favored by the Fundis and lend it the political form preferred by the Realos. In short, while less concerned with the various possibilities of coalitional arrangements with the SPD than the Realos, the Aufbruch people also spurned the categorical negativism exhibited with such regularity by the Fundis. In other terms, Aufbruch '88 aimed at reconciling the commitment (instead of the fanaticism) of the Fundis with the practicality (instead of the cooptation) of the Realos. Despite her misgivings about this role, Vollmer became the "mother" of the Greens.[200] While Vollmer's efforts to reconcile the two warring factions failed, the creation of a distinct, though heterogeneous, third force within the party did help to stabilize it. Aufbruch '88 became a weak but real middle in a party that had lost such a moderating internal balance. The Greens had developed into a three-winged creature which, though awkward and cumbersome, survived as a party."[201]

The Baden-Württemberg election of March 20, 1988 saw the Greens garner 7.9 percent of the vote, a loss of only 0.1 percent as compared to the result of 1984. While this was not a stellar showing, the returns indicated quite clearly that the Greens had become an established small party in Germany's most prosperous Land. Led by the prominent Realo, Rezzo Schlauch, a charismatic and rotund Marx lookalike with decidedly un-Marxist views, the Realos' position after the Baden-Württemberg election further solidified their long-held dominance in this German state, which in turn helped the Realo tendency in the country as a whole.[202]

But trouble was not far behind. On May 8, the Greens once again failed to surmount the 5 percent threshold in Schleswig-Holstein. Indeed, their 3 percent was lower than their previous showing in September 1987 when, as will be recalled, they garnered 4 percent.[203] Adding insult to injury, Willi Hoss, one of the Greens' most prominent Realo members of the Bundestag and a leading union activist from Stuttgart, taunted the fundamentalist tendencies of the Schleswig-Holstein Greens by declaring openly that he, a Green, would have voted for the SPD with no hesitation in this election.[204] The Fundis were not going to leave this provocation unchallenged. Indeed, they started a counteroffensive in which they not only demanded Hoss's resignation from the party, but once again blamed the Greens' poor showing on the Realos' accommodationism. The mediator between the two dueling factions was Aufbruch '88, whose spokesperson Ralf Fuecks judiciously assessed the defeat in Schleswig-Holstein as one for the whole party.[205]

The maturing of the Greens also brought with it the first signs of the pathologies which afflict all political parties. In June 1988, Germany's iconoclastic weekly, *Der Spiegel*, reported the discovery of financial improprieties at party headquarters. The tables were suddenly turned. In its early days, the party had won public legitimacy by exposing the improprieties of other parties, most notably in the infamous Flick scandal.[206] But now, *Der Spiegel* reported, green activists who were former members of the Frankfurt city council acknowledged and approved of the disappearance of two-thirds of DM 20,000 which were earmarked for a campaign against the chemical giant Hoechst. The money for this campaign came from the Greens' executive, the BuVo, which in turn had received it from the federal government's election campaign funds. This affair would not have attracted national attention had it not involved Manfred Zieran, Jutta Ditfurth's companion, who – like Ditfurth, a committed Fundi – used the money for "expense compensation." In yet another twist to this convoluted story, it appeared that the account from which this money originated had been set up in Ditfurth's name.[207]

In conformity with its tradition for relentless muckraking, *Der Spiegel* pursued the investigation further. According to the news weekly, members of the Green Party complained about checks being written without requisite receipts, thus making it virtually impossible to trace these financial transactions. Furthermore, reports emerged about some people using large sums of money from the party's petty cash account. In addition, it seems that the Fundi–Realo rivalry also determined who was compelled to repay loans and to whom they were forgiven. A Fundi, Ulrich Tost, and a Realo, Michael Merkel, borrowed DM 20,000 together for the printing of a calendar. When the project failed, only Merkel, the Realo, returned his share of the loan to the party while Tost, the Fundi, received dispensation from the Fundi-controlled BuVo from paying back the DM 10,000 which he owed.[208] Based on this and other misdeeds, Otto Schily demanded that Tost be expelled from the party. Not only did the Fundi-controlled BuVo spare Tost, it publicly reprimanded Schily.

The major financial problem featured by *Der Spiegel* involved the renovation of Haus Wittgenstein near Bonn, which was supposed to become the Greens' convention and meeting center. This mansion was bought for DM 1.4 million and by June 1988 had cost DM 3 million in renovations with the end not yet in sight. According to people involved in the project, the money for renovation went not only to *bona fide* workers, but also to party functionaries for their alleged overtime work. Haus Wittgenstein was supposed to be a showcase project for the Greens, built according to "ecological building principles" as part of a self-help project for former drug addicts.[209]

The BuVo's immediate reaction was denial. But the seriousness of the allegations and their corroboration by sources within the party continued to feed the scandal. As grass-roots pressure mounted, the BuVo reluctantly agreed to an investigation by a special internal party commission.[210]

But even before this commission could complete its work, "Glasnost in the Greens," a group under the leadership of former party manager Lukas Beckmann issued a 125-page report detailing the shady financial practices of the party in full detail. The Beckmann report concluded that the various denials and repeated cover-ups to which the party's leadership had contributed by its complete preoccupation with fighting the incessant battles between Fundis and Realos generated in the party an alarming degree of *Verfilzung*, that is, structural corruption and entanglement of offices and persons bordering on the illegal and the unethical.

Challenged by this report, the Green Party reluctantly issued its own findings on the scandal which, however, were not officially published until October 1988. Even then, it took the executive committee of the party four more months to accept full responsibility for the various financial misdeeds initially revealed by *Der Spiegel*. Still there were a number of green leaders, most notably among the Fundis, who continued to belittle the investigation's results. Some argued that it had been blown out of proportion. Others pointed to the help which the building renovation project of "Haus Wittgenstein" had offered to drug addicts and other marginalized youths. Jutta Ditfurth had even developed a social-theoretical justification for the Greens' wrongdoing by arguing that alternative businesses were not beholden to the profit-making logic of capitalism and thus rejected the rational, hierarchical structures of corporations.[211] Other Fundis tried to politicize the scandal by accusing the Realos of using it for political gain inside the party. But despite these spirited counterattacks, this was the beginning of the end of the Fundis, presaging their ultimate fall from the pinnacles of green power in the course of 1989 and 1990.

An early episode in what was to be a lengthy drama came in December 1988 at the Greens' congress in Karlsruhe. Originally convened to discuss party strategy for the European parliament elections slated for the spring of 1989, it developed into a public forum on the Greens' financial operations. Following a debate which was heated even by green standards, the congress delegates passed a vote of no confidence on the BuVo by a respectable margin of 214 to 186, leading to the BuVo's immediate resignation.[212] Considering the fact that the party activists, that is, a majority of the congress delegates, had at least been sympathetic to, if not consistently supportive of the Fundi position inside the party, the outcome of this vote was nothing short of sensational. After the vote the Fundis tried to block any further proceedings, arguing that such a momentous occasion called for the cessation of the congress. However, in yet another startling setback for the Fundi leadership, the delegates rejected this motion and voted to proceed with the original agenda. Moreover, before adjourning, the congress delegates empowered the party's extended executive committee (*Hauptausschuss*) to conduct the party's daily affairs until the election of the new BuVo on March 5, 1989.[213]

Yet when the temporary BuVo was elected in December 1988, the Realos once again found themselves in the minority. It appeared that the Fundis were so well ensconced in the party organization – as opposed to its electorate and its parliamentary wing – that even a scandal of this magnitude was not sufficient to dislodge them. Still, the Fundis had been gravely weakened. Growing pessimism, ongoing squabbles and a few key victories for the Greens in state and local elections brought about their downfall.

Following her ouster as a BuVo member, Ditfurth assailed the Realos with unusual vitriol. She not only chided them for acquiescing to the country's general rightward drift but charged them with actively supporting such a move. In addition to ruining the Greens, Realo-style politics had, in Ditfurth's view, contributed to a growing reaction in the Federal Republic as a whole.[214] She issued an impassioned plea to her Fundi followers to remain in the party. That such a plea was necessary indicated the rapidly souring mood within the party.[215] At a Fundi meeting in Bonn in early February 1989, a substantial rift developed between the radical ecologists and eco-socialists on the one hand and the undogmatic leftists on the other. The genealogy of this intra-Fundi rupture originated in Hamburg, where the Greens' two Fundi superstars, Rainer Trampert and Thomas Ebermann, made increasing noises about leaving the Greens altogether and starting their own radical party of the Left. Trampert even refused to be a candidate for the forthcoming BuVo election in March, arguing that the Greens had become part of the establishment. Despite their disgust with the Greens' "sell-out" (*Anbiederung*), Trampert and Ebermann were not to resign formally from the party for nearly another year. But cracks within the faction were already rapidly weakening the fundamentalists' position within the party.

Ironically, yet tellingly, it was a string of electoral victories for the Greens which dealt the Fundis their *coup de grace*. On January 29, 1989, the Greens attained 11.8 percent in the West Berlin state elections. This represented a 1.2 percent increase from the previous tally of 10.6 percent attained in 1985. Coupled with the CDU's embarrassing 8.6 percent loss and the SPD's 4.9 percent gain, West Berlin was poised for yet another experiment in red–green governance.[216] Similar results in Frankfurt's municipal elections catapulted another major German city into the realm of a red–green coalition. The red–green model of government, which had ended in abject failures in Hamburg and Hessen, was suddenly given another chance by the voters of West Berlin and Frankfurt. These convincing victories took the sting out of (yet another) failure to surmount the 5 percent threshold in the state of Saarland. Led by the youthful, energetic and greenish Oskar Lafontaine, the Social Democrats retained their absolute majority in the state legislature. This negative outcome for the Greens confirmed the pattern: where they were confronted with a left-leaning and ecology-conscious social-democratic leader such as Lafontaine, they fared poorly.

Although the Berlin Greens, known as the Alternative List (AL), were in many respects closer in substance and spirit to the Fundis than the Realos, their victory, just like that of the "super-Realos" in Frankfurt, nevertheless contributed to a weakening of the Fundis' cause. Successful elections, by their very nature, strengthened those in the party who pleaded for realism. And approval by the voters suggested that green politics could succeed *within* the existing framework of German politics.

At the Duisburg congress in early March, the flagging influence of the Fundis was translated into decreased power within the party apparatus. Rather than reinstating another fundamentalist majority in the BuVo, the Congress elected a diverse group representing virtually every shading which had come to exist inside the Greens. The three speakers of the executive committee, Ruth Hammerbacher, Ralf Fuecks and Verena Krieger represented the Realos, Aufbruch and Fundis, respectively, with the rest of the BuVo comprising a mixture of smaller tendencies. It should be added that Krieger – as an indication of the Fundis' imminent demise – hailed from the most moderate wing of this radical tendency.[217] Jutta Ditfurth, upset by these developments, berated the congress delegates with a bitter evaluation of her tenure. She announced that she would quit the party as soon as the Greens entered into a coalition with the SPD on the national level. Ditfurth accused the Realos of ruining the party's potential for effecting true societal change by systematically avoiding any real confrontation with capitalism and opting for the role of society's repairman instead. But in spite of Ditfurth's invective, the congress delegates voted by acclamation in support of a red–green coalition in Berlin.[218] The factional confrontation around which the party had been structured virtually since its founding suddenly dissolved as a wave of pluralism and pragmatism swept over the party.

The miraculous events of late summer and autumn 1989 changed Germany, Europe and the world. With the opening of the Berlin wall on November 9, German and European politics were never to be the same again. The landscape shaped by the agreement at Yalta in 1945 was dramatically altered. While no party in the Federal Republic was even remotely ready for the magnitude of these changes, the Greens seemed particularly slow to accept them and their consequences. Many of the premises defining the Greens' political parameters collapsed in the fall of 1989. At just the moment when they seemed to have found themselves at last, the Greens were plunged into yet another searching identity crisis.

The changes in East Central Europe led many within the party as a whole to "draw consequences." Wearied by the factional infighting of the 1980s, Otto Schily, a Realo mainstay and arguably one of the party's most original thinkers and innovative strategists over the years, left the Greens in the fall of 1989 and joined the SPD,[219] as Thea Bock, one of the Greens' most talented politicians from Hamburg, had done before. But among the Fundis the defections assumed the dimensions of an exodus. In the spring of 1990, the erstwhile Fundis from Hamburg, Thomas Ebermann and Rainer Trampert, decided to depart from the Greens in search of a genuine alternative to capitalism – which they felt the Greens had long ceased to be. Other Fundi stars such as the former members of the parliamentary leadership in Bonn, Christian Schmidt and Regula Schmidt-Bott, also left the party. To these and other Fundis, the Greens had become completely established and "social democratized." They had stopped offering a radical alternative to capitalism and bureaucracy. The Realos, so these Fundis believed, had rendered the Greens into a normal political party.[220]

At the party's Hagen congress held on April 1 and 2, 1990, the Fundis – or rather what remained of them – experienced a further setback. Ostensibly convened to discuss programmatic issues and to arrive at an overhaul of the party's program concerning a number of matters, it became a tribunal against the Fundis. Supported openly by the centrist Aufbruch, the Realos continued to dismantle the Fundis' organizational importance and ideological influence inside the party.[221]

The Fundi cause was hardly helped by the party's surprisingly strong showing in the Lower Saxony state elections of May 13, 1990. Coupled with the SPD's victory over the CDU, Lower Saxony became yet another experiment in the exercise of red-green governmental power. Headed by the SPD's Gerhard Schröder, like Lafontaine one of the Social Democrats' youthful and ecology-minded politicians, a coalition cabinet was established in Hanover in which the Greens became junior partners to the SPD.[222] With Lower Saxony joining Berlin, Saarland and Schleswig-Holstein as former CDU bastions suddenly ruled by the SPD alone or in coalition with the Greens, the forthcoming first Bundestag election of a united Germany looked hopeful for the Left, including the Greens.

Table 7.1 Results of the 1990 Bundestag election

	Votes (%)			Number of seats
	West	*East*	*Total*	
Christian Democrats (CDU/CSU)	44.3	41.8	43.8	319
Social Democrats (SPD)	35.7	24.3	33.5	239
Free Democrats (FDP)	10.6	12.9	11.0	79
Greens	4.8[a]	6.0[b]	5.1[c]	8
Party of Democratic Socialism (PDS)	0.3	11.1	2.4	17
Republicans	2.3	1.3	2.1	0
Other parties	2.0	2.6	2.1	0
Total	100	100	100	662

[a] Without 5 percent, the Greens of the West received no seats.
[b] With 6.0 percent, Alliance 90/Greens of the East received 8 seats.
[c] This 5.1 percent vote means that if the Greens of the West and the Alliance 90/Greens of the East had run in coalition they would have received around 40 seats in the Bundestag.

Sources: Reprinted from *Between Protest and Power: The Green Party in Germany*, by E. Gene Frankland and Donald Schoonmaker, 1992, by permission of Westview Press, Boulder, Colorado. Table adapted from Mannheim Forschungsgruppe Report no. 61 (Dec. 2, 1990), pp. 7–9.

These expectations proved to be cruel illusions. December 2, 1990 was a dark day indeed for the Greens. Exactly ten years after a tumultuous meeting in Karlsruhe established the party as a national force, the voters of a united Germany tossed all but a handful of newly arrived East German Greens into the cold (see the table). The chickens had come home to roost: the party's 4.8 percent in the former West Germany represented an electoral debacle which virtually no pollster or politician, green or otherwise, had predicted.[223] To list some observations about this bitter defeat:[224]

-   Almost a quarter of a million former voters for the Greens did not vote at all.
-   The core of the voters for the Greens never comprised more than 3–4 percent of the West German electorate, meaning that the decisive margins which catapulted the party over the 5 percent hurdles throughout the 1980s always emanated from a group of greenish sympathizers and floating voters who liked the party's appeal and ideas but lacked the commitment of the core. This group of "fellow travelers" never excluded the SPD as an option. Indeed, while the Social Democrats' electoral defeat was, if anything, even more severe than that of the Greens, the SPD did attract in excess of 600,000 votes from the Greens.
-   In addition to losing voters to the Social Democrats in a massive way, the Greens also lost a small, but crucially decisive, number of votes to a new rival on the Left, the Party of Democratic Socialism (PDS), the successor to the former East German Communist Party, SED. Especially in such green bastions as Bremen, Hamburg and Berlin, there occurred a quantitatively small (about 1 percent) but qualitatively important shift from the Greens to the PDS.
-   The Greens received a decreasing share of young (18–24 years) and first-time voters (one-third less than in 1987); they also lost voters in the 25–50 group, while they once again failed to gain any significant support in the over-50 category.
-   While it is true that, in a bizarre twist, the greens (quite uncharacteristic for any small party in Germany and rather untypical in light of their own past performance) received more first than second votes in the German two-ballot system, this remained a very small consolation for the party since it is only the tally of the second votes which determines a party's representational strength in the legislature. The most plausible explanation for this occurrence is that the voters in places like Bremen, Hamburg and Berlin "rewarded" individual Greens with their first vote but then gave their second vote – the one that really counted – to the SPD or some other party such as the PDS.

Though numerous, the reasons for this debacle can be summarized as follows. To begin with, more than any previous election in the history of the Federal Republic, this one was virtually monopolized by one single issue: unification. Understandably, the magnitude of this historical event simply displaced any other topic which would have been on the agenda of any normal German election. Issues such as peace, ecology, alternative lifestyles and others where the Greens had enjoyed a comparative advantage were all but crowded out by the salience of German unification.

Added to this quantitative predominance of German unification was also its qualitative side. Concretely, the very nature of the issue was either completely alien to the Greens – and to many of the Social Democrats as well – or met with their outright rejection. For obvious historical reasons, most of

the German Left – inclusive of Social Democrats and the Greens – has remained very uneasy about, indeed hostile to, anything even vaguely related
to German nationalism. This, of course, does not mean that either Social
Democrats or Green supporters have not repeatedly assumed positions which,
in their objective content as well as subjective ramifications, were profoundly
nationalistic. The reader needs only to be reminded of the SPD's neutralism
phase of the 1950s, in which the Social Democrats opposed Adenauer's pro-
NATO stance and western orientation with a heavy dosage of German nationalism in their quest to unify the recently divided country. In terms of the
Greens and their milieu, one needs only to look at the subtext of their
opposition to NATO's double-track decision and their pervasive anti-
Americanism to observe an array of themes which have been constant features of German nationalism. Yet, unlike the CDU and, to a much lesser
degree, even the FDP, the Greens and Social Democrats felt very ambivalent
about the whole unification complex, which evoked openly nationalistic
emotions, something quite alien and uncomfortable for the German Left
since 1945 and especially since 1968. While most Social Democrats and Greens
obviously favored the demise of the Stalinist and repressive SED regime in
East Germany, it was a much smaller number in either group who favored
that country's Anschluss-style disappearance into what amounted to an extended West Germany. To most Greens, this annexation was much too fast,
too undemocratic and, above all, market propelled. It bore the dangers of a
mighty and powerful Germany dominating the rest of Europe by virtue of its
economic prowess and its newly gained demographic, geographic and political
muscle.

The truth is that to most Greens, being a quintessential creation of the
Federal Republic, the German Democratic Republic had over the years become a foreign land. While its Stalinism was objectionable to most, though
certainly not all, Greens, the legitimacy of the GDR as a country was never
in doubt in the Federal Republic's green and social democratic milieus. As
such, the GDR was just another German-speaking country like Austria.
Moreover, even though its political rule was deformed by the excesses of a
Stalinist bureaucracy, to many a member of the Federal Republic's green
milieu, the GDR was in its own flawed way still a worthy socialist experiment.
As the self-styled successor to the "good" Germany of the old SPD and KPD,
the GDR – to many West German leftists – was the better of the two Germanies,
the one that confronted Germany's fascist past head on. Given this world-
view, it is understandable that most Greens were still hoping for the emergence of some sort of "third way" in a post-Stalinist GDR, while the vast
majority of East Germans had made the absorption of their country by West
Germany all but a *fait accompli*.

The Greens' disdain for unification, especially in such haste, manifested
itself in their programmatic stance and strategic miscalculation which insisted
that the two parties, the Green Party of the East and the Green Party of the
West, should not form an official alliance until one day *after* the Bundestag
election. Telling of the immense importance accorded to autonomy and

sovereignty as decisive moral categories by the Greens, the complete and official merger between East and West Greens did not occur until late January 1993. Then, in preparation for the Bundestag election of 1994, the two nominally separate entities decided to pool their resources in good part because both – East and West Greens – were determined to avoid the electoral disaster of 1990, which both viewed as self-inflicted. The reluctance on the part of both sides to merge at an earlier date once again solidified the Greens' opposition to unification *per se*, as well as to the actual form in which it was implemented by the CDU-led government. Moreover, it also confirmed the Greens' preoccupation with autonomy in that they were careful not to follow in the footsteps of all other West German parties in devouring their fledgling East German counterparts. Nevertheless, this upright and moral stance cost the West German Greens their parliamentary presence, since a united Green Party would have cleared the 5 percent hurdle which the West German Greens failed to do on their own.

Then the character of the party itself has to be taken into account. The Greens' preoccupation – some would say obsession – with democratic principles led them to "rotate" away most of their well-known public figures, such as Antje Vollmer. Rotation in effect meant that the Greens were unable – or unwilling – to field recognizable people in a media-dominated age. At the same time, their commitment to diversity within the party perpetuated the incessant battles between Fundis and Realos. Many green sympathizers showed their disillusionment with these fruitless quarrels by deserting the party, most typically, though not exclusively, for the SPD.

Lastly, the Greens suffered from their very own successes of the last ten years. In a sense, they had rendered all the other parties "green," leading to their own temporary demise in the process. Virtually all issues, be they women's rights or ecology, peace or nuclear energy, had been appropriated by all West German parties in the course of the 1980s. The most convincing evidence for the Greens' success was furnished by the party's loss of its uniqueness.

8

The East German Greens: From Underground Opposition to Bundestag Representation

With Susanne Altenburger

This is the story of relentless dissent. From their very origins to their current parliamentary representation, the East German Greens have consistently made antinomy the essence of their existence. But in notable contrast to the West German Greens, who emerged as the politically most significant legacy of the opposition to capitalism as represented by 1968, the East German Greens and their world emanated from the democratic resistance to the Stalinist dictatorship which ruled the German Democratic Republic for nearly 40 years. Moreover, it is a testimony to the lasting impact of Stalinist repression how life in the East German dissident community continues to shape the same people's political behavior and attitudes in the Federal Republic's liberal democracy.

This chapter begins by describing the origins of opposition in the German Democratic Republic. Among the most telling characteristics of this movement were its fragmentation and its ties to the Lutheran church. If at all, dissent occurred on the local level in a completely decentralized and uncoordinated manner. East Germany's early oppositionists were typical *Einzelkämpfer*, individual fighters who challenged the existing order by opposing it in the most varied ways. True to the compelling nature of their oppositionism, the dissidents who opposed the GDR's Stalinism continued their dissent during the days of the revolution in the fall of 1989, as well as during East Germany's transition regime. In the former, they emerged as the vocal advocates of what was then known as the "third way," a de-Leninized, democratic, real (as opposed to "real existing") socialism which was to be as decidedly anti-Stalinist as it was anti-capitalist. Like its West German counterpart, this milieu also proved the most hostile to any developments which, even if remotely, could in any way be linked to German nationalism. Democratic and oriented to the grass-roots through thick and thin, these dissidents continued to extol the revolution's original slogan of "We are the people." Thus it was no surprise that they opposed the GDR transition regime's preparations for self-sacrifice in the name of German unification. To its very end, the East German Greens and their milieu opposed the GDR's disappearance. They were particularly dismayed by the Federal Republic's Anschluss-like takeover of every aspect of East German life. The process of unification violated this group's sensibilities about democratic procedure, German nationalism and the politics of size, to mention but three important tenets of its overall belief system.

Needless to say, the East German Greens, their various predecessors and later-day allies have remained ardent critics of the united Germany. Opposed to unification in all its forms, these dissenters carried their politics of dissidence well beyond the established structures of the new Deutschland deeply into the country's green milieu. It is important to understand that the East German Greens became the sole representatives of the all-German Greens in the Bundestag following the election of December 2, 1990 precisely because they refused to be the subject of a takeover by the West German Greens paralleling the general incorporation of East Germany by the Federal Republic. This was the group of professional dissidents which found itself entering the Bundestag in Bonn, carrying the green cause without being fully part of it. Of course, their dissent has continued unabated in the Bundestag. They have remained vocal opponents of virtually all the government's policies vis-à-vis the former East Germany, in addition to assuming the West German Greens' traditional role of being the establishment's severe critics on issues related to the environment, the economy, foreign affairs, defense and social policy. Above all, they have been much-needed voices on behalf of the victims of Germany's increasing wrath against the large numbers of foreigners who have been granted asylum in the Federal Republic. In an era characterized by a growing brutalization of foreigners in Germany, which frequently includes killing and injuring of innocent people merely on account of their race, the color of their skin or the sound of their language, this handful of former East German dissidents turned green parliamentarians in a united Germany has championed a politics of tolerance and inclusion not matched in its scope and commitment by any of the other political actors in this increasingly xenophobic and intolerant country. The East German Greens' antinomy has attained such dimensions that – unlike their West German cousins and German parties in general – they and their allies have refused to vote as a bloc in the Bundestag. Hearkening back to the dark days of Stalinist repression in their former country, these dissidents developed such respect for the individual that – even at the cost of political expedience – they have chosen never to submit the individual to the will of the party or its parliamentary "faction." Risking marginality, perhaps even irrelevance, in an overly bureaucratized society defined by the political agenda of centralized party elites, these people's uncompromising commitment to something fundamentally democratic deserves at least our respect if it cannot escape our judgement.

On the Roots of the Independent GDR Opposition

The events of the summer of 1989, when waves of East Germans left the country through various means, not only put pressure on the regime of Erich Honecker in the East but also constituted a challenge to its opposition. Even in the aftermath of Mikhail Gorbachev's policies of liberalization, the East German government had maintained its traditional Stalinist approach in domestic politics. Whereas neighboring countries within the Soviet bloc were beginning to restructure their societies politically and economically, usually along liberal lines, Honecker's hesitation to adapt his government's position to the altered conditions in the East had resulted in growing dissatisfaction at home.

Public demonstrations against the regime and effectively organized political opposition had proved unfeasible in the past because of the regime's deployment of instant repression through its dense web of informers, the ubiquitous power of the Ministry of State Security (the dreaded Stasi), and ultimately, of course, the absolute monopoly of the state over the means of official communication. Of the increasing numbers of the public who were being informed about the changing conditions in neighboring "socialist brother-countries" (mostly through the West German media), those with the greatest sense of impatience and the least optimism for any kind of shift within East Germany decided to take advantage of the fundamental changes in neighboring countries in the only way that seemed possible. With loyalty to the regime barely a possibility, and with the choice of speaking out consistently stymied, often even punished, exit remained the only path of popular participation on a massive scale.[1] It is obvious that the presence of West Germany, and, above all, its citizenship laws which viewed every East German as a citizen of the Federal Republic, magnified the attraction of the decision to leave.

East Germans were allowed to travel only to countries in their Comecon trading bloc, so a growing number of determined souls chose to leave the German Democratic Republic with whatever they could carry in their suitcases or cars, entering Czechoslovakia, Poland and Hungary as summer tourists with the explicit goal of reaching the Federal Republic via its embassies in Prague, Warsaw and Budapest. The officials in those countries seemed to have little desire to stop the would-be defectors, and eventually "visiting" East Germans were allowed to continue into West Germany, where their enthusiastic welcome was duly reported over the airwaves for consumption in the GDR as well.

As a consequence the government in East Berlin was confronted by a de facto vote of no confidence in which its citizens expressed their disapproval of the regime with their feet. This not only undermined the system's authority but it further helped delegitimate the Honecker regime by demonstrating its increasing isolation even among the "socialist brother-countries" whose active assistance to the refugees made the whole thing possible. This avalanche of "tourists without return tickets" paradoxically exposed the very reasons for the Berlin Wall in the first place: the lack of loyalty to the regime, especially on the part of the educated and the skilled, which had led to a massive brain-drain. It was particularly in the eyes of this group that the Federal Republic embodied a panacea, the epitome of the good life consisting of personal freedom and economic prosperity. The external and internal pressures mounting on the Honecker regime assumed crisis proportions by the early fall of 1989, just when the GDR was to celebrate its fortieth birthday with much pomp. Even though thousands left the GDR daily in the late summer and early fall of 1989, with hundreds of thousands more getting ready to leave, there still remained many who might have been expected to go but who, for one reason or another, chose to stay. Prominent among them was a motley group of GDR dissidents who had emerged in positions of influence during the course of the fall revolution. It is to a discussion of their origins that we now turn.

Even though the Honecker regime's insistence on maintaining the political and economic status quo seemed to meet with increasing legitimacy problems, this did not mean that there existed no domestic political groups which were organized and ready to initiate discussion on systemic reform, potentially even to assume the reins of power. The regime's extensive mechanisms of repression and control had been very successful in suppressing any formation of national organization that could potentially evolve into a serious opposition movement not beholden to the government institutionally or ideologically. It is important to state this since the GDR always prided itself on actually having an opposition, albeit a government-sanctioned one. It consisted of what were called the bloc parties, a term derived from their membership in a body officially known as the Democratic Bloc. Its members were the Christian Democratic CDU, bearing the identical name and acronym as its mighty West German counterpart, the liberal LDPD (Liberal-Demokratische Partei Deutschlands), the national NDPD (National Demokratische Partei Deutschlands) and the farmer-based DBD (Demokratische Bauernpartei Deutschlands).[2] Of course, these bloc parties never challenged the complete monopoly of power wielded by the Communist-dominated SED (Sozialistische Einheitspartei Deutschlands). In the course of the events of 1989, these East German bloc parties soon matched up with their much more powerful corresponding sister-parties in the West, thereby foregoing any possibility of their providing leadership for a separate East German option without Communist rule. With the bloc parties rapidly folding into existing West German structures, East Germany's "third way" between its now discredited Marxism-Leninism and a market-driven western-style capitalism became all but impossible. Thus, while the foundations of Honecker's system began to show widening cracks under the effects of the soviet reforms of *perestroika* and *glasnost* spreading throughout the eastern bloc, any truly independent organizations representing opposition to both the systemic realities of Honecker's GDR and Kohl's Federal Republic had either not emerged from a state of infancy in the underground or had yet to be founded.

Despite the rigid control exercised by the state, there existed some underground oppositional activity with meetings and *samizdat* (self-publishing) publications. These groups had been numerically too insignificant to be easily detected by the regime. They certainly were too small to have had any political effect on it. Indeed, the conditions under which any form of dissent could survive permitted only the sporadic formation of minute groups. As a consequence of persecution by the state, communication among these groups was virtually impossible on either a national or a local level. The need to stay invisible to the authorities also condemned these oppositional groups to remain equally invisible to each other. The result was a high degree of organizational and ideological factionalism within the East German underground; while offering an interesting array of ideologies, visions and strategies, this proved very disadvantageous for the creation of a cohesive political coalition following the demise of the Honecker regime.

Systemic Legitimacy versus Dissent

Still, the persistence of unknown dissidents, their organizational experience in the underground, and the increasing relevance as well as legitimacy of their causes was to constitute much of the base for this unofficial opposition's role in the demise of the Honecker regime. A number of internal and external factors meant that small dissident groups continued to emerge under the GDR regime's system of control.

The pervasiveness of the GDR's secret police system and the regime's obsession with social and political control reflected in good part the regime's insecurities concerning the country's lack of legitimacy since its inception in 1949. Indeed, the severity of this control, which led to East German's abysmal civil and human rights record, was a major factor in contributing to the GDR's status of quasi-pariah among the community of nations. Even though the state apparatus, the SED and its ancillary organizations proved successful in quelling the popular uprising in East Germany in June 1953, the Soviet bloc's first genuine working-class revolt against the Communist ruling elite, the GDR establishment never trusted its manifest power, always fearing that the regime's serious deficit in legitimacy would ultimately undermine the country's existence as a whole. (Little did these elites know at the time how right they were.) The regime's paranoia was further stoked by the fact that over 80 percent of the GDR's population could receive West German television, which it watched with avid interest. Thus there arose a reality in the GDR which meant that a majority of its population lived a bifurcated existence: in the daytime people pretended to work just as hard as the regime pretended to pay them; at night they retreated into their private sphere to be tantalized by West Germany's consumer goods. In short, the whole system was based on lies, pretenses and fantasies which not only distorted, yet made bearable, the grim realities of life in the GDR, but also placed unrealistic expectations on the Federal Republic.

In an unsuccessful quest toward establishing what seemed to be a permanently elusive legitimacy[3] in the eyes of its citizens, the GDR's rulers pursued inherently contradictory strategies. On the one hand, they tried desperately to establish the country's legitimacy by attempting to be different from West Germany. They did this by claiming for the GDR the sole position of being the direct descendant of the "good" Germans and the moral Germany. The gist of this self-legitimating argument was that in notable contrast to the Federal Republic, which was the self-proclaimed successor of the horrible Third Reich, the GDR was the successor of its victims. Whereas by virtue of being capitalist the West German system embodied Nazi rule in what was merely a milder version, East Germany was the legacy of Germany's anti-fascist past, the political creation of the German working class and other progressive forces, as articulated especially by the KPD (Kommunistische Partei Deutschlands) during the Weimar Republic. The state attempted to create an East German identity which in its essence tried to be the exact opposite to the West German: socialist, anti-fascist, hence morally superior, indeed beyond reproach. The GDR's efforts in trying to establish a collective legitimacy by claiming the identity of a victim went so far as to have the country's schoolchildren believe that East German soldiers fought alongside the Red Army in trying to defeat the scourge of National Socialism. Jews were never acknowledged as particular victims of Nation Socialism. The Nazi genocide against the Jews was only mentioned in the context of Nazi repression of communists. Indeed, not until the fall of the SED-led communist regime in early 1990 did the GDR find it necessary to address the issues of restitution and reparation to the Jewish victims of National Socialism. Indeed, perhaps the only widely popular policy which the GDR's rulers pursued over the years was the silence on the Holocaust. East Germans were more than happy not to have to deal with that issue. They revelled in the state's myth that – miraculously – Nazis and fascists existed only to the west of the Elbe river. The Holocaust was purely a West German problem in the eyes of East Germany's political elite and, in this unique case, the population as well. The handful of Jews who lived in the GDR received some financial and other material support from the regime, but never as Jews, only as anti-fascist victims of fascism. Particularly heinous was the East German regime's position on Israel. To oppose policies of the Israeli government is one thing. But to be in the vanguard of eagerly assisting those whose expressed desire continues to be the annihilation of the Jewish state barely a few decades after Auschwitz is especially reprehensible. We are here referring to the GDR's massive aid in matériel and training to the Syrian and Iraqi governments, as well as to terrorist groups, both West German and Arab, explicit in their goal to cause harm to Israel and its population.

If the GDR's first strategy to attain legitimacy was predicated on establishing an identity in opposition to, almost in spite of, the Federal Republic and the West, the second aimed at the converse. In essence, this strategy tried to "buy" the citizens' loyalty, if not affection, by various conciliatory measures vis-à-vis the West. The deal was simple: in exchange for improving the lives of its citizens by allowing them to travel to the West (provided they were pensioners or Stasi informers), and by importing certain western status symbols such as blue jeans and Volkswagens for them, the GDR was accorded political respectability and economic aid. By hitching its fate to the Federal Republic and the international community, the GDR became, almost despite itself, part of an open transnational communications network. Increased border crossings in Berlin and elsewhere rendered German–German relations a daily reality in the lives of millions of East Germans. Barriers began to disappear. In a sense, the Berlin wall had started to crumble long before its opening on November 9, 1989. No matter how brutal and ubiquitous the regime's secret police had been, it simply was to prove no match for the increased contacts between East and West Germans. It is in this context that dissent began on a systematic and socially meaningful scale in East Germany. Despite the party's and the regime's most stringent efforts to the contrary, the exigencies of European politics, global developments and the advances in communication technology had pluralized East German society by the end of the 1980s. It is in this milieu that the precursors of what later became the East German Greens flourished.

The Lutheran Church vs the State: Dissent and its "Space" in a Repressive Society

If one looks at the social and occupational background of East German dissenters, the most telling observation pertains to the frequency of some sort of church-related affiliation or activity among them. There exists a sound structural reason for this clerical hegemony among the former GDR's dissidents and protesters. The East German Lutheran church was the only organization in the GDR which enjoyed the semblance of some independence from state and party. The Lutheran church thus provided an existential as well as spiritual space for activism whose philosophical underpinnings were deeply steeped in the church's ethics and therefore provided an automatic antinomy to the state's activities, if not necessarily its doctrine.[4]

Representing the vast majority of churchgoers in this highly secularized society, the church had been able to maintain its financial independence through support by its West German sister-church. It simultaneously took advantage of the regime's quest for international recognition through an improved civil rights record and established far-reaching connections with international church organizations. The church structured itself in a democratic fashion, in that it allowed its membership a certain degree of local autonomy. At a landmark meeting in March 1978, the church and the state agreed to respect each other's autonomy in particular areas, while making provisions for common action in others. Thus the church's internal structure was consolidated, while it retained the right to operate a number of independent theological institutions, above all its own publishing houses. It was the creation of these structures that allowed the forces of dissent to find a minimal degree of organization and the semblance of an autonomy on the level of the local parish.[5] Ironically, it was this "Concordat-style" agreement between the Leninist-Stalinist SED state and the traditional Lutheran church which furnished the necessary space for the dissidents to develop into a force which was eventually to destroy the GDR itself.

Two major areas of concern for these independent oppositional groupings were based on Protestant ideals which were particularly important to the East German Lutheran church: the assertion of any individual's civil rights as a prerequisite for the individual's capacity to act morally in the theological sense;[6] and the resistance against the degradation of the environment, which was viewed as a sin against God's creation.

The first principle had clearly constituted a philosophical challenge to the GDR's very understanding of its own legitimacy since its beginning. The likelihood of significant changes was more dependent on the GDR's desire for enhanced international standing and economic opportunity than on local or regional protests against the arbitrariness of the state in its refusal to grant basic individual rights. West Germany's insistence on humanitarian improvements as a condition for extending the GDR's credit line, for instance, appeared to be the more feasible path toward corresponding improvements than individuals risking their future and the church its precarious independence in a hopeless protest ignored by the media.

But environmental concerns could be presented as less fundamental. The Lutheran church had approached the environment and ecological matters as a theological problem since the early 1970s. It conducted research which remained internal to the church, but also produced position papers and periodicals on the issue. In this, the church followed a tradition of exploring Christianity's relationship to nature, a topic which had received particular attention in the Ecclesiastical Research Center in Wittenberg since 1927. Protected in its concerns and activities by the 1978 church–state agreement, this national effort concerning ecology emerged as a political force on the local level by the early to mid 1980s. Here, in keeping with the church's democratic structure, grass-roots activism by environmentally minded believers could be supported by the church's limited but still comparatively generous resources such as meeting facilities and mimeograph machines. This, of course, was only possible as long as the local pastor was sympathetic to the cause and strong enough to resist the local state authorities, a situation which varied tremendously from region to region.[7]

In light of the fact that environmental problems manifested themselves tangibly on a local level, small initiatives would often suffice to confront particular cases of environmental destruction. This, of course, is not to say that the state tolerated environmental protest at will. Private groups, meeting in members' houses, would eventually face harassment by the state authorities. Needless to say, any public protest against environmental degradation was immediately suppressed by the authorities, who claimed that socialist policies were by definition not ecologically harmful. The Lutheran church offered protection to many of these private protest groups. This, in turn, added to the radicalization of the church and spread the view that socialist policies – perhaps even more than capitalist one – produced significant environmental damage.[8]

The widening communication and travel channels to the West helped the flow of information and resources, allowed valuable personal contacts to be established and deepened, and lent increasing legitimacy to the independent opposition. Reports, eyewitness accounts, photographs and videos of the regime's repressive measures further undermined the state's feeble legitimacy in the eyes of its citizens. Once again, West Germany's presence proved fatal to the stability of the GDR's Communist regime since most of these videos and incriminating materials reentered East Germany via West German television. While this clearly proved insufficient to ease the state's continued repression of the oppositional forces, including environmental ones, it did contribute to a steady erosion of the Honecker regime's effectiveness and to a further reduction of its already low degree of legitimacy. Above all, it strengthened the resolve of the opposition. This, to be sure, remained factionalized and unable to coalesce on the national level. Constant fear of state informers and the growing vigilance by an increasingly defensive orthodox leadership rendered any meaningful collective action on the part of the dissidents impossible. The summer of 1989 proved particularly frustrating for the dissidents in the GDR, since they sensed that major historic changes were about to transform their lives, yet they found themselves still too weak to challenge the Honecker regime in a meaningful way. Still, by August of that year a movement was afoot which was to lead to the disappearance of the GDR and prove unique in the annals of German history, in the sense that it was to embody the origins of Germany's hitherto only successful "revolution from below."

Founding Fever

No other source reporting on these exciting events proved as thorough and insightful as the West Berlin alternative daily *Die Tageszeitung* (*Taz*), which has been, as already mentioned in this volume, a significant contribution by the Greens and their milieu to the enrichment and democratization of public discourse in the Federal Republic. Thus we have decided to rely very closely on the *Taz* in our presentation of the story of the East German revolution as it pertained to the eventual emergence of the East German Greens and their various ancillary groupings.

The *Taz* of August 15 best captured the nature of the GDR's burgeoning opposition on the one hand and the country's growing political vacuum on the other. The headlines read:

As a reaction to the wave of departures: the GDR
Opposition moves into a starting position

So far the manifold opposition groups constitute no
serious counterforce

Public call in East Berlin to establish an "identifiable
alternative" for the next elections

What followed in the two-page article was a comprehensive assessment of the
independent opposition's "vital statistics":

> The crisis of the system reveals the insufficiencies of its opposition: The
> scene in the GDR not only has increasing difficulty in acting under the
> umbrella of the church – it is only now beginning to emerge from
> factionalism, sectarianism and societal isolation. An attempt to create an
> alternative to the SED before the next election was initiated Sunday
> evening in an East Berlin church.
>
> . . .
>
> A personal or theoretical link that could span from the oppositional
> stirrings of the mid-fifties via the socialist critique of the system provided
> by the likes of Havemann or Biermann to today's approaches of the
> human rights and the ecology movements does not exist. What have
> established themselves as oppositional forces since the early eighties con-
> stitute essentially a new beginning. Due to the state's control the oppo-
> sition has so far not been able to create its own institutions. The broadest
> variety of groups act under the umbrella of the church.
>
> . . .
>
> But the liaison between opposition and church has by now become prob-
> lematic to all sides: the state increases its pressure on the church to
> restrict its activities exclusively to supposedly unpolitical tasks. The church,
> in turn, interested in the smoothest possible cooperation with the state,
> tries to keep its oppositional offspring within tolerable bounds.
>
> . . .
>
> The fact that up to now there exists no common platform either in an
> institutional or a programmatic perspective has something to do with the
> practices of the existing initiatives. Any form of institutionalization has so
> far quickly been suspected as an attempt toward an undemocratic
> hierarchization; demarcation – criticized as a characteristic of the "sys-
> tem" – is a defining element of the oppositional policies as well; the
> rigidity with which diverging opinions, evaluations, or actions are criti-
> cized is reminiscent of the left-sectarian feuds of the early seventies in the
> Federal Republic. . . .[9]

Still, early "symptoms of a founding fever," as the *Taz* would put it,[10] were
already observable, as indicated in the article's headlines. Following what
came to be known as a whisper campaign, 400 people assembled in the

parish hall of the Bekenntnis church in the Berlin district of Treptow on August 13. They heard the physicist Hans-Jürgen Fischbeck of the church group "Rejection of the Principle and Practice of Demarcation" (Absage an Prinzip und Praxis der Abgrenzung) call on the GDR opposition to found a countrywide "collective movement for renewal" in order to offer an "identifiable alternative" to the regime. Later, members representing several opposition groups in the GDR emphasized the need for innovation, though, tellingly, by asking Lenin's famous question "What is to be done?"[11]

Some notable GDR dissidents who had been expelled by the regime and now lived in the Federal Republic – Roland Jahn among them – supported these efforts vigorously in the hope of stemming the tide of refugees to the West and thus, at least implicitly, laying the groundwork for a two-state solution.[12] Also in August, leaders of the West German FDP met with East German opposition figures. The joint publication which emerged from this meeting was significantly entitled "United across Borders."[13] By the end of August, there were movements afoot to establish an East German SPD.[14] None of these political initiatives entertained even the faintest notion of a possible unification of the two Germanies.

Four major strains defined the political landscape of the GDR in early September 1989. On the official state and party level, a growing sense of frustration and insecurity developed concerning the regime's inability to control matters. It became increasingly obvious that the regime's lack of legitimacy was either to lead to more severe (and possibly violent) repression on its part, or to some structural changes toward a major shift in the country's power relations. Emanating especially from the Gorbachev-led Soviet Union, the international pressure experienced by the Communist leadership at the time further exacerbated the regime's predicament.

On the level of civil society, there emerged two countervailing trends. The first, described above as the origins of the dissident movement, formed the kernel of a new opposition which was clearly hostile to the existing regime yet believed in the validity of a continued East German entity under some form of "third way." In other words, these groups wanted a socialism which allowed different parties, permitted individual liberties and offered the right to travel anywhere in the world, while at the same time continuing the egalitarian protection offered by an extensive welfare state. This trend opted for increasing "voice" in the GDR which would then make growing "loyalty" to it feasible.

Opposed to this trend was the continued departure of thousands of GDR citizens to the Federal Republic; by voting with their feet, they were choosing a clear "exit" option as their preferred way to deal with the situation. This option dovetailed with the increasing sense of the presence of the Federal Republic and thus eventual unification. While nobody among the political class, the dissidents or the experts in the GDR or in the Federal Republic openly advocated, indeed believed in, the unification of the two countries in September 1989, it was clear that West Germany's sheer presence, its economic wealth and its professional competence rendered it a partner to the

GDR which was more than merely attractive. It was both overbearing and irresistible. Thus it was not by chance that many of the nascent East German political movements soon found themselves completely beholden to and controlled by their West German "helpers." This was the situation on September 12 when yet another reform-minded group entered the GDR's increasingly lively civil society. The group called itself the Initiativgruppe Neues Forum. It was to become one of the most significant direct precursors and constituents of the East German Greens.[15]

Neues Forum – a Third Way in a Second German State?

All efforts which the Neues Forum intends to muster are based on the desire for justice, democracy, peace, as well as the protection and conservation of nature. It is this impulse which we want to see realized in a vitalizing fashion during the coming restructuring of all areas of society.

We call upon all citizens of the GDR who want to participate in the restructuring of our society to become members of Neues Forum. The time is ripe.[16]

These concluding paragraphs of the Initiative's founding declaration constituted the first manifest assertion of an independent opposition's emergence from the GDR's hitherto fragmented and murky underground. Even though meek in character as revolutionary statements go, the opening manifesto of the Neues Forum (New Forum) nevertheless represented a clear challenge to the GDR's Stalinist rule. Indeed the statement's moderation was a consciously strategic step by the group's founders to render the whole project viable among a population still governed by a totalitarian system. Jens Reich, one of Neues Forum's most prominent founders and a respected East German scientist, asserted: "There is much need for calm voices in the current situation.[17]

Despite what it perceived as "troubled communication" between state and society, "insufficient representation of interests" by various groups and classes in state and economy, and other deficiencies due to the abusive nature of Leninist rule, the Neues Forum founders still appealed to dialogue with the regime instead of calling for its violent overthrow. Even at this early stage, it had become very evident that Neues Forum's founders and sympathizers were not interested in departing from socialism, let alone adopting western-style capitalism. Whereas the exact terminology of the "third way" had not yet entered this milieu's vernacular, the concept had clearly been established: retain the good, that is, pristinely socialist, features of the German Democratic Republic and develop them further in a second German state which was clearly independent of the Federal Republic. This new GDR was to protect and uphold civil rights, allow the formation of a multiparty system and foster the proliferation of diversity in opinion and lifestyles.

Neues Forum's strategy of conscious reformism genuinely hoped to enter into a dialogue with the guardians of the East German regime in an honest attempt to improve the crisis-ridden situation jointly. To that end, Neues

Forum went to great lengths to underline its acceptance of the GDR's legal framework which regulated the founding and activities of associations. It was via this kind of dialogue and formal loyalty vis-à-vis the regime that Neues Forum hoped to help legitimate the German Democratic Republic as an entity in the eyes of those who were contemplating joining the mass exodus to the Federal Republic. Thus, while profoundly system challenging in the content of its demands, Neues Forum remained in its essence quite loyal to the GDR.

Neues Forum's proliferation to a number of East German cities lent it the grass-roots appeal which the group relished. In a number of places, especially Leipzig, Neues Forum offered the GDR's opposition a forum which, for the first time, was beyond the confines of the Lutheran church. As coordinator Michael Arnold aptly put it, Neues Forum and its activists sought a "gradual emancipation from church protection" for the GDR's opposition by "moving outside the walls of the church."[18] By so doing, Neues Forum hoped to rally all independent opposition groups "to act together for the first time."[19]

In spite of this appeal to unity and inclusiveness, Neues Forum rejected explicitly any notion of becoming an umbrella organization for the GDR's opposition. Similar to the early days of the West German Greens and very much akin to the antinomian spirit of the West German social movements of the mid to late 1970s, Neues Forum explicitly rejected any developments which might potentially take it on the road to becoming a political party. Co-founder Baerbel Bohley stressed this milieu's antipathy toward all forms of conventional political organizations in an extensive interview with *Taz*.[20] Instead, she hoped to see Neues Forum become a loosely bound network of discussion groups which facilitated informal contacts among the GDR's citizens. It was only through such kind of informal and voluntary interaction that, in Bohley's view, any meaningful solidarity among citizens could be established.[21]

Much of this discussion still seemed rather academic at the time, since the regime had rejected Neues Forum's application for official recognition as a group.[22] Indeed, the ruling SED wasted little time in lambasting these developments as "counterrevolutionary" and "inimical to socialism." In an obvious attempt to foil Neues Forum's potential appeal to the country's young people, the party made a special effort to deploy its youth organizations as the most vocal critic of the increasingly visible dissident scene. At the same time, the SED leadership went to great lengths to have the country's bloc parties – which, after all, furnished the regime's loyal opposition – tow the official party line lest there be any fraternization between legal and illegal opposition.

But the dam had been cracked. Two new independent socialist groups, the Democratic Awakening (Demokratischer Aufbruch) and United Left (Vereinigte Linke) emerged in September. They made common cause with Neues Forum and the three groups agreed in late September "to break the SED's exclusive claim to representation."[23] The spirit of defiance spread rapidly into the streets. On October 3, 1989, more than 15,000 demonstrators marched in Leipzig's Karl Marx Square shouting "Democracy – now or never."[24] This proved to be the beginning of an increasingly vocal and active protest movement which was to undermine decisively the SED regime "from below." Like many elites in power, the GDR's elite, too, appeared just one step behind in its attempts to salvage the regime, and ultimately itself. When the protests had long departed from the Lutheran church, the SED finally appeared ready to negotiate with the church as equals. Then, following Erich Honecker's ignominious departure and his replacement by Egon Krenz (if anything an even more odious SED apparatchik) as the head of the SED and the republic, the party wanted to negotiate with opposition groups such as Neues Forum and its loosely structured "movement" allies. By now, however, the East German population's demands had long surpassed this milieu's reformist visions and become preoccupied with joining West Germany.

But the regime's collapse was ensured by concomitant pressure from above, when Mikhail Gorbachev informed Honecker and his henchmen that under no circumstances could they count on Soviet troops to bail them out of their predicament, as had happened in 1953. With no force at its disposal and with little, if any, legitimacy, the regime's fate was sealed. What made its exit from history interesting was the fact that its demise occurred without any bloodshed. This was perhaps the SED's only positive legacy.

The opening of the Berlin wall on the night of November 9 altered world history. It heralded the end of an era which had begun with the defeat of the Third Reich and continued with the division of Europe and Germany. As Harold James so aptly put it: "When the wall disappeared, Germany could reappear, and so could Europe. Germans, Poles, Czechs, and Hungarians could become Europeans, not merely 'East Europeans.'"[25] It also altered the fate of the East German opposition.

In an eerie parallel to the West German Left, the East German dissidents, too, misjudged the power of nationalism. Here, too, this was less of a strategic blunder than an inability to understand something which had become simply unacceptable to this milieu. Just like the West German Left, its East German counterpart, led by Neues Forum, continued its reformist course under the assumption of a two-state solution to the German question. Indeed, these progressive milieus, both East and West, did not even register the existence of a German question. To them, the reality of two German states was not only acceptable but in fact preferable from every point of view. It was in November that Neues Forum and its allies formulated concrete thoughts concerning the GDR's putative "third way." Reminiscent of Germany's tradition of council socialism of the period immediately following the First World War, the New Forum's third way was deeply anchored in a non-Leninist socialism based on popular participation, the absence of private property and an extensive welfare state. New Forum spurned the capitalism of the West, finding its excessive consumption habits particularly contemptible. This led to rather tasteless and elitist criticisms by some New Forum intellectuals of the East German public, whose attraction to West Germany's consumer goods they characterized as "mindless," "wanton" and "cheap."

Ironically, just as the Communist elite before them, East Germany's third-way leftists were one step behind the developments. Long after the GDR's former bloc parties had forsaken any meaningful role in governing an independent GDR, preferring to defer to their much wealthier and more experienced West German counterparts, Neues Forum and its loosely associated allies were still urging the GDR's population to take the road of independence and autonomy. Neues Forum warned the East German citizenry of the inevitable ills which would necessarily accompany any unification with West Germany. Urging the population "not to fall from confrontation into confederation", Neues Forum believed that unification might not only bring quick affluence but almost certain unemployment for many citizens of the GDR. Neues Forum also worried that unification might reduce the social accomplishments of the GDR, raise rents and – most bizarre of all concerns – lead to a reduction of participation and codetermination (as if the GDR had an abundance of either!). Yet again, it is obvious how deeply legitimate socialism and its values as a humanizing project had become for East German intellectuals, whose primary identity was formed by their bitter opposition to the so-called "socialist" regime of the GDR.

Once it was clear, even to Neues Forum and its sympathizers, that the two-state option was little more than a chimera, this major representative of the GDR's dissident milieu articulated the following conditions, among others, for a unified Germany: it had to be totally demilitarized and remain politically neutral; it was not to belong to any military alliance; it was to guarantee the Oder–Neisse line as a permanent border with Poland; it had to accord comprehensive social security, a decent home and a secure job to every citizen; it was to be governed by active popular participation via codetermination, referenda and other "direct" measures which, typically, were outside the conventional purview of political parties; it had to maintain equitable economic and cordial political relations with countries of the Third World.[26] Tellingly, these demands could have very easily emanated from any gathering or party platform of the West German Greens.

In early January 1990, Neues Forum issued a programmatic declaration which further clarified this group's grass-roots orientation and continued belief in the desirability (perhaps even possibility) of a democratic socialism, third-way style. Under the heading "citizen initiatives," Neues Forum once again affirmed its members' deep dislike of traditional parties which, so the argument ran, merely stifled individual initiative and democratic participation. While Neues Forum did not completely dismiss the validity of electoral politics as an expression of democracy, it viewed the upcoming elections for the Volkskammer, East Germany's parliament – the first (and, as it turned out, last) openly contested and free elections in the GDR's history – with much suspicion, even contempt. The section under "democracy in the economy" rejected any Leninist-style planning mechanism while simultaneously denouncing the evils of the market. Instead, Neues Forum advocated small democratically accountable business units whose prime mandate was to be social solidarity and ecological responsibility. The entry under "national question" still revealed Neues Forum's apprehensions regarding unification of the two German states. Instead, the group once again advocated the maintenance of two separate entities, bound together in a special condominium which would be based on the very promising – and mutually rewarding – treaty arrangements of the early 1970s which, among others, constituted a major aspect of Brandt's Ostpolitik, his opening to the East. It was essential in Neues Forum's view that both Germanies become completely demilitarized and leave their respective military alliances.

Neues Forum's official founding convention in late January 1990 was in many ways a sad event. What was supposed to have been a firm political statement of a new beginning, perhaps even the implementation of new politics on a hitherto unimaginable scale in East Central Europe, turned out to be a demonstration of historical irrelevance. Making matters worse was the fact that those who were clearly the "good guys" – the resisters, the regime dissidents, the oppositionists – were once again about to be marginalized, only this time not by an oppressive Stalinist dictatorship but by the dynamism of consumer capitalism and the appeals of national unity. Indeed, it was nothing short of tragic to see how the formal bloc parties which had been spineless backers of the SED regime for nearly forty years had suddenly emerged with massive West German assistance as the major political players in a West German dominated GDR. Once gain, opportunism had triumphed over idealism. The former dissidents became dissidents again.

While Neues Forum is clearly blameless for the unfortunate outcome of these events, its naiveté and faulty interpretation of the East German population's desires and state of mind contributed to the subsequent marginalization of this valiant organization and that of its dedicated activity in the political landscape of the new Germany. The group and its milieu emerged from a world which, very similar as well as beholden to that of the West German social movements, had no tolerance for and understanding of the kinds of human needs which were to render the GDR irrelevant. If these selfless dissidents are guilty of anything, then it would be a certain haughtiness, an elitist dismissal of ordinary citizens' wants and needs under the mental, if not verbally articulated, rubric of "false consciousness." Ironically, in this matter at least, the grass-roots oriented democrats of Neues Forum exhibited the top-down, know-it-all mentality which they so despised in the GDR's Stalinist rulers and which they have successfully criticized in the West Germans' patronizing demeanor vis-à-vis the former East Germans. The time proved to be ripe for a monumental restructuring of East German society. Alas, it was not to occur in the direction which Neues Forum had hoped and envisioned.

Regrouping under the Pressure of Pragmatism

However, Neues Forum's efforts were certainly not in vain. Even though the group adamantly refused to participate as a political party in the new world of East German politics, it actually proved remarkably successful in finding its niche among the East German public. Together with Initiative Democracy Now (Initiative Demokratie Jetzt, IDJ) and Initiative for Peace and Human Rights (Initiative für Frieden und Menschenrechte, IFM), Neues Forum formed on February 8, 1990, an electoral alliance which, though explicitly *not* a political party, was poised to contest the Volkskammer elections in March 1990. Thus developed Bündnis '90 (Alliance '90), what was later to become one of the key organizational constituents of the East German counterpart to the West German Green Party.

Just like the West German Greens, Bündnis '90 defined itself in the beginning more by what it was not than by what it actually was. It was decidedly not Stalinist and – singular among all the political actors in East Germany – it could claim an impeccable pedigree of dissent vis-à-vis the old regime. The Bündnis '90 activists were victims of the old order, not its secret service agents now masquerading as ardent Christian (on occasion even Social) Democrats. It was also emphatically independent of any West German parties, including the West German Greens, a virtual act of defiance in East Germany's political landscape at the time. "We have no partners and we are proud of it," stated Wolfgang Ullmann, one of the founders of Initiative Democracy Now. Indeed, he continued, "it would be a peculiar understanding of democracy if we had to let West German politicians tell us what to do."[27] Even if it was not the vaunted socialist third way, Bündnis '90 embodied a third way by its very existence: opposed to the old and the new order, trying to eke out an alternative to both.

Again, similar to the West German New Left and the Greens, especially in their formative years, Bündnis '90 was characterized by immense intra-organizational heterogeneity, turmoil and change. Even though Neues Forum was the largest of its three constituent groups, it exerted no particular dominance within Bündnis '90. The two other partners of Neues Forum forming this alliance possessed equally impressive credentials as Neues Forum in terms of being active opponents of the East German dictatorship. Initiative for Peace and Human Rights had in fact been one of the oldest human rights organizations in the GDR. Co-founded in 1985 by the well-known philosopher Wolfgang Templin, this organization's members were active participants in the revolution of 1989 in which they were among the first to demand that the opposition "leave its position" as a "petitioner" of the state for further reforms. Any successful opposition's task was to construct "bridges into society" by organizing groups and events, with its appeals to the state assuming secondary importance.[28] Given the excessive etatism of virtually all versions of the German Left, the group's emphasis on the primacy of civil society as the most essential locus of progressive politics certainly seems significant. Initiative Democracy Now had emerged from the GDR's seedbed of underground opposition at about the same time as Neues Forum. It had participated in the independent opposition's clandestine meeting of September 1989.[29] Its most articulate members were Wolfgang Ullmann and Konrad Weiss; the latter, together with Neues Forum's Jens Reich, has arguably been one of the East

German opposition's most democratically minded, soft-spoken, undogmatic, independent and committed participants.

Interestingly, a number of other organizations which had also belonged to East Germany's progressive opposition in the fall of 1989 stayed away from joining Bündnis '90. Most telling among them was the fate of Demokratischer Aufbruch (DA) which, in a matter of four months, had metamorphosed from being a radical member of the East German Left to becoming a close ally of the Deutsche Soziale Union (DSU), the East German sister-organization of the arch-conservative Bavarian CSU. Together with the East German CDU, the DSU and the Demokratischer Aufbruch comprised the so-called Allianz für Deutschland (Alliance for Germany), a conservative electoral alliance which proved to be the major winner in the GDR's one and only free parliamentary election. The East German SPD, which by March 1990 had become a virtual appendage of its West German counterpart, refused to enter any alliances since it was more than hopeful that it would emerge as the strongest party in East Germany. The Independent Women's Association (Unabhängiger Frauenverband, UFV) and the United Left (Vereinigte Linke), formerly distant allies of Neues Forum, decided against joining it in the electoral alliance of Bündnis '90. So did the Grüne Liga (Green League) and the Grüne Partei (Green Party). Apart from all these fundamentally anti-Leninist formations of the East German Left, there also existed the Partei des Demokratischen Sozialismus (PDS) which was nothing but a rechristened and repackaged version of the old SED.

At this juncture, a few words about the East German groups actually bearing the word "green" in their name is in order. Founded on November 6, 1989, the original East Greens had emerged from a combined effort by the Protestant church group Kirche International, by the European green movement, the Netzwerk Arche (Network Ark, as in Noah's), and by the Dritte Wurzel (Third Root) of the church-based environmental movement Gesellschaft für Natur und Umweltschutz (Society for Nature and Environmental Protection). Thus, just like Neues Forum and other elements of the East German non-Leninist Left, this early incarnation of the East Greens had been deeply rooted in the ethical and organizational world of the Lutheran church. The East Greens, too, pursued a politics of the third way which was as critical of the Stalinist practices of their own country's establishment as it was suspicious of anything western. The latter sentiment was eminently evident by the title of the Greens' founding document "Against the Freedom of Profit, Waste and Throw-Away Mentality." The East German Greens' concerns and overall orientation were very similar to those of the already mentioned groups comprising the East German progressive opposition. What distinguished the Greens from say, Neues Forum, was their greater emphasis on ecological issues and, perhaps, a more pronounced strain of radical feminism. If Neues Forum incorporated elements which rendered its politics similar to that of the West German Realos, this original version of the East German Green Party included movements which – at least at that juncture – betrayed certain kinship with the fundamentalist wing of the West German Greens.

Table 8.1 Results of the Volkskammer election, East Germany, March 18, 1990

Party	Percentage of the vote	Seats
Allianz für Deutschland	48.15	193
CDU	(40.15)	(164)
DA	(1.00)	(4)
DSU	(7.00)	(25)
SPD	21.84	87
PDS	16.33	65
Liberales Bündnis	5.28	21
Bündnis '90	2.90	12
Grüne/UFV	1.96	8
Others	3.57	16

Source: *Taz*, March 20, 1990, p. 1.

Attesting to the contentious, perhaps democratic, nature of green politics is the fact that there always exist rival organizations and movements claiming the sobriquet "green" for themselves exclusively. This was also the case in East Germany where the Green League derided the newly founded Green Party as hasty, dilettante, egoistic and without any consideration for the "entire green movement of the country as a whole."[30] What rendered this criticism of the Green Party by the Green League suspect was the latter's close alliance with the SED-sponsored Society for Nature and Environment (Gesellschaft für Natur und Umwelt, GNU). With the passage of time, most of the League's supporters joined the Green Party in one form or another, with only its orthodox members reemerging among the ranks of the PDS.

On March 18, 1990, the Volkskammer election was held. The course of events made it the German Democratic Republic's first and last democratically held, free parliamentary election. Voter turnout was high: 93.22 percent. The results are shown in table 8.1.

The westernization of East Germany had been accomplished. Perhaps more than the lure of material abundance and the possibilities accorded through freedom of travel and expression, it had been the promise of speed and expertise which had made the West German embrace so irresistible. East Germans knew instinctively that they were about to confront the most difficult period of their lives. They preferred to have West Germany shoulder this burden rather than face it alone. Above all, they knew that they were in desperate need of help which they believed only a complete merger with West Germany could provide. Thus the sad, though understandable, situation emerged in which a former bloc party and its allies, most of whom were loyal servants of the Communist regime, once again became the rulers of the country. This time, however, the real masters sat in Bonn's Konrad Adenauer

House rather than in the Kremlin. The East German Left's "movement intellectuals" were simply no match for the political professionals from the Federal Republic.

From East German Volkskammer to All-German Bundestag: A Continuation of Uneasy Alliances and Unchanged Dissent

The period between the Volkskammer election of March 1990 and the disappearance of the GDR as a political entity in October of the same year highlighted all the contradictions which had beset the East German opposition since its emergence as a major political force in the late summer of 1989. On the one hand, the process of this milieu's political marginalization accelerated. With the sudden – and completely unexpected – emergence of a CDU hegemony in East Germany, even the faintest hopes for a two-state solution had been rendered irrelevant. The dictates of the Federal Republic "colonized" the GDR, whose indigenous political forces were losing their independence and autonomy by the day. The dissenters' vision of a third way seemed like a distant chimera. And yet, on the other hand, just as the political presence of the West German Greens throughout the 1980s had changed the Federal Republic's public discourse, so too did the Neues Forum, the East German Greens and their fractious allies exert a certain public presence in the waning GDR which far exceeded their actual numbers in voters, sympathizers or members.

Thus, for example, it was mainly this milieu's activism which led the state first to dissolve and then to investigate the dreaded Ministry for State Security which oversaw the vast Stasi empire of the GDR. But unlike the revenge-driven cries for retribution which emanated from many a right-wing circle in the Federal Republic and the GDR, people such as Werner Fischer from IFM and Wolfgang Ullmann, now a Volkskammer representative for IDJ, wanted to proceed with caution lest the privacy of innocent people be unnecessarily jeopardized. The driving force behind this milieu's attacks on the Stasi was not so much revenge and retribution, as it was justice for victims and the sanctity of individual human rights. People like Fischer and Ullmann, as well as Jens Reich and Konrad Weiss, understood full well that the establishment of an enduring democratic mentality among the East German population necessitated a thoughtful and thorough coming to terms with the country's Stasi past – one devoid of any vengeance and retribution. Another mark of this milieu's presence in the GDR's public discourse was the fact that the GDR's new defense minister was tellingly rechristened Minister of Disarmament. Appropriately, its incumbent was a Lutheran clergyman.

With the GDR's demise becoming a certainty, the milieu faced the issue of linkages to western political organizations. Characteristic of the West German Greens' respect for autonomy, as well as their refusal to accept the unification of the two Germanies, they were the last of the West German parties to emerge on the East German political scene. Even though the West Greens had provided some financial assistance to the East Greens and likeminded groups as early as January 1990, it was not until May 1990 that an official delegation of westerners traveled to East Berlin to discuss possible joint actions between the two parties for the upcoming all-German elections set for December 2, 1990. In addition to meeting with their East German namesake – the aforementioned original East German Greens – the West Greens also held discussions with Neues Forum, Vereinigte Linke and the Unabhängiger Frauenverband.[31] As a result of these meetings, the West German Greens and their diverse and motley East German interlocutors decided to commence with the fusion process which would eventually lead to a unified all-German Green Party. While the West German Greens were much more sensitive in their approach to this convergence than other West German parties were in relation to their East German clients, the inherently unequal power relations between the two groups could not be denied in this instance either. By January, some members of the East German coalition were already voicing their frustration with the West German Greens for their allegedly overbearing manners, labeling them "eco-imperialism."[32] In addition to feeling less powerful (as well as less wealthy) than their West German counterparts, the East German Greens and their collaborators from the other related organizations had also emerged from a completely different political reality, so that the prospective partners looked at the world quite differently. Thus, for example, it does not seem surprising that some of the tensions centered on the westerners' perception of the easterners as much too conservative and anti-communist. Conversely, the westerners appeared to the easterners as naive and inexperienced, as people who really had no idea what a repressive system was.

Despite these obvious differences, the two partners, East and West, decided to form a confederation which was to lead to a permanent alliance following the Bundestag election of December 2, 1990, and to formal unity in early 1993. As an electoral strategy for the ballot, the two partners announced that, although uniformly called Die Grünen, they would run separately, each in their respective part of Germany. On the territories of the former East Germany, the original East Greens were to form a temporary electoral alliance with Bündnis '90. Following a favorable ruling by the Federal Republic's constitutional court in Karlsruhe, which in essence permitted the eastern part of the united country to conduct its balloting for this one occasion only under different rules from those pertaining to the West, the East German Greens and their allies from Bündnis '90 entered the Bundestag with eight members. A twist of fate would have it that as the East Greens and their Bündnis '90 colleagues made their entry into the first all-German parliament since the defeat of the Third Reich and Germany's subsequent division, the West Greens departed from this legislative body. With the 5 percent cut-off clause applying only to the country's western part, the East German Greens' participation in the new Bundestag was, at least in part, assured by the proper functioning of a liberal democracy, which in this case meant the implementation of an independent judgement by an autonomous judiciary.

Eight individuals would represent the Greens' cause in the 1990 Bundestag: Wolfgang Ullmann and Konrad Weiss (Initiative Demokratie Jetzt); Werner Schulz and Ingrid Koeppe (Neues Forum); Christine Schenck (Unabhängiger Frauenverband); Gerda Poppe (Initiative für Frieden und Menschenrechte); Vera Wollenberger and Klaus Feige (East Greens). In the course of less than two turbulent years, these dedicated and brave dissidents of the Honecker regime had become representatives in the freely elected parliament of Europe's most powerful country. Tellingly, their lives as dissidents did not diminish. From the very beginning of their entry into the Bundestag, these eight representatives continued their former activities as gadflies, critics and Cassandras. First, they waged a major battle against the Bundestag's rule on recognizing the status of a party on the parliament's floor. According to this rule, a party is only accorded the official status of a *Fraktion* – an official party delegation – if it seats a minimum of 34 members. This is important because only a party of official *Fraktion* status enjoys certain financial and personnel privileges, is offered appropriate physical space, and enjoys working conditions commensurate with those offered to the large parties. Above all, only *Fraktionen* are granted the all-important committee assignments which in essence define the Bundestag's daily existence. The Greens' initial protests against not being given the status of a *Fraktion* led to the Bundestag's extending to them the category of an "expanded group." Still feeling discriminated against, the Greens continued to voice their displeasure with this arrangement until they were granted the full-fledged status of a *Fraktion*, barring some budgetary adjustments as a consequence of their small size. Characteristic of the Greens' democratic commitment was the fact that they sought this upgrading in status to *Fraktion* also for their political rivals, the PDS, with whom they had little but past enmity in common.

However, being parliamentarians in a new country seemed not to diminish the oppositional zeal which each individual of this "gang of eight" exhibited under the East German dictatorship. They developed into the most ardent critics of the Treuhand, the government agency located in the eastern section of Berlin, empowered by the federal government to convert the former state-run and decrepit East German economy into a western-style economy driven by the market. The Treuhand's many detractors, among whom the Greens and members of Bündnis '90 have been very vocal, have accused the agency of running roughshod over people in quest of a quick conversion process to the market. Being driven by the profit motive and time considerations, the Treuhand, according to its critics, has generated massive unemployment in the former East Germany, much of which could have been avoided by a more gradual and tempered approach. In addition to attacking the Treuhand's wholesale "liquidation" of the East German economy, and its generation of millions of unemployed, the Greens have objected to this agency's dictatorial methods and the imperious manner in which it has behaved vis-à-vis the former East Germany.

The Greens and their allies have also been vocal critics of the government's environmental policy. Especially concerning their homeland, which had been environmentally ravaged by the obsessive industrialization of the Stalinist regime, the Greens have demanded much more stringent regulations concerning environmental protection. Above all, they have consistently urged the government to increase its investments and programs in the east of Germany to revitalize a seriously damaged environment.

The Greens have also demanded that the Stasi be classified as a criminal organization and be prosecuted accordingly. This is a very sensitive issue for Germans in general, but particularly so for the German Left, and one on which the Greens have assumed a thoughtful attitude. For Germans, the ubiquitous question of coming to terms with their past has once again reared its difficult head. The German Right in particular has taken the position of "this time we'll do it correctly", meaning that the massive "omissions" which occurred in dealing with the Nazis in the post-1945 period would be rectified by punishing the Communists in the post-1989 era. In other words, Communists and their henchmen were not to go unscathed as did the Nazis and their supporters. This position is cynical for two reasons: First, it conveys the image that the Right now harbors some kind of remorse concerning the leniency with which the Nazis were treated in the Federal Republic and the fact that they were fully integrated into the very fabric of its society. In reality, this travesty of justice occurred precisely at the behest of this very Right which is now clamoring for the punishment of Communists. Second, by turning on East Germany's Communists with an unprecedented vengeance, the German Right tries to convey to the world that Communism, if anything, was even worse than National Socialism, thereby once again trying to exculpate Germany from its Nazi past.

Juxtaposed to this position is the PDS-led view which is shared by many in left-liberal circles. Combining a certain post-1968, Ostpolitik-propelled acceptance of "real existing socialism" with the pervasive new phenomenon of a GDR nostalgia, many in Germany's leftist milieu would like nothing better than complete silence regarding the SED's and Stasi's crimes against the East German people. The Greens and Bündnis '90 disagree with the Left's attempted cover-up of the SED regime's crimes and abuses, just as they object to the Right's vengeance by instrumentalizing Communism as yet another instance to alleviate the memory of National Socialism's barbaric rule. Instead, they want to deal with this sordid chapter in German history for the sake of justice and the rights of individuals whom the East German regime victimized and not for the sake of politics, which in the Left's case has meant silence and in the Right's case has meant revenge.

As behooves their leftist credentials, the Greens and Bündnis '90 were vocal opponents of the American effort against Saddam Hussein in the Gulf war of 1991. Yet, unlike others on the Left, the East German Greens and their allies also objected to Hussein's treatment of the Kurds and Shiites in Iraq and the abuses of the Iraqui occupiers against the Kuwaiti people during Iraq's occupation of Kuwait. Unlike in certain circles of the green and left milieu in West Germany, where Saddam Hussein was extolled as a colorful Third World leader who dared the Americans, most such sentiments in East

Germany remained confined to the world of the PDS and its supporters, hard-line Communists, leaving the Greens and their political allies in the East largely untouched by such sordid sympathies.

Lastly, the "gang of eight" delighted in challenging any party discipline, including its own. Not being a real *Fraktion*, the Greens and their colleagues took advantage of their small size and spurned the conventional *Fraktionszwang* (parliamentary discipline) which has constrained many an initiative and much originality in the established German parties. The Greens and their parliamentary allies made their sparse numbers work to their advantage in that they once again became the collective voices of opposition and antinomy. True to their essence as critics and dissenters, the Greens and their partners found it impossible to convert themselves into conventional parliamentarians. "Once a dissenter, always a dissenter" seemed to be the motto by which they conducted their public lives.

Becoming a Party: Between Anti-Party Party and Establishment

With the passage of time, the East German Greens and Bündnis '90 soon realized that they, too, had to make certain accommodations with their new political environment. Playing the role of perpetual gadfly was certainly glamorous. It also had its occasional advantages. Moreover, being professional dissenters seemed to be an appropriate expression of their high sense of moralism. Enjoying unprecedented parliamentary autonomy by virtue of not being a full-fledged *Fraktion*, and being independent of the West German Greens due to the latter's absence in the Bundestag, undoubtedly offered the East German Greens and their colleagues a sense of freedom and a political forum which must have eluded even their wildest dreams during the Honecker regime. But was this enough? With the passage of time, yet another of their traditional traits – in addition to that of their dissenting ways – emerged. It was pragmatism.

This became especially salient in the East Green's increasingly rocky relations with the West Greens. By early April 1991, tensions between these two groups were so high that Vera Wollenberger, who had quickly established herself as one of the most prominent Bundestag representatives of the Greens, bemoaned the alliance between the two parties on election night as "rash."[33] Wollenberger voiced her contempt for and intolerance of the West Greens' constant internal bickering, terming it "political kindergarten." Expressing a particularly harsh judgement, she stated: "We of the citizen initiatives – helped, of course, by the East German population – attained something which the West Greens, beginning with the student revolts in 1968, never came close to: namely to change society in a most fundamental manner."[34] While this was far from a fair assessment of either of the two green parties, Wollenberger's views reflected the East Greens' longstanding frustrations with the internecine battles of the West Greens, which Wollenberger and her colleagues regarded as infantile. The East Greens and their colleagues also found the West Greens' ideological radicalism superfluous and counterproductive. Konrad Weiss was in agreement with Vera Wollenberger's frustrations concerning the West Greens: "Should it become necessary to found a party in the mode of the current 'alternative' scene, which, however, advocates value-conservative options, I would surely be part of it."[35] By early spring of 1991, a number of debates developed around the possibility of expanding Bündnis '90 from its East German base to all of Germany, thus in effect creating a rival party to the Greens.

Particularly disturbing to the East German Greens and their allies was the Neumünster convention of the West German Greens. Held in April 1991, this meeting exhibited the usual internecine battles which had become a trademark of the West Greens during the second half of the 1980s. Filled with mutual recriminations and the habitual dosage of venomous language, the West Greens simply could not agree on any long-term policies concerning their relations with the East Greens. Even though the Fundi wing of the party had suffered a serious setback with Jutta Ditfurth's departure, the Realos proved unable to convert this event to their permanent advantage. Instead, the new party leadership emerged as a weak, radical leftist, though not Fundi, coalition led by Hans-Christian Stroebele, whose anti-Semitic remarks during the Gulf war forced him to resign his position on the Greens' executive committee. The cleavages between East and West Greens which had been apparent from the very first meetings of these two groups in the late fall of 1989 had become, if anything, more pronounced by the spring of 1991. These differences were not only apparent on the federal level. Indeed, the Greens in the eastern province of Thuringia had become so outraged with the West-dominated Green Party that, by early May, they were seriously thinking about withdrawing from the Greens altogether and "leaving the West Greens simmering in their own juices until they 'conducted themselves in a civilized manner again.'"[36]

That the easterners' frustration was more than just talk became evident on September 21, 1991, when in Potsdam Neues Forum emerged as a fully fledged political party. Neues Forum, the party, intended still to maintain the "open structures" which characterized it during its movement phase. Moreover, it was, of course, to remain "non-hierarchical."[37] In essence, its purpose was to offer an alternative on the left which was to lie apart from the PDS's unabated Leninism, the Greens' factionalized radicalism and the SPD's drab "me-tooism". Above all, it was not to fall into nostalgia, a danger which was far from unreal, given an atmosphere on the German left which – as a consequence of its own failures as well as the German government's miserable record in unifying the two countries – increasingly glorified the GDR. Werner Schulz stated in his inaugural speech at the party's founding convention: "I do not want the GDR back. It is good that this state met with its demise. I am proud that we have decisively contributed to its ruin."[38] As an unmistakable jibe against the West German Left's continued nostalgia for the ever-elusive third way, Schulz said: "An alternative, which was none, has disintegrated."[39] Bündnis '90, as the party was to be called officially, was to remain close to the citizens' initiatives which created it in the first place. As such, it was to advocate democracy and humanism without any qualifications in a universalistic manner across all of Germany. Schulz warned the new party's members against behaving arrogantly toward anybody, least of all the Greens, whom he still viewed as the party's most natural – and probable – allies in the politics of change. The relationship of the green milieu in the East, now represented by Bündnis '90 as an independent party, and the West Greens had to be based on a "gradual approach, no fusion and no sub-mission."[40] These differences between Easterners and Westerners in the two Green milieus persisted all the way to the Hanover Congress in January 1993 when the two parties officially became one. Even at this congress of official unification where past misunderstandings were to be set aside in the quest of reentering the Bundestag – perhaps even as Germany's third largest party – the different, indeed partly contradictory, roots of these two milieus remained visible. Many Bündnis '90 people and their East German allies insisted in Hanover that they were not really leftists and that they felt uneasy about being absorbed by a party with decidedly leftist strategies and views. Many Westerners, in turn, saw this official (and one might add long overdue) merger with their East German colleagues as prima facie evidence for the Green Party's obvious turn to the right.

The frustrations of German unification have led to serious resentments on the part of the former East Germans vis-à-vis the dominant West Germans. These frustrations contributed to a certain post hoc legitimation of the PDS which many East Germans have come to see as an indigenous East German party which shows at least some pride and dignity, if little efficacy, in resisting the West German juggernaut. It is ironic that the PDS, the direct successor of the Stalinist SED, derives much support from an admittedly smallish percentage of the East German population (about 12 percent as averaged over the five Länder of the former GDR but as high as 30 percent in many parts of East Berlin) not so much by virtue of its little-changed hardline communist ideology, but by being a clear East German creation in a world where everything of substance seems to be West German.

This "local patriotism" (*Lokalpatriotismus*) also manifested itself in the politics of the East German Left. In the middle of July 1992, a group called the Committee for Fairness constituted itself to protest what East Germans consider their mistreatment at the hands of West Germans and the federal government. The committee, which in its initial stages perceived itself as an interest group and not a political party, comprised writers, professors, artists, and men and women of the Lutheran clergy – but, predictably, no blue-collar industrial workers. Led by the leader of the PDS, Gregor Gysi, and the well-known East German novelist Stefan Heym, the committee issued an appeal in which it deplored widespread unemployment, sharp increases in rent and other costs, reduced social services and the prospect of losing long-occupied homes. Above all, the appeal made it clear that the committee regarded all of these calamities befalling East Germans as direct results of the unification process, as well as the ensuing West German dominance. Even though the social composition of its membership and the content of its complaints made the committee quite similar to the East German Greens, Neues Forum and Bündnis '90, the undeniable closeness of some of its most prominent members to East Germany's former Communist regime rendered the committee untenable to East Germany's radical Left. Konrad Weiss, veteran of the East German revolution and member of the green delegation to the Bundestag, characterized the committee as a "'nostalgia club' in which 'former Communists now dressed as democratic socialists, together with former Stasi people, are trying to establish a new Politburo.'"[41]

Possibly, former East Germany's independent opposition had emerged far enough to become an autonomous player in the politics of a united Germany. Its role of expressing constructive dissent would now continue to be exercised in a framework in which it simultaneously became integrated into the institutional fabric of German politics and society. Whether this East German oppositional milieu could continue to play the role of the permanent dissenter depended in large part on its complex relationship with the West German dominated Greens with whom it united in 1993 in an atmosphere of antinomy on the one hand, yet from whom it continued to remain structurally separated by virtue of their different historical experiences, on the other. Regardless of the eventual outcome of this contentious relationship between the East and West Greens, there can be little doubt that the former's presence has altered the latter's political role in the Federal Republic. By so doing, Neues Forum, Bündnis '90 and all their East German allies have undoubtedly enriched the politics of the German Left. Indeed, their presence has enriched German democracy as a whole.

Conclusion

Conclusions have three functions: stocktaking, generalizing, predicting. We will concentrate on the former two, though we will not shy from the latter. While substantial parts of the empirical material comprising this book pertain to the Greens as party and movement (both in the former East and West Germany), we would like to turn in our concluding chapter to an evaluation of the Greens as the most prototypical representatives of the contemporary German Left as a whole. More than anything else, the Greens embodied the fundamental restructuring of Germany's progressive politics in the 1980s, a politics traditionally associated with the Left. Thus we regard this concluding section of our book as an interpretative statement not only of the Greens proper but also of their larger milieu, that is, the German, indeed European, Left. Briefly put, we argue that the Greens have been the most salient forerunners of a total reorganization and reconceptualization of what used to be a European left, anchored in the industrial working class and established roughly with the rise of its social and political institutions at the end of the nineteenth century. Coupled with the demise of Leninism in the former Soviet world and the concomitant transformation of European politics, the Greens' existence has initiated what amounts to a revolutionary reordering of progressive politics in the advanced industrial world. Just as occurred a century ago, the meaning, content and form of progressive politics, that is, of the Left, are in the process of being reconstituted. The Greens have done more than their share in initiating this worthy and long overdue process. As such, the Greens represent the end of an era while at the same time heralding a new one.

The Greens as Transformers of the German and European Left

The Greens have completely transformed the German Left. As our study argues, they were very much its creation and manifestation. As such, however, the Greens' decade as a party in the Federal Republic of the 1980s changed the existence and meaning of progressive (that is, left) politics in West Germany. As we argued throughout our study, the Greens – certainly by 1980 – had developed into a party and movement of the Left. Their success can be measured by the fact that the notion of "leftness," "left politics" or even of "the Left" will never be the same as it was before the advent of the Greens in German public life. Here the notion of a party is important. To be sure there existed many challenges to the two main institutional representatives of the traditional Left (social democracy and Leninist communism), with the New Left of the late 1960s being particularly prominent. But they all proved ephemeral in terms of their longevity and lasting impact. It took the Greens as a party to change the very notion of the Left as it had been basically established in most European societies by the 1880s, and in virtually all by the turn of the century. Until the theoretical advent of the New Left in the 1960s and the practical input of the Greens in the 1980s, "left" basically meant the politics of social and economic equality as conceptualized by the Left's major subject, namely the industrial working class and its political representatives in the form of social democratic and communist parties. There existed a sort of "crowding out" on the left in which the working class was not only the most important actor but also the sole legitimate reference point for any progressive politics. Everything happened in some relation to the working class, denoting in particular the collective of male, skilled, industrial, blue-collar, mainly unionized persons whose political identity was expressed by some sort of mass-based party. Indeed, for nearly one century "leftness" had been virtually monopolized by the organized working class and its politics. The whole "American exceptionalism" debate, questioning the existence of a genuine Left in the United States, was predicated on the virtually monopolized identification of the Left with an organizational and potent working class.[1]

About a hundred years later (from the 1880s to the 1980s) the Greens, as political representatives of the new social movements, succeeded in creating a whole new axis along which leftness will henceforth be measured. While the New Left of the 1960s had already provided the theoretical underpinnings to what would become a fundamental paradigm shift within the Left, it was not until the *Realpolitik* of the Greens (even that of the fundamentalists) that the orthogonality of this axis was placed into concrete political reality.

The traditional axis of the Left saw the working class as the paradigm's social carrier. Ideologically, it concentrated on the politics of production and equality in the framework of economic growth. Seeing the primary ills of capitalism in its system of private ownership and profit maximization, the old paradigm believed that with the abolition of both a new (and better) system of human relations called socialism would emerge. This axis provided the political framework for both the social democratic and the communist Left. This was the paradigm of the "materialist" Left representative of what Seymour Martin Lipset and Stein Rokkan termed the "owner-worker" cleavage.[2]

In contrast to this, the New Left and its successors pursued a project which was anchored in the "postmaterial" paradigm of "identity politics."[3] Still opposed to capitalism, the main axis of this political orientation centered on a rejection of growth for growth's sake as well as the bureaucratic exigencies associated with it. Carried by students, decommodified workers in salaried professions often associated with the public sector and – in a novel manner – women, this new collective identity received a well-defined, clear political articulation which led to the formation of a new cleavage structure in virtually all advanced industrial societies, and most certainly in the Federal Republic.

Thus the Greens added a major dimension in the thawing of the cleavages which, according to Lipset and Rokkan, were frozen by the end of the First World War and the Bolshevik revolution.[4] The Greens have thus contributed substantially to a fundamental alteration of the party system in Europe, most definitively in Germany, the dominant country in Europe. The decade of the Greens has led to a severe loosening, if not yet complete severing, of "leftness" from the working class. Always only an empirical rather than a stringently logical proposition, and largely confined to Europe, this century-old linkage cannot be taken for granted anymore. Indeed, in most advanced industrial countries there exists ample evidence that segments of the traditional working class have developed certain electoral affinities with parties of the radical Right. In France, a considerable percentage of workers who had previously voted for the Communist Party (PCF) joined the racist Front National led by Jean-Marie Le Pen in the course of the late 1980s.[5] Similar drifts could be observed in Austria, where – especially in "red" Vienna – workers who until the early 1990s had been solid supporters of the Austrian Socialist Party (SPÖ) opted for the rightist radical Freedom Party led by the populist demagogue Jörg Haider.[6] The concept of Reagan Democrats denoted a parallel development in the United States.

In Germany, too, one could observe a clear rightward drift by segments of the traditional working class during the 1980s.[7] It was not by chance that at the March 1983 election, which catapulted the Greens into the Bundestag, over one million largely blue-collar workers, hailing especially from the social democratic stronghold of the Rhine-Ruhr area, cast their support for the CDU led by Chancellor Helmut Kohl.[8] Even though most of them returned to the social-democratic fold in January 1987, when Johannes Rau, a traditional social democrat, was the SPD's top candidate, by December 1990 they had once again deserted the SPD in favor of the conservatives.[9] More troubling perhaps were the results of some Länder elections of 1992 where, particularly in Baden-Württemberg and Schleswig-Holstein, the far-rightist Republikaner and the extreme Deutsche Volksunion respectively received a smattering of working-class support in their successful quest for parliamentary representation.[10] Finally, in the former GDR, there are signs that former SED activists and former East German army officers are now supporters of the Republikaner.[11]

While it would be completely premature to argue that Europe's industrial working class might be in the process of drifting to the political right on a permanent basis, there seems little doubt that industrial workers, like other social groups, have become much more independent and unpredictable in their voting habits. The assumption of the past hundred years in which the Left was automatically identified – if not synonymous – with the organized working class has become tenuous, if not wrong, in the course of the 1980s. Perhaps Lipset's much-maligned concept of "working-class authoritarianism" may have some validity after all.[12] The working class will henceforth have to earn its place in the coalition of progressive politics; its mere existence will not make it belong to this coalition, let alone lead it.

In being the new torchbearers of progressive politics and the Left, the Greens have completely altered Germany's hitherto most eminent representative of the Left, namely the Social Democratic Party (SPD). Let us, for brevity's sake, only mention three crucial areas in which the presence of the Greens altered the very essence of the SPD's main post-Godesberg tenets and made the party in the course of the 1980s into something fundamentally different than it was before:

1 Foreign and defense policy. In 1983, the SPD renounced its support, arguably even its initiation, of NATO's double-track decision, thereby departing from the party's Atlanticist position of 25 years standing. This major shift occurred as a direct consequence of the growth of the Greens and their subculture immediately – and threateningly – to the SPD's left.
2 Energy policy and the logic of economic growth and technological advances. The SPD party congress in Nuremberg in 1986 decided in August to have the party renounce its century-old growth and technology fetish in favor of a greenish and alternative "soft" approach. Significantly, all forms of nuclear energy were denounced as dangerous. Nuclear energy, once a mainstay and hope for rapid and "clean" growth for the old Left, simply became unacceptable. In the meantime, nuclear energy has become so illegitimate as a concept that it in fact has since been eliminated from the boundaries of acceptable debate, perhaps even thought, in the world of social democracy and the organized labor movement. In the course of less than a decade, nuclear energy and other growth-oriented concepts of the old Left have become completely unmentionable in most social democratic circles.
3 Gender politics. Clearly compelled by the progressive position of the Greens, in 1988 the SPD passed a party-wide affirmative action regulation which postulated that by 1994, 40 percent of all party positions will have to be occupied by women.

Much more important than these concrete events has been the Greens' ability to dislodge the SPD from setting the agenda of leftist politics in the Federal Republic. The Greens became in the course of the 1980s at least conceptually, if not strategically, paradigmatic for the German Left. Leftness, until the 1980s always measured via some sort of – even if only implicit – dialogue with social democracy, has now been redirected into an entity defined by green hegemony. Now the dialogue occurs with the Greens – if not necessarily the party proper, then at least with a green-influenced social democracy. With all the issues defined by the Greens, the SPD had to put up with the rather ignominious position of presenting itself as the more efficient and politically seasoned of the two parties in terms of implementing the changes initiated by the Greens. It would not be completely erroneous to interpret social democracy's main activities throughout the 1980s as an attempt to realize green politics in a mediated manner.

This loss of the agenda setting role in progressive politics in the Federal Republic was particularly difficult for the SPD because – unlike in many continental countries – social democracy in Germany enjoyed a more or less unchallenged monopoly on the left throughout the postwar period. Throughout the 1980s, the Greens developed into the German Left's socializing agent in the sense that virtually all its new ideas, political innovations, strategic formulations, lifestyle – in short its entire habitus – originated from the Greens and their milieu. Since the 1980s the guiding principle of left politics in Germany has undoubtedly been green; methods of implementation, organizational manifestation and carrier opportunities may well have remained predominantly red. A convincing sign of the greening of the SPD has been the virtual disappearance of its formerly powerful *Kanalarbeiter* wing. Starting with the SPD's special party conference of 1983, the *Kanalarbeiter* and the party's centrists suffered one defeat after another, leading to their virtual insignificance. Former players such as Helmut Schmidt, Hans Apel and Hermann Rappe have been increasingly marginalized within the party.

Clearly, the crisis of social democracy goes much beyond the challenge represented by the Greens. Its sources are multiple, its causes varied. Among the most salient are the fundamental shifts in production and the labor market which, even in Germany (though to a lesser degree than in the United States and Great Britain), transformed a rather coherent industrially based Fordist labor force into a much more motley post-Fordist amalgam of groups and individuals dominated by the service sector. The breakdown of the Keynesian compact, the increase in floating voters, greater geographic mobility, the disappearance of a distinct working-class culture all led to the dissolution of the typical milieu in which social democracy flourished. Peter Lösche and Franz Walter are correct when they insist that the ideal type "social democrat" or the definitive image of the Social Democratic Party have long disappeared.[13] Just like the nemesis of social democracy, the Greens, so too has social democracy itself become "multicolored," shedding its uniform red in the process. Lösche and Walter speak of a "loosely coupled anarchy" when they characterize the SPD of the 1990s: home to the old industrial worker, but also to the yuppie executive, the radical peace activist and the office secretary, the pragmatist and the moralist.[14] Thus, just as in the case of the Greens, it has become virtually impossible to speak of one SPD. After all, there is the traditional labor-anchored SPD, just as much as there exists the professional-managerial SPD, the ecology and peace-oriented SPD and the power-holding SPD, the feminist SPD and the SPD of women, the latter two, of course, not being the same. In short, the heterogeneity of social democracy not only reflects the influence of the Greens and their milieu on the SPD and its world, but in and of itself is evidence for the substantial decomposition of the Left as it dominated the space of progressive politics in Germany and Europe for about a century. The SPD's transformation from the model of a rigidly led oligarchy described by Roberto Michels to that of a loosely coupled anarchy attests to the new era which the German – indeed European – Left is about to enter.[15]

Even more impressive evidence of the Greens' transformation of the German Left than their fundamental effect on the SPD has been their ability to alter the outlook of the German trade unions. The unions were on the whole extremely hostile to the New Left of the 1960s, far more so than the Social Democratic Party was. This animus by the unions continued vis-à-vis the New Left's legacy of the 1970s and the first half of the 1980s, that is, the new social movements and the Greens. The mutual antipathy between these two worlds was particularly acute since they clashed on virtually every level. In terms of their sociological background, the world of the unions consisted predominantly of skilled, male, industrial and blue-collar workers, whereas that of the new social movements and the Greens comprised university-educated, young, salaried employees, a large proportion of whom gained their livelihood through the country's decommodified sector. Ideologically, too, the difference between these two worlds could not have been starker. Unionists by and large extolled material growth, believed in the validity of industrial production as the primary guarantor of employment, disliked communism and all versions of progressive politics which were situated to the left of social democracy, and saw their role as being one of the essential participants in the creation of a wealthy and democratic Federal Republic. German labor prided itself on being one of the establishment's "players." Contrast to this the ideological orientation of the new social movements: profoundly anti-growth, deeply critical of modern production, especially in terms of its deleterious effects on the environment, decidedly anti-anti-communist (in notable distinction to being pro-communist), anti-western and thoroughly antinomian vis-à-vis virtually every aspect of the Federal Republic.[16]

Unionists were barred from attending Green Party meetings and barely concealed their utter contempt for a political formation whose protagonists they viewed as little better than spoiled rich kids motivated by naive, thus dangerous, phantasies masquerading as politics. And yet, by the mid to late 1980s, all of the DGB's "activist" unions – most important among them IG Metall, Germany's (and the capitalist world's) largest single union – had developed a world-view which had become decidedly "greenish."[17] Activist unions became enthusiastic supporters of the peace movement, something which they had still been guarded about as late as 1983; they developed strong interest in and support for various Third World liberation movements, notably the Sandinistas in Nicaragua; they cooled markedly in their formerly unmitigated pro-western and pro-American stance; and, denoting perhaps the most impressive metamorphosis, they developed into active ecologists and environmentalists.[18]

Organized labor's traditional fear of what it perceived as the zero–sum relationship between economy and ecology had, by the late 1980s, transformed itself into a view which argued that the compatibility of these two forces was not only possible but indeed in labor's best interest. Thus, according to the activist unions' altered position, a symbiotic relationship between economy and ecology had to furnish one of the decisive pillars of progressive politics in Germany and Europe. The fact that, among all of the country's social groups (barring farmers), the Greens' electoral failure has been the most pronounced among Germany's industrial working class does not contradict the success of the Greens' ideological conquest concerning the hearts and minds of union officials and bureaucrats, particularly of the younger and university-educated variety, which is rapidly becoming the norm among most union elites, particularly those belonging to the activist wing of labor.[19]

The Greens as Transformers of German Politics and Society

Maurice Duverger's famous concept of the "contagion from the left"[20] pertains to the Greens' influence on German politics and society well beyond the limits of the Left. Thus we argue that the Greens and their milieu have by and large enhanced the quality of democracy in Germany on the levels of elite competition, public participation and public debate. They created an atmosphere, as well as structures, which improved the democratic presence in the Federal Republic by facilitating a continued interaction between establishment and antinomy. Thus the fact that the Greens themselves have become part of the political establishment in the course of the 1980s does not detract from the validity of the argument which sees them as challengers of this very establishment. On the contrary: what has rendered the Greens so interesting – and politically meaningful – has been precisely the immense role that the established forces and institutions played in this whole development. After all, let us not forget that the Greens arose and flourished with the partial – though crucial – support on the part of the procedures and actors comprising the established political system of the Federal Republic. It has been precisely the Greens' tense, but substantial, relationship with the establishment which transformed them in the course of a decade into a serious force on the left and beyond, and meant that they did not disintegrate into the irrelevance of an ideologically pure but politically meaningless sect. Thus the Greens have been fertilizers and catalysts for the thought processes and programmatic reforms of the other parties. We give a couple of obvious examples.

The Greens have most definitely altered the interparty constellation of German politics and led it away from the two-and-one-half party system to a viable four-party configuration. Indeed, the fact that the topography of the German party system has begun to include a fifth player – thus far only on the state and local levels, but likely to occur on the federal one as well before too long – has something to do with the Greens' "vanguard" role in widening the political space for parties in the Federal Republic. Even though the newcomers, the far-right Republikaner party and the virtually national socialist Deutsche Volksunion (DVU) have little in common with the Greens

– representing, indeed, their antithesis in many ways – the pluralization of Germany's party space owes much to the Greens as democratizing agents of established politics in an advanced industrial society known for its high level of predictability and institutional stability.

Between the late 1950s and 1983, the topography of the Federal Republic's party landscape consisted of the two giants – CDU/CSU and SPD – together on the one hand, and the small but indispensable FDP on the other. The governing game was simple: Short of attaining an absolute majority, which happened only once in postwar German history in the case of Adenauer's memorable victory in 1957, the party which availed itself of the FDP's labile affections assumed power. Even though this constellation has continued on the national level in the early 1990s, the logic of coalitional politics on the state and local levels has been fundamentally transformed by the arrival of the Greens. There developed a four-party system which – simply by virtue of its combinatorial possibilities – augmented the governing options for either of the two giants. Various coloring schemes entered the vocabulary of German politics. While empirically speaking the most common color coordination emerged as a clearly leftist "red–green" versus an equally obvious center-right "black–yellow," there occured at various junctures speculations about the formations of so-called "traffic light coalitions" featuring Social Democrats (red), Greens (green) and Free Democrats (who in this case would presumably be represented only by the yellow of their otherwise bicolored blue and yellow.) The emergence of the Greens caused the clear demarcation of two distinct blocs in German politics, each with its own large party accompanied by a small, but cantankerous and difficult ally. The Greens pluralized the Federal Republic's party space.

Of course, it is certain that the petrification of the old party system, the cumbersome nature of the Big Two parties, and the sociological diversification of the German electorate constituted essential factors in the opening of Germany's party space. Parties other than the Greens emerged in the course of the 1980s. At present, there are indications of an even greater proliferation of parties, which, characteristically for the *zeitgeist* of the 1990s, will most likely occur on the far right of the political spectrum rather than on its left. Nevertheless, the Greens have contributed substantially to the structural transformation of the German party landscape.

Every party, including the CDU, CSU and FDP, has been devoting much attention to ecology as a crucial issue. There really has occurred a "greening" of the German party system on this question. Germany's stringent recycling law, Europe's strictest, is a consequence of the Greens' influence on the public discourse and ecological awareness of the German population. German industry joined the country's very costly recycling system not because it was compelled to do so by legislation, but because it is operating in a social environment with a fundamentally changed public consciousness which demands ecological vigilance. Being anti-ecological in contemporary Germany has become nothing short of blasphemous. It is most certainly politically suicidal.

The Greens have also changed the German public's discourse on women. Without becoming feminists, all the parties have developed a certain awareness of, even sensitivity to, the blatant inequality which women have thus far suffered in German public and private life. Every party has been sensitized to the women's question by the Greens.

This "contagion from the left" (or from the Greens) has affected German public life well beyond the realm of the parties, even though, of course, given the immense prominence of political parties in virtually every aspect of German public life, influencing the parties ensures a major presence in most dimensions of German politics. Thus it could well be argued that the Greens have rendered Germany more democratic, both in terms of procedure and of content. Inherent to their critical being and profound skepticism of all things capitalist and bureaucratic, the Greens challenged rules, regulations, conventions, all in the name of more openness, access – in short, democracy. Otto Schily's watchdog role in the Flick scandal is but one example of this whistle-blowing dimension of the Greens.[21] One should, of course, also add that by feminizing Germany's parties – at least to a degree – the Greens have further enhanced the democratization of the country's structures as a whole.

The Greens have made the German public more aware of risks in general. The term "risk society" (*Risikogesellschaft*) has become commonplace in public parlance in the Federal Republic.[22] Furthermore, the Greens have contributed substantially to a certain informalization of German life, something which could also be seen as part of a larger contribution to the democratization of German politics. The Greens have also been a liberal influence in the German public sphere. On issues such as personal freedom, the individual's relationship vis-à-vis institutions, most notably the state, of course, the Greens have played a key liberalizing role throughout the roughly dozen years of their existence.

The Greens' Shortcomings and Failures

By having to navigate a fine line between the Scylla of absorption and the Charybdis of isolation and irrelevance, the Greens committed a number of mistakes which impeded their political effectiveness and relevance. First and foremost, they never could reconcile the inherent (and internal) contradiction between a movement and a party. Most green activists remained very ambivalent about having become a party in 1980. The movement component informed the party's essence well beyond the obstructionist world of the fundamentalists.

Second, the Greens' daily world was dictated by a level of intolerance which rendered the whole project very painful to most of its protagonists. In the beginning of his fine study of the Greens, Joachim Raschke reports the telling fact that most of his interviewees, green activists of one kind or another, spoke with nothing but pain, disappointment, even hatred, about their experiences in and with the party.[23] In other words, the constant internecine struggles had consumed the party. Rather than being means to an end, the struggles had become an end in themselves. Strict adherence to mutually exclusive and rival beliefs, instead of a certain tolerance of ambivalences, ruled the world of most activists. Truth instead of tolerance, demarcation instead of mediation became the order of the day. Even though, of all German political parties, the Green Party was arguably the most distant from a Leninist model in its formal structure and general demeanor, the Greens' unbridled "culture of argumentation" (*Streitkultur*) created a sort of pluralized Leninism which was profoundly intolerant. Moreover there emerged a Leninism of the mind which, in turn, led to a behavioral Leninism as well. To continue using Duverger's categories, the Greens succeeded in concocting the strangest amalgam of party types one could imagine: on the one hand, they exhibited the characteristics of a classical "party of notables" in which a decentralized structure of personality-dominated fiefdoms coalesced for limited purposes; on the other hand, the Greens exhibited a zealotry and intolerance vis-à-vis each other which were reminiscent of a Leninist-style "cell party."[24] For a movement that thrived on informalism and for which dissent remained essential to its identity, the Greens and their milieu performed miserably in terms of tolerating ambiguities. They basically maintained a Manichean outlook, in which the world was divided into good and evil, with little or no room in between. Politics for this milieu was ultimately governed by categories of morality rather than by those of interest.

Third, the Greens failed to construct an economic policy worthy of the name. Here, too, the Greens proved once again that they have been, more than anything else, the immediate intellectual (in addition to sociological) successors of the New Left of the late 1960s. Just like the sixty-eighters, the Greens did not place much emotional or intellectual emphasis on economic policy. They were much more concerned with problems related to politics (state, class, power, bureaucracy, autonomy, hegemony, domination) and culture (self-actualization, emancipation, alienation, expression, sexuality), and it was in these areas that the intellectually innovative contributions of the New Left lay. Concerning the economy, the differences between the old and the new Left remained remarkably slim. While the latter was a good deal more suspicious of centralized planning than the former, and extolled various decentralized participatory models of workers' self-management such as "autogestion," plant-level codetermination, shop steward power and investment control, the New Left remained woefully inadequate on specifics and never established any viable alternatives which went beyond either Keynes (whom they rejected) or Marx (whom they lionized, especially in his younger and *Grundrisse* incarnation).

Because they were further distanced from Marx than the New Left, the Greens were, if anything even less concerned with issues of the economy than their intellectual predecessors. Beyond arguing that growth is detrimental, and that if it occurred it would have to be "qualitative," that all economic activities would ultimately have to be ecologically sound, and that conversion from a profit-driven market economy to an ecologically responsible social economy was only a matter of political will, the Greens offered very little in terms of concrete proposals related to economic policy. Thus, it is not by chance that their influence in this area on the Social Democratic Party and the trade unions remained ephemeral. Unlike in the realm of gender politics, foreign and defense policy, and environmental reforms, the unions and the SPD hardly bothered to attain any greenish hues in matters related to economic policy in the course of the 1980s. The Greens proved relatively irrelevant in this domain. If anything, it was they who imitated social democracy and the unions in this area, rather than the other way around, as was the case in virtually all other items of central concern to the Left.

The Greens as Representative of the Federal Republic

A key point in our overall assessment of the Greens centers on their inextricable ties with the pre-1990 Federal Republic. On the one hand, the Greens have been the Federal Republic's most prolific critics. Indeed, their very essence and identity has been a critique of everything that the Federal Republic represented: capitalism, the free market, industrial growth, parliamentary rule, bureaucratic domination, ties to the United States and NATO, the exercise of heteronomous power, material abundance, nondescript catch-all parties, corporate might and corporatist conflict management pursuant to the logic of technocratic criteria. It was an unforgettable morning in March 1983 when, following their stunning electoral victory of March 6, 28 green deputies entered the newly constituted Bundestag dressed in blue jeans and sweaters (with the exception of Gaby Potthast, a female delegate from Bochum, who wore a man's dark business suit with vest and tie) and carried large flowerpots to enliven this place of dark-suited old men aesthetically as well as politically. Few groups, if any, in postwar German history had their very identity as closely defined by their opposition to the Federal Republic as the Greens.

Yet, on the other hand, the Greens have been without any doubt one of the Federal Republic's most authentic and quintessential creations. To begin with, the Greens, more than any other of the Federal Republic's political parties with any significance, have been the construct of the Federal Republic's political reality. Unlike any other party in Germany, the Greens have not traced their origins to some previous development in German history. Of course there existed certain components in the Greens' ideology which had their roots in the pre-federal republican part of German history, both left and right. Yet, as our lengthy discussion in part I clearly demonstrates, the Greens emanated from the political, social and cultural constellation of the Federal Republic's progressive forces, most notably the Left. While the liberals (FDP), the two Christian parties (CDU and CSU), the Social Democrats (SPD), the Communists (KPD until 1957 and DKP after 1968; SED in the East and its succesor PDS since 1990) and, of course, all incarnations of the radical Right (SRP, NPD, Republikaner, DVU) continue to derive much of their legitimacy precisely by claiming roots in the Germany which existed before the Federal Republic, the Greens not only have no such claims but in fact prided themselves on being a "party of a new type." They understood themselves to be – and were in fact – total creations of the Federal Republic. By generation, outlook, spirit, behavior, total habitus (sociology of membership, structure of organization, programmatic outlook) the Greens were completely *bundes-republikanisch.*

It is thus more than mere coincidence that the election of December 2, 1990, which cemented the end of the old Bundesrepublik and represented the first major political event in the newly unified Deutschland also witnessed the relegation of the West German Greens from the Bundestag. Even though we are convinced as of now that this departure will prove to be merely temporary, and that the Greens will reenter the Bundestag in 1994, their failure to return to the first German (as opposed to federal republican) Bundestag symbolized, perhaps more than anything else, the definitive passing of the old Federal Republic and the beginning of a new Germany. After all, it was an attitude highly characteristic of the Federal Republic on the part of the West German Greens which led to their temporary parliamentary demise. Being suitably anti-nationalist, and particularly against nationalism of a German sort (both quintessential traits of the Federal Republic's identity, particularly as it concerned that of its intellectuals and its decommodified intelligentsia), the West German Greens disdained any of the growing nationalism which had accompanied the German unification process from the early spring of 1990. The West German Greens – just like their East German counterparts – wanted a two-state solution. They believed in the validity and legitimacy of another German state whose Stalinism they despised but whose existence they extolled. This federal republican identity of the Greens blinded them to the powers of national sentiment which, among many other factors, accelerated East Germany's voluntary absorption by West Germany.

The Greens' fear of "Deutschland" rendered them vociferous defenders of the "Bundesrepublik"; indeed, one still encounters many members of the new Germany's green milieu who remain reluctant to speak of the inherently national one and prefer the republican other. In virtually no other segment of German political life has Jürgen Habermas's notion of a "constitutional patriotism" (*Verfassungspatriotismus*) attained such a fundamental – indeed emotional and existential – acceptance as among the Greens and their ancillary world.[25] The Greens' liberalism has led them to disdain and mistrust the state in all its forms. Moreover, liberalism has taught the Greens to extol the individual's autonomy vis-à-vis all political power. The Greens' libertarian anarchism, derived from the New Left, rendered them the enemies of all mega-bureaucracies and technocratic strategies of problem solving. Lastly, the Greens' anchored socialism of the old Left made them bitter opponents of capitalism.

Despite all these antinomian positions, the Greens actually proved immensely loyal to the Federal Republic in their unbridled republicanism. It was the loyalty of the Greens and the German Left to the old Federal Republic's understated nationalism which rendered them blind to the new forces clamoring for Deutschland. Thus we disagree with those who view the debacle suffered by the Greens – as well as the SPD – in the first German elections of December 2, 1990 as a consequence of strategic errors committed by these two main representatives of the West German Left.[26] The reluctance of the West German Greens fully to incorporate their East German colleagues into one party prior to the election, which would have guaranteed the continued presence of the West German Greens in the Bundestag, had little to do with strategic miscalculation and everything with the Greens' (both East and West) fear of German nationalism. Similarly, the SPD's political leadership, which by 1990 had been furnished by the green-influenced Lafontaine generation, was reluctant to embrace East Germany in Anschluss-like fashion precisely because this generation had become deeply influenced by the Federal Republic's post-nationalist identity. To this milieu, the German Democratic Republic was merely another German-speaking state, like Austria, whose existence was not only legitimate but indeed welcomed by this milieu's members as a guarantee against a renewed and powerful German nationalism. "Constitutional patriotism" was inherently suspicious of anything which even vaguely resembled the reconstitution of a German nationalism. Alas, the West German Left's valiant position on this issue proved strategically erroneous and politically naive, and its two representatives (the Greens and the SPD) had to pay dearly at the ballot box for this miscalculation which, given their history, was inevitable.

In addition to being uneasy toward, even resentful of, German nationalism, it was yet another federal republican trait which led to the misreading of the situation by the West German Greens – and the Left – and their subsequent defeat at the polls. An essential part of the Federal Republic's public ethos had been its reluctance vis-à-vis the usage of power. Thus its characterization as "economic giant, political dwarf" was more than mere talk. While it clearly had a convenient side to it which allowed West Germany to enjoy the protection of US (as well as French) political and military power in the world (and Europe), the syndrome itself derived from the Federal Republic's burdened legacy which made West Germans cautious, indeed reluctant, to employ political power that would have been anywhere near commensurate to the Federal Republic's economic prowess. In other words, an essential part of the Federal Republic's identity was its caution with power, its willingness to defer to others (notably the United States and France) in matters related to political might. Here, too, the West German Greens and their leftist milieu internalized a trait which was quintessentially federal republican and also central to the core of the Left's identity. At least on the issue of flexing Germany's muscle in the international arena, the differences between the Federal Republic's political class and its antinomian greenish milieu were more of degree than kind.

Regarding the crucial topics of nationalism and power, there can be no doubt that 1989–90 formed an epochal turning point in the history of the Federal Republic as well as that of the Greens. Neither the republic nor the Greens will have disappeared, yet both will have emerged in a fundamentally different way in the politics of the 1990s. As they appeared in this study, they will be no more. The new Greens will operate in a Germany which already dominates all of Europe in a way which the Federal Republic could not even fathom. This new factor will inevitably alter the way the German Greens and the Left will have to relate to power and Germany's presence in Europe. It was one thing to be the progressive force in a rump Federal Republic tied to the United States. It is something entirely different to play this role in a united Germany within a transformed, and still changing, Europe. A new self-perception and a changed strategic presence are required of the German Left. The Greens and the Left will have to reevaluate their conventional, pre-1990 notion of nation and German power.

To take one example, Ostpolitik in this new world order will no longer mean the welcome accommodation with a formidable Communist foe for largely instrumental reasons and purposes of temporary detente. Instead, it will denote the projection of German power in an economically fragile, ethnically fragmented and politically volatile part of an otherwise wealthy and stable continent. A new era began in German politics in 1989–90, the politics of Deutschland instead of the Bundesrepublik. Whereas the latter's identity centered on concepts such as the social market economy, corporatist conflict management, para-public institutions and constitutionalism, the former's will be more actively defined by issues pertaining to power, history, hegemony and the nation. The future of the German Greens and the Left will depend on their ability to adjust to this enormous change.

The core of this change pertains to the manner in which this new Germany will balance the requisites of power and democracy in a completely altered global and European order. For 40 years democracy was easy for the Federal Republic and its citizens. West Germany was locked into an American-led western alliance. Its security did not allow it to fall out of step. The contentious issue of power remained unimportant as long as this power was deployed by its western allies, particularly the United States and France. But the days of limited authority, curtailed sovereignty and bridled power are gone. Germany will have to choose for itself. It will have to arrive at a *modus vivendi* between the often incompatible exigencies of democracy and power. In whichever manner this dilemma will be realized, it is clear that Germany's might in Europe and the world will render the outcome crucial to many beyond Germany's borders. That the German Left will be part of this process of choosing attests to the continued democratic nature of the enlarged Federal Republic as well as to the Left's vibrancy as a political actor. How these altered conditions will affect the Greens, the SPD and their shared milieu is currently anybody's guess. However, there can be little doubt that the Left will emerge substantially different in a united Germany than it had been in the "rump" Federal Republic as well as the GDR.

The Greens and the German Left: Future Prospects

When in April 1986 the Chernobyl disaster confronted the European public, many in Germany's green milieu – and beyond – believed that a true turning point in politics had arrived. Ecology was going to attain a salience which would transform the very nature of politics as we had come to know it during the industrial era. Yet it was three years later that the true epochal change in modern politics emerged, once again emanating from the East. The opening of the Berlin wall and the collapses of Leninist-style Communism, the German Democratic Republic and the Soviet Union proved once again that genuine historical conjunctures and epochal watersheds are still determined by politics rather than the economy or ecology. Thus, the real shift – or what the Germans love to call *die Wende* – occurred for the German and the European Left in 1989, not 1986.

While it is too early to tell how this new era will shape the German Greens, as well as the Left in Germany and Europe, it is rather safe to argue that most of the pre-1989 paradigms are at least up for substantial debate if not automatic change. Politics in the unified Germany will be different for the Left on all levels, and the differences will occur on an array of issues.

On the most technical level, the West German Greens will have to learn about coexisting with the East German Greens who, by the time the next electoral opportunity occurs on the federal level, will have represented green causes in the Bundestag for four years during the West German Greens' absence from parliamentary politics in Bonn. While the initial differences between these two green groups continue to diminish in the course of Germany's unification, the divergent nature of their respective origins still informs their political outlook and strategic behavior. Much less indebted to the New Left than the West German Greens, the East German representatives of the movement have a tendency to show little tolerance for what they regard as their western colleagues' overindulgence with ideological debates, factionalism and a tendency for self-righteous posturing. In turn, westerners might become a bit irritated by what they occasionally decry as the easterners' sense of entitlement and an oversensitivity vis-à-vis any western advice – which easterners, for understandable reasons, often interpret as condescending, patronizing and ill-informed. Moreover, western leftists have little tolerance for the easterners' continued hostility toward communism as practiced by the SED regime or in any other form. None of these impediments seem in any way insurmountable. But being aware of and sensitive to them will help both green groups overcome the inevitable difficulties which any arrangement of political cohabitation necessarily exacts from all parties involved. Conversely, the difference between these two groups, accentuated by the centrifugality of forces within each, might become so pronounced that the result could in fact lead to a definitive parting of the ways.

Moving from the technical/strategic to the substantive, most significant among the differences between the Greens' existence in the Federal Republic and in a united Germany will be the fundamentally altered German–US relationship. The pre-1990 Federal Republic owed its very existence and identity to the United States. More than in the case of any other country of the postwar US-dominated capitalist world, including such likely Americanized candidates as the defeated Japan and all the English-speaking states,

American hegemony witnessed its material concretization in the entity known as West Germany. The special nature of West German–American – as opposed to British–American, French–American, or Dutch–American – relations lay in the broken nature of Germany's national identity, its singularly burdened historical legacy resulting from Germany's National Socialist past and, as a consequence, West Germany's location on the front line, the place where the new war with the other superpower representing Communism could instantly turn from cold to hot. Until the fall of 1990, there simply could be no doubt that the United States played a qualitatively different role in West Germany's being than it did in the case of any other European country.[27]

As we argued elsewhere in this book, the special nature of this relationship also played an important role in the political life of the West German Left. The German Left of the 1950s, as represented by the SPD and the "activist" unions, opposed the Federal Republic's integration into a US-dominated North Atlantic economic and security system, preferring a neutral and independent unified Germany instead. Having lost this battle to Konrad Adenauer and the West German Right, Social Democrats and the labor movement became enthusiastic Atlanticists in the wake of their conversion at Bad Godesberg in 1959.

America proved central in the New Left's formation as well. Constructively speaking, the West German sixty-eighters saw themselves as closely related to the American student movement of the 1960s in terms of the strategy, tactics, content and style of their politics. With opposition to the Vietnam war a central ingredient of the identity formation of the West German New Left, the United States, of course, once again assumed a fundamentally negative image in the eyes of German progressives. This negative association grew stronger throughout the massive anti-missile demonstrations of the early to mid 1980s and the Gulf war of 1991.[28]

While anti-Americanism in its cultural as well as political form has been integral to all New Lefts and their descendants, it has had a unique quality in the West German case precisely as a consequence of America's special role as the Federal Republic's mentor, protector, founder and, of course, occupier. The special nature of this West German–American relationship no longer pertains to its German–American successor relationship. Even though NATO and the American presence in Germany will continue for the foreseeable future, the inherent inequality of the relationship has changed. Instead of having the United States always as the dominant partner and West Germany clearly as the subordinate one, the new relationship is that of two equally important and potent protagonists at the threshold of a new European and global order. America will not so much play a lesser role in the lives of Germans as it will assume a fundamentally different one. This will also apply to the German Left. While we do not expect anti-Americanism to abate in its most essential manifestation, namely as a fundamental critique of the evils of modernity – so that to the German Left, America will always be synonymous with pollution, brutality, exploitation, capitalism, imperialism, the megamachine – we are quite certain that the acuity with which America's special relationship to Germany found an identifying moment in the German Left's postwar existence will diminish in the years to come.[29] Thus, with Germany's autonomy from the United States complete and with its sovereignty fully restored, the German Left's disdain for America will in a sense become "purer", more *sui generis*: America will be hated for what it is and does, and less for its relationship (of domination and occupation) with Germany.

A companion to Germany's changed relationship with the United States is the disappearance of Communism, particularly as a threat to Germany emanating from a Soviet-dominated East. Just as America's particular postwar presence assumed special importance in West Germany's identity formation, so too did anti-communism and anti-Sovietism in the Federal Republic of the 1950s and 1960s. And once again, just as in the case of its opposition to the American war in Vietnam, it was the New Left's active antinomy which defined its identity in West German politics. In defiance of the accepted political norm, the New Left – in conjunction with the Willy Brandt-led SPD – began a policy of reconciliation with Communism and Soviet-dominated Eastern Europe which, under the term Ostpolitik, has become part of the political vernacular. In opposition to the hegemonic – often hysterical – anti-communism dominating the Federal Republic's public discourse for over 20 years, the New Left, together with its various political descendants as well as an increasing part of social democracy and the labor movement, developed positions and attitudes vis-à-vis Communism and "real existing socialism" which are best captured by the term "anti-anti-communism" which we used above. While never extolling "real existing socialism," the Federal Republic's leftist milieu learned to tolerate its abuses to the point of condoning them. By the 1980s, being a West German leftist meant never criticizing Communism or the Soviet East.[30]

The German Democratic Republic remained particularly immune from any criticism since it was, despite its faults and shortcomings, by virtue of its "socialism" the truly "anti-fascist" German state, thus morally superior to the capitalist Federal Republic.[31] Arguably one of the Greens' most notably antinomian (and admirable) positions was their open criticism of the Communist regimes and their active support of many East European, first and foremost East German, dissident groups in spite of hegemonic opinion in the West German Left which regarded them with hostility and suspicion. Clearly, it was the Greens' liberalism tinged with a good dosage of anarchism, as opposed to their Marxism, which rendered a number of them into such admirably active opponents to "real existing socialism."

Especially valiant in this context was the passionate engagement on the part of the late Petra Kelly on behalf of the victims of a number of brutal states legitimating their abuses in the name of "socialism." To the chagrin of many of her party comrades, Kelly devoted much of her energies to supporting dissidents in East Germany and criticizing the SED regime in no uncertain terms. During the last years of her life, Kelly developed into one of the most vocal advocates among the German Left supporting liberalization in China. In particular, she became a passionate defender of the Tibetan people in its struggle for independence from what is generally acknowledged as a brutal Chinese rule. Needless to say, Kelly found herself rather marginalized in her views and her passion among her green colleagues inside as well as outside the party.

With the disappearance of Communism and the Soviet world, anti-communism and anti-Sovietism disappeared as well. Thus the painfully contentious problem of communism/anti-communism, which plagued the Left in all western countries – and the West German Left in particular – will not assume any immediacy in the future political life of the German Left. As to the debate about Communism's legacy for the German – and European – Left, it has yet to begin.

With the collapse of the Soviet Union, the German Left will also have to redefine its relationship to the new Eastern Europe. As already argued, the previous relationship was dominated by some version of Ostpolitik, in other words an acceptance of the Communist status quo in return for normalization with the Federal Republic. This was the crux of the SPD's logic of "change through rapprochement," which in turn formed the centerpiece of the Social Democrats' strategy vis-à-vis Eastern Europe designed by Willy Brandt and Egon Bahr. Ostpolitik was progressive in the sense that it actively opposed the West German Right's revanchist designs on expanding Germany's territorial influence beyond the Federal Republic's political boundaries. In its attempts to normalize matters with the East, Ostpolitik also exacted concrete changes from these regimes which were not negligible. Borders became more open, travel increased and the flow of communication from the West to the East could not be blocked as easily as it had been before. Normalization most definitely entailed a gradual destabilization from below. In that sense, Ostpolitik – it could be argued – helped delegitimate, and ultimately dismantle "real existing socialism."

Yet Ostpolitik also had a reactionary side in that in its preoccupation with fighting the West German Right's territorial designs on East Central Europe and in its extolling of the geographical and political status quo in Europe, Ostpolitik paid only scant, if any, attention to the various dissident and opposition movements which were repressed by the established Leninist regimes for decades. One of the reasons for the West German Left's considerable suspicion of many East European dissidents was the latter's frequent attachment to ethnic and religious allegiances. Unable (perhaps also unwilling) to overcome its own historical experiences in which both religion and nationalism had few, if any, positive moments, the West German Left by and large rejected the East Europeans' attachments to either or both. Thus, unlike the Left in Italy and France, where Poland's Solidarity movement was accorded pride of place in discussions, many West German leftists viewed the developments in Poland as nothing but reactionary.[32] Again in contrast to other West European countries, the West German Left did not so much scold the oppositional movements in Eastern Europe as it ignored them.

The preceding analysis is important because it reveals a certain western as well as German prejudice in the Left's attitudes vis-à-vis Eastern Europe.

However, with Leninism gone and nationalism filling its place in many regions of the former Soviet empire, there can be no more doubt as to the staying power of certain collective identities which western leftists, especially those reared in the secular and anational Federal Republic, might see as primordial, reactionary or regressive. They very well may be, yet they comprise current reality in Europe's east. Perhaps this is as good a moment as any for the German Greens and the Left to rethink their long-held views on nationalism, conceding that in certain cases and under special conditions nationalism might indeed be worthy of a progressive's support even if it occurs outside the liberation struggles of an oppressed Third World people. Whatever the case, nationalism will continue to define the political reality of Eastern Europe and the successor states of the former Soviet Union. If the German Greens – as well as Social Democrats – do not want to cede this area completely to the German Right, then they must revise their preconceptions of the area as well as of nationalism as an expression of collective identity in Europe as a whole. It was a sign of utter confusion (or was it rather lack of interest?) that the German Left and its potent peace movement, so readily mobilized for any action when it involves the United States as the traditional bogeyman, remained completely invisible during months of butchery in the former Yugoslavia. Concretely speaking, we view it as arguably the most manifest sign of moral complacency and political irresponsibility for as potent a force as the German peace movement, the Greens, the Social Democrats, the trade unions – in short the Left in the Federal Republic – to have failed to demonstrate massively and with consistency against the genocide committed by ex-Leninist Serbs now turned national fascists a few hundred miles southeast of the German border. Conversely, of equal bankruptcy was this milieu's failure to raise its collective voice in opposition to its own government's haste in bullying Germany's partners in the European Community to extend a premature diplomatic recognition of Croatia, which, in turn, helped unleash the Serbian madness. In short, with the massive changes altering political life in Eastern Europe, the German Left has to rethink its previous premises or it will become irrelevant.

The collapse of the Soviet empire and Leninism will also necessitate a fundamental change in the Left's internal debate. The advent of the Greens provided a major shift in a helpful direction. But while key European countries and one nuclear superpower were officially governed in the name of Marxism-Leninism, any break with the past had to remain limited. Like a millstone, Leninism weighed on any debate, strategy or innovation which the Left entertained. Even in its negation, Leninism played a crucial part in the German Left's reality until 1990. Thus, for example, social democracy always had a facile excuse in that it could claim *not* to be like Leninism. Not even the Greens' presence stopped the endless debates among contemporary leftists which hearkened back to those conducted by their more illustrious predecessors during the first two decades of this century. Indeed, were the often brutal and ultimately so fruitless internecine battles between Realos and Fundis not reminiscent of earlier intra-Left altercations between Social Democrats and Communists? Was it not *déjà vu* when one group accused the other of "revisionism" or "dogmatism," as the case may be?

The disappearance of Leninist-style Communism will, of course, not impede battles between moderates and maximalists, realists and dreamers. These dichotomies are fundamental to all political life, reaching well beyond Leninism or any other political doctrine. What Leninism's disappearance will do, however, is put an end to the presence of a formidable paradigm of progressive thinking which, even if opposed, could simply not be ignored for over 70 years. *Every* leftist, Green or social democrat had to address Leninism, even if only implicitly. This, in a sense, meant the freezing of political content which long ago should have gone well beyond the debates that essentially defined the Second and Third Internationals. Communism's disappearance will also necessitate a fundamental change in social democracy if it, too, does not want to risk becoming irrelevant in a few years.

Thus, while it is true that Communism's demise has finally liberated social democracy from its long-term nemesis and rival on the left, it would be erroneous to see this development as an automatic boon to social democracy which now could finally bask in the glory of being the sole viable representative of the Left. Communism's fall presents also a fundamental challenge to social democracy. The redefinition and self-evaluation which social democracy began reluctantly and belatedly in the wake of the green challenge has to become much more thorough and complete if social democracy wants to remain a politically viable progressive force in the new Germany and Europe. Electoral gimmicks might suffice in the short run to return and even keep the SPD in power for a few years. The conservatives might prove so incompetent and corrupt that voters might turn to the Social Democrats for a lack of a better alternative. All of these developments, while possible, could in no way compensate for a fundamental redefinition of progressive politics and all that such a move entails at the latter part of the twentieth century. The social-democratic Left – very much a creation of the late nineteenth century – will have to rethink its relationship to the state, to culture, to the individual, to the collectives of class and nation, to Europe and the global economy. All of these complex structures will have undergone major changes in the wake of the revolution of 1989–90. Above all, they will have all become more diverse, pluralistic and differentiated. Following the demise of Leninism, social democracy would be well advised to shed its own dogmatism and adopt a flexibility and tolerance which it never had in over a century.

Progressive politics will by necessity mean plural politics. One danger of pluralization is complete fragmentation. Indeed, the Left – to a lesser extent in Germany and Europe than in the United States – has run the risk in the past decade of becoming particularized in good part because it has lost some of the key ingredients of its formerly universalizing principles and agents. The defeat of Leninism will only exacerbate these centrifugal tendencies, to which the rise of the new social movements and the Greens contributed quite considerably. Yet there clearly exists a universalizing principle around which social democracy and the Left could rally and redefine themselves. It is *democracy* pure and simple, without any qualifying adjectives such as "liberal," "constitutional," "parliamentary," "popular" and, yes, even "social."[33] Democracy in this case would denote the constant struggle for the weak and poor and disadvantaged wherever they might be, regardless of system and "ism." It would be a position of true antinomy and critique against *any* entrenched power anywhere. Thus, this democracy-defined Left would criticize American racism in the United States as vociferously as it would oppose Cuba's anti-gay policies, Serbian oppression of the Albanians in Kossovo, as well as Croatian discrimination against Serbs. This universalizing democracy would plead for more workers' control, more individual rights, more empowerment for regular citizens, more community responsibility, more egalitarianism, regardless of the "system." This project will be of a particularly tall order for most constituents of the German Left, Social Democrats included, who have by tradition been always more concerned with the "social" than with the "democrat." Here, too, the greening of German social democracy might prove beneficial in the long run to the necessary reorientation of progressive politics in the new Germany.

While the frequency and intensity of battles will in no way diminish among progressives, the lines will undoubtedly be drawn along different, much more fragmented and porous, axes than in the past. The days of the big schemes, the grand designs, the compelling "isms" are numbered. This is as true for social democracy as it was for Leninism. The Left's pluralization will not only enhance the Greens' presence in this debate but also render it much more open and exciting due to social democracy's inevitable defrosting as well.

Perhaps few issues will challenge social democracy and the Greens as fundamentally as their posture toward ethnic politics and the politics of European multiculturalism. Ethnic and national allegiances have always posed serious problems to most versions of the European left, be they mainly of the Leninist or the social-democratic variety. Emanating more or less from monoethnic societies, most notably Germany and Britain, Marxism bequeathed its descendants a preoccupation with class which rendered them virtually oblivious, even dismissive, vis-à-vis any collective identity beyond those of production. Collective identities associated with religion, nation or ethnic group were either viewed as epiphenomenal to that of class, or branded retrograde and reactionary by virtue of their being in potential conflict with class. The particularly woeful inadequacy of "false consciousness" as a concept for understanding political reality was nevertheless frequently used in this context. With the possible exception of Austro-Marxism, tellingly the political creation of a multiethnic society, the old Left had little useful to say about ethnic identity.[34] Worse still, it viewed nationalism as fundamentally irrelevant. The New Left fared only slightly better in that it recognized the importance of nationalism provided it occurred in the so-called developing world. Indeed, in the context of its Third World incarnation, nationalism attained a positively progressive dimension for the New Left. However, as far as Europe was concerned, the New Left's ignorance, disregard and contempt for nationalism as a legitimate, potentially even progressive, collective identity pretty much followed the perimeters delineated by the old Left.

The events of 1989–90 meant an end to this complacency. Even though the former Federal Republic had become a multicultural society in all but name by the early 1970s – by virtue of having "imported" more than two million "guestworkers" and their dependants to perform the country's most menial and demeaning jobs – it was not until the late 1980s that "multiculturalism" even became a public issue.[35] As in so many instances, here, too, the Greens deserve much credit for having made this problem a topic for public debate in the Federal Republic. Moreover, in notable contrast to the Social Democrats, the Greens remained the only progressive force which consistently confronted the barely veiled racism and xenophobia informing the actions of most conservative policy-makers on this issue. In particular, it was only the Greens who openly called for a complete integration of all foreigners in the Federal Republic by granting them full citizenship without any conditions and exceptions. Of course, the Greens' demand necessitates a different conception of citizenship than has been the case in Germany since 1913, a period of intense nationalism bordering on chauvinism which gave rise to what is basically a racist and culturally exclusive definition of who constitutes a German and thus a citizen of the German polity. The Federal Republic's current citizenship laws are much more restrictive than comparable laws in other western democracies.[36] Anchored in what is known as *jus sanguinis*, German citizenship is extended on the basis of lineage, blood ties, and a very particularistic and exclusive interpretation of culture instead of on the basis of political and legal criteria. Thus, millions of "guest workers" and their children – many of whom were born in Germany and speak only German – have been unable to obtain German citizenship, something granted routinely to any person from Russia, Romania, or Brazil for that matter, who can demonstrate German ancestry, even if he/she does not speak German and has nothing in common with the contemporary Federal Republic. Particularly disturbing have been those instances in which arrivals to the Federal Republic from Poland, Ukraine, Russia and other countries of the former Soviet empire successfully claimed German citizenship on the basis of proving their – or their ancestors' – collaboration with the German Nazis during the Second World War.

As has been the case with a number of issues, the Greens' sentiment in approaching multiculturalism in contemporary Germany has been commendable, whereas their politics has not. While the wish to include everybody in Germany on an equal footing which, among other things, also entails full citizenship is noble, it is politically unfeasible and naive. Once again, by having their sentiments and rigid ideologies define their political strategies, the Greens unnecessarily created a self-imposed limitation on the possibilities of their political activities in an area in which their engagement remains decisive for the enhancement of democratic rights in the new Germany.

But well beyond Germany, the politics of ethnicity has reemerged on the

European scene. With the opening of borders, both East and West, the creation of large internal markets and the challenges facing all existing political institutions, most notably the conventional nation-state, ethnic allegiances will become more pronounced all over the Continent. This means that progressives will have to take ethnic politics and the manifestations of national allegiance very seriously. Above all, they will have to be viewed on their own terms. Relegating them to various forms of epiphenomenality and false consciousness would not only demean them in an elitist manner, but also discount their political importance, thus threatening to render those committing such mistakes politically irrelevant.

The issue of nationalism as a potentially disruptive phenomenon need not remain confined to the eastern portion of the European continent. Even though part of Western Europe's postwar success story lay precisely in the taming of ethnic conflict, it is not inconceivable that there, too, inter-ethnic tensions might lead to forms of militant racism and violence. To the Greens and the German Left, "Europe" – meaning, of course, some sort of supranational political entity – was always desirable since it represented an international alternative to any versions of a disliked German state. The German Left's identification with Europe developed over the years into something akin to a substitute for German nationalism. Being European meant being anti-German, international, universalistic and – at least structurally – anti-Atlanticist, thus anti-American. With "Europe" becoming increasingly identified with a distant bureaucracy and a market-driven unification in which big business seems to be the only immediate beneficiary, the German Left's formerly enthusiastic "euroconsciousness" has given way to a "euroskepsis" if not yet "eurofatigue." Especially the Greens' criticism of the whole project following the Maastricht treaty borders on a wholesale rejection of European unification.[37]

As can be expected of a milieu for which local autonomy, grass-roots empowerment and hostility vis-à-vis distant bureaucracies has been fundamental to its identity, the Greens and their sympathizers have on the whole rejected what they consider to be an unnecessarily precipitous move to European unification. While the Greens' suspicion of and hostility toward German nationalism and the Federal Republic have continued to render them "good Europeans" and genuine internationalists, values equally dear to their hearts compelled them to oppose European unification as envisioned by the European Community's bureaucrats, especially in its accelerated version as annunciated in the Maastricht treaty. Here are some of the most salient objections which the Greens have brought to bear against Maastricht. In terms of the treaty's content, the Greens object to the woeful absence of social measures which are to guarantee the collective protection of the weak and disenfranchised. Further offending the Greens' traditionally socialist (that is "red") sensibilities is the absence of a powerful social component in the treaty and labor's clearly subordinate role in the Europe envisioned by the treaty. Irking the Greens' liberal, democratic as well as anarchist sides was the manner in which the Maastricht agreement came about. Instead of being the product of a "bottom up" process of democratic politics expressing the people's will, the whole treaty was – at least in the Greens' view – a "top down" concoction of state bureaucrats, technocratic modernizers and fat-cat capitalists whose interests alone were served by this precipitous arrangement. Lastly, the Greens' ecological (that is "green") sensibilities were also deeply offended by Maastricht's allegedly inadequate concerns for Europe's continuously deteriorating environment and by its very being as a huge, state-induced, though supra-statist, project extolling everything that the Greens believe to be wrong with modernity.

At least in the old Federal Republic positions such as these remained an exclusive prerogative of the radical Right. Even the SPD, formerly among the most ardent advocates of European unity on the Continent, voiced certain reservations concerning the content and speed of the post-Maastricht unification process. The German Left's criticism and skepticism vis-à-vis substantial parts of Europe's unification are completely justified. Thus there can be no doubt that many dimensions central to any left, such as for example social and economic protection of the weak, remain poorly articulated in the current unification blueprints. It very much behooves the German Left, as the most powerful in Europe, to criticize these deficiencies, and in so doing to exert its leadership where otherwise there would be none. The danger lies only in the possibility that the German Left, too, will develop an anti-European posture which would most certainly not stop Europe's unification but leave outside it the most powerful agent of opposition, criticism and antinomy.

Ultimately, the views of the Greens and the German Left on East and West European nationalism – as well as on the other issues discussed in this section of our conclusion – will greatly depend on their conceptualization of the new Germany's identity in a new European and global order. This, of course, entails a reconceptualization of their own identity in a fundamentally changed environment. While even speculative statements, let alone firm assessments, of this development would border on the irresponsible at this juncture, a few contours which have emerged might be worthy of mention. True to its pre-1945, but especially post-1945 traditions, the German Left continues to remain immensely skeptical of any power. In notable contrast to the situation in the old Federal Republic, the German Left will have to contend with the active projection of German power on the part of a united Germany. To its immense credit, the German Left seems determined to resist all temptations in this direction, which have already had considerable appeal to parts of the German political class. Helped by substantial public support on this issue, it seems that the Left has thus far been successful in rendering Germany into a large Switzerland or Austria. Yet there also lies the danger of naivety in this otherwise noble policy. Regardless of how reluctant Germany remains to deploy its armed forces anywhere in Europe – or the world for that matter – the country is by virtue of its economy, population size, geographic location and cultural legacy the uncontested hegemon in the European theater. This is a fact which Germany's progressive forces will have to recognize. Moreover, if their opposition and antinomy are to remain politically meaningful, the recognition of this fact also commits them to a politics of responsibility which goes beyond naive negations. Thus, wishing away German power by declaring Germany neutral, bloc-free, out of NATO – in short, by rendering it into an Austria – will simply not suffice. Making certain that German troops are never deployed under any circumstances, preferably not even as members of a multinational contingent under the command of the United Nations or the Conference of Security and Cooperation in Europe, is commendable but not quite sufficient. The German Left will have to pursue its opposition to all aspects of German hegemony with the vigor and passion it has directed against the United States and things American since the late 1960s. Whether it will be able to do that, or whether the German Left, too, will ultimately succumb to the irresistible charms of being once again part of a hegemonic power, only time will tell.

Appendix

Table 1 Votes for the Greens: national elections, 1980–1990

	Percentage of vote	Impact	Average vote
1980	1.5	no seats	1.5
1983	5.6	won 27 seats	5.6
1987	8.3	won 42 seats	8.3
1990	4.8(W)	no seats(W)	
	6.0(E)	won 8 seats(E)	5.1

Tables 1 and 2 are reprinted from *Between Protest and Power: The Green Party in Germany*, by E. Gene Frankland and Donald Schoonmaker, 1992, by permission of Westview Press, Boulder, Colorado. They are based on electoral statistics from Clause A. Fischer, ed., *Wahlhandbuch fur die Bundesrepublik Deutschland: Daten zu Bundestags-, Landtags-, und Europawahlen in der Bundesrespublik Deutschland, in den Ländern und in den Kreisen 1946–1989*, 2 vols (Paderborn: Schöningh, 1990). Tables 3 and 4 and figures 1 and 2 have been compiled by the authors.

Table 2 Votes for the Greens: state and city-state elections, 1978–1992

	State	Percentage of vote	Impact	Average vote
1978	Hamburg	4.5	(FDP out)	
	Lower Saxony	3.9	(FDP out)	
	Bavaria	1.8		(3.05)
	Hesse	2.0		
1979	Berlin	3.7		
	Schleswig-Holstein	2.4	SPD below 50%	(3.73)
	Bremen	5.1	won seats	
1980	Baden-Württemberg	5.3	won seats	
	Saar	2.9		(3.73)
	North Rhine Westphalia	3.0	(FDP out)	
1981	Berlin	7.2	won seats	(7.20)
1982	Lower Saxony	6.5	won seats	
	Hamburg (June election)	7.9	won seats	
	Hesse	8.0	won seats	(6.76)
	Bavaria	4.6		
	Hamburg (December election)	6.8	won seats	
1983	Rhineland Palatinate	4.5	(FDP out)	
	Schleswig-Holstein	3.6	(FDP out)	
	Bremen	7.8	won seats	(5.45)
	Hesse	5.9	won seats (coalition later)	
1984	Baden-Württemberg	8.0	won seats	(8.0)
1985	Saar	2.5		
	Berlin	10.6	won seats	(5.9)
	North Rhine Westphalia	4.6		
1986	Lower Saxony	7.1	won seats	
	Bavaria	7.5	won seats	(8.33)
	Hamburg	10.4	won seats	
1987	Hesse	9.4	won seats	
	Rhineland Palatinate	5.9	won seats	
	Hamburg	7.0	won seats	(8.13)
	Bremen	10.2	won seats	
1988	Baden-Württemberg	7.9	won seats	
	Schleswig-Holstein	2.9		(5.4)
1989	Berlin	11.8	in coalition; won seats	(11.8)
1990	Saar	2.6		

Table 2   (Cont.)

	State	Percentage of vote	Impact	Average vote
	Lower Saxony	5.5	in coalition; won seats	
	North Rhine Westphalia	5.0	won seats	
	Bavaria	6.4	won seats	
	Mecklenburg-West Pomerania	9.3	no seat; ran separately[a]	
	Brandenburg	9.2	in coalition; won seats	(6.48)
	Saxony Anhalt	5.3	won seats	
	Thuringia	6.5	won seats	
	Saxony	5.6	won seats	
	United Berlin	9.4	won seats	
1991	Hesse	8.8	in coalition; won seats	
	Rhineland Pfalz	6.4	won seats	
	Hamburg	6.2	won seats	(8.2)
	Bremen	11.4	in coalition; won seats	
1992	Baden-Württemberg	9.5	won seats	(7.78)
	Schleswig-Holstein	4.97		

[a] The three East German groups, Demokratischer Aufbruch/Vereinigte Linke, Initiative Demokratie Jetzt and the East Greens, not only ran separately but refused to pool their respective tallies, which combined amounted to 9.3 percent of the vote. By refusing to combine their forces, the three constituent elements of the Greens failed to attain any parliamentary seats in the legislature of Mecklenburg-West Pomerania.

The average votes for the city-states of Berlin, Bremen, and Hamburg are considerably higher than those of any other groups. The Greens and their counterparts in the East have jumped the 5 percent hurdle to win seats in all states except Saar and Schleswig-Holstein, where the SPD has strong party organizational strength.

Table 3 Green Party election results for the legislatures of the East German Länder, 14 October 1990 (percent)

Mecklenburg	4.2
Brandenburg	6.4[a]
Sachsen-Anhalt	5.3
Sachsen	5.6[a]
Thüringen	6.5

[a] Bündis '90 results

Table 4 Green Party election results for the Bundestag and the European Parliament (percent)

	17 Jun. 1979	21 Oct. 1980	6 Mar. 1983	7 Jun. 1984	25 Jan. 1987	8 Jun. 1989	2 Dec. 1990
European Parliament	3.2			8.2		8.4	
Bundestag		1.5	5.6		8.3		4.8

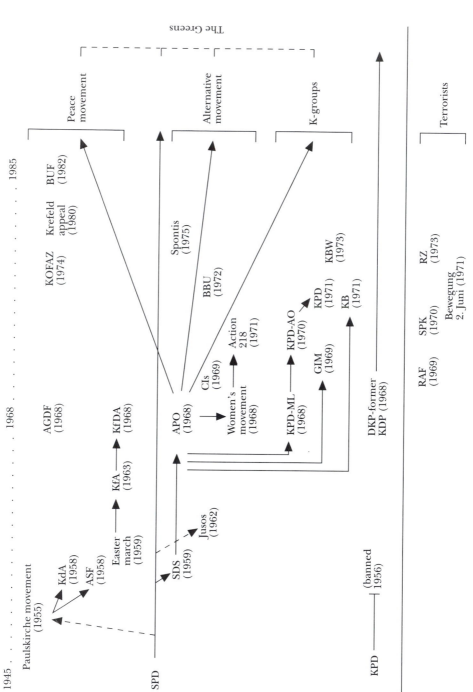

Figure 1 The genealogy of the West German Greens and a synopsis of the West German Left

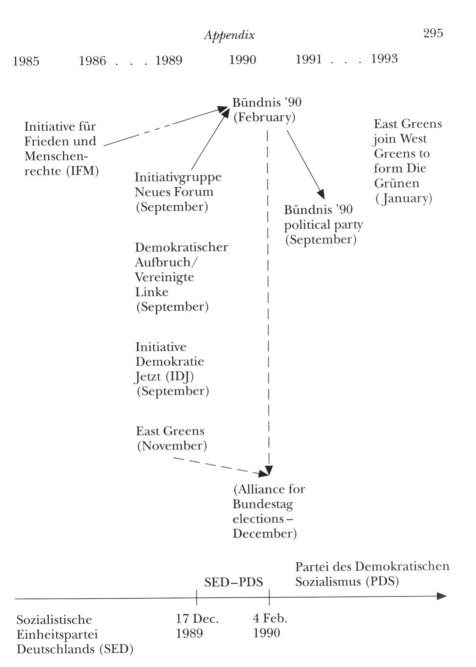

Figure 2 The genealogy of the East German Greens

Notes

Introduction

1 These recently formed parties should not be confused with the so-called "Green International" of the period between the two world wars. This loose federation of peasant parties was primarily focused in Eastern and Central Europe, with a central International Agrarian Bureau in Prague. Supposedly an organization of international peasant solidarity, the "Green International" chose its name to emphasize the contrast between itself and the "Red International" of the Communists on the one hand, and the "White International" of landlords and capitalists on the other. See Joseph Rothschild, *East Central Europe between the Two World Wars*, 1974, p. 18.

2 See Seymour Martin Lipset and Stein Rokkan, eds, *Party Systems and Voter Alignments: Cross-national Perspectives*, 1967, pp. 1–64. Also Anton Pelinka and Fritz Plasser, *The Austrian Party System*, 1989.

3 For a further explanation of this concept of "generation," see Karl Mannheim's *Ideology and Utopia*, 1936, or A. Belden Fields, *Student Politics in France: A Study of the Union nationale des étudiants de France*, 1970, and *Trotskyism and Maoism: Theory and Practice in France and the U.S.*, 1988.

4 For example, see Willy Brandt's "Mehr Demokratie wagen" from his *Regierungserklärung*, Oct. 28, 1969, in Willy Brandt, *Zum sozialen Rechtsstaat: Reden und Dokumente*, 1983, p. 10. Also see Karl-Werner Brant, "Cyclical Aspects of New Social Movements: Waves of Cultural Criticism and Mobilization Cycles of New Middle Class Radicalism," in Russell J. Dalton and Manfred Kuechler, eds, *Challenging the Political Order: New Social and Political Movements in Western Democracies*, 1990; and Charles Reich, *The Greening of America: How the Youth Revolution is Trying to Make America Livable*, 1970.

5 See John H. Goldthorpe et al., *The Affluent Worker in the Class Structure*, 1969; André Gorz, *Strategy for Labor: A Radical Proposal*, 1967; Alain Touraine, *The Workers' Movement*, 1987; Serge Mallet, *The New Working Class*, 1975.

6 Daniel Bell, *The End of Ideology: On the Exhaustion of Political Ideas in the Fifties*, 1988.

7 See Goldthorpe et al., *Affluent Worker,* Seymour Martin Lipset, ed., *The Third Century: America as a Post-industrial Society,* 1979.
8 See the study of white-collar workers in Weimar Germany in Richard F. Hamilton, *Who Voted for Hitler?* 1988.
9 See Philip G. Altbach, ed., *The Student Revolution: A Global Analysis,* 1970. See also Seymour Martin Lipset and Philip G. Altbach, eds, *Students in Revolt,* 1969; Seymour Martin Lipset and Sheldon S. Wolin, eds, *The Berkeley Student Revolt: Facts and Interpretations,* 1965; Seymour Martin Lipset, *Passion and Politics: The Dimensions of Student Involvement: Rebellion in the University,* 1972; *Seymour Martin Lipset, ed., Student Politics,* 1967.
10 Clark Kerr, *The Uses of the University,* 1963. For a good analysis of events in France, see Pierre Bourdieu, *Les heritiers: les etudiants et la culture,* 1964. For a look at Germany, see Stephan Leibfried, *Armutspolitik und die Entstehung des Sozialstaats,* 1985.
11 Steven Brint and Jerome Karabel, *The Diverted Dream: Community Colleges and the Promise of Educational Opportunity in America, 1900–1985,* 1989. See also Jerome Karabel and A. H. Halsey, eds, *Power and Ideology in Education,* 1977.
12 Claus Offe, *Disorganized Capitalism: Contemporary Transformations of Work and Politics,* ed. John Keane, 1985; Gøsta Esping-Andersen, *Politics Against Markets: The Social Democratic Road to Power,* 1985. Also by Esping-Andersen, *Social Class, Social Democracy and State Policy: Party Policy and Party Decomposition in Denmark and Sweden,* 1980.
13 See Werner Hülsberg, *The German Greens: A Social and Political Profile,* 1988, pp. 113–18.
14 See Solomon Barkin, ed., *Worker Militancy and its Consequences, 1965–75: New Directions in Western Industrial Relations,* 1975; Colin Crouch and Alessandro Pizzorno, eds, *The Resurgence of Class Conflict in Western Europe since 1968,* vols 1 and 2, 1978.
15 See Peter Gourevitch et al., *Unions and Economic Crisis: Britain, West Germany, and Sweden,* 1984; Andrei S. Markovits, *The Politics of the West German Trade Unions: Strategies of Class and Interest Representation in Growth and Crisis,* 1986.
16 See Daniel Bell, *The Coming of Post-industrial Society: A Venture in Social Forecasting,* 1973; Zbigniew Brzezinski, *Between Two Ages: America's Role in the Technocratic Era,* 1982; Alain Touraine, *The Post-industrial Society: Tomorrow's Social History, Classes, Conflicts and Culture in the Programmed Society,* 1971; Touraine, *Workers' Movement.*
17 See the recommendations of Paul McCracken et al., *Towards Full Employment and Price Stability: A Report to the OECD by a Group of Independent Experts,* 1977, pp. 167–72, 210–13.
18 On this "post-Fordism" see Michael J. Piore and Charles F. Sabel, *The Second Industrial Divide: Possibilities for Prosperity,* 1984.
19 One country where this model seems to have remained relatively intact is Sweden. See Esping-Andersen, *Politics Against Markets.*
20 On the concept of postmaterialism, see Ronald Inglehart, *Culture Shift in Advanced Industrial Society,* 1989, and *The Silent Revolution: Changing Values and Political Styles among Western Publics,* 1977. It is not by chance that the major rock 'n' roll bands of the late 1960s are still *the* major attractions in youth culture. Twenty years after their initial appearance, bands like the Rolling Stones, the Who and the Grateful Dead continue to enjoy youthful immediacy. It speaks for the cultural staying power of the late 1960s that many of these bands'

current followers were barely born when this genre of music first emerged as a distinct symbol of a "postmaterialist" life style.

21 Extensive literature on social movements in Europe includes the following. For France: Michel Tozzi, *Syndicalisme et nouveaux mouvements sociaux, régionalisme, feminisme, écologie,* 1982; Arthur Hirsch, *French New Left,* 1982; Philip G. Cerny, ed., *Social Movements and Protest in France,* 1982. For Italy: Paolo R. Donati, *Movimenti sociali contemporanei, bibliografia 1975–84,* 1984; Robert Lumpley, *States of Emergency: Cultures of Revolt in Italy from 1968 to 1978,* 1990; Mario Diani, *Isole nell'archipelago: il movimento ecologista in Italia,* 1988. For the United States the literature is vast, but among the best works are: Kenneth Clatterbaugh, *Contemporary Perspectives on Masculinity: Men, Women and Politics in Modern Society,* 1990; David de Leon, *Everything is Changing,* 1988; Alec Barbrook, *Power and Protest in American Life,* 1980; Judith C. Albert and Stewart E. Albert, eds, *The Sixties Papers,* 1984.

22 See Dieter Rucht, ed., *Neue soziale Bewegungen in der Bundesrepublik Deutschland,* 1987; Georg Haasken and Michael Wigbers, eds, *Protest in der Klemme: soziale Bewegungen in der Bundesrepublik,* 1986; Karl-Dieter Opp et al., *Soziale Probleme und Protestverhalten: Eine empirische Konfrontation des Modells rationalen Verhaltens mit soziologischen und demographischen Hypothesen am Beispiel von Atomkraftgegner,* 1987; Karl-Werner Brand et al., *Aufbruch in eine andere Gesellschaft: Neue soziale Bewegungen in der Bundesrepublik,* 1983; Robert Steigerwald, *Protestbewegung: Steitfragen und Gemeinsamkeiten,* 1982, Ernst Stracke, *Stadtzerstörung und Stadtteilkampf,* 1980, Claudia Mast, *Aufbruch ins Paradies?,* 1980.

23 Notably Claus Offe.

24 Clarles Perrow, *Normal Accidents: Living with High-Risk Technologies,* 1984.

25 Jost Halfmann, "Rights and Reciprocity: Social Movement Themes and Social Change in the Federal Republic of Germany," in *Praxis International,* 8. 1, 1987; also published as a paper from the annual meeting of the American Political Science Association, Chicago Sept. 3–6, 1987.

26 Of course, it would be ridiculous to paint green activists simply as "selfless" idealists. Many are indeed concerned with personal power and prestige. Instead, the point is that there are few material incentives for the green politician. This is because there are no institutionalized career paths within the green parties.

27 See Joachim Hirsch, *Der Sicherheitsstaat: Das "Modell Deutschland", seine Krise und die neue sozialen Bewegungen,* 1980.

28 Success is here understood in conventional terms as representation in legislatures (especially on the national level) and participation in government.

29 See Herbert Kitschelt, *The Logic of Party Formation: Ecological Politics in Belgium and West Germany,* 1989.

30 See Ferdinand Müller-Rommel, "New Political Movements and 'New Politics' Parties in Western Europe," in Dalton and Kuechler, *Challenging the Political Order,* and Ferdinand Müller-Rommel, ed., *New Politics in Western Europe: The Rise and Success of Green Parties and Alternative Lists,* 1989. See also a review by Philip Gorski in *German Politics and Society,* no. 22, Spring 1991.

31 See Müller-Rommel, "New Political Movements."

32 Obviously there are exceptions to any comparison of this kind. Thus, for example, Japan did not produce any "new politics" parties during the 1970s and 1980s, although it had virtually no labor strife. Conversely, the borderline cases of Finland and Italy, which did develop "new politics" parties, albeit of lesser significance than the European countries belonging to our first

group, also exhibited a fair amount of labor strife. It should be added, however, that in both countries, particularly in Italy, labor strife declined significantly during the 1980s, as compared to the 1970s. And it was in the 1980s that the Italian Greens emerged and eventually entered the Italian parliament in 1988.

33 Walter Korpi, *The Democratic Class Struggle*, 1983. According to Korpi, social democracy's major contribution to progressive politics has been its ability to divert the class struggle away from the market and into the state. In countries with strong social-democratic traditions, the labor movement succeeded in becoming institutionalized in state and society. In so doing, it attained benefits from both via established policy channels without having to resort to the much more costly and, usually, much less successful strike option. In short, the more labor could become institutionalized in the state and thus establish the state as a prime locus for the class struggle, the more it could increase its chances to gain victories against capital and thereby contribute to the democratization of the country's politics as a whole. The validity of Korpi's argument rests on the notion that in liberal democracies the state has proven to be a more democratic arena for conflict resolution than the market in good part because it has become a much more successful venue for those whose representation and power is weakened by the market, a grouping which clearly includes labor as a key constituency. Thus, in countries where labor remained weak, it failed to become institutionalized in state and society, leaving the market as the prime arena for labor's struggle against capital. Incapable of being a match for capital in this contest, labor in such countries remained excluded from the main areas of politics, and could never mobilize at least parts of the state for its purposes. Thus it had to resort to various militant steps in the industrial arena, most notably strikes. Strikes, following this logic, are symptoms of labor's weakness in a country, not of its strength. In a fine comparison of Scandinavian social democracies, Gøsta Esping-Andersen shows convincingly that the Swedish version weathered the crisis of the late 1970s much better than its Danish counterpart in good part because the former managed to remain anchored in the state much more thoroughly than the latter. See Esping-Andersen, *Politics Against Markets*.

34 For the concept of parapublic institutions, see Peter Katzenstein, *Policy and Politics in West Germany: The Growth of a Semi-sovereign State*, 1987.

35 On "organized capitalism" Rudolf Hilferding, *Finance Capital: A Study of the Latest Phases of Capitalist Development*, trans. Morris Watnick and Sam Gordon, 1981; Gerhard Lehmbruch and Philippe C. Schmitter eds, *Patterns of Corporatist Policy-making*, 1982, and *Trends Towards Corporatist Intermediation*, 1979; Philippe C. Schmitter, *Corporatism and Public Policy in Authoritarian Portugal*, 1975; Anton Pelinka, *Gewerkschaften im Parteienstaat*, 1980.

36 See Andrei S. Markovits, "German Social Democracy," *Studies in Political Economy*, no. 19, Spring 1986.

37 See Paul Byrne, "Great Britain: The Green Party," in Müller-Rommel *New Politics*. The first green party in the world was founded in New Zealand but never attained much political significance.

38 The Protestant predominance is only of recent (post-1990) vintage in Germany. The "old" Federal Republic – while basically evenly divided between Catholics and Protestants – still witnessed a separation of the two communities based on a geographic level with, roughly, the north Protestant, and the south Catholic.

39 Alice Holmes Cooper, "The West German Peace Movement of the 1980s: Historical and Institutional Influences," Ph.D. diss., 1988.

40 It is interesting to note that a disproportionately large number of West German terrorists of the 1970s, particularly among women, hailed from actively churchgoing and believing Protestant families, even from those with Protestant clergy.

41 The existence of the German past as a decisively weighty issue of the present is an excellent example of the reality and potency of latent phenomena in politics, and of the immense difficulty of their positive verification and measurability. See Peter Bachrach and Morton S. Baratz, *Power and Poverty*, 1970.

42 See Russell J. Dalton, *Politics in West Germany*, 1989, pp. 131–2.

43 Although he himself was not a German, Nicos Poulantzas's interpretation of fascism was hegemonic among the German student movement. See Nicos Poulantzas, *Fascisme et dictature*, 1974. For a Germany interpretation, see Wolfgang Haug, *Die Faschisierung des bürgerlichen Subjekts: Die Ideologie der gesunden Normalität und die Ausrottungspolitik im deutschen Faschismus*, 1986, and *Der hilflose Antifaschismus: Zur Kritik der Vorlesungsreihen über Wissenschaft und NS an deutschen Universitäten*, 1977.

44 Leo A. Muller, *Republikaner, NPD, DVU, Liste D . . .*, 1989; Gerd Knabe, ed., *20 Jahre NPD: Porträt einer junger Partei*, 1984; Siegfried Hergt, *Partei Programme: SPD, CDU, CSU, FDP, DKP, NPD*, 1975; Agnes Bruggeman, *Anhänger und Gegner der Nationaldemokratischen Partei Deutschlands (NPD)*, 1968; Josef Hindels, *NPD: Ein Alarmzeichen*, 1967; Clause Leggewie, *Die Republikaner: Phantombild der neuen Rechten*, 1989; Hajo Funke, *Republikaner: Rassismus, Judenfeindschaft, nationaler Grössenwahn*, 1989.

45 One of the flaws was – and still is – the reference only to "fascism," never to "National Socialism" or to "Nazism."

46 Alfred Dregger, *Freiheit in unserer Zeit*, 1989, and *Der Preis der Freiheit: Sicherheitspolitik im geteilten Europa*, 1985; Jutta Ditfurth, *Träumen, Kämpfen, Verwirklichen*, 1988.

47 On the German peace movement's "German" dimension, as expressed by its anti-Americanism, anti-West sentiments and neutralism, see Jeffrey Herf, *War by Other Means: Soviet Power, West German Resistance and the Battle of the Euromissiles*, 1991, and Robert Pfaltzgraf et al., *The Greens of West Germany: Origins, Strategies, and Transatlantic Implications*, 1983.

48 See Alice Schwarzer, "Bornierte Freund-Feind Muster," *Der Spiegel*, Apr. 29, 1991.

49 See Die Grünen's *Die Multikulturelle Gesellschaft: Für eine demokratische Umgestaltung in der Bundesrepublik. Positionen und Dokumentation*, 1990.

50 See Andrei S. Markovits, "On Anti-Americanism in West Germany," *New German Critique*, Winter 1985, pp. 3–27.

51 Peter Merkl et al., eds, *Development in West German Politics*, 1989.

Chapter 1   Reconstruction, Rearmament and Reintegration

1 Herbert Lilge, *Deutschland: 1945–63*, 1983, p. 17.

2 Hans Karl Rupp, *Politische Geschichte der Bundesrepublik Deutschland*, 2nd edn, 1978, p. 54.

3 Lilge, *Deutschland*, p. 19.

4 Ibid., pp. 29, 62, 131, 176.

5 Ibid., p. 167.

6 See Hans Karl Rupp, *Außerparlamentarische Opposition in der Ära Adenauers*, 1970, p. 64, and Rupp, *Politische Geschichte*, p. 64.
7 Andrei S. Markovits, *The Politics of the West German Trade Unions*, 1986.
8 Karl-Werner Brand, et al., *Aufbruch in eine andere Gesellschaft*, 1984, p. 4.
9 Hermann Kaste and Joachim Raschke, "Zur Politik der Volkspartei," in Wolf-Dieter Narr, ed., *Auf dem Weg zum Einparteienstaat*, 1977, p. 36; Lilge, *Deutschland*, p. 235.
10 The CDU, SPD and KPD each basically supported this goal with slightly different shadings, with proposals ranging from "self-administrating economic bodies" independent of state control in the case of the CDU, through the SPD's "economic democracy" of decentralized economic power with state oversight, to the KPD's more traditional Marxist views. In addition, clauses prescribing socialization and codetermination in various forms were written into almost every state constitution of the Federal Republic. However, even at this earliest, most sympathetic juncture of public sentiment, the recognition of codetermination and socialization was a (perhaps somewhat grudging) concession to the workers – in many cases, merely as a legalization of the power already won by spontaneously organized workers' councils right after the war. See Rupp, *Politische Geschichte*, pp. 63–4, and also Arno Klönne and Hartmut Reese, *Die deutsche Gewerkschaftsbewegung*, 1984, p. 183.
11 Through several grave strategic miscalculations, the opposition SPD had lost its foothold in the critical joint American-German Economic Control Committee of the Bizone, which had been entrusted with administering the economic recovery and restructuring in West Germany. Eberhard Schmidt, *Die verhinderte Neuordnung, 1945–52*, 7th edn, 1977, pp. 169–72.
12 While this strategy admittedly went some distance towards the original plans of "denazifying" the economy as well, it fell far short of the hopes of the Left. Ibid.
13 It became a part of the "Dusseldorf leading principles" which for all intents and purposes replaced the more "socialist" Ahlener program. Ibid., p. 174.
14 In August 1948, the SPD and KPD narrowly pressed a law through the Landtag in North-Rhine Westphalia which foresaw the conversion of the mining industry into a state-owned, self-administered concern. The military governor promptly replied that the law was inappropriate and that they could not recognize it. The unions suffered a second critical defeat in the raw materials industry, where many companies were confiscated from private owners. On May 5, 1950, the Allied High Command issued Law no. 27, which assured the former stock owners "an adequate and appropriate compensation and declared the managers of the firm overseers of the liquidation process, situating them, of course, quite ideally to regain control of their respective firms." See ibid., pp. 153, 177.
15 Ibid., p. 178.
16 See Dieter Schuster, *Die deutschen Gewerkschaften seit 1945*, 1973, p. 36.
17 In a general plebiscite among the IG Metall members, over 95 percent voted to strike in order to protect *Montanmitbestimmung*. See Schmidt, *Die verhinderte Neuordnung*, p. 184.
18 In general, the US occupation government suspended or failed to carry out many existing socialization or codetermination clauses, arguing that such fundamental decisions were subject to the popular decision of the German people, i.e., the *Bundestag*. Since However, Article F14 of the German Basic Law contained explicit guarantees of property rights and compensation in the

case of expropriation and since the Social Welfare clauses in Articles 20 and 28 contained only vague and ambiguous ruling about equity and democracy in the economy, the policy amounted to a concealed blockage of a more consequent socialization/codetermination policy. See Klönne and Reese, *Die deutsche Gewerkschaftsbewegung*, p. 193.

19 The debate broke out over the strike threat during the 1950 settlement in the iron and steel industry. Adenauer insisted that a strike such as the one threatened by IG Metall "could only have the goal of pressing the decision of the freely elected representatives of the people in the direction desired by the unions by threatening or inflicting economic damage that affects everyone." In essence, Adenauer argued that once the citizen had cast his or her vote, his or her say in policy had been exercised. Böckler, remembering the results when parliamentary democracy had been wed with economic authoritarianism during the Weimar Republic, insisted on the right to strike as a basic democratic freedom and one necessary to counter the influence of the economic elites and effect a genuine economic democracy. Perhaps the best instance of this analysis and self-criticism of the Weimar period can be found in Franz L. Neumann's writings. Compare, for instance, "Die soziale Bedeutung der Grundrechte in der Weimarer Verfassung" (1930) and "Der Niedergang der deutschen Demokratie," both in Franz L. Neumann, *Wirtschaft, Staat, Demokratie*, ed. Alfons Söllner, 1978. See also Schmidt, *Die verhinderte Neuordnung*, pp. 188–91.

20 Schmidt, *Die verhinderte Neuordnung*, p. 195.

21 See Klönne and Reese, *Die deutsche Gewerkschaftsbewegung*, pp. 74–5.

22 The anti-Hitler coalition (Britain, the United States and the USSR) proclaimed in the Potsdam Treaty of August 2, 1945: "German militarism and Nazism will be exterminated and the Allies will effect other measures by mutual agreement in the present and future, so that Germany can never again threaten her neighbors or the maintenance of peace throughout the world." Cited in Ulrich Albrecht, *Die Wiederaufrüstung der Bundersrepublik*, 1980.

23 Voices for rearmament within Germany were heard from 1948, and were given weight by Adenauer himself in December 1949, in his famous interview with the Cleveland *Plain Dealer*. In it, Adenauer expressed his support for the organization of a European army and professed his willingness to put a German contingent under its command. For excerpts from the interview, see Albrecht, *Die Wiederaufrüstung*, p. 88.

24 See for instance, Konrad Adenauer, *Erinnerungen* (*1945–53*), 1965, p. 382.

25 As preparatory measures, Adenauer created first "Schwerin's office" to engineer plans for an army and "Blank's office," a quasi-cabinet office under Theo Blank intended to assume the responsibilities of the defense ministry at the appropriate moment. Christoph Butterwegge and Heinz-Gerd Hofschen, *Sozialdemokratie: Krieg und Frieden*, 1984, p. 233.

26 The EDC was to include forces from Germany, Italy, France and the Benelux countries.

27 Before this, the Basic Law had included provisions prohibiting the rearmament of Germany, including the reinstitution of compulsory military service.

28 They provided that Germany and Italy be taken up into the "Brussels pact" of 1948 as well as into NATO. The former was to be called the West European Union and differed from the EDC only in including Britain. Lilge, *Deutschland*, p. 137.

29 See for instance Schumacher's arguments for the "Erhaltung der Volkssubstanz"

in his press conference of August 23, 1950, in Butterwege and Hofschen, *Sozialdemokratie,* p. 255.

30 Theo Pirker, *Die blinde Macht: Die Gewerkschaftsbewegung in Westdeutschland,* vol. 2, 1979, p. 116.

31 Schumacher said in 1950: "In Germany, every policy must be effected as if the country were still present as a unified whole." Ibid., p. 126.

32 Ibid., pp. 110–11.

33 In particular, the SPD under Schumacher had already abandoned the Marxist condemnation of parliamentary democracy as a subservient element of the capitalist system. As early as 1945, in his "Political Guidelines for the SPD," Schumacher had proclaimed: "As an intellectual and political foundation, democracy and socialism are inseparable." See Document 136 in Butterwege and Hofschen, *Sozialdemokratie,* p. 247.

34 See the analysis of the initial years after the 1949 election in Pirker, *Die blinde Macht,* esp. pp. 115–18.

35 Until the outbreak of the Korean war in 1950, the SPD maintained a position of categorical opposition to any German rearmanent, relying instead on the Allied occupation force for the defense of the Federal Republic in case of military attack and on the internal consolidation of a democratic popular consciousness as a bulwark against "subversion." Up until this point, the SPD even hoped that the establishment of democracy in the Federal Republic would be sufficient to bring about reunification, by "attracting" the East German population, the so-called "magnet theory". See Document 141 in Butterwege and Hofschen, *Sozialdemokratie,* p. 252. See also the SPD position paper from 1948 in Georg Benz et al., eds, *Rüstung, Entrüstung, Abrüstung,* 1982, p. 47. For a lengthier discussion of the magnet theory, see Joachim Hütter, *SPD und nationale Sicherheit,* 1975.

36 Cited from Schumacher's presentation, "Germany's Contribution to Peace and Freedom," Document 144, Butterwege and Hofschen, *Sozialdemokratie,* p. 257.

37 Schumacher insisted on German parity in the alliance with the West: "Europe cannot be the Americas' forward defense belt nor Germany Europe's … Military defense is only possible on the basis of commonality." See Schumacher's 1950 speech in the Bundestag in Benz et al., *Rüstung,* pp. 50–1.

38 See the SPD position paper against the EDC in Butterwege and Hofschen, *Sozialdemokratie,* Document 150, p. 267.

39 Letter reprinted in Benz et al., *Rüstung,* pp. 121–2.

40 It was not, strictly speaking, a movement. It lacked an organization or a clearly defined set of goals. Its existence can only be gleaned from posters and banners of the time. See facsimiles in Siegfried Thomas, *Zwischen Wehrmacht und Bundeswehr: Um die Remilitarisierung der BRD,* 1981, p. 135, and photo section.

41 In the Rhine-Ruhr coal-mining region, for instance, miners fought against the introduction of extra "tank-shifts" (*Panzerschichten*), which they argued were chiefly meant to satisfy the increased demands of arms manufacturers due to the Korean war.

42 These included the Committee of Peace Fighters (Komitee der Kämpfer für den Frieden) which had been founded in 1949 and the Central Committee for a Plebiscite against Remilitarization (Hauptausschuß für Volksbefragung gegen Remilitarisierung) upon whose founding in spring 1951 the KPD also exerted a strong influence. Thomas, *Zwischen Wehrmacht,* pp. 139–40.

43 Rupp, *Außerparlamentarische Opposition,* pp. 60–1.

44 The SPD regarded a plebiscite as an unacceptable subversion of democratic principles and an illegitimate detour around parliamentary process, reminiscent of Hitler's tactics in the Weimar Republic. Bundestag delegate Herbert Wehner went so far as to paint the plebiscite movement as a ploy of the Communists. See Wehner's speech in the Bundestag in April 1951, in Butterwege and Hofschen, *Sozialdemokratie*, p. 262.

45 Rupp, *Außerparlamentarische Opposition*, p. 61.

46 Firstly with respect to the constitutionality of various aspects of the EDC/General Treaty package, and secondly with regard to the power of the Bundestag to decide such issues by a simple majority vote.

47 In the Bundesrat, each state is represented individually and equally and the opposition parties had a majority.

48 See reprint of original in Benz et al., *Rüstung*, pp. 123–4.

49 In fact, a great deal of *potential* for a movement against rearmament could be documented in opinion surveys. Even in October 1950, four months after the outbreak of the Korean war, over 50 percent of those questioned answered "no" when they were asked whether they would don a soldier's uniform in the event of a Russian invasion. See Rupp, *Außerparlamentarische Opposition*, p. 46.

50 Pirker, *Die blinde Macht*, pp. 204–5.

51 Ibid., pp. 33–4.

52 Rupp, *Außerparlamentarische Opposition*, p. 36.

53 Ibid., p. 41.

54 The basic constellations remained more or less unchanged – the SPD in opposition, Adenauer in power – as did their overall programs. While the bomb itself had a shockingly greater destructive potential than conventional rearmament, its implications and use as a foreign policy instrument were also similar to rearmament. For Adenauer, nuclear weapons were another badge of great power status and equal status within the alliance, and a "necessary deterrent" directed at the East. For the SPD, nuclear weapons were an unacceptable restoration of German militarism, a threat to unification, and a bad alternative to a path of negotiation with the East. In short, the overall foreign policy framework of the chief political actors remained fairly constant, and the basic arguments put forward by both sides for and against nuclear armaments in Germany were almost identical to those of the rearmament debate.

55 See reprint of the SPD's agenda of questions in Benz et al., *Rüstung*, pp. 58–9.

56 Tactical nuclear weapons are ones intended for use against military targets on the battlefield.

57 Rupp, *Außerparlamentarische Opposition*, p. 77.

58 See reprint of Göttinger Erklärung in Benz et al., *Rüstung*, pp. 126–7.

59 Rupp, *Außerparlamentarische Opposition*, pp. 80–3.

60 Ibid., p. 89.

61 In a seven-point statement on May 9 and during a Bundestag debate the following day, the SPD restricted itself to dramatic but insubstantial warnings about the danger of nuclear bombs, on the one hand, and to demands that the path of negotiation be exhausted before any actual stationing of the weapons, on the other hand.

62 A list of ten theses with the title "Security for Everyone" (*Sicherheit für alle*), in which the SPD's commitment to private property, economic prosperity and stability, and the free market were explicitly and heavily underlined, was then drafted for the election.

63 Rupp, *Außerparlamentarische Opposition*, p. 89.
64 The proposal was supported in a radio broadcast by George F. Kennan, former US ambassador to Moscow. SPD leaders, among them Carlo Schmid and Fritz Erler, reacted positively to the proposal. See reprints of press statements in Benz et al., *Rüstung*, p. 65.
65 Rupp, *Außerparlamentarische Opposition*, p. 122.
66 See reprint in Benz et al., *Rüstung*, pp. 65–6.
67 The organizational meeting on February 23 in Bad Godesberg included not only the other opposition parties, but the EKD, DGB, and ex-GVP members. Rupp, *Außerparlamentarische Opposition*, p. 130.
68 The opening rally was held in Frankfurt on March 23 right in the middle of a four-day foreign policy debate over the NATO communiqué in the Bundestag. On April 24, the SPD brought a bill before the Bundestag calling for a general plebiscite on nuclear arms. At the level of the states, talks were conducted with the FDP where the SPD and FDP had a numerical majority in the Landtag. In the Hanseatic cities of Bremen and Hamburg, where the SPD possessed an absolute majority, laws calling for a local plebiscite were actually passed. Ibid., pp. 182, 200.
69 As in 1955, the parliamentary initiatives were blocked by the Adenauer government. The Federal Constitutional Court issued a court order blocking all planned plebiscites, and on July 30 officially rejected the Hamburg and Bremen initiatives. The various FDP Landtag fractions fell into line with the Bonn coalition, and the Adenauer government was able to push through passage of the NATO communiqué. Ibid., p. 220.
70 In March, DGB chairman Willi Richter spoke of the "necessity of a struggle" and the "total 'no'" of the unions with respect to Adenauer's rearmament plans. See reprints in Benz et al., *Rüstung*, pp. 132–4. The initial response of the DGB to the Göttingen declaration had been overwhelmingly positive – the DGB had cooperated in the organization of the KdA. Ibid., p. 83.
71 Ollenhauer declared his support for "work stoppages," as did the young leftist delegate, Helmut Schmidt. Rupp, *Außerparlamentarische Opposition*, p. 167. Even the SPD's moderate proposal of a five-minute demonstrative work stoppage was rejected. For an interesting analysis of this episode see Pirker, *Die blinde Macht*.
72 Spontaneous walk-outs and isolated strikes following the Bundestag debate on March 20 was evidence of a willingness among the rank-and-file to apply extreme measures.
73 According to opinion polls a startling 52 percent of the population advocated a strike, if necessary, to prevent the Federal Republic's atomic armament. Rupp, *Außerparlamentarische Opposition*.
74 Ibid., p. 216.
75 See for instance the KdA's "Aufruf zum Kampf" on March 10, 1958, in Benz et al., *Rüstung*, p. 130.

Chapter 2 "Anabaptists in the Affluent Society"

1 During the fall of 1962, several editors and journalists from the news magazine *Der Spiegel* were arrested on charges of "treason" for having purportedly published defense secrets vital to national security. In the course of investigations, it became clear not only that the magazine had published nothing a

researcher could not find out in any decent library, but that the arrests had been ordered by the then defense minister Franz-Josef Strauß in a clear breach of his constitutional powers. The subsequent scandal which forced Strauß to resign was an important test of democracy in West Germany. For more on the role of the Spiegel affair in the political normalization of the Federal Republic, see Aline Kuntz, "From Spiegel to Flick: The Maturation of the West German *Parteienstaat*," in Andrei S. Markovits and Mark Silverstein, eds, *The Politics of Scandal: Power and Process in Liberal Democracies*, 1988.

2 Hans Karl Rupp, *Außerparlamentarische Opposition in der Ära Adenauers*, 1970, pp. 216, 235.

3 The Easter march had first been invented and used by the British Campaign for Nuclear Disarmament and was imported by German activists who had observed Easter marches in England.

4 Karl A. Otto, *Vom Ostermarsch zur APO*, 1977, p. 73.

5 Ibid., p. 120.

6 The only organizations allowed to send delegates to the organizational meetings of the movement's central committee were those approved by the committee itself. Applications from various organizations suspected of associations with or infiltration by the KPD were refused. Ibid., pp. 79–80.

7 Ibid., pp. 80, 92.

8 Ibid., p. 104.

9 Ibid., p. 93.

10 The KfA's new look extended so far as to include the distribution of balloons, pens, stickers and calendars with the KfA logo. Ibid., p. 92.

11 In preparation for the party's 1959 refurbishing, reformist forces within the SPD gathered around treasurer Alfred Nau and Berlin Mayor Willy Bandt fastened their designs on disciplining or dispensing with the SDS's left wing, centered around the Hamburg magazine *konkret*, Wolfgang Abendroth's Marxist orthodoxy in Marburg, and Max Horkheimer and Theodor Adorno's burgeoning "Frankfurt school."

12 See Ernst Richert, *Die Radikale Linke*, 1969.

13 In somewhat greater chronological detail: On February 5, 1960, the SPD executive committee handed the SDS an ultimatum and a veiled threat – the SDS must formally recognize the Bad Godesberg program, and any organization which did would receive equal support from the SPD. On May 9, the SPD set up the alternative social democratic youth organization, the SHB, whose leadership positions were quickly occupied by the SDS right wing. Finally, on November 6, 1961, in the face of the SDS's continued intransigence, the SPD formally forbade simultaneous membership in the SPD and SDS. See Tilman Fichter and Siegward Lönnendonker, *Kleine Geschichte des SDS*, 1977, pp. 67, 70; for the finest account of SDS–SPD relations and the SDS's radicalization within and eventual expulsion from the SPD, see Tilman Fichter, *SDS und SPD: Parteilichkeit jenseits der Partei*, 1988.

14 Richert, *Die Radikale Linke*, p. 88.

15 At its 18th delegate conference. Fichter and Lönnendonker, *Kleine Geschichte des SDS*, p. 78.

16 Even the "traditionalist" current in the SDS, which felt itself more linked to proletarian socialism, conceded that the working class was "subjectively" depoliticized, maintaining only that it was "objectively" a revolutionary class.

17 Otto Wilfert, *Lästige Linke*, 1978, p. 45.

18 For a superb comparison of the German SDS with its counterpart and namesake

in the United States, see George Katsiaficas, *The Imagination of the New Left: A Global Analysis of 1968*, 1987.

19 The classical German university has often been called Humboldtian after Wilhelm von Humboldt (1767–1855). He was a Prussian nobleman and a career diplomat who, among numerous diplomatic posts and high-level administrative positions, also served as Prussian Privy Councillor in charge of culture and education from February 20, 1809 to June 14, 1810. During this time, Humboldt was influential in developing the ideas which underpinned the University of Berlin and which, emanating from that institution, were eventually to define German higher education until the student revolts of the late 1960s. For a fine discussion of the German university system, the Humboldtian reforms, and democratization of the 1960s, see Rosalind M. O. Pritchard, *The End of Elitism? The Democratization of the West German University System*, 1990.

20 The radical program behind these actions can be seen in the SDS's 1964 "Reflections on the University Reform" (*Denkschrift zur Hochschulreform*), which argued that "either [the university] works along on the dynamic and continued development towards democracy and democratization of society, or it turns into an instrument in a development toward authoritarian social formations." Cited after Gerhard Bauß, *Die Studentenbewegung der sechziger Jahre*, 2nd edn, 1983, p. 228.

21 In February of that year, over a dozen Nazi war criminals were convicted in highly publicized trials in Frankfurt.

22 The twentieth anniversary of the absolute surrender on May 8, 1965 was drawing perilously close, and the Basic Law prescribed a statue of limitations (*Verjährungsklausel*) of 20 years for all crimes.

23 In 1966 in Hessen, Bavaria, Rheinland-Pfalz, Schleswig-Holstein and Niedersachsen, the NPD cleared the 5 percent hurdle with shares of the vote ranging from 5.8 to 7.9 percent. Ernst Deuerlin, *Deutschland 1963–70*, 1972, pp. 199–200.

24 This was to begin at the grass-roots level of the repression of the history of the Third Reich in school lessons and the silence of parents about their lives from 1933–45.

25 For Adenauer, the *Wirtschaftswunder* had been the litmus test of his policy's rightness and the fruits of its prosperity the basis on which he was able to politically and historically carry them through.

26 The recession in West Germany had much the same sources as those in other western industrial democracies. On the one hand, wage gains had outpaced GNP growth, resulting in inflation. On the other, increases in government spending exceeded expansion of the tax base, producing a serious fiscal crisis for the Erhard government.

27 The recession had greatly exacerbated the structural crisis of the mining and steel industries in the Ruhr area, leading to the first major strike actions in some years.

28 Erhard described the *formierte Gesellschaft* as a society which "rests on the working together of all groups and interests. This society . . . does not form itself through authoritarian force but out of its own power." From Erhard's speech before the 13th CDU party congress, see Document 2 in Irmgard Wilharm, ed., *Deutsche Geschichte 1962–1983: Dokumente in zwei Bänden*, 1985, pp. 32–3.

29 Passage of such laws, argued the Right, was a prerequisite to fully reestablishing national sovereignty because of a clause in the German Treaty of 1952 in

which the Allies reserved the right for their troops stationed in Germany to take up arms in self-defense if no provision for their defense through the German government existed for a state of emergency. The Left, including the unions, warned that similar "emergency laws" in Weimar had smoothed Hitler's path to power, and the they condemned them as inimical to a democratic order.

30 Rudi Dutschke et al., *Rebellion der Studenten*, 1968, p. 18.

31 This identification on the part of the western student radicals with the Vietcong is described well by Ruth Rosen, a professor of history at the University of California, in the documentary film *Berkeley in the Sixties*. During a particularly vicious police action against striking students sitting on Sprout Plaza of the Berkeley campus, the authorities used helicopters to frighten and photograph the students from the air. Rosen recounts how she and many demonstrators believed that they were in fact Vietcong and that the choppers would open fire on them just like they would have battling the Vietcong in Vietnam.

32 In line with the internal political realignment within the KfA several years before, these statements abandoned pacifist moral criticisms for a social-theoretical criticism of the connection between militarism and the contradictions of western industrial societies. See Bauß, *Die Studentenbewegung*, p. 175, and Otto, *Vom Ostermarsch*, p. 145.

33 Fichter and Lönnendonker, *Kleine Geschichte des SDS*, p. 89.

34 At its 20th delegate conference that year, the SDS rejected the US portrayal of the war as military assistance for South Vietnam to preserve freedom and democracy and for the first time characterized it as an imperialist war. See excerpts from the protocol in Bauß, *Die Studentenbewegung*, p. 176.

35 The SDS was no longer content with vague attempts at "influencing" debate, but began to think of itself as a "free-standing (*eigenständige*), third, political force" over and against social democracy and communism. This was strongly manifested on February 5, 1966, in a demonstration by Free University students against the "dirty war in Vietnam." A sit-down strike by the 2,500 demonstrators blocked traffic for 20 minutes on Berlin's central boulevard, the Kurfürstendamm. See Fichter and Lönnendonker, *Kleine Geschichte des SDS*, pp. 91–2.

36 Gerd Langguth, *Protestbewegung: Entstehung, Entwicklung, Renaissance*, 1977, p. 26.

37 The animosities began over an incident after the anti-Vietnam war demonstration in February, 1966. Following the protest, a number of participants marched to the nearby America House and one protester bombarded the facade with six eggs. The conservative public was outraged.

38 Herbert Marcuse, a leading representative of the Frankfurt School and godfather of the German student movement, was the main speaker. Although extraparliamentary organizations from outside the university arena were represented, the congress, as well as the anti-Vietnam war protest in general, was dominated by students and professors.

39 Bauß, *Die Studentenbewegung*, pp. 178–80.

40 Cited from Bauß, *Die Studentenbewegung*, p. 183.

41 Maren Krohn, *Die gesellschaftlichen Auseinandersetzungen um die Notstandesgesetze*, 1981, pp. 109–12.

42 Ibid., p. 109.

43 Fichter and Lönnendonker, *Kleine Geschichte des SDS*, p. 85.

44 Krohn, *Die gesellschaftlichen Auseinandersetzungen*, p. 122.

45 See citation from 18th SDS delegate conference, 1963, in Bauß, *Die Studentenbewegung*, p. 127.
46 Ibid., p. 128.
47 Fichter and Lönnendonker, *Kleine Geschichte des SDS*, p. 84.
48 Krohn, *Die gesellschaftlichen Auseinandersetzungen*, p. 126.
49 Ibid., p. 124.
50 Bauß, *Die Studentenbewegung*, p. 129.
51 Ibid.
52 See a listing of action committees in Krohn, *Die gesellschaftlichen Auseinandersetzungen*, p. 344.
53 Werner Hofmann, cited after Krohn, *Die gesellschaftlichen Auseinandersetzungen*, p. 181.
54 Krohn, *Die gesellschaftlichen Auseinandersetzungen*, p. 183.
55 See ibid., pp. 184, 190, and Bauß, *Die Studentenbewegung*, p. 137.
56 Krohn, *Die gesellschaftlichen Auseinandersetzungen*, p. 196.
57 Ibid., pp. 198–9.
58 Ibid., p. 190.
59 Otto, *Vom Ostermarsch*, pp. 147, 157.
60 Krohn, *Die gesellschaftlichen Auseinandersetzungen*, p. 204. For detailed eye-witness accounts and descriptions of the planned provocation of the students exercised by the Iranian secret service and West Berlin police, see Kai Harmann, "Die Polizeischacht von Berlin," *Die Zeit*, no. 23, June 9, 1967.
61 Ibid.
62 Bauß, *Die Studentenbewegung*, p. 53.
63 Fichter and Lönnendonker, *Kleine Geschichte des SDS*, p. 106.
64 See Bauß, *Die Studentenbewegung*, p. 56.
65 Ibid., p. 55.
66 Knut Nevermann, ed., *Lokal 2000: Berlin als Testfall*, 1983, p. 5.
67 See Bauß, *Die Studentenbewegung*, p. 57.
68 See Autorenkollektiv, ed., *Bedingungen und Organisation des Widerstandes*, 1967, and by the same, *Die Linke antwortet Jürgen Habermas*, 1968.
69 Jürgen Habermas first recognized this phenomenon and provocatively described it as "leftist Fascism". See Jürgen Habermas et al., *Protestbewegung und Hochschulreform*, 1969, especially pp. 136–49.

Chapter 3   Revolutionary Cadre Politics and Terrorism

1 Helmut Billstein et al., *Organisierter Kommunismus in der Bundesrepublik Deutschland*, 1977, p. 15.
2 Ibid.
3 Of the 3,360 members belonging to the new party's nine state districts, 2,360 had also been members of the former KPD. Ibid., p. 17.
4 Ulrich Probst, *Die kommunistischen Parteien der Bundesrepublik Deutschland*, 1980, p. 23.
5 Ibid., p. 24.
6 According to its own 1979 records, the DKP financed itself from the following sources: DM 5.6 million generated by contributions from the Federal Republic; DM 3.15 million stemming from membership dues; and DM 50 million received from the GDR in 1977. It should be added that West German authorities gauged that figure to be much too low. See ibid., pp. 23–4.

7   It would be well beyond the scope of this chapter to give a full account of the
     West German Communist Party's role vis-à-vis the unions. Suffice it to say that
     the Deutsche Kommunistische Partei (DKP) had a strong presence in certain
     unions during the latter half of the 1970s and the first part of the 1980s.
     Recognizing the futility of its electoral activities, which yielded consistently
     abysmal results, and rejecting any form of violent or clandestine strategy against
     the existing parliamentary order, the DKP's activism within certain unions
     represented the sole possibility for the party to lend at least some significance
     to its existence. Moreover, the party also opted for the approach because it
     regarded the unions as the only institutions within West German capitalism
     capable of initiating and implementing social change. Indeed in viewing the
     DGB and its constituent unions as the only effective organizations of the West
     German working class, the DKP pursued from the very beginning an exceed-
     ingly pro-DGB line which bordered on subservience with one major excep-
     tion: the DGB's traditional ties to the SPD. In attempting to woo the organized
     working class away from its strong SPD allegiance, the DKP activists within the
     unions gradually developed into model "organization men" on the rank-and-
     file level. Their unselfish behavior often met with great success among work-
     ers, who welcomed the activism of these people not because they belonged to
     the DKP but in spite of that fact. By the end of the 1970s, the situation had
     become sufficiently widespread in some of the activist unions to incur the
     wrath of their SPD-dominated leadership, directed especially at the DGB and
     its accommodationist members. The intra-union tensions reached such di-
     mensions by 1979 that leading union officials accused the DKP of infiltrating
     the unions in order to make them the party's transmission belt of Leninist
     dogma. In short, the "subversion" theme, so readily used by the employers
     and the conservative media in their attacks against labor, also found its enthu-
     siastic supporters within the union movement itself. The issue was compli-
     cated by the fact that part of the DKP's pro-DGB strategy entailed active
     denunciations by the Communists of other leftists within the unions who –
     unlike the DKP's members – were *personae non gratae* according to the union's
     "clauses of incompatibility." Thus in addition to the SPD vs DKP rivalry there
     was a concomitant DKP vs "undogmatic leftist" tension which intensified con-
     siderably in the last few years of the 1970s.
         The first area of major conflict concerned the interpretation of union his-
     tory, particularly the very sensitive era of the last few years of the Weimar
     Republic. Central to the debate was a widely used and very thorough book on
     the history of the German labor movement authored by a number of histor-
     ians from the University of Marburg, whose history department had a re-
     putation for representing views which were close to – though not identical
     with – those advocated by the DKP. The book was edited by Frank Deppe,
     Georg Fülberth and Jürgen Harrer, and entitled *Geschichte der deutschen
     Gewerkschaftsbewegung.* Published by the Cologne-based firm of Pahl-Rugenstein,
     which specialized in publishing studies in the social sciences and history that
     expounded views bearing similarities to the ones put forth by the DKP, the book
     aroused immediate suspicions on the part of many an accommodationist union
     leader by virtue of the institutional affiliation of its authors and the reputation
     of its publisher. The book's severe criticism of the labor movement's social-
     democratic leadership and its close alliance with the SPD during the Weimar
     Republic irked many DGB leaders. Accompanied by the book's virtual silence
     on the divisive strategies pursued by the Communist Party (KPD) within the

union movement during the latter years of the Weimar Republic, the Deppe et al. volume served as prima facie evidence for many unionists that the DKP and its intellectual allies were trying to use a one-sided interpretation of history to make a negative statement about the continued ties between the SPD and the labor movement during the Bonn republic as well. The reaction to the book and its larger implications was wide-ranging and engaged the interest of many unionists as well as a number of leftist intellectuals. For the three most authoritative attacks against the books emanating from the official union press, see Manfred Scharrer, "Eine die Geschichte verfälschende 'Gewerkschaftsgeschichte,'" *Die Quelle*, 29.11 (Nov. 1978), pp. 606–8; Gerhard Beier, "Leninisten führten die Feder," *öTV-Magazin*, no. 3 (Mar. 1978), pp. 33–7; and Hermann Weber, "Kommunistische Gewerkschaftspolitik in der Weimarer Republik," *öTV-Magazin*, no. 4 (Apr. 1979), pp. 39–42. See also "'Hier wird Geschichte gefälscht' – Kritik aus der öTV an Historikern aus Marburg," *Frankfurter Allgemeine Zeitung*, Apr. 10, 1979. For the "undogmatic Left's" intermediate position on this important debate, see Edgar Weick, "Aus der Geschichte lernen," *express*, 17.4 (Apr. 23, 1979), pp. 8, 9; Peter von Örtzen, "Wie lässt sich Geschichtsschreibung' im DKP-Stil messen?", *Frankfurter Rundschau*, Apr. 11, 1979; and "Zwei Linien und ein roter Faden," *Frankfurter Rundschau*, Oct. 6, 1979. The issue was sufficiently important and divisive for the DGB to organize a major conference on the matter with all sides invited to present their views. While the Munich conference held on October 13–14, 1979 eliminated some of the sharper edges of the underlying hostilities, it failed to alleviate them completely, and they thus continue to linger. See "Mit den Experten konnten die Veteranen nichts anfange," *Frankfurter Rundschau*, Oct. 15, 1979: "Das Signal zum Widerstand blieb aus," part 1 published in *Frankfurter Rundschau*, Oct. 13, 1979, and part 2 published in *Frankfurter Rundschau*, Oct. 18, 1979, and the proceedings of the conference in Heinz O. Vetter, ed., *Aus der Geschichte lernen – die Zukunft gesalten: Dreissig Jahre DGB*, 1980.

The Deppe et al. book would most likely not have become such an issue of contention had it not been for the fact that it was adopted in many union schools' curricula, thereby giving it extensive exposure. The form and content of youth education within the unions represented the second area of intra-union conflict involving the DKP. The controversy gained public attention over the so-called "Oberurseler Papier" in which union leaders from the DGB's education center in Oberursel, just outside of Frankfurt, accused the DKP and its supporters of trying to undermine the existing political conditions within the unions, with the aim of making them subservient to the DKP. It is important to point out that the main author of the Oberurseler paper, the director of the DGB's education center in Oberursel, Hinrich Otjen, perceived himself as a member of the independent or "undogmatic" Left and professed to be as critical of the SPD-dominated union establishment as were his major targets in the paper. The ensuing intra-DGB feuds were very heated, resulting in further exacerbations of the already considerable differences between accommodationist and activist unions within the federation. The activist unions led by IG Metall and IG Druck und Papier vowed never to send any of their young officials to a DGB-run education center whose director engaged in red-baiting. The accommodationists led by IG Bergbau und Energie and IG Chemie-Papier-Keramik embraced the paper's accusation and viewed it as an excellent corroboration of their long-held fears concerning the DKP's "cadre politics" designed to undermine the existing union structures solely for the party's benefit. Thus an interesting anti-DKP alliance developed within the labor movement in which right-wing social democrats joined independent leftists, often of a very radical sort, in opposing the communists' operations, which remained almost exclusively confined to the activist unions. It is quite clear that the two members of this tenuous alliance opposed the DKP's presence within West Germany's trade unions for very different reasons. For the Oberurseler Papier, see "Erst Posten erobern und dann gegen Kritik abschotten" in the documentation section of the *Frankfurter Rundschau*, May 5 and May 7, 1979. For the most pronounced statements by the accommodationists on this matter, see "Kommunisten an 'Knotenpunkten' in der DGB-Jugend fest verankert? Die DGB-Bundesjugendschule warnt vor DKP-Einflüssen," *Einheit*, Apr. 1, 1979. For IG Metall's irritated response to the accusations implicitly leveled at it and other activist unions by the accommodationists see "IG Metall wirft DGB Bundesjugendschule Diffamierung vor," *Frankfurter Rundschau*, Jan. 4, 1980; "IG Metall Jugend will Härte," *Frankfurter Rundschau*, Jan. 12, 1980; and "Preiss; 'In der Gewerkschaft zählt nicht das Trennende sondern die Solidarität'" *Die Neue*, May 16, 1979. For good documentation on the direct debate between accommodationists and activists regarding this matter see "Schmuddlife Kampagne gegen Kommunisten," *Frankfurter Allgemeine Zeitung*, Apr. 26, 1979; "Bild von der Gewerkschaftsjugend hängt schief links," *Frankfurter Rundschau*, June 1, 1979; "Vorwurf der Verniedlichung kommunistischer Ziele gegen Detlef Hensche," *Frankfurter Rundschau*, Sept. 29, 1979; "Schon einmal dienten Feindbilder dazu, Verfolgungen einzuleiten," *Frankfurter Rundschau*, Oct. 22, 1979; and "Der Unterwanderweg ist lang," *Der Spiegel*, Jan. 14, 1980. The most comprehensive treatment of all these matters regarding the DKP's role in the education of union youth, the interpretation of labor history and the intra-labor battles between activists and accommodationists can be found in Ossip K. Flechtheim et al., *Der Marsch der DKP durch die Institutionen: Sowjetmarxistische Einflussstrategien und Ideologien*, 1980; as can be readily gauged from the title of this book, its authors are extremely critical of the DKP and its numerous sympathizers among the activist wing of the DGB, and find the communist presence in the unions worrisome and counterproductive. The book represents a joint effort by the ephemeral anti-DKP coalition consisting of right-wing social democrats and "undogmatic" – that is, non-communist – leftists.

The third area of union politics in which the DKP's existence played a crucial role during the crisis of the late 1970s was the formulation of economic policy. Centered around the so-called "memorandum" which was originally published by a number of radical economists with DKP leanings at the University of Bremen, the debates once again concerned both the form and the content of the Communist Party's engagement in union affairs during the crisis. In this case, too, there existed a coalition of right-wing social democrats and non-communist radicals who opposed the memorandum's strategies for diametrically opposite reasons.

Taken from Andrei S. Markovits, *The Politics of the West German Trade Unions*, 1988, p. 478, n. 208.

8 See Probst, *Die kommunistischen Parteien*, p. 26.

9 The most prominent event being the storming of the Bonn city hall, April 10, 1973, as a result of a demonstration against the visit of the South Vietnamese

president. Thirty-four were wounded. See Billstein et al., *Organisierter Kommunismus*, p. 80, n. 133.

10 Ibid., p. 80.
11 Ibid., p. 82.
12 Probst, *Die kommunistischen Parteien*, p. 49.
13 Frank Karl, *Die K-Gruppen*, 1976, p. 18.
14 Probst, *Die kommunistischen Parteien*, p. 60.
15 Ibid.
16 Ibid., p. 70.
17 The name was taken from an Apache Indian tribe, perhaps an indication of the fascination of the German middle class with American Indians. This fascination goes back to the writings of Karl May, whose novels about the Wild West are still enormously popular in Germany. There exist, of course, two much less innocuous interpretations of the Germans' infatuation with American Indians than Karl May's, with its immense influence on the formative experiences of middle-class Germans, especially boys. One is the German penchant for the romantic, the extolling of the "noble savage" as virtue incarnate. The other explanation focuses on the Germans' interest in American Indians as a self-exculpatory act for the Germans' genocidal behavior against the Jews. Native Americans – or Indians as they continue to be steadfastly known and referred to in Germany – were exterminated by white settlers, just as Jews were by the Germans. This view robs the Holocaust of its uniqueness and renders it one of the many massacres committed by human beings against each other. For German leftists, with their unmitigated identification with Third World peoples, the extermination of native Americans at the hand of First World dominated white Anglo-Saxon men is, if anything, a crime of greater proportions than the Holocaust. Thus, Americans – in the eyes of many Germans, especially leftists – are at least as guilty of genocidal murder as are Germans. Crudely put, the Germans' fascination with native Americans is part of a psychological self-exoneration of the Germans' heinous past. See Andrei S. Markovits, "On Anti-Americanism in West Germany", *New German Critique*, no. 34, Winter 1985, p. 11, n. 21.
18 See *Der Spiegel*, Aug. 15, 1977, p. 27.
19 Herbert Jäger et al., *Lebenslaufanalysen*, vol. 2 of *Analysen zum Terrorismus*, 1981, pp. 82ff. Of those who became terrorists, 37 percent had lived in a commune and 36 percent in a living cooperative (*Wohngemeinschaft*); 43 percent had at one time been enrolled in a university. Living in a *Wohngemeinschaft* was one of the main selection criteria for recruiting members to a terrorist organization.
20 Iring Fetscher, *Terrorismus und Reaktion*, 1977, p. 104.
21 See Hans Josef Horchem, *Die verlorene Revolution: Terrorismus in Deutschland*, 1988, p. 48.
22 See Carlos Marighella, *The Mini-Manual of the Urban Guerilla*, 1978.
23 Horchem, *Die verlorene Revolution*, p. 49.
24 Ibid., pp. 51–6.
25 Ibid., p. 20.
26 Ibid., p. 43.
27 Iring Fetscher and Günter Rohrmoser, *Ideologien und Strategien*, vol. 1 of *Analysen zum Terrorismus*, 1981, p. 43.
28 Meinhof, as quoted in Michael Horn, *Sozialpsychologie des Terrorismus*, 1982, p. 39.

29 Mahler was eventually expelled from the group for his dissensions from this view.
30 Another controversy concerned the social composition of the vanguard. For Baader, it was the working class, while Meinhof placed her hopes in the students. The prison experience led Baader and Meinhof to the theory that prisoners might indeed become the new revolutionary subject as a consequence of their blatant oppression by the state.
31 Horchem, *Die verlorene Revolution*, p. 141.
32 Ibid., pp. 164–5.
33 Ibid., p. 41.
34 See ibid., pp. 41–2.
35 Ibid.
36 See Gerard Braunthal, *Political Loyalty and Public Service in West Germany: The 1972 Decree against Radicals and its Consequences*, 1990, pp. 154–5.
37 Ibid., pp. 155–7.
38 Ibid., p. 156.
39 Gerard Braunthal, *The West German Social Democrats, 1969–1982: Profile of a Party in Power*, 1983, pp. 214–15.
40 This derogatory name was given to the functionaries of the right-wing of the SPD.
41 See Andrei S. Markovits, "German Social Democracy," *Studies in Political Economy*, no. 19, Spring 1986, p. 96 and p. 111, n. 26.

Chapter 4   Revolution, Retreat, Reform

1 See Jürgen Miermeister and Jochen Staadt, eds. *Provokationen: Die Studenten und Jugendrevolte in ihren Flugblättern, 1965–1971*, 1980, pp. 69–72.
2 Bernd Guggenberger defines a citizens' initiative as follows: "Citizens' initiatives are spontaneous, organizationally loose alliances of citizens who gather for a limited period. They articulate demands which arise principally from concrete personal grievances outside the venues of traditional institutions and channels of representative democracy. These groups seek support for their cause be it by way of self-help or by exercising political pressure." From *Bürgerinitiativen in der Parteiendemocratie*, 1980, p. 19.
3 See Miermeister and Staadt, *Provokationen*, pp. 140–1.
4 See Miermeister and Staadt, *Provokationen*, p. 128.
5 Tilman Fichter and Siegward Lönnendonker, *Kleine Geschichte des SDS*, 1977, p. 136.
6 See Meermeister and Staadt, *Provokationen*, p. 129.
7 See Gerhard Bauß, *Die Studentenbewegung der sechziger Jahre*, 2nd edn, 1983, p. 99.
8 Ibid., pp. 101–3.
9 Fichter and Lönnendonker, *Kleine Geschichte des SDS*, p. 136.
10 Miermeister and Staadt, *Provokationen*, pp. 198–9.
11 Karl-Werner Brand, et al., *Aufbruch in eine andere Gesellschaft*, 1983, p. 155.
12 Marie-Luise Weinberger, *Aufbruch zu neuen Ufern?*, 1984, p. 77.
13 Never was the *Taz*'s open irreverence more pronounced than during the Gulf war and its aftermath, when the newspaper – to the chagrin of much of its readership – published a number of pieces supporting the Allies in their war against Iraq. Above all, the newspaper printed a number of articles and letters

favorable to Israel's predicament. Judging from the letters to the editor published by *Taz*, few of the newspaper's readers had anything positive to say about articles arguing for anything short of Israel's annihilation. The vicious anti-Zionism of a substantial segment of the German Left, which was such an integral part of its identity from the late 1960s, was once again corroborated during the Gulf war. Saddam Hussein became a hero for this part of the Left in good part because he threatened to annihilate Israel. It is on some level beyond comprehension that such hatred for Israel and the Jews emanates from the sons and daughters of those who built and operated Auschwitz. As the saying goes: "The Germans will never forgive the Jews for Auschwitz."

14 Weinberger, *Aufbruch zu neuen Ufern?*, p. 77.
15 The *Taz's* excellent reporting on the East German revolution and the dissident scene in the GDR confirmed its independence of mind. As will be evident in chapter 8, we relied very closely on *Taz's* reporting in our analysis of the emergence of the East German Greens and their allies.
16 Brand et al., *Aufbruch in eine andere Gesellschaft*, p. 173.
17 Cited after Weinberger, *Aufbruch zu neuen Ufern?*, p. 89.
18 See Walter Hollstein and Boris Penth, *Alternativprojekte: Beispiel gegen der Resignation*, 1980, pp. 191–7.
19 See Gerd Langguth, *Protestbewegung: Enstehung, Entwicklung, Renaissance*, 1977, p. 255, and Hollstein and Penth, *Alternativprojekte*, p. 177.
20 See Brand et al., *Aufbruch in eine andere Gesellschaft*.
21 Hollstein and Penth, *Alternativprojekte*, p. 180.
22 See Langguth, *Protestbewegung*, and Uwe Schlicht, *Vom Burschenschafter bis zum Sponti: Studentische Opposition gestern und heute*, 1980, p. 133.
23 Johannes Schütte, *Revolte und Verweigerung: Zur Politik und Sozialpsychologie der Spontibewegung*, 1980, p. 92.
24 Ibid., p. 38.
25 Ibid., pp. 26–8.
26 See ibid., p. 25, and Schlicht, *Vom Burschenschafter*, pp. 128–30.
27 Schlicht, *Vom Burschenschafter*, pp. 130–4.
28 Schütte, *Revolte und Verweigerung*, pp. 28–9.
29 Ibid., p. 64.
30 Alice Schwarzer, *So fing es an! Die neue Frauenbewegung*, 1983, p. 13.
31 See Gisela Brandt, et al., *Zur Frauenfrage im Kapitalismus*, 1973.
32 Herrad Schenk, *Die feministische Herausforderung: 150 Jahre Frauenbewegung in Deutschland*, 1981, p. 22.
33 Ibid., p. 85.
34 See facsimile of declaration in Schwarzer, *So fing es an!*, p. 124.
35 Schenk, *Die feministische Herausforderung*, p. 87.
36 Ute Frevert, *Frauengeschichte: Zwischen bürgerlicher Verbesserung und neuer Weiblichkeit*, 1987, p. 278.
37 Ibid.
38 See especially Gisela Brandt et al., *Zur Frauenfrage im Kapitalismus*.
39 Schenk, *Die feministische Herausforderung*, p. 86.
40 For a superb discussion of the issue of abortion and other subjects pertaining to gender politics in the two Germanies as well as the United Germany, see the articles in the double issue of *German Politics and Society* entitled "Germany and Gender," nos 24–5, Winter 1991–2. See also Jeremiah M. Riemer, "Reproduction and Reunification: The Politics of Abortion in United Germany," in Michael G. Huelshoff et al., eds, *The New Germany in the New Europe*, 1993.

41   Schwarzer, *So fing es an!*, p. 28.
42   Frevert, *Frauengeschichte*, p. 280.
43   Ibid., p. 281.
44   Gisela Brandt et al., *Zur Frauenfrage im kapitalismus*, p. 131.
45   Schwarzer, *So fing es an!*, p. 35.
46   Ibid., p. 37.
47   Ibid., p. 52.
48   Ibid., pp. 54–5.
49   Ibid., p. 41.
50   Schenk, *Die feministische Herausforderung*, p. 88.
51   The conferences had titles like "Women and Science" (1976), "Women as Paid and Unpaid Labor Power (1977), "Women and Mothers" (1978), "Autonomy and Institutions" (1979). See ibid., pp. 100, 102.
52   Ibid., p. 99.
53   Schwarzer, *So fing es an!*, p. 75.
54   See reprint in H. Billstein and K. Naumann, eds, *Für eine bessere Republik: Alternative der demokratischen Bewegung*, 1981, pp. 216–20.
55   See the group's call in Billstein and Naumann, *Für eine bessere Republik*, pp. 220–1.
56   Ibid., p. 225.
57   Reprinted in Schwarzer, *So fing es an!*, pp. 188–92.
58   Reprinted in ibid., pp. 193–4.
59   Schenk, *Die feministische Herausforderung*, p. 216.
60   On the importance of this group for the 1969 and 1972 elections, see Horst W. Schmollinger and Peter Müller, *Zwischenbilanz: 10 Jahre sozialliberale Politik, 1969–1979*, 1980, pp. 39–42.
61   Ibid., p. 126.
62   Karlheinz Schonauer, *Die ungeliebten Kinder der Mutter SPD: Die Geschichte der Juso von der braven Parteienjugend zur innerparteilichen Opposition*, 1982, p. 128.
63   Juso-Bundesausschuß letter to SPD executive committee in October 1969, cited after Schonauer, *Die ungeliebten Kinder*, p. 138.
64   Schonauer, *Die ungeliebten Kinder*, pp. 129–30.
65   Ibid., pp. 133–4.
66   Dieter Stephan, *Jungsozialisten: Stabilisierung nach langer Krise? 1969–79*, 1980, pp. 26–7.
67   Norbert Gansel, ed. *Überwindet den Kapitalismus oder Was wollen die Jungsozialisten?*, 1971, p. 22.
68   Stephan, *Jungsozialisten*, p. 28.
69   Schonauer, *Die ungeliebten Kinder*, p. 255.
70   Ibid., p. 279.
71   Stephan, *Jungsozialisten*, p. 31.
72. See Wolfgang Roth, *Kommunalpolitik für wen? Arbeitsprogramm der Jungsozialisten*, 1971, pp. 54–131.
73   For descriptions of three model actions which ended successfully, see Schonauer, *Die ungeliebten Kinder*, pp. 285–90.
74   Schonauer, *Die ungeliebten Kinder*, p. 248.
75   Ibid.
76   Ibid., p. 257.
77   Wolfgang Roth, *Kommunalpolitik für wen?*, p. 25.
78   Schonauer, *Die ungeliebten Kinder*, p. 315.

79 Norbert Gansel, "Die Strategie in der Diskussion der Jungsozialisten," in Gansel, ed. *Überwindet den Kapitalismus*, p. 81.

80 Stephan, *Jungsozialisten*, p. 33.

81 Schonauer, *Die ungeliebten Kinder*, p. 317.

82 Stephan, *Jungsozialisten*, p. 64.

83 Schonauer, *Die ungeliebten Kinder*, p. 267.

84 They concerned the state's function and level of autonomy and the potential socialist content of investment steering. Franz Osterroth and Dieter Schuster, *Chronik der deutschen Sozialdemokratie*, vol. 3: *Nach dem zweiten Weltkrieg*, 2nd rev. edn, 1963, pp. 610–11.

85 Ibid., pp. 612–13.

86 Stephan, *Jungsozialisten*, p. 56.

87 Osterroth and Schuster, *Chronik*, p. 620.

88 Ibid., p. 627.

89 Stephan, *Jungsozialisten*, p. 58.

90 Schonauer, *Die ungeliebten Kinder*, p. 291.

91 Ibid.

92 See for instance the contribution by Karl-Hein Naßmacher in Gansel, *Überwindet den Kapitalismus*.

93 Schonauer, *Die ungeliebten Kinder*, pp. 295–8; and for the first study of this sorry episode in social democractic history, see Gerard Braunthal, *Political Loyalty and Public Service in West Germany*, 1990.

94 Brand et al., *Aufbruch in eine andere Gesellschaft*, p. 85.

95 Thus, as Peter Mayer-Tasch puts it, "one must emphasize that 'the' citizens' initiative in itself doesn't exist." C. P. Mayer-Tasch, *Die Bürgerinitiativbewegung*, 5th rev. edn, 1985, p. 20.

96 Guggenberger, *Bürgerinitiativen in der Parteiendemokratie*, p. 87.

97 Among all variables analyzed, educational level appears to coordinate most strongly with participation in CIs: according to a study conducted by the respected public opinion outfit INFAS and cited by Wolfgang Rüdig, 9 percent of those with a university or pre-baccalaureate degree (*Abitur*) are/were active in a CI. Wolfgang Rüdig, "Bürgerinitiativen im Umweltschutz: Eine Bestandsaufnahme der empirischen Befunde," in Volker Hauff, ed., *Bürgerinitiativen in der Gesellschaft*, 1980, pp. 163–4.

98 Ibid., pp. 164–6.

99 Ibid., p. 164.

100 Due to their financial autonomy and education, and in contrast to the working class, these people have the security, leisure and intellectual equipment to perceive, evaluate and be moved by problems which do not threaten their share of the material necessities of life. Many analyses have rightly noted how certain social-structural processes have swelled the "protest reservoir," the population pool fitting the above profile: factors such as the post war standard-of-living explosion, expansion of the service sector and, to a lesser degree, of educational opportunities. However, this in and of itself cannot explain the emergence and content of political phenomena such as the new social movements, CIs and the Green Party. The impulses and content for them originate elsewhere. The most notable and misleading diagnosis is perhaps Ronald Inglehart's famous "post material values" thesis. Ronald Inglehart, *The Silent Revolution: Changing Values and Political Styles among Western Publics*, 1977. And for the best German treatment of the "value change" thesis see also Helmut

Klages, *Wertorientierungen im Wandel*, 1985. However scant its intellectual value may be, the thesis receives almost obligatory mention in almost all German treatments of the CIs, new social movements and Greens and a catchword dropped by many activists and leaders – neo-conservatives and Leftists alike. For an empirical attack on the "value-change thesis," see Wilhelm Bürklin, *Grüne Politik*, 1984.

101   Mayer-Tasch, *Die Bürgerinitiativbewegung*, p. 14.
102   Ibid., pp. 59, 60.
103   Ibid., p. 64.
104   Ibid., p. 50, and for more complete statistics, p. 84.
105   Ibid., pp. 18–25.
106   Brand et al., *Aufbruch in eine andere Gesellschaft*, p. 89.
107   Karl-Werner Brand, ed., *Neue soziale Bewegungen in Westeuropa und den USA*, 1985, pp. 44.
108   Ibid., pp. 93, 46.
109   The first CIs around Wyhl were organized as early as 1971 against French plans to build a nuclear reactor and lead plant on the left bank of the Rhine.
110   Dieter Rucht, *Von Wyhl nach Gorleben: Bürger gegen Atomprogramm und nukleare Entsorgung*, 1980, pp. 81–2.
111   Nina Gladitz, ed., *Lieber heute aktiv als morgen radioaktiv*, 1976, p. 36.
112   Ibid., pp. 48–9.
113   Rucht, *Von Wyhl nach Gorleben*, p. 83.
114   A brochure jointly distributed by the power company executives and state and federal authorities and entitled "Project Information" tried to bolster public confidence. It trivialized the dangers of the proposed reactor and played up potential economic benefits.
115   "International" because it included French members from the left bank of the Rhine.
116   For the full text of the declaration, see Billstein and Naumann, *Für eine bessere Republik*, pp. 172–6.
117   Rucht, *Von Wyhl nach Gorleben*, p. 86.
118   In the referendum held in January, 1975, a narrow majority of the population, some 55 percent, voted for the sale of the building plot. The vote had been preceded by a campaign with "sugar dough and a whip." The power company had offered extravagant sums to the individual landowners and DM 2 million, a swimming pool, water-processing plant, and many jobs to the community. And the state government had made threats which were less than veiled to seize the land without compensation to the owners. See Gladitz, *Lieber heute aktiv*, p. 50.
119   Ibid.
120   Rucht, *Von Wyhl nach Gorleben*, pp. 84–7.
121   Stefan Aust, ed., *Brokdorf: Symbol einer politischen Wende*, 1982, p. 21.
122   The presents they promised – a swimming pool, a water-processing plant, a kindergarten – were also much the same as in Baden-Württemberg.
123   Of 1,551 ballots, 784 were marked "no," 202 "yes," and the rest were not returned. Aust, *Brokdorf*, p. 22.
124   In August 1974, the power company applied for a building and operation approval and in the following four-week period allowed for raising objections, the BUU collected over 31,000 signatures. Again, the reason for the tenacity and success of the pro-nuclear forces in the face of clear popular opposition

was the fact that those in charge of evaluating the building and operation of the plant also sat on the board of the power company. Ibid., p. 25.

125 CI headquarters were raided and flyers confiscated. Telephones were bugged and local residents followed. In an act of unmitigated provocation in October 1976, construction machines were moved on to the reactor site under heavy police protection – *although* the project as a whole was still tied up in legal proceedings. Ibid., pp. 25–6, and Rücht, *Von Wyhl nach Gorleben*, p. 89.

126 Bürgerinitiative Umweltschutz Unterelbe (Brokdorf), *Der Bauplatz muß wieder zur Wiese werden!*, 1977, p. 102.

127 Ibid., p. 113.

128 Two weeks later, on November 13, a second demonstration crossed the line to open combat. Stones were thrown by both sides and batons applied liberally. The police succeeded in breaking the demonstration only by flying in members of the border patrol police and dropping tear-gas canisters into the crowd from helicopters. Aust, *Brokdorf*, pp. 30–1.

129 Rucht, *Vom Wyhl nach Gorleben*, p. 90.

130 Ibid.

131 See for instance the 1978 flyer from the CIs against the planned processing plant in Gorleben, in Billstein and Naumann, *Für eine bessere Republik*, pp. 180–4.

132 Erhard Eppler, *Ende oder Wende? Von de Machbarkeit des Notwendigen*, 1975, and Herbert Gruhl, *Ein Planet wird geplundert*, 1975.

133 Rucht, *Vom Wyhl nach Gorleben*, p. 98.

134 In 1976, Willy Brandt headed a commission which drafted a report on energy policy and the anti-nuclear movement. Hans Mathöffer summoned several thousand party functionaries to a conference on energy policy held in April, 1977. The CDU emulated the SPD. The Hamburg SPD party congress in November 1977 also stood under the shadow of the energy policy debate. See Brand et al., *Aufbruch in eine andere Gesellschaft*, p. 95, and Rucht, *Vom Wyhl nach Gorleben*, p. 92.

135 The BBU, founded in 1972, rapidly became the most important umbrella organization for CIs in the Federal Republic with the advent of the anti-nuclear movement in 1975. Though no exact figures on its membership exist, conservative estimates count some 300 member CIs and over 100 within the organization's sphere of influence. The only systematic study of the various environmental organizations in the Federal Republic is, to our knowledge, Martin Leonhard, *Umweltverbände: Zur Organizierung von Umweltinteressen in der BRD*, 1986, esp. pp. 131ff., 156ff.

136 BBU, "Für eine ökologische Kreislaufwirtschaft," in Billstein and Naumann, *Für eine bessere Republik*, pp. 164–7.

137 By this time, in 1977–8, the first green electoral initiatives were forming in Lower Saxony, Schleswig-Holstein, Hamburg and Berlin. These early documents generally also revolve around the concept of an ecologized "circulatory economy." Many of them are reprinted in Anna Hallensleben, *Von der Grünen Liste zur Grünen Partei*, 1984.

138 See Hans-Christoph Binswanger, "Qualitatives Wachstum: Strategie und Ausgestaltungsprobleme," in Harald Müller-Witt, ed., *Arbeitsplätze contra Umwelt: eine rot-grüne Kontroverse*, 1980.

139 Though much has since been written on the relationship between ecology and socialism, these are some of the early works. From the communist spectrum:

the imaginative book by Hellmuth Schehl, *Vor uns die Sintflut?: Ökologie, Marxismus und die herrschende Zukunftsgläubigkeit*, 1977; the less self-critical more orthodox books by Alfred Leonhardt, *Umweltreproduktion im staatsmonopolistischen Kapitalismus: Zur Kritik bürgerlicher Konzeptionen einer marktwirtschaftlichen Lösung des Umweltprobleme*, 1977, and, somewhat later, Horst Paucke, *Umweltprobleme: Herausforderung der Menschheit*, 1980; and an assessment of the green movement itself from the communist spectrum, Harry Tallert, *Eine grüne Gegenrevolution*, 1980. From the social-democratic perspective: the indispensable book by Müller-Witt, *Arbeitsplätze contra Umwelt;* Volker Ronge, *Die Gesellschaft an den Grenzen der Natur: Aufsätze zur politischen Ökologie*, 1978; and the interesting critique of social-democratic statism and technocracy by Gerda Zellentin and Günter Nonnenmacher, eds, *Abschied von Leviathan: Ökologische Aufklärung über politische Alternativen*, 1979.

140 See the groundbreaking article by Gabrielle Kuby, "Ende der partriarchalen Herrschaft," in *Frauenoffensive*, no. 2, April 1975.

141 See Carola Parniske-Kunz, "Ökologie – eine Angel des Feminismus?" in Norbert W. Kunz, ed., *Ökologie und Sozialismus: Perspektiven einer umweltgründlichen Politik*, 1986, p. 116. The eco-feminism discussion has been hotly condemned by radical feminists, who insist on the cultural roots of differences between men and women, as a dangerous re-biologization of the gender difference which must ultimately play into the hands of the male ideology and patriarchal repression. And indeed many eco-feminists have sought an "objective" basis for magic and witchcraft as "alternative models" to male rationality within ecology. See for instance Sarah Jansen, "Magie und Technik – Auf der Suche nach feministischen Alternativen zur patriarchalen Naturnutzung," *Beiträge zur feministischen Theorie*, no. 12, Dec. 1984, pp. 76ff.

142 See the book published by the Achberg circle, Wilfried Heidt, ed., *Abschied vom Wachstumswahn: Ökologischer Humanismus als Alternative zur Plünderung des Planeten*, 1980, and also the work by the future green leaders in Baden-Württemberg, Wolf-Dieter and Connie Hasenclever, *Grüne Zeiten*, 1982.

143 For an overview of the Christian discussion of ecology, see Klaus Meyer-Abich, ed., *Frieden mit der Natur*, 1979.

144 Brand et al., *Aufbruch in eine andere Gesellschaft*, p. 213.

145 Lorenz Knorr, *Geschichte der Friedensbewegung in der Bundesrepublik*, 1983, p. 169.

146 Begun in the 1950s and conducted with state support in the Federal Republic, peace research did not place itself entirely or unambiguously behind the peace movement, but did analyze peace on an intellectual rather than a purely ethical level, helping to popularize and illuminate the opaque, statistics laden debates of nuclear strategists. See Egbert Jahn, "Friedensbewegung und Friedensforschung," in Reiner Steinweg, ed., *Die neue Friedensbewegung. Analysen aus der Friedensforschung*, 1982, pp. 146–65.

147 Thomas Leif, *Die professionelle Bewegung; Friedensbewegung von innen*, 1985, p. 39.

148 KOFAZ's organizational backbone consisted of "two professed disciples of the Soviet security policy position," see Rüdiger Schlaga and Hans-Joachim Spanger, "Die Friedensbewegung und der Warschauer Pakt: Ein Spannungsverhältnis," in Steinweg, *Die neue Friedensbewegung*, pp. 54–85, 64. Consequently, KOFAZ refused for instance, despite great pressure from the rest of the peace movement, to take a position on the imposition of martial law in Poland, ibid., p. 66.

149 With the exception of Communist groupings, who agitated for detente and East/West cooperation, the West German peace movement during the early to mid-70s remained diffusely "anti-militarist" and busied itself mostly with vague

moral denunciations, thematization of the military-industrial complex, and the promotion of conscientious objectors. See Leif, *Die professionelle Bewegung*, p. 40, Knorr, *Geschichte der Friedensbewegung*, pp. 145, 150, 154, 160, and Brand, *Neue soziale Bewegungen*, p. 215.

150 It was entitled "Stop the Arms Race" and was attended by some 40,000 people, including prominent political and literary figures. See Knorr, *Geschichte der Friedensbewegung*, pp. 168, 170, 172, 177.

151 The Soviets, drumming as usual on the "the indissoluble bond between socialism and peace" and the "Soviet people's love of peace," had successfully pressed for the round of negotiations. But in 1979 there were plenty of reasons for a European to doubt their goodwill at least as much as that of the Americans. It was the Soviet modernization of their mid-range missile systems though deployment of the SS-20 which allowed portrayal of the euromissiles as an "arms chase" or *Nachrüstung*. And the open militarism and aggression apparent in the Soviet invasion of Afghanistan and the institution of martial law in Poland in 1979 were enough to shake many even among the neutralist and pro-Soviet currents in the traditional West German peace organizations. And not to be forgotten, 1979 was also the year of the Iranian revolution, escalating tensions in the Middle East, and of first whispers of American intervention in the Persian Gulf. Importantly, this conjuncture in world events fell together with a period of worldwide recession. This made it hard for even politically apathetic individuals to numb themselves to an electric air of crisis. On this, see Berthold Meyer's article below. Employing a battery of statistics on postwar Germany, Meyer concludes that "fear of war clearly emerges more easily in situations experienced as economically problematic than when the economic development is judged positively." Berthold Meyer, "Neutralistische Träumereien? Öffentliche Meinung, Frieden und Friedensbewegung," in Steinweg, *Die neue Friedensbewegung*, pp. 113–44, esp. p. 124.

152 A comprehensive survey on peace conducted by the respected EMNID organization and commissioned by Germany's leading weekly magazine *Der Spiegel* showed that the arms race greatly decreased the trust of SPD and green voters in the United States. See "Jeder dritte hofft auf die Null-Lösung," *Der Spiegel*, no. 48, 1981, p. 56.

153 In late 1979, Mechtersheimer, a former air-force colonel and member of Franz-Josef Strauß's ultra-right CSU, published a paper warning that the "Europeanization of an East/West war" and the stationing of weapons with first-strike capability on German soil could provoke the Soviet Union to initiate a preventive nuclear attack on Germany. Several months later, Bundeswehr General Gert Bastian published a statement in which he argued along similar lines. Subsequently forced to take early retirement, Bastian became an outspoken peace activist and companion to peace movement leader Petra Kelly. Both Bastian and Mechtersheimer went on to serve as green MPs, Bastian after the 1983 elections, Mechtersheimer after the 1987 elections.

Mechtersheimer's vicious hatred of all things American – not an uncommon trait among many on the German right as well as left, especially among so-called "value conservatives" who extol Germany's supposedly pristine, untarnished pre-American existence and decry all things modern as evil impositions by the United States on an unwilling Germany – led him to advocate the formation of an internationally linked movement of anti-Americanism, to be led presumably by Mechtersheimer and his followers. An enthusiastic supporter of Saddam Hussein during the Gulf War, Mechtersheimer's influence declined in the Green party by the early 1990s. Mechtersheimer's political career and convictions serve as a good illustration of the possible merger between radical Right and Left in the context of German anti-modern conservatism, anti-liberalism and anti-Western views.

Much more tragic and infinitely sadder was Gert Bastian's fate. Disillusioned by the Greens' permanent factionalism and internecine battles, Bastian left the party in 1984 but completed his term in the Bundestag as an independent until January 1987. He remained a sort of vocal gadfly, a one-man moral wrecking crew, who admonished the German public – including his former green friends – of failing to show sufficient commitment in the quest of righting the world's many wrongs. Together with his companion Petra Kelly, one of the most important founding figures of the green movement and the Green Party, Bastian tirelessly advocated social justice on behalf of the forgotten and unpopular. An example was the Tibetans, who continue to suffer under their Chinese yoke; their cause was never picked up by the left-leaning Greens in good part because their subjugators were Communist, indeed Maoist, Chinese, who, after all, represented many a Green's idol in her/his political socialization during the late 1960s and early 1970s. Typically, Bastian had become very concerned with the rightward drift of German politics after unification. He was particularly shocked by the brazenness of right-wing violence against foreigners all over Germany and the conservative government's failure – and perhaps unwillingness – to counter these heinous crimes with the full force of the law. Bastian's last published words, appearing in the Green Party's magazine *Bundnis 2000* sounded dire and hopeless. He wrote: "The glamor is gone from the Federal Republic. The makeup of democratic prosperity has been washed away; the mask of rejecting violence, of tolerance and solidarity with the weak has been laid aside, revealing once again the grimacing mug of ugly Germany, which holds itself as important and worthy of life, which with hate persecutes and mercilessly destroys all 'aliens' who disturb the picture of a 'pure' Fatherland." (as quoted in the *New York Times*, October 21, 1992). For reasons which remain still unclear, and certainly still tragic, Bastian killed Petra Kelly with a gunshot in early October 1992, and then proceeded to take his own life. Since the bodies were not discovered until nearly three weeks after the deed and no written notes were found, it is uncertain as to when exactly the murder and suicide occurred. It also remains unknown whether Bastian committed the murder of Kelly on his own or whether she had been his accomplice in a shared murder-suicide pact. Whatever the case, there can be no doubt that the German Left lost two of its most sincere and committed figures.

154   Bastian's statement, cited from Georg Haasken and Michael Wigbers, *Protest in der Klemme: Soziale Bewegungen in der Bundesrepublik*, 1986, pp. 84–5.

155   Some merely criticized the abandonment of deterrence in favor of "flexible response" and the euromissiles. Like Mechtersheimer, they pointed to the first-strike capability of the Pershings as provocation for a preemptive Soviet first strike. (The Pershing IIs were capable of reaching Soviet soil in approximately five minutes and are highly accurate, making it possible to reach and take out Soviet missiles before they could have been launched from their silos.) Others rejected nuclear deterrence and war-fighting strategies straight away and worked out a range of "alternative defense concepts," including plans for gradual, unilaterally taken steps toward disarmament, and schemes for non-nuclear "social defense" based on passive resistance and civilian militias ("autonomous tech-commandos") after the Swiss model, which would be so highly dispersed

as to be immune to a centralized blitz attack. The peace researchers' proposals were not meant as utopias, but were often genuinely aimed at winning a majority of politicians and voters. On gradualism and unilateral disarmament, see Peter Schlotter, "Strategien der Konfliktentspannung: Vorschläge für die achtziger Jahre," in Hessische Stiftung Friedens- and Konfliktforschung, ed., *Europa zwischen Konfrontation und Kooperation: Entspannungspolitik für die 80er Jahre*, 1982, and also Reiner Steinweg, ed., *Das kontrollierte Chaos: die Krise der Abrüstung*, 1980. The most famous version of "alternative defense" is Horst Afheldt and Jochen Löser's. For a short discussion, see Horst Afheldt, "Friedenspolitik – naiv oder realistisch?" in Hans A. Pestalozzi et al., eds, *Frieden in Deutschland: die Friedensbewegung, wie sie wurde, was sie ist, was sie werden kann*, 1982, pp. 59–62. For a good summary with criticisms, see also Thomas Trempnau, "Afheldts Konzept einer defensiven, reaktiven Verteidigung," *Antimilitarismus Information*, no. 3, 1981, pp. 17–22. And on the "realist" character of peace research, see Jahn, "Friedensbewegung und Friedensforschung," p. 151.

156 Brand et al., *Aufbruch in eine andere Gesellschaft*, p. 213.
157 Ibid., p. 206.
158 This phrase is patterned on Ernst Bloch's famous "principle of hope." On the "eco-pax" synthesis, see especially Petra Kelly, "Wie sich die Ökologiebewegung zur Friedensbewegung entwickelte" in Petra Kelly and Joe Leinen, eds, *Prinzip Leben – Ökopax, die neue Kraft*, 1982.
159 As early as October 27–28, 1979, in the shadow of the double-track decision, a joint congress in Kassel sponsored by the DFG-VK and BBU undertook a first exploration of common concerns; see the declaration, "Zusammenarbeit und Handlungseinheit fördern!" in Billstein and Naumann, *Für eine bessere Republik*, p. 184. This was followed by a joint rally, "Stop the increase of atomic arms in Europe! Lift the NATO missile decision" held in the Lingen on October 25, 1980. See Knorr, *Geschichte der Friedensbewegung*, p. 183. Shortly thereafter, the BBU issued a "nuclear-site map" showing the location of missile bases and nuclear plants in the Federal Republic and commissioned studies of the potential ecological consequences of a nuclear war in West Germany. On this subject, see Harald Müller, "Ökologiebewegung und Friedensbewegung: Zur Gefährdung des Lebensraums," in Steinweg, *Die neue Friedensbewegung*, p. 177.
160 See K. D. Ernst et al., *Umweltkrieg und Abrüstung*, 1976.
161 On this subject, see Elmar Römpczyk, *Internationale Umweltpolitik und Nord-Süd Beziehungen*, 1979.
162 For a clear example of this sort of analysis, see the declaration of the BBU and DFK-VG entitled "Gegen Rüstung und Atom," in Billstien and Naumann, *Für eine bessere Republik*, pp. 65–8.
163 See Müller, "Ökologiebewegung und Friedensbewegung," p. 185.
164 See Hans-Jürgen Benedict, "Auf dem Weg zur Friedenskirche? Entstehung und Erscheinungsformen der neuen Friedensbewegung in der evangelischen Kirche," in Steinweg, *Die neue Friedensbewegung*, p. 232.
165 Haasken and Wigbers, *Protest in der Klemme*, p. 119.
166 See Benedict, "Auf dem Weg zur Friedenskirche?", p. 230.
167 Leif, *Die professionelle Bewegung*, p. 31.
168 The position it embodied was, until the dissolution of the social-liberal coalition in 1982, the only one which did not risk Schmidt's wrath and exclusion from the party. It insisted that two of the intermediate positions leading to deployment, ratification of the Salt II treaty and "serious" negotiations with the

Soviets had not been fulfilled, and, on that basis, called for nullification of the NATO decision. See the reprint of the appeal in Hans Apel et. al., *Sicherheitspolitik contra Frieden? Ein Forum zur Friedensbewegung*, 1981, pp. 146–7.

169   "Friedenssicherung ist nicht an das Gleichgewicht der Rüstungen gebunden ... Landgestützte Mittelstreckenraketen auf deutschen Boden sind militärisch, politisch und moralisch nicht zu verantworten ... Das im NATO-Doppelbeschluß enthaltene Verhandlungsangebot muß in Erstschlagswaffen und Entwaffnungssystem destabilisieren. ..." Cited from reprint in "Erklärung der Klausurtagung der Gustav Heinemann Initiative in Bonn am 12. Juni, 1981 zur Sicherheitspolitik," in Apel et al., *Sicherheitspolitik*, pp. 152–4.

170   They not only demanded renunciation of the NATO double-track decision and the continuation of further East–West negotiations but called for unilateral NATO troop reductions. The Jusos also took up the peace movement's association of the arms race with domestic unemployment and with poverty in the Third World. See reprint of "Resolution des Jungsozialisten-Bundeskongresses in Lahnstien vom 26. bis 28. Juni, 1981" in Apel et al., *Sicherheitspolitik*, pp. 155–6.

171   Leif, *Die professionelle Bewegung*, pp. 34–5.

172   The Krefeld appeal criticized the inadequacy of East–West negotiations and the refusal by the Reagan administration to sign or obey the SALT II Treaty and demanded that the "Chancellor keep his word" and not station the missiles. "The SALT Treaty is dead. ... The opponents of any arms chase (*Nachrüstung*) ... therefore expect ... courage and firmness from the Federal Government by the keeping of the Chancellor's word: namely, the retraction of the approval given with the 'arms catch-up' decision for the future stationing of American intermediate range nuclear missiles on the soil of the Federal Republic of Germany." For a complete reprint of the "Krefelder Appel," see Georg Benz et al., eds, *Rüstung, Entrüstung, Abrüstung*, 1982, pp. 140–1.

173   See Brand et al., *Aufbruch in eine andere Gesellschaft*, p. 216.

174   The 1981 convention was held in Hamburg under the slogan "Fear not. ..." On the final day of the meeting, some 40,000 participants in the Church Day marched under the banner "Have fear, nuclear death threatens us all." Ibid.

175   Among those in attendance were Jo Leinen, Lukas Beckman, Roland Vogt, Volkmar Deile, Gregor Witt, Achim Maske, Manfred Kühel, Ulrich Frey, Eva Quistorp. Beckmann, Vogt and Quistorp later became prominent Greens. See Leif, *Die professionelle Bewegung*, p. 59.

176   The charges of the federal government were not entirely false but were highly exaggerated. While the KOFAZ exerted a significant influence on the movement during the late 1970s, its influence had since been dwindling. Nevertheless, the defense ministry had even gone so far as to publish a diagram "proving" a direct chain of command from the central committee of the Soviet Communist Party to the organizers of the Krefeld forum, which it was later forced to withdraw. See the reprint in Apel et al., *Sicherheitspolitik*, p. 185.

177   Leif, *Die professionelle Bewegung*, p. 60.

178   See reprint of flyer, "Aufruf zur Bonner Demonstration," in Benz et al., *Rüstung*, pp. 144-5. On the Russell Foundation see Knorr, *Geschichte der Friedensbewegung*, p. 192.

179   Knorr, *Geschichte der Friedensbewegung*, p. 197.

180   The *Spiegel*-Emnid survey. Against this, only 29 percent expressed a negative stance toward the peace movement, and the percentage was even lower among the young. Among those 35 years or younger with a high level of education,

40.9 per cent could be reckoned to be "potential activists" of the peace movement. See *Der Spiegel*, no. 48, 1981, pp. 63, 68.

181 The members were Lukas Beckmann, Wolfgang Biermann, Rudolf Hartung, Jo Leinen, Klaus Mannhardt, Achim Maske, Gunnar Mathiesen, Gerd Pflaumer, Eva Quistorp, Werner Rätz, Andreas Buro, Bernd Vallentin, Klaus Waiditschka, Helga Weber, Harald Jansen, Michael Gerber, Godecke von Bremen, Rudolf Steinecke, J. Bernd Runge and Jochen Dietrich. See Leif, *Die professionelle Bewegung*, pp. 62–3.

182 Ibid., p. 68.

183 On the press work of the coordinating committee, see ibid., pp. 77–83, 135–44, 146–53.

184 Knorr, *Geschichte der Friedensbewegung*, p. 202, and Haasken and Wigbers, *Protest in der Klemme*, p. 96.

185 See Knorr, *Geschichte der Friedensbewegung*, p. 203, and Haasken and Wigbers, *Protest in der Klemme*, pp. 91–2.

186 On the positions of the various parties on the double-track decision and disarmament, see the cover story, "Raketenwahlkampf," *Der Spiegel*, no. 5, 1983.

187 As *Der Spiegel* put it: "When it comes to the core questions of West German policies, the majority of the Federal Republic's citizens are green to the Greens." According to a survey ordered by the Kohl government and conducted by the Sinus Institut (which was not released to the public, presumably because of its results) and leaked to *Der Spiegel*, 54 percent of the CDU/CSU voters and 70 per cent of FDP sympathizers were for postponing the stationing of the euromissiles should the Geneva negotiations fail. According to the same survey, 85 percent of all voters were for a continuation of détente policy (*Entspannungspolitik*), and many more expressed trust toward the Soviet Union than several years before. While this clearly indicates the message of the elections was *not* a moratorium on the euromissiles, it also makes clear the level and generality of opposition to them in the general population. The survey results were excerpted in "Nichts geändert," *Der Spiegel*, no. 1, 1983, pp. 30–1, and "Kein Kardinal," *Der Spiegel*, no. 2, 1983, pp. 27–8.

188 Despite police precautions, a small band of militant anarchists succeeded in pelting Bush's limousine with rocks. Over 100 demonstrators were injured in struggles with the police. See "Wie in Chicago," *Der Spiegel*, no. 27, 1983.

189 In August, a Federal Conference of Autonomous Peace Initiatives was held, attended among others by the Greens, the BBU, the Hamburg GAL, the AL-West Berlin and the DFG/VK. See Haasken and Wigbers, *Protest in der Klemme*, pp. 95, 10; Leif, *Die professionelle Bewegung*, pp. 200–2, "Woche des Zorns," *Der Spiegel*, no. 46, 1983. For details of the plans they developed for the fall, see "Der Herbst wird organisiert," *Antimilitarismus Information*, no. 8, 1983.

190 Some 8,000–10,000 demonstrators participated in a blockage of streets and intersections near the Bundestag. The final toll in the conflicts was 500 arrests and 100 injuries. See Haasken and Wigbers, *Protest in der Klemme*, p. 100.

191 Exercised against a Pershing II transportation vehicle in the tiny town of Schwäbisch-Gmündl. See "Zerstörungswerk am Zerstörungswerkzeug," *Der Spiegel*, no. 50, 1983.

192 See the course of events at the fifth "action conference" of the coordinating committee in early 1984, described in Leif, *Die professionelle Bewegung*, pp. 209–23.

193 On the "Fall '84 Action", see "Rühig und Still," *Der Spiegel*, no. 40, 1984, pp. 41–4, and "Herbst '84," *Antimilitarismus Information*, no. 8, 1984.

Chapter 5   Ideology

1 Even though the only faction within the party openly to profess a Marxist ideology was that of the eco-socialists, we interpret the essence of the Greens' project in its totality as a complete reconstruction of Marxian socialism.

2 See Andrei S. Markovits and David S. Meyer, "Green Growth on the West German Left: Cultivating Political Space," paper presented at the 13th world congress of the International Political Science Association, Paris, July 15–21, 1985.

3 We are not here depicting the "Aufbruch" section of the Greens since we deem this group not to have contributed much to the ideological diversity of and controversy within the party. In contrast to the four groups discussed in this chapter, Aufbruch '88 represented purely a parliamentary maneuver and a compromising step led by Antje Vollmer to keep the various tendencies together as something resembling one party called "The Greens."

4 During a debate between Eckhard Strattmann and Helmut Wiesenthal moderated by *Taz* reporter Jakob Sonnenschein in Bochum, May 1985, attended by Philip Gorski.

5 Helmut Wiesenthal, "Grün-Rational: Vorschläge für eine zeitgemässe Strategie," reprinted in Gabriel Falkenberg and Heiner Kersting, eds, *Eingriffe im Diesseits*, 1985, p. 3.

6 See especially, Thomas Ebermann and Rainer Trampert, *Die Zukunft der Grünen*, 1985, pp. 242–54.

7 See Jutta Ditfurth, "Radikal und phantasievoll gesellschaftliche Gegenmacht organisieren! Skizzen einer radikalökologischen Position," in Thomas Kluge, ed., *Grüne Politik*, 1984, p. 63.

8 See Antje Vollmer's speech in "Perspektive grüner Politik," *Grüner Basis-Dienst*, no. 1, 1985, p. 61.

9 See "Veto-Partei: Gegen den hundischen SPD-Bezug," in Rudolf Bahro, *Pfeiler am anderen Ufer*, 1984, pp. 8–10.

10 See interview with Thomas Ebermann in Sabine Stamer, ed., *Von der Nachbarkeit des Unmöglichen*, 1985, p. 102.

11 See Ditfurth, "Radikal und phantasievoll," p. 67.

12 Ibid., p. 57.

13 See Petra Kelly, "Wir müssen die Etablierten entblössen wo wir können," in Jörg Mettke, ed., *Die Grünen*, 1982, p. 31.

14 See Ditfurth, "Radikal und phantasievoll," p. 64.

15 See Ebermann interview in Stamer, *Von der Nachbarkeit*, pp. 94–5.

16 See interview with Joschka Fischer, "Zieran hat mit grüner Kultur so viel zu tun wie die Curry-Wirscht mit dem Müsli," *Pflasterstrand*, no. 169, Oct. 22, 1983, p. 15.

17 Ibid., p. 16.

18 See interview with Norbert Mann in Brigitte Jäger and Claudia Pintl, eds, *Zwischen Rotation und Routine: die Grünen im Bundestag*, 1985, p. 144.

19 See Otto Schily, "Vor unvergleichlichen Möglichkeiten," in Wolfram Bockerioch, ed., *SPD und Grüne: Das neue Bündniss?*, 1985, p. 148.

20 See interview in Stamer, *Von der Nachbarkeit*, p. 114.

21 See "Jutta ist jetzt die Kaiserin," *Der Spiegel*, May 11, 1987.

22 See Joschka Schmiere, "Weichenstellungen," *Kommune*, no. 12, 1983, p. 8.

23 See Gabriel Falkenberg, and Erhard Müler, "Thesen für eine systemüberwindende Realpolitik," *Kommune*, no. 7, 1984, p. 36.

24 See Hendrik Auhagen, "Skizze eines sozio-ökologischen Kompromisses," *Kommune*, no. 10, 1984, p. 33.
25 See Kelly, "Wir müssen die Etablierten entblössen, p. 32.
26 See Rudolf Bahro, "Hinein oder hinaus," in Mettke, *Die Grünen*, p. 45. Helmut Wiesenthal summarizes the fundamentalist position well: "thus when playing along 'in the system' as well as a passivity amounting to toleration count as an affront against the goal of overcoming the system, only the alternative of consequent opposition remains, that uses its participation to represent its own standpoint and to show the limits of the legitimacy and formative power of parliament . . ." Helmut Wiesenthal, "Grün-Rational," in Falkenberg and Kersting, *Eingriffe im Diesseits*, p. 6.
27 Bahro, "Hinein oder hinaus."
28 Joachim Raschke, arguably the Federal Republic's most eminent authority on the Greens, also sees Rudolf Bahro and his ideas as particularly representative of a major strain in green thinking. See Joachim Raschke, *Krise der Grünen: Bilanz und Neubeginn*, 1991.
29 *Mitteleuropa* included principally Germany and the Austro-Hungarian empire: what are now the united Germany, Austria, Hungary, Czechoslovakia, Poland, the Hungarian-speaking and German-speaking areas of Romania, and Croatia, Slovenia and Bosnia-Herzegovina.
30 The better studies on the history and politics of early German romanticism, oddly enough, are in French. See the fine study by Henri Brunschwig, *Société et romantisme en Prusse au XVIIIe siècle*, 1973, and also the introduction in J. Droz, ed., *Le romantisme politique en Allemagne*, 1963. For a sampling of critical texts, see Paul Kluckhohn, ed., *Weltanschauung der Frühromantik*, 1966.
31 See the groundbreaking, finely written scholarship of Michael Löwy on this subject, especially *Rédemption et utopie*, 1988. Also useful is his study of Lukács, *Pour une sociologie des intellectuels révolutionaires*, 1976, pp. 9–106. Another fine piece is Anson Rabinbach, "Benjamin Bloch and Modern German Jewish Messianism," *New German Critique*, no. 34, Winter 1985, pp. 78–125.
32 See Fritz Stern, *The Politics of Cultural Despair*, 1961.
33 See Robert Wohl, *The Generation of 1914*, 1978, and Jeffrey Herf, *Reactionary Modernism: Technology, Culture and Politics in Weimar and the Third Reich*, 1984.
34 Fritjof Capra, *The Turning Point: Science, Society and the Rising Culture*, 1982, p. 21.
35 See Murray Bookchin, *The Ecology of Freedom: the Emergence and Dissolution of Hierarchy*, 1982, p. 3.
36 The term is Marilyn Ferguson's. See Marilyn Ferguson, *The Aquarian Conspiracy: Personal and Societal Transformation in the 80s*, 1980.
37 See Capra, *Turning Point*, p. 27; Ferguson, *Aquarian Conspiracy*, p. 51; Rudolf Bahro, *Die Logik der Rettung*, 1987, p. 11.
38 See Capra, *Turning Point*, p. 26.
39 For a brief history, see E. Mayr, *The Growth of Biological Thought*, 1982.
40 See Carl Amery, *Natur also Politik: Die ökologische Chance des Menschen*, 1976.
41 Capra, *Turning Point*, p. 92.
42 Two recent attempts which have received some attention in the Federal Republic are Frederic Vester, *Neuland des Denkens: Vom technokratischen zum kybernetischen Zeitalter*, 1980, and Joël de Rosnay, *Le macroscopie: Vers une vision globale*, 1975. The best-known exponent of systems theory in West Germany is, of course, Niklas Luhmann.

43   See Vester, *Neuland des Denkens*, pp. 19–21.
44   See de Rosnay, *Le macroscopie*, pp. 24–36. See also the revealing diagram in Vester, *Neuland des Denkens*, p. 19, in which biology is placed at the center of all branches of natural and social science.
45   Amery, *Natur also Politik*, p. 13.
46   Ibid., p. 65.
47   Ibid., p. 183.
48   Ibid., p. 92.
49   Ibid., p. 167.
50   Ibid., p. 37.
51   Ibid., pp. 129–32.
52   Ibid., p. 46.
53   Ibid., p. 36–7.
54   Ibid., p. 166.
55   Ibid., p. 184.
56   From Jochen Reiche's critical article on Amery and his relation to the West German ecology movement, "Ökologie und Zivilisation: Der Mythos von der den natürlichen Kreisläufen," in Thomas Schmid, ed., *Die Linke neu denken*, 1984, p. 42.
57   See Manon Maren-Griesbach, *Philosophie der Grünen*, 1982, p. 32.
58   See Ludwig Trepl, "Ökologie – eine grüne Leitwissenschaft? Über Grenzen und Perspektiven einer modischen Disziplin," *Kursbuch*, no. 74, Dec. 1983, p. 7.
59   Ibid., p. 12.
60   Ibid., p. 6.
61   Bookchin, *Ecology of Freedom*, p. 315.
62   The model character of the American Indians has played a central role for the German middle-class Left. One of its most obvious functions is an implicit relativization of the Nazi horrors and yet another demonstration of evil America. If the Americans did to the Indians what the Germans did to the Jews, then clearly there could be no singularization of the Holocaust. Moreover, the analogy places the much-hated Americans into a similar category with the Nazis. The romanticization of the Indians by a large number of Germans derives from the extremely popular books written by Karl May. Hardly any German-reading middle-class child, especially male, of the 1950s and 1960s has grown up without reading a few of May's "classics" about the Wild West with its Indians, both "good" and "bad." Thus, it is fascinating to see that one of the most popular "alternative" German-language guidebooks of the United States starts the presentation of each of the 50 states with an account of the destruction of the Native American population. For more on May's enormous popularity, see Gerhard Armanski, "Yankees, Indsmen, und Sachsen," in *Dollars und Träume*, no. 10, Oct. 1984, pp. 83–105.
63   As Bookchin puts it: "Wholeness compromises the variegated structures, the articulation, and the mediation that impart to the whole a rich variety of forms and thereby add unique qualitative properties to what a strictly analytic mind often reduces to 'unnumerable' and 'random' details." Bookchin, *Ecology of Freedom*, p. 23.
64   Maren-Griesbach, *Philosophie der Grünen*, p. 33.
65   See Bookchin, *Ecology of Freedom*, ch. 2, "The Outlook of Organic Society," pp. 42–61.

66   Ibid., p. 319.
67   Naturally, since these ecological theorists tend to concern themselves with these issues only from the "superstructural" standpoint of culture and consciousness, it generally remains unclear just how much of the base of modern, industrial civilization they would retain in their ecotopias. The concrete experimentation with "life-reform" and "soft technologies" has been undertaken by the alternative movement itself. Perhaps the only attempt at conceiving and painting out an alternative, ecological utopia in rich descriptive detail is still Ernest Callenbach's imaginative novel about the secession of the West Coast from the United States and its ecotopia. See *The Notebooks and Reports of William Weston*, 1975. For an attempt to evaluate an alternative living experiment in light of the movement's theoretical claims, see Bernd Leinweber and Karl-Ludwig Schibel, "Die Alternativebewegung: Ein Beitrag zu ihrer gesellschaftlichen Bedeutung und politischen Tragweite, ihren Möglichkeiten und Grenzen," in Wolfgang Kraushaar, ed., *Autonomie oder Getto? Kontroversen über Alternativebewegung*, 1978, pp. 95–128. For more general accounts of the various branches of the alternative movement, see Robert Jung and Norbert R. Müller, *Alternatives Leben*, 1980.
68   Dieter Duhm, *Aufbruch zur neuen Kultur: Von der Verweigerung zur Neugestaltung: Umrisse einer ökologischen und menschlichen Alternative*, 1984, p. 43.
69   Ibid., p. 50.
70   Ibid., p. 29.
71   See Horst von Gizycki, *Aufbruch aus dem Neandertal: Entwurf einer neuen Kommune*, 1974. The idea of the *aufrechte Gang*, of course, is Ernst Bloch's.
72   Ibid., p. 38.
73   Bookchin, *Ecology of Freedom*, p. 323.
74   Reprinted in "Notes on Exterminism, the Last Stage of Civilization," in E. P. Thompson, *Beyond the Cold War*, 1982, pp. 41–80. It first appeared in German translation as "Exterminismus als letztes Stadium der Zivilisation," *Befreiung: Zeitschrift für Politik und Wirtschaft*, no. 19/20, 1980, and later under the same title in *Arbeitskreis atomwaffenfreies Europa* (Berlin: Alternativen Europäischer Friedenspolitik), 1981.
75   See Thompson, *Beyond the Cold War*, pp. 44–5.
76   Ibid., pp. 64–5.
77   Günther Anders, "Über die Seele im Zeitalter der zweiten industriellen revolution," in Anders, *Die Antiquiertheit des Menschen*, 7th edn, vol. 1, 1987, p. 243.
78   Günther Anders, "Über die Zerstörung des Lebens im Zeitalter der dritten industriellen Revolution," in Anders, *Die Antiquiertheit*, vol. 2, p. 20.
79   Ibid., p. 2.
80   Ibid.
81   Anders, *Die Antiquiertheit*, vol. 2, p. 33. In its provocative thesis of "total domination" and "mediatization," Anders's analysis strongly resembles Horkheimer and Adorno's analysis of the "administered world."
82   For Anders's analysis of the bomb, see *Die Antiquiertheit*, vol. 1, pp. 233–324.
83   Anders, *Die Antiquiertheit*, vol. 2, p. 9.
84   Mumford's work has had an especially great impact on Rudolf Bahro, as we will see below.
85   Lewis Mumford, "The Pentagon of Power," *The Myth of the Machine*, vol. 2, 1970, pp. 236–7.
86   Ibid., p. 251.

87   Ibid., p. 267.
88   Ibid., p. 258.
89   Ibid., p. 183.
90   Ibid., p. 201.
91   Ibid., p. 127.
92   Ibid., p. 228.
93   Ibid., p. 303.
94   Anders, *Die Antiquiertheit*, vol. 1, p. 271.
95   Anders, *Die Antiquiertheit*, vol. 2, p. 17.
96   See Anders, *Die Antiquiertheit*, vol. 1, pp. 233–9.
97   Ibid., p. 268.
98   Ibid., p. 273.
99   The argument for a reconstructed humanism, for a reclamation of the moral intentions of the Enlightenment has been made most forcefully and systematically by Jürgen Habermas. See the Conclusion in Jürgen Habermas, *Theorie des kommunikativen Handelns*, vol. 2, 1981.
100 Jeffrey Herf, *War by Other Means: Soviet Power, West German Resistance, and the Battle of the Euromissiles*, 1991, and Alice Cooper, "The West German Peace Movement of the 1980s: Historical and Institutional Influences," Ph.D. diss. 1988.
101 See Klaus Bitterman, ed. *Liebesgrüsse aus Bagdad: Die "edlen Seelen" der Friedensbewegung und der Krieg am Golf,* 1991.
102 See articles by Marion Gräfin Dönhoff: "Wirklich ein gerechter Krieg?" *Die Zeit,* Feb. 15, 1991, and "Ein dubioser Sieg: Lieber Drückberger als Mittäter," *Die Zeit,* Mar. 15, 1991.
103 See "Ein amerikanischer Jude und eine deutsche Fridensrede: Ein Briefwechsel unter den linken Freunden Andrei Markovits und Jürgen Hoffman, aus dem eine Grundsatzdebatte wurde," *Frankfurter Rundschau*, Feb. 16, 1991; Rainer Erd, "Deutsche Linke an die Front?", *Frankfurter Rundschau*, Feb. 20, 1991; Andrei Markovits, "Eine ernüchternde Erfahrung," *Die Zeit*, Feb. 22, 1991; Andrei Markovits, "Die Linke gibt es nicht – und es gibt sie doch," *Frankfurter Rundschau*, Mar. 7, 1991.
104 See Alice Schwarzer, "Bornierte Freund-Feind Muster," *Der Spiegel,* Apr. 29, 1991.
105 See Henryk Broder, "Unser Kampf," *Der Spiegel*, Apr. 29, 1991. In many ways Stroebele's views are not surprising if one takes into account the rabid nature of anti-semitism which – masquerading under the guide of anti-terrorism – became commonplace in the West German Left of the 1970s and 1980s. On this sorry topic, see the brilliant book by Martin Kloke, *Israel und die deutsche Linke: Zur Geschichte eines schwierigen Verhältnisses,* 1990.
106 "Fundamentalism can never prove itself constructive or destructive through the objects negotiated in parliaments, because it aims at attitudes (*Haltungen*)." Bahro, *Die Logik der Rettung,* p. 10.
107 Ibid., p. 307.
108 Ibid., p. 15.
109 Ibid., p. 111.
110 For the diagram, see ibid., p. 107.
111 Ibid., p. 185.
112 Ibid., p. 181.
113 Ibid., p. 103.
114 Ibid., p. 186.
115 Ibid., p. 188.
116 Ibid., p. 193.

117 Ibid., p. 208.
118 Ibid., p. 237.
119 Ibid., p. 304.
120 Ibid., p. 284.
121 Ibid., p. 431.
122 Ibid.
123 Ibid., p. 316.
124 Ibid., p. 452.
125 Ibid., p. 329.
126 Ibid., p. 436.
127 Just as in Bahro's case, our discussion of the ideas expressed by the Bielefeld sociologists is not based on the political importance of these people inside the Green Party. Rather, it is our judgement that the writings of Offe, Wiesenthal and Kostede offer the most salient examples of a particularly important strain in green ideology and *Weltanschauung*, which we chose to characterize as the realist version of reformist humanism.
128 See Claus Offe, "Griff nach der Notbremse. Bewirken oder Bewahren – der Aufstieg der Grünen bringt zwei Politikbegriffe ins Spiel, die einander widersprechen," *Die Zeit*, Aug. 20, 1982. Also reprinted in Wolfgang Kraushaar, ed., *Was sollen die Grünen im Parliament?*, 1983, pp. 85–92.
129 Offe, "Griff nach der Notbremse", in Kraushaar, *Was sollen die Grünen*, p. 87.
130. Ibid., pp. 89–90.
131 Wiesenthal, "Grün-Rational," pp. 14–15.
132 Ibid., p. 26.
133 Ibid., p. 30.
134 Ibid., p. 22.
135 Ibid., pp. 3–6.
136 Ibid., p. 27.
137 Again, just as in the case of Bahro and the threesome of the Bielefeld school, Thomas Schmid's salience has less to do with his positional presence inside the Green Party and green movement that it does with the clarity of his articulated positions, which we deem important as constituent elements in the Greens' overall ideology and world-view.
138 See Thomas Schmid, "Nicht sozial, aber bürokratisch, über die Vergesell-schaftung der Ohnmacht," in Schmid, ed. *Das pfeifende Schwein: Über weitergehende Interessen der linken*, 1985, p. 127.
139 See Thomas Schmid, "Plädoyer für einen reformistischen Anarchismus," in Kluge, *Grüne Politik*, p. 75.
140 See "Vorbemerkung" in Thomas Schmid, ed., *Die Linke neu denken*, 1984, p. 7.
141 "Einigkeit und Grüne und Freiheit, ökolibertäre Grüne. Gründungserklärung," reprinted in *Kommune*, no. 4, 1984, p. 51.
142 Ibid.
143 Ibid., p. 52.
144 Ibid., p. 54.
145 Schmid, "Plädoyer," p. 78.
146 Ibid., p. 76.
147 Schmid, "Nicht sozial," p. 135.
148 See Thomas Schmid, "Reform-Absolutismus und Basis-Bürokratie?", *Die Zeit*, Feb. 6, 1987.
149 Ibid.
150 "Einigkeit und Grüne und Freiheit," p. 54.

151 In notable contrast to our previous "ideal" types – Bahro, Wiesenthal and Schmid – Ebermann and Trampert were major "players" in the Green Party throughout all of the 1980s until the decisive defeat of the fundamentalist wing in 1990–1. Tellingly, both Ebermann and Trampert departed from the Greens in anger and disappointment, because they perceived the Greens to have become an accommodationist group kowtowing to the Social Democrats and obsessed with exercising governmental power. Their attempt to start a new, genuinely green party ended in failure.

152 See Johanno Strasser and Klaus Traube, *Die Zukunft des Fortschritts: Der Sozialismus und die Krise des Industrialismus*, 1984, p. 284.

153 Ebermann and Trampert, *Die Zukunft der Grünen*, p. 209.

154 Strasser and Traube, *Die Zukunft des Fortschritts*, p. 25.

155 Ebermann and Trampert, *Die Zukunft der Grünen*, p. 128.

156 Strasser and Traube, *Die Zukunft des Fortschritts*, pp. 32–3. Also Ebermann and Trampert, "Sozialistischer Industrialismus," in Ebermann and Trampert, *Die Zukunft der Grünen*, pp. 136–40.

157 See Strasser and Traube, *Die Zukunft des Fortschritts*, p. 23.

158 Ibid., p. 43. See also Ebermann and Trampert, *Die Zukunft der Grünen*, p. 7.

159 Of course, left mavericks such as Ernst Bloch and Herbert Marcuse also presented a critique of science and technology, attacking the idea of their neutral and emancipatory character. See Ernst Bloch, *Das prinzip Hoffnung*, 4th edn, 1977, pp. 778ff., and Herbert Marcuse, *One-Dimensional Man*, 1983.

160 See Ebermann and Trampert, *Die Zukunft der Grünen*, p. 147.

161 See Ernst Bloch, *Geist der Utopie*, 2nd edn, 1985, pp. 240–1.

162 The neologism, is, of course, John Kenneth Galbraith's. See J. K. Galbraith, *The New Industrial State*, 1967.

163 See Strasser and Traube, *Die Zukunft des Fortschritts*, pp. 186–9.

164 Ibid., p. 166.

165 Ibid., pp. 258–60. For a similar criticism of real, existing socialism, see also Rudolf Bahro, *Die Alternative: Zur Kritik des real-existierenden Sozialismus*, 1981.

166 Here the eco-socialists borrow particularly heavily from the work of Ivan Illich; see especially *Tools for Conviviality*, 1973.

167 See Ebermann and Trampert, *Die Zukunft der Grünen*, p. 220.

168 Strasser and Traube, *Die Zukunft des Fortschritts*, pp. 290, 295.

Chapter 6 Policy

1 Die Grünen, *Das Bundesprogramm*, 1980, p. 4.

2 Of its 46 pages, energy policy receives 2, "space, settlement and traffic" 2, peace and the Third World 4, environment and nature 6, democracy and civil rights 4, women 4, "social outsiders" 2, and health policy 2. Not only do the various policy headings correspond to the movements of the late 1970s, but each policy statement represents, in essence, a brief account of the movements' essential positions. Little wonder, since leaders from the respective movements were charged to draft them.

3 Renewed growth has not, as in the past, produced new jobs. Businesses have used their profits to expand investment portfolios and finance rationalization measures.

4   Die Grünen, *Umbau der Industriegesellschaft, Schritte zur Überwindung von Erwerbslosigkeit, Armut und Umweltzerstörung (Umbauprogramm)*, 1986, p. 7.
5   The Greens believe that the industrialists' desire for profit and the consumers' desire for material goods feed on one another, and both feed on the environment. The consumers' desire is not natural, but a displacement because of unfulfilling work, social estrangement and – of late – the absence of a livable environment. In the eyes of the Greens, the engine of this self-destructive cycle is economic growth. A powerful societal consensus behind growth exists, which assures, on the one hand, continued capital accumulation and, on the other hand, buys off potential social unrest by assuring an ever-increasing standard of living for the majority. Increasingly, the state, caught between the burden of a swollen welfare system and spiraling public needs and demands, becomes increasingly coopted into the "growth cartel." By promoting growth, political leaders hope to generate tax revenue and new jobs, thereby boosting welfare resources and cutting demands on them. In the classic Marxist scenario of capitalist crisis, overproduction results in bankruptcies and falling wages. Decreased competition and cheap labor, in turn, renew the conditions for the valorization of capital and business expansion. This results in the creation of new jobs to expand output and the (re)hiring of the unemployed at lower wages. The disappearance of the "employment effect" from "capitalist crises" has been much discussed by Marxist and neo-Marxist social scientists in the Federal Republic. For a good discussion, see Michael Opielka, "Vom Sozialstaat zum ökologischen Gemeinwesen – Für eine neue Sozialpolitik," in Niels Beckenbach et al., *Grüne Wirtschaftspolitik: Machbare Utopien*, 1985, pp. 106–226, and also Georg Vobruba, *Politik mit dem Wohlfahrtstaat*, 1983, especially pp. 83–129.
6   See Die Grünen, *Bundestagswahlprogramm 1987*, 1986, p. 33, and Christian Leipert, "Die Grünen auf der Suche nach einem neuen ökonomischen Leitbild," in Beckenbach, et al., *Grüne Wirtschaftspolitik*.
7   Leipert, "Die Grünen auf der Suche," p. 21. This view is obviously an economic rendering of the exterminism thesis, proffered by E. P. Thompson and propagated among the Greens by Rudolph Bahro.
8   In the pursuit of profit, the industrialist reduces nature to an input in economic calculations. Nature, like labor, is thereby reduced to a commodity, whose value is not intrinsic but quantified in a price. The effects of production on nature – pillaging and pollution of irreplaceable resources – are externalized from the calculation.
9   Growth industries such as the medical and pharmaceutical branches are little more than repair services for the psychological stress and life-threatening environmental contamination which have resulted from past growth. The causes of many illnesses are not to be seen principally in the individual behavior of people, but rather in the increasing destruction of natural conditions of life, and in the societal relations in which people must live. Prevention, in the context of green health policy, means first of all decontamination of soil, water, air and food, prohibition and replacement of poisonous substances, combating work pressure and other factors in work and daily life which make people sick. Die Grünen, *Gesundheitspolitische Vorstellungen der Grünen*, 1986, p. 6. See also Opielka, "Vom Sozialstaat," pp. 206–7.
10 *Bundestagswahlprogramm*, 1987, p. 34.
11 *Umbauprogramm*, p. 9.
12 *Bundesprogramm*, p. 6.

13 In opposition to unemployment and poverty, the ecological dangers do not take the form of class oppression but "ein . . . askriptives Gefährdungsschicksal" (an ascriptive fate of endangerment). "Dangers become blind passengers of normal consumption. They travel with the wind and water, hide in everything and everyone and pass with the most necessary things of life – the air we breathe, food, clothes, the apartment furniture. . . ." The impacts of the ecological crisis cannot be deflected by the happy majority on to the unfortunate remainder. It affects or rather endangers everyone more or less equally. See Ulrich Beck, *Risikogesellschaft: Auf dem Weg in eine andere Moderne*, 1986, pp. 8, 10.

14 *Umbauprogramm*, p. 10.

15 Ibid.

16 Ibid., p. 103.

17 Ibid., p. 10.

18 See Opielka, "Vom Sozialstaat," pp. 36–7. This differentiation between "genuine" and "artificial" or "manufactured" needs stems from Herbert Marcuse's *One-Dimensional Man* and has, with justice, been frequently and violently criticized. It appears, nevertheless, quite frequently in green and alternative writing, most often as theoretical windowdressing for an essentially moralistic argument against consumerism based on asceticism and anti-materialism.

19 *Bundesprogramm*, p. 7.

20 Other areas include agriculture, traffic and the food industry.

21 By green reckonings, in the course of a single year the "poison kitchens" pump some 5.1 million tons of sulfate, 53,000 tons of ammonia, 500,000 tons of phenol, 1,700 tons of chrome, 1,200 tons of lead and 320 tons of arsenic into the Rhine alone, which still serves as a source of household and drinking water for a good portion of Germany. In addition, some 30,000 tons per year of pesticides are used by West German agriculture and 155,000 tons per year are exported abroad, a significant share of which eventually trickle into ground water. "The chemical industry is one of the most significant economic sectors and the branch which produces at the greatest costs to the environment. . . . Only one-seventh of the production is designated for direct use. This gives the chemical industry the character of a modern key industry. It is the starting point for an increasing chemicalization of production and consumption." Particularly baleful are non-biodegradable chemicals such as the chlorohydrates which are not broken down or processed by nature. Once in the water supply, they soon enter the food chain and are deposited in fat cells where they may cause cancer and birth defects in animals and humans. German control legislation generally prohibits only sales and applications in the Federal Republic, but not manufacture for export. Die Grünen, "Der Rhein ist tot – es lebe die Chemie?" (n.d.), and *Umbauprogramm*, p. 48.

22 *Umbauprogramm*, p. 49; "soft chemistry" means that "substances are produced which are not foreign to nature and for which life-destroying (*lebensfeindliche*) effects can be ruled out . . . that substances occurring in nature may only be produced or manufactured in quantities and in ways and fashions which do not bring natural material cycles out of balance."

23 This includes canceling the numerous product lines whose synthesis employs the supertoxin dioxin and the heavy metal cadmium, and prohibiting the manufacture, application, import and export of known carcinogens (such as asbestos, PCB and formaldehyde). See Die Grünen, "Umweltpolitisches Entgiftungsprogramm" (n.d.).

24 Above all, the authorities would acquire the right to inspect all files and documents, including the firms' "ecological" accounting. New and/or untested products would be subject to strict environmental impact studies.

25 A "plausibility principle" would replace the "causality principle" as the legal foundation for consumers" claims to financial compensation. Workers would receive the right to refuse to do work they deemed dangerous, including that with chemicals. See ibid., and Die Grünen, "Vorschläge der Grünen zur Veränderung des Betriebverfassungsgesetzes," 1987.

26 *Umbauprogramm*, p. 50; Die Grünen, "Entgiftung – sanfte Chemie ist keine Utopie," 1986.

27 Die Grünen, "Entgiftung."

28 As a consequence of this heritage, green anti-nuclear policy has possessed an elaborate critique of status quo energy politics and a sophisticated array of counterproposals from the very beginning. Even in the somewhat delirious and formulaic 1980 federal program, the energy policy section contains, in addition to the usual abstract and exclamatory demands, a long list of ambitious but politically realizable proposals which address the political, economic and social side-effects and consequences of a rapid shutdown of the nuclear power industry.

29 Submitting to extreme public pressure following Chernobyl, the SPD Right submitted to a proposal for an "exit" over a period of ten years, while the CDU/CSU and FDP have stubbornly held fast to their claims for the technological safety and economic necessity for nuclear energy. The detailed proposal is outlined in Die Grünen, "Der sofortige Ausstieg ist möglich," 1986.

30 This axis normally revolves around conserving existing structures or redressing existing dysfunctions. The most incisive analyst of this problem in Germany is undoubtedly Niklas Luhmann. For an abstract theoretical treatment, see the chapter "System und Umwelt" in his *Soziale Systeme*, 1987, pp. 242ff.

31 In the words of the 1980 program: "Nuclear energy is not safe, since the operation of nuclear installations leads to creeping radioactive contamination, and the catastrophe potential of the nuclear power plants and other nuclear installations represents an irresponsible, unanswerable risk (*ein nicht verantwortbares Risiko*), and because so far atomic waste cannot be disposed of." From *Bundesprogramm*, 1980, p. 10.

32 This is, of course, one of the principal dilemmas of green politics: they represent "universal" risks and interests which are hard to mobilize and organize. We will return to this issue below.

33 The technical term GAU – *größter, anzunehmender Unfall* – that is, "greatest, imaginable accident" or "worst-case scenario," has increasingly entered popular parlance since the meltdown of the nuclear reactor at Chernobyl.

34 Die Grünen, "Der sofortige Ausstieg," p. 27.

35 What makes this polemic particularly volatile is the fact that levels of risk and consequences demonstrate an inverse relation to each other – a meltdown is the least likely event but the one with the furthest reaching consequences.

36 This does not mean that the Greens completely abjure these sorts of cost–benefit calculations. They have been forced to engage conservative proponents of nuclear energy on their own terms. Obviously, conservative proponents of nuclear energy do not simply deny the existence of these risks – indeed, their risk projections and statistics sometimes form the basis of green arguments. (For instance, the "Sofortiger Ausstieg" pamphlet employs data from the notorious Rheinisch-Westfälisches Elektrizitätswerk and the SPD report on "Sichere

Sorgung ohne Atomenergie?") While pro-nuclear arguments do downplay and minimize risks, their strategy consists principally in stressing (and often exaggerating) the costs of eliminating nuclear power. The Greens have moved to guard this flank by contesting the existence or level of these costs and consequences. While some contentions, such as the oft-heard "the lights would go out," have been reliably disproved by the Greens, others lead to knottier arguments. For instance, abandoning nuclear energy would, at least in the short run, shift the full burden of producing electric power back on to the heavily polluting fossil fuel plants largely responsible for acid rain and diseased German forests. The Green exit scenario therefore foresees a strict clean-up program for coal- and oil-burning power plants. To the argument of increased energy prices, the Greens respond with a spartan calculation of an additional 7 DM per month per three person household. To the "lost jobs" argument used to mobilize union support, the Greens adduce the fact that a single conventional power plant employs as many workers as the entire German nuclear energy industry. See Die Grünen, "Der sofortige Ausstieg," pp. 4, 6–8, 11–12.

37   "Der sofortige Ausstieg," p. 14.
38   *Umbauprogramm*, p. 43.
39   The first step would be a four-year decontamination program for existing plants burning fossil fuels, using existing resources, such as high-tech filters and low-sulphur coal. In addition, all power plants would be required to have heat-coupling systems designed to pipe the warmth released in electricity production for home use. *Umbauprogramm*, p. 44.
40   *Bundestagswahlprogramm*, 1987, p. 37.
41   To encourage energy conservation by private consumers, the Greens advocate energy education for architects and building contractors; the creation of energy conservation agencies to dispense advice and financial support; organization of a special research and development program; and stricter building regulations. In addition, existing power rate structures would be changed so as to penalize heavy consumption. See ibid.
42   "Local [energy] networks would be transformed into communal property . . . essentially different from traditional energy provision in the following four points: need principle instead of acquisition principle; utilization orientation instead of supply orientation; democratization instead of continuing enterprise autonomy (*unternehmerische Verselbständigung*); participation instead of planning." In order to introduce a successful process of communalization, several intermediate steps would also be necessary: separating energy production and distribution by putting the power-line network in public hands and breaking up the energy monopolies. *Umbauprogramm*, pp. 43–5, and "Der sofortige Ausstieg," p. 14.
43   They are "ecological" because they are renewable. They are "democratic" because they lend themselves to decentralized application: even individual households can produce their own power cleanly and efficiently. And because of the underdevelopment of a corresponding industry and the labor intensity of alternative energy techniques, it would have "positive job market effects." As a positive political measure, the Greens therefore demand government provision of DM 4 billion over a four-year period for research programs and tax breaks to encourage the development and use of alternative energy technologies. Additionally, legislation would be passed legally obligating power companies to buy any surplus of privately produced power. "Der sofortige Ausstieg," pp. 18, 45, and *Umbauprogramm*, pp. 45–6.

44 "Der sofortige Ausstieg," p. 30.
45 It is the very incorporation of energy production into the capitalist relations of production which creates a "need" for atomic energy. Energy is not perceived as a limited social resource but as a commodity available in unlimited quantities. Thus, the power industry releases enormous amounts of irreplaceable energy in the form of warmth not because it would not be technologically feasible to trap and use it, but because it would not be "profitable." The industry price structure, decreasing unit prices with increased consumption, also serves to encourage public waste and the illusion of unlimited energy resources. See *Umbauprogramm*, pp. 42–3.
46 A book often cited in this context is E. F. Schumacher's *Small is Beautiful*, 1973, and to a lesser extent Kirkpatrick Sale's *The Human Scale*, 1980. Almost all of Ivan Illich's writings rest on this sort of industry/technology critique; see, for instance, *Tools for Conviviality*, 1973. For a more sober, empirically and historically grounded variant, see Michael Piore and Charles Sabel, *The Second Industrial Divide*, 1984, especially the sections on "flexible specialization."
47 Recent histories of the concept and history of German *Sozialpolitik* are Volker Hentschel, *Geschichte der deutschen Sozialpolitik, 1880–1980*, 1983; H. Lampert, *Sozialpolitik*, 1980; G. W. Brück, *Allgemeine Sozialpolitik*, 1976; and – unquestionably the most scrupulous and authoritative work – V. V. Bethusy-Huc, *Das Sozialleistungssystem der Bundesrepublik Deutschland*, 1976.
48 It objects that the classic liberal rights of free self-determination and full self-realization are not fulfilled in a classic liberal free-market – read "capitalist" – economy, except for the bourgeoisie. The existence of the worker as "wage laborer" remains bound to the labor market and his/her will as "abstract labor" is subjugated to the capitalist's organization of production.
49 *Umbauprogramm*, p. 11.
50 CDU ideologue Heiner Geißler discovered a "new social question," a conspiracy of organized capital and labor against the "non-organized, large families, single mothers with children, old people" and decried the plight of the "administered citizen" beset by an interventionist social bureaucracy. Heiner Geißler, *Verwaltete Bürger: Gesellschaft in Fesseln*, 1978.
51 One of the best analyses of the German variant of the neo-conservative ideology is Jürgen Habermas in *Die neue Unübersichtlichkeit*, 1986.
52 The two chief representatives of the steering/legitimation crisis thesis were Claus Offe, *Strukturprobleme des kapitalistischen Staates*, 1972, and Jürgen Habermas, *Legitimationsprobleme im Spätkapitalismus*, 1973. Both, like the German Left in general, have since rejected this thesis.
53 This classic analysis by Schumpeter was revived in Germany above all through James O'Connor's book, *The Fiscal Crisis of the State*, 1973.
54 For the SPD standpoint, see Johanno Straßer, *Grenzen des Sozialstaats?*, 2nd rev. edn, 1983. For the DGB position, see Erich Standfest, "Die Zukunft des Wohlfahrtstaates aus der Sicht der Gewerkschaften," *Sozialer Fortschritt*, 4, 1980, pp. 79ff.
55 This thesis of a commodification or functionalization of the reproductive sphere is advanced principally by the post-Fordist school in Germany and the regulationist school in France. See Joachim Hirsch and Roland Roth, *Das neue Gesicht des Kapitalismus*, 1985.
56 Although Habermas's provocative phrase falls often in the green milieu, the ambitious analysis behind it is not known or is regarded with great suspicion. See Jürgen Habermas, *Theorie des kommunikative Handelns*, vol. 2, 1981, pp. 489ff.

57 Michael Opielka, "Von der Krise zur Zukunft des Sozialstaats: Ansatzpunkte einer ökologischen Sozialpolitik," in Die Grünen, Baden-Württemberg, *Die Zukunft des Sozialstaats*, 1983, p. 30. The book offers a wide variety of green and left opinion.

58 In the document published after the Greens' congress in Sindelfingen, near Stuttgart, thus called "Sindelfingen program": Die Grünen, "Gegen Arbeitslosigkeit und Sozialabbau. Sinnvoll arbeiten solidarisch leben," 1983, p. 8.

59 Michael Opielka et al., "Umbau statt Abbau des Sozialstaats!" in Die Grünen, Baden-Württemberg, *Die Zukunft des Sozialstaats*, p. 288.

60 The Greens fix this minimal need at some DM 1,000 per month plus rent costs, to which an additional DM 200 per month supplement is reckoned for the elderly and the young. This is substantially above private levels, which may lay beneath the "poverty line" of DM 650 per month for many, such as working class widows or students. See ibid., pp. 96–7, and Die Grünen, "Freiheit von Armut."

61 *Umbauprogramm*, p. 95. The use of the word *entwürdigend* is a clear allusion to Article 1, Paragraph 1 of the Basic Law ("Die Würde des Menschen ist unantastbar"), often cited by leftist critics as an indictment of the existing order in the Federal Republic and interpreted as the foundation of the *Sozialstaatsgebot*.

62 For instance, because women receive wages considerably below their male counterparts, or none at all as housewives (although they make an equal work contribution to the household) they are structurally disadvantaged vis-à-vis men by the existing old-age pension system based on years in the work force and final salary. Secondly, the structural and financial gap between private sector and civil servant (*Beamten*) pensions would be evened out. Private sector pensions would also be structured as tax-financed benefits (rather than insurance based on premiums) and "excessive" civil service pensions reduced from a "reward" to a guarantee.

63 In order to remedy the discrepancies between the relatively good social benefit claims of privileged sections of the population . . . and the lesser claims of underprivileged sections . . . the social insurance system is to be unified." Sindelfingen program, p. 7.

64 Die Grünen, "Freiheit von Armut," 1988. A welfare recipient, for instance, may be subject to compulsory apartment searches to evaluate whether the living space exceeds their "needs" or whether the number of private possessions suggests outside aid or income. Similarly, a person receiving unemployment compensation who turns down work deemed "reasonable" (*zumutbar*) by the Arbeitsamt may be refused further benefits.

65 This applies especially to private health insurance. Opielka, et al., "Umbau statt Abbau," in Die Grünen, Baden-Württemberg, *Die Zukunft des Sozialstaats*, p. 294.

66 Sindelfingen program, p. 5.

67 *Bundestagswahlprogramm*, 1987, p. 47.

68 *Bundesprogramm*, p. 5.

69 *Umbauprogramm*, p. 10.

70 At present, most health insurance companies (*Krankenkassen*) which sell only health insurance charge a fixed rate. Although one may choose which firm one is insured by, one is legally obligated to purchase full coverage. The employer also pays a prescribed share of the insurance premium. However, white-collar employees, professionals and the rich in general often evade paying the full percentage of their income by purchasing private insurance, whose

premiums are more expensive than the payments to a normal *Krankenkasse* on an average income but lower than those for someone with a high income. Additionally, beyond a certain maximal premium one often no longer pays a fixed percentage. This, the Greens feel, is not only socially inequitable, but also robs the public healthcare system of considerable and needed funds.

71 Die Grünen, *Gesundheitspolitische Vorstellungen,* p. 10. For a more detailed analysis and representation of the Greens' stance on social distribution as a "money transfer from the social budget to capital incomes," see especially Michael Wunder and Jose Qaldueza's contributions in Die Grünen, *Die Grünen im Bundestag: Kritik des Gesundheitswesens und Alternativen,* 1986, pp. 33–41, 44–53.

72 *Gesundheitspolitische Vorstellungen,* p. 13.

73 *Bundestagswahlprogramm,* '87, p. 46.

74 *Gesundheitspolitische Vorstellungen,* p. 6.

75 *Umbauprogramm,* p. 86.

76 *Gesundheitspolitische Vorstellungen,* p. 19.

77 Ibid., p. 6.

78 Ibid., p. 7.

79 Ibid., p. 14.

80 *Gesundheitspolitische Vorstellungen,* p. 24.

81 Established under the guidance of the Keynesian SPD finance and economics minister, Karl Schiller, the "concerted action" (*konzertierte Aktion*) was a round-table gathering of representatives from the state, labor and capital. It was formally dissolved by labor's departure in 1978, when capital tried to have the Codetermination Act of 1976 declared unconstitutional. On "concerted action", see Rolf Seitenzahl, *Einkommenspolitik durch konzertierte Aktion and Orientierungsdaten,* 1974.

82 It was framed in a bundle of legislation stemming from the Allied occupation and the first years of the Adenauer government.

83 Rainer Erd, *Verrechtlichung industrieller Konflikte: Normative Rahmenbedingungen des dualen Systems der Interessenvertretung,* 1978.

84 Ibid., p. xi. A certain legal orientation and consciousness has long been an element of German trade-union politics. The union policy of legalism first emerged during the Weimar republic. See Klaus Schönhoven, *Die deutschen Gewerkschaften,* 1987, pp. 161–80.

85 On the concept of *kooperativer Gewerkschaftspolitik,* see Otto Jacobi, ed., *Kritisches Gewerkschaftsjahrbuch 1978,* 1978.

86 See Schönhoven, *Die deutschen Gewerkschaften,* p. 225.

87 On the basis of an empirical model, Adam Przeworski even claims that the German Social Democrats were the only European party which pursued this strategy optimally; see *Capitalism and Social Democracy,* 1985, esp. ch. 3.

88 This is of course the famous Piore/Sabel thesis.

89 "In the decade between 1970 and 1979, the number of those who participated in labor disputes [strikes] more than doubled in comparison to the previous ten years and the number of work days lost climbed threefold." Schönhoven, *Die deutsche Gewerkschaften,* p. 237.

90 For an extensive assessment of the politics of German labor relations and of the structure of trade unions in a historical perspective, see Andrei S. Markovits, *The Politics of the West German Trade Unions,* 1986.

91 IG Metall is the largest and among the most radical of the unions in the DGB.

92 Despite a growing ecology consciousness among progressive unionists, DGB top brass advanced an argument of a primacy of economy over ecology and of

jobs over pollution control. See *Deutscher Gewerkschaftsbund,* "Umweltschutz und qualitatives Wachstum," Mar. 1985, and *Gewerkschaftliche Monatshefte* 2/1985 with contributions from D. Wunder, H. Rappe, K. von Haaren and G. Döding. The IG Metall chief at the time, Hans Mayr, said in 1985: "When an ecological problem is only solvable by putting jobs in danger, then the jobs have first priority for me"; in *Frankfurter Rundschau,* Jan. 14, 1985.

93   The Greens have long denounced what they perceive as the longstanding alliance between capital and labor against the environment, based on a common and unmitigated commitment to economic growth to achieve higher wages and profits.

94   It ranks alongside Britain, the Netherlands and Belgium in this respect.

95   Roland Czada demonstrates econometrically that the national economy in the Federal Republic has undergone "the highest degree of modernization in which the adaptation of the labor market was accomplished by layoffs." This is in contrast to other countries, such as Great Britain, where the high level of unemployment is due to backward infrastructure and where the means of adapting the labor market was "cheapening labor." "Wirtschaftlicher Strukturwandel und Arbeitslosigkeit," *Leviathan,* 8, 1987, pp. 63–4.

96   For a fine empirical approach to this these see Gøran Therborn, "Nationale Politik der international Arbeitslosigkeit: Der Fall Bundesrepublik im Lichte der OECD-Daten von 1973–1985," *Leviathan,* 8, 1987, pp. 39–56. Since the Schmidt regime, faced with the trade-off between high inflation/monetary instability and high unemployment, the West German federal government has consistently opted for the latter. Contrary to popular opinion, this policy of sacrificing full employment for growth and stability did not begin with the fall of the Schmidt government and the ascension of the Kohl-led coalition in September 1982. Kohl continued Schmidt's policies in a more concrete way allowed by his different electoral constituency. See Douglas Webber, "Eine Wende in der deutschen Arbeitsmarktpolitik?, *Leviathan,* 8, 1987, pp. 74–85; Dieter Vesper, "Der Beitrag der Finanzpolitik zur Beschäftigungssicherung – Ein empirischer Befund" and Rüdiger Pohl, "Bundesbankpolitik in der Krise – Krise der Bundesbankpolitik," in Heinz Markmann and Diethard B. Simmer, eds, *Krise der Wirtschaftspolitik,* 1978. At the same time, the private economy, with massive financial support from the government, undertook a massive rationalization campaign which drastically increased productivity. In the area of job creation, the Federal Republic turned in one of the poorest performances of all major industrialized nations. The other nations with the poorest results were Belgium and the UK. See Therborn, "Nationale Politik," table 3, p. 45. In part, the overcrowding on the labor market has been ameliorated, or rather masked, by slowing and blocking new entries – for instance, by encouraging deficient training measures for young people and discouraging housewives from entering the labor market. See Blanke, et al., "Staatliche Sozialpolitik und die Regulierung der Nichterwebstätigkeit," *Leviathan,* 8, 1987, pp. 297–313.

97   It has relegated them to "marginal work groups" (*Randbelegschaften*), parttime employment and joblessness. This process of marginalization as a means of instilling and inspiring labor discipline is executed above all through the interventionary mechanisms of the social security system. The brutal effectiveness of this strategy is matched by its political invincibility, for these groups can be politically discredited and defamed, and it is difficult to mobilize them. For an excellent collection of analyses, see Stephan Leibfried and Florian Tennstedt, eds., *Politik der Armut und die Spaltung des Sozialstaats,* 1983.

98   Karl Hinrichs et al., "Der Streit um die Zeit: Die Arbeitszeit im gesellschafts-
     politischen und industriellen Konflikt," in Claus Offe et al., eds, *Arbeitszeit-
     politik: Formen und Folgen einer Neuverteilung der Arbeitszeit*, 1982, p. 8.
99   This rate of growth has been consistently estimated at 6 percent, a rate not
     achieved since the "economic miracle" or *Wirtschaftswunder.*
100 See Industriegesellschaft Metall, "Einheitsgewerkschaft: Solidarisches Handeln
     – Soziale Gegenmacht. Protokoll des 13. Ordentlichen Gewerkschaftstages der
     IG Metall in Berlin," 1980.
101 The volume by Offe et al., *Arbeitszeitpolitik*, based on a conference on the
     politics of working hours at the Center for Interdisciplinary Research at the
     University of Bielefeld is the best-known, most comprehensive and incisive
     Left/socialist treatment of this topic available.
102 The Greens do not view the 35-hour week as a "long-term final goal, but
     a short-range goal, which has to be reached as soon as possible." "Sofortmaßnah-
     men zur Arbeitsumverteilung", in Sindelfingen program.
103 Helmut Wiesenthal, "Arbeitszeitverkürzung – Arbeitsumverteilung," in Becken-
     bach, *Grüne Wirtschaftspolitik*, 1985.
104 *Umbauprogramm*, p. 58.
105 A gradual reduction in working hours spread out over a number of years
     would allow businesses to subvert the goal of job creation by introducing further
     rationalization measures to reduce total need for manpower – as advocated by
     steel-mill owners and printing managers during the tumultuous labor conflict
     of 1984 over the 35-hour week in which both the IG Metall and IG Druck und
     Papier (the printer's union) struck for over seven weeks in the spring and
     summer of 1984.
106 Eckhart Strattmann's speech in German Bundestag during the second reading
     of the Work Promotion Act on Mar. 29, 1984.
107 *Mehrarbeit* occurs when a worker's regular, contractual working time exceeds
     the normal, legal working week.
108 The bill is reprinted in Die Grünen, "Arbeitszeit-Forum – Arbeitszeitpolitik,"
     1984, pp. 76–81.
109 Statistical surveys for the Federal Republic have repeatedly confirmed that 90
     percent of those working in this category of job are women. See for instance
     Hinrichs, et al., "Der Streit um die Zeit."
110 Reprinted with supporting documents in Die Grünen, "Antidiskriminie-
     rungsgesetz," 3rd edn, 1986, pp. 14–67.
111 Marielouise Janssen-Jurreit, "Gesetze gegen die katastrophale Bescheidenheit
     der deutschen Frau," *Taz*, Mar. 5, 1986.
112 Appeals to the constitutional guarantee of equality between the sexes – which
     is confined to the household and does not extend to the public sector – have
     generally been unsuccessful. Specific legal guarantees as established first in the
     United States and Britain, later in Italy and France, were not then instituted
     in the Federal Republic. It was not until 1980 that the social–liberal coalition
     government passed a law adopting the European Community norms of sexual
     discrimination.
113 Paragraph 1, Article 2.
114 Ibid.
115 The controversy occurred within and round congresses held by women in the
     Greens during the final drafting of the bill in March and June, 1986. For a
     good overview of the conflicts and issues, see Tina Stadlmayer, "Wie stark darf
     Quotierung sein?", *Taz*, June 25, 1986.

116 Article 1.
117 Put into practice, it is clear that the highly leveraged legal machinery of the quota regulation would unleash no less than a revolution in the distribution of life chances, virtually excluding men from certain traditionally male career paths for decades. New entries to these professions would have to be all-female for many years to balance of the existing preponderance of men. Until the present generation of men in these professions retired, they would be effectively barred to men.
118 See "Begründung zur Generalklausel," in Die Grünen, "Antidiskriminierungsgesetz," p. 19.
119 Feminist lawyer Vera Slupik in Stadlmayer, "Wie Stark darf Quotierung sein?"
120 The law would require that all public and private employers submit yearly reports on their hiring and trading decisions to control agencies. It also sets harsh financial penalties for non-compliance. See Articles 10, 11, and 12 of the bill. Oversight and grievance processing would be placed under the jurisdiction of autonomous "women's agencies" (*Frauenbeauftragten*), Frauenbeauftragtengesetz, Article 1.
121 The "general justification" in Die Grünen, "Antidiskriminierungsgesetz," p. 17.
122 See the "justification for the Working Time Act" in "Arbeitszeitforum," p. 82.
123 Preamble to the Working Time Act in ibid.
124 In fact, the Greens have drafted a lengthy culture program entitled "Dem Struwelpeter durch die Haare gefahren: Auf dem Weg zu einer Grünen Kulturpolitik," 1987. It provides an interesting and occasionally frightening glimpse into "green culture," ranging from a Berlinesque anarchist underground to a revamped proletarian cultural policy.
125 Although its substantive discussion began earlier in the IG Metall, the phrase itself was first coined at the 9th federal congress of the DGB in June 1972. Deutscher Gewerkschaftsbund, "Protokoll des 9. Ordentlichen Bundeskongress des DGB, 25–30.6.1972."
126 See the documentation on the IG Metall's workshop: G. Friedrichs, ed., "Aufgabe Zukunft: Qualität des Lebens," 1972.
127 From Deutscher Gewerkschaftsbund, "Protokol des 9. Ordentlichen Bundeskongress," p. 181. And, at its 10th Federal Congress in 1975, the DGB formally incorporated the humanization of labor into its collective bargaining agenda. Deutscher Gewerkschaftsbund, "Protokol des 10. Ordentlichen Bundeskongress des DGB."
128 Among those concrete union demands which lie within the purvey of parliamentary responsibility (and not that of the "social partners"), most have been incorporated into either the Greens' anti-discrimination or labor time bills. They include extra breaks for assembly-line workers, longer and more frequent work pauses for everybody; and communal break times and spaces to promote interchange and discussion. They do not, however, get at the causes of boredom and strain in the work process itself; rather they try to make them more bearable.
129 From a purely constitutional point of view, the state could not legislatively compel a humanizing reorganization of the production process, nor would any set of general legal norms be sufficient to encompass the multiplicity of different situations.
130 *Umbauprogramm,* p. 64.
131 Ibid.
132 Ibid.
133 Die Grünen, "Vorschläge der Grünen." These rights, while anchored in the

Basic Law, do not fully apply within the context of the workplace. Hence the need to explicitly extend their validity.

134 Item 3 of the proposed revision of the Codetermination Act 1976, in ibid., p. 5.

135 They would include considerable influence on corporate planning as well as technical, organizational and temporal changes in the labor process. In ibid., p. 7.

136 In Rainer Erd's words, the juridification of collective bargaining means that "legislation and court rulings (*Rechtsprechung*) determine . . . what the unions and works' councils can agree upon under what specific question and with which means." Erd, *Verrechtlichung industrieller Konflikte*, p. 16. In practice, this has meant an orientation toward wage increases, the use of strikes only under tightly prescribed legal conditions, and the restriction of negotiations to the central organization; ibid., p. 22.

137 From the commentary accompanying the proposed revision of the Codetermination Act 1976 and the Works Constitution Act 1972 in Die Grünen, "Vorschläge der Grünen," p. 10.

138 This argument has had its proponents in both the Weimar and Bonn republics. On the former, see for instance, Otto Kirchheimer's essays, "Weimar – und was dann? Analyse einer Verfassung" in Otto Kirchheimer, *Politik und Verfassung*, 2nd edn, 1981, pp. 9–56, and "Legalität und Legitimität" in Kirchheimer, *Politische Herrschaft: Funf Beiträge zur Lehre vom Staat*, 4th edn, pp. 7–29. For a contemporary advocate of this position, see Ulrich K. Preuß, *Legalität und Pluralismus: Beitrage zum Verfassungsrecht der Bundesrepublik Deutschland*, 1973.

139 On the plant level, this means above all eliminating the clause in the Codetermination Act obligating the works council to "trustful cooperation" and prohibiting it from employing conflict measures (so-called *Friedenspflicht*) which "make works council activities in the interests of wage labor more difficult." See introduction to revision proposal, "Vorschläge der Grünen," p. 2.

140 Die Grünen, *Weder Waffenrock noch Schwesterkleid*, 1988.

141 See *Bundestagswahlprogramm*, p. 27, and Bundes-Arbeitsgemeinschaft Frieden der Grünen, "Einseitig abrüsten – wir machen den ersten Schritt. Friedenskonzept, 1987," 1986, p. 7.

142 First proclaimed by Pentagon pundits in 1973, it was caused among other things by the Soviets' achievement of strategic nuclear parity and the defeat in Vietnam. The nuclear deterrence of "mutual assured destruction" was no longer credible psychologically or technologically.

143 Richard Nixon's Secretary of Defense James Schlesinger had already broached a discussion on the "crisis of deterrence" during the early 1970s, which led to a turnaround of defense outlays under the Carter administration in 1977. Henry Kissinger, likewise, did much to bring this theme into public discussion during the late 1970s.

144 "Counterforce" means, most broadly, targeting military installations, missile silos and other strategic points to knock out the enemy's retaliatory capability. Its predecessor and antinomy was the "countervalue" strategy, which aims at having sufficient retaliatory capacity after any attack to inflict an equal amount of damage on the enemy by hitting civilian targets such as population centers.

145 By definition, a counterforce strategy implies the option of a first strike. And the principles of horizontal escalation and flexible response necessarily imply the option of choosing the location and scale of any military action.

146 The first to capture national attention was the leak of the Fiscal Year 1984–85 Defense Guidance papers to the *New York Times* in October, 1981.

147   Since it was not reasonable to expect the United States to risk its own existence in an all-out nuclear war to defend Europe, defense options at a lower level of escalation had to be created. By stationing American missiles in the Federal Republic, it became possible for the United States to be bound into a conflict to defend Europe without the immediate risk of sacrificing its own territory. It is important to recall, however, that the policy discussion which led to the double-track decision had begun much earlier and had been initiated by a West German. It was the then chancellor Helmut Schmidt who discovered the "missile gap" or "eurostrategic imbalance." It was supposed to have been brought about by the Soviet achievement of intercontinental nuclear parity. Schmidt launched the missile gap discussion which culminated in the double-track decision in a 1977 speech before the Institute for Strategic Studies in London. Correspondingly, the Pershing itself was tailored principally with the aim of strengthening the alliance. Since it was "use or lose" and under exclusive American control, the US would be automatically pulled into any showdown with the Soviets in Central Europe. By offering intermediate threats, they made it possible for America to engage in a nuclear exchange below the threshold of total, thermonuclear warfare, that is, to defend Europe without committing suicide.

148   In the Greens' pamphlet, "Necessary Footnotes to the NATO Double Decision," Gert Bastian, ex-Bundeswehr general turned green parliamentarian, debunked the official allied claims of Soviet military superiority in Europe used to legitimize the "modernization" of NATO's intermediate nuclear forces: the NATO figures represented not a different interpretation of the facts but a conscious distortion of them to sell the missiles to the western public. Die Grünen (Gerd Bastian), "Notwendig Anmerkungen zum NATO Doppelbeschluß," 1981.

149   The analysis entitled "Der Atomkrieg rückt näher" in the mini-book by Die Grünen, Baden-Württemberg, *Schlachtfeld Europa*, 1983, is one of the most extensive technical critiques of the euromissiles. See p. 28.

150   Ibid., p. 21.

151   Marie-Louise Beck-Oberdorf, "Wehrt euch gegen die Bedrohung – Wir wollen leben," in *Schlachtfeld Europa*, p. 7.

152   The Germans being like the victim African tribes tie to a tree to catch a lion; when the lion comes, the victim is killed, but the lion is trapped. The metaphor stems from Horst Afheldt and is cited in *Schlachtfeld Europa*, p. 46.

153   In Die Grünen, "Wir wollen leben!", 1983, p. 21.

154   Die Grünen, Baden-Württemberg, *Schlachtfeld Europa*, p. 12.

155   On this see Hedley Bull's fine article, "European Self-reliance and the Reform of NATO", *Foreign Affairs*, Spring 1983, pp. 874–92. On the crisis of NATO, see Earl C. Ravenal, "Europe without America: the Erosion of NATO," *Foreign Affairs*, Spring 1983, pp. 1020–35.

156   Indeed a group of Germans, including ex-SPD Minister of Defense Georg Leber, and CDU defense expert Alois Mertes violently opposed American voices calling for a no-first-use policy as a form of "decoupling." See Karl Kaiser et al., "Nuclear Weapons and the Preservation of Peace," *Foreign Affairs*, Summer 1982, pp. 1157–70. The Greens have often ignored the fact that first use (not to be confused with first strike) has been part of every American defense doctrine – "balanced collective forces," "massive retaliation," "mutual assured destruction," "flexible response" and "seamless web" – and supported above all by the West Germans.

157 This meant interspersing the ladder of escalation with more rungs to allow a response short of the irrational, premature and suicidal step of all-out nuclear confrontation. The US needed a war-fighting strategy capable of countering Soviet aggression or enforcing American interests without repeating the mistakes of Vietnam. This meant maximizing the comparative advantages of the US military, which consisted not in manpower but in technologically superior weaponry.

158 See the masterfully written and high influential article by McGeorge Bundy, F. Kennan, Robert S. McNamara and Gerard Smith, "Nuclear Weapons and the Atlantic Alliance," *Foreign Affairs*, Spring 1982, pp. 753–66, and Robert S. McNamara, "The Military Role of Nuclear Weapons: Perceptions and Misperceptions," *Foreign Affairs*, Fall 1983, pp. 59–80.

159 See above all the report of the ESECS leadership group, *Wege zur Stärkung der konventionellen Abschreckung in Europa: Vorschläge für die 80er Jahre*, 1983, and the Wörner-Wurzbach study commissioned by the CDU/CSU Bundestag delegation in May, 1982.

160 It was followed by a second, revised version, the "Rogers plan," trimmed in accord with various European grievances and named after the then NATO general commander General Rogers. In the following, we will refer only to ALB for the sake of simplicity.

161 ALB elaborated three new strategic principles: (1) the "integrated battlefield" meant that conventional, chemical and tactical nuclear weapons (grenades, mines, shells, etc.) would be used in a coordinated attack; (2) the "extended battlefield' meant that the offensive would extend beyond the front lines into preemptive attacks in the "enemy hinterlands"; (3) this was complemented by the "deep attack" against strategic targets – nuclear delivery systems, reserves, control and command installations.

162 See Department of the Army, *Field Manual 100–5*, Operations, Washington DC, Aug. 20, 1982, pp. 8–1, 10–1.

163 The coordinating committee chose ALB as one of its focal points for the time after deployment. The Greens held a conference and published a lengthy documentation on ALB. And the *Taz* began a concerted media campaign to publicize the new US strategy.

164 Strategically speaking, the Greens argue that the increased flexibility afforded by conventional, sub-theater strategies like ALB heightens rather than lowers the chance of escalation to nuclear conflict in Europe. This view is at variance with one of the main rationales behind the new conventional strategies, at least in the eyes of military planners, which was that it raised the threshold for a general, thermonuclear war, ironically, by lowering the threshold of military engagement.

165 Die Grünen, Baden-Württemberg, *Schlachtfeld Europa*, p. 8.

166 Ibid., p. A86.

167 Ibid., p. A69.

168 Although they also occasionally denounced the aggressiveness of Soviet leaders and strategists in the same tones, they did so less frequently, whereas they rarely failed to cite the militant posture of the Reagan administration, designating America as the "aggressive" and "warmongering" superpower. See "Angriff als Verteidigung", pp. 85–6, and *Schlachtfeld Europa*, pp. 50–6.

169 "The prospects for large sectors of US capital in this competitive battle are poor. In such a situation, it is tempting to instrumentalize the area in which

one always undisputedly played 'first fiddle,' namely the military, in order to bring oneself into a better position in the economic realm. And that is exactly the present US policy." See *Schlachtfeld Europa*, ch. 6, "US Weltmachtpolitik – US Globalstrategie und Kriegführungskonzepte für Europa," p. A66.

170 Behind the arms race and its "conventionalization," the Greens claim to espy a familiar constellation of interests: international capital, the arms industry, the military and their political allies. See ibid., esp. ch. 5, "Profit für den Frieden: ökonomische Aspekte der 'Konventionalisierung,'" pp. A51–A64.

171 In order to survive, capitalism must continually expand its markets and increase its profits. And in the face of "awakening national consciousness" and the "struggle for liberation" in the Third World, capitalism increasingly requires the support of an aggressive foreign policy to maintain the export of raw materials.

172 On this phenomenon, see Andrei S. Markovits, "On Anti-Americanism in West German," *New German Critique*, no. 34, Winter 1985, pp. 3–27.

173 Jean Pauer lays out the chain of thought on the USSR which follows from the Greens' revamped capitalist imperialism theory in four points:

1 In contrast to western capitalism, there is no economic mechanism in the so-called real, existing socialist countries which would produce a systemically determined interest in the maintenance of the armament complex.

2 Unlike under capitalism, which under pain of extinction must espouse economic growth and thereby an economically motivated expansion, there is no such immanent force in the real existing socialist states . . . .

3 The undeniable expansion of the Soviet Union after the World War II is explained by the suffering of the Soviet Union [under German attack and occupation] and the excessive anxiety complex of the Soviet power elite which emerged from it . . . .

4 The Soviet Union does not act exploitatively toward the Third World, but rather makes an "objectively" anti-imperialist contribution.

See Jean Pauer, "Wie Friedliebend ist die UdSSR? Die Grünen und Osteuropa. Anmerkungen zu einer laufenden Diskussion," *Kommune*, July 1985, p. 38. In this nicely written article, Pauer examines the unreflected "transport of old left *Weltbilder* from the pre-ecological period into green policy" from a critical but sympathetic leftist perspective.

174 The Soviet gerontocracy, so this argument went, was mainly interested in maintaining a geopolitical buffer zone around the "motherland." Competing with the United States, far from benefiting the Soviet Union, was destroying its economy. The arms race was therefore a consciously planned economic war against the Soviet people. The ascent of the USSR to second world power was of course completed in the form of militarily closing ranks with the US. "Angriff als Verteidigung", p. A66.

175 Petra Kelly, Torsten Lange, Henning Schierholz and Roland Vogt in Die Grünen, "Statt Krieg der Sterne, Abrüstung auf der Erde. SDI, EUREKA, und 'Europäische Verteidigungsinitiative,'" 1985.

176 See in ibid., Henning Schierholz, "SDI, EUREKA und das 'Europäische Raketenabwehrsystem,'" pp. 18–22.

177 See in ibid., "Reaktionsmöglichkeiten der UdSSR auf ein umfassendes BMD-System der USA aus technischer Sicht," pp. 64–8.

178 Die Grünen, "Ohne Waffen aber nicht wehrlos: Das Konzept der Sozialen Verteidigung", 2nd edn, 1987, p. 4.
179 Die Grünen, *Bundestagswahlprogramm 1990*, 1990, p. 4.
180 Ibid., p. 5.
181 Ibid., pp. 8–10.
182 Ibid., pp. 11–12.
183 Ibid., p. 16.
184 Ibid., p. 12.
185 Ibid., p. 13.
186 Ibid., pp. 14–15.
187 With the inevitable decline of NATO's importance as a consequence of the Cold War's demise, the Western European Union has enjoyed a hitherto unparalleled prominence. Central to it is, of course, the Franco-German axis which has attained a new military dimension with the formation of a joint brigade. There are plans to have this brigade become the origin of a fully fledged European army which presumably would render NATO completely redundant. For the Greens' criticism of the WEU and the Franco-German military alliance in general, see Regenbogenfraktion im Europaparlament der Grünen. *Bundesrepublik und Frankreich: Nicht Militärkumpanei, sonder Völkerfreundschaft!* (n.d.).
188 *Bundestagswahlprogramm*, 1990, pp. 20–1.
189 Ibid., p. 23.
190 Ibid., p. 22.
191 Ibid., p. 24.
192 Ibid.
193 On the debate between the trade unions and the Lafontaine wing of the Social Democratic Party concerning the deregulation of work time, see Christopher S. Allen, "Trade Unions, Worker Participation, and Flexibility: Linking the Micro to the Macro," *Comparative Politics*, 22. 3, April 1990, pp. 253–73; Andrei S. Markovits and Christopher S. Allen, "The Trade Unions," in Gordon Smith et al., eds., *Developments in West German Politics*, 1989, pp. 289–307.
194 *Bundestagswahlprogramm, 1990*, p. 25.
195 Ibid., p. 25.
196 Ibid., pp. 26–7.
197 Ibid., p. 28.
198 Ibid., pp. 30–1.
199 Ibid., p. 32.
200 Ibid., pp. 32–5.
201 Ibid., p. 36.
202 Ibid. The Verfassungsschutz is the rough German equivalent to the American Federal Bureau of Investigation. One of a number of German policing organizations, its special mandate has been the tracking of people whom the state deemed dangerous to the Federal Republic's constitutional order. Hence the name which translates literally into "Protection of the Constitution." By placing the word "Schutz," i.e. protection, between quotation marks, the Greens convey their rather cynical view and negative feelings regarding the protective nature of this organization.
203 Ibid., p. 37.
204 Ibid.
205 Ibid., p. 37.
206 Ibid., pp. 38–9.

Chapter 7 Politics

1   The term is borrowed from Werner Hülsberg, *The German Greens*, trans. Gus Fagan, 1987.

2   The preceding three phases have been examined in Hülsberg, *German Greens*, pp. 77–107; Lillian Klotzsch and Richard Stöß, "Die Grünen," in Klotzsch and Stöß, eds, *Parteienhandbuch*, 1983.

3   Anna Hallensleben, *Von der Grünen Liste zur Grünen Partei*, 1984, p. 62. Hallensleben's book is the only genuinely comprehensive study of the formation of a green regional party and despite a sometimes excessive detail and thoroughness which distracts from the narrative is an indispensable resource for an understanding of the deeper roots of the movement for a green party.

4   They were generally over 30 – in some local organizations the average age was even between 40 and 60 – and most were integrated into working life. See ibid., pp. 50, 54, 141.

5   Ibid., p. 63.

6   As KdA veteran Georg Otto suggested at the founding convention, "electoral participation" was to be seen as "an additional means of the citizens' initiatives," working as a pressure group by "channeling off votes." See Hallensleben, *Von der Grünen Liste*, p. 62.

7   Ibid., p. 25.

8   Hülsberg, *German Greens*, p. 82.

9   Ibid., p. 84.

10 Hallensleben, *Von der Grünen Liste*, pp. 90–2.

11 Ibid., p. 92.

12 Hulsberg, *German Greens*, p. 84.

13 Hallensleben, *Von der Grünen Liste*, p. 150.

14 Ibid., p. 132.

15 For a more detailed history and documentation on the Alternative List, see Michale Bühnemann, et al., *AL: Die Alternative Liste Berlin*, 1984.

16 Hülsberg, *German Greens*, p. 92.

17 Ibid., p. 90.

18 Hallensleben, *Von der Grünen Liste*, p. 170.

19 See Rold Meyer and Günter Handlögten, "Die Grünen vor der Wahl," *Aus Politik und Zeitgeschichte*, no. 3, 1981, p. 7.

20 See Aline Kuntz, "From *Spiegel* to Flick: the Maturation of the West German *Parteienstaat*," in Andrei S. Markovits and Mark Silverstein, eds, *The Politics of Scandal*, 1988.

21 "Für SPD-Dialog mit Grünen: Grundwerte Kommission legt ihr Diskussionpapier vor," *Frankfurter Rundschau*, Dec. 3, 1982.

22 Reprinted as "Kanzler: Für SPD sind Grünen kein Partner," *Frankfurter Rundschau*, Mar. 17, 1982.

23 Richard Löwenthal, "Identität und Zukunft der SPD," *Gewerkschaftliche Umschau*, Jan./Feb. 1982.

24 "SPD im Bundestag sperrt sich gegen Grünen; Roth: chaotisch; Ehmke: Kein Koalitionspartner . . ." *Frankfurter Rundschau*, Mar. 20, 1983.

25 "Ravens bringt Grüne ins Gespräch," *Frankfurter Allgemeine Zeitung*, Feb. 23, 1982.

26 SPD 55 seats, CDU 56, GAL 9, FDP 0. "Klose: Mit GAL kooperieren," *Frankfurter Rundschau*, June 11, 1982.

27 "GAL-Angebot an die SPD," *Frankfurter Rundschau*, June 14, 1982.

28 "Hamburger SPD ziert sich noch: Gespräche mit GAL erst nach Kieps Scheitern," *Frankfurter Allgemeine Zeitung,* June 18, 1982.

29 "Hamburgs SPD lädt Grüne ein," *Frankfurt Rundschau,* July 2, 1982.

30 "Nur strapaziös oder ruinös? Die Verhandlungen der Hamburger SPD mit den Grün-Alternativen."

31 "Der Sonderfall Hamburg," *Frankfurter Rundschau,* Aug. 13, 1982.

32 "Wenn SPD bis dahin keine dicken Hirsche schieBt . . . GAL und SPD in Hamburg. Gespräche über Sachfragen Aufgenommen," *Frankfurter Rundschau,* July 8, 1982.

33 "Dohnanyi läßt sich von Schmidt u. Börner nicht beirren; Hamburgs Bürgermeister verteidigt Gespräche mit GAL," *Frankfurter Rundschau,* Aug. 17, 1982.

34 "Forderung nach Neuwahlen bringt Dohnanyi um die Contenance; GAL und SPD beschließen Kreditermachtigung," *Frankfurter Allgemeine Zeitung,* Aug. 17, 1982.

35 "Hamburger SPD in Zerreissprobe; GAL will Hamburg zu einer atom-waffenfreien Zone erklären," *Frankfurter Allgemeine Zeitung,* Sept. 1, 1982.

36 "GAL bringt Dohnanyis SPD größte Verlegenheit," *Frankfurter Allgemeine Zeitung,* Aug. 9, 1982.

37 "Für Gespräche mit GAL," *Frankfurter Rundschau,* Aug. 4, 1982.

38 "Hafenausbau kamm zum größten Zankapfel werden," *Frankfurter Rundschau,* Aug. 13, 1982.

39 "Neuwahlen lediglich eine Flucht (Dohnanyi)," *Frankfurter Rundschau,* Aug. 18, 1982.

40 "Dohnanyi u. Kose verlangen von Klose Kompromisse," *Frankfurter Rundschau,* Oct. 8, 1982.

41 "SPD ist nicht lemfähig; GAL entäuscht," *Frankfurter Rundschau,* Oct. 9, 1982.

42 "Hamburger SPD billigt Entscheidung für Wahlen im Dezember Entschiedene Absage an Grosse Koalition," *Frankfurter Rundschau,* Oct. 13, 1982.

43 "Mehrheit für Auflösung der Hamburger Bürgerschaft; Auch GAL für Neuwahlen am 19. Dezember," *Frankfurter Rundschau,* Oct. 25, 1982.

44 "GAL für Gesprache mit SPD weiter offen," *Frankfurter Allgemeine Zeitung,* Oct. 19, 1982.

45 "SPD zum Tanzen bringen; Im Hamburger Wahlkampf legen GAL neu gefasste Forderungen vor," *Frankfurter Allgemeine Zeitung,* Dec. 2, 1982.

46 Ibid.

47 "Absolute Mehrheit für SPD in Hamburg," *Frankfurter Allgemeine Zeitung,* Dec. 20, 1982; "Berliner Abgeordnete gewählt; Erstmals Vertreter der AL im Bundestag," *Frankfurter Rundschau,* Mar. 7, 1983.

48 "Grüne vom Ergebnis überrascht," *Frankfurter Allgemeine Zeitung,* Dec. 21, 1982.

49 "Genscher ärgert SPD-Flirt mit Grünen," *Frankfurter Rundschau,* July 5, 1982.

50 "Thema Koalition mit Grünen erregt Bonner Parteien," *Frankfurter Rundschau,* July 5, 1982.

51 Ibid.

52 "Skandalöse Äußerungen, Grüne contra Börner," *Frankfurter Rundschau,* July 5, 1982.

53 "Hessische Grüne wollen keine Koalition eingehen," *Frankfurter Rundschau,* Feb. 8, 1982

54 "Grüne Grundsätze," *Frankfurter Rundschau,* Aug. 16, 1982.

55 The distribution of seats was as follows: CDU 52, SPD 49, Greens 9. See "Realität

verdrängt bald Freude über Erfolg; Hessens Grüne nach Wahl; Viel ist von SPD die Rede," *Frankfurter Rundschau*, Sept. 28, 1982.

56   "Wiesbaden macht sich auf die Suche nach der Mehrheit," *Frankfurter Rundschau*, Sept. 28, 1982.

57   Ibid.

58   "Hessens Grüne strecken Fühler zu Landtagsparteien aus," *Frankfurter Rundschau*, Oct. 9, 1982.

59   "Börner signalisiert Grünen Einlenken," *Frankfurter Rundschau*, Oct. 21, 1982.

60   "Grüne: Börners Schwenk um 180 Grad . . ." *Frankfurter Rundschau*, Oct. 22, 1982.

61   Börner was not compelled to have a formal coalition partner under the Hessian constitution. When no majority exists and no new prime minister is elected, the previous prime minister may remain in office as "chief parliamentary executive" (*parlamentarischer Geschäftsführer*).

62   State elections in the spring would coincide with the Bundestag election, yielding low electoral participation which tends to hurt the Social Democrats more than the CDU/CSU or the FDP.

63   "Grüner Apfel u. Bauchschmerzen der Umweltschützer," *Frankfurter Rundschau*, Jan. 22, 1983.

64   "SPD in Hessen setzt auf Sieg," *Frankfurter Rundschau*, Aug. 15, 1983.

65   "Kritik an Fuhrung der hessischen SPD," *Frankfurter Allgemeine Zeitung*, Mar. 29, 1983.

66   "Öko-soziale Alternative wichtiger dennje," *Frankfurter Rundschau*, May 14, 1983.

67   "Südhessische SPD denkt an Koalition mit Grünen," *Frankfurter Allgemeine Zeitung*, May 30, 1983.

68   "Hessens SPD will Zusammenarbeit mit Grünen," *Frankfurter Allgemeine Zeitung*, May 30, 1983.

69   The SPD improved its share of seats by 2 to 51. The Greens lost 2, slumping to 7. The FDP reentered the Landtag again with 8 of the CDU's seats, bringing the conservative-liberal bloc's total to 54. "Mit dem Schwenk der FDP fing alles an," *Frankfurter Rundschau*, Nov. 22, 1984.

70   "Hessens Grüne bieten SPD Zusammenarbeit an," *Frankfurter Rundschau*, Oct. 3, 1983.

71   "Der Chef garantiert Solidarität des Experimentes," *Frankfurter Rundschau*, Nov. 7, 1983.

72   "SPD u. Grüne in Hessen beginnen Verhandlungen," *Frankfurter Rundschau*, Nov. 15, 1983.

73   The SPD's pre-negotiation statement contained a revised investment program favoring smaller – read decentralized – firms as well as a temporary, perhaps even permanent, stay on construction of the Biblis nuclear reactor. See "Nassrasieren u. kontinuierliche Zusammenarbeit," *Frankfurter Allgemeine Zeitung*, Nov. 12, 1983.

74   As Horst Winterstein elaborated some of their demands: "Vocational training for young people, active employment policies and consequential environmental protection." See "Spierlraum für Verhandlung nicht eingeengt," *Frankfurter Rundschau*, Nov. 12, 1983.

75   "SPD u. Grüne verhandeln in gereizter Atmosphäre," *Frankfurter Allgemeine Zeitung*, Nov. 15, 1983.

76   "Hektik vor historischem Moment," *Frankfurter Rundschau*, Jan. 11, 1984.

77   "Börner: In Wiesbaden bald wieder eine gewählte Regierung," *Frankfurter Allgemeine Zeitung*, Jan. 2, 1984. They included dropping two proposed garbage dumps, "more humanized" policies toward foreigners, cancellation of

construction of two new prisons, less money for road construction and a rule against night flights at the Frankfurt airport. See "Sechs Bedingungen der Grünen für SPD-Bündnis," *Frankfurter Rundschau*, Mar. 15, 1984.

78 "Hessens Grüne stellen neue Forderungen an SPD," *Frankfurter Allgemeine Zeitung*, May 9, 1984.

79 "Zu geständnisse Börners an Grünen," *Frankfurter Allgemeine Zeitung*, May 16, 1984.

80 The Minister of Finance, Herbert Reitz, publicly announced his resignation, giving a personal analysis but not openly challenging Börner's course. Further dissent, also on a small scale, was evident during the long-awaited election of Börner as prime minister on June 7, 1984. Several invalid ballots were reasoned to have been cast by SPD members. See "SPD u. Grüne wählen Börner zum Ministerpräsident," *Frankfurter Allgemeine Zeitung*, June 8, 1984.

81 "Grüne sprechen Börner das Vertrauen aus," *Frankfurter Allgemeine Zeitung*, July 5, 1984.

82 This was the view of Paul Giani, one of the powerful rightists in the Hessian SPD. See "SPD u. Grüne: Hörden werden kleiner," *Frankfurter Allgemeine Zeitung*, July 27, 1984.

83 Halting their construction had been one of the Green's six demands for passing the 1984 budget. As green delegate Kem had said ominously about the demands: "Even if just one single prison is built, then there won't be any votes for Börner."

84 "Wilde Beziehungskiste in Wiesbaden," *Frankfurter Rundschau*, Oct. 18, 1984.

85 See "Zunächst einmal Werbung für rot-Grüne Bundnis in Wiesbaden," *Frankfurter Allgemeine Zeitung*, Nov. 19, 1984; "Nach dem Bruch in Hessen," *Frankfurter Allgemeine Zeitung*, Nov. 22, 1984; "Kaum Chancen für Neubeginn des Bündnisses," *Frankfurter Allgemeine Zeitung*, Nov. 23, 1984.

86 "Die Reifeprüfung" and "Den Grünen ihre Widersprüche vorhalten," *Frankfurter Rundschau*, Dec. 1, 1984.

87 See "Grüne wollen Bündnis retten," *Frankfurter Rundschau*, Dec. 3, 1984; "Absage oder Angebot?" *Frankfurter Rundschau*, Dec. 3, 1984.

88 "Börner ruft Grüne zu Bündnissen auf," *Frankfurter Rundschau*, Mar. 12, 1985.

89 "Börners Regierungserklärung," *Taz*, May 13, 1985.

90 See: "Platzt Koalition in Hessen doch noch?" *Taz*, May 12, 1985; "Zweckbündnis unter hessischen Verhältnissen," *Frankfurter Allgemeine Zeitung*, Oct. 18, 1985; "Börner Koalition sieht ein Lehrstück für sozialdemokratisches Verhalten," *Frankfurter Allgemeine Zeitung*, Oct. 18, 1985.

91 The entire Fundi-controlled federal executive committee with the single exception of Norbert Kostede expressed positions ranging from skepticism to opposition. See "Bundesvorstand der Grünen hält nichts von Wiesbadener Koalitionsabsprache," *Frankfurter Allgemeine Zeitung*, Oct. 22, 1985.

92 "In Wiesbaden nicht die Vision eines Kompromisses am Horizont," *Frankfurter Allgemeine Zeitung*, Oct. 16, 1985.

93 On October 30, 1984.

94 Erhard Eppler insisted that "wherever one can accomplish constructive work with the Greens one should do so"; and Brandt chimed in again with his formula about the majority left of the Union once more. See "Brandts Rechenexempel hat zuviele Unbekannte," *Frankfurter Allgemeine Zeitung*, Nov. 22, 1984.

95 The survey appeared on June 19, 1984.

96 In the *Rheinische Post*, Aug. 7, 1984.

97 Richard Niehoff said, "I am firmly proceeding from the assumption that the Greens will get into the state parliament." In *Westdeutsche Allgemeine Zeitung,* Apr. 16, 1985.

98 As subsequently related to the author during interviews with business-manager Martin Pannan, June 15, 1985, Düsseldorf and party-speaker Thomas Hoof, May 27, 1985, Düsseldorf.

99 See *Bonner Rundschau,* Aug. 1, 1984.

100 It also included a "middle-range end to expanding power plants burning brown coal," a program against unemployment, and opposition to Bonn's plans for a cable television network. See *Frankfurter Rundschau,* Dec. 17, 1984.

101 *Rheinische Post,* Feb. 2, 1985.

102 *Frankfurter Rundschau,* Mar. 16, 1985.

103 Ibid.

104 Such as *Bild* and Cologne's *Express.*

105 Henrich Schnoor, NRW's Minister of the Interior, proclaimed it further proof of the "complete political incompetence" of the Greens. *Frankfurter Rundschau,* Mar. 16, 1985.

106 See *Die Tageszeitung,* Dec. 15 and 18, 1984.

107 *Die Tageszeitung,* May 17, 1985.

108 William R. Doemer, "Key Vote for Kohl," *Time,* June 30, 1986.

109 Günter Bannas, "Je linker, desto aussichtsreicher," *Frankfurter Allgemeine Zeitung,* May 21, 1986.

110 Chernobyl, combined with positive results in the local elections in Schleswig-Holstein finally claimed the mood of impending crisis which had prevailed since the electoral catastrophes in NRW and the Saar. See Ursel Sieber, "Aufwind durch die Katastrophen? – Die Grünen vor ihrem Bundesparteitag," *Die Tageszeitung,* May 15, 1986.

111 An allusion to Günter Anders's well-known book, *Hiroshima is Everywhere,* this phrase later won great currency within the West German Left and the anti-nuclear movement.

112 See the text of Ditfurth's speech in the hefty protocol of the congress in *Grüner Basis Dienst,* nos 7–9, 1986, p. 18.

113 See Trampert's speech in ibid., p. 22.

114 See Joachim Wille, "Das Neue Testament war nicht gefragt," *Frankfurter Rundschau,* May 20, 1986.

115 Biblis was the largest nuclear plant in Hesse and was undergoing a considerable expansion at that time. The firms which have a monopoly on producing fuel rods and processing and transporting nuclear waste in the Federal Republic are in Hanau.

116 See *Grüner Basis-Dienst,* nos 7–9, 1986, p. 5.

117 As in the United States, the German federal system assigns different legal purviews to the states (Länder) and the federal government. In both countries nuclear power falls predominantly under federal jurisdiction.

118 The final compromise on the "Hessen statement" demanded little more than "concrete steps" before the end of 1986 and a shutdown of state nuclear plants by the end of the legislative period. "It was mainly a vote of mistrust for the Realist politicians within one's own party." See "Dauerkonflikt," *Die Zeit,* May 23, 1986.

119 See Oliver Tolmein, "Grüne radikale Mehrheit auf Kompromißkurs," *Tageszeitung,* May 20, 1986.

120 Ibid.

121 Ibid. NATO was still characterized as the alliance which steadily propelled the arms race; yet rather than be destroyed, it was only to be "weakened." In terms of public relations, however, the nuances were for naught.

122 *The Frankfurter Allgemeine Zeitung* headlined "NATO-Austritt und Abschaffung der Bunderswehr im Wahlprogramm der Grünen." The *Suddeutsche Zeitung* declared "Austritt der Bundesrepublik aus der NATO gefordert." The foreign press – *The Times* of London, *International Herald Tributne, Le Figaro and Le Monde* – also emphasized green opposition to NATO in their reports to the exclusion of all other issues.

123 Interview in the German television news program "Heute," May 20, 1986.

124 The rumor went back to a bogus news agency report wildly exaggerated in subsequent reports. See Martin Winter, "Verletzung nicht beklatscht," *Frankfurter Rundschau*, July 3, 1986.

125 See Matthias Naß, "Wir haben einen Elfmeter vergeben," *Die Zeit*, June 20, 1986.

126 See for instance "Grüne ruinieren das Land: Harte Attacken der Koalition vor der Niedersachsen Wahl," *Frankfurter Rundschau*, June 5, 1986.

127 "Wir haben gewonnen, aber eben nicht gesiegt." Interview on "Heute," June 15, 1986.

128 Interview in Suddetusche Rundfunk program "Journal," June 16, 1986.

129 See Jürgen Voges, "Die geplatzten Träume der Grünen," *Die Tageszeitung*, June 18, 1986.

130 See the summary of the Infas Institut analysis, "Der Wähler hielt sich an vertaute Muster," *Süddeutsche Zeitung*, June 18, 1986.

131 See Voges, "Die geplatzten Träume."

132 See "Auf der Party der Grünen wurde es still", *Die Welt*, June 16, 1986.

133 See Naß, "Wir haben einen Elfmeter vergeben." For Jütta Ditfurth, the election was a "good success but not an overwhelming one." See Günter Bannas, "Die Grünen sind mit sich unzufrieden," *Frankfurter Allgemeine Zeitung*, June 18, 1986. Lukas Beckmann argued somewhat perlexingly that the gap between the 80– 90 percent of the population upset over Chernobyl and the 7 percent who voted for the Greens represented a "lack of democracy." See Klaus Hartung, "Mangel an Demokratie," *Die Tageszeitung*, June 18, 1986.

134 See Hartung, "Mangel an Demokratie."

135 See interview with Fischer by Hans-Helmut Kohl, "Mehr auf die Leute zugehen," *Frankfurter Rundschau*, June 18, 1986.

136 See Günter Bannas, "Die Grünen sind mit sich unzufrieden," *Frankfurter Allgemeine Zeitung*, June 18, 1986.

137 See Hans-Helmut Kohl's interview with Fischer, *Frankfurter Rundschau*, June 18, 1986.

138 "Stahlkügelfraktion" is an allusion to the use of steel balls as sling-shot ammunition by the anarchist Autonomen during demonstrations. At the same time, it implicitly places them on the same level as the so-called far-right "Stahlhelmfraktion" of the CDU, known for its authoritarian tendencies. The Autonomen and other groupings who approve of violent resistance are particularly strongly represented in the German anti-nuclear movement. This "steel-ball faction" was subjected to especially harsh criticism in a Realo paper by Helmut Wiesenthal and Norbert Kostede. For a summary, see Voges, "Die geplazten Träumen."

139 Ruth Hammerbacher, top candidate for the Greens in the Lower Saxony election in a group interview, "Umarmen bis ihnen die luft augeht," *Die Tageszeitung*, July 2, 1986.

140 See Bannas, "Die Grünen sind mit sich unzufrieden."
141 See Naß, Wir haben einen Elfmeter vergeben."
142 See Oliver Tolmein, "Das kleinste gemeinsame Radikale," *Die Tageszeitung*, May 20, 1986.
143 See "Prominente Grüne sollen nach Bonn zurück," *Süddeutsche Zeitung*, July 14, 1986; Dieter Bauer, "Grüne gönnen Petra Kelly nur dem fünften Platz," *Süddeutsche Zeitung*, July 28, 1986.
144 See Martin Winter, "Die alte Streitlüst kam erst beim Thema SPD auf," *Frankfurter Rundschau*, Sept. 29, 1986; Bernd Siegler, "Kein Demoaufruf – der Wahl zuliebe," *Die Tageszeitung*, Sept. 29, 1986.
145 See Astrid Hölscher, "Neuer Geist der Grünen," Frankfurter Rundschau, Sept. 29, 1986.
146 See Winter, "Die alte Streitlust."
147 See Siegler, "Kein Demoaufruf."
148 The Bavarian state party had already repeatedly distanced itself from demonstrator violence at the Wackersdorf site. See Max-Hermann Bloch, "Bayers Grünen wollen gewaltfrei auftreten," *Augsburger Allgemeine*, June 2, 1986.
149 See Hölscher, "Neuer Geist der Grünen."
150 Ibid.
151 See Ursel Sieber, "Realos wollen abwarten," *Die Tageszeitung*, Sept. 25, 1986.
152 See Ursel Sieber and B. Siegler, "Mit angelegten Flügeln in der Wahl," *Die Tageszeitung*, Sept. 29, 1986.
153 Ibid.
154 Excerpt from "Bündnispolitische Erklärung," in Bernd Siegler, "Rot-grünes Blockdenken irreal," *Die Tageszeitung*, Sept. 27, 1986. A favorite Fundi tactic in NRW and Hamburg had been to vote for a formal coalition offer but to set the preconditions so high as to make negotiation impossible, thereby showing how "reactionary" the SPD "really" was. Helmut Wiesenthal, NRW Realo and professor of sociology in Bielefeld had rejected this tactic for theoretical reasons earlier that spring. See Helmut Wiesenthal, "Vorschläge zur Wahrnehmung politischer Chancen," *Die Tageszeitung*, Apr. 2, 1986.
155 The formally liberal right to political asylum and immigration in the Federal Republic, a constitutional legacy of the Holocaust, has been progressively limited through bureaucratic means. Ultra-rightist forces such as Strauß's CSU and Schönhuber's Republicans in Bavaria had propagated a "Germany for Germans" policy during the election under the pretext of abuses and labor surpluses, proposing for the first time actual constitutional and legislative changes in the right to asylum. Moderate forces within the CDU, such as Heiner Geißler and Rita Süssmuth, vehemently opposed Strauß, as did Genscher's FDP. As already discussed in chapter 6 under the Greens' position on "multicultural democracy," the issue of asylum and foreign immigration had become the most politically salient issue in Germany by 1992, well beyond anything imaginable in 1987.
156 The number of candidates from each state party's electoral list who actually receive a mandate depends on the percentage received by the party in the national election. This means that in all those cases where the total number of candidates from a state list who receive mandates is odd, women will automatically constitute the majority of the delegates.
157 They had narrowly missed the critical margin for entering the Bavarian legislature in 1983 when they received 4.6 percent. See Klaus Ott, "Gedämpfte

Freude bei den Grünen," *Süddeutsche Zeitung*, Oct. 14, 1986; "Erfolg der Grünen im zweiten Anlauf," *Die Welt*, Oct. 13, 1986.

158 See Andrei S. Markovits, *The Politics of the West German Trade Unions*, 1986.

159 Thomas Ebermann flatly stated the Greens' fears to the SPD manager Peter Glotz: "The present strategy of the SPD is designed to destroy the Greens." See the interview with Glotz and Ebermann, "Es wird keine rot-grüne Mehrheit geben," *Stern*, Nov. 27, 1986.

160 See interview with Antje Vollmer and Christa Nickels, "Warten auf Willy," *Wirtschaftswoche*, Nov. 27, 1986.

161 See "Grüne: Man wählt das Abenteuer," *Der Spiegel*, Jan. 12, 1987.

162 See Horst Bieber, "Auf die Promis kommt es an," *Die Zeit*, Jan. 16, 1987.

163 See "Grüne: Man wählt das Abenteuer," *Der Spiegel*, Jan. 12, 1987.

164 See Michael Stiller, "Hinüber zum anderen Ufer," *Süddeutsche Zeitung*, Jan. 15, 1987; Christian Schneider, "Wahlkämpfer ohne Zwangsjacke," *Süddeutsche Zeitung*, Jan. 16, 1987.

165 See Ursel Sieber, "Wenn das Spielbein zum Standbein wird . . ." *Die Tageszeitung*, Jan. 13, 1987.

166 Ibid.

167 For a list of the new green delegates, see "Die neuen Bundestags-Grünen," *Die Tageszeitung*, Jan. 27, 1987.

168 See Günter Bannas, "Die Grünen sprechen von einer historischen Wahl," *Frankfurter Allgemeine Zeitung*, Jan. 27, 1987.

169 See Günter Bannas, "Otto Schily ist der Mann des Abends," *Frankfurter Allgemeine Zeitung*, Jan. 26, 1987.

170 See the fine article by Claus Offe, "Zwischen Protest – und Parteipolitik," *Die Zeit*, Oct. 10, 1986.

171 See Günter Bannas, "Schily fühlt sich als Mohr, und Ebermann strahlt," *Frankfurter Allgemeine Zeitung*, Feb. 6, 1987.

172 Schily in a radio interview, quoted in *Frankfurter Allgemeine Zeitung*, Feb. 6, 1987.

173 Ibid.

174 "Wenn wir untergehen, dann aufrecht," *Der Spiegel*, Feb. 16, 1987.

175 "Die Grünen drohen mit Aufkundigung der Koalition in Wiesbaden," *Frankfurter Allgemeine Zeitung*, Feb. 9, 1987.

176 "Börner entläßt Umweltminister Fischer: Neuwahlen im Frühjahr wahrscheinlich," *Süddeutsche Zeitung*, Feb. 10, 1987.

177 "Börner gibt auf. Verzicht auf den Landesvorsitz und auf die Kandidatur als Regierungschef," *Frankfurter Allgemeine Zeitung*, Feb. 11, 1987.

178 See text of Börner's letter to Fischer, *Süddeutsche Zeitung*, Feb. 10, 1987, and the interview with Börner in *Der Spiegel*, Feb. 16, 1987.

179 See Gerhard Spörl, "Ein Vatermord auf Raten," *Die Zeit*, Feb. 13, 1987.

180 See Gerhard Spörl, "Die Macht fest im Blick," *Die Zeit*, Feb. 27, 1987.

181 Ibid.

182 See Claus Brill, "Spaltet Aussicht auf Mitregierung?" *Süddeutsche Zeitung*, Mar. 7–8, 1987, and an interview with Fundi Manfred Zieran in *Der Spiegel*, Mar. 9, 1987.

183 See Herbert Riehl-Heyse, "Die Akrobaten mit der Atom Nummer," *Süddeutsche Zeitung*, Mar. 31, 1987.

184 "Die wollen doch nur Ängste schüren," *Der Spiegel*, Mar. 30, 1987, and an interview with Walter Wallman in *Der Spiegel*, Mar. 30, 1987.

185 "Machtwechsel in Hessen: Wallman wird Regierungschef," *Süddeutsche Zeitung*, Apr. 6, 1987.
186 "Keine Große Koalition in Hamburg: Dohnanyi spricht sich für Neuwahlen aus," *Süddeutsche Zeitung*, Mar. 4, 1987.
187 See Volker Skierka, "GAL bleibt beim Nein zu einer Koalition," *Süddeutsche Zeitung*, Mar. 30, 1987.
188 See Volker Skierka, "Im weißen Lammfell auf Stimmenfang," *Süddeutsche Zeitung*, Apr. 15, 1987.
189 See "SPD und CDU in Hamburg setzen auf die FPD," *Süddeutsche Zeitung*, Apr. 13, 1987, and an interview with Klaus von Dohnanyi in *Der Spiegel*, Mar. 9, 1987.
190 "Wo sind sie geblieben?" *Die Tageszeitung*, May 19, 1987. It is interesting that only 6.4 percent of women voters opted for the GAL's all-female list whereas 8.5 percent of men did so.
191 "Die 'Versuchung' der GAL zog nicht," *Die Welt*, May 18, 1987.
192 "Jutta findet's 'schade' und 'schön,'" *Die Rheinpfalz*, May 18, 1987.
193 "Trotz Erfolgs bleiben Grüne in der Opposition," *Die Welt*, Sept. 14, 1987.
194 The Barschel affair, or "Waterkantgate" as some of the media dubbed it, represented one of the most bizarre scandals in the history of the Federal Republic. Uwe Barschel, the youthful and popular Prime Minister of Schleswig-Holstein, engaged in a number of dirty tricks to discredit his Social Democrat challenger, Björn Engholm, who, equally youthful, seemed even more popular. Confronted by the media and investigators regarding these tricks, which included paying private detectives to follow Engholm in the hopes of uncovering material that could be used in a smear campaign, Barschel gave his word of honor in public that he had nothing to do with them. When the evidence against Barschel became irrefutable, he committed suicide in the bathtub of a hotel in Switzerland. See "Waterkantgate: Beschaffen Sie mir eine Wanze," *Der Spiegel*, Sept. 14, 1987; "Waterkantgate: Einer hat beim Beten gelogen," *Der Spiegel*, Sept. 21, 1987; "Waterkantgate: Das Kartenhaus fällt," *Der Spiegel*, Sept. 28, 1987; "Waterkantgate: Sterben nach Methode 1," *Der Spiegel*, Oct. 19, 1987.
195 "Grüne reden von Stalins Methoden," *Bonner Rundschau*, Sept. 15, 1987.
196 "Grünes Streitritual nach der Wahl," *Die Tageszeitung*, Sept. 15, 1987.
197 For an excellent article depicting the "show" character of green politics, especially the ritualized battles between Fundis and Realos, see "Krise ohne Untergang," *Die Zeit*, Dec. 11, 1987.
198 "Die Grüne Waltraud Schoppe schüttelt Reck ihren roten Haarschopf," *Frankfurter Allgemeine Zeitung*, Nov. 21, 1987.
199 "Vermitteln, damit es einen nicht selber zerreist," *Brigitte*, Jan. 24, 1990.
200 "Getrennt laufen, zusammen raufen," *Die Zeit*, Nov. 20, 1987.
201 "Von nun an mit drei Flügeln," *Süddeutsche Zeitung*, Jan. 28, 1988.
202 "Per Ritterschlag vom Landesfürsten," *Die Zeit*, Mar. 11, 1988; "Der Bart allein macht keinen 'jungen Marx,'" *Stuttgarter Zeitung*, Mar. 9, 1988; "Es wurde nichts aus acht plus X," *Frankfurter Allgemeine Zeitung*, Mar. 21, 1988.
203 "Den Grünen ist man im Norden nicht grün," *Die Welt*, May 9, 1988.
204 "Niederlagen haben keine Väter," *Die Tageszeitung*, May 10, 1988.
205 "Grüne bangen um ihre zukunft," *Frankfurter Rundschau*, May 11, 1988.
206 See Kuntz, "From Spiegel to Flick."
207 "Einmalig schweinische," *Der Spiegel*, Oct. 24, 1988.
208 Ibid.
209 Ibid.

210 "Alle durchgeknallt," *Der Spiegel*, Oct. 24, 1988.
211 Ibid.
212 "Nach der Abwahl des Bundesvorstandes verstärken sich dei Flügelkämpfe bei den Grünen," *Süddeutsche Zeitung*, Dec. 5, 1988.
213 See Giovanni di Lorenzo, "Ich wollte einfach nur reinen Tisch," *Süddeutsche Zeitung*, Dec. 5, 1988.
214 "Jutta Ditfurth warnt vor Rechtstruck," *Süddeutsche Zeitung*, Dec. 6, 1988.
215 See Günter Bannas, "Zwischen Radikalität und Kompromiß," *Frankfurter Allgemeine Zeitung*, Feb. 10, 1989.
216 Election figures are from *Süddeutsche Zeitung*, Jan. 30, 1989.
217 "Fundamentalisten verlieren Mehrheit bei den Grünen," *Süddeutsche Zeitung*, Mar. 6, 1989.
218 See Klaus Dreher, "Abschied unter Tränen und Buh-Rufen," *Süddeutsche Zeitung*, Mar. 6, 1989.
219 "Enttäuschte Gefühle," *Der Spiegel*, Apr. 16, 1990.
220 "Völlig irre," *Der Spiegel*, Apr. 16, 1990.
221 See Günter Bannas, "Resigniert nicht, arbeitet weiter!" *Frankfurter Allgemeine Zeitung*, Apr. 2, 1990.
222 "Machtwechsel in Hannover nach 14 Jahren CDU-geführter Regierung," *Süddeutsche Zeitung*, Mar. 14, 1990.
223 See "Nach dem Wahldebakel streiten die Grünen über ihren künftigen Kurs," *Frankfurter Allgeimeine Zeitung*, Dec. 4, 1990; Günter Bannas, "Nicht an der Weggabelung, sondern im Nebel," *Frankfurter Allgemeine Zeitung*, Dec. 5, 1990; "Fischer: Grüne zwischen Neubeginn und Exitusverwaltung," *Frankfurter Allgemeine Zeitung*, Dec. 5, 1990; Giovanni di Lorenzo, "Rettungsversuche nach dem Untergang," *Süddeutsche Zeitung*, Dec. 7, 1990; "Dagobert vom Fleischerladen," *Der Spiegel*, Dec. 10, 1990.
224 See: "Wähler honorierten Architekten der deutschen Einheit," and election statistics pp. 10–11 in *Frankfurter Rundschau*, Dec. 4, 1990.

Chapter 8   The East German Greens

1 For an insightful application of Albert O. Hirschman's influential analytic framework of "exit, voice and loyalty" to the GDR, its collapse and relationship vis-à-vis the Federal Republic, see Albert O. Hirschman, "Exit, Voice, and the Fate of the German Democratic Republic: An Essay in Conceptual History," in *World Politics*, 45.2, Jan. 1993, pp. 173–202. The whole exit option was only made possible by the decision on the part of the Hungarian government in early May 1989 to dismantle the Iron Curtain of minefields and barbed wire which constituted the Hungarian border with Austria. Six months later, this little-noticed action would render the Berlin wall irrelevant.
2 Peter Joachim Lapp, *Die "befreundeten Parteien" der SED: DDR-Blockparteien Heute*, 1988. It is important to note that thousands of Nazi sympathizers and former Wehrmacht officers were given a political home in the form of the NDPD by the state, so that it became a sort of officially sanctioned "reservation" for ex-Nazis under Communist rule.
3 See Merrill Elaine Jones, "Greens under God and the Gun: the East German Environmental Movement, the Lutheran Church and the East German State," B. A. Hons thesis, 1991, pp. 19–22.
4 Ibid., p. 10.
5 Ibid., p. 15.

6   Ibid., pp. 15–16, 54–5.

7   Ibid., p. 16. For the role of the Lutheran church in the creation of environmentalism is the GDR, see Carol Hager, "Environmentalism and Democracy in the Germanies," *German Politics*, 11, April 1992, pp. 95–118.

8   See ibid., ch., 3, "The Early Movement."

9   *Taz*, Aug. 15, 1989, p. 2.

10   *Taz*, Aug. 30, 1989, p. 8.

11   *Taz*, Aug. 15, 1989, p. 3.

12   *Taz*, Aug. 15, 1989, p. 9.

13   *Taz*, Aug. 19, 1989, p. 2.

14   *Taz*, Aug. 30, 1989, p. 8; Aug. 31, 1989, p. 8.

15   *Taz*, Aug. 13, 1989, p. 8.

16   Ibid.

17   *Taz*, Sept. 13, 1989, p. 7.

18   *Taz*, Sept. 20, 1989, p. 6.

19   Ibid., p. 7.

20   *Taz*, Sept. 28, 1989.

21   Ibid.

22   *Taz*, Sept. 23, 1989, p. 1.

23   *Taz*, Sept. 25, 1989, p. 1.

24   *Taz*, Oct. 4, 1989, pp. 1 and 3.

25   Harold James, "Introduction," in Harold James and Marla Stone, eds, *When the Wall Came Down: Reactions to German Unification*, 1992, p. 1.

26   *Taz*, Dec. 20, 1989, p. 2.

27   *Taz*, Feb. 8, 1990, p. 6.

28   *Taz*, Sept. 6, 1989, p. 3.

29   *Taz*, Sept. 25, 1989, p. 1.

30   *Taz*, Nov. 27, 1989, p. 5.

31   *Taz*, May 22, 1990, p. 6; May 25, 1990, p. 6.

32   *Taz*, Jan. 29, 1990, p. 5.

33   *Der Spiegel*, Apr. 15, 1991, pp. 26–30.

34   Ibid.

35   Ibid.

36   *Taz*, May 7, 1991.

37   *Taz*, Sept. 23, 1991, p. 5.

38   Ibid.

39   Ibid.

40   Ibid.

41   As quoted in Stephen Kinzer, "In Germany, too, an Effort to Mobilize Political Outsiders," *New York Times*, July 19, 1992.

Conclusion

1   Some have perceived the United States as an "exception" precisely because its working class has not articulated its collective political identity by forming a party of its own, which *ipso facto* would be classified as "left." The literature dealing with American exceptionalism, or at least certain aspects of it, is vast. Of particular importance are the following: Louis Hartz, *The Liberal Tradition in America: An Interpretation of American Political Thought since the Revolution*, 1955; Frederick Jackson Turner, *The Frontier in American History*, 1947; John M. Laslett

and Seymour Martin Lipset, eds, *Failure of a Dream? Essays in the History of American Socialism*, 1974; Seymour Martin Lipset, *Political Man*, 1960; Lipset, *The First New Nation*, 1967; Lipset, *Agrarian Socialism*, 1968; Lipset, *Revolution and Counterrevolution*, 1968; the exchange between Sean Wilentz and Michael Hanagan in *International Labor and Working Class History*, no. 26; Gwendolyn Mink, *Old Labor and New Immigrants in American Political Development: Union, Party, and State 1875–1920*, 1986; and Jerome Karabel, "The Failure of American Socialism Reconsidered," in *The Socialist Register*, 1979, pp. 204–27.

2   See Seymour Martin Lipset and Stein Rokkan, "Cleavage Structures, Party Systems, and Voter Alignments: an Introduction," in Seymour Martin Lipset and Stein Rokkan, eds, *Party Systems and Voter Alignment: Cross-National Perspectives*, 1967, pp. 1–64.

3   The term "postmaterial" has been closely associated with the pioneering work of Ronald Inglehart. See especially his article "Post-materialism in an Environment of Insecurity," *American Political Science Review*, no. 75, 1981, pp. 880–900, and ch. 2, "The Rise of Postmaterialist Values," in Ronald Inglehart, *Culture Shift in Advanced Industrial Society*, 1989, pp. 66–103.

4   Lipset and Rokkan, "Cleavage Structures."

5   Reinhard Kühnl, "Der Aufstieg der Extremen Rechten in Europa," *Blätter für deutsche und internationale Politik*, June 1992, pp. 730–41.

6   Ibid.

7   Claus Leggewie, *Die Republikaner: Phantombild der neuen Rechten*, 1989; Hans Georg Betz, "Politics of Resentment: Right-wing Radicalism in West Germany," *Comparative Politics*, 23, Oct. 1990, pp. 45–60.

8   See Ursula Feist and Klaus Liepelt, "Die Wahl zum Machtwechsel: Neuformierung der Wählerschaft oder Wählerkoalition aus Hoffnung? Eine Analyse der Bundestagswahl vom 6. März 1983," *Journal für Sozialforschung*, 23.3, Fall 1983.

9   Thomas Koelble, "After the Deluge: Unification and the Political Parties in Germany", *German Politics and Society*, no. 22, Spring 1991, pp. 45–59.

10 The DVU won 6.18 percent of the vote in Bremen in September 1991. In April 1992, the DVU won 6.3 percent of the vote in Schleswig-Holstein, while the Republikaner won 10.9 percent of the vote in Baden-Württemberg. See *Der Spiegel*, Apr. 13, 1992.

11 See "Feine Jungs," *Der Spiegel*, May 4, 1992, pp. 102–5.

12 See Lipset, *Political Man*, esp. ch. 4, "Working-Class Authoritarianism."

13 Peter Lösche and Frans Walter, *Die SPD: Klassenpartei-Volkspartei-Quotenpartei*, 1992, pp. 379–86.

14 Ibid.

15 It is clear that not all parties of the European Left have conformed to the Michelsian model of oligarchic organization. In that sense, the difference between, say, the German SPD and the French Socialist Party (and its precursor) have been gigantic. And yet all parties of the traditional European Left had a certain Michelsian oligarchic rigidity, at least in their world-view and general habits, if not necessarily in their organizational framework proper. It is this which has been challenged in all parts of the traditional European Left, regardless of country and exact ideological orientation.

16 The concept of anti-anti-communism was first conveyed to us by Helmut Dubiehl, who developed it in a brilliant book published together with Ulrich Rödel and Günter Frankenberg. See Ulrich Rödel et al., *Die demokratische Frage*, 1989, pp. 11–17.

17 On the concept of activist vs accommodationist unions, see Andrei S. Markovits, *The Politics of the West German Trade Unions: Strategies of Class and Interest Representation in Growth and Crisis*, 1986.

18 On the greening of the German trade unions in the course of the latter part of the 1980s, see Tom Harsanyi, "The New Left and the Dilemmas of Social Democracy in the Federal Republic of Germany: Leftism in an Affluent Society," unpublished dissertation prospectus, Harvard University, May 29, 1992.

19 On the Greens' failure to make any meaningful inroads into the ranks of the industrial working class, see Russell J. Dalton, *Politics in West Germany*, 1989, pp. 287–8.

20 Maurice Duverger, *Political Parties: Their Organization and Activity in the Modern State*, trans. Barbara North and Robert North, 1954, p. xxvii.

21 See Roland Roth, "Eine korrupte Republik? Konturen politischer Korruption in der Bundesrepublik," in Rolf Ebbighausen and Sighard Neckel, eds, *Anatomie des Politischen Skandals*, 1989, pp. 201–33.

22 It is not by chance that one could hardly read any publications in macrosociology or any of the related "qualitative" social science in the Germany of the late 1980s without encountering at least a few citations to Ulrich Beck's book *Risikogesellschaft*, 1986. While Beck's is a very fine analysis of the risk problems haunting any advanced industrial society at the end of the twentieth century, it is the "Beckism" or "Beckmania" which are much more telling than the work itself. One had the impression that citing Beck's work was simply de rigueur for any German social scientist with a "critical" bent.

23 Joachim Raschke, *Krise der Grünen: Bilanz und Neubeginn*, 1991, pp. 7–9.

24 Duverger, *Political Parties*, pp. 27–36.

25 Jürgen Habermas coined the term of "constitutional patriotism" in an attempt to extol and affirm the Federal Republic's western values and virtues against an increasingly loud chorus of conservative voices which bemoaned the alleged lack of national feeling and pride in the Federal Republic, interpreting this perceived lacuna as detrimental to Germany's self-perception. See "Über den doppelten Boden des demokratischen Rechtsstaates," in Jürgen Habermas, *Eine Art Schadensabwicklung*, 1987, pp. 18–23.

26 See for example Lösche and Walter, who, among many others, lay the blame for the SPD's abysmal showing in the December 2, 1990, Bundestag elections on Oskar Lafontaine's faulty strategy rather than on his perfectly explicable inability to understand, let alone coddle, the forces of nationalism. See Robert Leicht, "Bleibt einfach alles, wie es ist?" *Die Zeit*, Dec. 7, 1990.

27 For a more detailed development of this idea, see Andrei S. Markovits, "Anti-Americanism and the Struggle for a West German Identity," in Peter H. Merkle, ed., *The Federal Republic of Germany at Forty*, 1989, pp. 35–54. See also Karen Donfried, "West German Youth Protest and Anti-Americanism," unpublished B.A. Hons thesis, Wesleyan University, 1984.

28 On the anti-Americanism of the German demonstrators against the Gulf war, see Andrei S. Markovits, "Die Linke gibt es nicht – und es gibt sie doch," *Frankfurter Rundschau*, Mar. 7, 1991; Markovits, "Ein Amerikanischer Jude und eine deutsche Friedensrede," *Frankfurter Rundschau*, Feb. 16, 1991; Markovits, "Eine ernüchternde Erfahrung: Die Friedensbewegung aus der sicht eines amerikanischen Juden," *Die Zeit*, Feb. 15, 1991. See also the collection of essays in Klaus Bittermann, ed., *Liebesgrüsse aus Bagdad: Die "edlen Seelen" der Friedensbewegung und der Krieg am Golf*, 1991.

29 On anti-Americanism as a critique of modernity, see Paul Hollander, *Anti-Americanism: Critiques at Home and Abroad, 1965–1990*, 1992.
30 Of course, there were exceptions. Thus, for example, it is important to mention Peter von Oertzen's engaged commitment on behalf of many East German dissidents, as well as his participation at the conference in support of Rudolf Bahro's freedom in Berlin in November 1978. Tellingly, however, Peter von Oertzen was the only member of the SPD's executive committee to have participated in this conference. Equally worthy of being mentioned as an exception to social democracy's silent approval of "real existing socialism" was the cultural journal *Logo*, which was close to the SPD and an ardent advocate of the cause of Eastern European dissidents. Yet, again, it is noteworthy that this journal folded *before* the events of 1989. See Tilman Fichter, "Die SPD und die nationale Frage," in Cora Stephan, ed., *Wir Kollaborateure*, 1992, pp. 107–24. That the issue of social democracy's position on nationalism and its attitude vis-à-vis "real existing socialism" is a particularly contentious one for the German Left is best exemplified by the numerous debates which have emerged concerning this topic. Thus, for example, see the reply of Peter Glotz, one of social democracy's and the Left's most original thinkers and prolific writers, to Fichter tellingly entitled "Fichter und Fichte," in ibid., pp. 125–30. For a similar debate on this topic, see Andrei S. Markovits, "The West German 68-ers Encounter the Events of 1989," *German Politics*, 1. 1, Apr. 1992, pp. 13–30; Melanie Drane, "A Divided Left Faces German Unity: A Response to Andrei Markovits," *German Politics*, 1. 2, Aug. 1992, pp. 274–81.
31 For an exceptionally perceptive treatment of the GDR's legitimacy in the eyes of the West as a consequence of its "anti-fascist" origins, see Chaim Noll, "Treue um Treue: Linke Gefühlslagen und die literarische Beschwörung der besseren DDR," in Stephan, *Wir Kollaborateure*, pp. 90–106.
32 For some particularly egregious examples of the hostility of the West German Left, particularly on the part of some activist unions, toward Solidarity and its ally among the intelligentsia, KOR, see Peter Schneider, "Man kann ein Erdbeben auch verpassen," *Die Zeit*, Apr. 27, 1990.
33 For the most eloquent appeal for a progressive politics based on democracy, see Paul Berman, "My Version of DSA's Vision and Mission," *Socialist Forum: Discussion Bulletin of the Democratic Socialists of America*, no. 19, Spring 1992, pp. 9–14.
34 For a useful collection of Austro-Marxist writings, including some on nationalism, see Tom Bottomore and Patrick Goode, eds, *Austro-Marxism*, 1978.
35 For a nice treatment of this topic, see Claus Leggewie, *Multikulti: Spielregeln der Vielvölkerrepublik*, 1990.
36 The issue of citizenship, multiculturalism and refugees are crucial in all of Europe, not only in Germany. Germany has, in fact, become Europe's premier country of immigration in the past few years. In 1992 alone, over 600,000 individuals arrived in the Federal Republic as refugees. For example, of the 425,000 refugees who managed to leave the borders of the former Yugoslavia by early August, Germany accepted more than 200,000. In comparison, Austria and Hungary each gave shelter to 50,000, with Switzerland trailing at 17,500. The figures for Britain (1,200), France (1,200), Belgium and Finland (fewer than 1,000), Spain (120) and Greece (97) are very disappointing, to say the least. (See "Germany Chides Europe about Balkan Refugees," *New York Times*, July 29, 1992.) In other words, Germany – as has often been the case

since 1945 – proved much more humane in its reception of refugees than any other European country. And yet there is a serious problem. On the one hand, Germany has far and away the most liberal policy in terms of providing a haven for refugees in Europe. Article 16.2.2 of the Basic Law states it clearly: "Persons persecuted on political grounds shall enjoy the right of asylum." Because this article's authors were former second World War exiles who had been given refugee status in other countries, this article of the Basic Law is considered to be a more liberal statute than the 1951 United Nations (Geneva) Convention, which was targeted primarily at dissidents and minorities oppressed by Soviet-style regimes in the postwar period. During the asylum process, the Länder and local authorities (Kommunen) provide seekers with housing, medical services, an allowance to cover living expenses, help with job searches and German language lessons. Under legislation that went into effect on July 1, 1992, the federal government has sought to centralize and streamline the process by taking matters away from the Länder and local authorities. The federal government is expecting to make a decision on asylum seekers within three months of their arrival in the Federal Republic. It allocated approximately 3 billion dollars per year for refugee resettlement.

On the other hand, Germany's tolerant acceptance policy is countered by a very exclusive notion of citizenship, which has already been discussed in this book.

Even though quota refugees are not mentioned in the Basic Law, the government has on occasion resorted to quotas to have certain people accepted in the country on a collective rather than an individual basis as mandated by Article 16.2.2. The Vietnamese "boat people" were the most prominent examples of quota refugees who were resettled in the Federal Republic in 1979. Chileans, Argentineans, Cubans, Kurds, and most recently Jews from the Soviet Union and its successor states have also been treated as quota refugees. (Much of this information stems from a superb research proposal written by Madeleine Tree entitled "Germany's New 'Jewish Question' or German Jewry's 'Russian Question'? The Resettlement of Jews from the Former Soviet Union in the Federal Republic of Germany," unpublished Ms, Refugee Resettlement Department, Council of Jewish Federations, 1992).

37 In the Dutch town of Maastricht, the twelve members of the European Community met in December 1991 to delineate clear stages leading to the unification of this community by the end of the millennium. Ostensibly, the Maastricht treaty was yet another of the numerous steps and measures taken by countries of the European Community in their quest of creating ultimately some sort of United Europe. In that, it seemed merely an extension of the Single Act which, implemented as of January 1, 1993, is to dismantle gradually all political and economic borders among the 12 members of the European Community. But Maastricht proved qualitatively different from all previous agreements concerning European unity. For unlike any of its predecessors, Maastricht went to the core of things. It demanded nothing short of a general relinquishing of national sovereignties which have historically been the exclusive prerogatives of nation-states. In other words, Maastricht envisioned a three-step process of integration; if implemented, it would go well beyond the integrative measures of the Single Act by, in fact, actually limiting the autonomy and sovereignty of nation-states in their decision-making ability in key areas of public life, ranging from economic policy to social reforms. Thus,

to nobody's surprise, excepting the bureaucrats in Brussels (the so-called "eurocrats"), resistance to the essence of Maastricht has been substantial in virtually every country of the Community. The Danes' aversion to Maastricht's design led them to reject the treaty by a bare majority in the spring of 1992. The French almost followed suit but at the last minute a paper-thin majority of the French public approved Maastricht in September 1992. Resistance to the treaty has been so fierce on the grass-roots level in every European country that the treaty's initiators have in the meantime returned to the drawing board with the mandate not to rescind Maastricht's original intent, but to retard and cushion its implementation.

It was in good part such measures of mitigation and a general willingness to slow things down which helped the Danes reverse their initial rejection of Maastricht in a second vote held in May 1993. Still, over 40 percent of the Danish public continued to oppose the country's joining even a less compelling and less accelerated Europe. While Maastricht may not be dead, it certainly has lost its initial attraction and urgency among all Europeans, including the Germans.

Bibliography

Books

Adamschek, Helmut, and Alexander Sprom, eds, *Die Macht und ihr Preis: Grün-Alternative Bewegung und Parlamentarismus*. Berlin: Clemens Zerling, 1984.

Adenauer, Konrad, *Erinnerungen (1945–53)*. Stuttgart: Deutsche Verlagsanstalt, 1965.

Albert, Judith C., and Stewart E. Albert, eds, *The Sixties Papers*. New York: Praeger, 1984.

Albrecht, Ulrich, *Die Wiederaufrüstung der Bundesrepublik*. Cologne: Pahl-Rugenstein, 1980.

Altbach, Philip G., ed., *The Student Revolution: A Global Analysis*. Bombay: Lalvani, 1970.

Amery, Carl, *Natur also Politik: Die ökologische Chance des Menschen*. Reinbeck: Rowohlt, 1976.

Anders, Günther, *Die Antiquiertheit des Menschen*, 7th edn, vols 1 and 2. Munich: C. H. Beck, 1987.

Apel, Hans, et al., *Sicherheitspolitik contra Frieden? Ein Forum zur Friedensbewegung*. Berlin: Dietz, 1981.

Aust, Stefan, ed., *Der Baader-Meinhof Komplex*. Hamburg: Hoffmann and Campe, 1985.

—— *Brokdorf: Symbol einer politischen Wende*. Hamburg: Hoffman and Campe, 1982.

Autorenkollektiv, ed., *Bedingungen und Organisation des Widerstandes*. West Berlin: Der Kongress von Hannover-Protokolle, 1967.

—— *Die Linke antwortet Jürgen Habermas*. Frankfurt: Europäische Verlagsanstalt, 1968.

Bachrach, Peter, and Morton Baratz, *Power and Poverty*. New York: Oxford University Press, 1970.

von Baeyer-Katte, Wanda, et al., *Gruppenprozess: Analysen zum Terrorismus*, vol. 3 Opladen: Westdeutscher Verlag, 1981.

Bahro, Rudolf, *Die Alternative: Zur Kritik des real-existierenden Sozialismus*. Cologne: Europäische Verlagsanstalt, 1981.

—— *Building the Green Movement*. Philadelphia: New Society, 1986.

—— *Elemente einer neuen Politik: Zum Verhältnis von Ökologie und Sozialismus.* Berlin: Vielfalt, 1980.

—— *From Red to Green.* London: Verso, 1984.

—— *Die Logik der Rettung.* Stuttgart: K. Thienemanns, 1987.

—— *Pfeiler am anderen Ufer.* Berlin: Wagenbach, 1984.

—— *Socialism and Survival.* London: Heretic, 1982.

Barbrook, Alec, *Power and Protest in American Life.* Oxford: Martin Robertson, 1980.

Barkin, Solomon, ed., *Worker Militancy and its Consequences, 1965–75: New Directions in Western Industrial Relations.* New York: Praeger, 1975.

Bauss, Gerhard, *Die Studentenbewegung der sechziger Jahre,* 2nd edn. Cologne: Pahl-Rugenstein, 1983.

Beck, Ulrich, *Risikogesellschaft: Auf dem Weg in eine andere Moderne.* Frankfurt: Suhrkamp, 1986.

Beckenbach, Niels, et al., *Grüne Wirtschaftspolitik: Machbare Utopien.* Cologne: Kiepenheuer and Witsch, 1985.

Bell, Daniel, *The Coming of Post-industrial Society: A Venture in Social Forecasting.* New York: Basic Books, 1973.

—— *The End of Ideology: On the Exhaustion of Political Ideas in the Fifties.* Cambridge: Harvard University Press, 1988.

Benz, Georg, Bernt Engelmann and Detlef Hensche, eds, *Rüstung, Entrüstung, Abrüstung,* Bornheim: Lamuv, 1982.

Bethusy-Huc, V. V., *Das Sozialleistungssystem der Bundesrepublik Deutschland.* Tübingen: J. C. B. Mohr, 1976.

Billstein, H., and K. Naumann, eds, *Für eine bessere Republik: Alternative der demokratischen Bewegung.* Cologne: Pahl-Rugenstein, 1981.

Billstein, Helmut, et al., *Organisierter Kommunismus in der Bundesrepublik Deustchland.* Opladen: Leske, 1977.

Bitterman, Klaus, ed., *Liebesgrüsse aus Bagdad: Die "edlen Seelen" der Friedensbewegung und der Krieg am Golf.* Berlin: Tiamat, 1991.

Bloch, Ernst, *Geist der Utopie,* 2nd edn. Frankfurt: Suhrkamp, 1985.

—— *Das Prinzip Hoffnung,* 4th edn. Frankfurt: Suhrkamp, 1977.

Bockerioch, Wolfram, ed., *SPD und Grüne: Das neue Bündniss?* Reinbeck: Rowohlt 1985.

Boggs, Carl, *Social Movements and Political Power.* Philadelphia: Temple University Press, 1986.

Bookchin, Murray, *The Ecology of Freedom: The Emergence and Dissolution of Hierarchy.* Palo Alto: Cheshire Books, 1982.

de Boor, Wolfgang, *Ursachen des Terrorismus in der Bundesrepublik Deutschland.* Berlin: Walter de Gruyter, 1978.

Borgwardt, Peter, *Abschied von den Grünen.* Dusseldorf: Neuer Weg, 1988.

Bottomore, Tom, and Patrick Goode, eds, *Austro-Marxism.* Oxford: Clarendon, 1978.

Bourdieu, Pierre, *Les heritiers: les étudiants et la culture.* Paris: Éditions de Minuit, 1964.

Brand, Karl-Werner, ed., *Neue soziale Bewegungen in Westeuropa und den USA.* Frankfurt: Campus, 1985.

Brand, Karl-Werner, Detlef Büsser and Dieter Rucht, *Aufbruch in eine andere Gesellschaft: Neue soziale Bewegungen in der Bundesrepublik.* Frankfurt: Campus, 1983.

Brandt, Gisela, Johanna Kootz, and Gisela Steppke, *Zur Frauenfrage im Kapitalismus.* Frankfurt: Suhrkamp, 1973.

Brandt, Willy, *Zum sozialen Rechtsstaat: Reden und Dokumente.* Berlin: Berlin Verlag, 1983.

Braunthal, Gerard, *Political Loyalty and Public Service in West Germany: The 1972 Decree against Radicals and its Consequences.* Amherst: University of Massachusetts Press, 1990.

—— *The West German Social Democrats, 1969–1982: Profile of a Party in Power.* Boulder: Westview, 1983.

Brint, Steven, and Jerome Karabel, *The Diverted Dream: Community Colleges and the Promise of Educational Opportunity in America, 1900–1985.* New York: Oxford University Press, 1989.

Brück, G. W., *Allgemeine Sozialpolitik.* Cologne: Bund, 1976.

Bruggeman, Agnes, *Anhänger und Gegner der Nationaldemokratischen Partei Deutschlands (NPD).* Bonn, 1968.

Brunschwig, Henri, *Société et romantisme en Prusse au XVIIIe siècle.* Paris: Flammarion, 1973.

Brzezinski, Zbigniew, *Between Two Ages: America's Role in the Technocratic Era.* Westport: Greenwood, 1982.

Bühnemann, Michael, Michael Wendt and Jürgen Witüschek, *AL: Die Alternative Liste Berlin.* Berlin: LitPol, 1984.

Bürklin, Wilhelm, *Grüne Politik.* Opladen: Westdeutscher Verlag, 1984.

Butterwegge, Christoph, and Heinz-Gerd Hofschen, *Sozialdemokratie: Krieg und Frieden.* Fulda: Distel, 1984.

Callenbach, Ernest, *The Notebooks and Reports of William Weston.* Berkeley: Banyan Tree, 1975.

Capra, Fritjof, *The Turning Point: Science, Society and the Rising Culture.* New York: Simon and Schuster, 1982.

Capra, Fritjof, and Christine Spretnak, *Green Politics: The Global Promise.* New York: E. P. Dutton, 1984.

Cerny, Philip G., ed., *Social Movements and Protest in France.* New York: St Martin's, 1982.

Clatterbaugh, Kenneth, *Contemporary Perspectives on Masculinity: Men, Women and Politics in Modern Society.* Boulder: Westview, 1990.

Cooper, Alice Holmes, "The West German Peace Movement of the 1980s: Historical and Institutional Influences," Ph.D. dissertation, Harvard University, 1988.

Crouch, Colin, and Alessandro Pizzorno, eds, *The Resurgence of Class Conflict in Western Europe since 1968,* vols 1 and 2. New York: Homes and Meier, 1978.

Dalton, Russell J., *Politics in West Germany.* Glenview: Scott Foresman, 1989.

Dalton, Russell J., and Manfred Kuechler, eds, *Challenging the Political Order: New Social and Political Movements in Western Democracies.* New York: Oxford University Press, 1990.

Deppe, Frank, Georg Fülberth, and Jürgen Harrer, *Geschichte der deutschen Gewerkschaftsbewegung.* Cologne: Pahl-Rugenstein, 1978.

Deuerlin, Ernst, *Deutschland, 1963–70.* Hanover: Verlag für Literatur und Zeitgeschehen, 1972.

Diani, Mario, *Isole nell'archipelago: il movimento ecologista in Italia.* Bologna: Il Mulino, 1988.

Ditfurth, Jutta, *Lebe wild und gefährlich. Radikalökologische Perspektiven.* Cologne: Kiepenheuer and Witsch, 1991.

—— *Träumen, Kämpfen, Verwirklichen.* Cologne: Kiepenheuer and Witsch, 1988.

Dittmers, Manuel, *The Green Party in West Germany: Who are they? and What do they really want?* Buckingham: Dimen Corporation, 1986.

Donati, Paolo R., *Movimenti sociali contemporanei, bibliografia 1975–84.* Milan: UNICOPLI, 1984.

Donfried, Karen, "West German Youth Protest and Anti-Americanism," unpublished B.A. Hons thesis, Wesleyan University, 1984.

Dräger, Klaus, and Werner Hülsberg, eds, *Aus für Grün? Die Orientierungskrise zwischen Anpassung und Systemopposition.* Frankfurt: Sp-Verlag, 1986.

Dregger, Alfred, *Freiheit in unserer Zeit.* Munich: Herbig, 1989.

—— *Der Preis der Freiheit: Sicherheitspolitik im geteilten Europa.* Munich: Universitas, 1985.

Droz, J., ed., *Le romantisme politique en Allemagne.* Paris: Armand Colin, 1963.

Duhm, Dieter, *Aufbruch zur neuen Kultur: Von der Verweigerung zur Neugestaltung: Umrisse einer ökologischen und menschlichen Alternative.* Munich: Kösel, 1984.

Dutschke, Rudi, Wolfgang Lefèvre and Bernd Rabehl, *Rebellion der Studenten.* Reinbeck: Rowohlt, 1968.

Duverger, Maurice, *Political Parties: Their Organization and Activity in the Modern State,* trans. Barbara North and Robert North. London: Methuen, 1954.

Ebbighausen, Rolf, and Sighard Neckel, eds, *Anatomie des politischen Skandals.* Frankfurt: Surhkamp, 1989.

Ebermann, Thomas, and Rainer Trampert, *Die Zukunft der Grünen.* Hamburg: Konkret Literatur, 1985.

Eppler, Erhard, *Ende oder Wende? Von der Machbarkeit des Notwendigen.* Stuttgart: W. Kohlhammer, 1975.

Erd, Rainer, *Verrechtlichung industrieller Konflikte: Normative Rahmenbedingungen des dualen Systems der Interessenvertretung.* Frankfurt: Campus, 1978.

Ernst, K. D., M. M. Schneider and Karlheinz Lohs, *Umweltkrieg und Abrüstung.* Berlin: Akademie, 1976.

ESECS Lenkungsgruppe, *Wege zur Stärkung der konventionellen Abschreckung in Europa: Vorschläge für die 80er Jahre.* Baden-Baden: Nomos, 1983.

Esping-Andersen, Gøsta, *Politics Against Markets: The Social Democratic Road to Power.* Princeton: Princeton University Press, 1985.

—— *Social Class, Social Democracy and State Policy: Party Policy and Party Decomposition in Denmark and Sweden.* Copenhagen: Institute of Organization and Industrial Sociology, 1980.

Falkenberg, Gabriel, and Heiner Kersting, eds, *Eingriffe im Diesseits.* Essen: Klartext, 1985.

Ferguson, Marilyn, *The Aquarian Conspiracy: Personal and Societal Transformation in the 80s.* Los Angeles: J. P. Tarcher, 1980.

Fetscher, Iring, *Terrorismus und Reaktion.* Cologne: Europäische Verlagsanstalt, 1977.

Fetscher, Iring, and Günter Rohrmoser, *Ideologien und Strategien, vol. 7 of Analysen zum Terrorismus.* Opladen: Westdeutscher, 1981.

Fichter, Tilman, *SDS und SPD.* Opladen: Westdeutscher Verlag, 1988.

Fichter, Tilman, and Siegward Lönnendonker, *Kleine Geschichte des SDS.* Berlin: Rotbuch, 1977.

Fields, A. Belden, *Student Politics in France: A Study of the Union nationale des étudiants de France.* New York: Basic Books, 1970.

—— *Trotskyism and Maoism: Theory and Practice in France and the U.S.* New York: Praeger, 1988.

Fischer, Joschka, *Der Umbau der Industriegesellschaft.* Frankfurt: Eichborn, 1989.

—— *Von grüner Kraft und Herrlichkeit.* Hamburg: Rowohlt, 1984.

Flechtheim, Ossip K., Wolfgang Ruzio, Fritz Vilmar and Manfred Wilke, *Der Marsch der DKP durch die Institutionen: Sowjetmarxistiche Einflussstrategien und Ideologien.* Frankfurt: Fischer, 1980.

Frankland, E. Gene, and Donald Schoonmaker, *Between Protest and Power: The Green Party in Germany.* Boulder: Westview, 1992.

Frevert, Ute, *Frauengeschichte: Zwischen bürgerlicher Verbesserung und neuer Weiblichkeit.* Frankfurt: Suhrkamp, 1987.

Funke, Hajo, *Republikaner: Rassismus, Judenfeindschaft, nationaler Grössenwahn.* Berlin: Aktion Sühnezeichen, 1989.

Galbraith, J. K., *The New Industrial State.* Boston: Houghton Mifflin, 1967.

Gansel, Norbert, ed., *Überwindet den Kapitalismus oder Was wollen die Jungsozialisten?* Reinbeck: Rowohlt, 1971.

Geissler, Heiner, *Verwaltete Bürger, Gesellschaft in Fesseln.* Frankfurt: Ullstein, 1978.

von Gizycki, Horst, *Aufbruch aus dem Neandertal: Entwurf einer neuen Kommune.* Neuwied: Luchterhand, 1974.

Gladitz, Nina, ed., *Lieber heute aktiv als morgen radioaktiv.* Berlin: Wagenbach, 1976.

Goldthorpe, John H., et al., *The Affluent Worker in the Class Structure.* London: Cambridge University Press, 1969.

Gorz, André, *Strategy for Labor: A Radical Proposal*, trans. Martin Nicolaus and Victoria Ortiz. Boston: Beacon, 1967.

Gourevitch, Peter, et al., *Unions and Economic Crisis: Britain, West Germany, and Sweden.* London: Allen and Unwin, 1984.

Gruhl Herbert, *Ein Planet wird geplundert.* Frankfurt: Fischer, 1975.

Grupp, Joachim, *Abschied von den Grundsätzen?* Berlin: Clemens Zerling, 1986.

Guggenberger, Bernd, *Bürgerinitiativen in der Parteiendemokratie.* Stuttgart: W. Kohlhammer, 1980.

Haasken, Georg, and Michael Wigbers, eds, *Protest in der Klemme: Soziale Bewegungen in der Bundesrepublik.* Frankfurt: Neue Kritik, 1986.

Habermas, Jürgen, *Eine Art Schadensabwicklung.* Frankfurt: Suhrkamp, 1987.

—— *Legitimationsprobleme im Spätkapitalismus.* Frankfurt: Suhrkamp, 1973. Trans. as *Legitimation Crisis.* Cambridge: Polity, 1988.

—— *Die neue Unübersichtlichkeit.* Frankfurt: Suhrkamp, 1986.

—— *Theorie des kommunikativen Handelns*, vol. 2. Frankfurt: Suhrkamp, 1981. Trans. as *The Theory of Communicative Action*, vol. 2. Cambridge: Polity, 1988.

Habermas, Jürgen, et al., *Protestbewegung und Hochschulreform.* Frankfurt: Suhrkamp, 1969.

Hallensleben, Anna, *Von der Grünen Liste zur Grünen Partei.* Göttingen: Muster-Schmidt, 1984.

Hamilton, Richard F., *Who Voted for Hitler?* Princeton: Princeton University Press, 1988.

Hartz, Louis, *The Liberal Tradition in America: An Interpretation of American Political Thought since the Revolution.* New York: Harcourt, Brace and World, 1955.

Hasenclever, Wolf-Dieter, and Connie Hasenclever, *Grüne Zeiten.* Munich: Kösel, 1982.

Hauff, Volker, ed., *Bürgerinitiativen in der Gesellschaft.* Villingen-Schwenningen: Neckar, 1980.

Haug, Wolfgang, *Die Faschisierung der bürgerlichen Subjekts: die Ideologie der gesunden Normalität und die Ausrottungspolitiken im deutschen Faschismus.* Berlin: Argument, 1986.

—— *Die hilflose Antifaschismus: zur Kritik des Vorlesungreihen über Wissenschaft und NS an deutschen Universitäten.* Cologne: Pahl-Rugenstein, 1977.

Heidt, Wilfried, ed., *Abschied vom Wachstumswahn: Ökologischer Humanismus als Alternative zur Plünderung des Planeten.* Langnau: Achberger, 1980.

Heller, Agnes, *Theorie der Bedürfnisse bei Marx.* Cologne: Europäische Verlagsanstalt, 1981.

Hentschel, Volker, *Geschichte der deutschen Sozialpolitik, 1880–1980.* Frankfurt: Suhrkamp, 1983.

Herf, Jeffrey, *Reactionary Modernism: Technology, Culture and Politics in Weimar and the Third Reich*. Cambridge: Cambridge University Press, 1984.

—— *War by Other Means: Soviet Power, West German Resistance and the Battle of the Euromissiles*. New York: Free Press, 1991.

Hergt, Siegfried, *Partei Programme: SPD, CDU, CSU, FDP, DKP, NPD*. Opladen: Heggen, 1975.

Hermand, Jost, *Grüne Utopien in Deutschland: Zur Geschichte des ökologischen Bewusstseins*. Frankfurt: Fischer, 1991.

Hesse, Gunter, and Hans-Hermann Wiebe, ed., *Die Grünen und die Religion*. Frankfurt: Athenäum, 1988.

Hessische Stiftung Friedens- und Konfliktforschung, ed., *Europa zwischen Konfrontation und Kooperation: Entspannungspolitik für die 80er Jahre*. Frankfurt: Fischer, 1982.

Hilferding, Rudolf, *Finance Capital: A Study of the Latest Phases of Capitalist Development*, trans. Morris Watnick and Sam Gordon. London: Routledge and Kegan Paul, 1981.

Hindels, Josef, *NPD: Ein Alarmzeichen*. Vienna: Bund Sozialistische Freiheitskämpfer, 1967.

Hippler, Jochen, and Jürgen Maier, eds, *Sind die Grünen noch zu retten? Krise und Perspektiven einer ehemaligen Protestpartei*. Cologne: Förtner and Kroemer, 1988.

Hirsch, Arthur, *French New Left*. Montreal: Black Rose, 1982.

Hirsch, Joachim, *Der Sicherheitsstaat: Das "Modell Deutschland", seine Krise und die neue sozialen Bewegungen*. Frankfurt: Europäische Verlagsanstalt, 1980.

Hirsch, Joachim, and Ronald Roth, *Das neue Gesicht des Kapitalismus*. Bonn: EVA, 1985.

Hollander, Paul, *Anti-Americanism: Critiques at Home and Abroad, 1965–1990*. New York: Oxford University Press, 1992.

Hollstein, Walter, and Boris Penth, *Alternativprojekte: Beispiel gegen der Resignation*. Reinbeck: Rowohlt, 1980.

Horchem, Hans Josef, *Die verlorene Revolution: Terrorismus in Deutschland*. Herford: Busse Seewald, 1988.

Horn, Michael, *Sozialpsychologie des Terrorismus*. Frankfurt: Campus, 1982.

Heulshoff, Michael G., Andrei S. Markovits, and Simon Reich, eds, *The New Germany in the New Europe*. Ann Arbor: University of Michigan Press, 1993.

Hüllen, Rudolf van, *Ideologie und Machtkampf bei den Grünen*. Bonn: Bouvier, 1990.

Hülsberg, Werner, *The German Greens: A Social and Political Profile*, trans. Gus Fagan. London: Verso, 1988.

Hütter, Joachim, *SPD und nationale Sicherheit*. Meisenheim am Glan: Anton Hain, 1975.

Illich, Ivan, *Tools for Conviviality*. New York: Harper and Row, 1973.

Inglehart, Ronald, *Culture Shift in Advanced Industrial Society*. Princeton: Princeton University Press, 1989.

—— *The Silent Revolution: Changing Values and Political Styles among Western Publics*. Princeton: Princeton University Press, 1977.

Jacobi, Otto, ed., *Kritisches Gewerkschaftsjahrbuch 1978*. Berlin: Rotbuch, 1978.

Jäger, Brigitte, and Claudia Pintl, eds, *Zwischen Rotation und Routine: die Grünen im Bundestag*. Cologne: Kiepenheuer and Witsch, 1985.

Jäger, Herbert, Gerhard Schmidtchen and Lieselotte Süllwold, *Lebenslaufanalysen*, vol. 2 of *Analysen zum Terrorismus*. Opladen: Westdeutscher Verlag, 1981.

James, Harold, and Marla Stone, eds, *When the Wall Came Down: Reactions to German Unification*. New York: Routledge, Chapman and Hall, 1992.

Jones, Merrill Elaine, "Greens under God and the Gun: The East German Environmental Movement, the Lutheran Church and the East German State", B. A. Hons thesis, Harvard University, 1991.

Jung, Robert, and Norbert R. Müller, *Alternatives Leben*. Baden-Baden: Signal, 1980.

Kahl, Werner, *Vorsicht Schusswaffen! von kommunistischen Extremismus. Terror und revolutionärer Gewalt*. Munich: G. Olzog, 1986.

Kallscheuer, Otto, ed., *Die Grünen – Letzte Wahl? Vorgaben in Sachen Zukunftsbewältigung*. Berlin: Rotbuch, 1986.

Karabel, Jerome, and A. H. Halsey, eds, *Power and Ideology in Education*. New York: Oxford University Press, 1977.

Karl, Frank, *Die K-Gruppen*. Bonn: Neue Gesellschaft, 1976.

Katsiaficas, George, *The Imagination of the New Left: A Global Analysis of 1968*. Boston: South End Press, 1987.

Katzenstein, Peter, *Policy and Politics in West Germany: The Growth of a Semi-sovereign State*. Philadelphia: Temple University Press, 1987.

Kelly, Petra, and Joe Leinen, eds, *Prinzip Leben – Ökopax, die neue Kraft*. Berlin: Colloquium, 1982.

Kerr, Clark, *The Uses of the University*. Cambridge: Harvard University Press, 1963.

Kirchheimer, Otto, *Politik und Verfassung*, 2nd edn. Frankfurt: Suhrkamp, 1981.

—— *Politische Herrschaft: Funf Beiträge zur Lehre vom Staat*, 4th edn. Frankfurt: Suhrkamp.

Kitschelt, Herbert, *The Logic of Party Formation: Ecological Politics in Belgium and West Germany*. Ithaca: Cornell University Press, 1989.

Klages, Helmut, *Wertorientierungen im Wandel*. Frankfurt: Campus, 1985.

Kleinert, Hubert, *Aufstieg und Fall der Grünen: Analyse einer alternativen Partei*. Bonn: Dietz, 1992.

Kloke, Martin, *Israel und die deutsche Linke: Zur Geschichte eines schwierigen Verhältnisses*. Frankfurt: Haag and Herchen, 1990.

Klönne, Arno, and Hartmut Reese, *Die deutsche Gewerkschaftsbewegung*. Hamburg: VSA, 1984.

Klotzsch, Lilian, and Richard Stoss, eds, *Parteienhandbuch*. Opladen: Westdeutscher Verlag, 1983.

Kluckkohn, Paul, ed., *Weltanschauung der Frühromantik*. Darmstadt: Wissenschaftliche Buchgesellschaft, 1966.

Kluge, Thomas, ed., *Grüne Politik*. Frankfurt: Fischer, 1984.

Knabe, Gerd, ed., *20 Jahre NPD: Porträt einer junger Parteien*. Knullwald-Nausis: Winkelberg, 1984.

Knorr, Lorenz, *Geschichte der Friedensbewegung in der Bundesrepublik*. Cologne: Pahl-Rugenstein, 1983.

Kofler, Leo, *Zur Kritik der "Alternativen"*. Hamburg: VSA, 1983.

Kolinsky, Eva, ed., *The Greens in West Germany: Organization and Policy Making*. Oxford: Berg, 1989.

Korpi, Walter, *The Democratic Class Struggle*. London: Routledge and Kegan Paul, 1983.

Kraushaar, Wolfgang, ed., *Autonomie oder Getto? Kontroversen über Alternativebewegung*. Frankfurt: Neue Kritik, 1978.

—— *Was sollen die Grünen im Parliament?* Frankfurt: Neue Kritik, 1983.

Krieger, Verena, *Was bleibt von den Grünen?* Hamburg: Konkret Literatur, 1991.

Krohn, Maren, *Die gesellschaftlichen Auseinandersetzungen um die Notstandesgesetze*. Cologne: Pahl-Rugenstein, 1981.

Kunz, Norbert, ed., *Ökologie und Sozialismus: Perspektiven einer umweltgründlichen Politik.* Cologne: Bund, 1986.

Lacqueur, Walter, *Terrorism: A Study of National and International Political Violence.* Boston: Little, Brown, 1977.

Lampert, H., *Sozialpolitik.* Berlin: Springer, 1980.

Langguth, Gerd, *The Green Factor in German Politics: From Protest Movement to Political Party.* Boulder: Westview, 1984.

—— *Protestbewegung: Entstehung, Entwicklung, Renaissance.* Cologne: Wissenschaft und Politik, 1977.

Lapp, Peter Joachim, *Die "befreundeten Parteien" der SED: DDR-Blockparteien Heute.* Cologne: Wissenschaft und Politik, 1988.

Laslett, John M., and Seymour Martin Lipset, eds, *Failure of a Dream? Essays in the History of American Socialism.* Garden City: Anchor, 1974

Leggewie, Claus, *Multikulti: Spielregeln der Vielvölkerrepublik.* Berlin: Rotbuch, 1990.

—— *Die Republikaner: Phantombild der neuen Rechten.* Berlin: Rotbuch, 1989.

Lehmbruch, Gerhard and Philippe C. Schmitter, eds, *Patterns of Corporatist Policymaking.* London: Sage, 1982.

—— *Trends towards Corporatist Intermediation.* London: Sage, 1979.

Leibfried, Stephan, *Armutspolitik und die Entstehung des Sozialstaats.* Bremen: Forschungsschwerpunkt Reproduktionkrisen soziale Bewegungen und Sozialpolitik, 1985.

Leibfried, Stephan, and Florian Tennstedt, eds, *Politik der Armut und die Spaltung des Sozialstaats.* Frankfurt: Suhrkamp, 1983.

Leif, Thomas, *Die professionelle Bewegung: Friedensbewegung von innen.* Bonn: Forum Europa, 1985.

de Leon, David, *Everything is Changing.* New York: Praeger, 1988.

Leonhard, Martin, *Umweltverbände: Zur Organizierung von Umweltinteressen in der BRD.* Opladen: Westdeutscher Verlag, 1986.

Leonhardt, Alfred, *Umweltreproduktion im staatsmonopolistichen Kapitalismus: Zur Kritik bürgerlicher Konzeptionen einer marktwirtschaftlichen Lösung des Umweltprobleme.* Berlin: Akademie, 1977.

Lilge, Herbert, *Deutschland: 1945–63.* Hanover: Fackelträger, 1983.

Lipset, Seymour Martin, *Agrarian Socialism.* Garden City: Anchor, 1968.

—— *The First New Nation.* Garden City: Anchor, 1967.

—— *Passion and Politics: The Dimensions of Student Involvement: Rebellion in the University.* Boston: Little Brown, 1972.

—— *Political Man.* Garden City: Doubleday, 1960.

—— *Revolution and Counterrevolution.* New York: Basic Books, 1968.

—— ed., *Student Politics.* New York: Basic Books, 1967.

—— *The Third Century: America as a Post-industrial Society.* Stanford: Hoover Institution Press, Stanford University, 1979.

Lipset, Seymour Martin, and Philip G. Altbach, eds, *Students in Revolt.* Boston: Houghton Mifflin, 1969.

Lipset, Seymour Martin, and Stein Rokkan, eds, *Party Systems and Voter Alignments: Cross-national Perspectives.* New York: Free Press, 1967.

Lipset, Seymour Martin, and Sheldon S. Wolin, eds, *The Berkeley Student Revolt: Facts and Interpretations.* Garden City: Anchor, 1965.

Lösche, Peter, and Frans Walter, *Die SPD: Klassenpartei-Volkspartei-Quotenpartei.* Darmstadt: Wissenschaftliche Buchgesellschaft, 1992.

Löwy, Michael, *Pour une sociologie des intellectuels révolutionaires.* Paris: Presses Universitaires de France, 1976.

372   *Bibliography*

—— *Rédemption et utopie*. Paris: Presses Universitaires de France, 1988.

Lüdke, Hans-Werner, and Olaf Dinné, eds, *Die Grünen: Personen, Projekte, Programme*. Stuttgart: Seewald, 1980.

Luhmann, Niklas, *Soziale Systeme*. Frankfurt: Suhrkamp, 1987.

Lumpley, Robert, *States of Emergency: Cultures of Revolt in Italy from 1968 to 1978*. London: Verso, 1990.

McCracken, Paul, et al., *Towards Full Employment and Price Stability: A Report to the OECD by a Group of Independent Experts*. Paris: OECD, 1977.

Mallet, Serge, *The New Working Class*, trans. Andrée and Bob Shepherd. Nottingham: Bertrand Russell Peace Foundation for Spokesman Books, 1975.

Mannheim, Karl, *Ideology and Utopia*. San Diego: Harcourt Brace Jovanovich, 1936.

Marcuse, Herbert, *One-Dimensional Man*. Boston: Beacon, 1983.

Maren-Griesbach, Manon, *Philosophie der Grünen*. Munich: Günter Olzog, 1982.

Marighella, Carlos, *The Mini-Manual of the Urban Guerilla*. San Francisco: Patrick Arguello, 1978.

Markmann, Heinz, and Diethard B. Simmer, eds, *Krise der Wirtschaftspolitik*. Cologne: Bund, 1978.

Markovits, Andrei S., *The Politics of the West German Trade Unions: Strategies of Class and Interest Representation in Growth and Crisis*. Cambridge: Cambridge University Press, 1986.

Markovits, Andrei S., and Mark Silverstein, *The Politics of Scandal: Power and Process in Liberal Democracies*. New York: Holmes and Meier, 1988.

Mast, Claudia, *Aufbruch ins Paradies?* Zurich: Interfrom, 1980.

Mayer-Tasch, Peter, *Die Bürgerinitiativbewegung*, 5th rev. edn. Reinbeck: Rowohlt, 1985.

Mayr, E., *The Growth of Biological Thought*. Cambridge: Harvard University Press, 1982.

Merkl, Peter, ed., *The Federal Republic of Germany at Forty*. New York: New York University Press, 1989.

Merkl, Peter, William E. Paterson, and Gordon Smith, eds, *Development in West German Politics*. Houndmills: Macmillan, 1989.

Mettke, Jörg, ed., *Die Grünen*. Reinbeck: Rowohlt, 1982.

Meyer, Thomas, *Am Ende der Gewalt? Der deutsche Terrorismus, Protokoll eines Jahrzehnts*. Frankfurt: Ullstein, 1980.

Meyer-Abich, ed., *Frieden mit der Natur*. Freiburg: Herder, 1979.

Miermeister, Jürgen, and Jochen Staadt, eds, *Provokationen: die Studenten und Jugendrevolte in ihren Flugblättern, 1965–1971*. Darmstadt: Luchterhand, 1980.

Mink, Gwendolyn, *Old Labor and New Immigrants in American Political Development: Union, Party, and State, 1875–1920*. Ithaca: Cornell University Press, 1986.

Muller, Leo A., *Republikaner, NPD, DVU, Liste D . . .* Göttingen: Lamuv, 1989.

Müller, Emil-Peter, *Die Grünen und das Parteiensystem*. Cologne: Deutscher Instituts Verlag, 1984.

Müller-Rommel, Ferdinand, ed., *New Politics in Western Europe: The Rise and Success of Green Parties and Alternative Lists*. Boulder: Westview, 1989.

Müller-Witt, Harald, ed., *Arbeitsplätze contra Umwelt: eine rot-grüne Kontroverse*. Freiburg: Dreisam, 1980.

Mumford, Lewis, *The Myth of the Machine*, vol. 2. New York: Harcourt Brace Jovanovich, 1970.

Narr, Wolf-Dieter, ed., *Auf dem Weg zum Einparteienstaat*. Opladen: Westdeutscher Verlag, 1977.

Neumann, Franz L., *Wirtschaft, Staat, Demokratie*, ed. Alfons Söllner. Frankfurt: Suhrkamp, 1978.

Nevermann, Knut, ed., *Lokal 2000: Berlin als Testfall.* Reinbeck: Rowohlt, 1983.

O'Connor, Jim, *The Fiscal Crisis of the State.* New York: St Martin's, 1973.

Offe, Claus, *Disorganized Capitalism: Contemporary Transformations of Work and Politics,* ed. John Keane. Cambridge: Cambridge University Press, 1985.

—— *Strukturprobleme des kapitalistischen Staates.* Frankfurt: Suhrkamp, 1972.

Offe, Claus, Karl Hinrichs and Helmut Wiesenthal, eds, *Arbeitszeitpolitik: Formen und Folgen einer Neuverteilung der Arbeitszeit.* Frankfurt: Suhrkamp, 1982.

Opp, Karl-Dieter, et al., *Soziale Probleme und Protestverhalten: Eine empirische Konfrontation des Models rationalen Verhaltens mit soziologischen und demographischen Hypothesen am Beispiel von Atomkraftgegner.* Opladen: Westdeutscher Verlag, 1987.

Osterroth, Franz, and Dieter Schuster, *Chronik der deutschen Sozialdemokratie,* vol. 3: *Nach dem zweiten Weltkrieg,* 2nd rev. edn. Bonn: Dietz 1963.

Otto, Karl A., *Vom Ostermarsch zur APO.* Frankfurt: Campus, 1977.

Paucke, Horst, *Umweltprobleme: Herausforderung der Menschheit.* Frankfurt: Marxistische Blätter, 1980.

Pelinka, Anton, *Gewerkschaften im Parteienstaat.* Berlin: Duncker and Humbolt, 1980.

Pelinka, Anton, and Fritz Plasser, *The Austrian Party System.* Boulder: Westview, 1989.

Perrow, Charles, *Normal Accidents: Living with High-Risk Technologies.* New York: Basic Books, 1984.

Pestalozzi, Hans A., Ralf Schlegel and Adolf Bachmann, eds, *Frieden in Deutschland: die Friedensbewegung, wie sie wurde, was sie ist, was sie werden kann.* Munich: W. Goldmann, 1982.

Pfaltzgraf, Robert, et al., *The Greens of West Germany: Origins, Strategies, and Transatlantic Implications.* Washington: Institute for Foreign Policy Analysis, 1983.

Piore, Michael J., and Charles Sabel, *The Second Industrial Divide: Possibilities for Prosperity.* New York: Basic Books, 1984.

Pirker, Theo, *Die blinde Macht: Die Gewerkschaftsbewegung in Westdeutschland,* vol. 2. Berlin: Olle and Wolter, 1979.

Poulantzas, Nicos, *Fascisme et dictature.* Paris: Maspero, 1974.

Preuss, Ulrich K., *Legalität und Pluralismus: Beiträge zum Verfassungsrecht der Bundesrepublik Deutschland.* Frankfurt: Suhrkamp, 1973.

Pritchard, Rosalind M. O., *The End of Elitism? The Democratization of the West German University System.* New York: Berg, 1990.

Przeworski, Adam, *Capitalism and Social Democracy.* Cambridge: Cambridge University Press, 1985.

Probst, Ulrich, *Die kommunistischen Parteien der Bundesrepulik Deutschland.* Munich: Ernst Vogel, 1980.

Raschke, Joachim, *Krise der Grünen: Bilanz und Neubeginn.* Marburg: Schüren, 1991.

Reich, Charles, *The Greening of America: How the Youth Revolution is Trying to Make America Livable.* New York: Random House, 1970.

Richert, Ernst, *Die radikale Linke.* Berlin: Colloquium, 1969.

Rödel, Ulrich, Günter Frankenberg, and Helmut Dubiehl, *Die demokratische Frage.* Frankfurt: Suhrkamp, 1989.

Römpczyk, Elmar, *Internationale Umweltpolitik und Nord-Süd Beziehungen.* Saarbrücken: Breitenbach, 1979.

Ronge, Volker, *Die Gesellschaft an den Grenzen der Natur: Aufsätze zur politischen Ökologie.* Bielefeld: AJZ-Druck und Verlag, 1978.

de Rosnay, Joël, *Le macroscopie: Vers une vision globale.* Paris: Seuil, 1975.

Roth, Wolfgang, *Kommunalpolitik für wen? Arbeitsprogramm der Jungsozialisten.* Frankfurt: Fischer, 1971.

Rothchild, Joseph, *East Central Europe between the Two World Wars*. Seattle: University of Washington Press, 1974.

Rucht, Dieter, ed., *Neue soziale Bewegungen in der Bundesrepublik Deutschland*. Frankfurt: Campus, 1987.

—— *Von Wyhl nach Gorleben: Bürger gegen Atomprogramm und nukleare Entsorgung*. Munich: C. H. Beck, 1980.

Rupp, Hans Karl, *Ausserparlamentarische Opposition in der Ära Adenauers*. Cologne: Pahl-Rugenstein, 1970.

—— *Politische Geschichte der Bundesrepublik Deutschland*, 2nd edn. Stuttgart: W. Kohlhammer, 1978.

Sale, Kirkpatrick, *The Human Scale*. New York: Coward, McCann and Keoghegan, 1980.

Schehl, Hellmuth, *Vor uns die Sintflut?: Ökologie, Marxismus und die herrschende Zukunftsgläubigkeit*. Berlin: Rotbuch, 1977.

Schenk, Herrad, *Die feministische Herausforderung: 150 Jahre Frauenbewegung in Deutschland*. Munich: C. H. Beck, 1981.

Schlicht, Uwe, *Vom Burschenschafter bis zum Sponti: Studentische Opposition gestern und heute*. Berlin: Colloquium, 1980.

Schmid, Thomas, ed., *Die Linke neu denken*. Berlin: K. Wagenbach, 1984.

—— *Das pfeifende Schwein: Über weitergehende Interessen der linken*. Berlin: Klaus Wagenbach, 1985.

Schmidt, Eberhard, *Die verhinderte Neuordnung, 1945–52*, 7th edn. Frankfurt: Europäische Verlagsanstalt, 1977.

Schmitter, Philippe C., *Corporatism and Public Policy in Authoritarian Portugal*. London: Sage, 1975.

Schmollinger, Horst W., and Peter Müller, *Zwischenbilanz: 10 Jahre sozialliberale Politik, 1969–1979*. Hanover: Fackelträger, 1980.

Schonauer, Karlheinz, *Die ungeliebten Kinder der Mutter SPD: Die Geschichte der Juso von der braven Parteijugend zur innerparteilichen Opposition*. Bonn: Selbstverlag-Karlheinz Schonauer, 1982.

Schönhoven, Klaus, *Die deutschen Gewerkschaften*. Frankfurt: Suhrkamp, 1987.

Schroeren, Michael, ed., *Die Grünen: 10 bewegte Jahre*. Vienna: Ueberreuter, 1990.

Schumacher, E. F., *Small is Beautiful*. New York: Harper and Row, 1973.

Schuster, Dieter, *Die deutschen Gewerkschaften seit 1945*. Stuttgart: W. Kohlhammer, 1973.

Schütte, Johannes, *Revolte und Verweigerung: Zur Politik und Sozialpsychologie der Spontibewegung*. Giessen: Focus, 1980.

Schwarzer, Alice, *So fing es an! Die neue Frauenbewegung*. Munich: Deutscher Taschenbuch Verlag, 1983.

Seitenzahl, Rolf, *Einkommenspolitik durch konzertierte Aktion und Orientierungsdaten*. Cologne: Bund, 1974.

Smith, Gordon, William E. Paterson and Peter H. Merkl, eds, *Developments in West German Politics*. London: Macmillan, 1989.

Stamer, Sabine, ed., *Von der Nachbarkeit des Unmöglichen*. Hamburg: Junius, 1985.

Steigerwald, Robert, *Protestbewegung: Streitfragen und Gemeinsamkeiten*. Frankfurt: Marxistische Blätter, 1982.

Steinweg, Reiner, ed., *Das kontrollierte Chaos: die Krise der Abrüstung*. Frankfurt: Suhrkamp, 1980.

—— *Die neue Friedensbewegung: Analysen aus der Friedensforschung*. Frankfurt: Suhrkamp, 1982.

Stephan, Cora, ed., *Wir Kollaborateure*. Reinbeck: Rowohlt, 1992.

Stephan, Dieter, *Jungsozialisten: Stabilisierung nach langer Krise? 1969–79*. Bonn: Neue Gesellschaft, 1980.

Stern, Fritz, *The Politics of Cultural Despair*. Berkeley: University of California Press, 1961.

Stracke, Ernst, *Stadtzerstörung und Stadtteilkampf*. Cologne: Pahl-Rugenstein, 1980.

Strasser, Johanno, *Grenzen des Sozialstaats?*, 2nd rev. edn. Cologne: Bund, 1983.

Strasser, Johanno, and Klaus Traube, *Die Zukunft des Fortschritts: Der Sozialismus und die Krise des Industrialismus*. Berlin: Dietz, 1984.

Tallert, Harry, *Eine grüne Gegenrevolution*. Frankfurt: Ullstein, 1980.

Thomas, Siegfried, *Zwischen Wehrmacht und Bundeswehr: Um die Remilitarisierung der BRD*. Berlin: Dietz, 1981.

Thompson, E. P., *Beyond the Cold War*. New York: Pantheon, 1982.

Tolmein, Oliver, *Ökorepublik Deutschland. Erfahrungen und Perspektiven rot-grüner Zusammenarbeit*. Hamburg: Konkret Literatur, 1986.

Touraine, Alain, *The Post-industrial Society: Tomorrow's Social History, Classes, Conflicts and Culture in the Programmed Society*, trans. Leonard F. Mayhew. New York: Random House, 1971.

—— *The Workers' Movement*, trans. Ian Patterson. Cambridge: Cambridge University Press, 1987.

Tozzi, Michel, *Syndicalisme et nouveaux mouvements sociaux, régionalisme, feminisme, écologie*. Paris: Editions ouvrières, 1982.

Turner, Frederick Jackson, *The Frontier in American History*. New York: 1947.

Vester, Frederic, *Neuland des Denkens: Vom technokratischen zu kybernetischen Zeitalter*. Stuttgart: Deutsche Verlags-Anstalt, 1980.

Vetter, Heinz O., ed., *Aus der Geschichte lernen – die Zukunft gesalten: Dreissig Jahre DGB*. Cologne: Bund, 1980.

Vobruba, Georg, *Politik mit dem Wohlfahrtstaat*. Frankfurt: Suhrkamp, 1983.

Vollmer, Antje, ed., *Kein Wunderkind für Alice? Frauen-Utopien*. Hamburg: Konkret Literatur, 1986.

Wallach, H. G. Peter, and George K. Romoser, eds, *West German Politics in the Mid-Eighties*. New York: Praeger, 1985.

Weinberger, Marie-Luise, *Aufbruch zu neuen Ufern?* Bonn: Neue Gesellschaft, 1984.

Wilfert, Otto, *Lästige Linke*. Mainz: Barbara Asche, 1968.

Wilharm, Irmgard, ed., *Deutsche Geschichte, 1962–1983: Dokumente in zwei Bänden*. Frankfurt: Fischer Taschenbuch, 1985.

Wohl, Robert, *The Generation of 1914*. Cambridge: Harvard University Press, 1978.

Zellentin, Gerda, and Günter Nonnenmacher, eds, *Abschied von Leviathan: Ökologische Aufklärung über politische Alternativen*. Hamburg: Hoffman and Campe, 1979.

Articles

Afheldt, Horst, "Friedenspolitik: naiv oder realistisch?" in Hans A. Pestalozzi, Ralf Schlegel and Adolf Bachmann, eds, *Frieden in Deutschland: die Friedensbewegung, wie sie wurde, was sie ist, was sie werden kann*. Munich: W. Goldmann, 1982.

Allen, Cristopher S., "Trade Unions, Worker Participation, and Flexibility: Linking the Micro to Macro," *Comparative Politics*, 22. 3, Apr. 1990.

Armanski, Gerhard, "Yankees, Indsmen, und Sachsen," *Dollars und Träume*, no. 10, Oct. 1984.

Auhagen, Hendrik, "Skizze eines sozio-ökologischen Kompromisses," *Kommune*, no. 10, 1984.

Bahro, Rudolf, "Hinein oder hinaus," in Jörg Mettke, ed., *Die Grunen*. Reinbeck: Rowohlt, 1982.

Beier, Gerhard, "Leninisten führten die Feder," ö *TV-Magazin*, no. 3, Mar. 1979.

Benedict, Hans-Jürgen, "Auf dem Weg zur Friedenskirche? Entstehung und Erscheinungsformen der neuen Friedensbewegung in der evangelischen Kirche," in Reiner Steinweg, ed., *Die neue Friedensbewegung: Analysen aus der Friedensforschung*. Frankfurt: Suhrkamp, 1982.

Berman, Paul, "My Version of DSA's Vision and Mission," *Socialist Forum: Discussion Bulletin of the Democratic Socialists of America*, no. 19, Spring 1992.

Betz, Hans Georg, "Politics of Resentment: Right-wing Radicalism in West Germany," *Comparative Politics*, 23, Oct. 1990.

Binswanger, Hans-Christoph, "Qualitatives Wachstum: Strategie und Ausgestaltungsprobleme," in Harald Müller-Witt, ed., *Arbeitsplätze contra Umwelt: eine rot-grüne Kontroverse*. Freiburg: Dreisam, 1980.

Blanke, Bernhard, et al., "Staatliche sozialpolitik und die Regulierung der Nichterwerbstätigkeit," *Leviathan*, 8, 1987.

Brandt, Willy, "Mehr Demokratie wagen," in Willy Brandt, *Zum sozialen Rechtsstaat: Reden und Dokumente*. Berlin: Berlin Verlag, 1983.

Brant, Karl-Werner, "Cyclical Aspects of New Social Movements: Waves of Cultural Criticism and Mobilization Cycles of New Middle Class Radicalism," in Russell J. Dalton and Manfred Kuechler, eds, *Challenging the Political Order: New Social and Political Movements in Western Democracies*. New York: Oxford University Press, 1990.

Braunthal, Gerard, "Social-Democratic–Green Conditions in West Germany: Prospects for a New Alliance", *German Studies Review*, 9, 1986.

Bull, Hedley, "European Self-reliance and the Reform of NATO," *Foreign Affairs*, Spring 1983.

Bundy, McGeorge, F. Kennan, Robert S. McNamara and Gerard Smith, "Nuclear Weapons and the Atlantic Alliance," *Foreign Affairs*, Spring 1982.

Bürklin, Wilhelm P., "The Greens: Ecology and the New Left," in H. G. Peter Wallach and George K. Romoser, eds, *West German Politics in the Mid-Eighties*. New York: Praeger, 1985.

—— "Social Integration and the Future of the Greens", *ASGP Journal*, 15, 1987.

Byrne, Paul, "Great Britain: The Green Party," in Ferdinand Müller-Rommel, ed., *New Politics in Western Europe: The Rise and Success of Green Parties and Alternate Lists*. Boulder: Westview, 1989.

Chandler, William M., and Alan Siaroff, "Postindustrial Politics in Germany and the Origins of the Greens," *Comparative Politics*, 18. 3, 1986.

Czada, Roland, "Wirtschaftlicher Strukturwandel und Arbeitslosigkeit," *Leviathan*, 8, 1987.

Ditfurth, Jutta, "Radikal und phantasievoll gesellschaftliche Gegenmacht organisieren! Skizzen einer radikalökologischen Position," in Thomas Kluge, ed., *Grüne Politik*. Frankfurt: Fischer, 1984.

Dominick, Raymond, "The Roots of the Green Movement in the United States and West Germany," *Environmental Review*, 12. 3, 1986.

Drane, Melanie, "A Divided Left Faces German Unity: A Response to Andrei Markovits," *German Politics*, 1. 2, Aug. 1992.

Dunn, Keith A., and William O. Staudenmeier, "Strategy for Survival," *Foreign Policy*, Fall 1983.

"Einigkeit und Grün und Freiheit, ökolibertäre Grüne: Gründungserklärung," reprinted in *Kommune*, no. 4, 1984.

Ely, John "The Greens: Ecology and the Promise of Radical Democracy," *Radical America*, 17. 1, 1983.

―― "The Greens between Legality and Legitimacy," *German Politics and Society*, no. 14, 1988.

―― "Marxism and Green Politics in West Germany," *Thesis Eleven*, no. 13, 1992.

Falkenberg, Gabriel, and Erhard Müler, "Thesen für eine systemüberwindende Realpolitik," *Kommune*, no. 7, 1984.

Feist, Ursula, and Klaus Liepelt, "Die Wahl zum Machtwechsel: Neuformierung der Wählerschaft oder Wählerkoalition aus Hoffnung? Eine Analyse der Bundestagswahl vom 6. März 1983," *Journal für Sozialforschung*, 23. 3, Fall 1983.

Fichter, Tilman, "Die SPD und die nationale Frage," in Cora Stephan, ed., *Wir Kollaborateure*. Reinbeck: Rowohlt, 1992.

Frankland, E. Gene, "Green Politics and Alternative Economics," *German Studies Review*, 11. 1, 1988.

―― "Parliamentary Politics and the Development of the Green Party," *Review of Politics*, 51. 3, 1989.

Gansel, Norbert, "Die Strategie in der Diskussion der Jungsozialisten," in Norbert Gansel, ed., *Überwindet den Kapitalismus oder Was wollen die Jungsozialisten?* Reinbeck: Rowohlt, 1971.

Gorski, Philip, review of Ferdinand Müller-Rommel, ed., *New Politics in Western Europe*. In *German Politics and Society*, no. 22, Spring 1991.

Hager, Carol, "Environmentalism and Democracy in the Two Germanies," *German Politics*, 1.1, April 1992, pp. 95–118.

Halfmann, Jost, "Rights and Reciprocity: Social Movement Themes and Social Change in the Federal Republic of Germany," *Praxis International*, 8. 1, 1987.

Harsanyi, Tom, "The New Left and the Dilemmas of Social Democracy in the Federal Republic of Germany: Leftism in an Affluent Society," unpublished dissertation prospectus, Harvard University, May 29, 1992.

Hill, Phil, "The Crisis of the Greens," *Socialist Politics*, no. 4, 1985.

Hinrichs, Karl, Claus Offe and Helmut Wiesenthal, "Der Streit um die Zeit: Die Arbeitszeit im gesellschaftpolitischen und industriellen Konflikt," in Offe, Hinrichs and Wiesenthal, eds, *Arbeitszeitpolitik: Formen und Folgen einer Neuverteilung der Arbeitszeit*. Frankfurt: Suhrkamp, 1982.

Hirsch, Joachim, "Between Fundamental Opposition and *Realpolitik*: Perspectives for an Alternative Parliamentarism," *Telos*, no. 56, 1983.

―― "Fordist Security State and New Social Movements," *Kapitalstate*, no. 10–11, 1983.

Hirschman, Albert O., "Exit, Voice, and the Fate of the German Democratic Republic," *World Politics*, 45.2, Jan. 1993.

Hülsberg, Werner, "The Greens at the Crossroads," *New Left Review*, no. 152, July–Aug. 1985.

Inglehart, Ronald, "Post-materialism in an Environment of Insecurity," *American Political Science Review*, no. 75, 1981.

Jahn, Egbert, "Friedensbewegung und Friedensforschung," in Reiner Steinweg, ed., *Die neue Friedensbewegung: Analysen aus der Friedensforschung*. Frankfurt: Suhrkamp, 1982.

Jansen, Sarah, "Magie und Technik – Auf der Suche nach feministischen Alternativen zur patriarchalen Naturnutzung," *Beiträge zur feministischen Theorie*, no. 12, Dec. 1984.

Kaiser, K., G. Leber, A. Mertes and F.-J. Schulze, "Nuclear Weapons and the Preservation of Peace," *Foreign Affairs*, Summer 1982.

Karabel, Jerome, "The Failure of American Socialism Reconsidered," in *The Socialist Register*, 1979.

Karapin, Roger, "Social Movements and Democracy in Western Germany: Creating Coalitions for Policy Reform, 1969–89," unpublished Ph.D. thesis, Department of Political Science, Massachusetts Institute of Technology, 1993.

Kaste, Hermann, and Joachim Raschke, "Zur Politik der Volkspartei," in Wolf-Dieter Narr, ed., *Auf dem Weg zum Einparteienstaat*. Opladen: Westdeutscher Verlag, 1977.

Kelly, Petra, "Wir müssen die Etablierten entblössen wo wir Können," in Jörg Mettke, ed., *Die Grünen*, Reinbeck: Rowohlt, 1982.

—— "Wie sich die Ökologiebewegung zur Friedensbewegung entwickelte," in Petra Kelly and Joe Leinen, eds, *Prinzip Leben – Ökopax, die neue Kraft*. Berlin: Colloquium, 1982.

Kitschelt, Herbert, "Left Libertarian Politics: Explaining Innovation in Competitive Party Systems," *World Politics*, 40. 2, 1988.

Klotzsch, Lilian and Richard Stöss, "Die Grünen," in Klotzsch and Stöss, eds, *Parteienhandbuch*. Opladen: Westdeutscher, 1983.

Koelble, Thomas, "After the Deluge: Unification and the Political Parties in Germany," *German Politics and Society*, no. 22, Spring, 1991.

Komer, Robert W., "Maritime Strategy vs. Coalition Defense," *Foreign Affairs*, Summer 1982.

Kuby, Gabrielle, "Ende der patriarchalen Herrschaft," *Frauenoffensive*, no. 2, Apr. 1975.

Kühnl, Reinhard, "Der Aufstieg der Extremen Rechten Europa," *Blätter für deutsche und internationale Politik*, June 1992.

Kuntz, Aline, "From *Spiegel* to Flick: The Maturation of the West German *Parteienstaat*," in Andrei S. Markovits and Mark Silverstein, eds, *The Politics of Scandal: Power and Process in Liberal Democracies*. New York: Holmes and Meier, 1988.

Leinweber, Bernd, and Karl-Ludwig Schibel, "Die Alternativbewegung: Ein Beitrag zu ihrer gesellschaftlichen Bedeutung und politischen Tragweite, ihren Möglichkeiten und Grenzen," in Wolfgang Kraushaar, ed., *Autonomie oder Getto? Kontroversen über Alternativbewegung*. Frankfurt: Neue Kritik, 1978.

Leipert, Christian, "Die Grünen auf der Suche nach einem neuen ökonomischen Leitbild," in N. Beckenbach et al., *Grüne Wirtschaftspolitik: Machbare Utopien*. Cologne: Kiepenheuer and Witsch, 1985.

McNamara, Robert S., "The Military Role of Nuclear Weapons: Perceptions and Misperceptions," *Foreign Affairs*, Fall 1983.

Markovits, Andrei S., "Anti-Americanism and the Struggle for a West German Identity," in Peter Merkl, ed., *The Federal Republic of Germany at Forty*. New York: New York University Press, 1989.

—— "German Social Demoracy," *Studies in Political Economy*, no. 19, Spring 1986.

—— "On Anti-Americanism in West Germany," *New German Critique*, no. 34, Winter, 1985.

—— "The West German 68-ers Encounter the Events of 1989", *German Politics*, 1. 1, Apr. 1992.

Markovits, Andrei S., and Christopher S. Allen, "The Trade Unions," in Gordon Smith, William E. Paterson and Peter H. Merkl, eds, *Developments in West German Politics*. London: Macmillan, 1989.

Markovits, Andrei S., and David S. Meyer, "Green Growth on the West German Left: Cultivating Political Space," paper presented at the 13th World Congress of the International Political Science Association, Paris, July 15–21, 1985.

Meyer, Rold, and Günter Handlögten, "Die Grünen vor der Wahl," *Aus Politik und Zeitgeschichte*, no. 3, 1981.

Müller, Harald, "Ökologiebewegung und Friedensbewegung: Zur Gefährdung des Lebensraums," in Reiner Steinweg, ed., *Die neue Friedensbewegung: Analysen aus der Friedensforschung.* Frankfurt: Suhrkamp, 1982.

Müller-Rommel, Ferdinand, "New Political Movements and 'New Politics' Parties in Western Europe," in Russell J. Dalton and Manfred Kuechler, eds, *Challenging the Political Order*. New York: Oxford University Press, 1990.

Neumann, Franz L., "Der Niedergang der deutschen Demokratie," in Franz L. Neumann, *Wirtschaft, Staat, Demokratie*, ed. Alfons Söllner. Frankfurt: Suhrkamp, 1978.

——"Die soziale Bedeutung der Grundrechte in der Weimarer Verfassung," in Franz L. Neumann, *Wirtschaft, Staat, Demokratie*, ed. Alfons Söllner. Frankfurt: Suhrkamp, 1978.

Noll, Chaim, "Treue um Treue: Linke Gefühlslagen und die literarische Beschwörung der besseren DDR," in Cora Stephan, ed., *Wir Kollaborateure*. Reinbeck: Rowohlt, 1992.

Offe, Claus, "Griff nach der Notbremse," in Wolfgang Kraushaar, ed., *Was sollen die Grünen im Parlament*. Frankfurt: Neue Kritik, 1983.

Opielka, Michael "Vom Sozialstaat zum ökologischen Gemeinwesen – Für eine neue Sozialpolitik," in N. Beckenbach et al., *Grüne Wirtschaftspolitik: Machbare Utopien*. Cologne: Kiepenheuer and Witsch, 1985.

——"Von der Krise zur Zukunft des Socialstaats: Ausatzpunkte einei ökologischen Sozialpolitik," in Die Grünen, Baden Württemberg, *Die Zukunft des Sozialstaats.* Stuttgart: Die Grünen, 1983.

Parniske-Kunz, Carola, "Ökologie – eine Angel des Feminismus?" in Norbert W. Kunz, ed., *Ökologie und Sozialismus: Perspektiven einer umweltgründlichen Politik.* Cologne: Bund, 1986.

Pauer, Jean, "Wie Friedliebend ist die UdSSR? Die Grünen und Osteuropa. Anmerkungen zu einer laufenden Diskussion," *Kommune*, July 1985.

Pohl, Rüdiger, "Bundesbankpolitik in der Krise – Krise der Bundesbankpolitik," in Heinz Markmann and Diethard B. Simmer, eds, *Krise der Wirtschaftspolitik*. Cologne: Bund, 1978.

Rabinbach, Anson, "Benjamin Bloch and Modern German Jewish Messianism," *New German Critique*, no. 34, Winter 1985.

Ravenal, Earl C., "Europe without America: the Erosion of NATO," *Foreign Affairs*, Spring 1983.

Reiche, Jochen, "Ökologie und Zivilisation: Der Mythos von der den natürlichen Kreisläufen," in Thomas Schmid, ed., *Die Linke neu denken*. Berlin: K. Wagenbach, 1984.

Riemer, Jeremiah M., "Reproduction and Reunification: The Politics of Abortion in United Germany," in Michael G. Huelshoff, Andrei S. Markovits and Simon Reich, eds, *The New Germany in the New Europe*. Ann Arbor: University of Michigan Press, 1993.

Roth, Roland, "Eine korrupte Republik? Konturen politischer Korruption in der Bundesrepublik," in Rolf Ebbighausen and Sighard Neckel, eds, *Anatomie des politischen Skandals*. Frankfurt: Suhrkamp, 1989.

Scharrer, Manfred, "Eine die Geschichte verfälschende 'Gewerkschaftsgeschichte'," *Die Quelle*, 29. 11, Nov. 1978.

Schiller, David, "Germany's Other Terrorists," *Terrorism: an International Journal*, 9. 1, 1987.

Schily, Otto, "Vor unvergleichlichen Möglichkeiten," in Wolfram Bockerioch, ed., *SPD und Grüne: Das neue Bündniss?* Reinbeck: Rowohlt, 1985.

Schlaga, Rüdiger, and Hans-Joachim Spanger, "Die Friedensbewegung und der Warschauer Pakt: Ein Spannungsverhältnis," in Reiner Steinweg, ed., *Die neue Friedensbewegung: Analysen aus der Friedensforschung.* Frankfurt: Suhrkamp, 1982.

Schlotter, Peter, "Strategien der Konfliktentspannung: Vorschläge für die achtziger Jahre," in Hessische Stiftung Friedens- und Konfliktforschung, ed., *Europa zwischen Konfrontation und Kooperation: Entspannungspolitik für die 80er Jahre.* Frankfurt: Fischer, 1982.

Schmid, Thomas, "Nicht sozial, aber bürokratisch, über die Vergesellschaftung der Ohnmacht," in Thomas Schmid, ed., *Das pfeifende Schwein: Über weitergehende Interessen der linken.* Berlin: Klaus Wagenbach, 1985.

—— "Plädoyer für einen reformistischen Anarchismus," in Thomas Kluge, ed., *Grüne Politik.* Frankfurt: Fischer, 1984.

Schmierer, Joschka, "Weichenstellungen," *Kommune*, no. 12, 1983.

Schwarzer, Alice, "Bornierte Freund-Feind Muster," *Der Spiegel*, Apr. 29, 1991.

Standfest, Erich, "Die Zukunft des Wohlfartstaates aus der Sicht der Gewerkschaften," *Sozialer Fortschritt*, 4, 1980.

Therborn, Gøran, "Nationale Politik der internationale Arbeitslosigkeit: Der Fall Bundesrepublik im Lichte der OECD-Daten von 1973–1985," *Leviathan*, 8, 1987.

Trempnau, Thomas, "Afheldts Konzept einer defensiven, reaktiven Verteidigung," *Antimilitarismus Information*, no. 3, 1981.

Trepl, Ludwig, "Ökologie – eine grüne Leitwissenschaft? Über Grenzen und Perspektiven einer modischen Disziplin," *Kursbuch*, no. 74, Dec. 1983.

Tress, Madeleine, "Germany's New 'Jewish Question' or German Jewry's 'Russian Question'? The Resettlement of Jews from the Former Soviet Union in the Federal Republic of Germany," unpublished MS, Refugee Resettlement Department, Council of Jewish Federations, 1992.

Vesper, Dieter, "Der Beitrag der Finanzpolitik zur Beschäftigungssicherung – Ein empirischer Befund," in Heinz Markmann and Diethard B. Simmer, eds, *Krise der Wirtschaftspolitik.* Cologne: Bund, 1978.

Webber, Douglas, "Eine Wende in der deutschen Arbeitsmarktpolitik?", *Leviathan*, 8, 1987.

Weber, Hermann, "Kommunistische Gewerkschaftspolitik in der Weimarer Republik," *öTV-Magazin*, no. 4, Apr. 1979.

Weick, Edgar, "Aus der Geschichte lernen," *express*, 17. 4, Apr. 23, 1979.

Wiesenthal, Helmut, "Arbeitszeitverkürzung – Arbeitsumverteilung," in N. Beckenbach et al., *Grüne Wirtschaftspolitik: Machbare Utopien.* Cologne: Kiepenheuer and Witsch, 1985.

—— "Grün-Rational: Vorschläge für eine zeitgemässe Strategie," *Kommune*, no. 4, 1984. Also in G. Falkenberg and H. Kersting, eds, *Eingriffe im Diesseits.* Essen: Klartext, 1985.

Primary Sources

Bundes-Arbeitsgemeinschaft Frieden der Grünen, "Einseitig abrüsten – wir machen den ersten Schritt. Friedenskonzept, 1987." Bonn: Die Grünen, 1986.

Bürgerinitiative Umweltschutz Unterelbe (Brokdorf), *Der Bauplatz muss wieder zur Wiese werden!* Hamburg: Association, 1977.

Department of the Army, *Field Manual 100–5*. Washington, DC, Operations, Aug. 20, 1982.

Deutscher Gewerkschaftsbund, "Protokoll des 9. Ordentlichen Bundeskongress des DGB, 25–30.6.1972."

—— "Protokoll des 10. Ordentlichen Bundeskongress des DGB."

Friedrichs, G., ed., "Aufgabe Zukunft: Qualität des Lebens." Frankfurt: IG Metall, 1972.

Die Grünen, "Antidiskriminierungsgesetz," 3rd edn. Bonn: Die Grünen, 1986.

—— "Arbeitszeitforum – Arbeitszeitpolitik." Bonn: Die Grünen, 1984.

—— *Das Bundesprogramm*. Bonn: Die Grünen, 1980.

—— *Bundestagswahlprogamm 1987*. Bonn: Die Grünen, 1986.

—— *Bundestagswahlprogramm 1990*. Bonn: Die Grünen, 1990.

—— "Entgiftung – sanfte Chemie ist keine Utopie." Bonn: Die Grünen, 1986.

—— "Euromilitarismus – Zur Bedeutung der Europäisierung der Sicherheitspolitik." Bonn: Die Grünen, 1985.

—— "Freiheit von Armut," Bonn: Die Grünen, 1988.

—— "Gegen Arbeitslosigkeit und Sozialabbau: Sinnvoll arbeiten – solidarisch leben" (Sindelfingen program). Bonn: Die Grünen, 1983.

—— *Gesundheitspolitische Vorstellungen der Grünen*. Bonn: Die Grünen, 1986.

—— *Die Grünen im Bundestag: Kritik des Gesundheitswesens und Alternativen*. Bonn: Die Grünen, 1986.

—— *Grüner Basis-Dienst*, no. 1, 1985.

—— *Grüner Basis-Dienst*, nos 7–9, 1986.

—— "Militärgrossmacht Westeuropa? Zur Bedeutung der Europäisierung der Sicherheitspolitik und der Belebung der Westeuropäischen Union." Bonn: Die Grünen, 1985.

—— *Die multikulturelle Gesellschaft: Für eine demokratische Umgestaltung in der Bundesrepublik. Positionen und Dokumentation*. Bonn: Die Grünen, 1990.

—— "Notwendige Anmerkungen zum NATO Doppelbeschluss." Bonn: Die Grünen, 1981.

—— "Ohne Waffen aber nicht wehrlos: Das Konzept der sozialen Verteidigung," 2nd edn. Bonn: Die Grünen, 1987.

—— "Der Rhein ist tot – es lebe die Chemie?" Bonn: Die Grünen, n.d.

—— "Der sofortige Ausstieg ist möglich." Bonn: Die Grünen, 1986.

—— "Statt Krieg der Sterne, Abrüstung auf der Erde: SDI, EUREKA, und 'Europäische Verteidgungsinitiative.'" Bonn: Die Grünen, 1985.

—— "Dem Struwelpeter durch die Haare gefahren: Auf dem weg zu einer Grünen Kulturpolitik." Bonn: Die Grünen, 1987.

—— *Umbau der Industriegesellschaft, Schritte zur Überwindung von Erwerbslosigkeit, Armut und Umweltzerstörung (Umbauprogramm)*. Bonn: Die Grünen, 1986.

—— "Umweltpolitisches Entgiftungsprogamm." Bonn: Die Grünen, n.d.

—— "Vorschläge der Grünen zur Veränderung des Betriebverfassungsgestzes." Bonn: Die Grünen, 1987.

—— *Weder Waffenrock noch Schwesterkleid*. Bonn: Die Grünen, 1988.

—— "Wir wollen leben!" Bonn: Die Grünen, 1983.

Die Grünen, Baden-Württemberg, *Schlachtfeld Europa*. Bonn: Die Grünen, 1983.

—— *Die Zukunft des Sozialstaats*. Stuttgart: Die Grünen, 1983.

Die Grünen im Bundestag, eds, *SPD-Sicherheitspolitik. Ein halber Frieden. Was uns von der SPD trennt*. Hamburg: Die Grünen, 1986.

—— *Vergesellschaftung der Stahlindustrie – eine Alternative zur Stahlkrise?* Bonn: Die Grünen, 1983.

Industriegesellschaft Metall, "Einheitsgewerkschaft: Solidarisches Handeln – Soziale Gegenmacht. Protokoll des 13. Ordentlichen Gewerkschaftstages der IG Metall in Berlin." Frankfurt: IG Metall, 1980.

Regenbogenfraktion im Europaparlament du Grünen, *Bundesrepublik und Frankreich: Nicht Militärkumpanei, sondern Völkerfreundschaft!* Bonn: Die Grünen, n.d.

Newspapers and Magazines

Augsburger Allgemeine Zeitung
Bonner Rundschau
Brigitte
Frankfurter Allgemeine Zeitung
Frankfurter Rundschau
Gewerkschaftliche Umschau
The New York Times
Pflasterstrand
Rheinische Post

Der Spiegel
Stern
Süddeutsche Zeitung
Die Tageszeitung (Taz)
Die Welt
Westdeutsche Allgemeine Zeitung
Wirtschaftswoche
Die Zeit

Index

Organizations which are known by acronyms can be found under the acronym or under the English form of the name.

abortion, 80, 87–90, 180, 196
Achberg Circle, 193, 194
Action Community Service for Peace (Aktionsgemeinschaft Dienst für den Frieden, AGDF), 107, 109, 110
Action for a Third Way (Aktion 3. Weg, A3W), 193
Action Sühnezeichen/Service for Peace (Aktion Sühnezeichen/Friedensdienst, ASF), 107, 109, 110
Adenauer government, 35, 36, 37, 38–9, 41, 42–3, 46, 304n54
  see also CDU, W. German
AGDF (Action Community Service for Peace), 107, 109, 110
Air Land Battle (ALB), 171–2
AL (Alternative List), 68, 195, 196, 197, 231, 325n189
Albania, 63
All-German People's Party (Gesamtdeutsche Volkspartei, GVP), 41
Alliance '90 see Bündnis '90
Allianz für Deutschland (Alliance for Germany), 254, 255
Alternative List (AL) see AL
alternative movement, 81–5, 172
  see also Spontis
Amery, Carl, 127, 128–9
anarchism, 58, 81, 87, 216, 276, 281
  and anti-nuclear protest, 103, 104, 109, 325n188, 353n138
  see also autonomists

Anders, Günther, 133, 135
anthroposophic organizations, 105, 193
anti-anti-communism of Left, 270, 281
anti-communism, 9, 25, 52, 98
  see also Communism
anti-imperialism, 109, 167, 171
Anti-Imperialist Struggle, 74
anti-militarism, 38, 40, 48, 109, 167, 251, 252, 289
  see also disarmament; peace
antimodernism, 26, 27, 93–4, 171, 280, 322n153
anti-nuclear movement see nuclear power
antisemitism, 20, 137
  see also Holocaust; Jews
Apel, Hans, 269
APO (extraparliamentary opposition), 47–58, 59, 80, 81, 87, 94, 95, 171
apocalypse, Greens and, 177
arms race see nuclear weapons
arms trade, Greens and, 177
Arnold, Michael, 249
ASF (Action Sühnezeichen/Service for Peace), 107, 109, 110
A3W (Action for a Third Way), 193
AUD (Independent Germans' Action), 193, 194, 195, 196
Aufbruch '88 (New Beginning '88), 228, 229, 233, 326n3
ausserparlamentarische Opposition see APO
Aust, Ernst, 62
Austria, 19, 22, 267

autonomists (Autonomen), 81, 111, 213, 353n138
autonomy *see* individual

Baader, Andreas, 68–9, 71, 72, 314n30
Baden-Württemberg, 228, 267
  see also Wyhl
Bahr, Egon, 282
Bahro, Rudolf, 120, 124, 126, 127, 138–41, 361n30
Ban on Careers (Berufsverbot), 98–9
Basic Law, 34, 36, 38, 40, 54, 159, 183, 301n18, 307n22, 361n36
Basic Principles on the Question of Anticonstitutional Personnel in the Public Service, 98–9
Bastian, Gert, 108, 344n148
Battle against Nuclear Death (Kampf dem Atomtod, KdA), 43–5, 47, 153
Baumann, Michael 'Bommi', 66
Bavaria, 197, 213, 217, 219
BBU (Federal Association of Citizens' Initiatives for Environmental Protection), 102, 105, 108, 323n159, 325n189
BDA (Bundesverband der Deutschen Arbeitgeberverbände), 71
Beck-Oberdorf, Marie-Louise, 172, 196
Beckmann, Lukas, 198, 212, 214, 230, 324n175, 325n181, 353n133
Beddermann, Karl, 189, 193
Benjamin, Walter, 142
Berlin, 60, 195, 197, 231, 292
  Free University, 51–4, 61, 90
Berlin Action Committee for Women's Liberation (Berliner Aktionsrat zur Befreiung der Frau), 87
Berlin Student Congress against Nuclear Arms, 50
Berlin Wall, opening of, 232, 243, 250, 279
Bewegung 2. Juni, 66–7, 73
Bielefeld appeal, 109
Black Help, 74
Bloch, Ernst, 130, 136, 148
Bock, Thea, 232
Böckler, Hans, 36, 302n19
Bohley, Baerbel, 249
Bonn peace demonstrations, 110–11
Bookchin, Murray, 131
Börner, Holger, 190, 200, 203, 204–8, 222, 223
Brand, Karl-Werner, 35
Brandt, Willy, Brandt administration, 22, 81, 98–9, 190, 202–3, 306n11, 319n134, 351n94

Ostpolitik, 22, 25, 34, 252, 281, 282
  see also SPD
Bremen, 189, 197, 226, 292
Bremen Green List, 195, 196
Brockmann, Heinz, 66
Brokdorf anti-nuclear protest, 103–4, 213, 215, 217
Brownmiller, Susan, 92
Buback, Siegfried, 65, 71
BUF (Federal Conference of Independent Peace Groups), 109
Bundesverband der Deutschen Arbeitgeberverbände (BDA), 71
Bündnis '90 (Alliance '90), 253–4, 255, 257, 258, 259, 260, 261, 262, 263
BUU (Citizens' Initiative for Environmental Protection on the Lower Elbe), 103, 318n124

Callenbach, Ernst, 130
Campaign for Democracy and Disarmament (Kampf für Demokratie und Abrüstung, KfDA), 47, 48
Campaign for Disarmament (Kampf für Abrüstung, KfA), 48–9, 53, 55
Capra, Fritjof, 126, 127
CDU (Christian Democratic Union, East German), 240, 254, 255, 256
CDU (Christian Democratic Union, West German), 34, 35, 36, 54, 120, 193, 197, 198, 201, 202, 214, 221, 224, 231, 233, 272, 275, 325n187, 335n29, 354n155
CDU/CSU/SPD grand coalition, 53, 54, 55, 94
  see also Adenauer; Erhard; Kohl
Central Committee for a Plebiscite against Remilitarization (Hauptausschuss für Volksbefragung gegen Remilitarisierung), 303n42
chemical industry, 156–7, 175, 176, 219, 229
Chernobyl nuclear disaster *see under* nuclear power
China, 62, 63, 281–2, 322n153
  see also Maoism
Christian Democratic Students' Circle (Ring Christlich Demokratische Studenten), 52
Christian Democratic Union (Christlich Demokratische Union, CDU, East Germany), 240, 254, 255, 256
Christian Democratic Union (Christlich Demokratische Union, W. Germany) *see* CDU
Christian Social Union *see* CSU
Christianity and peace movements, 107, 109, 110
  see also Protestantism

Citizens' Initiative for Environmental
Protection on the Lower Elbe
(Bürgerinitiative Umweltschutz
Unterelbe, BUU), 103, 318n124
Citizens' Initiative Weisweil, 102
citizens' initiatives (Bürgerinitiativen), 30,
80, 96, 99–105, 193, 194
E. Germany, 251, 262
citizenship rights, 239
Green policy, 24, 182–3, 218, 286
see also foreigners; immigration
class, 4–5, 15–16, 46, 50–1, 70, 97, 285
see also middle class; working class
codetermination, 7, 34, 35–7, 158, 166–7,
182, 251
Codetermination Acts, 167, 339n81, 343n139
Cohn-Bendit, Daniel, 203
Cold War, 9, 34, 38
see also nuclear weapons
Committee for Disarmament and
Cooperation (Komitee für Abrüstung
und Zusammenarbeit, KOFAZ), 107,
324n176
Committee for Fairness (E. Germany), 262–3
Committee of Peace Fighters (Komitee der
Kämpfer für den Frieden), 303n42
communes, 66, 82, 84, 92
Communism, 17
collapse of E. European, 3, 9–10, 20,
279, 281–4
see also East Germany
Communist Federation (Kommunistischer
Bund, KB), 64, 194
Communist Federation of West Germany
(Kommunistischer Bund
Westdeutschlands, KBW), 63
Communist Party of Germany *see* KPD
Communist Party of Germany/Marxist-
Leninist (Kommunistische Partei
Deutschlands/Marxisten-Leninisten,
KPD/ML), 62–3
Communist Party of Germany–
Reconstruction Organization
(Kommunistische Partei Deutschlands–
Aufbau Organisation, KPD-AO), 57, 61
Communist Party of West Germany
(Kommunistische Partei
Westdeutschlands, KPW), 63
Communist Workers' Federation
(Kommunistischer Arbeiterbund,
KAB), 64
Communists, W. German, 33, 48, 53, 96,
98, 103, 104, 196, 260
see also K-groups; KPD
Conference for Security and Cooperation
on Europe, 177

consumerism
E. Germany and, 250, 252
Greens and, 148, 154, 156, 158, 171,
333n5, 334n18
Contact Ban Law (Kontaktsperre-Gesetz), 75
corporatism, 16, 17, 18, 147
Corterier, Peter, 94
Courage, 91
Croatia, 283
CSU (Christian Social Union), 43, 197,
198, 254, 272, 275, 325n187, 335n29,
354n155
Czechoslovakia, 239

DA (Democratic Awakening), 249, 254,
255, 292
DBD (German Democratic Farmers' Party),
240
Decree against Radicals (Radikalenerlass),
98–9
demilitarization of unified Germany, 251,
252, 289
democracy, 101, 145, 146, 152, 181–2, 236,
278, 285
Greens' role in development of , 187–8,
263, 271–3
Neues Forum and, 251
and society *see* social policy
Democratic Awakening (Demokratischer
Aufbruch), 249, 254, 255, 292
Democratic Front for the Liberation of
Palestine (DFLP), 76
Democratic Women's Initiative group, 92, 107
Demokratischer Aufbruch (DA), 249, 254,
255, 292
Deppe, Frank, 310–311n7
Deutsche Volksunion (DVU), 184, 267, 271
DFG/VK (German Peace Society/United
Conscientious Objectors), 107,
323n159, 325n189
DGB (German Trade Union Federation),
36, 37, 39, 41, 42, 43–4, 45, 47, 48,
160, 166, 219, 270, 305n67, 305n70,
310–11n7, 339n92
disarmament, SPD and, 34, 35
see also peace policy, Green; rearmament
Ditfurth, Jutta, 119, 121, 123, 124, 203, 212,
220, 223, 225, 229, 230, 231, 232,
353n133
DKP (German Communist Party),
60–1, 85, 86, 87, 98, 105, 107, 275
Dohnanyi, Klaus von, 190, 191, 200, 201,
205, 216, 224, 226
Drenckmann, Günter von, 67
DSU (German Social Union), 254, 255
Duhm, Dieter, 131

Dutschke, Rudi, 50, 57, 68
Duverger, Maurice, 271, 274
DVU (German People's Union), 184, 267, 275

East German Communist Party
    (Sozialistische Einheitspartei
    Deutschlands) see SED
East Germany, 235
    bloc parties, 240, 249, 252
    defection to West, 239–40, 247
    democratic opposition, 237–45, 281,
        360–361n30; emergence of opposition
        movements, 245–8; opposition trends
        1989-March 1990, 247–56;
        Volkskammer to Bundestag elections
        1990, 251, 255, 256–60
    Honecker regime's search for legitimacy,
        242–3, 245, 247
    Stasi (Ministry of State Security), 239,
        256, 259
    support for terrorism in W. Germany,
        77–8
    view of Nazism, 19–20, 242, 357n2
    see also Greens, E. German
Easter March of the Opponents of Atomic
    Weapons (Ostermarsch der
    Atomwaffengegner), 47–8, 57, 110, 153
Eastern Europe, 174, 175, 232, 279, 281,
    282–4
Ebermann, Thomas, 122, 147, 148, 149,
    150, 200, 201, 202, 222, 225, 231, 232,
    355n159
eco-feminism, 105
eco-libs, 117, 118, 145–7
ecological humanism, 105
ecological policy, Green, 154–8, 174–7
    see also environment(al)
ecology
    development of parties' interest in, 272
    Green ideology, 116, 117, 125–41, 152–3,
        195, 196, 288
    unions and, 270–1
ecology movement, 99–106, 108–9, 133, 198
economic growth, 7, 8, 80, 101–2, 147, 153,
    155, 266–7, 268, 333n5
economic policy
    Green, 155–67, 182, 196, 274–5
    Neues Forum and, 251–2
economy, 34, 35–8, 52–3
eco-pax movement, 108–9, 142, 143, 152
eco-socialism, 117, 118, 147–50, 216
ecotopia, 130–2
EDC (European Defence Community), 38
education, higher see universities
EKD (Protestant Church), 40, 41, 42,
    305n67

elections
    Bundestag, 290, 293; in 1980, 190; in
        1983, 190, 197, 275; in 1987, 191,
        217–20, 225, 226, 228; in 1990, 24–5,
        174–85, 192, 233–6, 238, 257–8,
        276, 277
    European Parliament, 17, 189–90, 191,
        195, 209, 293
    state and city-state, 291–2; in 1978–9,
        189; in 1982, 200–2; in 1984, 208; in
        1985, 190, 191, 209–11; in 1986, 191,
        211–17, 219; in 1987, 191, 225, 226; in
        1988, 228–9; in 1989, 231; in 1990,
        233, 293; in 1992, 267
    Volkskammer 1990, 251, 255
Emergency Laws, 53, 54–5, 57, 65, 120, 182
Emergency Society for European Peace
    (Notgemeinschaft für den Frieden
    Europas), 40, 41
Emma, 91
energy policy, 156, 157–8, 268
Engholm, Björn, 227
Enlightenment, attitudes to, 126, 129, 136,
    139, 141, 145, 153
Ensslin, Gudrun, 68, 69, 71, 72
Entebbe hijacking, 74, 76
environment, Lutheran Church, and, 244–5
    see also ecology
environmental policy, E. Green, 258–9
Environmental Protection Party
    (Umweltschutz Partei, USP), 189, 193–4
Enzensberger, Hans Magnus, 146
Eppler, Erhard, 104, 109, 147, 199, 351n94
Erd, Rainer, 163, 343n136
Erhard, Ludwig, 36, 46, 53
ethnic politics, 285–7
euromissiles, opposition to see under nuclear
    weapons
Europe, Left and, 177, 287–8
European Defence Community (EDC), 38
European Parliament elections, 17, 189–90,
    191, 195, 209, 293
extraparliamentary protest, 12, 35, 38, 39,
    40, 41, 43, 44, 45, 121–2, 213
    see also APO

Fatah, Al, 68, 69, 76
FDP (Free Democratic Party), 37, 54, 75,
    83, 94, 191, 192, 197, 198, 202, 213,
    224, 233, 247, 272, 275, 325n187,
    335n29, 350n69
Federal Association of Citizens' Initiatives
    for Environmental Protection
    (Bundesverband der Bürgerinitiativen
    für Umweltschutz, BBU), 102, 105,
    108, 323n159, 325n189

Federal Conference of Autonomous Peace Initiatives, 325n189
Federal Conference of Independent Peace Groups (Bundeskonferenz Unabhängiger Friedensgruppen, BUF), 109
Feige, Klaus, 258
Feigenwinter, Grunhild, 89
feminism *see* women's movement
Fischbeck, Hans-Jürgen, 247
Fischer, Joschka, 13, 122, 123, 198, 203, 208, 212–13, 214, 215, 220, 222, 223, 225
Fischer, Werner, 256
Flechtheim, Ossip K., 147
Flick scandal, 198, 229, 273
foreigners, right-wing extremism and, 77, 238
   see also citizenship rights; immigration
France, 18, 267
Frankfurt, 231
   airport demonstration, 203–4, 206
Frankfurt School, 59
Frauen für den Frieden (Women for Peace), 92–3
Frauenoffensive (Women's Offensive), 91
Free Democratic Party *see* FDP
Freitag, Walter, 36
Frevert, Ute, 88
Fritsch, Ronald, 67
Fuecks, Ralf, 229, 232

GAL (Green Alternative List) Hamburg, 197, 200–2, 219, 224–5, 325n189
GAZ (Green Action Future), 194, 195, 196
Geissler, Heiner, 211, 337n50, 354n155
gender politics, 13, 268, 273
   see also women, green policy
General Agreement on Tariffs and Trade, 184
German Communist Party *see* DKP
German Democratic Farmers' Party (DBD), 240
German Peace Society/United Conscientious Objectors (Deutsche Friedensgesellschaft/Vereinigte Kriegsdienstverweigerer, DFG/VK), 107
German Peace Union (Deutsche Friedensunion), 107
German People's Union (Deutsche Volksunion, DVU), 184, 267, 275
German Social Union (Deutsche Soziale Union, DSU), 254, 255
German Trade Union Federation *see* DGB
German Women's International, 93
Gesellschaft für Natur und Umweltschutz (Society for Nature and Environmental Protection), 254

Gewerkschaft Handel, Banken, Versicherungen, 61
GIM (Group of International Marxists), 64–5
Global 2000, 80, 101, 132
Glotz, Peter, 121, 199, 214, 355n159
GLU (Green List for Environmental Protection), 193, 194–5, 196
GLU-NRW (Green List for Environmental Protection–NRW), 195
GNU (Society for Nature and Environment), 255
Gorbachev, Mikhail, 213, 250
Göttingen declaration on nuclear weapons, 42
Grashof, Manfred, 68
grass-roots groups, 55, 109–10
   see also citizens' initiatives; Spontis
Green Action Future (Grüne Aktion Zukunft, GAZ), 194, 195, 196
Green Alternative List (GAL) Hamburg, 197, 200–2, 219, 224–5, 325n189
Green International, 296n1
Green League (Grüne Liga), 254, 255
Green List Bremen, 195, 196
Green List for Environmental Protection (Grüne Liste fur Umweltschutz, GLU), 193, 194–5, 196
Green List for Environmental Protection–NRW (GLU-NRW), 195
Green List Schleswig-Holstein, 195, 196
Green Party (Grüne Partei), E. Germany, 254, 255
green protest movement, 79–112
Greens, 1, 29–30, 115–16
   difficulties of transformation to party, 187
   Fundi/Realo struggle, 29, 116, 117–25, 187, 190–1, 192, 203, 210, 214–17, 220, 222–8, 230–3, 261, 273–4
   future prospects, 278–89
   genealogy, 294
   ideology, 113, 115–51
   Marxism, Marxism/Leninism and *see under* Marxism
   policies, 113–14, 152–85
   political involvement, 189–236
   reasons for development of green parties, 14–18
   reasons for prominence in Federal Republic, 18–28
   relationship with SPD *see under* SPD
   as representative of Federal Republic, 275–8
   shortcomings and failures, 273–5
   support for dissidence in Communist societies, 281–2

transformers of German and European
    Left, 265–71
transformers of German politics and
    society, 188, 271–3
Greens, East, 24, 188, 234, 237–8,
    253–63, 292
    genealogy, 295
    precursors, 239–52
    relationship with W. German Greens,
        235–6, 256–7, 260–3, 279
    state election results, 293
Greens, The (Die Grünen, W. German
    federal party), 190
    BuVo (Bundesvorstand), 225, 229–31, 232
Group of International Marxists (Gruppe
    Internationale Marxisten, GIM), 64–5
Gruhl, Herbert, 104, 115, 193, 194, 196
Grüne Liga (Green League), 254, 255
Grüne Partei (Green Party, E. Germany),
    254, 255
Grünen see Greens
Guerilla Diffusa, 74
Gulf War, 23, 26, 136–8, 171, 172, 259,
    280, 314n13, 321n153
    see also Iraq
Gustav Heinemann Initiative, 109
GVP (All-German People's Party), 41,
    305n67
Gysi, Gregor, 262

Haag, Siegfried, 71
Habermas, Jürgen, 135, 276, 309n69,
    337n52, n56
Haibach, Marita, 208
Hamburg, 190, 191, 192, 194, 195, 200–3,
    219, 222, 224–6, 231, 292
Hamburg GAL, 197, 200–2, 219,
    224–5, 325n189
Hamburg Rainbow List, 195, 196
Hammerbacher, Ruth, 232
Hash Rebels (Haschenrebellen), 66
Hausner, Siegfried, 71
health policy, Green, 161–2, 179, 333n9
Heinemann, Gustav, 40, 41, 60
Herrhausen, Alfred, 72
Hessen, 119, 190, 191, 192, 203–8, 212–13,
    222–4, 231
Heym, Stefan, 262
Holocaust, 2, 18–21, 52, 133, 136, 137, 138,
    313n17, 328n62
    see also Nazism
Honecker, Erich, 239, 250
Horleman, Jürgen, 61
Hoss, Willi, 228
Huber, Wolfgang, 73
Hungary, 239, 357n1

IDJ (Initiative Democracy Now), 253, 256,
    258, 292
IFM (Initiative for Peace and Human
    Rights), 253, 256, 258
IG Bergbau und Energie, 36, 311n7
IG Druck und Papier, 61, 85, 163, 311n7,
    341n105
IG Medien, 163
IG Metall, 36, 42, 54, 61, 85, 163, 164, 165,
    270, 302n19, 311n7, 341n105
immigration, 183–4, 196, 361n36
Independent Germans' Action (Aktion
    Unabhängiger Deutscher, AUD), 193,
    194, 195, 196
Independent Women's Association
    (Unabhängiger Frauenverband, UFV),
    254, 257, 258
individual, individual rights, 10–11, 16, 153,
    161, 181–2, 235, 236, 238, 244, 256,
    273, 276
industrial conflict and new politics parties, 15
industrial relations, Green policy, 158,
    162–7, 182
    see also codetermination; unions
Initiative Democracy Now (Initiative
    Demokratie Jetzt, IDJ), 253, 256, 258, 292
Initiative for Peace and Human Rights
    (Initiative für Frieden und
    Menschenrechte, IFM), 253, 256, 258
Initiativgruppe Neues Forum see Neues Forum
International Committee of the 21 Citizens'
    Initiatives of Bad-Elsass, 102
international relations, Green policy for,
    184
    see also peace policy
internationalism, 23, 25, 167, 287
Iraq, E. Germany and, 242, 259
    see also Gulf War
Israel, 19, 76, 137, 138, 242, 315n13

Jaeckel, Monika, 93
Jahn, Roland, 247
Janssen, Hans, 164
Jews, 19, 20, 52, 76, 133, 137, 138, 242, 315n13
    see also Holocaust
June 2 Movement, 66–7, 73
Jusos (Jungsozialisten, Young Socialists),
    58, 79, 85, 86, 94–9, 100, 105, 109,
    119, 153, 205, 211

KAB (Communist Workers' Federation), 64
KB (Communist Federation), 64, 194
KBW (Communist Federation of West
    Germany), 63
KdA (Campaign against Nuclear Death),
    43–5, 47, 153

Kelly, Petra, 93, 108, 121, 123, 124, 170, 193, 198, 212, 217, 220, 222, 281, 321–322n153
Kerschgens, Karl, 203, 208
KfA (Campaign for Disarmament), 48–9, 53, 55
KfDA (Campaign for Democracy and Disarmament), 47, 48
K-groups, 30, 55, 57, 59–65, 81, 86, 98, 105, 115, 120, 153
Kirche International, 254
Kitschelt, Herbert, 14, 15
Klöpper, Gerald, 67
Knoll, Peter, 66
Koeppe, Ingrid, 258
KOFAZ (Committee for Disarmament and Cooperation), 107, 324n176
Kohl, Helmut, Kohl government, 154, 160, 164, 183, 198, 211, 213, 219, 223, 267
Kommune 1, 58, 68
König, Jörg, 200
Konkret, 69
Konkret Berlin, 69
Kostede, Norbert, 142, 353n138
KPD (Communist Party of Germany), 33, 34, 35, 39, 40, 50, 60, 61–2, 242, 275, 301n14, 310n7
KPD-AO (Communist Party of Germany–Reconstruction Organization), 57, 61
KPD/ML (Communist Party of Germany/Marxist-Leninist), 62–3
KPW (Communist Party of West Germany), 63
Krabbe, Hana, 73
Krahl, Hans-Jürgen, 87
Krefeld forum and appeal, 109–10
Krenz, Egon, 250
Krieger, Verena, 232
Kukielka, Christina, 225
Kunzelmann, Dieter, 68

Lafontaine, Oskar, 109, 121, 178, 190, 202, 209, 216, 231, 277, 360n26
Laing, R. D., 73
LDPD (Liberal Democratic Party of Germany), 240
Leinen, Jo, 108, 324n175, 325n181
Liberal Democratic Party of Germany (Liberal-Demokratische Partei Deutschlands, LDPD), 240
Liberales Bündnis, 255
liberalism, 9, 12–13, 125, 145, 276, 281
libertarianism, Greens and, 14, 145, 184, 276
Lipset, Seymour Martin, 266, 267, 268
Live Without Armaments (Ohne Rüstung Leben), 109

Lorenz, Peter, 67, 73
Lösche, Peter, 269
Löwenthal, Richard, 199
Lower Saxony, 193–5, 211–17, 233
Luhmann, Niklas, 142
Luther, Angela, 66
Lutheran Church, 237, 243–5, 246, 247, 249, 250, 254

Maastricht Treaty, 287–8
Mahler, Horst, 67, 68, 69, 70
Maoism, 60, 62, 63, 64, 149, 322n153
Marcuse, Herbert, 50, 53, 54, 308n38, 334n18
Maren-Griesbach, Manon, 129
Marighella, Carlos, 67
Marxism, Marxism-Leninism, 6, 9, 53, 70, 97, 105, 266, 285
  Greens and, 14, 274; ideology, 115, 116–18, 119, 123–5, 144, 145, 147, 148, 149, 150, 216; policy, 152, 154, 159, 166, 167, 168, 172
  see also Communism; K-groups
Mechtersheimer, Alfred, 108, 171, 217
mega-machine, 12, 133–4, 139, 140
Meinhof, Ulrike, 69, 70
Meins, Holger, 69, 71
Merkel, Michael, 229
Meyer, Roland, 71
Meyer, Till, 67
Michalik, Regina, 225
Michels, Roberto, 270
middle class, 79, 100, 101, 104, 106, 146, 149, 150
Mini-Manual of the Urban Guerilla (Marighella), 67
Miscellaneous Political Union–The Greens (Sonstige Politische Vereinigung–Die Grünen, SPV), 189–90, 191, 195, 196
modernity *see* antimodernism
Mohnhaupt, Brigitte, 71
MSB Spartakus, 60
Müller, Gerhard, 69
Müller-Rommel, Ferdinand, 14
multiculturalism, 182–4, 218, 285–6
Mumford, Lewis, 133–4, 139

National Democratic Party of Germany, E. German (National Demokratische Partei Deutschlands, NDPD), 240
National Democratic Party of Germany, W. German (Nationaldemokratische Partei Deutschlands, NPD), 21, 52, 193, 275
National Socialism *see* Nazism
nationalism, 23–5, 170–1, 235, 237, 250, 276–8, 283, 285–8
  see also reunification

NATO, 72, 111, 280
    double-track decision, 23, 106, 107, 120,
        198, 235, 268, 323n159, 324n168,
        n170, 344n147
    Greens and, 26, 168, 169, 170, 177, 213,
        214, 353n121
    see also nuclear weapons
Nazism, 3, 19, 21–2, 52, 137, 193, 198, 259,
    286
    E. Germany and, 19–20, 242, 357n2
NDPD (National Democratic Party of
    Germany), 240
Netzwerk Arche (Network Ark), 254
Neue, Die, 84–5
Neue Heimat housing corporation, 219, 226
Neues Forum, 248–53, 254, 257, 258, 261, 263
New Left, 13, 14, 17, 21, 22, 153, 210, 266,
    270, 274, 276, 280, 281, 285
    compared with old, 8, 76, 164, 266–7
"new politics parties", 14–18
new social movements, 10–14, 18, 22, 25,
    26, 30, 65, 101, 153, 193, 270
new spirituality, 125, 136, 138–41
Nickels, Christa, 211, 217
Niemöller, Martin, 40
non-violence *see* pacifism; peace
North-Rhine Westphalia, 119, 190–1, 192,
    208–11, 221
    GLU-NRW, 195
Notgemeinschaft für den Frieden Europas
    (Emergency Society for European
    Peace), 40, 41
NPD (National Democratic Party of
    Germany), 21, 52, 193, 275
nuclear power, 8, 12, 63, 80, 100, 101–4,
    157, 193, 204, 206, 217, 268, 350n73
    Chernobyl disaster, 135, 155, 157,
        212–15, 278, 335n29
    NUKEM and ALKEM projects, 207, 208,
        222–3, 224
nuclear weapons, 22–3, 26, 38, 42–5, 133,
    168–73, 177, 213, 280
    opposition to euromissiles, 80,
        106–12, 136, 168, 198, 201
    SPD and, 42–5, 48, 106, 109, 268, 280
    see also Easter March; NATO

Oberrheinisches Aktionskomitee gegen
    Umweltgefährdung durch
    Kernkraftwerke (Upper Rhine Action
    Committee against Environmental
    Endangerment through Nuclear Power
    Plants), 102
Offe, Claus, 6, 142–3, 337n52
Ohne Rüstung Leben (Live Without
    Armaments), 109

Ohnesorg, Benno, 56, 66, 68
oil crises, 7, 8, 101, 163
Ollenhauer, Erich, 42, 43, 305n71
Ostermarsch der Atomwaffengegner, 47–8,
    57, 110, 153

pacifism, 22, 40, 107, 136–8, 169
    see also peace
Palestinians, 72, 74, 76, 137, 182
Pannen, Martin, 210
parliament, 33, 36, 37, 39–40, 41, 44,
    121–3, 124, 142–4, 146, 192
Party of Democratic Socialism (Partei des
    Demokratischen Sozialismus, PDS),
    233, 234, 254, 255, 258, 259, 260, 262,
    275
Paulskirche Bewegung (Paul's Church
    Movement), 41
PDS (Party of Democratic Socialism), 233,
    234, 254, 255, 258, 259, 260, 262, 275
peace, commitment to, 65, 104, 152
    see also pacifism
peace movements, 23, 26, 40, 133, 136–8,
    171, 172, 173, 270, 283
    opposition to euromissiles, 80, 106–12,
        136, 168, 198
peace policy, Greens', 167–73, 177, 196,
    213, 325n189
PFLP (Progressive Front for the Liberation
    of Palestine), 74, 76
Pirker, Theo, 39
Plembeck, Juliane, 67
Plogstedt, Sibylle, 93
Poland, 239, 282, 286
political asylum *see* foreigners
Ponto, Jürgen, 71
Poppe, Gerda, 258
post-Fordism, 3, 6–7, 8, 10
postmaterialism, 10, 14, 135, 164, 266–7
Potthast, Gaby, 275
power, Left and, 277–8, 288–9
press, 84–5, 89, 90, 91
    see also Tageszeitung, Die
progress, 3, 116, 117, 126, 131, 132, 142,
    145, 153, 158
Protestant Church (Evangelische
    Kirchengemeinschaft Deutschlands,
    EKD), 40, 41, 42, 305n67
Protestantism, 17–18, 105
    see also Christianity; Lutheran Church

quality of life, 102, 156, 166
quota regulation, 165–6, 178–9, 342n117

Rabehl, Bernd, 50
RAF (Red Army Faction), 58, 66, 67–8

Rainbow List of Hamburg, 195, 196
Rapacki, Adam, 43
Rappe, Hermann, 199, 269
Raschke, Joachim, 273
Raspe, Jan-Carl, 69, 71, 72
Rau, Johannes, 190, 202, 209, 213, 217, 218, 219, 267
Rauch, Georg von, 66
Reagan, Ronald, 108, 111, 169, 173
rearmament of Germany, 38–41
Red Army Faction (Rote Armee Fraktion, RAF), 58, 66, 67–73
Red Cells (RZ), 58, 61, 66, 73–5
Red Help, 74
Reents, Jürgen, 137
reformist humanism, Greens', 117, 141–50
refugees *see* foreigners
Reich, Jens, 248, 253, 256
Reiche, Annerose, 66
Reinders, Ralf, 66, 67, 73
religion *see* Christianity; Protestantism
Republikaner, 184, 233, 267, 271, 275, 354n155
Republikanischer Club, 68
reunification
    E. German Left and, 238, 251, 252, 262–3
    Greens and, 24, 175, 234–6
    SPD and, 34, 39, 42
Revolutionärer Zorn, 74
Revolutionary Struggle, 74
Revolutionary Union Opposition (Revolutionäre Gewerkschafts-opposition, RGO), 62
Rhineland-Palatinate, 197, 225, 226
Right, 8, 160, 175, 184, 259, 267, 288, 322n153
    anti-Americanism, 171, 321n153
    attacks on foreigners, 77, 322n153
    role in formation of Greens, 193–6
    value conservatives, 13, 81, 193, 321n153
Röger, Sigrid, 87
Rohwedder, Detlef, 72–3
Rokkan, Stein, 266, 267
Rollnick, Gabriele, 67
romanticism, German, 26, 29, 119, 126, 141, 153
Rosenbaum, Helga, 63
Rote Presse Korrespondenz, 69
RZ (Red Cells), 58, 61, 66, 73–5

Saarland, 119, 190–1, 192, 211, 221, 231
SALZ (Socialist Workers' and Apprentices' Center), 64
Sander, Helke, 87
SB (Socialist Office), 193, 203
Schelm, Petra, 68

Schenck, Christine, 258
Schily, Otto, 68, 198, 217, 220, 222, 225, 229, 232, 273
Schlauch, Rezzo, 228
Schleswig-Holstein, 197, 226, 227, 228–9, 267
    see also Brokdorf
Schleswig-Holstein Green List, 195, 196
Schleyer, Hanns-Martin, 71, 72, 75
Schmid, Thomas, 145–7, 150
Schmidt, Christian, 225, 232
Schmidt, Helmut, Schmidt government, 70–1, 75–7, 81, 95, 97, 99, 104, 106, 154, 160, 164, 198, 199, 200, 202, 269, 305n71, 344n147
    see also SPD
Schmidt-Bott, Regula, 232
Schmierer, Joschka, 63
Schoppe, Waltraud, 217, 225
Schröder, Gerhard, 121, 211, 214, 215, 216, 233
Schubert, Alexander, 193
Schulz, Werner, 258, 261, 262
Schumacher, Kurt, 39–40
Schumann, Bodo, 201
Schütte, Johannes, 85
Schwarzer, Alice, 88, 90, 136
SDS (Socialist German Students' League), 47, 49–52, 53, 54, 55, 56, 171
SED (Socialist Unity Party of Germany), 50, 234, 240, 249, 250, 267, 275
Semler, Christian, 61
SHB (Social Democratic University League), 50
sixty-eighters, 4, 21, 79, 82, 274
    see also New Left
social democracy, 7–8, 9, 10, 15, 16–17, 30, 147, 153, 266
Social Democratic Party of Germany *see* SPD
Social Democratic University League (Sozialdemokratischer Hochschulbund, SHB), 50, 86
Social Democratic Voter Initiative, 100
social policy, 16–17, 152, 158–67, 177–9, 287, 288
socialism, 10, 14, 24, 53, 145, 147, 250, 251
Socialist Aid Society (Sozialistische Förderergesellschaft), 50
Socialist German Students' League *see* SDS
Socialist League (Sozialistischer Bund), 50
Socialist Office (Sozialistisches Büro, SB), 193, 203
Socialist Patients' Collective (Sozialistisches Patienten Kollektiv, SPK), 66, 73
Socialist Unity Party of Germany *see* SED
Socialist Women's League of West Berlin, 87

Socialist Workers' and Apprentices' Center (Sozialistisches Arbeiter- und Lehrlingszentrum, SALZ), 64
Society for Nature and Environment (Gesellschaft für Natur und Umwelt, GNU), 255
Society for Nature and Environmental Protection (Gesellschaft für Natur and Umweltschutz), 254
Sonnenschein, Jakob, 210
Soviet Union, 62, 240, 247, 279, 286
  and arms race, 170, 173, 321n151, 343n142, 345n168
  implications of collapse for Left, 9–10, 281–4
Sozialistische Förderergesellschaft (Socialist Aid Society), 50
Sozialistischer Bund (Socialist League), 50
Sozialpolitik *see* social policy
SPD (Social Democratic Party of Germany), 33–5, 37–8, 39–41, 47, 58, 83, 115, 197, 198, 267, 272, 275, 301n14
  Bad Godesberg program, 34, 44, 50, 53, 97, 280
  effect of Greens on, 268–70
  and Emergency Laws, 54–5
  and European unification, 288
  future prospects, 284
  and immigration, 183
  Kanalarbeiter, 75–6, 96, 121, 208, 269
  Long-Term Program 1975–1985, 97
  and nationalism, 235, 277
  and nuclear power and ecology, 104, 105, 157, 268
  and nuclear weapons and defense, 42–5, 48, 106, 109, 173, 201, 268, 280
  politics in 1970s, 79–81
  relationship with Greens: ideology, 119, 120–1, 123, 147, 149; politics, 190, 191, 192, 199–219, 221–5, 227, 231, 232, 233; role in formation of, 189, 193
  and terrorism, 75–6
  see also Jusos; SDS
SPD (Social Democratic Party, East Germany), 247, 254, 255
Spiegel, Der, 46–7, 90, 213, 229, 230
SPK (Socialist Patients' Collective), 66, 73
Spontis, 85–7, 100, 153, 193, 203
Springer press empire, 54, 57, 68
Springmann, Baldur, 193
SPV (Miscellaneous Political Union–The Greens), 189–90, 191, 195, 196
SRP (Socialist Reich Party), 275
Stamokap (state monopoly capitalism), 61, 85, 97
Star Wars (SDI) program, 173

Stark, Eva-Maria, 93
Stasser, Johanno, 147
Steger, Ulrich, 223
Stockholm embassy, terrorist attack on, 70–1, 73
Strattmann, Eckhart, 120, 210
Strauss, Franz-Josef, 38, 42, 46, 218, 219
Stroebele, Hans-Christian, 136–7, 261
student movement, 5, 6, 14, 21, 30, 47, 51–4, 56, 57, 59, 66, 73, 81, 87, 100, 106
Syria, E. German aid to, 242
systems theory, 125, 127–8, 142, 143–4

Tageszeitung, Die (*Taz*), 82, 84–5, 137, 210, 245–6, 249, 345n163
Temple, Hans-Konrad, 47–8
Templin, Wolfgang, 253
terrorism, 57–8, 65–78, 242, 300n40
Teufel, Fritz, 67, 68
Third World, 70, 168, 172, 177, 181, 184, 185, 251, 270, 285, 324n170
Thompson, E. P., 132–3
Tost, Ulrich, 229
trade unions *see* unions
Trampert, Rainer, 120, 124, 147, 148, 149, 150, 212, 214, 220, 225, 231, 232
transport policy, Greens', 156, 175, 176
Trepl, Ludwig, 129–30

UFV (Independent Women's Association), 254, 257, 258
Ullmann, Wolfgang, 253, 256, 258
Unabhängiger Frauenverband (United Womens' Association, UFV), 254, 257, 258
Union of Independent Socialists (Vereinigung Unabhängiger Sozialisten), 50
unions, 6, 35–7, 54, 61, 62, 63, 147–8, 163–7, 178, 182, 270–1, 280
  see also codetermination; DGB
United Left (Vereinigte Linke), 249, 254, 257
United Nations, Greens and, 184
United States of America, 9, 18–19, 266, 267
  Native Americans, Germans and, 130, 313n17, 328n62
  and German economy, 35, 36, 301–302n18
  Left and, 171–3, 280, 328n62
  and rearmament, 38
  relationship of FR with, 25–6, 279–81
  Right and, 171, 321n153
  weapons on German soil *see* nuclear weapons
  see also Gulf War
universities, 5–6, 59–60, 65
  see also student movements

Unruh, Trude, 217
Upper Rhine Action Committee against
    Environmental Endangerment through
    Nuclear Power Plants (Oberrheinisches
    Aktionskomitee gegen
    Umweltgefährdung durch
    Kernkraftwerke), 102
USP (Environmental Protection Party), 189,
    193–4
utopianism, 125, 130–2, 141

Vereinigte Linke (United Left), 249, 254,
    257, 292
Vereinigung Unabhängiger Sozialisten
    (Union of Independent Socialists), 50
Vielhauer, Jochen, 223
Vietnam, War, 18–19, 53–4, 56, 171, 280,
    343n142
Viett, Inge, 67
Vogel, Hans-Jochen, 96, 111, 141, 206
Vogt, Roland, 108, 324n175
Voigt, Karsten, 98
Vollmer, Antje, 211, 217, 218, 219, 220,
    228, 236, 326n3
Vollmer, Ludger, 214, 220
Voters' League, Nuclear Power, No
    Thanks! (Wählergemeinschaft,
    Atomkraft, Nein Danke!, WGA), 194

Wackersdorf nuclear reprocessing plant,
    213, 217
Wallman, Walter, 223, 224
Walter, Franz, 269
Wartime Host National Support agreement
    with US, Greens and, 177

Wegener, Friedrich, 195
Wehner, Herbert, 44, 75, 304n44
Weimar Republic, 37, 76, 81, 242,
    310–311n7
Weiss, Konrad, 253, 256, 258, 261, 263
Weissbekker, Thomas, 66
welfare state *see* social policy
Western European Union, Greens and,
    177
WG (living communes) *see* communes
WGA (Voters' League, Nuclear Power, No
    Thanks!), 194
Wiesenthal, Helmut, 120, 142, 143, 150,
    327n26, 353n138, 354n154
Wollenberger, Vera, 258, 260, 261
women, green policy, 161, 165–6, 168,
    178–9, 184, 185, 218, 273
Women for Peace (Frauen für den
    Frieden), 92–3
Women's Congress against Nukes and
    Militarism, 93
women's movement, 13, 80, 87–94
Women's Offensive (Frauenoffensive), 91
Work Group for Employee Affairs, 200
working class, 3, 50–1, 59, 61, 147–50, 164,
    209–10, 211, 221, 266, 267–8
Works Constitution Act, 37, 163, 167, 182
World Bank, 185
Wyhl anti-nuclear protest, 102–3, 104, 193

Young Socialists (Jungsozialisten) *see* Jusos
Yugoslavia, 138, 283, 361n36

Zieran, Manfred, 119, 203, 229
Zionism *see* Israel

Index by Mary Madden